NIXON'S PIANO

THE FREE PRESS
New York London Toronto Sydney Tokyo Singapore

NIXON'S PIANO

Presidents and Racial Politics from
Washington to Clinton

KENNETH O'REILLY

The Free Press
A Division of Simon & Schuster Inc.
1230 Avenue of the Americas
New York, N.Y. 10020

Printed in the United States of America

printing number

1 2 3 4 5 6 7 8 9 10

Text design by Carla Bolte

Library of Congress Cataloging-in-Publication Data

O'Reilly, Kenneth.
    Nixon's piano : presidents and racial politics from Washington to
Clinton / Kenneth O'Reilly.
        p. cm.
    Includes bibliographical references and index.
    ISBN 0-02-923685-1
    1. Presidents—United States—Attitudes—History. 2. United
States—Race relations. 3. Afro-Americans—Politics and government.
4. Afro-Americans—Civil rights. 5. Public opinion—United States—
History. I. Title.
E176.1.074 1996
306.2'4—dc20   95-24095
                                                           CIP

For M.A.O.

CONTENTS

ACKNOWLEDGMENTS

Thanks are due family first. Maureen Alice and Eamon have now lived through all four books, Teddy three, and Sam two and a half. All seem to be doing fine.

This book started out at the Free Press under the guidance of Joyce Seltzer, who moved on to Harvard University Press just as the first draft neared completion. Beth Anderson took over from there. Both editors deserve unimaginable riches for their many skills—not the least of which is stamina.

Colleagues and students at the University of Alaska Anchorage helped out on physical and intellectual matters alike. Especially Jean Agha, Caroline Anunsen-Ahrens, B. J. Bradshaw, Jeanne Brookshire, John Edmunson, Steve Haycox, Patricia Hodges, Will Jacobs, Kent Pegg, Denise Vania, Janice Willman, and Aharon Zorea. My University also provided a faculty development grant.

Other financial support came from the Herbert Hoover Library Association, the Franklin and Eleanor Roosevelt Institute, the Harry S. Truman Library Institute, the John F. Kennedy Foundation, and the Moody Grant program of the Lyndon B. Johnson Foundation.

Among the many librarians and archivists who kept me up and running, I am in particular debt to Mildred Mather, Shirley Sondergard, and Dwight Miller of the Hoover Library; Mark Renovitch of the

Roosevelt Library; Dennis Bilger and Raymond Geselbracht of the Truman Library; David J. Haight of the Eisenhower Library; Ronald Whealan of the Kennedy Library; Mary K. Knill of the Johnson Library; Bonnie Baldwin, William Joyner, and Scott Parham of the Nixon Presidential Materials Project; Karen Holzhausen, William McNitt, and David Horrocks of the Ford Library; Gary Foulk, David Stanhope, Keith Shuler, Albert Nason, Martin Elzy, and James Yancey at the Carter Library; and Avril Madison at Howard University's Moorland-Spingarn Research Center.

On research trips to America, support of a different kind came from Pat and Mary Delehanty, George Eddy, Elizabeth Moore, and my parents and brothers and sisters.

NIXON'S PIANO

BONES AND TAMBO

Roger Wilkins never expected to be coming to dinner. In the fifteenth month of Richard M. Nixon's presidency he was thirty-seven years old, co-opted scarcely a whit, and prematurely PC sensitive; and this dinner was no place even for an Uncle Tom.

Nephew of NAACP giant Roy Wilkins, Roger Wilkins had been born into the civil rights movement but neither followed his staid uncle's path nor took to the streets with Martin King's nonviolent protestors. He chose the system route and worked himself up to director of the Justice Department's Community Relations Service. When Lyndon B. Johnson needed an emissary to visit Watts with the fires still burning, he picked Roger Wilkins. Los Angeles Police Department officers called their nightsticks "niggersticks" then, and when they greeted Wilkins that first night only White House credentials and the protestations of the white men Johnson had sent with him prevented him from getting what Rodney King got a quarter century later.

In 1970 Wilkins worked for McGeorge Bundy at the Ford Foundation in New York, and he sat in his office there when Tom Wicker of the *New York Times* called with the dinner invitation. "The notion of hobnobbing with the nation's elite," he confessed, "turned me on." So he accepted with the delight of a 1940s' kid who had stood all day, nose

1

plastered against a candy store window, and then suddenly come into a nickel.

A few days later Wilkins received another unexpected invitation. The White House called this time asking if he might attend a prayer break-fast on the Sunday following the dinner.[1] His first inclination was to decline because not even the yet to come Watergate scandal could push Nixon's reputation in black America lower than it stood in 1970. His principles would not allow him to break bread with a politician lacking a moral compass on matters of race, and Wilkins considered telling the world that with a movement-style flourish (meaning a press confer-ence). An occasion not to pray but to denounce. Given that he was more of a policy guy than a militant, Wilkins suppressed this impulse and delayed his response to the president's invitation until he could con-sult with Uncle Roy, Bundy, and Kenneth Clark (the psychologist who helped the Supreme Court justices hearing arguments in *Brown* under-stand the harm segregation did to black schoolchildren). They told him he couldn't turn down the president of the United States and the first lady (Pat Nixon also wanted him to come). Wilkins's curiosity further balanced his activist appetite. "It was like being invited to an Andy Warhol happening," he said. "I wanted to see the latest tacky trend."

So when Wilkins finally decided it was with mixed emotions. He telephoned the White House to decline the invitation and lay out his prayer-breakfast objections (an unconstitutional waste of taxpayer dol-lars). "Besides," he told the woman in the White House social secretary's office who answered the phone, "I think Mr. Nixon's policies are damaging to blacks." "Oh, that's a shame," she responded. "You know, we have lots of coloreds at these occasions. Sometimes they're even the preachers."

Wilkins later learned that President Nixon had invited all the big dinner's out-of-town guests to the prayer breakfast. On the evening of March 14, shortly before walking into the ballroom of the Washington Statler Hilton, he also learned that he would have to violate his prin-ciples if he were to hobnob. To get in he had to cross what the handful of women demonstrating out front called (with some exaggeration) a picket line. Once inside Wilkins nearly asphyxiated on the overwhelm-ing white maleness. The only other black was someone they had to invite, District of Columbia Mayor Walter Washington. This was "white folks' night," and two of the only three pleasant memories Wilkins could remember best measured his discomfort. One was the warm embrace of Deputy Attorney General Richard Kleindienst, scarcely known as a civil rights friend even in John Mitchell's Justice Department. The other was a long conversation with Cartha D. DeLoach, deputy director of the Federal Bureau of Investigation.

DeLoach, a native Georgian, had come up in that crook-, commie-, and coon-fighting bureaucracy as the protege of Louis B. Nichols, the Hoover man whose chores included leaking tidbits to Senator Joseph R. McCarthy. DeLoach himself had tried (and failed) to peddle the FBI's Martin Luther King tap and bug recordings to Ben Bradlee, then *Newsweek*'s Washington bureau chief, and several other reporters. If a black man found the Kleindienst/DeLoach encounters the high point of his Statler Hilton visit, something was terribly wrong that evening.

The dinner itself was an annual affair of the Gridiron Club, an enterprise that Hedrick Smith, in his book on how Washington works, called, simply, "an elitist social club of sixty print journalists." This early spring gathering was probably the Beltway royalty's closest match to Oscar night glitter both on the Hollywood-ish front end (with white-tied and -tailed guests from the political and corporate arenas stepping from limos into a sidewalk crowd) and on the back end (with postevent parties hosted by students of the legendary Swifty Lazar bash). "One of the high tribal rites of Washington insiders," Smith continued. "A mark of making it."[2] Gridiron men had been carrying on the tradition with only slightly less fanfare since 1885, managing to coax Harrison and every other president except Cleveland out of the White House for libations and a gourmet menu. When not focused on Terrapin Maryland served amid spotlights and red roses, the guests passed time with vaudevillian speeches, skits, songs, dances. All off-the-record. The red-jacketed Marine Corps band played Sousa marches. Pedantry permitted no member to forget that John Philip Sousa had been the club's first music director.

Eleanor Roosevelt staged the initial demonstration against Gridiron exclusiveness in 1933 after the club fractured its own tradition of inviting all cabinet members to maintain the higher tradition of men only. The president's wife held a "Gridiron Widows' Party" in the East Room of the White House for Labor Secretary Frances Perkins and those women whose husbands made the big show. It was not much of a protest. By 1935 the affair had grown into a full-blown imitation that differed only in favoring tamer stuff than what Mrs. Roosevelt's husband sat through at the official dinner.

While the Gridiron Widows dined and clowned, the Gridiron men across town performed a skit for Mrs. Roosevelt's husband that featured "the Southern nightshirt trade." These newspaper reporters in Ku Klux costume poked fun at former Alabama Klansman Hugo Black, the president's nominee to the Supreme Court. Instead of "K-K-K-Katy," FDR got:

> K-K-K-Klansman
> Beautiful Klansman,
> You're the same old K-K-K-Klux I knew before,
> When the m-m-m-moon shines,
> Over the White House,
> We'll be watching at the K-K-K-Kourthouse door!

Franklin Roosevelt was not amused; Eleanor even less so when she learned of this classic.[3]

If race rivaled gender in the Gridiron hierarchy of exclusiveness, members occasionally enlisted blacks for their skits. A Spanish-American War item entitled "Uncle Sam's Yellow Kids," for example, featured a clubber who dressed up as "Uncle Sam" and brought in six "colored boys of the complexion that the negroes call 'yaller.'" They did a dance, a Gridiron chronicler noted, and "were meant to represent the Filipinos." Members and their dinner guests more often had to settle for blackface actors in the routines. After *Plessy v. Ferguson* (1896) made segregation the land's law, the club even formed its own "Supreme Court" consisting of nine newspapermen "in black robes who were to all intents and purposes minstrels, for they had their interlocutor, bones, and tambo, jokes and songs."[4]

On Roger Wilkins's night out at the Gridiron Club, roasters and roastees included Robert Finch, Ralph Nader, John Mitchell, Richard Helms, Walter Mondale, Edmund Muskie, George McGovern, Henry Kissinger, Tom Clark, William Westmoreland, and some 550 other luminaries. Some thought Julian Bond and Andrew Young were on hand. But "Bond" and "Young" turned out to be Roger Wilkins, who knew how to take they-all-look-alike episodes in stride. Once, when Wilkins was ringing a lady's doorbell at an precipitous hour, Merv Griffin popped out of the opposite apartment, gave him a puzzled look, and asked, in a quizzical voice, "Andy?" "No," Wilkins responded just as his friend opened the door. "I'm Julian Bond."

Wilkins and the other Gridiron dinner guests were no doubt unaware that a club speaker some sixty-three years earlier had screamed, in a voice famous for its strident pitch and dental emphasis but suddenly angrier than ever before: "All coons do *not* look alike to me!"[5] That speaker was President Theodore Roosevelt, and he protested too much—having recently dismissed without honor all 167 men in the Twenty-fifth U.S. Infantry's three Negro companies. The offense was an apparent anti–Jim Crow rampage that left one white resident of Brownsville, Texas, dead. Roosevelt punished every last man even though only a handful could have possibly participated in that night's violence and no hard evidence identified any culprit. Fourteen soldiers were subsequently reinstated, but the dishonorable discharges stood for the rest of the men until Nixon's Defense Department changed them to honorable on the grounds that mass punishment contradicted Army policy.

Richard Nixon attended the March 14, 1970, Gridiron dinner, too. Wilkins looked up from his terrapin to catch "the President—all dressed up in white tie and tails, sitting about twenty feet away—staring at me intently. Our eyes locked only briefly before the President turned away, his eyes blinking in a rapid, nervous way. Though we had never met, he had to know that I was the black who had turned down his [prayer breakfast] invitation with those rude comments, because I was one of only two blacks in the group of more than five hundred men in the room." It was of no comfort here that Nixon could tell one black face from the next.

Gridiron rules allowed the roasting of the president of the United States if not his portrayal on stage. Most but by no means all past occupants of the office loved the attention, with Lyndon Baines Johnson being among the more direct objectors. "About as much fun as throwing cowshit at the village idiot," he once said. Nixon, in contrast, hoped to earn a reputation as a good sport and thus sided with the majority. Democratic Senator Edmund Muskie of Maine gave what Wilkins called "a very funny and exquisitely partisan speech"—observing that the Republicans' three problems were the war, inflation, and what to say on Lincoln's birthday. Nixon laughed, and so did Wilkins.

Muskie's line was among the rare bits that Wilkin's enjoyed. Overall, he said, "the humor made me think I had stumbled into the locker room of a segregated country club." Most songs and skits spoofed Nixon's so-called southern strategy of reaching white voters at black expense. For this president race was a tool for breaking the "solid South" and tipping those white voters out of their traditional Democratic party nest. Even Gridiron president Jack Steele, Washington bureau chief for Scripps-Howard newspapers, joined in. President Nixon could fulfill the Republican promise to stop "court-ordered busing" and otherwise protect "neighborhood schools," Steele deadpanned. "All he has to do is get Ralph Nader to get General Motors to recall all the school buses."

A newspaper reporter on the card, in the role of HEW chief "Bob Finch," sang, to the tune of "A Dixie Melody," a summary of this Republican party tack that Wilkins found a bit too cute:

> Rock-a-bye the voters with a southern strategy;
> Don't you fuss; we won't bus children in ol' Dixie!
> We'll put George Wallace in decline
> Below the Mason-Dixon line.
> We'll help save the nation
> From things like civil rights and inte-gra-tion!
> Weep no more, John Stennis!
> We'll pack the court for sure.
> We will fight for voting rights—
> To keep them white and pure!
> A zillion Southern votes we will deliver;
> Move Washington down on the Swanee River!
> Rock-a-bye with Ol' Massa Nixon and his Dixie strategy!

A singing "Carswell" developed the court-packing reference:

> Nobody knows the trouble I've seen,
> Nobody knows but Haynesworth.

President Nixon had tried and failed to put Florida's G. Harrold Carswell and South Carolina's Clement F. Haynesworth, Jr., both outstanding segregationists, onto the Supreme Court in hope of courting Alabama Governor George Wallace's constituency.[6]

Things got no better at the Gridiron that night. Absolutely determined that a good time would be had by all, and equally determined to bring down the house, Richard Nixon appeared as the final act. The curtain pulled back to reveal the president and Vice President Spiro Agnew seated at two modest black pianos (Dwight Chapin at the White House had requested grand pianos or at least baby grands but the Statler Hilton could only manage uprights). This was the first time a chief executive had appeared on the Gridiron stage, and Nixon opened by asking: "What about this 'southern strategy' we hear so often?" "Yes suh, Mr. President," Agnew replied, "Ah agree with you completely on yoah southern strategy." The dialect, as Wilkins observed, got the biggest boffo.

After more banter with the "darky" Agnew, Nixon opened the piano duet with Franklin Roosevelt's favorite song ("Home on the Range"), then Harry Truman's ("Missouri Waltz"), then Lyndon Johnson's ("The Eyes of Texas Are Upon You"). Agnew drowned him out a few bars into each with a manic "Dixie" on his piano, and the Gridiron crew got louder and louder. "The crowd ate it up," Wilkins observed. "They roared." Nixon ended with his own favorite songs, "God Bless America" and "Auld Lang Syne," and here Agnew played it straight. The Gridiron dinner faded with five hundred men suddenly solemn and on their feet, many with tears in their eyes, all singing along, all celebrating their nation.[7]

Even before Watergate, Richard Nixon knew something about scandal; and he knew as well that his boffo keyboard bit was no scandal among the made men of how-it-really-works Washington. Those Gridiron members and their distinguished guests laughed and sang and cried not because they considered the president's southern strategy in the nation's best interest. Many in fact condemned his politics as opportunistic, divisive, even immoral. They cheered the president because they respected the electoral results. Simply put, southern strategy worked. It put Nixon in the White House. And nothing in the political culture symbolized by the Gridiron Club is more honored than a grand strategy that can carry a man to the Oval Office.

Nixon and his southern strategy braintrust created and then exploited a message identifying the "new liberalism" as a doctrine sympathetic to the "excessive demands" of blacks (feminists, too, for that matter). As they portrayed it, the new liberalism opposed the modest aspirations of white working-class and middle-class families while forcing those families to pay taxes for programs like affirmative action that undermined their own values and placed them at an economic disadvantage. Unlike the New Deal's old liberalism, which supposedly favored universal or class-based programs, new liberalism supposedly favored special interest programs. The demand for racial justice is thus dismissed as the exclusive prerogative of the special interest group in question (blacks) and their benefactors in the courts and bureaucracies and other orbs favored by the new liberalism.[8]

Nixon was not the first candidate to refine and then ride a southern strategy into the White House. The words themselves ("southern strategy"), though a relatively recent construct, can be better understood as regionless code for "white over black." That racist policy dates back not to Nixon's campaign in 1968 (or as some argue to Barry Goldwater's run in 1964), but to the Constitutional Convention of 1787. Slavery was the unwritten code then (the word appears only in the Constitution's Thirteenth Amendment added in 1865 to abolish the peculiar institution formally and forever), and it affected the Philadelphia debates on such key issues as representation in Congress, interstate commerce, and the method of choosing the president. No matter how elliptical, discussion of the slave question influenced things far more than the divisions between "big states" and "small states" that all schoolchildren read about in their texts.

William Lloyd Garrison and his *Liberator* condemned the Constitution as "A Covenant with Death and an Agreement with Hell" because the Founders sought to preserve their young republic and its economic health by providing explicit and implicit protections for the South's labor system. Explicit protections include the Constitution's three-fifths clause (Art. I, Sec. 2); the "such Persons" (slave importation) clause (Art. I, Sec. 9, Par. 1); the capitation tax clause (Art. I, Sec. 9, Par. 4); the "Person held to Service or Labour" (fugitive slave) clause (Art. IV, Sec. 2, Par. 3); and Article V prohibiting any amendment of the slave-trade and capitation tax clauses before the year 1808. Implicit protections include the amendment structure for changing the document (Art. V), requiring approval of three-fourths of the states (in 1860 slave states still made up nearly half the nation); prohibition on export taxes (Art. I, Secs. 9 and 10), meaning that slave-produced products (tobacco, rice, and later cotton) could not be taxed; and the insurrection clause (Art. I, Sec. 8) and domestic violence clause (Art. IV, Sec. 4), assigning federal responsibility for suppressing slave revolts.

Because the Electoral College structure included the three-fifths compromise (Art. II, Sec. 1, Par. 2), slaveowners got a disproportional say in choosing the person charged with enforcing the domestic violence clause in the worst-case event that the task of controlling slaves proved too much for these otherwise die-hard states' righters. It ought to come as no surprise, then, that from 1789 to 1861 nine of the fifteen commanders-in-chief were slaveowners; or that all five two-term presidents during those years claimed human property rights; or that even Abraham Lincoln, before battlefield woes forced a reappraisal, promised only to keep slavery from spreading. Lincoln made no promise to move against slavery in the states where it already existed. Careful, as ever, to distinguish between what the Union's people should do (abolish slavery everywhere) and what they could not do, he said that "the peace of society, and *the structure of our government* both require that we should let it alone [in the states], and we insist on letting it alone [emphasis added]." For the pre-Gettysburg Lincoln, the Constitution's articles, sections, and paragraphs regarding slavery were "guards which our forefathers have placed around it."[9]

Of the forty-two presidents of the United States only Lincoln and Lyndon Johnson stand out for what they ultimately did on the matter of civil rights for all. But even they brought baggage to their great accomplishments: Lincoln with his white supremacist caveats, closet dream of sending the slaves he freed back to Africa, and faint Reconstruction notion of building a decent Republican party home for the South's poor white trash at the expense of any freedman he could not ship to Liberia; and Johnson with his surveillance state (that gave the FBI et al. free run at an entire race by ranking blacks alongside Communists and criminals) and Vietnam draft boards (that always came first for the people at the bottom he otherwise seemed so intent on helping).

Collectively, the nation's forty-two chief executives have exercised little leadership on any civil rights front. This includes all but the two bright stars whose positive accomplishments were aided by the flow of history. From the Quaker pleas of George Washington's time to the post–Jim Crow litigations and consent decrees of Bill Clinton's time, African Americans have slid about in white America's consciousness as property, dilemma, threat, inconvenience, and cause for guilt and shame. Black citizens occasionally represented a mere patronage or diversity headache for the post–Civil War presidency; more often they served as a permanent opponent for the domestic security community's war games and especially as a tool for dividing the electorate.

Southern strategy in our time remains what it has always been: the gut organizing principle of American politics. At root it is nothing more than a belief that presidential elections can be won only by following the doctrines and rituals of white over black. The pecking order has stayed that way through the death of slavery and Jim Crow, and notwithstanding Lincoln and Johnson our presidents have in nearly every other case made it their job to keep that order.

All three of the nation's two-party systems have accommodated white over black and respected White House responsibilities to ensure that the nation's politics remains organized according to that dictate. In the era of Federalists v. Republicans, our presidents enforced by example the gentlemen's agreement that kept slavery removed from public discourse. While the Whigs continued that increasingly difficult duty from the 1820s to the 1850s, the Jacksonian movement invented a party and a style of presidential leadership that knew no higher purpose than protecting slavery forever. Our third and still functioning two-party system has been largely shaped since the Civil War by a Republican struggle to capture the white southern vote and a Democratic struggle to keep that vote. For the former this meant a presidential charge to transform the Republican party into a white man's party. For the latter it meant a peaceful coexistence between the White House and the worst extremes of southern racism until the coming of Lyndon Johnson and the Second Reconstruction. For post-Johnson Democrats it has meant an effort to counter the GOP's exclusionary racial status. To put it bluntly, Republicans seeking election or re-election to the land's highest office are expected to solidify their hold on the angry white male vote while Democratic presidential candidates are expected to win that vote back.

The most surprising and ultimately disturbing thing in all this is how little the personal values of our presidents mattered. Nearly every pre–Civil War chief executive who owned slaves privately admitted that the practice was a sin. A "stain," to use Madison's chilling word. In their public lives, of course, those slaveowners honored the Constitution. In more recent times we have had presidents contradict their own heart-felt values by implementing blatantly racist electoral strategies and policies. One candidate actually organized his campaign around the great taboo of American race relations, the black man who raped a white woman. That such a thing could still cut a path to the White House exactly two hundred years after Washington's election is the sort of troubling reality that needs to be confronted if we are to understand the nature of our democracy and where that democracy will take us all, whatever our color, in the future.

Such a conclusion seems especially alarming when contrasted with more conventional wisdom. The latter holds that presidential or any other sort of leadership requires followers first and foremost, and thus if the electorate holds racist notions then the men who would be president must inevitably bow to those notions. This is truly a more numbing formulation because it locates the problem in the American people themselves and not in governmental structures. Equally alarming is the historical evidence that the men who ran our political institutions worked so hard to nurture and support the nation's racism. These men, including our presidents, in all too many cases had no great confidence that white over black would rule so absolutely without proper guidance from above.

That lack of confidence was present before the Constitutional Convention and continues to hold to this day. "If Negro slavery came to Virginia without anyone having to decide upon it as a matter of public policy," as historian Edmund S. Morgan has shown, "the same is not true of racism. By a series of acts, the assembly deliberately did what it could to foster the contempt of whites for black and Indians." Similarly, C. Vann Woodward demonstrated that segregation was not a time-honored tradition even in the deep South but a relatively recent construct of the late nineteenth and early twentieth centuries.[10] In the history of American racism, stateways have influenced folkways far more deeply than the reverse; and the men who came to the Oval Office were as responsible for seeing to this as any Jamestown slave-owner or Jim Crow architect or practitioner of the segmented racial politics that dominates presidential elections today.

Whether in theory and practice or in creation and maturation, the nation's executive branch of government has remained remarkably fixed on the Founders' so-called original intent. An urge to confront problems of race and racism head on has appeared in the Oval Office about as often as a famous named comet cuts the earth's heavens. Structure and nature, however, explain only in part this White House institutionalization of white over black. History shows what the presidency can accomplish when the stars are properly aligned, yet all too often the choices that could have been made to improve things were not made. To write of the forty-two chief executives and their deeds and dreams on matters of race yields few profiles in courage and a great many profiles of men who agonized and analyzed only in search of more perfect ways to protect slavery or Jim Crow or a life expectancy that in the mid-1990s is lower in Harlem than Bangladesh. The story of the presidency and the politics of race is thus largely a story of choices made to acquiesce in, preserve, and adapt the original intent of 1787 to modern times.

All too often the quality of the decisions made by the honorable men who lived in the White House was no better than Nixon's decision at the Gridiron Club to follow Spiro Agnew's darky patter with "Dixie" and then "God Bless America" on his piano. It was indeed a Mr. Bones spectacle that Roger Wilkins witnessed when he came to dinner that evening, and aside from a few unscheduled breaks it rates as the nation's saddest and longest running show.

: 1 :

OWNERS

America's War for Independence ended on October 19, 1781, when Cornwallis and 7,000 British troops stacked their weapons at Yorktown with the bands playing "The World Turned Upside Down." Some eighteen months later the two great freedom fighters of that Revolution plotted another. "Let us unite in purchasing a small estate," Lafayette proposed, "where we may try the experiment to free the negroes, and use them only as tenants. Such an example as yours might render it a general practice. . . . If it be a wild scheme, I had rather be mad this way, than to be thought wise in the other task." "To encourage the emancipation of the black people of this Country from that state of Bondage in wch. they are held," Washington responded, "is a striking evidence of the benevolence of your Heart. I shall be happy to join you in so laudable a work; but will defer going into a detail of the business, 'till I have the pleasure of seeing you." When meeting at Mount Vernon a year later they discussed the issue in some detail. The new revolution, however, proved beyond their grasp. They began no joint venture to establish a plantation for free blacks.[1]

Lafayette could not let go. He launched his plan not in Virginia in 1783 but near Cayenne in French Guiana in 1786 and pleaded once more with the great man to lend his name. Washington again declined with enthusiasm. "Would to God a like spirit might diffuse itself generally into the minds of the people of this Country. But I despair of seeing it. . . . To set the slaves afloat at once would, I really believe, be productive of much inconvenience and mischief; but by degrees it certainly might, and assuredly ought to be effected; and that too by legislative authority." Washington listed among his "first wishes," no matter how perplexing the details, the desire "to see some plan adopted, by which slavery in this country may be abolished by slow, sure and imperceptible degrees." Meanwhile he could only make a qualified promise. "I never mean (unless some particular circumstance should compel me to it) to possess another slave by purchase." When writing those words in 1786 he held 111 dower Negroes from his marriage to Martha Curtis and another 105 slaves outright.[2]

Washington, like most of his contemporaries, knew right from wrong here. "All America acknowledges the existence of slavery to be an evil," a young Henry Clay said in 1798, the year before the general's death. Even if Clay exaggerated, the Quakers had no moral monopoly on this question in the eighteenth century.[3] Washington became an owner at age eleven when his father died and left him ten slaves. From childhood to manhood slavery was part of everything he knew and understood. Yet he realized it was wrong, pledged not to buy slaves, fantasized about freeing them, believed the great planters of the tidelands had no more right to rule "the blacks . . . with such arbitrary sway" than the British had to "make us . . . tame and abject slaves." Still, his holdings grew. At his inaugural on March 4, 1789, he owned more slaves than the 216 claimed while plotting with Lafayette. The public man, when pressed, said that he did "not like even to think, much less talk of [slavery]."[4] But the private man brooded and always knew exactly what was right. The hero who risked all in crossing the Delaware froze up on this problem, never lifting a public voice or pen, let alone a musket, to throw out the thing that ate at him.

Washington had no doubt that slavery should perish. "[This] troublesome species of property ere many years pass over our heads," he predicted, would lead to a terrible and perhaps bloody tragedy. The first order of business for the first president of the United States, however, was to protect his rights to the household slaves brought to Philadelphia. (Pennsylvania law required adult bondsmen to be freed six months after the owner moved into the commonwealth.) "As all except

Hercules and Paris are dower negroes," Washington explained, "it be-
hooves me to prevent the emancipation of them, otherwise I shall not
only lose the use of them but may have them to pay for." (That is, he
might owe his wife's family the fair market value of any dower Negro
he freed.) The nation's greatest soldier and greatest white father saw
slavery as a moral abomination and a looming political horror, and kept
silent. Because pecuniary interest balanced conscience.[5]

Not that ownership meant unrestricted wealth. For Washington,
who vowed to "never turn [tobacco] Planter," financial pressures were
particularly vexing since he could quite balance the number of slaves
owned with the amount of work to be done. At Mount Vernon, he
often complained, "I have more working negroes by a full moiety, than
can be employed to any advantage in the farming system." Yet during
busier times he found himself forced to lease slaves from neighboring
farms and plantations. The institution's economic tangle thus contributed to Washington's closet abolitionism. Yet he remained unwilling,
and in his mind unable, to strike a political blow against the hated institution that defined his profession and the nation he worked so hard
to construct.[6]

Another missed opportunity for the first president involved the
Pennsylvania Abolition Society. In what was probably his final public
act, eighty-five-year-old Benjamin Franklin signed and transmitted a
society petition in early 1790 asking Congress to "step to the very verge
of the power vested in you for discouraging every species of traffic in
the persons of our fellow men." While southerners shook the House
and Senate with predictions of "tumults, seditions, and insurrections,"
Washington kept his own counsel. "I was not inclined to express my
sentiments on the merits of the question," he explained after a Quaker
called to discuss "the immorality—injustice—and impolicy of keeping
these people in a state of slavery." He considered "the memorial of the
Quakers . . . very malapropos." "Not only *ill-timed*" but "a great waste
of time."

Relief from the dissension of abolitionist ideas floating about the
political arena for all to see (as opposed to private letters to Lafayette
and like-minded men) came soon enough. "The memorial of the
Quakers . . . has at length been put to sleep," Washington noted on that
day, March 28, 1790, "and will scarcely awake before the year 1808."

The Constitution (Art. I, Sec. 9) prohibited Congress from regulating "the Migration or Importation of such Persons [slaves]" until that year, and that settled the matter.[7]

Citizen Washington told Lafayette that he hoped the "legislative authority" would someday abolish slavery; President Washington would not tell Congress that he thought slavery wrong. He declined to lend his name or his office's prestige at a time when the words of the Declaration of Independence ("all men are created equal") were still resonate, a time when egalitarian political ideas and pre–cotton gin economic forces conspired to make slavery vulnerable. Washington addressed slavery in the first term only once with a request that Spain return runaways who had crossed from Georgia to Florida by the tens and hundreds. In the second term he devised a plan to free his own slaves and kept that plan secret for "reasons of a political and indeed imperious nature."

Washington never quite figured out how to circle the financial hardship either. "To liberate a certain species of property which I possess, very repugnantly to my own feelings; but which imperious necessity compels," was no easy task. He would simply wait "until I can substitute some other expedient"—he considered "importing Palatines" (German indentured servants)—"by which expences not in my power to avoid (however well disposed I may be to do it) can be defrayed."[8] Intermarriage between his own slaves and the dower Negroes complicated outright emancipation. So did slave resistance which increased the financial burden that blocked both the slaves' and Washington's freedom. "When an overlooker's back is turned," he complained, "the most of them will slight their work, or be idle altogether; in which case correction cannot retrieve either but often produces evils which are worse than the disease."[9] The moral issue was clear if unactionable; the economic utility of slavery on the Mount Vernon farms debatable. Unable to work out the numbers, Washington preferred to muddle along with slave labor rather than confront free labor's unknown economic risks and predictable political risks.

This private accounting might have achieved a perverse balance had Washington been willing to take black men and women to market. "Were it not then, that I am principled against selling Negroes, as you would cattle," he wrote a friend in 1794, "I would not in twelve months from this date, be possessed of one as a slave."[10] So he pressed on, ignoring slavery in office and tending to the master's responsibilities in private life. When returning to Virginia at the second term's end he freed his household slaves quietly, in effect covertly, by leaving them in Philadelphia. He kept the 317 slaves on his five Mount Vernon farms.[11]

Washington was a good owner within the limits of that particular myth. He knew most of his slaves by name (though he had a reputation for keeping a distance from "my people"), and unlike most Virginia big holders occasionally freed field slaves (sometimes taking the bother to provide tenancy or apprenticeship).[12] He also left a will that freed upon his wife's passing the 124 slaves he held outright. In the whole of his public life, however, he moved in the right direction only in the long-ago 1770s by supporting the British slave-merchant boycott; and, citing military necessity, by reversing his Continental Army policy of refusing enlistment to "any stroller, negro, or vagabond." He recruited and commanded free blacks solely to prevent them from seeking "employ in the ministerial army." This fear of an enemy determined to "arm our slaves against us" remained throughout his presidency.[13]

No rut cut by the first president went deeper than the idea that the slave issue ought not intrude on democracy's grand experiment. This first and most enduring southern strategy elevated expedience over morality and for the nation's sake commanded whoever happened to occupy the land's highest office to take that sin to the grave. Slavery did not so much earn its keep as it was protected by Washington and the presidents who followed. All men of their time, and nearly all convinced, like Washington, that slavery was wrong, yet they stood and watched, usually in silence, always in the name of order and stability, as the institution corrupted their country and slowly split it apart.

From John Adams came only dead silence. Southern strategy demanded not one utterance during his presidency (1797–1801), and he made none. His long career included a single bombast in the rarefied air of 1776 against the slave trade.[14] So cautious that he opposed black enlistment in the Continental Army (for fear it would make southerners "run out of their Wits at the least Hint of such a measure"), Adams summed up the view that would rule his political life in a private comment in 1777 about a Massachusetts emancipation proposal: "The Bill for freeing the Negroes, I hope will sleep for a Time. We have Causes enough of Jealousy Discord and Division, and this Bill will certainly add to the Number." The words foreshadowed Washington's on the Quaker memorial all the way down to the put-to-sleep imagery.[15]

In the privacy of his home and in his personal correspondence, Adams agreed with his wife, Abigail, who thought slavery "allways appeard a most iniquitous Scheme" fit only for the "daily robbing and plundering from those who have as good a right to freedom as we have."[16] "Although I have never sought popularity by any animated speeches or inflammatory publications against the slavery of the black," he wrote, "my opinion against it has always been known, and my practise has been so conformable to my sentiments that I have always employed free men; both as domestics and laborers and never did I own a slave." Slavery, however, was not iniquitous enough to stifle complaints about "Franklin and his Quakers." Adams the diplomat pressed Britain for reparations covering slaves liberated and carried off during the Revolution. Adams the president pressed nothing one way or the other. Even his qualified thoughts on abolition remained private. The freeing of the slaves must proceed, if at all, "with much caution and circumspection." No one should "venture an exertion which would probably excite insurrections among the blacks to rise against their masters, and imbue their hands in innocent blood."

With his presidency about to end Adams said he would "always be ready to cooperate" with the proponents of emancipation "as far as my means and opportunities can reasonably be expected to extend." No opportunities arose; no means extended. Thirteen years later he warned against abolition while holding that his soul remained antislavery. "What would follow?," he asked in yet another private missive. "Would the democracy, nine in ten, among the negroes, be gainers? Would not the most shiftless among them be in danger of perishing for want . . . go back to their masters, best of them work at horrible jobs, become squatters, incorporate with Indians, commit crimes in bands. . . . Will the poor simple, democratical part of the people gain any happiness by such rash revolution?" He answered "no," remaining, as ever, opposed to slavery, but only within the limits of his own four walls.[17]

With Thomas Jefferson keeping to the rut, the silence of the presidency thundered. For the eight years beginning March 4, 1801, Jefferson was chief executive of the world's largest slave-holding nation. Nine-hundred thousand slaves in all. One-hundred thousand more than the entire British empire. One of seven Americans woke, worked, and died a slave, while Jefferson pretended it was not so.[18] The government came to Washington, D.C., in 1801, the same year that he came to office, and with Congress placing the District and its 3,244 slaves under Virginia and Maryland law one could stand in the Capitol Building doorway and watch processions of chained men, women, and children shuffling to the pens to await sale and new southern homes. On Pennsylvania Avenue the St. Charles Hotel catered to visiting owners by advertising the wall rings adorning six basement cells. Ignoring these sights as well, the new president brought his household slaves up from Monticello. This property included Fanny and Eddy, whose baby was born in the White House. The baby died there, too, before its second birthday.[19]

Jefferson's silence thundered because this president had written the great words of the Declaration of Independence. In an early draft (what he called "the original paper"), Jefferson described slavery as "cruel war against human nature itself." "This piratical warfare, the opprobrium of *infidel* powers," he charged, "is the warfare of the CHRISTIAN king of Great Britain. Determined to keep open a market where MEN should be bought and sold, he has prostituted his negative for suppressing every legislative attempt to prohibit or to restrain this execrable commerce; and that this assemblage of horrors might want no fact of distinguished die, he is now exciting these very people to rise in arms among us, and to purchase that liberty of which he deprived them, by murdering the people upon whom *he* also obtruded them."[20]

More an attack on the African slave trade than slavery itself, the lines never made the Declaration's final draft. "Struck out in complaisance to South Carolina and Georgia," Jefferson grumbled, and perhaps also at the insistence of "our Northern brethren . . . [who] felt a little tender under those censures; for though their people had very few slaves themselves, yet they had been pretty considerable carriers of them to others."[21] The charge itself (that the British crown bore sole responsibility and guilt for American slavery) was implausible. At the time Jefferson ranked as Albemarle County's second largest owner with 175 slaves on his books. No doubt some of them wanted to know, with Samuel Johnson, "how is it that we hear the loudest yelps for liberty from the drivers of negroes?"[22]

Political rhetoric about a Christian king aside, Jefferson's emphasis on slaves as *men* transcended his ownership of men. The wondrous five words of equality that remained in the Declaration of Independence would prove an eighty-four-year burden for his southern brethren. Even the peculiar institution's Virginian advocates would distance themselves from their own giant as the nation crept toward civil war. They called him a feeble man of "strange eccentricities, quaint expressions, gleaming paradoxes, and sweeping assertions."[23]

Jefferson knew that slavery violated every imperative of nature and every natural law of God and man. He called it, in the privacy of his correspondence, a "moral and political depravity," an "abominable crime," a "hideous blot." With North Carolina's Hugh Williamson, he was one of two southerners to support a bill in 1784 to exclude slavery from the Northwest Territory. Exclusion triumphed three years later with the Northwest Ordinance.[24] Public condemnation of the institution as a whole came, if only for a non-American audience, in *Notes on the State of Virginia.* He tried to prevent publication in the United States of the only book he ever wrote because "the terms in which I speak [against] slavery . . . may produce an irritation."[25]

It did produce an irritation though not in the way Jefferson suspected. *Notes on the State of Virginia* first appeared in Paris (1785) and London (1787) before a pirated edition surfaced in Philadelphia and alerted the American public to Jefferson's advocacy of both emancipation and colonization (that is, the costly proposition of freeing the slaves and then sending them back to Africa or some other "congenial" place). Having raised the question ("why not retain and incorporate the blacks into the State, and thus save the expense"), Jefferson answered it: "Deep-rooted prejudices entertained by the whites; ten thousand recollections, by the blacks, of the injuries they have sustained; new provocations; the real distinctions which nature has made; and many other circumstances . . . which will probably never end but in the extermination of one or the other race."

Jefferson then moved to the "physical and moral" spheres, continuing what one scholar called "a semi-Joycian" screed that carried a single paragraph for six pages. He asked "whether the black of the negro resides in the reticular membrane between the skin and the scarf-skin, or in the scarf-skin itself; whether it proceeds from the color of the blood, the color of the bile, or from that of some other secretion." Next came "the circumstance of superior beauty" which the slaves confirmed in "their own judgment in favor of the whites, declared by their preference of them, as uniformly as is the preference of the Oranootan for the black woman over those of his own species." Finally, intelligence: "In memory they are equal to whites; in reason much inferior . . . in imagination . . . dull, tasteless, and anomalous."[26]

For all its qualifications, Winthrop Jordan observed, *Notes on the State of Virginia* constituted the most "extreme formulation of anti-Negro 'thought' offered by any American in the thirty years after the Revolution."[27] While Jefferson's God created all men equal, his science "proved" blacks inferior to whites. Even as he stoked abolition's great engine (the printed word) with his own timeless words from the Declaration, he stoked slavery's great engine (cotton) with the Louisiana Purchase and his mind-boggling "diffusion" theory. That theory held that slavery would shrivel and die if allowed to extend to all territories. The president proposed to kill the "malign twins" (the plantation system and slavery) by giving them free run across the entire continent.

The Federalists, vowing to make an issue in the election of 1800, accused Jefferson of degrading "the blacks from the rank which God hath given them in the scale of being" and otherwise advancing "the strongest argument for their state of slavery!" They tried again in the 1804 elections. Clement Moore, who went on to write "A Visit from St. Nicholas," asked "where Mr. Jefferson learnt that the orang-outang has less affection for his own females than for black women." "No doubt from some French traveller," he suggested, in true Federalist spirit.[28] The Federalists may have mocked these "scientific" musings, but Jefferson's words mattered (because of who he was) and were deeply disturbing (because they fed the racist myths that roared through his time and into ours). "Mr. Jefferson's remarks respecting us," Boston's black radical David Walker wrote in 1829, "have sunk deep into the hearts of millions of the whites and never will be removed this side of eternity."[29]

In 1788, when asked to join the Society for the Abolition of the Slave Trade, Jefferson said "nobody wishes more ardently to see an abolition not only of the trade but of the condition of slavery: and certainly nobody will be more willing to encounter every sacrifice for that object."[30] For the next twelve years and the eight years after that in which he served as the nation's third president, however, Jefferson sacrificed nothing. When several religious sects advocated Negro education, he showed no interest. He also made no effort to persuade Congress to exclude slavery from the Louisiana Territory in its entirety. Or to accept slavery in Orleans in exchange for exclusion in the remainder of the Louisiana Purchase. The coming struggle between the free-labor North and the slave-labor South for primacy in the national domain was, as the historian John Chester Miller noted, perhaps "the immediate, and probably the only truly irrepressible, cause of the Civil War." Either Jefferson did not see the chance or lacked the courage to act. Perhaps he believed that his incredible diffusion theory would actually work.[31]

The French sold their North American empire largely because General Charles Leclerc's troops in St. Domingo (Haiti) failed to crush Toussaint Louverture's slave army. That revolt convinced Napoleon that the cost of empire in this hemisphere was too high, and convinced Jefferson that the race issue was primarily a security issue. Thousands died in St. Domingo from yellow fever, from the British blockade's grim efficiency, from battle and massacre. Even the massacre of white men by black men. On New Year's Day 1804 black revolutionaries proclaimed Haiti the hemisphere's second independent nation—a declaration that terrified the white men in this country who surrounded themselves with slaves.

Jefferson feared Haiti as the spark that might ignite race war in the South. The president defended his country by tracking Haitians who came to the United States, always believing that they were plotting insurrection. He warned Madison, on a bill calling for trade with Toussaint, to "expect therefore black crews, and supercargoes and missionaries thence into the southern states. . . If this combustion can be introduced among us under any veil whatever, we have to fear it." Republicans even accused Federalists of supporting Haiti's blacks. (Adams had sent warships to blockade the island and bombard Toussaint's enemy; but Federalist guns fought for Britain against its enemy and not for black revolutionaries.) Congress banned trade with Haiti in 1806 and withheld *de facto* and *de jure* recognition until 1862 when southern owners no longer sat in the House and Senate to block such things. The irony is that without Haiti's blacks and their struggle for independence the United States would not have doubled in size when it did. And slavery would not have spread as quickly or dug its roots as deeply.[32]

Whether the subject was Haiti's revolutionaries or the American South's chattel, demands of security and property always dominated. Jefferson intended to free his own slaves. He could scarcely call them slaves (preferring "servants" or even "family"), and hoped to transform them into tenants. Once he "cleared off" his debts he would "try some plan of making their situation happier, determined to content myself with a small portion of their labour." But financial considerations blocked manumission as did Jefferson's belief that "to abandon persons whose habits have been formed in slavery is like abandoning children." He was nonetheless wealthy enough to include "25 negroes little and big" in daughter Martha's dowry. Also master enough to work slave children in the nailery and small textile factory he ran in retirement.

For every dream of manumission blocked only by personal debts, it should be noted, the Monticello aesthete offered a thought that could have come from an accountant's pen. "I consider the labor of a breeding woman as no object, and that a child raised every 2. years is of more profit than the crop of the best laboring man," he wrote. "In this, as in all other cases, providence has made our interests and our duties coincide perfectly." He disliked slavery only in theory.[33]

Jefferson did not engage, in his father-in-law's manner, in the commercial slave trade. He sold slaves most often if they habitually stole or ran away. On occasion he would also take men, women, and children over the age of ten to market if he needed to raise capital. More charitably, he sometimes bought the husbands, wives, or children of his own slaves, declaring himself "always willing to indulge connections seriously formed by those people, when it can be done reasonably." Between 1784 and 1794 Jefferson sold or gave away 161 people. When he died thirty years later $100,000 in debt, his daughter auctioned off slaves with little thought to family ties ("connections seriously formed"). The sale eased the debt but not by much, and eventually the house had to go, too.[34]

Jefferson freed no slaves in his will either (unlike Washington), with detractors charging that he was loathe to free anyone besides the children born to the slave Sally Hemmings. Supposedly, these were Jefferson's children. John Adams, who never mentioned the allegation publicly and gave it no credence in private (calling it "a natural and almost inevitable consequence of the foul Contagion in the human Character, Negro Slavery"), took comfort nonetheless in realizing that it would remain "a blot on his [Jefferson's] Character." Those miscegenation and bastardy charges, first raised in 1802 by the scandalmonger and luckless federal office seeker James T. Callender, echoed in the anti-Jefferson press and dragged after his memory, as Adams predicted and historian Winthrop Jordan noted, "like a dead cat through the pages of formal and informal history."[35]

If Jefferson's words in the Declaration earned his memorial, his actions did little to honor that vision. Jefferson found no way to move against slavery in the first term and conceded as much to the Quaker George Logan while simultaneously promising not to give up the fight: "I have most carefully avoided every public act or manifestation on that subject. Should an occasion ever occur in which I can interpose with decisive effect, I shall certainly know and do my duty with promptitude and zeal."[36] In the second term he found one (uncontroversial) occasion to act. With only South Carolina permitting entry of slaves from outside the United States and with a growing slave population already here, he asked Congress in March 1807 to abolish the foreign slave trade. Little opposition arose. On the first day permitted by the Constitution, January 1, 1808, Congress rid the land of this blight, enacting a law, Jefferson said, to which "the morality, the reputation, and the best interests of our country have long been eager to proscribe."

Direct involvement never went beyond the suggestion that Congress move on the question. It never occurred to Jefferson for posterity's sake that this achievement ought to be among the things inscribed on his tombstone. It might be more accurate, on the broader subject of slavery in all its vices, to remember him as a chief executive who could dismiss an antislavery poem, *Avenia, or a Tragical Poem on the Oppression of the Human Species*, by Thomas Brannagan of Philadelphia, as "one of those little irritating measures." An endorsement, the president claimed, would "only lessen my powers of doing them [the slaves] good in the other great relations in which I stand to the public." Yet he sat rather than stood, and sat dead still. He moved only to tremble, and only then when he remembered that "God is just; that his justice cannot sleep forever."[37]

For his own generation Jefferson was especially pessimistic. "I have long since given up," he wrote in 1805, "the expectation of any early provision for the extinguishment of slavery among us." But things would be easier for future generations! "Interest is really going over to the side of morality. The value of the slave is everyday lessening; his burthen on his master dayly increasing. Interest is therefore preparing the disposition to be just; and this will be goaded from time to time by the insurrectionary spirit of the slaves. This is easily quelled in its first efforts; but from being local it will become general, and whenever it does it will rise more formidable after every defeat, until we shall be forced, after dreadful scenes and sufferings to release them in their own way, which without such sufferings we might model after our own convenience." Always the revolutionary and president for eight years of a nation born in revolution, he proposed that other generations of Americans fight a winnable battle later as opposed to an impossible battle now—completely unaware that the coming cotton culture, already evident in South Carolina if not in his native Virginia, would make it unimaginably harder for his descendants to root out slavery. He had it exactly backwards.[38]

Perhaps the most disturbing element of Jefferson's tacit support of slavery was that this brilliant and eloquent leader raised all the central questions and by his day's moral calculus or ours often had the right answers. Could the Revolution of 1776 be considered complete while blacks remained enslaved? No. "[Could] the liberties of a nation be thought secure when we have removed their only firm base, a conviction in the minds of the people that these liberties are of the gift of God? That they are not to be violated but with his wrath?" He knew they could not. Was slavery "the unremitting despotism" not only for what it took from the slave but for what it required of the master? Yes. Because slavery sucked freedom from everyone. From his first memory on this earth of a house slave carrying him on a pillow to the slave carpenter who made his coffin, Jefferson relied on slaves.[39] That he sometimes rose above circumstance, asked his questions, and answered right is less a comment on his greatness than the situation's obviousness. Its hopelessness, too, everyone with power agreed. It took no great man to recognize that slavery was morally wrong if politically and economically confounding.

These contradictions immobilized Jefferson in the presidency, leaving a legacy that is, in any century, both wonderful and appalling. In his own century the only consistency lay in a refusal to lead or join any moral crusade. "It shall have all my prayers," Jefferson wrote a young abolitionist who tried to budge him one last time in 1825, "and these are the only weapons of an old man." A year later he was dead.[40]

Madison, the fourth president (1809–1817) and fourth great man, agonized, and froze, deepening the rut in the manner of his predecessors. An owner who knew slavery put an "unfortunate stain" on self, family, state, and nation, he sold three of his farms and thereby risked financial ruin "to avoid the sale of Negroes."[41] When preparing to leave the Continental Congress he had trouble with a slave named Billey who had spent time among Philadelphia's free black community. "Too thoroughly tainted to be a fit companion for fellow slaves in Virginia," Madison told his father. "I do not expect to get near the worth of him; but cannot think of punishing him by transportation merely for coveting that liberty for which we have paid the price of so much blood, and have proclaimed so often to be right, and worthy the pursuit, of every human being."

Realizing that slavery would corrupt the nation's soul, Madison railed in *The Federalist No. 54* against the Constitution's three-fifths compromise. That compromise debased "by servitude below the equal level of free inhabitants, which regards the *slave* as divested of two fifths of the *man*." The Founders put a number on black people. A fraction. The northerners opposed it, and in their humanity so did the Virginians—Washington, Jefferson, Madison. Still, the number stayed.[42] Madison fought the good fight in *The Federalist*, lost, and accepted defeat like a gentleman. For the next twenty years he rarely had anything to say about matters of race, remaining silent even when General Andrew Jackson, himself an owner, commended the courage of the free blacks who fought at New Orleans. Jackson said he recruited those men for the War of 1812's great battle with "the sincerity of a Soldier." He acted more like Washington during the Revolutionary War. Negroes were a security problem, and Jackson brought them into the army to keep them from joining the British.[43]

Madison broke his silence in his second message to Congress by condemning violations of the prohibition against the foreign slave trade and calling for "further means of suppressing the evil." (It was permissible for the president or anyone else to call the slave trade an evil but not slavery itself.) Madison spoke out because the law in question was largely unenforceable and the source of some embarrassment. States' rights doctrine, read into the legislation, required that captured slave traders and their black cargoes be turned over to the states (most of which had little means or interest in handing out punishments to whites and liberty to blacks). Under another doctrine, freedom of the seas, Jefferson, then Madison, refused to permit British war ships to search American crews and cargoes. With Britain having the only navy capable of policing this commerce, the result was that the stars and stripes became a symbol of slavery in the Atlantic world. Slave runners of every nationality flew that flag.

So in December 1816, with his second term about to end, Madison again asked Congress to amend the law for more effective use against "unworthy citizens."[44] Congress acted nearly four years later by declaring participation in the slave trade an act of piracy punishable by death and funding a naval squadron to patrol the African coast. Even that law went largely unenforced until 1862, however, when Britain and the remaining United States finally came to terms on the matter of running down and boarding slave ships sailing the Atlantic under the American flag.

For the greater evil, slavery itself, Madison dreamed of emancipation and colonization either to the American continent's western expanse or Africa. Upon retiring to the privacy of his Montpelier estate in 1817 he worked on the scheme; bled over the details ("supposing the numbers of slaves to be 1,500,000, and their price to average 400 dollars . . ."); commiserated with Washington's confidante, Lafayette ("the Negro slavery is, as you justly complain, a sad blot on our free country"). In private life he kept at the numbers and kept searching for a plan to take out the stain. As president he made no effort. He did the right thing in speaking against the slave trade, but it required no courage and inspired none of the libertarian rhetoric for which he is so rightly remembered.[45]

Harriet Martineau, the English author, found Madison in retirement obsessed with slavery. His concern, however, seems strangely distant from his earlier recognition of slavery's injustice. Now he expressed his "deep feeling of the sufferings of ladies under the system, declaring that he pitied them even more than their negroes, and that the saddest slavery of all was that of conscientious Southern women. They cannot trust their slaves in the smallest of their own orders; and they know that their estates are surrounded by vicious free blacks, who induce thievery among the negroes and keep the minds of the owners in a state of perpetual suspicion, fear." After Madison died Daniel Webster bought the freedom of his body servant, Paul Jennings, for $120, which Jennings worked off at eight dollars a month as Webster's man. Webster acted out of charity for Dolly Madison who needed the money desperately. Jennings, now in the class of "vicious free blacks," brought vegetables and butter to Madison's penniless widow at Webster's direction. At his own, he gave her money from his pocket.[46]

Missouri erupted a year after Madison returned to Montpelier and threatened to destroy both the first southern strategy and perhaps the Union itself. Before 1820 eleven free states balanced eleven slave states. Now, with Missouri seeking admission as a slave state, the calm broke with New York Congressman James Tallmadge's proposed amendment (to a bill authorizing Missouri to frame a constitution) prohibiting the introduction of additional slaves and requiring the gradual emancipation of those already there. It passed in the House and died in the Senate. With neither side willing to budge, slavery rocked the political process for the first time since the Constitutional Convention—showing the bitterness of sectional rivalry and the bankruptcy of leadership committed to keeping the slave question dormant. Missouri, to put it bluntly, raised the specter of civil war.

James Monroe, another Virginia owner, had clear ideas about slavery and surrounding issues of morality and security. The nation's fifth president (1817–1825) favored emancipation and "asylum" (his preferred word for colonization). More so than most owners, Monroe knew firsthand the fear of slave revolt—having served as Virginia's governor in 1800 during Gabriel's insurrection. He mustered the militia, ordered a three-hundred-dollar reward for the capture of Gabriel Prosser and Jack Bowler, and eventually paid fifty dollars to Peter Smith, the black who convinced Bowler to surrender (explaining that the hundred-dollar reward was for whites only). While captured slaves were hanged, Monroe dreamed as never before of asylum for every last black. Seventeen years later, while president, he supported the formation of the American Colonization Society and sent a ship to the West Africa territory acquired in that society's name. In 1824 Liberia's inhabitants named their capital Monrovia in recognition of the president's efforts on behalf of their cause. "Unhappily," he said, "while this class of people exists among us we can never count with certainty on its tranquil submission."[47]

Monroe remained in the background while Missouri played out. He discussed the crisis with fellow owners William Crawford of Georgia and John C. Calhoun of South Carolina, and did little more than watch as Kentucky's Henry Clay, among others, negotiated the compromise that brought Missouri into the Union as a slave state and Maine as a free state. Monroe commended those he ignored once the peculiar balance had been restored. The plot to dismember the Union, he wrote Jefferson, owed its death to "the patriotic devotion of several members in the non slave-owning states, who preferred the sacrifice of themselves at home, to a violation of the obvious principles of the Constitution."[48]

From the comforts of Monticello, Jefferson dismissed the Missouri Compromise as "a mere party trick" performed by decaying Federalists. Privately, however, he shared Monroe's obsession with slavery's continuing threat to the nation's tranquility. Could the nation continue indefinitely half slave and half free? Jefferson did not think so. "This momentous question, like a fire bell in the night, awakened and filled me with terror," he wrote. "We have the wolf by the ears; and we can neither hold him, nor safely let him go. Justice is in one scale, and self-preservation in the other." The Union would ultimately break apart, Jefferson predicted. "All, I fear, do not see the speck on our horizon which is to burst on us as a tornado, sooner or later. The line of division lately marked out between different portions of our confederacy is such as will never, I fear, be obliterated."[49] Colonization represented the last best hope to avoid race war and save white lives. Whether to the West Indies, Latin America, or Africa, Jefferson never stopped thinking, like Madison and Monroe, of sending blacks "beyond the reach of mixture." A far-away place where the Negro could never shed "the blood of his master."[50]

John Adams, the other ex-president, was also moved more by a fear similar to Jefferson's than a desire for freedom and justice for all regardless of color. He hoped "the Missouri question . . . will follow the other Waves under the Ship and do no harm," but predicted the slave issue was more likely to "rend this mighty fabric in twain . . . [and] produce as many Nations in North America as there are in Europe." This did not mean that Adams counseled any immediate action on abolition's behalf. "Slavery in this Country," he wrote Jefferson, "I have seen hanging over it like a black cloud for half a Century. If I were as drunk with enthusiasm as Swedenborg or Westley, I might probably say I had seen Armies of Negroes marching and countermarching in the air, shining in Armour. I have been so terrified with this Phenomenon that I constantly said in former times to the Southern Gentlemen, I cannot comprehend this object; I must leave it to you. I will vote for forcing no measure against your judgements. What we are to see, *God* knows, and I leave it to him, and his agents in posterity."[51]

This was a telling illusion. Utterly frozen during his presidency, Adams now thought it might be best, at some unspecified day, for Congress to take "every constitutional Measure" to prevent the institution's spread. Slavery on the loose would move like "gangrene," bar free labor's "middling classes" from the territories, and "stamp our National Character and lay a foundation for Calamities, if not disunion." Negro freedom might produce "severer Calamities," Adams reasoned, listing, in repetition of an earlier theme, "despair, or the necessity of robbery, plunder, and massacre to preserve their lives." Yet there was no choice. "Humanity" demanded abolition "more, it would seem, for the welfare of society than out of justice for the Negro."

John Adams's solution (emancipation and "eventual total extirpation") required "every measure of prudence" and "all possible humanity . . . consistent with public safety." The only alternative was race war. "[An] Insurrection of the Blacks" and a predictable counter-attack by a white majority "exasperated to Madness" and "wicked enough to exterminate the Negroes." Adams had finally found his voice and place to stand in the midst of the Missouri crisis. Unfortunately his focus was primarily on domestic security and his words carried no further than the eyes of Jefferson and those others who received his ventings in the post.[52]

The next Adams, John Quincy, came to the presidency (1825–1829) believing that "slavery in a moral sense is an evil, but as connected with commerce it has its uses."[53] Business rated higher than morality so he left slavery alone. (He would reject the first southern strategy and earn a place in abolitionist lore only in the decade after turning his office over to the hated Andrew Jackson.) Adams cared little whether the West was settled by free soilers or slavers, only that it be settled. To impede western progress was "to condemn vast regions of territory to perpetual barrenness and solitude that a few hundred savages might find wild beasts to hunt upon it." Adams and the Jacksonians found common ground here. They all dreamed of an alliance made up of one or more of the basic parts (artisan, farmer, slaveowner) marching West, expropriating Indian land and exterminating the Indians themselves. "Westward the star of empire takes its way," Adams said. "In the whiteness of innocence."[54]

Andrew Jackson, the second general and fifth owner of the first seven chief executives, was the first (and arguably the only chief executive in American history) not to consider slavery a moral evil. He traded in men, became master of the Hermitage in Tennessee, counted eighty-three slaves on his "Black Polls" when plotting both a run for the highest office and the more sordid land deals that placed him among the southwest's biggest slave holders. At best the movement to which he gave his name was casual in its acceptance of slavery. Ownership, his biographer noted, "was as American to these Jacksonians as capitalism, nationalism, or democracy." At worst the movement sought to structure a political party with no greater goal than protecting slavery forever.[55]

Jackson's presidency (1829–1837) was a contradictory one, and contradictions were apparent even on racial matters. Jackson the slave trader could nonetheless condemn this "barbarous traffic" when such a condemnation proved useful in acquiring land from the Spanish in Florida. He called the Missouri Compromise "the entering wedge to separate the union . . . It is a question of political ascendancy, and power, and the Eastern interests" planned to "excite those who is [*sic*] the subject of discussion to insurrection and massacre."[56] Ten years later, in 1830, he attacked the other side ("nullifiers in the South") for endangering the Union in the name of states' rights. This was in reference to defiance of a federal tariff law in South Carolina, where politicians tended to blame all their state's problems, including such things as soil exhaustion, on the so-called tariff of abominations. Yet the man who threatened to invade South Carolina and hang Calhoun over that defiance sat out the most notable battle of his administration's last years (Texas annexation). He shied away because the slave issue, unmasked and foremost in debate, might upset the Union's delicate balance.[57]

"I could not bear the idea of inhumanity to my poor negroes," Jackson said of his own human property. Yet he advertised in the press for the return of runaway slaves (with a greater reward for those captured *and* whipped), and concocted stories if discipline crippled or killed a slave. Of a beaten woman, he wrote to a partner in one such cover-up: "You may say to Dr. Hogg, that her lament was occasioned by a stroke from Betty [another slave], or jumping over a rope, in which her feet became entangled, and she fell." Such stories protected the president of the United States. If Jackson had no qualms of his own he knew many new voters in this common-man age would not understand this sort of blood on the hands of their great general—the hero of New Orleans.[58]

Once the tariff crisis passed Jackson predicted a "coalition between Calhoun, Clay, Poindexter, and the nullifiers in the South intended to blow up a storm on the subject of the slave question." This cabal would stop at "[no] act to destroy the union, and form a southern confederacy bounded north by the Potomac River."[59] Fearing that the Union faced a more immediate threat from abolitionist literature flooding the South, the president embraced the southern solution ("a most fearful surveillance of the postoffice"). He ordered Postmaster General Amos Kendall to deny the abolitionists the use of the mail and asked Congress for a federal law prohibiting circulation of antislavery propaganda. Only southern subscribers who demanded abolitionist literature ought to receive it, he noted, and the newspapers ought to publish the recipients' names. "[For] those in the South, who were patronizing these incendiary works," Jackson would deliver, along with the mail, "such disrepute with all the South, that they would be compelled to desist, or move from the country." Abolitionists, the president held, were "monsters" sent by moneyed masters to "stir up amongst the South the horrors of servile war." They intended to free the Negro and drive him North to drive down working-class wages.[60]

This was Jackson's counsel at a time when abolitionists were pariahs North and South and antiabolitionist mobs roamed the land, destroying printing presses, threatening lynching. One mob even murdered Elijah Lovejoy, editor of an abolitionist newspaper in Alton, Illinois. Slaveholders hated the abolitionists. So did northern businessmen who wanted stable trade with the South, nationalists who had no higher law than the Union, reactionary churchmen who feared their kingdoms would break on sectional lines, and those common people who held racist attitudes. Jackson threw his words into a tinderbox.

An unlikely champion, the former appeaser John Quincy Adams, led the abolitionist fight in Congress. Adams came to the House in 1830 and presented antislavery petitions that first year. He acted here only because his Massachusetts constituents asked him to do so. Initially, he thought no more of the abolitionists' work as a congressman than he had as president. It could only bring the country "to ill-will, to heartburning, to mutual hatred . . . without accomplishing anything else."[61] When petitions calling for abolition of slavery in the District of Columbia deluged Congress in 1836, however, Adams had to pick a side. Southerners again raised the stakes by pushing a gag rule through the House requiring the tabling of such petitions. (They were not printed, referred to committee, or debated.) While Jackson stood with the South, Adams stood with the abolitionists and eventually made even Negrophobes in the North see that slavery eroded everyone's civil liberties. He did so by demonstrating the price that the gag-rule advocates were demanding: To protect slavery every American had to surrender the right to petition their government, a right guaranteed in the Constitution's First Amendment.

Adams realized that his stance made him an abolitionist by default. But he never considered himself more than a half-baked one who came up short of "the true faith," and he never stopped criticizing those who had the true faith. He condemned the American Anti Slavery Society, for example, for "pouring oil into the summit of a smoking crater." Yet he carried the battle against the gag rule nearly alone until 1841 when an abolitionist bloc formed in the House. And he never lost sight of the issue: How slavery violated "the Constitution of the United States . . . the rules of the House, and the rights of my constituents." Slavery, he concluded long after winning the gag-rule fight, was sinking the Union into "a military monarchy" and turning the Constitution into "a menstruous rag" by slowly bleeding away the rights of white America in the peculiar institution's defense.[62]

Jackson, president when ex-president Adams began his fight, stood with the South all the way down. In the years that followed his second term, however, he did not intrude. Content to rely on a favorable majority in the House and a lieutenant (New York's Martin Van Buren) in the presidency, the general continued his contradictory ways in retirement. He had much to say about Texas, but always denied that slavery was the primary issue. He also began using the word "abolitionist" (as he did the word "Federalist)" as a pejorative, a weapon in the name-calling game to which politics occasionally descends. Even on his deathbed he remained contradictory—telling his slaves that he would meet them in heaven, telling them that "Christ hath no respect to color."[63]

The eighth president (1837–1841), second Jacksonian, and third non-owner, Van Buren, promised, with a professional politician's joy, to keep to the deeper southern-strategy rut cut by the hero of New Orleans. Though Van Buren once favored sending antislavery petitions in the House to committee (to give abolition "its quietus"), he came round like a good Jacksonian to support the gag rule. Abolition, he said, was no more than a movement "of evil disposed persons to disturb the harmony of our happy Union through its agency."[64] As the Jacksonians' candidate he took the pledge: "I must go into the presidential chair the inflexible and uncompromising opponent of any attempt on the part of Congress to abolish slavery in the District of Columbia, against the wishes of the slaveholding states; and also with a determination *equally* strong, to resist the slightest interference with the subject in the states."

Opponents said Van Buren "went South," and, minutes after taking the oath of office, the new president confirmed that view by taking the pledge again. The first chief executive to use the word "slavery" in an inaugural address, he promised to veto any bill concerning the institution that the South opposed and to mark every abolitionist as a threat to the Union. "So then it has come to this," a *Colored American* editor roared. "The President of the United States, clothed in the constitutional power of his high office, in the contest now waging between Liberty and Slavery, plants *himself* in the breach."[65]

Van Buren understood the role of the presidency. Abolitionists were to be harried, owners appeased. Slavery would not otherwise intrude. Even if Van Buren had been of another mind there were headaches enough on other fronts. Not that he was well prepared to accomplish much regarding the depression that brought down Jacksonian prosperity, attributing the economic troubles to "over banking" and "over trading"—an explanation no more sophisticated than his thoughts on abolitionist motives. He spoke out on the other side of the slave issue only when condemning the continuing violation of the Slave Trade Act. Perhaps the most serious problem encountered along the color line, beyond John Quincy Adams's tireless arguments, occurred during the reelection campaign. Van Buren's running mate Richard M. Johnson of Kentucky, another War of 1812 hero (who supposedly killed by his own hand the chief Tecumseh), had lived with a black mistress, claiming two daughters from that union. Rumors spread that Johnson had renewed the affair.[66]

Van Buren lost the election to William Henry Harrison, a man descended from Virginia aristocrats and now an Ohio country gentleman. (He passed in the campaign as a frontiersman complete with log cabin and cider barrel symbols.) Pneumonia took Harrison's life a month after the inauguration and brought a current Virginia aristocrat, Vice President John Tyler, to the presidency (1841–1845). A former Democrat who broke with Jackson over nullification and the bank war, Tyler made an odd Whig. He sided with the owners and opposed almost everything the Whig majority proposed. He addressed the slavery issue only in 1841 when nineteen slaves on the brig *Creole* bound for New Orleans from Virginia mutinied, made Nassau in the British Bahamas, and gained liberty for themselves and the 116 other slaves on board. In response Tyler sent Daniel Webster, then secretary of state and always the lawyer, to demand the return of all human property. "One can not conceive how any other counsel could justly be adopted," Webster pleaded. Known in Massachusetts as a barrister who could break even the devil's contract for a soul, Webster had less success with the British. They returned no free blacks to slavery.[67]

After the Whig disaster came Tennessee's James K. Polk, a Democrat, unabashed champion of territorial expansion, and yet another owner who spent his single term (1845–1849) hoping antislavery hot heads would simply go away. "The abolition agitation," he said, "is now as it has ever been, political in its object and design." The "opposing extremes" fared no better. Polk attributed the rising militants of the slavery-as-a-positive-good school "no other or higher motives" even as wife Sarah, in an economy move, replaced White House servants with slaves and rearranged the White House basement into slave quarters.[68]

Polk's first great triumph was the December 1845 admission of Texas as a slave state. This came merely by his election on an expansionist plank and the lame-duck Tyler's acquiescence. More territory came in Oregon through negotiations with the British, then more still through war with Mexico. Polk sided with those who hoped to carve this last bit into three or four new slave states. His blissful notion (that "slavery was one of the questions adjusted in the compromises of the Constitution . . . and can have no legitimate connection with the War with Mexico"), died suddenly on August 8, 1846, three months after hostilities commenced, when Pennsylvania Congressman David Wilmot offered a proviso to a two-million dollar appropriation to facilitate a Mexican land purchase. This prohibited slavery or involuntary servitude in any acquired/conquered territory. It passed twice in the House and died in the Senate.[69]

Polk called the Wilmot Proviso a "mischievous and foolish" product of "demagogues and ambitious politicians" bent on promoting "their own prospects."[70] But the support for Wilmot's proviso was of course much broader. Geography and imagination divided the United States into three main parts: The North with its diversified free-labor economy; the South, with its cotton- and slave-driven economy; and the West, which represented less a region than *the future*. Whichever system (free or slave labor) moved into the West would control the nation's destiny.

Zachary Taylor, the Whig's old-rough-and-ready professional soldier who followed Polk to the presidency (1849–1850), saw things a bit clearer. A Louisiana slaveholder, Taylor nonetheless deemed slavery in the Mexican cession (California and New Mexico) the most dangerous issue facing the nation. "The intemperate zeal of the fanatics of the North, and the intemperate zeal of a few politicians of the South," he said, prevented "calm discussion, neither in the pulpit or Congress, in the newspapers or in primary assemblies of the people." In practice he tried to avoid discussion altogether (much as he tried to hide from public view his fifteen White House slaves who labored in the family's private quarters upstairs and slept in eight attic rooms).[71] Taylor had merely advised the people of California and New Mexico to frame constitutions and apply for admission as states. California, bursting with gold-seeking "forty-niners," did so immediately. New Mexico was ready by May 1850. Both territorial constitutions prohibited slavery. With New Mexico and southern California below the Missouri Compromise line (which supposedly protected slavery forever), southerners attacked Taylor as an abolitionist tool and threatened secession. Civil war loomed once more.

Henry Clay quickly worked out a compromise that Congress debated for seven months until the last obstacle disappeared on July 9 with Taylor's sudden death after a monstrous bowl of cherries and chilled buttermilk.[72] Absent the threat of a presidential veto it still took another two months for the Compromise of 1850 to move through Congress piece by piece, and for the new president, Millard Fillmore (1850–1853), to sign each piece into law. For those who opposed slavery the Compromise in final form included California's entry into the Union as a free state and the interstate slave trade's banishment from the District of Columbia; and for those who supported slavery a tough new Fugitive Slave Law and the peculiar institution's protection in the remainder of the Mexican cession. No one was happy. The crisis of 1850 was simply the opening round in a decade of crises that jerked the nation ever closer to war, ending only with Lincoln's election and Beauregard's bombardment of Fort Sumter.[73]

Fillmore, a New York Whig and free-soil sympathizer, considered the Fugitive Slave Law repugnant but supported it anyway. The Constitution required the return of escaped slaves, and he would do his duty, ignoring the "vials of wrath" that the abolitionists would "draw down upon [my] head." There was no cabinet discussion. He simply gave the bill to Attorney General John J. Crittenden for an opinion then signed it into law. Privately he worried about race war based on his projections of black and white birth rates, and to avoid this horror dreamed of colonization. In the manner of Madison he worked out the details of a plan, in private, to send "100,000 per annum" back to Africa. Fortunately he never took a single step to implement this scheme.[74]

New Hampshire's Franklin Pierce followed Fillmore to the White House and provided even less leadership in an even more troublesome time (1853–1857). This Jacksonian had stood in the Senate with Calhoun on the slave question. Once in the White House he reached out to Mississippi's Jefferson Davis, a friend, ally, and confidante, and made him secretary of war. Pierce was a doughface's doughface (that is, a northern man with southern principles) who acted against the slave interest on only two occasions. The first came when he called the Fugitive Slave Act enforceable if inhumane and immoral. When horrified southerners objected to that significant qualification, Pierce claimed they had misrepresented his remarks. The second occasion came when he backed off his own administration's policy of acquiring Cuba by any means necessary. "By every law human and divine," the oddly named Ostend Manifesto declared, "we shall be justified in wresting it from Spain, if we possess the power." The boast delighted southerners, who saw the Caribbean as a natural place for their plantation system to expand; and enraged the abolitionists. Secretary of State William L. Marcy repudiated the Ostend Manifesto when the European powers also objected.[75]

Reverting to his proslavery form in Kansas, Pierce pressed Congress to pass Illinois Senator Stephen Douglas's Kansas-Nebraska Bill calling for popular sovereignty. This let-the-people-decide strategy, designed to remove from Congress the explosive issue of slavery in the territories, instead brought chaos to Congress and Kansas both. While Free-Soilers recruited some 1,200 settlers through Eli Thayer's Emigrant Aid Company, border ruffians from Missouri crossed over to supplement proslavery votes. Kansas ended up with rival governments, one favoring slavery and the other free soil; a visit from John Brown, with his tribe of sons and their sharpened broadswords; and guerrilla warfare between roaming border ruffians and Free-Soil settlers armed with "Beecher Bibles." These guns were named in honor of Henry Ward Beecher, the antislavery preacher who said only rifles could bring order to Kansas.

Things were scarcely better in Washington after Charles Sumner, the antislavery senator from Massachusetts, attacked the Pierce administration for its "Crime Against Kansas." Of the southerners insulted in this two-day speech, one, Andrew P. Butler, the old and infirm senator from South Carolina, had a young cousin, Congressman Preston Brooks, who steamed for a few days and then walked into the Senate with his cane to beat Sumner unconscious. Admirers sent "Bully" Brooks walking sticks in the post. Sumner took years to recover.[76]

President Pierce rooted for Butler, Brooks, and the owners in bleeding Kansas. In a special message to Congress on January 24, 1856, he condemned the territory's entire Free-Soil movement as good for "nothing but unmitigated evil, North and South." He refused to blink even when the territory's proslavery government announced a slave code that set the death penalty for anyone aiding a fugitive slave. Blaming the violence, in true conspiratorial style, on the Emigrant Aid Company (outside agitators), Pierce ignored the Missouri border ruffians. After he declared the Free-Soilers' constitution illegal (the so-called Topeka constitution), Missourians raided the free-state capital at Lawrence. Although it was not his intention, the president's statement, in part, at least, incited the attack.[77]

Popular sovereignty had failed miserably. So much so that when Pierce's successor, James Buchanan (1857–1861) of Pennsylvania, asked Congress to admit Kansas into the Union as a slave state, Stephen Douglas, progenitor of the let-the-people-decide strategy, stood against him. Douglas did so knowing full well that the Democratic party might break into northern and southern wings and that the nation might also break apart. He lost the battle in the Senate, but the House blocked admission of Kansas as a slave state. Douglas's stance all but assured his reelection to the Senate in the great campaign of 1858 against the ex-Whig and now Republican Abraham Lincoln; and also assured him that he would lose the presidency to Lincoln two years later.

The Republican party itself was born a month after Douglas introduced his Kansas-Nebraska Bill. Its presidential candidate in 1856, John C. Fremont, a soldier and explorer, ran on a platform calling for territorial exclusion. The new party proposed to leave slavery alone where it already existed but to stop the peculiar institution from spreading one more inch. This was a containment policy, a frank attempt to bottle up the thing until it expired under its own weight. The party platform also favored a stronger tariff, homestead laws, and federal funding for a Pacific railroad and other internal improvements. Legislative initiatives, in other words, that southerners, intent on their plantation system marching into the West, routinely blocked in Congress.[78]

Republican strategists made no effort to attract a single southern vote. They lost the presidency to Buchanan but could have won without one such vote if their candidate had carried Pennsylvania and either New Jersey, Illinois, or Indiana. (Freemont took every free state but five.) Because power in the United States had shifted irrevocably, northerners would soon be making decisions regarding slavery without even bothering to consult those who owned slaves. The irony is that under Buchanan the planter South had a stranglehold on the federal government. "The Slave power," Henry Adams would later write, "took the place of Stuart kings and Roman popes," driving "the whole Puritan community back on its Puritanism."[79] With a Georgian in Treasury and a Virginian running the War Department, the cabinet spoke for the South nearly with one voice. Even Secretary of State Lewis Cass of Michigan, the first prominent proponent of popular sovereignty, had opposed the Wilmot Proviso. On the Supreme Court, moreover, five of nine justices came from slaveholding states.

It was here, in the Court, with the *Dred Scott* case, that Buchanan tried to resolve the question of slavery in the territories. While still president-elect he conspired with three of those southern justices and one compliant northern justice to guarantee a favorable ruling. In his inaugural address he mentioned a momentous case pending before the Court, predicted that it would settle the matter, and counseled all Americans to accept the verdict, whatever it might be, as final. He told southern friends in private that they would be pleased with the decision. They were. Five justices concurred with Chief Justice Roger B. Taney of Maryland that Scott, a black man suing for his freedom, was part of a race ("beings of an inferior order") whose members had "no rights which any white man was bound to respect."

Because the Fifth Amendment denied Congress the right to deprive persons of their property without due process of law, Taney asserted that the Missouri Compromise prohibition against keeping slaves north of the 36 degree 30' line was unconstitutional. Owners could take their slaves into a free state as readily and with as much impunity as the shoes on their feet. This absolute prohibition against congressional regulation of slavery in the territories also questioned whether even territorial legislatures could exclude slavery. Southerners were delighted, northerners enraged. Rather than settle the question, as the dim, plotting Buchanan hoped, *Dred Scott* made civil war that much more likely.[80]

Buchanan and the southern Democrats counted on the Supreme Court, got what they wanted, but failed anyway. They had no other prospects. To prop up declining representation they could only think to revive the Ostend Manifesto. To counter the abolitionists they could only demand more systematic enforcement of the Fugitive Slave Law. The Republicans, already with a numerical majority, benefited from the Democratic party's split into a northern wing and a southern wing. (In true Whig spirit the Democrats also split into a border-state wing.) South Carolina left the Union upon Lincoln's election, followed by Mississippi, Florida, Alabama, Georgia, Louisiana, and Texas. The lame-duck Buchanan counseled patience and inaction. While denying any state the right to secede he claimed that no president had the right to use force to prevent secession. He fired no states' righter from his cabinet. Only when they resigned did he replace them with Union men.

No chief executive from Washington forward understood the office's southern-strategy duties better than Buchanan or otherwise worked harder to keep the slave issue dormant. Unfortunately no president had less luck. No president did so much, if in unintentional design, to make the politics of race explode. Yet another president who knew slavery was wrong (admitting as much in his memoir though he was never much troubled by moral questions), he did not understand his own country. He did not understand that his own people back in Pennsylvania were willing to pick up guns over this issue. In the end he convinced the South that the North did not have the stomach to fight, and he convinced Ulysses Simpson Grant and a good many other northerners that they had voted for the wrong man.[81]

Lincoln, the sixteenth president (1861–1865), was the first to act his conscience on matters of race. The signer of the Emancipation Proclamation was also the first chief executive to grant an official audience with free blacks and to admit men and women of color to White House social functions. A singular man who became singularly great in the presidency, he grew in the office from the day Beauregard's guns rained down on Fort Sumter. A child at Elizabeth Hyde Botume's school for freedmen, when asked after the war "Who is Jesus Christ?," answered, "Him's Massa Linkum." Black preachers called him "our 'dored Redeemer an' Savior an' Frien'! Amen!" He was a messiah figure in slave narratives—half Moses, half Yankee, a man next to the Lord.[82]

The South left the Union and Lincoln stepped forward, willing to take the nation to war and unwilling to retreat on the expansion of slavery. A year into what remains the most bloody conflict in American history, he made the first of a series of decisions that ultimately led him to abandon containment in favor of a more direct approach. He would kill slavery, and he would tell the country of that final decision to make over this war of rebellion into a war against slavery. In the process he made over a nation and a Constitution that protected slavery into a nation where Jefferson's words in the Declaration of Independence were primary. At Gettysburg he defined "a new nation conceived in Liberty, and dedicated to the proposition that all men are created equal." He used patronage and army bayonets to force compliance in occupied territory, advocated the abolition amendment to the Constitution, took steps to insure the freedmen would have the right to vote. If circumstance made Lincoln great, circumstance had much to work with.[83]

To achieve what he did, Lincoln had to overcome his own caution. "If slavery is not wrong, nothing is wrong," he said. Yet he made the distinction between "is" and "ought to be" so often that he developed a case of "the slows" (something he would complain about in General George B. McClellan). A pragmatist, not an abolitionist, Lincoln's opposition to slavery was not always evident. In the 1830s he signed a resolution stating that "the promulgation of abolition doctrines tends rather to increase than to abate its evils." In the 1850s he favored restoration of the Missouri Compromise and opposed the effort to repeal the Fugitive Slave Law. His basic belief (that slavery was inevitably doomed) made him patient enough to sit and wait until the abomination died a natural death.

"A universal feeling, whether well or ill-founded, can not be safely disregarded," Lincoln explained repeatedly when a candidate for the Senate in 1858 and the presidency in 1860, adding, for emphasis: "I am not, nor have ever been in favor of bringing about in any way the social and political equality of the white and black race—that I am not nor ever have been in favor of making voters or jurors of negroes, nor of qualifying them to hold office, nor to intermarry with white people." He also felt compelled, like Jefferson, to comment on "the physical differences" which "will forever forbid the two races living together on terms of social and political equality. And inasmuch as they cannot so live, while they do remain together there must be the position of superior and inferior, and I as much as any man am in favor of having the superior position assigned to the white race." He evoked memories of Van Buren, too, by offering the South promises ("I do not now, nor ever did, stand in favor of the unconditional repeal of the fugitive slave law . . . I do not now, nor ever did, stand pledged against the admission of any more slave states into the Union . . . I do not stand pledged to the prohibition of the slave trade between the states," etc.) He spoke as a candidate here, in his great debates with Stephen Douglas, completely aware of the risks and uses to which racism could be put in politics.[84]

Lincoln promised while president-elect to enforce the Fugitive Slave Law and during the war's first years demonstrated an ambivalence on emancipation profound enough to incite abolitionist carping. Frederick Douglass, runaway slave and movement giant, attacked Lincoln's "slave-hunting, slave-catching and slave-killing pledges." Wendell Phillips called him "the slave-hound of Illinois."[85]

The president nonetheless opposed slavery and he did so for reasons stretching to the peculiar institution's adverse impact on American foreign policy. ("[It] deprives our republican example of its just influence in the world," he said. "Enables the enemies of free institutions to taunt us as hypocrites.")[86] He stood foremost against slavery, however, because it threatened white labor. Because it interfered with "the right to rise." Lincoln blurred the distinction between owners and workers, emphasized social mobility, saw economic success as the standard upon which all men ought to be judged, believed that social class was not fixed. He held that hard work could make today's wage earner tomorrow's capitalist, that everyone had a right to own a farm or business, that nothing ought to stand in the way. The moral consensus that allowed the North to mobilize in modern warfare came from Lincoln's faith that "the man who labored for another last year, this year labors for himself, and next year he will hire others to labor for him."[87]

Slavery shaped and threatened the Republican's thoroughly middle-class ideology. Lincoln, "the child of labor," said that "advancement, improvement in condition—is the order of things in a society of equals," a society in which there can be no class who "are always to remain laborers." The South equated all labor, even paid white labor, too closely with slavery, claiming northern wage earners were "fatally fixed in [their] condition for life." If the South had its way in the West, moreover, its claim might prove true.[88] The West was nothing less than the Republican solution to the problem of poverty, the rock of Republican faith in social mobility. Lincoln favored homestead legislation with tracts small enough (160 acres) and cheap enough to be within the common peoples' grasp and thus aid them in achieving economic independence. Economic independence itself was tied directly to land ownership, and only one part of the nation had enough surplus land to keep the dream of independence alive. Western land, in other words, assured social mobility in the North. Only slavery, which degraded all labor, and the slave power, which sought the prize for itself and its plantations, barred the door.

Republican ideology also had imperial and racial elements because it rested on the nineteenth century's basic national themes of democracy, economic growth, and westward expansion, all of which were tied up in race. An increasingly racial definition of citizenship emerged on the heels of northern state abolition of indentured servitude and slavery and then nationwide abolition of the property caveat on the (male) suffrage. Every state except Maine that joined the Union after 1800 restricted the vote to white males. Economically, the nation entered the century on the backs of the slaves who produced tobacco and then rode the slaves who produced cotton. These commodities gave the North the where-withal to industrialize when and in the manner in which it did; and gave the North's armies, whether of soldiers or farmers, the wherewithal to move ever further West. By 1860 the Republican party dream for the West was in some ways an honorable one and in other ways a dishonorable dispossession and brutal conquest of Indians and Mexicans.

Many Republicans (Lincoln among them at times) wanted to keep all blacks, whether slave or free, out of the West.[89] "Who believes that the Whites and Blacks can ever amalgamate?," Walt Whitman asked in 1856 when commenting on the new state constitution in Oregon that excluded Negroes. "Nature has set an impassable seal against it. Besides, is not America for the Whites? And is it not better so?" For poets and politicians alike it came down to a question of who would do the nation's work. The South proposed black slaves, the North free white labor. Only a few Republicans spoke of the dignity of all free labor (black or white), and Lincoln was rarely among them because he suspected what "the great mass of white people" thought about blacks and the risks inherent in any politician's attempt to challenge that prejudice.

One solution to the race problem involved colonization. If that scheme was immoral and impractical (and there is evidence that he thought it was), Lincoln could see utility nonetheless and so clung to the idea until his death. Colonization if implemented might promote racial harmony by removing the source of irritation (blacks). Even if colonization remained a mere idea it might nonetheless preclude political opponents from smearing Republicans. Advocacy would show that the party was a white man's party and not a black man's party. Lincoln saw colonization as an issue with no down side, in other words. "It will take with the people," as one Ohio Republican told Senator Benjamin F. Wade. "If we are to have no more slave states what the devil are we to do with the surplus niggers? Your plan will help us out on this point. But practically I have no faith in it. You could not raise twenty five cents from a Yankee to transport a Nigger to South America."[90]

Lincoln spoke of sending blacks "to Liberia—to their own native land." (Such comments prompted the anti-administration press to suggest that Lincoln himself go there or some other more "congenial" place like Haiti.) The president, determined as ever to link colonization with Republican free-labor doctrine, advised Congress that "emancipation, even without deportation, would probably enhance the wages of white labor. . . . With deportation, even to a limited extent, enhanced wages to white labor is mathematically certain." More ambitious Republicans thought blacks could not only be removed to good political effect at home but put to use abroad as agents of empire. (That is, the United States would no doubt acquire colonies in the future and might send freed slaves to those colonies for the purpose of doing whatever manual labor was required.) All colonization schemes, whether those of Lincoln or anyone else, remained what they had always been. Racist, opportunistic, absurd, unworkable fantasies.[91]

Lincoln plotted emancipation simultaneously. The Confiscation Act of 1861 freed captured slaves who had been used by their owners to support the Confederacy's war effort, and the second Confiscation Act of 1862 declared all slaves of rebellious masters to be free. In practice, however, these measures meant little as the United States lacked military control and therefore jurisdiction. Lincoln finally decided, with the war going badly, to reverse his original strategy of leaving slavery alone. (He had hoped to hold the border states for the Union and perhaps crack the confederacy by appealing to slave holders who opposed secession.) Once the decision for emancipation had been made only the timing of implementation remained in question. After McClellan's defeat in the Peninsular Campaign, Secretary of State William Seward advised the president to wait for a victory before making the announcement. Lincoln agreed. The act ought not appear a desperate one.

Lincoln's reasons for freeing the slaves involved a mix of public opinion, humanitarianism, and especially military necessity. Emancipation would solve problems. It would clarify the status of fugitive slaves, boost troop strength, remove forever the possibility of British recognition of the enemy, destroy the Confederacy's workforce, kill the cancer that caused the war in the first place, and square the nation with its own ideals. This is what the abolitionists had advised all along. "Massa Linkum he great man, and I'se poor nigger," underground railroad hero Harriet Tubman said. "But dis nigger can tell Massa Linkum how to save de money and de young men. He do it by setting de niggers free. . . . De snake he spring up and bite you agin, and so he keep dwine, till you kill him. Dat's what Massa Linkum orta know."[92]

Lincoln understood. Still, he believed the races could not coexist peacefully. Thus he clung to colonization, explaining the hard facts to Frederick Douglass and a committee of free blacks. The president first harangued the group, in effect blamed the black presence for the war. He then tried to convince Douglass and the others to go among their people and recruit for the coal mines of Central America. When Lincoln looked into the future he saw perpetual racial conflict. He saw no hope or place for black Americans even while acknowledging that "your race [suffer] . . . the greatest wrong inflicted on any people." Sinking as low (or lower) as he had on that day spent proving to the people of Illinois that he was as white as Stephen Douglas, he said: "You are cut off from many of the advantages which the other race enjoy. The aspiration of men is to enjoy equality with the best when free, but on this broad continent, not a single man of your race is made the equal of a single man of ours. Go where you are treated the best, and the ban is still upon you." Underneath "the tone of frankness and benevolence" Frederick Douglass found no "genuine spark of humanity" or "sincere wish to improve the condition of the oppressed." Lincoln had only "the desire to get rid of them," a desire consistent with the "canting hypocrisy" of "a genuine representative of American prejudice and Negro hatred." A man with his own "pride of race blood."[93]

The president's decision to free the slaves nearly stood Frederick Douglass's view on its head. (Douglass could not forget that the president advocated colonization.)[94] On September 22, 1862, after a narrow victory (of sorts) at Antietam, Lincoln issued the Emancipation Proclamation. Slaves in all Confederate states would be forever free after January 1, 1863. Of course this stroke of a presidential pen freed only those slaves who had made their way to Union lines. Congress had directed northern officers in March 1862 not to return runaways, and in the six-month period from that act to the Emancipation Proclamation increasing numbers of slaves had come over. While freeing only those slaves who could help the war effort as laborers or soldiers, Lincoln nonetheless kept the nation fixed on the higher morality. He went to Gettysburg two months after signing the Emancipation Proclamation and made Jefferson's words into the nation's new creed.

Unsure of the Emancipation Proclamation's constitutionality, Lincoln kept coming back to the document's utility. Before colonizing the blacks he would enlist them. "The bare sight of fifty thousand armed, and drilled black soldiers on the banks of the Mississippi," he wrote Andrew Johnson, then military governor of Tennessee, "would end the rebellion at once. And who doubts that we can present that sight, if we but take hold in earnest?" Black soldiers would join the Union war effort by the thousands, and white enlistments would also rise with the nobler cause.[95]

Draft riots in New York and the tendentious 1864 elections proved that deep divisions remained. Democrats ignored Republican advocacy of colonization and instead charged that their rivals favored absolute racial equality. Broadsides targeting "Abraham Africanus The First" were common; and the *New York World*, backing the canned general and now Democratic party nominee, McClellan, against Lincoln, came out with an anonymous pamphlet entitled *Miscegenation: The Theory of the Blending of the Races.* The supposed Republican authors of this hoax, besides coining the word, proposed "miscegenation" as a solution to the race problem. A solution that would benefit the Irish especially, it was said.

If few believed this crude fare represented a legitimate Republican program, charges of race mixing remained a campaign staple. Democratic editors called the nation's most important document "the Miscegenation Proclamation" while editorial cartoons depicted black men kissing white women and dancing at "the Miscegenation Ball." A few editors asked if Lincoln was a product of a mixed marriage. Fortunately the war on slavery overrode race-baiting. Lincoln even joked about it, predicting that miscegenation would produce good Union men. The people put Lincoln back in the White House and a block of Radical Republicans in the House and Senate who were more committed to black rights than the emancipator himself.[96]

Those Radicals had no use for Lincoln's Reconstruction plans (so far as those plans were known). The president apparently intended to use patronage to build up the Republican party in the South with an appeal based on class and race in that order. This appeal would aim for the mass of southern whites who had never owned slaves while ignoring planters *and* freedmen. Lincoln's Reconstruction dream was arguably the first populist hint of the southern strategy that remains with us today. Even as he destroyed slavery, the emancipator plotted his party's growth in the white South and pocket vetoed the Radicals' Wade-Davis Bill. (He considered that proposed legislation vindictive, too insensitive to the needs and fears of those southerners he hoped to recruit into the Republican party.) This president had the twin high hopes of sending the freedmen back to Africa and building a decent white man's party "below the line," and those hopes held fast nearly to the day Booth made his shot and his leap. Only in his last speech on April 11, 1865, when discussing Reconstruction in Louisiana, did Lincoln publicly support Negro suffrage if only for "the very intelligent" and "those who serve our cause as soldiers."[97]

It would be difficult to exaggerate Abraham Lincoln's legacy. Yet that legacy never quite escaped his advocacy of colonization to spare future generations racial agony by geographically separating blacks and whites. While colonization collapsed under its own weight, a bargain-basement version would emerge in the postwar decades. Lincoln's advocacy of separation was such that a hundred years later, in the time of Martin Luther King, Jr., and the great southern war on Jim Crow, integrationists and segregationists alike claimed the great man, perhaps the greatest of our presidents, for their side.[98]

If the racist whirlwind of his own day repeatedly knocked him off course, Lincoln always righted himself and pressed forward on the front that counted most: The freeing of the slaves. That one grand thing outweighed what he wanted to do on colonization and Reconstruction (if only because he never got the chance to act on those matters). This chief executive cut a new rut into the nation's imagination. By the time the assassin killed "Massa Sam," the president of the United States and the government of the United States were already one in the minds of many freedmen.

When Lincoln lived those freedmen saw this as cause for joy. With the last Jacksonian now in the White House (1865–1869), it was cause for despair. Incredibly, Andrew Johnson saw himself as the freedmen's best hope. He once promised Nashville's black residents, "Humble and unworthy as I am, if no other better shall be found, I will be your Moses, and lead you through the Red Sea of War and Bondage to a fairer future of Liberty and Peace." "For the colored race," he claimed on another occasion, "my means, my time, my all has been periled." Unfortunately this Moses acted like Pharaoh, advocating white supremacy, pardons for ex-Confederate leaders, restoration of political and economic power to the planter class, denial of all civil rights for blacks.[99] He fired Freedmen's Bureau agents who did their job with any degree of enthusiasm and had soldiers take land from freedmen and give that land back to the master class. He called the Radicals in Congress traitors and vetoed their bills, and the Radicals impeached and tried him for it (finding an excuse in an alleged violation of the Tenure of Office Act). Moses remained in office when the Senate fell one vote short of the two-thirds majority required to convict.

Johnson was a self-made man in the extreme.[100] Born to illiterate parents in North Carolina, he was apprenticed at age ten to a tailor (his father already dead seven years). He ran away at fifteen and settled in Tennessee where he opened a tailor shop, taught himself to read with his wife's help, made money, bought a few slaves, became alderman, mayor, state legislator, governor, United States congressman, senator. Those charitable comments to Nashville's blacks aside, Johnson was better known as a Negrophobe. Blacks were best prepared for "drudgery and hardship." Abolitionists were determined to "place every splay-footed, bandy-shanked, hump-backed, thick-lipped, flat-nosed, woolly-headed, ebon-colored negro in the country upon an equality with the poor white man." He became a hero in the North (being the only senator from the eleven Confederate states who stayed at his post), and Lincoln showered rewards (naming him Tennessee's military governor and exempting the state's slaves from the Emancipation Proclamation). Recognizing slavery was everywhere doomed regardless, Johnson came out in August 1863 for emancipation. Lincoln put him on the ticket a year later.

Johnson fought the Radicals because he was an absolute white supremacist. "This is a country for white men," he said, "and by God, as long as I am President, it shall be a government for white men." His own private secretary, William G. Moore, who was no less white in most matters, worried about the president's "morbid distress and feeling against negroes." When meeting with a group of blacks headed by Frederick Douglass, Johnson said the freedmen's fate ("this thing") would be decided by "the [white] people of the states . . . for themselves." He would merely observe this process because he did "not want to be engaged in a work that will commence a war of races." After the delegation left Johnson said "those damned sons of bitches thought they had me in a trap. I know that damned Douglass; he's just like any nigger, and he would sooner cut a white man's throat than not."[101]

Johnson stood above all else against those "who are wild upon Negro franchise." This obsession first rose in the 1850s when he suddenly realized that the Constitution's three-fifths clause no longer worked to the South's advantage. "Do not you get representation for all your negroes—all your slaves without masters?," he asked northern senators in a speech on Harper's Ferry. "We have sixteen Representatives on the floor less than we should have if all our negroes were free men of color. We can understand that. . . . Where, then, is this great hardship to you; where is the wrong in the Constitution to you?" The senator from Tennessee not only wanted to count "five-fifths" but to insure that all "free negroes" North and South were "shorn of every franchise that constitutes a freeman."[102]

So President Johnson proposed that Mississippi adopt literacy tests to keep black suffrage down and vetoed a voting rights bill for the District of Columbia. "It is within their power, in one year," he warned (with one-third of Washington's population already black), "to come into the District in such numbers as to have the supreme control of the white race, and to govern by their own officers."[103] Here and elsewhere Johnson's voice was unique only in degree. Of all the chief executives who came before and all who followed he was the most unabashedly and prolifically racist. It was bad enough that this mean-spirited, barely literate monomaniac rose so high. Worse to realize that before long the nation would scarcely note the existence of the thing that Lincoln's successor wanted most: Black disenfranchisement in the former confederacy.

Ulysses S. Grant, the next president (1869–1877) and in a limited way the last owner (having worked slaves briefly and unsuccessfully on his farm), pushed Reconstruction forward cautiously. The Democrats called Grant a black Republican, an unrepentant abolitionist, and a nigger lover in the 1868 campaign because he adopted a strategy of harmonious silence on the divisive issue of black enfranchisement in the North while seeking black votes in the South. He would have won a majority in the electoral college anyway but the southern black vote guaranteed him a popular victory. When a Negro delegation from Nashville called before the inauguration to ask his support for the Fifteenth Amendment (guaranteeing United States citizens the right to vote regardless of "race, color, or previous condition of servitude"), he listened politely and made no commitment.[104]

Grant, the soldier, had no doubt that the war would end slavery. One result of the effort to send "the secession army howling," he told wife Julia, would be that "negroes will depreciate so rapidly in value that no body will want to own them and their masters will be the loudest in their declamations . . . The nigger will never disturb this country again." He had one worry (the possibility of "negro revolts" as his soldiers marched forward and Robert E. Lee's rebels fled), yet had "no doubt but a Northern army would hasten South to suppress anything of the kind." When President Johnson sent him on a southern fact-finding tour after the war he reported to the cabinet that blacks should have no role in Reconstruction. The task belonged to "the thinking people of the South," he said, an observation that encouraged Johnson in his pitiless work.[105]

Looking to annex Santo Domingo as a haven for blacks, Grant dreamed of colonization. He sent a commission to the island with Frederick Douglass as its secretary after his annexation treaty died in the Senate, then failed to invite Douglass to the White House dinner for the commissioners on their return. Grant also tolerated his family's white supremacist values. "There were people who believed in the 'divinity' of human slavery," he once complained, and his wife was probably among them. Julia Dent Grant grew up with slaves around her, apologized for slavery even in the White House, and mourned the passing of the peculiar institution's "comforts." When son Fred, a West Point cadet, joined in the racist verbal assaults on the black cadet James Smith, Grant made no attempt to discipline the officers who ran the academy with the weapon he had at his disposal—the promotions list (an awesome club in that career-climbing world). The son said "no damned nigger will ever graduate from West Point." The father's silence made sure that this would be true for at least a little while longer.[106]

From the day General Robert E. Lee surrendered at Appomattox Court House to the middle of his second term as president, Grant helped construct every part of the Reconstruction machine—the Thirteenth, Fourteenth, and Fifteenth Amendments to the Constitution, the civil rights and Ku Klux Klan-control legislation of 1866, 1870, 1871, and 1875, and the creation of the Justice Department. But the determination "Captain Sam Grant" had demonstrated before Lee surrendered did not follow him to the White House. If the South refused to cooperate with the Radical Republican plan for Reconstruction and the North soon proved more interested in the misadventures and corruptions of the administration itself, Grant lacked the will to enforce the things added in the name of equality to the Constitution and federal statutes. In 1871 he sent the army after the Ku Klux Klan in South Carolina. By 1876, more fearful of race war, he gave white supremacy free reign. Where freedmen gained even a semblance of physical safety it was at the expense of their economic and political rights.

The president allowed the revolution to end—what W. E. B. Du Bois called "the battle of all the oppressed and despised humanity of every race and color, against the massed hirelings of Religion, Science, Education, Law, and brute force." Whether he could have reversed this course and finished the business of Reconstruction is doubtful. The point is that he would not try. On a field of battle this human bulldog would not surrender. On matters of race he would not fight. For the soldier frozen by the idea of race war this was the price of peace. Grant again spoke of Santo Domingo in his last message to Congress, looking as ever for "a congenial home" for the slaves he freed.[107]

When Reconstruction ended with the Compromise of 1877 that brought Ohio Republican Rutherford B. Hayes to the presidency (1877–1881), Du Bois said "the slave went free; stood a brief moment in the sun; then moved back again toward slavery."[108] Reconciliation ruled. Reconciliation between conservative northern Republicans and southern Democrats. This states' rights approach, another early inkling of the GOP's modern southern strategy, promised to leave the race problem in each of the former Confederate states to the white majority. It was Andrew Johnson's policy without the vulgarity, transparent stupidity, and Democratic affiliation. "The constitutional rights of the negro shall be as safe in the hands of one party as it is in the other," another Ohio Republican, James A. Garfield, wrote Hayes, while Hayes waited to see if the deal to make him president would be struck. "And that thus in the south as in the north men may seek their party associates on the great commercial and industrial questions rather than on questions of race and color." In Grant's day the press and the politicians called this "the let alone policy," and even before the election Hayes said it "seems now to be the true course."[109]

The let alone policy did not fit the new president's personal values. Hayes had defended fugitive slaves as a Cincinnati lawyer and could make a claim that he was an abolitionist. By the last of Grant's years the word "abolitionist" was of course a political pejorative once more with so many now agreed that the slaves were freed prematurely—fit as they were for nothing but vile corruptions and defilements of the South's politics and belles. Never willing to go that far, Hayes had no trouble identifying the former master class as the real monsters. The day after the election, when he thought he had lost the presidency, he wrote a friend: "I don't care for myself; and the party, yes, and the country, too, can stand it; but I do care for the poor colored men of the South . . . the colored man's fate will be worse than when he was in slavery."[110]

President Hayes occasionally acted on this concern. He appointed Frederick Douglass marshal of the District of Columbia and for the next four years spoke out often against "an oligarchy of race" in the South and the continued violation of the freedman's constitutional rights. After leaving the White House he sat as a trustee of the Slater Fund, established by the Norwich, Connecticut, textile industrialist John F. Slater to aid "the emancipated population of the Southern states and their posterity, by conferring on them the blessings of Christian education."[111]

Hayes reconciled his actions and inactions with his own values by keeping Reconstruction's rhetoric and symbolism while abandoning the intent. Douglass's appointment, for example, was part of a strategy to conceal the details of the let-alone policy. Douglass suspected as much even as he took the job and (with the Republican message of social mobility taken to heart) moved into a twenty-one room house just outside the District of Columbia.[112] Hayes told Douglass that he would not sacrifice black rights for white southern support and otherwise promised to uphold the Thirteenth, Fourteenth, and Fifteenth Amendments. From time to time he urged Congress to take any action necessary to support the rights guaranteed in those amendments. But such promises were hollow. Hayes had consciously abandoned "the poor colored people of the South" to the "honorable and influential Southern whites."

The president stood still out of no laissez-faire principle. If there would be no enforcement of Reconstruction laws and doctrines, there would be enforcement on another front. Three months after Reconstruction collapsed Hayes intervened in the Great Strike of 1877, a bloody explosion of class warfare, by sending troops into four states to protect the rights of property. Capital needed the state in this age of social Darwinism. The money men and industrialists who ran the emerging trusts and corporations prescribed rugged individualism for workers, women, Indians, farmers, Negroes. Everyone, it would seem, but themselves.[113]

James Garfield (1881), following Hayes, promised to be more forceful in protecting black rights. "We have seen white men betray the flag and fight to kill the Union," he said, "but in all that long, dreary war, we never saw a traitor in black skin." He had acted on that view while in Congress, often standing with Thaddeus Stevens and other Radicals. During the 1880 campaign he told black audiences that they should have no illusions. Slavery was killed only "because it was dangerous to the peace and prosperity of the white race and to the stability of the Republic." He also told black voters not to turn the other cheek: "Permit no man to praise you because you are black, nor wrong you because you are black." In his inaugural address he warned white supremacists in the South that there was no middle ground between slavery and equal citizenship. The nation would permit no "permanently disfranchised peasantry." Implications were clear. The new policy of Grant's last years and Hayes's four would be reversed.[114] In private, however, Garfield quoted Coleridge:

> Habitual evils change not on a sudden,
> But many days will pass and many sorrows.

"Time is the only cure for the Southern difficulties," he said two months before taking up (or seeming to take up) the black cause at his inauguration. "In what shape it will come, if it comes at all, is not clear."[115]

Things became clearer after the inauguration. In the new policy's name Garfield revoked Douglass's appointment as marshal of the District of Columbia, naming him in the process to a lesser position (recorder of deeds). He told a delegation of South Carolina blacks headed by Robert Brown Elliott, former congressman and graduate of Britain's Eton College, that they ought to go home and study Webster's speller. Of African Americans in general he admitted that he "never could get in love with [the] creatures," that Capitol Hill was too "infested" with their presence for his comfort. He hoped they could be "colonized, sent to heaven or got rid of in any decent way."[116]

Another assassin put Chester A. Arthur, a New York machine politician, into the White House (1881–1885), and his first message to Congress had the distinction of being the first presidential address since the war not to mention the Negro question. He found race a "constantly" boring subject involving little more than "office begging" by black Republicans. His southern strategy thus wrote off the Negro vote in favor of alliance building among Readjusters, Independents, Greenbackers, anti-Bourbon Democrats.[117] Arthur was not bored, however, when the National Convention of Colored Men scheduled a meeting in Washington, D.C. His request that Frederick Douglass move the gathering prompted T. Thomas Fortune, the black newspaperman, to ask: "Is Arthur a Negro?" Fortune was amazed that the White House would bother to involve itself. Douglass knew better. He moved the meeting to Louisville because the Supreme Court was considering the constitutionality of the Civil Rights Act of 1875—specifically, whether the Fourteenth Amendment protected black rights to enter privately owned places of public accommodation or whether the owners' property rights permitted exclusion. Douglass's discretion was in vain. The Supreme Court held for property in the so-called Civil Rights Cases.[118]

That such a decision came down with Arthur in the White House was ironic. As a young lawyer in 1854 he represented Elizabeth Jennings, the black woman who brought the test case that integrated New York City's streetcar system. But President Arthur never moved beyond symbolic gestures. He donated money to a black church, handed diplomas to graduates of a black Washington high school, called for federal aid to Negro education in his last three annual messages to Congress, and invited the Fisk University choir to perform at the White House. None of this interfered with southern strategy pursuits. For black Americans, hope, aspiration, social and economic status, even prospects for physical safety sank ever lower during Arthur's three-and-a-half years. Even as the Fisk choir moved this president to tears.[119]

Under Grover Cleveland (1885–1889 and 1893–1897), the first Democrat in the White House since Buchanan, the politics of race never moved beyond platitudes and occasional patronage for professional Negro officeholders. At that the administration tolerated discriminatory hiring and firing practices in various government agencies (notably the Bureau of Engraving and Printing), while Secretary of State Richard Olney told the president that it would be a mistake to appoint "colored men" as consuls in South America or anywhere else.[120] The president and his southern lieutenants acted on the assumption that the former master class was best equipped to protect black interests. Cleveland criticized the Reconstruction era's carpetbag governments and even when promoting education as the solution to the nation's race problem called for "separate schools." He would get his wish in his second term when the Supreme Court, in *Plessy v. Ferguson* (1896), established the separate-but-equal doctrine that held in the public schools for fifty-eight years.[121]

A year before *Plessy*, Cleveland spent an hour in the Negro Building at the Cotton States and International Exposition in Atlanta—shaking blacks hands and huddling with Booker T. Washington, the Negro leader who told his people to give up the Reconstruction dream of equality and accept the white desire for segregation. Washington's critics said his famous Atlanta Compromise looked more like a capitulation. Cleveland found the man to be a reasonable, responsible Negro. Washington, in turn, admired Cleveland's "simplicity, greatness, and rugged honesty." They would meet and talk again, assuring each other of the wisdom of their respective and often parallel courses even as Jim Crow rolled across the South like a pea-soup fog and lynching became the preferred way to control a hated and despised race.[122]

Cleveland, in the manner of Hayes, rose not in defense of black lives and limbs but property. He sent some 2,000 troops to Chicago to bust the Pullman strike and countenanced the use of the Sherman Antitrust Act against Eugene Debs and the American Railway Union. This was a time when the politicians and jurists looked for any excuse not to bring blacks under the protection of the Fourteenth or any other constitutional amendment while finding every excuse to bring the new corporate entities under those protections.[123]

Indiana's Benjamin Harrison, grandson of former President William Henry Harrison, interrupted Cleveland's two terms in the White House (1889–1893) but not, to any great degree, Cleveland's racial policies. Initially it looked like dramatic change would come. For the first time since 1875 the Republicans controlled both Houses and with the shock of Cleveland's win fresh in mind they pushed again for the black vote by introducing two major pieces of legislation to protect voting rights and expand educational facilities. Meanwhile, Harrison met with a delegation of Mississippi blacks to discuss the pending disenfranchisement in that state through poll taxes and literacy tests. But the Republican Congress repudiated the party pledges and turned down the elections bill, and the president himself came around to the new policy of deference to the South.[124]

Harrison, like Arthur, repudiated his own past. In response to the Civil Rights Cases of 1883 he had said the Republican party would if necessary again amend the Constitution to guarantee the black rights that the Supreme Court had so casually disregarded. And he had spoken movingly of slavery's horror, recalling a boyhood romp through his grandfather's orchard at North Bend, Ohio, the natural boundary of the slave state of Kentucky, and coming suddenly upon "a colored man with the frightened look of a fugitive in his eye." President Harrison, however, had a different message. Reminding southern whites of his Virginia ancestors, he pledged to respect his party's Lily-White wing by appointing blacks only to minor positions. These positions, he reiterated, would involve no "personal contact with and official authority over white citizens . . . which you and your people find so offensive."

Harrison was more respectful of white authority over black citizens no matter what the form. In 1891, a year that saw 184 lynchings in the United States, he proposed an antilynching bill not to protect southern blacks (the usual victims) but foreign nationals. This was the result of a complaint filed by the Italian government after eleven of its citizens had been lynched.[125]

The next Republican president, Ohio's William McKinley (1897–1901), more than matched Harrison's retreat. Again there was cause for hope early on. McKinley condemned lynching in his inaugural address and in his first year appointed thirty blacks to a variety of offices. But he always acted in a utilitarian manner, using the race issue to advance a more questionable cause. Black appointments, for example, had less to do with merit or justice than the straightforward southern strategy orchestrated by the political boss Marcus Alonzo Hanna. With little immediate hope of attracting white southern voters, patronage could be useful nonetheless in controlling the nominating process at the Republican National Convention. This, Henry Cabot Lodge said, "[is] what southern delegates are good for"—that is, nominating a president, not electing one. McKinley opted for this strategy after losing the 1892 nomination to Harrison. Hanna went South to secure the 1896 nomination and literally bought the appropriate faction in each state (whether Black and Tan or Lily White).[126]

McKinley rarely moved beyond a stunted view of racial justice as something encompassing only a fair share of jobs for black office seekers. He looked to Booker Washington for advice on whom to appoint and had advice of his own for the students at Washington's Tuskegee Institute. "The best aspirations of your people," he counseled during his visit, would only be won with "patience, moderation, self-control."

For people ruled by the rope, the president counseled such virtues. Lincoln told Frederick Douglass's group more than thirty years before that "the ban is still upon you." It remained there eight presidents later.[127]

In his sole dramatic gesture on the race issue McKinley organized two all-black Army regiments and sent them to take up the white man's burden in the Philippines. The Spanish-American War had thrust the United States into the global race for empire—a race that historian John Hope Franklin called the industrial world's "program to dominate the backward areas of the world. Invariably, these backward peoples were dark; and frequently, they were Negroid." The American Negro as agent of that empire, the president told a delegation of black leaders at the White House, would now have a chance "to make a record for himself." He agonized over the Forty-eighth and Forty-ninth, his black regiments, confiding to Secretary of War Elihu Root that "this subject is always one of difficulty, but I feel very much inclined to organize a colored regiment making the field officers (white) all regulars, and the line officers all colored."[128] Integration of those agents would not come for another half century, and for another half century after that we would still hear that military service provides the best chance for this nation's darker peoples to make something of themselves.

While sending Negroes to kill Filipinos and otherwise march behind the flag, McKinley kept silent as disenfranchisement swept the black belt. He said nothing when Louisiana adopted the grandfather clause and North Carolina amended its state constitution to deny the vote. He said nothing about the Wilmington, North Carolina, race riot either. For yet another chief executive, the race problem at home was one for the states to settle for themselves by whatever chosen means.[129]

This was a time of deeds and dreams of empire for much of white America. An old century had ended, a new one had begun, and the issues were fixed. Whites feared that blacks were out to get their jobs, violate their women, cut their throats on country roads and city streets, and go over to their enemies on whatever battlefield. One or more of these racist notions confounded every chief executive from the Fillmores, Pierces, Buchanans, Garfields, and Arthurs at the bottom to the Washingtons, Adamses, Jeffersons, Madisons, Jacksons, and Lincolns at the top. By the time the old century's third assassin took McKinley's life Reconstruction was long dead, states' rights again triumphant on matters of race (if not secession), and white racist terror a mode of governance. This was the time that a new man, the first great man since Lincoln, stood ready to bring the presidency into the twentieth century. And this great man, the first modern president, could see only white recruits for his Republican party when he looked South. He saw southern black men only when the subject was lynching, and then only in the context of white women raped by Negroes freed too soon.

: 2 :

PROGRESSIVES

When Theodore Roosevelt became the twenty-sixth president (1901–1909) of the United States the pace of change brought on by industrialization threatened to overwhelm society. Democracy demanded informed and active citizens yet the late nineteenth century's complexity inspired a more deferential, less democratic politics. Technological advances, corporate dominance, finance capitalism, and a quickening urbanization complete with slums and ghettos had created a dramatically different country. Jefferson's agrarian dream of a self-sufficient Republic had long been discarded; and Lincoln's dream, with its emphasis on social mobility and labor's inherent dignity, had given way to the McKinley-Hanna courtship of big business and attendant war on the farmers and their Populist movement. If individualism and free competition remained the announced values, in practice the culture was becoming more corporate and its markets were becoming increasingly oligopolistic.[1]

While recognizing the inevitability of change, Theodore Roosevelt and many of his fellow Americans refused to be fatalistic. It was their energetic if sometimes tortuous, contradictory, and confused response to the changes that had already taken place and the promise of more to come that produced the Progressive movement. Progressivism promised a revolt against profit-gouging corporations, corrupt political machines, and reactionary politicians intent on minimizing the differences between the two parties and thus insulating themselves from popular protest. It included a humanitarian commitment to protect the emerging new order's victims and thrived (unlike earlier social reform movements) because small business and the professional classes embraced it as their own. By legitimizing the call for reform the urban middle class made the early twentieth century a bit more democratic and benevolent than it otherwise might have been and helped break ground for the New Deal of another Roosevelt.

Both Theodore Roosevelt and the Progressive movement were complex and above all dissonant. For every action taken by the great trust-buster to earn that name, another action helped solidify a new and even more predatory order. For every federal or state regulation to curb corporate power and its attendant threat to democracy, another came at the specific request of Wall Street's new finance capitalists. If the progressive idea had room enough for Wisconsin Senator Robert M. LaFollette's ambitious program to smash corporate power, its practice on the federal level rarely moved beyond Roosevelt's view that there were good and bad trusts (the former to be nurtured, the latter to be negotiated with). The movement encompassed both the humanitarianism of settlement house worker Jane Addams and an elitist and intolerant strain. Roosevelt and many mainstream progressives had an affinity for administrative solutions that imposed change from above.[2]

These contradictions bureaucratized and rule-bound the nation. In immigration policy the progressives rejected an essentially "open door" tradition in favor of exclusive and racialist legislation based on pseudo-scientific arguments and intended to weed out political and social undesirables (radicals, Jews, Catholics). A preference for order and professionalism also lead to the birth of the first national police force, the Bureau of Investigation (later renamed the Federal Bureau of Investigation), a progressive response to the problems of subversion and lawlessness. Having served as New York City police commissioner, Roosevelt knew something about crime and how to attack it. Walk softly and carry a big stick, TR said. Sailors and marines solved foreign policy problems in the name of the white man's burden.

Whether at home or abroad questions of race and racism influenced Roosevelt and progressivism as much as anything else. The great yellow peril thrived (Roosevelt called the Japanese "lacquered half-monkeys") along with black, brown, and off-white (immigrant) perils leading to endless speculations and predictions about race purity and race suicide. At the same time the trust busting and child labor laws came about Jim Crow sped up, lynching became even more routine, disenfranchisement spread like prairie fire. A thinking man's racism even burrowed into the academy, finding a home in the sciences, social sciences, and the humanities. Roosevelt, himself a historian and ornithologist, got a dose at Columbia Law School under John W. Burgess, the political theorist who said "[only] the Teuton really dominates the world by his superior political genius."[3]

A few Progressive Era politicians and their allies in academe and elsewhere actually tried to float the colonization panacea. The Philippines, it was said, might make a proper home for America's blacks, and some thought Roosevelt himself entertained the idea of colonizing the Pacific possessions with Negroes. This was particularly true after he appointed the black newspaperman T. Thomas Fortune special commissioner to Hawaii and the Philippines. Fortune's mandate aside (to study "sociological questions"), in all probability the appointment was merely a patronage matter. As the new century pushed forward only the fringe kept the colonization dream alive.[4]

Roosevelt was nonetheless among those obsessed with race. He carried a gene hierarchy in his head and spent endless hours compiling and cataloguing "stronger races" and "weaker races." Negroes found themselves placed near rock bottom among the "most utterly underdeveloped." "Suffering from laziness and shiftlessness" and prone to "vice and criminality of every kind," blacks threatened white citizens and "race purity." Roosevelt studied the problem scientifically, in the progressive manner, and concluded that Negro "evils" were "more potent for harm to the black race than all acts of oppression of white men put together." "[This] perfectly stupid race can never rise," he added on another occasion. "The Negro . . . has been kept down as much by lack of intellectual development as by anything else." "Mentally," William James observed, this cowboy trust-buster remained "in the *Sturm und Drang* period of early adolescence."[5]

Rather than push educational opportunity, Roosevelt, a patrician and at forty-two America's youngest chief executive, championed white reproduction and motherhood against black birth rates, appearance, and odors. In an odd way he also championed segregation, yet another scientific solution to racial problems. "As a race and in the mass they are altogether inferior to the whites," he noted. Observation not only proved this but located "the real problem"—namely, the "presence of the negro." Slavery itself had been "merely the worst possible method of solving the problem." Before Lincoln the problem (blacks) and the solution (slave holders) had been joined. The progressive Roosevelt's more humanitarian approach would merely segregate the races. Yet his record on race was not one dimensional. TR took pride in being man enough to open his home to black guests, to sit at a table and break bread with a black man in the executive mansion when governor of New York and to put up overnight at Oyster Bay the lawyer and ex–Harvard footballer William H. Lewis.[6]

Roosevelt knew slavery indirectly from the Bullochs of George. The half brother of his mother's grandmother, Daniel Stuart Elliot, once killed a slave. Only a child at the time, he shot his "little shadow" in a rage, and the family sent him abroad for a year hoping Europe would cure his remorse. Of the tales heard from this side of the family the one that influenced Roosevelt most involved a dead-of-night struggle between a Florida panther and one of great-grandfather Daniel Stewart's slaves. The slave had been cutting his way through a swamp on the way to "see his sweetheart," and the family found his body the next day lying alongside the dead cat.[7]

Roosevelt always described the slave as "a man of colossal strength" when telling the story of that terrible encounter. But he saw only cowardice in the performance of black troops when reflecting on his Rough Rider tour in Cuba during the Spanish-American War. While editors and politicians debated the wisdom of using Negro soldiers in the Philippines, he attributed a poor performance in San Juan Hill environs to "the superstition and fear of the darkey." When this criticism became an issue in the 1900 campaign, he explained, as ever, that he was no racist. His children "sat in the same school with colored children," and colored men "eat at my table and sleep in my house." TR failed to mention that blacks from the Ninth and Tenth Cavalries had saved the Rough Riders from annihilation at the battle of Las Guasimas.[8]

Early on in his presidency Roosevelt brought in experts, white and black, to talk about "the question of the colored race." They included Lyman Abbott and Silas McBee, editors of the *Outlook* and the *Churchman* respectively; and especially Booker T. Washington, who he called "the most useful, as well as the most distinguished, member of his race in the world," a perfect example of the "occasionally good, well-educated, intelligent and honest colored men" who ought to have the right to vote.[9] This courtship was mutual. "When you come up North next I particularly want to see you," Roosevelt wrote in November 1900 while still vice-president. "I have had some long talks recently with my friend Lewis at Harvard. There are some points where I do not entirely agree with him and I want to consult you about them."

Consultation invariably involved patronage. Roosevelt was always asking Washington for "the names of one or two first-class colored men," "the kind of colored man who reflects credit upon his people— the kind that I want to see given the recognition to which they are entitled; that is, given the recognition which would come to them naturally if they were not colored." Washington's critics were not pleased. "How does he know anything about the fitness of people for office?," asked William Monroe Trotter, the militant Harvard-trained lawyer. "It is simply an insult to every Negro to have such a trimmer made a boss by President Roosevelt."[10]

Roosevelt was delighted with Washington as confidante. Though patronage remained at the relationship's heart he sought advice on numerous other fronts. Washington occasionally edited the president's speeches, always changing the word "black" to "colored." "I used the term," Roosevelt explained, "because you used it in the memorandum you sent me." (Even Tuskegee's wizard could slip.) On other occasions the two men pondered the patriotism of militants like Trotter. Roosevelt told Washington that Henry M. Turner, southern bishop in the African Methodist Episcopal Church Zion, ought to be indicted for treason because he had called the American flag a "bloody rag." Both men were no doubt unaware that John Quincy Adams had called the Constitution, more than a half century earlier, a menstruous rag.[11]

Roosevelt would visit Tuskegee during his second term and eventually become a trustee. But he pursued his relationship with Washington largely through the mails and not personal contact, the result of the biting southern reaction to his White House dinner with the black leader. On the day McKinley died, September 14, 1901, the new president wrote Washington to come North "as soon as possible" to discuss southern patronage. At the last minute he extended a dinner invitation. So on the evening of October 16, in his presidency's first month, TR sat with Washington to break bread. The meal merely drew asides from Washington's black critics. Trotter, for example, emphasized the hypocrisy of a black Alabama advocate of Jim Crow at the president's table. Die-hard segregationists, in contrast, went after Roosevelt ruthlessly for the crime of aiding and abetting "social intercourse between blacks and whites." The White House, Mississippi Senator James K. Vardaman said, was "so saturated with the odor of the nigger that the rats have taken refuge in the stable."[12]

Initially, Roosevelt paid no attention to such comments. A few days after the White House dinner he marched with Washington in the Yale Bicentennial procession. The two men received honorary degrees and attended Yale President Arthur Hadley's dinner afterward (where Washington sat by Roosevelt's daughter, Alice). Even as late as December 1901, at the Gridiron Club dinner, the president could see some humor in the situation (however much in poor taste). Guests received a cartoon featuring a grinning "king of hearts" (Roosevelt) dining with "the ace of spades" (Washington). A skit also began with a commotion at the door and explanation that "Booker Washington" was trying to crash the affair. One "particularly Southern" member protested, but "Washington" came in anyway (because "he has been invited by the President") and sang "one of his inimitable coon songs."[13]

Southern reaction to the real Roosevelt/Washington dinner, however, did not let up. Washington's visit kept popping up in the press, with newspaper editors and politicians blaming it for every problem arising in the South from spot shortages of domestic servants to the lynching and burning of blacks at the stake. One critic said the dinner tinged "for the South every subsequent act of [Roosevelt's] in which the Negro was involved." Another Harvard man (from Alabama, this time), the historian William Garrott Brown, explained the depth of this reaction to Harvard president Charles W. Eliot. "It is not that intelligent Southerners any longer fear that 'social equality' will be, or ever can be, forced

upon them. It is that they Know from experience the effect on the negroes of such utterances, and of such incidents as President Roosevelt's
dining with Booker Washington at the White House. These effects are
apparent in the criminal courts, in the behavior of domestic servants,
and in other very disagreeable ways; and it would be hard to name any
countervailing good effects."14

Dumbfounded by this "condition of violent chronic hysteria," which
he explained by reference to the same "combination of Bourbon intel-
lect and intolerant truculence of spirit . . . which brought on the Civil
War," Roosevelt and his partisans recast the Washington dinner. To
minimize fallout from the breach of racial etiquette they downgraded
the dinner to a luncheon, told the press that the Roosevelt women did
not sit and eat with the black man, and reminded everyone that black
women were not welcome at the first lady's weekly teas and biweekly
musicals. Friends and enemies alike floated so many versions of what
happened that the details clouded up. Even today's textbooks sometimes mistakenly refer to a White House lunch. Either way, as the
segregationist newspaperman Josephus Daniels observed at the time, "it
is not a precedent that will encourage southern men to join hands with
Mr. Roosevelt."15

After Booker Washington's White House call Roosevelt made two
more gestures on behalf of blacks during his first term. The first involved Minnie M. Cox, the Fisk-educated postmistress of Indianola,
Mississippi, who served under Harrison and McKinley with few incidents until 1902 when a mob pressured her into resigning and she fled
to Birmingham. Roosevelt refused to accept the resignation and when
protests continued shut down the post office rather than give in—forcing the residents to nearby Heathman for their mail. "They sent to the
next town for theirs, and for this task they selected a *Negro*," cousin
Kermit Roosevelt marveled. Only when Cox's term expired did the
president replace her—with a white man who had stood up for her.
(Trotter listed the entire affair among the president's "bravest acts.")
Thereafter, Washington kept Roosevelt informed of Cox's fate on her
return to Indianola and attempt to organize the Delta Penny Savings
Bank. The president noted the irony: The white people who would not
let her handle their mail put their money in her bank. At bottom,
nonetheless, TR acted not on behalf of any racial justice principle but

because Indianola had challenged national supremacy and the authority of his office.[16]

In his third and last gesture Roosevelt stood by another black appointee in South Carolina, William D. Crum, a physician named collector of customs for the port of Charleston. Ben Tillman, the South Carolina Populist ("Pitchfork Ben") and now incurable Negrophobe, rose to cut Crum off in the Senate (filibustering against the nomination until it died). But Roosevelt consulted with Washington and then gave Crum an interim appointment—which he continued to do for the next seven years. "I can not consent to take the position that the door of hope—the door of opportunity—is to be shut upon any man, no matter how worthy, purely upon the grounds of race or color," the president explained to the city's mayor. "Such an attitude would, according to my conviction, be fundamentally wrong." For his part Crum served without pay, the result of a highly technical Treasury Department ruling that he was not entitled. In effect, the president offered that fact as a bone to Charleston whites.[17]

Washington's meal and the Cox and Crum battles all suggested that Roosevelt's Square Deal applied to black Americans. At least TR got the symbols and rhetoric right no matter how crudely put. "Inasmuch as [the Negro] is here and can neither be killed nor driven away," he once wrote Albion Tourgée, author of a well-known book on Reconstruction (*A Fool's Errand*), "the only wise and honorable and Christian thing to do is to treat each black man and each white man strictly on their merits as a man." Unfortunately the Square Deal had more than four even sides. Trotter said the president "stood his ground in most cases against the assault of southern color prejudice, even when practically deserted by his own party."[18] In fact Republican party politics and not an abstract commitment to opportunity dictated Roosevelt's actions. As much as anything else Roosevelt based his racial politics on a fear that archenemy Marc Hanna would steal the 1904 presidential nomination.

Roosevelt and Hanna both viewed the northern black vote as relatively unimportant in deciding the outcome of presidential elections. Running for the White House as Lincoln's heir, Republican candidates simply had a lock on those votes. The votes of black southern delegates to the Republican National Convention, in contrast, were immensely important in determining the party's nominee. With Hanna controlling Lily-White delegations in certain southern states and black delegations in others, Roosevelt responded in kind—though he rarely resorted to the Hanna method (cash payments to Negro delegates). He prepared to fight Hanna's southern machines even before McKinley's assassination. It made little difference thereafter, as one historian observed, that the new president "found himself in command of the very troops he had set out to fight." He still had to counter a persistent Hanna organization. So he moved through the South state-by-state. In Alabama, for example, he opposed the antiblack group that favored Hanna. In North Carolina he gave grudging, gradual support to the racist group that opposed Hanna. On occasion he would even support white supremacy Democrats. The Cox affair in Mississippi and the Crum affair in South Carolina were strategic moves in this game. Booker Washington, who provided advice on the right type of Negro appointments to help break the remnants of Hanna's ring in any given state, was also a player.[19]

Roosevelt's logistical twists and turns obscured a fundamental consistency. Eventually incumbency's growing weight and Marc Hanna's death allowed the president to abandon the game before his first term ended to begin a new game of wooing southern whites to the Republicans by loosening party ties with blacks. This meant a more consistent approach to the racist factions, and it led to opposition from the Republican National Committee. (The RNC, in contrast to TR, thought the Negro vote in the North relatively important and potentially decisive in a close election.) Roosevelt went to Booker Washington for sympathy. "The National Committee has thrown over the Williams-Clarke organization just because it was tainted with the Lily White business," he wrote Washington after that "organization" was purged from the Louisiana Republican party. "Politically, I think this may be of momentary advantage. I wish I were as sure that it was a good thing, both for white and black men." For Roosevelt, "the safety for the colored man in Louisiana is to have a white man's party which shall be responsible and honest." This was a southern strategy with no interest in black citizens' safety and a great interest in using race to break the one-party South.[20]

Trotter said Roosevelt "went over to the South." In practice the new policy mostly demanded silence. "In my position," TR wrote about racial issues to Carl Schurz, the Republican reformer and once Hayes's secretary of the interior, "I have seen nothing that could be gained by my saying anything in public on these subjects at the present time." With the nomination secure in 1904 he told Lyman Abbott that "I have nothing to gain and everything to lose by any agitation of the race question. . . . You will notice that in my speech of acceptance I did not touch upon this matter at all. If I can avoid touching upon it and retain my self-respect, I shall do so." The new policy required one to speak softly and carry no stick.

On those rare occasions when Roosevelt did touch and agitate, he did so for the other side. "Race purity must be maintained," he exhorted at a 1905 Lincoln Day dinner. In a trip South after the inauguration he reminded audiences of his mother's southern birth. In his message to Congress in 1906 he implied that black assaults on white women caused lynchings. "In a certain proportion of these cases," he told the governor of Indiana two years later, "the man lynched has been guilty of a crime horrible beyond description." With an average of eighty lynchings of black men in each of his White House years, one wonders what proportion TR had in mind—or what he thought of a 1903 Gridiron Club burlesque on southern politics that included "a lynching."[21]

If Roosevelt brought joy to the presidency and promised to use his office as a "bully pulpit" to rally the nation to progressive causes, on racial issues he refused to even stand in the pulpit. He remained silent when the Booker Washington dinner story broke; kept as quiet as possible when supporting Minnie Cox and William Crum; and, in perhaps the only move he ever made for black rights that was free from partisan consideration, kept his tongue for fear of "embitter[ing] the people." This last involved peonage in the South, and "people" meant white southerners. Convinced that a "partially successful movement to bring back slavery" was underway in at least three southern states, TR wrote the historian and scourge of Reconstruction, James Ford Rhodes, to ask that he speak against this evil. In another quiet move he encouraged Attorney General Charles J. Bonaparte to move against peonage. (Bureau of Investigation agents quickly headed South to gather the evidence needed to prosecute cases.) Bonaparte also pursued an *amicus curiae* strategy on behalf of civil rights for blacks in cases that came before the Supreme Court.[22]

Roosevelt stepped into the bully pulpit only to further his Lily-White politics. In August 1906 soldiers assigned to three companies of the black Twenty-fifth U.S. Infantry supposedly shot up Brownsville, Texas, leaving one civilian dead, one wounded, and the police chief injured. Roosevelt dismissed every last man without honor that November, disqualifying its members from military or civil service forever. Booker Washington made a brief attempt to get the president to change his mind and then counseled acceptance. "One thing the American people will not stand for any length of time," he said, "is abuse by any group of people of the President of the United States, and if our people in the North make a mistake of going too far there will be a reaction." Others would not let go. Monroe Trotter attacked Roosevelt's "monstrous breach of equity." No more than ten or twelve soldiers could have been involved, and given the scant evidence it is possible that no member of the Twenty-fifth participated. Still, the Army concluded that the culprits ran through Brownsville's streets at midnight firing guns before disappearing into their barracks. With no trial nor chance for appeal, the president punished the entire Twenty-fifth because no one identified the guilty parties.[23]

It made no difference that five of the 167 Brownsville soldiers held the Congressional Medal of Honor. With an eye on the black vote Roosevelt held news of the dismissal order until Tuesday, November 6 (the evening of election day). Though he had no plans to seek reelection in 1908, the president acted with a view to the future. His long-run goal was to build a Republican party in the South and to do this the Civil War and Reconstruction Era images had to be destroyed. The message that he wanted to get across was this: No longer the party of Lincoln, Sumner, and Stevens, the Progressive Era's Republican party was as much a white man's party as the Democratic party.[24]

Roosevelt failed to find humor when he heard of the Brownsville skits at the Gridiron Club that fall. (TR did not attend this dinner.) One club member, appearing as "an old nigger from down Tuskegee way" who "had a boy in dem colored troops," asked to see the president and Inspector General Ernest A. Garlington, who had compiled the report on Brownsville and issued the president's order that all soldiers would be punished unless they identified the guilty parties. "I'se got a reception for [Garlington]," the blackface actor said, and with that pulled out what a Gridiron chronicler called "one of those big pieces of pocket artillery which the James-Younger gang had made famous." Another Gridiron member appeared as "Mingo Saunders," a Twenty-fifth Infantry veteran with a quarter century service. "I trust you have said your prayers, Mingo," said a character portraying John D. Rockefeller. "Deed I has, boss," came the response. "I'se been prayin' dat I might be as lucky as Booker Washington, but my number hasn't come out yet."

As it turned out this was tame stuff compared to the fare Roosevelt himself offered at the next Gridiron dinner on January 26, 1907. The president took his seat at the head table and thumbed through a souvenir booklet of cartoons, two of which related to Brownsville. The first had TR saying: "I'm busy with things night and day . . . killing bears, firing coons." The president took it in good humor but then exploded at a spoof aimed at the foremost Senate critic of the Brownsville dismissals:

'All coons look alike to me,'
J. B. Foraker, says he, says he,
'Even if they is black as kin be,
An' is dressed in blue or yaller
    khaki.
All coons look alike to me,
Since 'mancipation set 'em free,
Nigger vote hold de balance,
All coons look alike to me.'

Roosevelt looked up and saw Senator J. B. Foraker, an Ohio Republican, among the Gridiron guests, along with such traditional enemies as J. P. Morgan and E. H. Harriman. "He was angry of the implications of the 'all coons' line," Gridiron president Samuel G. Blythe said, "and he found facing him not only his principal antagonists on his Brownsville policy, but ten or twelve of the plutocratic gentlemen on whom he had regulatory designs. He was in a forum where he could say what he liked, without fear of publication, and he just couldn't wait." While Foraker squirmed and Morgan sat dead still with a cigar clenched in his teeth, the president, according to Blythe's account, outlined his Brownsville record and then moved on to attack Wall Street. His voice, another Gridiron reporter noted, was "high," "strident," and "sandwiched with gestures more than emphatic."

When Roosevelt finished the entire dinner was as still as J. P. Morgan. Blythe's voice broke the calm and upped the ante. "Now is the time to bridge the bloody chasm," he said when inviting Foraker to the podium for a reply. No one was more shocked than TR or Foraker himself. But egged on "by the occupants of Millionaires' Row," the latter recovered and gave a rousing speech that brought the bankers and Standard Oil magnates crowding "to the front or standing on chairs cheering the defiances" and "waving their napkins at him." Blythe had "no doubt that this was the first time J. Pierpont Morgan ever waved a napkin at any speaker, but he made a flag out of his that night. So did his plutocratic companions, and so did far more than half the guests."

Foraker, known as "Fire Alarm Joe" for good reason, got the best of Roosevelt that evening. TR tried to respond once more, but for once appeared a feeble figure at the podium. Still, the mass discharge of Brownsville's troops held. "Some of the men were bloody butchers— they ought to be hung," the president had shouted only minutes before Morgan picked up his napkin. "It is not the business of the House. It is not the business of the Senate. All talk on the subject is academic. If they pass a resolution to reinstate these men, I will veto it; if they pass it over my veto, I will pay no attention to it. I welcome impeachment."[25]

What Rev. Clayton Powell of Harlem's Abyssinian Baptist Church called "the awful march of events since the famous Roosevelt-Washington luncheon [sic]" culminated in a congressional investigation of the Brownsville riot during Roosevelt's last White House year.[26] With Republicans split and southern Democrats committed to white supremacy, the Senate Committee on Military Affairs sided (more or less) with the president. In a compromise measure the Army appointed five officers to a Court of Inquiry that took testimony from eighty-two of the 167 discharged soldiers before announcing that no further cases could be heard. Fourteen of the eighty-two were reinstated and eleven of those reenlisted. Whether any of the Brownsville troops fired their guns in town that night remained an open question. Roosevelt had Secretary of War William Howard Taft hire a Negro detective, William G. Baldwin, to conduct a secret investigtion, with the goal of proving the soldiers guilty. Unfortunately Baldwin and his partner, the journalist Herbert J. Browne, lied when claiming to have the specific names of guilty parties. Like everything else on Brownsville these spies only brought the president more grief.[27]

Taft, never a friend to the black fighting man, carried out the Brownsville soldiers' discharge. Earlier, when serving as governor general of the Philippines, he said that McKinley's black troops "got along fairly well with the natives . . . too well with the native women." So he had them withdrawn "out of their regular turn." When Taft ran for the presidency in 1908 as Roosevelt's hand-picked successor, Trotter said that any black who supported him "puts himself in eternal disgrace. He is branded with the mark of Cain." Determined to protect his man and keep the black vote, Roosevelt said Brownsville was his affair and Taft had nothing to do with it. Memories and resentments remained but were insufficient to pull those voters from Lincoln's party. Those half million blacks who could vote, a number cut in half over the past ten years, continued to support Republican candidates.[28]

Taft followed Roosevelt's lead on the campaign trail, too, avoiding race whenever possible and minimizing the issue whenever necessary. "The problem of the colored race," he said at Fisk University, "is a problem which . . . is solving itself" with the help of "sympathy . . . among the southern white men." Even if proved wrong on this, Taft believed things would improve anyway because everyone would soon recognize that prejudice was not in their "pecuniary" interests. Also in the manner of Roosevelt, he courted Booker Washington—sending him "a tentative passage from my acceptance speech for your criticism and suggestion." "What [would] you . . . think of the wisdom of having Lewis, of Massachusetts, as one of those who second my nomination in the Chicago Convention," he asked the wizard of Tuskegee on another occasion. Taft thought "it would be better to have a colored man from the north do it," but did not move until he got Washington's approval.[29]

The reference to William Lewis was not coincidental. This "Boston Bookerite" and Harvard-crowd friend of TR had performed a service and deserved a reward. Roosevelt, Lewis explained, "appointed me assistant United States attorney . . . and in return I defended the discharge of the Brownsville soldiers, a thing which no other colored Federal office-holder did." But Henry Cabot Lodge blocked Taft's plan to reward Lewis again by naming him an assistant attorney general "on the ground that he is an office holder," and it would be three years before Taft got the appointment through the Senate. The president had the narrow focus throughout of controlling the southern delegations at the Republican National Convention in order to counter his chief rival for the nomination, fellow Ohioan J. B. Foraker. Taft was remarkably successful here, lining up 128 of 194 southern delegates. Roughly a quarter of the total convention vote.[30]

With Roosevelt off hunting big game in Africa, Taft (1909–1913) settled into the White House with his own southern strategy agenda. He called black disenfranchisement in the South a "turn for the better"; supported voting rights only "in such small numbers . . . as not to threaten control by the baser element of the community"; promised to exclude blacks from patronage; and saw nothing wrong constitutionally or otherwise with election laws which barred "an ignorant electorate." In his inaugural address he outlined "a policy of not making Southern appointments from Negroes" in any "community in which the race feeling is so widespread and acute." The always obliging Gridiron Club parodied this, too, with a Sambo bit entitled "Uncle Joe's Cabin or Life Among the Insurgents":

'What's that last?,' cried 'Uncle Tom.'
   'Patronage will be restored.'
   'Hooray,' he cried, 'we'se 'mancipated. Didn't I tole ye' I could see dem pearly gates.'

Taft defended his policy of not appointing southern Negroes to office as being in the best interest of the Negroes themselves in that it might prevent lynching or some other tragedy. "Personally, I have not the slightest prejudice or feeling," he claimed. "I [merely] question the wisdom of a policy that is likely to increase [white southern violence against blacks]." In line with this logic the president removed the black postmaster of Port Gibson, Mississippi, because "the presence of a number of female schools there seems to increase the friction due to his remaining." Lynching itself merited no official concern. Murders of southern blacks by white mobs merely provided the Justice Department an opportunity to explain that it lacked "authority . . . to protect citizens of African descent in the enjoyment of civil rights generally." Again this echoed the inaugural address. "It is not the disposition or within the province of the Federal Government," Taft said, "to interfere with the regulation by the Southern States of their domestic affairs."[31]

With the utterly frank goal of building "a decent white man's party" below the Mason-Dixon line, Taft understood the nature of the white man's burden at home and abroad. "Our little brown brothers" would need "fifty or one hundred years . . . to develop anything resembling Anglo-Saxon political principles and skills," he once said of the Filipinos. His view of American blacks was scarcely different. For this president the politics of race never moved beyond an attempt to break the black Republican machines in the South. The National Civil Service Reform League kept the White House posted on its investigations in Alabama and other states to this end, basing its findings on the reports of former Confederate soldiers turned private eyes. Taft concluded that "fatally corrupt" black Republicans were interested only in the patronage that would come with being on the winning side every four years at the Republican Convention. For advice on building up a different GOP the president went to William Garrott Brown, who described "the disenfranchisement of the mass of the negroes, and the practical acquiescence of the Republicans therein . . . [as] the necessary preliminary to any substantial and permanent Republican gains in the distinctly Southern states."[32]

For this task Taft was a better man than Roosevelt, Brown concluded. "In these thoroughly Southern quarters, where there are many negroes and prejudice is strong, what is needed is fuller and fuller proof of an entirely sympathetic attitude on the part of the Republican party and its national leaders. Mr. Roosevelt did much in this direction, but the effect of it was largely marred by the Crum appointment, the Booker Washington dinner, and the Indianola incident. The President has done much, and so far has made no such mistake. I trust he will make more visits to the South, and keep the tone he has hitherto taken."[33] Taft kept to the rut so well that the black press said "there is not much to choose between [the Negrophobic] Ben Tillman and Bill Taft." The White House even expected complaints from Booker Washington and tried to head them off by warning him that there would "probably be grief below the [Mason-Dixon] line." When Washington complained anyway the president said there might be a city or two where the policy of not making black appointments need not apply. Washington suggested New Orleans.[34]

More old guard than progressive, Taft backed off his Lily-White southern strategy in 1911 when trying to hold the Republican party together against Roosevelt's insurgents. The former president, who objected to Taft's so-called dollar diplomacy abroad and antitrust policy at home, had come out of retirement in 1910 to lead the charge against this betrayer of the progressive spirit, delivering his famous "New Nationalism" speech at the dedication of the John Brown Memorial Battlefield in Osawatomie, Kansas. (Among those on the platform were Mary Langston, last surviving widow of the Harper's Ferry Force, and her eight-year-old grandson, Langston Hughes.) Roosevelt put all his effort into taking the nomination, but the Republican National Convention threw him aside. Taft got fifty-four of the sixty-two black delegates, and these were the votes TR would remember. With the white South watching this courtship of black Republicans in anger, Taft made amends after he had the nomination in hand. He hit the region's patronage-driven Republican politics on election eve by placing fourth-class postmasters (about 16,000 nationwide) under civil service. The irony is that the president used patronage to line up the black delegates in the first place.[35]

At their own convention in Chicago, Progressive party activists nominated Roosevelt and with surprisingly little debate selected an explicitly Lily-White campaign strategy. This took Joel Spingarn of the three-year-old National Association for the Advancement of Colored People (NAACP) by surprise. Spingarn had brought a plank to Chicago calling for repeal of Jim Crow laws and complete black enfranchisement, but with Roosevelt and white southern delegates objecting the convention excluded the NAACP lines from the Progressive party platform. The convention also voted to ban several blocs of black delegates.[36]

Roosevelt's logic was consistent with the electoral strategies he pursued while a Republican president. As a Progressive party candidate, however, he was more straightforward and extreme on racial issues. With industrialization coming to the South (however slowly), Roosevelt argued, the Democratic party's agrarian, low-tariff doctrines were hopelessly dated. But no third party could reach southern whites unless it somehow transcended or exploited the race issue, courting those whites at the expense of blacks. So Roosevelt consulted with John M. Parker of New Orleans and other southern advisers who told him to forget the black vote and go after the white vote—the very politics he had dabbled in while president. He had always thought that this was the "formula best designed for party success." His message (that each state's residents settle race questions for themselves) was at bottom an absolute surrender to a states' rights doctrine that included everything from disenfranchisement to lynching as ways and means for controlling black people. The obvious problem was that the Progressive party needed Negro support to mount a credible challenge. TR was vaguely aware of this, having beaten Taft in the Maryland primary largely on the strength of the black vote.[37]

Not all Progressive party members and supporters accepted a Lily-White politics. If Roosevelt embraced segregation as a scientific solution to racial tensions, other progressives, like Joel Spingarn, considered segregation a moral evil. A small group saw segregation as a political concession that would ultimately dim their party's long-term prospects because it strengthened reactionary forces in the South and elsewhere. With these divergent opinions requiring at least a perfunctory explanation from the candidate, TR looked for a chance to do so at the Chicago convention. "Nobody can ask me a question I am afraid of," he said during his acceptance speech, veering off from the prepared text at the first hoot from a delegate. "I heard over there, did I not, some query about the negro question." To applause and cries of "don't answer him," he pushed on "fearlessly and conscientiously" into a brief history of the Republican party since the Civil War.

What had the party accomplished, Roosevelt asked, besides irreparable harm to southern blacks and whites alike? A policy that cannot see beyond race and patronage could only breed corruption and bring "to crushing disaster the death of the great Republican party itself." (This was a veiled reference to Taft's control of the party apparatus and thus the nomination process.) Of the new Progressive party's segregationist policy, TR said "we are in the first place beginning where all charity must begin—at home . . . . I have advocated the action which, as far as I am able to judge my own soul, I believe with all my heart is the only action that offers any chance of hope to the black man in the south, to the white man in the south . . . . The old policy of attempt-

ing to impose on the southern states from without a certain rule of conduct toward the negro has, in fact broken down. . . . The American
people is a mighty good people to lead and a mighty poor people to
drive." Whites were to be led, blacks driven.[38]

While Roosevelt gave this somewhat convoluted explanation his
men distributed to the delegates a more detailed briefing in the form of
a letter to Julian Harris (son of "Uncle Remus" creator Joel Chandler
Harris). A great many "sad and unpleasant facts," the letter read, made
it "much worse than useless" for the Progressive party to seek even one
southern black vote. During Reconstruction the Republicans had
merely built "a party in which the Negro should be dominant, a party
consisting almost exclusively of Negroes," a "ghost party . . . lamentable
from every standpoint" and capable of producing only "evil to the colored men themselves." By looking "facts in the face," Roosevelt
reiterated, it became clear that "the racial issue . . . always works harm
to both races, but immeasurably most harm to the weaker race. . . .
Therefore I feel that we have to adapt our actions to the actual conditions . . . and feelings of each community."[39]

Roosevelt looked into the future and saw the white southern vote as
the key to the nation's politics. "In the South the Democratic machine
has sought to keep itself paramount by encouraging the hatred of the
white man for the black; the Republican machine has sought to perpetuate itself by stirring up the black man against the white; and surely
the time has come when we should understand the mischief in both
courses, and should abandon them both." The vehicle for this would
be the Progressive party because "colored members" had ruined the
Republican party. "In the convention at Chicago last June," he told
Harris, "the break-up of the Republican Party was forced by those
rotten-borough delegates from the South. . . . Colored men, or whites
selected purely by colored men, were sent to the convention, representing nothing but their own greed for money or office."

"Seven-eighths of the colored men . . . [voted against] me," Roosevelt
thundered, defying and betraying "the will of the mass of the plain
people of the party. . . . It would be not merely foolish but criminal to
disregard the teachings of such a lesson . . . It would be criminal for the
Progressive Party to repeat the course of action responsible for such disaster, such failure, such catastrophe." "The real problem," in Roosevelt's

mind, remained what it had always been (the "presence of the negro"). Neither slavery ("the worse possible method of solving the problem") nor Civil War and Reconstruction had worked. The solution lay somewhere between slavery and freedom.[40]

Roosevelt championed a progressive movement and nation for whites only, calculating that advocacy of white over black would put him back in the White House. Again he guessed wrong. America's Bull Moose candidate had his campaign manager disavow the only movement started in South Carolina on his behalf because it was all black, and then watched in dismay as his segregationist support washed away with a news story that he had taken a meal with two black Progressive party members in Providence, Rhode Island. He could only confess his bewilderment when the white southern voter creamed him at the polls in November. "Ugh! There is not any more puzzling problem in this country than the problem of color." TR had come back to where he had started, squaring the circle. The "ugh" in 1912 echoed a confession made in his presidency's second month to former carpetbagger Albion Tourgée: "I too have been at my wits' ends in dealing with the black man."[41]

Another progressive from another party, Woodrow Wilson, won the election of 1912—the first Democrat since Cleveland and the first southern-born president (1913–1921) since the Civil War. Born in 1856 in Virginia, he grew up in Georgia, son of a Presbyterian minister and son of the South. "The only place in the country, the only place in the world where nothing has to be explained to me," he explained, adding that his interest in politics dated from the day he heard news of Lincoln's election and the coming war.[42] He earned a doctorate and became a scholar of national reputation with a sweeping if hardly original view of the nation's people and their political institutions. Slavery was part of the civilizing process; Reconstruction nothing more than "a host of dusky children untimely put out of school."[43]

Having invited Booker Washington to his 1902 inauguration as president of Princeton University, Wilson spent the next eight years working to keep every other Negro off campus and out of the student body altogether (not wishing to make uncomfortable any southern white who happened to enroll for classes).[44] Having closed off Princeton, Wilson had confidence in his ability to manage the Negro problem. While visiting Grasmere, according to a young woman who drank tea with the scholar, "he told of a coloured cook they had who needed winding up about every three weeks; then he would go down and artificially get into a raving bad temper. She would be frightened, and for a week after would be superb, the next one, fair, and the next abominable again. It is the only way to deal with coloured servants." Or colored people in general. Wilson assured his British friends that he would not follow Roosevelt's lead. "Dr. W. thought it an unwise piece of bravado . . . to put that negro [Crum] over white wholesale traders—too much for them to stand." Wilson then told a "darky" joke about the Booker Washington dinner. His racial views were as prejudiced as those of TR's southern critics.[45]

Wilson was nonetheless the first Democratic presidential candidate in history to receive widespread endorsement from prominent blacks (though largely in protest against the alternative candidates, Roosevelt and Taft). W. E. B. Du Bois considered him "a cultivated scholar" of "farsighted fairness." "He has brains," Du Bois said. "He will not seek further means of 'jim crow' insult." Wilson told Bishop Alexander M. Walters of the African Methodist Episcopal Church Zion that blacks "may count on me for absolute fair dealing. . . . My earnest wish [is] to see justice done them in every matter, and not merely grudging justice. My sympathy with them is of long standing." That got Walters's endorsement. Wilson got Monroe Trotter's by promising "to be a President of the whole nation—to know no white or black."

Although Wilson received no more than 5–7 percent of the total Negro vote, the election of 1912 marked the first significant defection from the Republican party. While the mass of African Americans still cast their ballots for the party of Lincoln either directly or indirectly, with TR and Taft receiving a roughly equal share of their ballots, black leadership, alienated by the competing whiter-than-thou posturing of those two candidates, went over to the party of Calhoun and Davis.[46]

While Negro servants at the White House caught glimpses of Wilson wandering the halls with a Bible under his arm, the hopes of Du Bois and the talented tenth crashed. The new president appeared religiously determined to bring the Princeton way to federal patronage.

Consultation on appointments with Bishop Walters, who headed the National Colored Democratic League, was a mere formality. Policy dictated a purge of black office holders extending to William Lewis, the lawyer who stood by Roosevelt on Brownsville. While one should not expect a Democratic president to keep holdover Republican appointees, Wilson invariably replaced blacks with whites and made no attempt to do otherwise until the second term—when the demands of world war and the contradictions of his own global vision dictated the occasional gesture.[47]

More troubling was Wilson's push to institutionalize segregation within the federal civil service. This created such an uproar that the president tried to disperse blame among overzealous southerners in the cabinet. That effort fooled no one. "My distrust and dislike of the attitude of the Administration centered upon Woodrow Wilson," the NAACP's James Weldon Johnson said, "and came nearer to constituting keen hatred for an individual than anything I have ever felt."[48] Johnson knew that nothing could be more destructive in the world of political symbolism than Jim Crow as United States government policy. Nothing could be more debilitating to Wilson's own democratic vision for the nation and the world than the sight of workers tacking up "White Only" or "Colored" signs over District of Columbia toilets. Yet this is what Wilson and his people set out to do from the administration's first days.

Segregation within the federal bureaucracy, hardly a novel idea, had occurred under the last Democrat (Cleveland) and also under Wilson's two Republican predecessors (Roosevelt and Taft). And it would inch forward again under his two immediate Republican successors (Harding and Coolidge). Only the *Washington Bee*, a black newspaper, paid much attention before Wilson's time because segregation crept in almost imperceptibly.[49] Wilson created a national debate by elevating the practice to the level of "reform" and proceeding under the progressive banner. Coming after Roosevelt's Lily-White campaign, Wilsonian segregation suggested that progressivism and racism were somehow interdependent.

Wilson and his cabinet saw segregation as a rational, scientific policy. The Negro press, in contrast, speculated that the administration launched its crusade at the prodding of First Lady Ellen Axson Wilson who was shocked, apparently, at the sight of black and white clerks eating lunch together at the Bureau of Printing and Engraving. With a distinctly southern twist to the cabinet, the administration needed little encouragement from the president's wife. Secretary of the Treasury William Gibbs McAdoo, a native Georgian, emerged as the policy's chief spokesman and defender. Other southern cabinet members included Postmaster General Albert S. Burleson (Texas), Secretary of the Navy Josephus Daniels (North Carolina), and Attorney General James C. McReynolds (Kentucky). All were militant segregationists who enjoyed the (unscientific) "darky stories" that Wilson sometimes told (in dialect) at their meetings.[50]

At one of those meetings, on April 11, 1913, Burleson said he could separate Railway Mail Service employees in "an easy way." There was little discussion and no written commitment for formal action. Neither Wilson nor any cabinet member objected. The policy simply began and spread Jim Crow most rapidly in the Post Office and the Treasury and Interior Departments.[51] The scope of Wilsonian segregation became known during debate on a rare black appointee, Oklahoma lawyer Adam E. Patterson. Nominated for Register of the Treasury, Patterson had the support of Bishop Walters and the blind Oklahoma Senator Thomas P. Gore, and the predictable opposition of Ben Tillman, James K. Vardaman, and other southern senators. Wilson and McAdoo defended Patterson by emphasizing the plan for segregation in the federal bureaucracy and making the case that the Registry (already 40 percent black) was a perfect place to start. Tillman and Vardaman failed to see the logic in Negroes running their own department and the nomination died. The general plan kept to schedule regardless.[52]

Wilson was primarily worried about white women working under the same roof with black men. His progressive solution (what he called "a plan of concentration") "will put them all together and will not in any one [federal] bureau mix the two races."[53] Segregation moved forward (though not in the grand design of McAdoo and Burleson), spreading beyond the Post Office and Treasury with the administration requiring photographs on all civil service applications. A young assistant secretary of the navy would be embarrassed years later by his role in this business—specifically, for introducing segregated toilets in the

State, War, and Navy Department Building. On October 15, 1932, the *Chicago Defender* ran a story under the title "[Franklin D.] Roosevelt Exposed as Rabid Jim Crower."[54]

Oswald Garrison Villard, grandson of the abolitionist and NAACP board chairman, tried to convince Wilson to abandon the segregation project. Armed with the facts that came out during the Patterson nomination fight and the more detailed investigations of NAACP secretary May Childs Nerney, Villard succeeded only in engaging the president in a private dialogue. If Wilson's progressive mind opened to Villard's call for a national race commission, his political mind warned that this would lead to another divisive Senate debate. So he simply advised Villard that it would be "a blunder." "The segregation of the colored employees in the several departments," he explained, was "as much in the interest of the negroes as for any other reason, and with the idea that the friction, or rather the discontent and uneasiness, which had prevailed in many of the departments would thereby be removed. It is . . . [not] a movement *against* the negroes. . . . We are rendering them more safe in their possession of office and less likely to be discriminated against."[55]

Villard and the NAACP persisted, and since Villard was also editor of the *New York Evening Post* the carping could not be ignored. Growing more exasperated with each editorial outburst, Wilson eventually tried to back out of his own Jim Crow policy. "The delicacy and difficulty of the situation . . . with regard to the colored people," he told Villard, required "the greatest possible patience and tact." Casting blame on others, he said he wanted to do the right thing but found himself "absolutely blocked by the sentiment of Senators; not alone Senators from the South, by any means." The issue itself led to wild mood swings. At one moment Wilson was "not without hope that I may succeed in certain directions." At the next he was ready to give up and leave racial dilemmas to others: "I never realized before the complexity and difficulty of this matter in respect of every step taken here. I not only hope but pray that a better aspect may come upon it before many months." In the end, the president always returned to segregation, the progressive's only logical and scientific solution to a vexing social problem. He never outgrew the idea.[56]

Wilson wanted to be left alone first and foremost. His experts were McAdoo and Burleson (not Villard and the NAACP), and they knew best how to attack the race problem's debilitating aspects. The president thus tried to end his private dialogue with Villard by appealing for help "in holding things at a just and cool equipoise until I can discover whether it is possible to work out anything or not." "Either now or at any future time," he warned, progress will not come "if a bitter agitation is inaugurated and carried to its natural ends." The problem, in other words, lay not in the administration's segregation policy but in the policy's critics.[57]

With Villard keeping at it Wilson finally requested a personal interview in the controversy's fifth month (October 1913). When the two men sat down together the president promised to wash his hands. "I say it with shame and humiliation, with shame and humiliation, but I have thought about this thing for twenty years and I see no way out. It will take a very big man to solve [it]." Four years later he would have visions of a global democratic order free from autocracy, militarism, colonialism, communism. He did not shrink from plotting for a new world but claimed his own nation's racial landscape was beyond his ability.[58]

Having disposed of Villard, Wilson next received Monroe Trotter and a delegation from the National Independent Political League. These African Americans, less polite than Villard, condemned federal Jim Crow as "a new slavery of caste" with no possible justification. Trotter asked if the president considered blacks "diseased or indecent as to their persons"? "Inferior beings of a lower order"? Or had the president merely deferred to "other employees [who] have a class prejudice which is to be catered to or indulged"? Wilson listened politely and made a few half-hearted attempts to defend his administration. "I do not think that the spirit of discrimination has been shown in any essential manner," he said. Besides, working conditions had been altered "but very slightly. . . . In the first place, a great deal has been exaggerated. . . . In the second place, there is no policy on the part of the administration looking to segregation." The few things done, he reiterated, merely served "the convenience and agreeable feelings of everybody concerned."

Trotter could not believe his ears. He had supported Wilson in the New Jersey gubernatorial election of 1910 and the presidential election of 1912, and now here he was quoting Wilson's own words: "I shall be a Christian gentleman in the White House." Didn't he remember promising to enforce the law with equal rights and justice for all regardless of race or color? "Mr. President," Trotter tried to explain, "it is true in almost every case that we who suffer know as even you can't know." "To plead benevolence for such a policy," he added, was simply "preposterous." Wilson took these words as an insult but remained calm. He accepted the group's petition, showed Trotter the door, and then ignored Trotter's follow-up letters and the continuing coverage in the black press of "officially marked and ordered Jim-Crow toilets" and other segregationist outrages.[59]

Trotter, like Villard, was persistent. He somehow arranged another group meeting with Wilson in November 1914, a meeting for which the president was ill-prepared given his preoccupation with the European war and his own grief. (His wife had died in August.) Trotter opened with a direct challenge to the president: "Have you a 'new freedom' for white Americans and a new slavery for your Afro-American fellow citizens?" The discussion subsequently degenerated into a forty-five-minute argument with Wilson ordering Trotter to "leave politics out of it" because "we are dealing with a human problem, not a political problem." If black people objected to administration policy they had the right to vote for another candidate at the next election.

Wilson made it clear that he would not be threatened. "Politics must be left out," he repeated, "because don't you see, to put it plainly, that is a form of blackmail." Getting back to the "human problem," he defended segregation without apology. "We are all practical men. We know that there is a point at which there is apt to be friction, and that is in the intercourse between the two races. Because, gentlemen, we must strip this thing of sentiment and look at the facts. . . . It is going to take generations to work this thing out. And . . . it will come quickest if these questions aren't raised." "We can't blink the fact," the president closed, then bid Trotter's group goodbye.

Trotter refused to budge, saying segregation was unbearable. "If you take it as a humiliation, which it is not intended as," Wilson responded, "and sow the seed of that impression all over the country, why the consequences will be very serious." When Trotter called this reasoning "an insult," the president shook with rage. "If this organization wishes to approach me again, it must choose another spokesman. I have enjoyed listening to these other gentlemen. They have shown a spirit in the matter that I have appreciated, but your tone, sir, offends me." Those other blacks, of course, barely said a word since Trotter was the spokes-person. The spirit that the president admired was silence.

"You are the only American citizen that has ever come into this office," Wilson continued, "who has talked to me in a tone with a back-ground of passion that was evident." Trotter tried to explain, saying "I am from a part of the people, Mr. President." Wilson would not have it. He accused Trotter of spoiling "the whole cause from which you came." Trotter again tried to explain. "Mr. President, my whole desire is to let you know the truth we know." Wilson wanted to know why he did not "come to me in a Christian spirit." Trotter said "we are not wards."[60]

A newspaperman in his own right (editor of the *Boston Guardian*), Trotter had walked out of the meeting and into the arms of the black press. "The main issue for us was to force from the President, after two years effort, an expression of his views," he told reporters and the crowd that gathered at Washington's Second Baptist Church. "The President declared in favor of race segregation as beneficial to both whites and Negroes." Trotter recounted an earlier meeting with an Equal Rights League delegation when Wilson was governor of New Jersey. "We were received open-handed, we Afro-Americans, over the heads of a score of 'non-Afro-Americans' who were waiting in the ante room. The gov-ernor had us draw our chairs right up around him, and shook hands with great cordiality. When we left he gave me a long handclasp, and used such a pleasant tone that I was walking on air. What a change be-tween then and now!"[61]

Things changed because Wilson's constituency shrank when he moved from the New Jersey governor's mansion to the White House— that is, it narrowed to exclude minorities. "It would not be right for me to look at this matter in any other way than as the leader of a great national party," he explained to arch-segregationist Thomas Dixon. "I am trying to handle these matters with the best judgment but in the spirit of the whole country, though with entire comprehension of the considerations which certainly do not need to be pointed out to me." The president promised to handle "the force of colored people who are now in the departments in just the way in which they ought to be handled."[62]

Three months after meeting with Trotter, Wilson did more for Thomas Dixon than provide words of comfort. He permitted a private White House screening of *Birth of a Nation*, the D. W. Griffith Reconstruction epic inspired by Dixon's novel (*The Clansman*), and encouraged cabinet members and their families to attend. "History written with lightning," the president said of that racist film as the last reel closed.[63] With *The Leopard's Spots* and *The Traitor*, Dixon's *Clansman* completed a trilogy of race and sex which depicted black men crawling after southern belles and Ku Klux Klansmen riding to the rescue. The stage version of *The Clansman* appeared in Atlanta in 1906 and some credited it with sparking the race riot that hit shortly thereafter. Griffith's film version was even more powerful, a movie-making masterpiece by any definition. Its genius made the content and message all the more frightening. A campaign of opposition, led by Villard and another NAACP founder, American Bar Association president Moorfield Storey, had some success in preventing screenings in New York and Boston. While Dixon's lawyers went to court to force theater owners to show the film, Dixon went to his White House friend.

After the White House show, Dixon took the film (and the president's endorsement) to the Supreme Court where Josephus Daniels helped him talk his way into Chief Justice Edward D. White's chambers. White, a Confederate veteran from Louisiana, listened to the pitch then said, "I was a member of the Klan, sir." He agreed to see the film at the Raleigh Hotel ballroom and for company took along several justices and congressmen. With the president's assistance, Dixon got more than he expected.[64]

Given *Birth of a Nation*'s racist message and the controversy it generated, Wilson gradually backed off his initial praise. For those who bothered to complain that the president of the United States had no business saying kind things about the Klan, the White House mailed out a disclaimer drafted by Wilson himself: "The President was entirely unaware of the character of the play before it was presented and at no time expressed his approbation of it. Its exhibition at the White House was a courtesy extended to an old acquaintance."[65]

A complete reevaluation of the film came when America entered World War I and wartime race riots swept the land. Now demands of security and Jeffersonian doubts about Negro loyalty took precedence.

In *Notes on the State of Virginia* the third president predicted that slavery's bitter memories would render the race permanent subversives, and the current president seemed to agree with that assessment. What Wilson once called "history written with lightning" now became an "unfortunate production." Where the president once stood with Dixon against Villard and the NAACP, he now wished "most sincerely" that *Birth of a Nation* be banned "particularly in communities where there are so many colored people." This divisive film, which Wilson considered an "all so true" depiction of Reconstruction evils and Klan heroism, had no place in wartime.[66]

Ironically, Wilson helped create the climate for the first major wartime riot by accusing the Republicans of "colonizing" black voters in East St. Louis, Illinois, and other cities. These voters, largely migrants from Mississippi and West Tennessee, were lured North by factory jobs and not Republican party manipulations. Local employers often hired black migrants at wages low enough to undercut white wages or used them as strikebreakers against white union members. At the president's urging, nonetheless, the Justice Department and its Bureau of Investigation opened voting fraud cases, a decision that stirred up racial hatred in places that had problems enough. In May 1917 minor rioting occurred in East St. Louis leaving one black dead, dozens of blacks and whites injured, and hundreds of blacks homeless; and in Waukegan, where some 150 recruits from the Great Lakes Naval Training Station roamed through the black area throwing rocks and breaking windows. Police fired on that mob, wounding two. Five weeks later, on July 2, white mobs burned East St. Louis's black section, killing at least thirty-nine persons and driving 6,000 from their homes. One police officer and seven other whites also died.[67]

Questions of loyalty and security came to the front. When William English Walling complained, incredibly, that the East St. Louis riot was part of "the German plot to prevent conscription of negroes and keep large sections of American troops in America," Wilson had Tumulty tell "Mr. Walling that we are making a rigid investigation."[68] Bureau of Investigation agents, still in hot pursuit of voting fraud in East St. Louis and other cities, now looked into Negro attitudes toward the draft. The most bizarre rumor that the Wilson administration pursued had German agents organizing a Mexican/African American army to fight a rear-guard action in the southwest on Kaiser Wilhelm's behalf. Germany's offer in the Zimmermann telegram to help Mexico regain territory lost seventy years before in the Mexican war inspired this rumor. The Houston riot of August 1917 kept it alive. That riot involved a clash between black soldiers and local police officers at Fort Logan resulting in twenty deaths (two blacks and eighteen whites) and dozens of courts-martial (eighteen soldiers executed and fifty-one given life sentences). Secretary of War Newton D. Baker blamed the Houston violence on the arrival of Negro troops and "more or less continuous trouble over the enforcement of so-called Jim Crow laws."[69] Segregation, Wilson learned, might not be a progressive, scientific solution to racial problems after all.

Elsewhere the riots continued. In 1918 five people died in Chester, Pennsylvania, and another four in Philadelphia. In 1919 minor rioting hit Knoxville and Omaha, and major riots hit Chicago, Washington, D.C., and Elaine, Arkansas. Twenty-five blacks and five whites died in the latter. In Chicago thirty-eight people died after a white man threw rocks at a black boy who had crossed to the Caucasian side of an invisible line at a public beach. The boy drowned. In Washington soldiers and sailors roared through a black area setting fires and otherwise destroying property—a rampage ignited by newspaper stories about black assaults on white women and stopped only by a cavalry charge.[70]

President Wilson agreed to see James Weldon Johnson and three other NAACP men and accept their petition asking executive clemency for Fort Logan's condemned soldiers. When this group also asked Wilson to speak out against mob violence and lynching, the president "demurred," according to Johnson's account, "saying that he did not think any word from him would have special effect." When the NAACP men said "his word would have greater effect than the word of any other man in the world," the president meekly "promised that he would 'seek an opportunity' to say something." The meeting itself, nonetheless, was a far cry from the Trotter confrontation. "The official air had been dropped," Johnson said. "The sternness of his face relaxed and, occasionally in a smile, became completely lost. . . . When I came out, it was with my hostility toward Mr. Wilson greatly shaken; however, I could not rid myself of the conviction that at bottom there was something hypocritical about him." Johnson would not forget the growth of segregation under this president.[71]

Rather than grant executive clemency to Fort Logan's soldiers Wilson reconsidered the requested antilynching statement. Black spokespersons and organizations across the country pressured the White House on this issue. "While making [the] world safe for democracy," the ubiquitous Monroe Trotter asked, why not "make us safe"? Even the secretary of war joined the call. "My anxiety is growing at the situation in this country among the negroes," Baker said, and a statement by the president condemning lynching would have a "wholesome effect." He also suggested a more aggressive Department of Justice policy to protect civil rights because "the negroes . . . feel that Federal agencies alone will be able to deal with such a situation." If Wilson was too much a states' righter on racial questions for this last suggestion, he did, finally, speak out on lynching—though only on the grounds of military necessity and at Baker's prodding.[72]

Wilson spoke no more on race despite the constant pleadings of Baker and other administration officials. George Creel, the former Denver newspaperman who ran the Committee on Public Information, said "the colored population . . . has been torn by rumor and ugly whisperings ever since we entered the war. Their leaders have been working with the Administration splendidly in combatting this dangerous unrest." Wilson nonetheless rejected Creel's suggestion that he meet a delegation of forty-five black newspaper editors and commend them for their support of the war. "I have received several delegations of negroes and I am under the impression that they have gone away dissatisfied," he explained. "I think probably it would be best just to carry out the programme without me for the present, until I am able to act in a way that would satisfy them."[73]

Wilson gave Creel and other home-front bureaucrats in the Committee on Public Information, the Bureau of Investigation, and Military Intelligence a free hand to collect information on virtually all prominent black citizens, groups, publications, and causes.[74] In theory the reports compiled by the intelligence community supplied leads for possible prosecution under the Espionage and Sedition Acts, but in practice the great bulk of the information gathered merely sat in agency files. On occasion reports circulated through other federal bureaucracies and on up to the White House. Often conspiratorial in tone with their warnings of subversive bogeys manipulating plain black folk, these intelligence reports nonetheless contained a sociological slant and recognized a legitimacy in the call for equality under the law. This slant was rare in the Bureau of Investigation, common in the Creel Committee and especially Military Intelligence—where NAACP leader Joel Spingarn and other racial liberals served and where even W. E. B. Du Bois sought a commission.

For his part the president never moved beyond the idea of segregation as policy. If the opposition's bitterness during the first term and the race riots of the second made him question the timing of segregation in the federal bureaucracy, he never let go the idea. Political scientist Clinton Rossiter described Wilson as "the best prepared President, intellectually and morally, ever to come to the White House."[75] Yet this best-prepared man could not see over segregation's hump. At his direction Jim Crow within the federal bureaucracy grew every day of his eight White House years, and at the direction of others Jim Crow had swept the entire capital by the second term's end. In 1920, the year the nation returned a Republican to the land's highest office, blacks and whites could mingle only in the buses and trolleys, the libraries, Griffith Stadium's grandstands, and for one day a year on the White House lawn (where black and white children joined in the Easter egg rolling events). The Easter Sundays this president spent in office where the only eight days when he did not applaud Jim Crow.

Wilson stuck to segregation to the end, and critics like Monroe Trotter stuck to him. Trotter kept reminding the president of his grand plan to bring democracy to the world and his grand silence on the lack of democracy for African Americans at home. With Wilson persisting in his silence, Trotter turned to Senator Henry Cabot Lodge, the man who stood between the president and his legacy, the League of Nations. At the time Wilson was on a national tour to drum up support for the League. After his health gave out during a stop in Colorado he returned to Washington too tired to work and too nervous to rest. A stroke followed. And as the president lay in the White House a sick and broken man, Trotter asked Lodge to read the Thirteenth, Fourteenth, and Fifteenth Amendments to the United States Constitution into the Treaty of Versailles.[76]

While the Senate debated Wilson's League of Nations the campaign of 1920 occasionally touched on questions of race. The Democratic party's vice-presidential nominee, Franklin Roosevelt, accused the Republicans of appealing to hatreds and prejudices. Presidential nominee James M. Cox said the Republicans were "the Afro-American party, whose hyphenated activity has attempted to stir up troubles among the Negroes upon false claims that it can bring social equality." A few white supremacists even circulated the rumor that Republican candidate Warren G. Harding was actually a Negro.[77] If Harding had little interest in race he occasionally received black spokesmen at his Marion, Ohio, home. That was enough to inspire Roosevelt and Cox let alone the race baiting of unabashed white supremacists.

James Weldon Johnson, Harding's most prominent black guest, proposed that the candidate speak out on Haiti. The issue here was a simple one—what Johnson called "the contradiction in the preachments of President Wilson about self-determination of small nations and the military seizure under his administration of a weak but friendly republic." American marines had gone in to establish a protectorate, a task that left many dead and homeless, and in a fact-finding trip to Haiti for the NAACP (made with TR's approval) Johnson estimated some 3,000 Haitian casualties. Harding listened carefully, breaking a chain of cigarettes only to cut off a big plug of chewing tobacco and stick it in his mouth. Later, when he used this Wilsonian contradiction in the campaign, Johnson said it "struck Washington like a bombshell." Harding agreed. "We certainly made a good shot [on Haiti]," he said.[78]

Harding continued to meet black leaders at the request of Johnson and Robert Moton, Booker Washington's successor at Tuskegee. One member of a Florida delegation reported that the president-elect was an incredibly ignorant man who had probably never heard of Washington. "If you'd eliminate 'damn' from that fellow's vocabulary," the delegate commented on yet another flaw, "he couldn't do anything but stutter." The group had come to discuss Haiti, a pardon for the Houston rioters, the Ku Klux Klan, and race problems in the South generally; but Harding apparently thought they were job-seeking politicians. This reflexive response only hardened over his time in the White House (1921–1923). "The Negroes are very hard to please," the president complained. "If they could have half of the Cabinet, seventy-five percent of the Bureau Chiefs, two-thirds of the Diplomatic appointments and all the officers to enforce prohibition perhaps there would be a measure of contentment temporarily, but I do no think it would long abide." Like his Republican predecessors going back to Garfield, he saw nothing in the race issue beyond patronage headaches.[79]

Harding barely did more than meet with Johnson and other black leaders for five minutes here and there.[80] He ignored Republican National Committee pleas to cultivate the black press and counter the Democratic party's "strong, effective propaganda to alienate our colored friends." He made only one speech on the race question, giving a Birmingham, Alabama, audience a contradictory message by simultaneously condemning economic, political, and educational discrimination and noting the "fundamental, eternal, and inescapable difference" between the two races that made social equality impossible. To his credit he also noted that racial problems, having infected "democracy everywhere," were hardly unique to the South. While Senator Pat Harrison of Mississippi called the Birmingham speech "a blow to the white civilization," more favorable commentators praised it as a rare example of political courage. It was neither. The speech merely represented this unprogressive president's view of "normalcy" on the subject of American race relations.[81]

Not the sort to strike a blow for or against anything, Harding ultimately emphasized promise over performance. He called for early military withdrawal from Haiti, then watched as Secretary of State Charles Evans Hughes squelched that idea. He encouraged the formation of an interracial commission, then dropped that idea. He first supported a Justice Department investigation of the resurgent Ku Klux Klan, then grew increasingly silent on the Klan as it continued to grow in size and strength. He opposed a Lily-White Republican party in the South, then said all Republican organizations on the Mason-Dixon line's far side ought to have white leadership. He supported the Dyer antilynching bill, then made no move to force it out of the Senate Judiciary Committee.[82]

An Alaska king crab feast and misdiagnosed heart attack ended Harding's presidency in August 1923 with the Ohio-gang administration falling apart amid scandal and official corruption that would culminate a year later with Teapot Dome. Harding came to the White House with the rumor circulating that he had Negro blood in his veins, a rumor that he could joke about with the NAACP's Johnson.[83] After his death an equally ridiculous if more persistent rumor circulated that he had been given a Ku Klux Klan burial in Marion. In office he had neither a black man's soul nor a Klansman's hate. He was simply a common man with neither vision nor courage who somehow rose from the bosses' caucus smoke when the Republican National Convention deadlocked.

Harding's death brought Calvin Coolidge to the presidency (1923–1929), and for the first of his five-and-a-half White House years the Ku Klux Klan emerged as a force in national politics. The Klan issue split delegates nearly fifty-fifty at the New York Democratic National Convention. A motion not to include a plank in the platform condemning the Klan passed by one vote, prompting the *New York Times* to conclude that "the Ku Klux problem has blackened the entire Democratic sky."[84] It took 103 ballots to nominate John W. Davis. If the Klan was not an issue at the Republican National Convention that nominated Coolidge, it should be noted that a chicken-wire screen kept black delegates separated from white delegates. Coolidge, the Massachusetts governor who had come to prominence by breaking the Boston police strike, ignored the Klan. He kept to this strategy during the campaign and after, even as Klansmen paraded through Washington's streets and constituents flooded the White House with mail imploring him to condemn such spectacles.[85]

Coolidge kept the politics of race stuck in the usual rut. Segregation of the federal bureaucracy spread to at least eleven departments and probably peaked under this "most Yankee of presidents." Coolidge's secretary, Bascom C. Slemp, an admitted proponent of "the Jim Crowing of negroes" and a segregationist Republican party in the South, was said to be a secret Klansman.[86] Jim Crow stalled in only one federal agency under Coolidge. After the NAACP's Washington chapter and other black groups filed complaints with the Commerce, Interior, and Treasury Departments, Interior and Treasury issued immediate denials. Secretary of Commerce Herbert Hoover, in contrast, asked his staff for a report, read it, then ordered segregation abolished in the Census Bureau where some sixty black workers had been kept apart from their white colleagues. For a time Hoover was a hero in the black press. Coolidge barely noticed. With an eye on the black vote he allowed Hoover to proceed; but this would be the only example of segregation marching backwards during his tenure.[87]

Coolidge went after black votes with the sort of energy that caused him to spend half his presidency asleep in bed. The administration based its strategy on the assumption, in Slemp's words, that "the northern negro is commonly a good deal more interested in promoting his own concerns than in making himself serviceable to his confreres of the south." This merely required GOP orators to seek party loyalty by reminding blacks "that when they live in the north, where the Republican Party generally dominates, they have their political and civil rights completely assured, but in the south where the Democratic Party dominates, these are denied to them." Neither Coolidge nor his secretary made any attempt to square such an approach with the Lily-White Republican dream.[88]

The president had no other civil rights policy beyond gestures and an occasional meeting with black leaders. He knew James Weldon Johnson and for those black leaders or groups he had not heard of turned for approval to Tuskegee's Robert Moton. Moton, who had passed information on black radicals to Military Intelligence during World War I, let Coolidge know who was a responsible Negro and who was not. A. Philip Randolph, who would visit the White House often over the next four decades, described what a meeting with this president was like: "We went in and it was an interesting conference. Monroe Trotter was known; he knew Coolidge and Coolidge knew him from Boston. And so President Coolidge told Trotter, 'All right, Mr. Trotter, you present your matter.' He did and he made a fiery talk, you know. And when he finished, President Coolidge said, 'Have you finished, Mr. Trotter?' So Trotter says, 'Yes.' He says, 'All right, thank you very much,' and he sat down and Trotter turns right around with his group and we walked out." Coolidge neither asked a question nor made any statement.[89]

In the manner of the Klan issue of 1924–1925, three events near the end of Coolidge's presidency almost knocked him from the rut. The first involved requests to pardon Marcus Garvey, the Universal Negro Improvement Association's Jamaican-born founder and arguably among the century's most important black leaders. The Justice Department and its Bureau of Investigation had gone after Garvey during the Wilson and Harding years with a young J. Edgar Hoover leading the charge and making the decision to imprison Garvey even before he was suspected of any specific crime. Eventually sentenced to five years for using the mails to defraud in raising back-to-Africa money for his Black Star Steamship Line, Garvey had served two by 1927 when Coolidge commuted his sentence for all the wrong reasons.

"[A] most unusual [case]," Attorney General John Sargent advised the president. "Notwithstanding the fact that the prosecution was designed for the protection of the colored people, whom it was charged Garvey had been defrauding by means of exaggerated and incorrect statements circulated through the mail, none of these people apparently believe that they have been defrauded." "This is by no means a healthy condition of affairs," Sargent continued, because Garvey's imprisonment not only made him a martyr for "the race" but drew attention to the prosecution's questionable nature. Even the attorney general admitted that the Justice Department's "facts . . . are perhaps somewhat severly stated and susceptible of modification and explanation in many respects." To rid the land of a martyr and avoid an exposé of prosecutorial misconduct, Coolidge took Sargent's advice, commuted the sentence, and ordered Garvey's immediate deportation.[90]

The second event that stretched beyond the usual involved flood relief after the Mississippi River crested its banks. Walter White of the NAACP discovered that federal relief administrators were actually helping Mississippi planters exploit "a terrible disaster to force Negroes into peonage." Blacks were segregated in the camps set up for people forced from their homes and sometimes held at gunpoint by plantation owners determined to insure an adequate labor supply once things returned to normal. With White charging federal relief agents with little concern beyond protecting "ownership of Negroes," Coolidge passed the complaint to Herbert Hoover who belatedly asked the Red Cross and Tuskegee's Robert Moton to file a report. "With [a] view," the secretary of commerce said, "to making certain as to the proper treatment of the colored folks."[91]

"My first of many bitter clashes with Herbert Hoover," Walter White recalled. It was more bitter than he knew. While Hoover patiently explained that the Coolidge administration's intervention in the Mississippi Valley had saved two hundred thousand Negro farmers and sharecroppers whose "gratitude is pathetic and overwhelming," other Commerce Department officials labeled the NAACP findings a "catalogue of misrepresentations" and "communist propaganda." "[We managed] to call [off] most of the dogs," one White House aide noted, "except one Walker [sic] White . . . a Negro who looks like [a] white man and has set himself up as a champion of his race. . . . Literally the nigger in the wood pile."[92]

Coolidge's third major civil-rights event involved Perry Howard, the black Republican national committeeman from Mississippi who was indicted for buying and selling public offices. (Similar charges were also brought against Benjamin Davis, the black national committeeman from Georgia.) The Justice Department sent J. Edgar Hoover's agents after Howard, and the director himself called the case "bigger than Teapot Dome. It could wreck this Administration." With scant evidence making Howard a hard man to convict, however, the white South suspected a cover-up. "In order that the Republican party," as one of Hoover's special agents explained, "will be in a position to retain millions of votes from the negroes at the fall election."

Coolidge, as ever, remained low key. He wanted those black votes; but he also wanted, like TR and Taft, a decent white man's party in the South. On this last point he acted as in the Mississippi disaster, leaving the details to someone else—namely, Mabel Walker Willebrandt, a Justice Department official. Willebrandt was as obsessed with Howard as J. Edgar Hoover had been with Garvey, and many political observers saw her pursuit as an attempt to foster a segregationist GOP. Howard was neither convicted nor stripped of his delegate credentials. But by 1928 the Republican National Committee purged all but four black delegates. After the convention, the party tried to oust three of the four, including Howard.⁹³ The Republicans did all this with their candidate's approval. Hoover objected only to the overly zealous Willebrandt, who also happened to be the RNC's credentials committee chair. In addition to her pursuit of Howard, Willebrandt tried to indict delegate Mary Booze and her husband, both of whom were personal friends of the president.⁹⁴

Walter White, a force in the NAACP since his battle with Herbert Hoover during the Mississippi flood relief, observed these events and concluded that political alignments were changing. "Eventually," he told Moorfield Storey, "the Republicans will absorb the anti-Negro South and become, through compromises necessary to gain that end, the relatively anti-Negro party, while the Negro will find refuge in the Democratic Party controlled by the North where in ten states the Negro today holds the balance of power."⁹⁵ Belle Moskowitz, an emissary of New York governor and Democratic presidential candidate Al Smith, told White that Smith had come to the same conclusion and planned to "make the first open and aggressive campaign to win the support of the Negro vote for the Democratic ticket." White found Moskowitz, a power in the city's philanthropic and political life, hard to resist. "One of the most colorful and forceful individuals I have ever known," he said. But he declined her offer to campaign for Smith "among Negroes" because his NAACP position demanded nonpartisanship. He also objected to the candidate's decision to organize a "racially segregated campaign bureau." Moskowitz then asked if he would advise Smith "on what Negroes were . . . thinking." White agreed with the condition that he not be considered a campaign aide.

When the two men met in Albany the governor opened in the traditional way—by offering a job in return for support. White declined. Smith then spoke "of his ambition to see Congress enact legislation to wipe out the vast inequalities in income and status among the American people, which, he feared, would inevitably lead to conflict which would destroy America if not resolved." What Smith wanted from White, short of paid campaign work, was a statement saying that the governor would not bow to "the anti-Negro South." "We Northern Democrats have a totally different approach to the Negro," he said. White wrote the statement and sent it to the governor's mansion but heard nothing in response. Belle Moskowitz told him a few months later that Mississippi Senator Pat Harrison and the vice-presidential nominee, Arkansas Senator Joseph T. Robinson, insisted that it be killed.[96]

Al Smith played both ends here. "This whole campaign," adviser George Fort Milton of Tennessee explained, "is predicated on the political theory that Smith can be elected by adding the wet, alien, negro voters of the East to the stupid, somnolent yellow-dog votes of the South. In other words, that nothing Smith can do or say can alter the traditional party regularity of the Southern states." If Smith took the South for granted he did make the occasional gesture to demonstrate that he was "reliable." His refusal to sign White's statement was one such gesture. Eleanor Roosevelt, making another on his behalf, assured an Alabama reporter that the New York governor "does not believe in intermarriage . . . and would never try to do violence to the feelings of the Southern people." Southern white people, that is.[97]

Walter White had no empathy whatsoever for the other candidate, Herbert Hoover (1929–1933), who showed nothing to indicate "that he regarded Negroes as citizens and human beings."[98] Running a segregationist campaign against a Roman Catholic from the sidewalks of New York who promised to repeal prohibition, Hoover took seven southern states (Florida, Kentucky, North Carolina, Tennessee, Texas, Virginia, and West Virginia). Leaving nothing to chance he even denied having abolished Jim Crow in the Commerce Department during his tenure in the Coolidge cabinet. "He issued no order respecting segregation of colored employees and made no changes in existing practice," administrative assistant Harold N. Graves falsely explained. Not everyone bought it. Mississippi Governor Theodore Bilbo saw integrationist taint of an even worse sort, charging that Hoover had danced with a black woman at Mound Bayou during a flood relief trip. Another aide, George Akerson, called this charge "the most indecent and unworthy statement in the whole of a bitter campaign."[99]

Hoover and his people were so careful not to offend the white South that they alienated much of their own party in key states where blacks held the balance of power. The *Chicago Tribune* accused the new president of turning the GOP into "a socially acceptable mansion for southern gentlemen. "The Republican party will sacrifice its Negroes,"

the paper's editors predicted, and woo the white vote in the only possible way—by becoming more antiblack than the Democratic party's
southern wing. An enraged Hoover told publisher Robert McCormick
that his paper "grossly misrepresents my position to the colored community in Chicago." "It is not a question of negroes or whites," he
explained, merely a matter of shutting out Republican organizations in
southern states that sell public offices and then opening up the party
"to other organizations where progress and endeavor are moving toward
clean public service." Corruption and not race, Hoover reiterated, dictate "my intent and the action I have taken." The president positioned
the campaign as a progressive move for clean government rather than a
transparent racial appeal.[100]

This obsession with "corrupt Negro office holders" was in part the
result of the Reconstruction mythology of carpetbaggers and scalawags.
To some degree it was also a legitimate issue. Offices were bought and
sold by black Republicans in the South, though the degree of corruption was in all probability no greater than among white politicians
from either party in any area of the country. More important, the obsession was the predictable result of the way in which the GOP
organized black politics from the Civil War forward. That politics
never moved beyond patronage. To court the southern white vote,
however, black patronage in the South had to be rolled back, which
Hoover sought to do in the name of clean government and not in the
name of white supremacy.

Matters of race and racism, nonetheless, pulled Hoover both ways
in his personal and political life. An engineer who had "much observation and experience in working Asiatics and negroes as well as
Americans and Australians in mines," he thought "one white man
equals from two to three of the colored races, even in the simplest
forms of mine work such as shoveling or tramming." Yet Hoover and
his wife, Lou Henry, refused to sign a restrictive covenant against
blacks and Jews on their S Street home in Washington.[101] As secretary
of commerce he abolished segregation in his department and then as a
presidential candidate denied having done so. Once in the White
House he wavered between trying to hold the black vote for the Republican party and building a base in the white South at the expense
of blacks who could not vote.

Hoover's indecision during the Oscar DePriest incident dealt an early blow to his Lily-White plottings. DePriest, a black man elected to Congress from Illinois in 1928, arrived in Washington amidst a minor southern protest. When he moved into a House Office Building room next to George M. Pritchard of North Carolina, Pritchard moved out (remaining officeless for a few weeks because all rooms had been assigned and no one would trade with him). The grumbling of Pritchard and a few other southerners erupted when Hoover's wife held a White House tea for the families of congressmen and DePriest's wife showed up. Southern fury had not been seen on this scale since Booker Washington came to dine with Theodore Roosevelt.

Hoover learned something from TR's handling of that dinner. The administration and its supporters in the press inspired "stories" to minimize the breach of racial etiquette, telling reporters that Mrs. DePriest remained on the outer lawn among the black servants and did not mingle with the white ladies. Other administration officials dismissed the tea furor as "another well-planned attack upon President Hoover by the wet newspapers." Eventually, Hoover jettisoned this strategy. He had his staff search the record of the Taft and Wilson administrations to see if the wives of black diplomats had ever attended diplomatic dinners, and when done that report noted that they had and further that some of these women "were mulattoes—some were exceedingly dark." In a final attempt to shift the attack from the first lady, Hoover invited Robert Moton to the White House for dinner (the first African-American dinner guest since Washington).[102]

For black citizens in general Hoover offered little. He had few contacts beyond Moton and Associated Negro Press chief Claude Barnett and no civil rights policy to speak of beyond greetings routinely sent to various organizations in the Booker Washington tradition (National Negro Bankers Association, National Negro Business League, National Negro Insurance Association, National Association of Teachers in Colored Schools, and Colored Masons). He called the National Urban League's work "fundamental to the progress of the race" because "economic independence . . . is the soil in which self respect takes root, and from which may then grow all the moral and spiritual enrichments of life." He also sent $500 to the Urban League. But as with other pro-

Negro actions, the president shied from credit or blame by insisting that the gift be given no publicity.[103]

Predictably, Hoover was most cautious with regard to the NAACP and its explicit civil rights agenda. James Weldon Johnson's request in May 1929 for the president to send a message to the groups's annual conference included a reminder that every chief executive for the past ten years had done so. Still stinging from Walter White's assault during the Mississippi flood relief project, Hoover ignored Johnson and the decade-long precedent.[104] The NAACP proved troublesome again in 1930 when White organized opposition to John J. Parker's nomination to the Supreme Court. White went after Parker, a Circuit Court judge from North Carolina, because he had a record of antiblack statements. ("The participation of the Negro in politics," he once said, "is a source of evil and danger to both races.") "The opposition to Parker made Hoover furious," recalled Roy Wilkins, who served as White's principal assistant.[105]

Hoover fought for the Parker nomination in a particularly bitter way. White House aide Walter Newton and Virginia Congressman Carl G. Bachmann encouraged New York Congressman Hamilton Fish's Special Committee to Investigate Communist Activities to look at the NAACP.[106] Newton also discussed the Parker nomination over lunch with the director of the Bureau of Investigation. J. Edgar Hoover subsequently ordered background checks on Joel Spingarn and other NAACP leaders. Mostly the bureau's findings were bland. White, Spingarn, and their associates, one report noted, disseminated "propaganda against the Ku Klux Klan"; supported "the so called Dyer Anti-Lynching Bill"; demanded withdrawal of troops from Haiti; and lobbied for "the liberation of those members of the 24th United States Infantry . . . imprisoned in the Leavenworth Federal Penitentiary for participation in the race riots in Houston."[107]

Not all Bureau of Investigation items were this soft. Another report, based on a wiretap, suggested the extent to which J. Edgar Hoover's agents supported the White House effort to push through the Parker nomination. "Mrs. Willebrandt yesterday telephoned to Mrs. Mary Wright Overton, of New York, who has been engaged for some years in philanthropic work and endeavored to have Mrs. Overton bring pressure to bear upon the N.A.A.C.P. to withdraw its opposition to Judge Parker," the report concluded. "Mrs. Overton is alleged to have told Mrs. Willebrandt that she was in full sympathy with the activities of the N.A.A.C.P. and would not accede to Mrs. Willebrandt's request. Mrs. Overton reported the conversation in detail to White of the N.A.A.C.P."[108]

The Hoover White House established a troubling precedent here by turning to the Bureau of Investigation for assistance in dealing with the NAACP. J. Edgar Hoover extended an open-ended offer to gather information, and from time to time the administration requested file checks on other black groups. One involved the separatist Moorish Science Temple of America, a precursor of sorts to the Nation of Islam's so-called Black Muslims. On other occasions the bureau simply volunteered information about such things as Communist party sponsorship of an interracial dance where young Jewish girls reportedly mingled with blacks.[109] From their early peonage investigations under Theodore Roosevelt to their wartime security work under Woodrow Wilson and now special services for the Hoover White House, Hoover's agents would remain part of the presidential arsenal for dealing with problems along the color line. All too often the FBI would be used not to protect black civil rights or even the national interest but to serve the president by gathering derogatory political information on his opponents.[110]

By the time the John J. Parker fight ended Walter White and the NAACP were a modest force in American politics. With help from American Federation of Labor leaders, who joined the opposition because Judge Parker had upheld yellow-dog contracts in a coal-mining dispute, the NAACP played a major role in the Senate's decision to reject the nomination by a two-vote margin. Herbert Hoover had said during the Mississippi flood that he had never heard of White, and his staff could not even get the name right (calling him "Walker"). Now when White called Hoover "the man in the lily-White House," the criticism stuck. "The N.A.A.C.P. had taken to slugging under White's direction," Roy Wilkins said. "Here at last was a fighting organization, not a tame band of status quo Negroes."[111]

"Hoover's intransigence in the Parker case," White realized, "permanently alienated Negroes." Roy Wilkins said the president "seemed immune to learn anything from such affairs, and his thickheadedness cost him dearly two years later." Hoover learned enough, however, to make one last bid for the black vote. With the Great Depression ratcheting the economy down every day and the segregationist politicking of the past driving "the colored people . . . off the reservation" (that is, away from the Republicans and toward the Democrats), he took pains to make symbolic gestures during his presidency's last eighteen months.[112]

When Interior Secretary Ray L. Wilbur asked for "a helpful word . . . to the negroes who are having difficulty at the present time in making social adjustments," Hoover did so. "Apparently," Wilbur said, "whatever the President has to say weighs with them more than anything else." (By "the President," Wilbur meant "any president.")[113] Other gestures included praise for the remarkable Mary McLeod Bethune, a commencement address at Howard University, and a meeting on the White House lawn with more than one hundred black leaders. (By meeting outside, the president avoided the repercussion of Negroes under the White House roof.)[114] Hoover also tried to be more aggressive on patronage. With the Perry Howard stink still in the air he looked for a black attorney for the Justice Department, finally settling on David E. Henderson, a deputy county attorney in Kansas City.[115]

In what was no doubt his most difficult gesture on a personal level, Hoover swallowed his pride and sent greetings to the hated NAACP's annual conference. He did so only after much soul searching and pressure from Theodore Roosevelt, Jr., the former president's son. Roosevelt could not understand why Hoover would hesitate. "We don't care what they have done in the past—it is what they are going to do next year," he said. "They have convinced me that they have no contribution from Raskob at all. Their books are audited by a public accountant every year, and they will account for every penny and the books have been so audited right along." Roosevelt pleaded for a message and "a statement against lynching."[116]

The Parker nomination and a new embarrassment, the so-called Gold Star Mothers outrage, combined with the Depression's relentless pressure to erode much of Hoover's belated effort to keep blacks on the reservation. The Gold Star women were wives and mothers of servicemen killed during World War I, and when they left to visit Europe's cemeteries the thirty-eight blacks sailed on their own boat. Stories about widows and mothers condemned to "a Jim Crow cattle ship" proved a major election-eve headache for the president. If nothing could have put Hoover in the White House for a second term at this point, his handling of racial politics could scarcely have been worse.[117]

With his administration and the nation in shambles Hoover sat in the White House waiting for President-elect Franklin D. Roosevelt to take over. Among the things he worked on during these dark days was the problem of lynching, something he had generally ignored in the past. (He had refused Walter White's repeated requests for a meeting on the subject; his aides asked White to send a memorandum instead, which he did, and which they promptly filed, apparently unread.)[118] Now the lame-duck Hoover, always the engineer, dreamed of attacking the lynch mob "with the modern expedition, through aerial and motor forces of Federal troops located at all important centers throughout the country." Unfortunately, nothing ever came of this dream.[119]

In sum, Herbert Hoover failed to achieve either of his competing goals. He was unable to recast the Republican party as lily-white, nor was he able to keep black Americans in the Republican camp. At one minute he deferred to the southern rope and courted the votes of the great white race; at the next he offered his hand to the NAACP and declared himself willing (in theory, at least) to send soldiers after the Klan. When Hoover left office the United States stood on the verge of a revolution in its political alignments. The next president would bring black people by the millions to the Democratic party, once the party of Calhoun and Davis. Five presidents down another Republican with another lily-white southern strategy would complete the work of Theodore Roosevelt and Herbert Hoover and bring the white South to the Republican party, once the party of Lincoln, Sumner, Stevens, and Wade.

: 3 :

NEW DEALER

Franklin D. Roosevelt presided over the United States during one of the most difficult periods in history. His four terms (1933–1945) spanned much of the Great Depression and Second World War, and his accomplishments during those trying times were impressive by any measure. Roosevelt's New Deal, certainly the most famous and arguably the most important and ambitious reform movement ever undertaken, undermined traditional states' rights attitudes by legitimizing the idea of federal responsibility to solve economic problems and promote (in a nonracial sense) social equality.[1] Roosevelt also presided over the emergence of a realigned Democratic party that would dominate American politics for thirty-six years. The so-called Roosevelt coalition had an urban, liberal, and northern base with ethnics, Catholics, Jews, and blacks coexisting with conservative southern Democrats (who went from a minority party's majority faction to a majority party's minority faction). Black Americans joined the Roosevelt coalition last, but once in would prove over the next six decades to be the most committed to the things the New Deal stood for.

Blacks came to the Democratic party for reasons of economic interest and not because the New Deal had a significant record of promise or performance on civil rights issues.[2] Roosevelt had charisma and wealth, a prominent family name, a professional machine headed by

Louis Howe and James Farley, and national prominence through his battle with polio and record as governor of New York. Lacking was an appreciation of or sympathy for problems of race and racism in American life. From the governor's mansion in Albany this Roosevelt reminded white voters, in his speeches and by his example, that he did not, like distant cousin Theodore, dine with blacks. "He was a New York patrician," the NAACP's Roy Wilkins would later write. "Distant, aloof, with no natural feel for the sensibilities of black people, no compelling inner commitment to their cause."[3]

Roosevelt had few contacts with African Americans beyond the odd jobs done for an elderly widow while a student at Groton. The servants at the Hyde Park estate where he grew up were all English and Irish. When serving in the New York State Senate he scribbled a note in the margin of a speech to remind himself about a "story of a nigger." Telling jokes about how some "darky" contracted venereal disease was a habit never outgrown. He used the word "nigger" casually in private conversation and correspondence, writing Mrs. Franklin Delano Roosevelt of his trip to Jamaica and how "a drink of coconut water, procured by a naked nigger boy from the top of the tallest tree, did much to make us forget the dust."

Eleanor Roosevelt, who had some exposure to black poverty through Progressive Era work at College Settlement on Rivington Street in New York's Lower East Side, was only marginally more sensitive. Following her husband's 1919 appointment as assistant secretary of the navy, she set up house in Washington "amid a world of people who are having fearful domestic trials . . . [But] I seem to be sailing along peacefully," having "acquired . . . a complete darky household." (In fact she kept an English nurse and Scottish governess.) In contrast to the Irish girls brought in from New York City, Eleanor found Washington's black domestics "pleasanter to deal with and there is never any question about it not being their work to do this or that." She was also something of a romantic here, having fond memories of her Auntie Gracie's "tales of the old and much-loved colored people on the plantation."[4]

Serious matters of race intruded only once in those early days. Franklin Roosevelt spent the summer of 1919 in Washington alone while his family vacationed in Fairhaven, and the four days of rioting that rocked the capital in July proved unnerving. "Though I have troubled to keep out of harm's way," he wrote Eleanor, "I have heard occasional shots during the evening and night." The Washington riot, part of the post-war black scare that brought interracial violence to more than a dozen cities, pushed Roosevelt toward law and order. "I only wish *quicker* action had been taken to stop it," he complained, admitting that he found something to admire in the "handling of Africans in Arkansas." This was a reference to the Elaine riot in which roving bands of whites drove past the fields and shot at cotton pickers.[5]

Race was scarcely a cork in this patrician's ocean, something that could pop up now and then to cause a minor inconvenience or embarrassment. Roosevelt promised everything to nearly everyone in the 1932 campaign with one speech calling for a redistribution of income and the next advocating a balanced budget. But when Walter White and the NAACP sent a questionnaire asking where he stood on eleven subjects ranging from segregation to Haitian independence, the candidate did not respond.[6] He kept silent after White reminded him that he had once bragged, when assistant secretary of the navy, about writing Haiti's constitution. When White and Joel Spingarn kept trying to establish contact after the election, the president-elect eventually sent the persistent NAACP men a short note begging off "due to pressure of work."[7]

FDR had other priorities (notably the economic emergency) and a political instinct that told him not to risk any capital on black America's behalf or otherwise antagonize southern Democrats. "I just can't take the risk," he said repeatedly. Those words summed up his southern strategy. In four White House terms he neither advocated a single piece of civil rights legislation nor scarcely spoke a single word against Jim Crow. Nor did he even seem to think about or discuss privately the issue of race. Franklin and Eleanor's son James could not remember "a single discussion" among family members "with respect to, say, voting rights in the South."[8]

Ambivalence and outright fear dictated most assumptions about African Americans throughout the Roosevelt administration. "We really weren't aware of their problems," admitted Elizabeth Wickenden, director of the Federal Emergency Relief Administration's transient program. Thomas ("Tommy the Cork") Corcoran, the political fixer and sometime White House aide, said "there *wasn't* any race problem in the Thirties." "We weren't concerned with civil rights," he added. "[It wasn't] a primary consideration of the guy at the top. He does his best for it, but he ain't gonna lose his votes for it." Secretary of Labor Frances Perkins "dreaded" the issue's mere mention. Jonathan Daniels, the White House "Negro question" specialist during the war years, said he did not "know anybody around the president who was a strong Negrophile." Will Alexander, the liberal white southerner who succeeded Rexford Tugwell as Farm Security Administration chief, said Secretary of Agriculture Henry Wallace was "terribly afraid" of anything concerning race. "[He] just wouldn't stand up under it," preferring to tell his own "darky" jokes and to ask, "Will, don't you think the New Deal is undertaking to do too much for negroes?"9

Remarks of Corcoran and the others indicate the general New Deal approach to ignore civil rights, or when that proved impossible, to push civil rights issues to the periphery. Yet the New Deal was nothing if not complex and contradictory, and its civil rights policies fit that pattern. A few of Roosevelt's key appointments were in fact civil rights advocates, notably National Youth Administration director Aubrey Williams and Interior Secretary Harold Ickes (who briefly served as president of the NAACP's tiny Chicago chapter). Henry Wallace would come around, too, especially during his tenure as FDR's second vice-president and his third-party run for the presidency against Truman. And the president had no problem with Negro patronage. After the August 1933 appointment of Clark Foreman, a white man, as "adviser on the economic status of the Negro," this was best symbolized by the New Deal's "black brains' trust" or "black cabinet" culled from the hundred-plus men and women appointed as "advisers," "assistants," and "directors" of Negro affairs in relief and recovery agencies and a few cabinet offices.

Several appointments fell within commonly accepted Negro patronage standards. *Pittsburgh Courier* editor Robert Vann, who received a Justice Department post, had been active in black politics for some time and was best known for his 1932 campaign suggestion that black voters turn Lincoln's portrait to the wall. The debt to the Republican party had been paid in full, he said. It was time to join FDR's Democrats. Another appointee, Edgar Brown, secured a Civilian Conservation Corps (CCC) position with the help of his brother-in-law, Irwin H. McDuffie, who happened to be the president's valet. Both men were largely ignored once on the job. Vann sat in a Justice Department office for a month "before they knew I was there," and he probably never even met Attorney General Homer Cummings. Brown said his CCC office was made with a "panel placed across a space at the end of a corridor."[10]

The New Deal also recruited black middle-class, college-educated, highly trained professionals with little prior involvement in Democratic party politics. Mary McLeod Bethune, president of the National Council of Negro Women and a force in the National Youth Administration, was the acknowledged leader; but the black cabinet actually divided into two informal groups. One met at Bethune's office or apartment. The other, younger and smaller, met at Robert Weaver's house. Ickes and Foreman had brought Weaver into the New Deal in 1933 during the National Recovery Administration code hearings. With William Hastie, an assistant solicitor in the Interior Department, he integrated the department's lunchroom—calling this "the first break in the cafeteria services in the federal establishments."[11] (Interior had offered a separate lunchroom for "messengers.") With a doctorate in economics from Harvard, Weaver served under Ickes and then Nathan Straus (Housing Authority) and Will Alexander (Office of Production Management). Thirty years later he joined the Lyndon B. Johnson cabinet as secretary of housing and urban development.

Roosevelt's New Deal did something for blacks through government appointments, general aid to the dispossessed, and symbolic gestures. And at least one alphabet agency, the Public Works Administration, occasionally approached the ideal of equal treatment for all. More often than not, however, the New Deal came up short. Of the National Recovery Administration (NRA), the centerpiece of the administration's economic program, some blacks said the acronym stood for "Negroes Ruined Again." Its Blue Eagle, they added, was more "a predatory bird" symbol than "a messenger of happiness." "After a thorough discussion of race prejudice, relative inefficiency, and cost of living," NRA officials concluded that their disparate treatment of blacks "was a problem more far reaching than any of these, and that there seemed to be no existing human solution of it." New Deal optimism gave way here to the faint echo of TR's "ugh."[12]

African Americans found themselves barred from the Tennessee Valley Authority's model town (Norris) and discriminated against in most relief and recovery agencies. This was especially true in the Civilian Conservation Corps (CCC), the Federal Emergency Relief Administration (FERA), and the Agricultural Adjustment Administration (AAA). If southern Negroes voted in AAA crop referendums, many of whom had never cast any sort of ballot before, they also saw policies implemented that drove tenant farmers and sharecroppers off the land while white landowners pocketed government checks. Roosevelt himself rarely displayed an interest in any of it. An exception was a complaint to CCC director Robert Fechner about the paucity of "colored chaplains" and medical facilities "for colored boys." "In the CCC Camps, where the boys are colored," the president wanted Fechner, conservative and southern born, "to put in colored foremen, not of course on technical work, but on ordinary manual labor." Even when his heart was in the right place, as it usually was, he rarely got past his own prejudices let alone those of his party's southern wing.[13]

With Louis Howe counseling the president to favor "our southern brethren" and not "our anxious colored brethren," FDR did exactly that. He managed to receive the votes of both groups while satisfying neither. The Negro press supported the New Deal while grumbling about a "Dirty Deal" and reminding the president that "in some sections, the administration of relief . . . could just as well be handled by the K.K.K." "Roosevelt!," marveled a black character in Chester Himes's novel, *Lonely Crusade*. "How he done it I do not know—starve you niggers and made you love 'im."[14]

At the advice of Howe, Farley, and other members of the palace guard, especially appointments secretary Marvin McIntyre and press secretary Stephen Early, Roosevelt initially closed off the White House. Black newspaper editors and NAACP officials could not get in, let alone an International Labor Defense delegation whose members wanted the president to meet with the mothers of the Scottsboro boys—the nine Alabama teenagers sentenced to death for the alleged rape of two white women. McIntyre and Early either referred everyone to Howe, who looked at communist involvement in the Scottsboro boys' legal defense as a convenient excuse for refusing White House involvement, or turned them back in the waiting room. The president's men would ask black visitors, whether newspaper editors or NAACP officials, "What do you *boys* want?"[15]

To further avoid offending white southerners, Roosevelt banned black reporters from his first press conference in 1933 and every other press conference for the next eleven years. His idea of communicating with blacks, concluded John H. Sengstacke, publisher of the *Chicago Defender* and founder of the Negro Newspaper Publishers Association, was to tell Walter White and "Walter would tell everybody else." When Attorney General Francis Biddle "suggested that the President admit Johnson of the Associated Negro Press . . . he said I should take it up with Early, but I rejoined that Steven certainly would be against it. He has in mind that this might run into unfavorable congressional opinion as they have excluded Negroes from the Press Gallery."[16]

Early, Howe, and the rest of the palace guard preferred to share racist drivel; minimize patronage for black party regulars; and keep the quest for black votes confined to the Democratic National Committee's loosely organized and neglected Colored Division (formed during the campaign's early months to handle the heavy correspondence from blacks eager to flee the Republican party of Herbert Hoover and the Great Depression). Called to explain an expense account, Joseph L. Johnson, the Colored Division chief for West Virginia, Ohio, Michigan, Indiana, and Illinois, told Howe that "during the two years in which we have been in power not one thing . . . has been given to the Colored Democrats of this district. Not even a messenger has been appointed. The Colored Democratic leaders of these states know this and some of them were mad and threatening to bolt. The expense account represents a part of the amount I spent holding them in line." Unimpressed by this plea, Howe kept Johnson's people shut out.[17]

With more than patronage in mind Walter White and the NAACP sought access to FDR with an end run around the Oval Office guard. "It was Walter's idea to reach him through the First Lady. We courted her for several years," Roy Wilkins recalled. "I had never used so much soft soap on anyone in my life." Though White and Wilkins selected Eleanor early on because they sensed she was a good and decent person, they knew her commitment to civil rights was questionable. "Even after she moved into the White House," Wilkins said, "there was gossip that she referred to Negroes as 'darkies.' " (That word would remain part of her vocabulary for the next three decades.) Once in the White House the first lady trimmed domestic staff in economy's name by dismissing the whites and keeping the blacks—a decision that devastated two Irish maids, Nora and Annie. Eleanor again took pride in her "all darky" household, assembling what Missouri Senator Harry S. Truman called, after a White House meal, "an army of coons." She also insisted that maids and cooks visit the beauty parlor once a month to get their "kinky" hair straightened. This strained their budgets, particularly after FDR cut wages 25 percent as a further economy.[18]

White and Wilkins nonetheless made a wise choice in Eleanor Roosevelt. "She took up the blacks," Jonathan Daniels said, and soon ranked among the twentieth century's great champions of equal opportunity.[19] She also became a target for the right-wing's anti–New Deal assaults with native fascist Gerald L. K. Smith predicting that race mixing would lead the white South to give way to "a sort of Miami tan." Modernist churchmen, academic sentimentalists, Communists, and New Dealers participated in this "campaign of mongrelization," Smith said. "All operating under the leadership of Eleanor Roosevelt. . . . God save us!" About the only thing the first lady could not do was get through to the president. She pestered him about everything, even tried (and failed) to get him to read Du Bois's *Black Reconstruction*. "If only F.D.R. would listen to his wife," Wilkins lamented.[20]

The New Deal rarely moved beyond racial symbolism. A black Boy Scout stood with the inaugural honor guard on the White House lawn even as the president respected the Jim Crow line on Pennsylvania Avenue that separated 150,000 blacks from 450,000 whites. In his first year Roosevelt pardoned the black Industrial Workers of the World leader Ben Fletcher, who had been tried under the Espionage Act of 1917 (Harding had commuted Fletcher's sentence in 1923); invited black artists and college glee clubs to perform for the first family; entertained former Harvard classmates without respect to color; and for the first time treated Haiti's president like any other head of state. In 1934 Franklin and Eleanor spent fifteen minutes in Nashville listening to the Fisk University glee club sing Negro spirituals with some 25,000 blacks jamming the hall and the streets outside. In Atlanta the president inspected a low-cost housing project and spoke briefly to 20,000 blacks assembled on Atlanta University's athletic field. On other trips South he dedicated the Eleanor Roosevelt School House in Warm Springs, Georgia, and met with George Washington Carver at the Tuskegee Institute. For her part the first lady refused to respect Jim Crow seating at a Southern Conference for Human Welfare meeting in Birmingham.[21]

Back in Washington, recalled C. R. Smith, Eleanor Roosevelt's long-time friend and later president of American Airlines, "I was over at the White House one night and the place was running over with blacks—you never saw so many blacks in your life."[22] The New Deal's excursions into the politics of racial symbolism may have been low key and low risk, but Mrs. Roosevelt had at least overcome, with no direct help from her husband but with his amused approval, the Howe-Farley policy of closing off the White House. Access to the president himself, nonetheless, was still problematic. The NAACP remained dependent on the first lady's manipulations, and within the so-called black cabinet only Mary McLeod Bethune could command an occasional audience.

Despite Eleanor's advocacy, the administration continued to defer to southern sensibilities. When Walter White asked Roosevelt in 1933 to send a message to the NAACP's twenty-fourth annual conference in Chicago, Stephen Early declined. The president did send a message in subsequent years but not without considerable debate among his advisers. "This should be checked carefully, considering the possible political reaction from the standpoint of the South," Early told Charles Michelson, the Democratic National Committee's publicity director. "I am a little hazy about the Association for the Advancement of Colored People," Michelson responded. "There have been some uncomfortable instances concerning intermarriage between races, etc., that concern some of the extremists in the organization."[23] When Walter White's twenty-fifth anniversary with the NAACP came around and White House staff prepared a draft of a testimonial, FDR's secretary, Grace Tully, relayed the boss's caution: "The President doesn't think too much of this organization—not to be to [sic] fulsome—tone it down a bit." Even J. Edgar Hoover wrote a testimonial for White with less trepidation.[24]

Franklin Roosevelt considered the NAACP a nuisance. Nowhere was this more apparent than in his response to the organization's antilynching campaign. The administration proposed and Congress approved ambitious crime-control legislation in 1933 aimed at John Dillinger and the Depression Era's other flamboyant criminals who exploited local police jurisdiction simply by fleeing across city, county, or state lines. These laws, radically expanding federal jurisdiction (especially over racketeering, bank robbery, and kidnapping), included no anti-lynching statute. "Not favored at this time," Louis Howe noted, in a bow to southern Democrats who considered lynching a local issue. "May create hostility to other crime bills."[25] Having remained silent through twenty-five lynchings, Roosevelt finally condemned such crimes, after a mob executed two white men in San Jose, California, as "a vile form of collective murder." Two days later in St. Joseph, Missouri, when vigilantes tortured, burned, and hanged a nineteen-year-old black man, the president returned to a policy of silence.[26]

With the support of Senators Edward Costigan of Colorado and Robert Wagner of New York, Walter White spent the next six years seeking Roosevelt's unqualified endorsement of antilynching legislation. Upon learning that "the lean and saturnine Marvin McIntyre . . . had intercepted my letters and telegrams, showing none of them to the President," White once more "turned in desperation to Mrs. Roosevelt" who deluged her husband with notes and memoranda on the Costigan-Wagner antilynching bill. She also talked to him "rather at length." "I do not think you will either like or agree with everything that he thinks," she later advised White. That would prove to be an understatement.[27]

Eleanor Roosevelt managed to arrange two White House meetings. At the first, held in 1934 on the south portico on a warm spring Sunday, White found the first lady and Mrs. Sara Delano Roosevelt, FDR's mother, waiting for him. Delayed in returning from a Potomac cruise, the president arrived late and immediately began telling anecdotes. When White cornered him on the Costigan-Wagner bill Roosevelt said "[Senate Majority leader] Joe Robinson tells me the bill is unconstitutional." White countered this and a string of other objections, prompting Roosevelt to conclude: "Somebody's been priming you. Was it my wife?" White simply "smiled and suggested we stick to our discussion of the bill." FDR then asked Eleanor if she had coached White. She told him to focus on the antilynching bill. Roosevelt finally turned to his mother, pleading, "Well, at least I know you'll be on my side." When she also told him to stick to the subject he roared with laughter and confessed defeat. "The charm and informality of the conversation there on the porch" aside, White knew this was "only a moral victory . . . because the President was frankly unwilling to challenge the Southern leadership of his party." Roosevelt would not fight for the bill, issue a statement calling for its passage, or raise a finger to break a threatened filibuster if the legislation ever came to the Senate floor for a vote.[28]

White pushed harder for FDR's support in fall 1934 after Claude Neal's particularly gruesome lynching. (This Marianna, Florida, murder, advertised beforehand in the press, drew thousands of spectators carrying picnic lunches.)[29] When queried at a press conference a few days later whether he would support antilynching legislation, Roosevelt ducked the question by asking for time "to check up and see what I did last year. I have forgotten." This incredible response led Roy Wilkins to conclude that the president suffered from "expedient cowardice." Roosevelt admitted as much in private. He considered the Marianna lynching "a horrible thing," telling his wife "that he hoped very much to get the Costigan-Wagner Bill passed" but continued to have doubts about its constitutionality. The president's real doubts concerned the political wisdom of challenging the widespread southern belief that states' rights doctrine precluded Congress from punishing civil rights violations by private individuals.[30]

With Eleanor Roosevelt's help Walter White spent much of 1935 battling Marvin McIntyre and Stephen Early who rose to shield FDR from this "very delicate situation." Early, a Virginian and grandson of Confederate General Jubal A. Early, was particularly vexing. He considered White the "most continuous of trouble makers" with the bad habit of "bombarding" the White House with "insulting" correspondence "demanding passage of the Costigan-Wagner Anti-Lynching Bill." He also made much of White's moral fiber by emphasizing his recent incarceration for protesting segregation. "I realize perfectly that he has an obsession on the lynching question and I do not doubt that he has been a great nuisance," the first lady tried to explain. "However . . . if I were colored, I think I should have about the same obsession. . . . It is the same complex which a great many people belonging to minority groups have, particularly martyrs. The type of thing which would make him get himself arrested in the Senate Restaurant is probably an inferiority complex. . . . It is worse with Walter

White because he is almost white. If you ever talked to him, and knew him, I think you would feel as I do. He really is a very fine person with the sorrows of his people close to his heart."[31]

Eleanor Roosevelt realized her words were wasted on Early and McIntyre. "There was no use in my trying to explain," she later wrote, "because our basic values were very different." Early would go on, five years later, to show something of his own moral fiber by putting a black New York City policeman in the hospital with a knee to the groin. The assault proved a major embarrassment. Roosevelt was concluding the third-term campaign at the time and hurrying to catch the Washington train after a Madison Square Garden speech, and Early thought the officer was needlessly delaying the presidential party.[32]

Even Eleanor Roosevelt was occasionally infected with caution on lynching and other questions of race. On the same day that the 1935 congressional hearings on the Costigan-Wagner bill began, the NAACP opened "An Art Exhibit Against Lynching" in a New York gallery and invited the first lady to attend. "The more I think about going to the exhibition the more troubled I am," she confided to White. "So this morning I went in to talk to my husband about it and asked him what they really planned to do about the bill because I was afraid that some bright newspaper reporter might write a story which would offend some of the southern members and thereby make it even more difficult to do anything." FDR told Eleanor to go anyway. She thought "it would be safer if I came without publicity or did not come at all." While Mrs. Roosevelt agonized, Tom Connally of Texas led a six-day filibuster against the antilynching measure. The Senate laid the bill aside on May 1 by a 48–32 vote in favor of majority leader Robinson's motion to adjourn. Neither the president nor the northern Democrats in Congress considered the measure important enough to divide the party and risk the New Deal's entire legislative agenda.[33]

Roosevelt and Walter White met again on January 2, 1936, with the president suggesting that the NAACP give up the antilynching bill in favor of a less controversial Senate investigation of mob violence in the United States. Unfortunately, southern senators lead by South Carolina's James Byrnes opposed that as well. For the remainder of the year White continued to work through Eleanor Roosevelt and to push for an antilynching law, and FDR continued to beg off responsibility. "In

view of the simple fact that I keep repeating to Senate and House leaders that the White House asks only three things of this Congress
(appropriations, a tax bill, and a relief bill), and that all other legislation
is in the discretion of the Congress," he told Eleanor, "I think that no
exceptions can be made at this session. If an exception is made in one
case it would have to be made in many others." When the first lady
"asked . . . if there were any possibility of getting even one step taken,"
her husband "said the difficulty is that it is unconstitutional apparently
for the Federal Government to step in in the lynching situation." "The
President," Mrs. Roosevelt wrote when briefing White, "feels that
lynching is a question of education in the states, rallying good citizens,
and creating public opinion so that the localities themselves will wipe
it out. However, if it were done by a Northerner, it will have an antagonistic effect."[34]

Rather than speak out Roosevelt secretly ordered Attorney General
Homer Cummings to meet with Joel Spingarn and other NAACP representatives and hammer out a new antilynching bill. "Distinct progress
is being made," Cummings reported back, "and the prospect of formulating a bill that will meet constitutional tests is encouraging."
"Knowing of your deep interest," Cummings added, "I would suggest
that these papers be regarded as strictly confidential. It would seem to
me altogether best that we should limit our approach to this matter to
oral discussions. We can give all the necessary help in this way without
putting the Department in the position of having given advice to any
private group."[35] Ultimately the new bill satisfied neither man. "We
gave what help we could in the preparation of the Wagner-Van Nuys
bill," Cummings concluded, but "Constitutional uncertainties" persisted. In an off-the-record note to Senator Wagner, Roosevelt refused
to support this latest round in the antilynching fight. True to his word,
he merely watched in February 1938 as a bitter filibuster led by Georgia Senator Richard Russell, among others, killed the Wagner-Van
Nuys bill.[36]

The fight against lynching had positive effects nonetheless. Lynchings diminished (from twenty-eight in 1933 to six in 1938 and two in
1939), and several southern states enacted legislation to head off the
federal effort. The NAACP increased its membership rolls and fund-
raising capacity, gained experience in the intricacies of public relations

and lobbying, and publicized the great horror at the center of race relations in the American South—a horror made more painful with news
of Japanese and German racial atrocities in Asia and Europe.

The Marian Anderson affair ended both the 1930s and the New
Deal's excursions into the politics of racial symbolism during that
decade. When the Daughters of the American Revolution (DAR) refused to permit Howard University to use its Constitution Hall for a
concert by Anderson, Eleanor Roosevelt resigned her DAR membership
in protest. Walter White and Assistant Secretary of the Interior Oscar
Chapman then proposed a free public concert at the Lincoln Memorial,
and Harold Ickes convinced FDR that it was the right thing to do. Plus
it was good politics with more than two-thirds of those questioned in a
Gallup Poll approving Mrs. Roosevelt's slap at the DAR. (Her protest
did little political harm even in the South because she was already seen
as a rabid civil rights advocate.) "Tell Oscar," the president replied, after
listening to Ickes's arguments, "he has my permission to have Marian
sing from the top of the Washington Monument if he wants it." Anderson gave her concert on Easter Sunday before a crowd of 75,000 that
included congressmen, cabinet members, and Supreme Court justices.[37]

Attorney General (and former NAACP board member) Frank
Murphy moved beyond symbolism later in the year. In response to
labor and civil rights demands that the Roosevelt administration do
something about violence against union organizers in particular and
Negroes in general, Murphy established a special Civil Liberties Unit
(renamed the Civil Rights Section in 1941) within the Justice Department's Criminal Division. Murphy relied on two statutes from the
Reconstruction Era that were intended to guarantee a permanent rights
equality and to control Ku Klux Klan terrorism. This new Civil Rights
Section legitimized the idea, for the first time in the twentieth century,
that the federal government had the right and duty to investigate, me-
diate, and if necessary prosecute civil rights violations.[38]

Civil Rights Section attorneys acted aggressively on occasion. This
was particularly true during the war years after Attorney General Francis Biddle ordered FBI agents to investigate the Cleo Wright lynching
in Sikeston, Missouri. Of nearly 4,000 lynchings in the United States
between 1889 and 1941 this was the first to attract official Justice Department involvement.[39] Roosevelt himself asked Biddle to draft a bill

allowing "the United States . . . [to] immediately investigate any instances of mob violence resulting in death or injury." The hope was that "this would stop lynchings if FBI men were on the scene automatically." Though ultimately deciding against legislation, the president implemented the proposed policy on his own executive authority.[40]

Administration officials remained cautious nonetheless. When Alain Locke recommended Howard Law School dean Charles Houston for a Civil Rights Section post, Biddle objected. Houston, who led the NAACP's legal fight against segregation in the public schools and recruited Thurgood Marshall and other star pupils who would triumph more than a decade later in *Brown v. Board of Education*, did not measure up. "I do not think that Houston would do on account of the FBI report," Biddle advised the White House, in a reference to the bureau's wartime loyalty investigations and view of civil rights work as subversive. Biddle also suggested that White House aide James Rowe talk to Civil Rights Section chief Victor Rotnem and "consider whether it is wise to put a Negro in. . . . I have some doubts."[41]

A starker example of the Roosevelt administration's caution was the decision to balance the Civil Rights Section's more aggressive approach on lynching with a passive approach on Negro suffrage. The administration had a few radicals on this issue, including Victor Rotnem, who recommended a "Federal prosecutive" assault on the various "trickeries, devices and tests and exclusions" used to deny the vote to blacks, accompanied by "the most careful national publicity." "The South will respond," he concluded, in a burst of wild optimism, "only with a realization of the importance of the war issues in relation to these cases."[42] Ignoring this, the president instead ordered Biddle to study the problem and come up with a way to attack "unreasonable restriction" on the suffrage without alienating the white South.

If Congress would not act, the president reasoned, then the attorney general becomes "the guardian of the Constitution" with a duty to intervene. "Would it be possible," he asked Biddle in a carefully drafted memorandum, "to bring an action against, let us say, the State of Mississippi, to remove the present poll tax restrictions?" He focused on the poll tax because it also restricted, in theory at least, the voting rights of poor whites. Thus "the question of race need not be raised in any way." Always sensitive to political realities, the president ordered Biddle to destroy the only memorandum he ever wrote on voting rights (some-thing the attorney general either forgot or refused to do).[43]

Rotnem's voting rights campaign never materialized. White House and Justice Department officials stayed out of the poll tax fight, largely limiting their involvement to reading FBI reports that suggested the whole thing was a communist plot. (The administration's response to the anti–poll tax bills introduced in Congress had much in common with its earlier response to the antilynching bills.) Biddle also refused to enter the Texas primary case (where the NAACP had filed a chal-lenge to the all-white Democratic party primary laws), a decision that Thurgood Marshall called especially hard to take because the attorney general was a "liberal . . . who has always been considered a good friend of our cause."[44]

The president's decision was strictly political. "Should we . . . make a gesture which cannot fail to offend many others, in Texas and the South generally," Solicitor General Charles Fahy asked. "I think not." Biddle agreed. "You suggested to me that there had been a 'good deal of a howl' because the Department of Justice did not participate 'amicus' in the Texas primary case," he told the president. "The ques-tion is purely political. . . . If we intervened it would be widely publicized and Texas and the South generally will not understand why we are taking sides." Still, Biddle said "the question is a close one and should you be inclined the other way, a brief will of course be filed." Roosevelt was not so inclined. No brief was filed.[45]

Another opportunity to enter a voting rights case arose on election eve 1944 in Alabama. After consulting Senator Lister Hill, Jonathan Daniels reported back to Roosevelt: "I strongly share his sentiments that any such action by the Federal government at this time might be the fact which would translate impotent rumblings against the New Deal into an actual revolt at the polls." Justice Department advocacy of voting rights for Alabama blacks, Daniels concluded, "would be a very dangerous mistake." Again, Roosevelt agreed.[46]

Roosevelt and Biddle hoped to placate both African Americans (by sending Justice Department attorneys and FBI agents south to investi-gate lynchings) and white southerners (by refusing to support voting rights in the black belt). Previous presidents had responded by ignoring both lynchings and voting rights, but after 1939 FDR did not have that option. He had to pursue a balancing act. This can be explained by World War II's pressures and the security issues posed by the nation's race problem. Lynching and other terrorism against blacks were especially troublesome, as one Justice Department official reminded Rotnem, because such incidents "have been utilized by [Japanese] enemy propagandists in international broadcasts particularly directed to members of the Negro race with the allegation that the Democracies are insincere and that the enemy is the true friend of the people of this race." The Japanese were especially troublesome because they urged a nonwhite racial solidarity. German propagandists merely compared their segregation of Jews with southern segregation of blacks. Hitler's SS even learned a bit by studying Jim Crow structures and rituals.[47]

Rotnem's Civil Rights Section focused on "Negro Cases . . . in view of the importance of Negro morale to the war effort." The nation's factories desperately needed black labor and to a lesser degree black recruits for its segregated armed forces. Rotnem's unit was particularly troubled by "the apparent effectiveness [among African Americans] of Nazi-propaganda, especially the Japanese. . . . It would seem that our work has taken on an obligation of being almost 'anti-Nazi' propagandists." Although the Axis line never penetrated deeply into black communities, the argument made government officials nervous: If the United States treated Negroes as second-class citizens, why then should Negroes fight for the United States? The Civil Rights Section's attorneys responded by defining "anti-Axis work" broadly enough to include "confidential checks" on prominent segregationists who might be spreading the enemy's message inadvertently or otherwise. Among others, Georgia Governor Eugene Talmadge and Congressmen John Rankin of Mississippi and Martin Dies of Texas were investigated "to ascertain . . . connections . . . with fascist groups." Such probes revealed that White House press secretary Stephen Early had said that "the Japanese were truly friendly with the negroes."[48]

Neither the president nor prominent administration officials like Biddle shared Early's well-known prejudices. Still, those officials had something in common with the White House press secretary on this issue. Roosevelt told Walter White that southerners in Congress were pressuring the administration to prosecute black newspaper editors for "sedition" and "interference with the war effort." This pressure led to investigations of the black press by the FBI, the Post Office, the Office of Facts and Figures, the Office of War Information, the Office of Censorship, the Military Intelligence Agencies, and the War Production Board. (This last agency cut newsprint supplies to several papers.) While black editors generally escaped indictment others were not as fortunate. Justice Department prosecutors filed sedition charges in 1942 against eighty blacks, including Nation of Islam leader Elijah Muhammad, chiefly because they had a "pan-colored" identification with the nation's non-white enemy (Japan). OWI complained that the FBI, in its press release announcing the arrests, "created the impression that most Negroes were Jap sympathizers."[49]

Neither the Roosevelt administration's actions nor the endless intelligence community investigations of African Americans had much of an impact. Criticism of the nation's dismal race relations continued unabated. Sometimes the civil rights advocates who voiced these criticisms could be dealt with quietly. Secretary of the Treasury Henry Morgenthau, Jr., for example, simply ordered a Bureau of Internal Revenue probe of the great Negro baritone Paul Robeson after Robeson made one too many comments about the administration's tolerance of racism.[50] At other times civil rights advocates could be simply ignored. This was always Roosevelt's preferred method for dealing with racial problems, and one easy-to-ignore problem involved his wife's reminder of how he had once praised heavyweight boxing champion Joe Louis after the second Schmeling fight: "Joe, we need muscles like yours to beat Germany." When Eleanor suggested a commission, however, Franklin declined. "I very much doubt," he said, "if Joe Louis has the necessary educational qualifications to be a Lieutenant in the Army." That ended the matter.[51]

Not all racial problems could be dealt with quietly or ignored. From the president's perspective the most disturbing of these problems involved NAACP and other civil rights groups' complaints about segregation in the Army and Navy and in the booming defense industries. In September 1940 Eleanor Roosevelt helped Walter White, Arnold Hill, and A. Philip Randolph arrange a New York meeting with Secretary of War Henry Stimson in an effort to convince the administration to do something about these problems. Ironically, the difficulties White, Hill, and Randolph faced were symbolized by the secretary of war himself. Stimson was an uncompromising opponent of integration who railed against "foolish leaders of the colored race" in hot pursuit of "race mixture by marriage." Like the New Deal's far-right critics, he even traced the carping for racial justice to the first lady's "intrusive and impulsive folly."

"We have got to use the colored race to help us in this fight and we have got to officer it with white men," Stimson later explained. "Better to do that than to have them massacred under incompetent officers." That was Stimson's position: The Army could not train black soldiers as officers or otherwise employ them in "technical units" because they lacked innate intelligence and were suited only for West Africa's oppressive climate. If Stimson did not get his way here exactly (black troop deployment was not confined to Africa), the president tilted in the secretary of war's direction. He would press for integration only in the War Department, and only gently. Always the Navy man, he would scarcely press for integration in that service whatsoever.[52]

Getting nowhere with Stimson, White, Randolph, and Hill pressed for and got a White House audience with Roosevelt, Secretary of the Navy Frank Knox, and Undersecretary of War Robert Patterson. Although White thought the idea of "non-segregated units in the Army" had never even dawned on the president, he found FDR generally receptive—full of suggestions about how "the Army could 'back into' the formation of units without segregation." Patterson also seemed receptive. Knox, in contrast, said the problem "was almost unsolvable" in the Navy "since men have to live together on ships." Roosevelt could only suggest that the Navy "organize Negro bands . . . an opening . . . which in time might help to . . . accustom white sailors to the presence of Negroes on ships." That was as far as he was willing to push his beloved Navy. The meeting ended with the president's promise to confer with additional government officials and report back to White's group.[53]

Roosevelt neither conferred nor reported. With Knox threatening to resign if the administration made the slightest move to desegregate the Navy and Stimson refusing to embrace even modest changes in Army policies, the president opted for the status quo. He scribbled "OK" on a memorandum reaffirming the War Department's 1937 plan "not to intermingle colored and white personnel in the same regimental organizations." Stephen Early then released this document to the press, falsely telling reporters that White, Randolph, and Hill had approved the existing policy. "Negro leaders 'played ball' by not mentioning the segregation problem in the Army," presidential aide James Rowe noted, "until the unfortunate misconstruction placed on the White House announcement. . . . To protect themselves with their own people [that is, to counter the charge in the black press that they had sold out], they felt they had to attack the White House statement." Criticism of the administration's segregationist policies was so widespread that FDR thought it might cost him the election.[54]

With the North's war production industries drawing migrants from the South's cotton fields, the Negro vote was becoming increasingly important as a swing vote in a dozen northern states. It had already influenced FDR's choice of a running mate. Eleanor Roosevelt, for example, was startled by the bitterness of Walter White and other civil rights leaders when Senator James Byrnes of South Carolina, an outspoken segregationist, was mentioned as a possible candidate. Edward Flynn, Democratic national committeeman, repeatedly warned that Byrnes's "nomination would cost the President 200,000 Negro votes in New York [alone]." (Roosevelt ran with Henry Wallace instead and put Byrnes on the Supreme Court.) Meanwhile, White and the ostensibly nonpartisan NAACP flirted with Republican presidential candidate Wendell Willkie. "Over cocktails he made the usual offers of jobs for myself and other Negroes if I would support [him] and he were elected," White said.[55]

Roosevelt had good reason to worry about the black vote even though he had little reason to fear an NAACP defection. (White told Willkie privately he had no faith in any "candidate who could obtain the nomination of a party so committed to the interests of big business.")[56] But White could not be sure about the level of "pro-Willkie sentiment among Negroes," the result of discrimination in the armed forces and defense industries, the president's silence during the anti-lynching fight, and the "continued domination by Southerners of Administration policies so far as the Negro is concerned." White took every opportunity to remind the White House that black voters held the balance of power in New York, Pennsylvania, Massachusetts, Ohio,

Indiana, Illinois, and Michigan. "A total of 188 electoral votes which, in the popular slang of the day," he said, "'ain't hay.'"[57]

Two weeks before the election James Rowe advised Roosevelt to make eight moves in dealing with the Negro problem. Most were cosmetic, designed to finesse the issue of segregation in the Army. Among other things the president could order the Selective Service to modify its strict quota calls based on race and follow "the lottery system . . . impartially, insofar as the first quota call of 35,000 men is concerned." The promotion of Colonel Benjamin O. Davis, Sr., "a Negro West Point graduate," to the rank of brigadier general would also help. Particularly if accompanied by a few other strategic appointments—notably, William Hastie as an assistant to Secretary of War Stimson; and Campbell Johnson, the head of the Washington Negro YMCA, as advisor on Negro affairs to General Clarence A. Dykstra, director of Selective Service. Finally Rowe suggested that Roosevelt "announce . . . a gradual beginning to end segregation," reminding him that "Army Officers will oppose this bitterly. Their stock argument is that they make some concessions but the President never forces his pet, the Navy, to take on any colored men."[58]

Hoping "to turn the protest meetings on segregation into Roosevelt meetings," Rowe promised "to let all the negro leaders in the close states know what we are doing." The idea was to publicize the administration's initiatives in the black press (not the white press), but the policy of barring black reporters from the White House made this difficult to do. As a dig at Stephen Early, Rowe also suggested that the president or the first lady, on their next campaign trip to New York, inquire about the groin-injured policeman.[59]

Concern about civil rights did not end with a few cosmetic changes in the military establishment. Protests against segregation coalesced after the election into a massive March on Washington Movement led by A. Philip Randolph of the Brotherhood of Sleeping Car Porters. A former socialist and twenty-five year veteran of the civil rights struggle, Randolph began the March on Washington Movement in New York. "I had a program of going down the avenue," he said. "Going into all the stores on that avenue—the barber shops, the saloons, the poolrooms—and saying to the men, 'Are you satisfied with the jobs you've got?' They said, 'No.' I said, 'Do you want more jobs? Are you willing to march to Washington for them?' And the response would be 'Yes! We'll go anywhere!'"[60]

Randolph anticipated that the government would try to dismiss his movement, as it had other protestors who invaded Washington (notably the Bonus March of 1932), as a collection of communist dupes. To avoid that problem Randolph kept his movement all black. "I never called on the whites for this reason," he explained:

> The communist had a policy of infiltrating *every* movement for the business of taking it over. They would build up fifth columns. . . . We had a public rally at the Madison Square Garden. We had one white man to speak. That was Father [John] LaFarge, he was Catholic, and I knew him very well, so I decided that we, at least, have one white person. But we never enrolled any whites. . . . I told them frankly, I said, 'Now, we don't want any Communist in this movement. And I'm not going to ask any Socialist because, as a matter of fact, you then will not be able to discriminate as to who's who. . . . So I'm drawing the line . . . against our white brothers because . . . they'll be more of a hindrance than a help.'

The greatest antidiscrimination event in the twentieth century's first half began by adopting discrimination as its own policy.[61]

When "Walter White said . . . I think we ought to try it," Randolph threw all his energy and incredible talents into the March on Washington Movement. Given the plans for an all-black march, White's pledge of NAACP support was crucial. Even though the NAACP was an interracial organization, its staunch anticommunism made it sympathetic to Randolph's all-black movement. The NAACP also gave the March a ready-made organizational base across the country. "Many of our chapters . . . [met] at nine o'clock," Roy Wilkins recalled, "and at ten thirty they would change over and become a March on Washington chapter." It looked like Randolph would keep his promise to bring 100,000 people to Washington.[62]

The White House saw Randolph, White, and the other members of the March on Washington Committee as crude blackmailers. At a time when they thought the nation needed stability and unity above all else these Negroes threatened "a monster mass meeting" on the capital mall unless Roosevelt granted a series of demands. Randolph's six-point program called on the president to lobby for legislation denying National Labor Relations Act protections to unions that discriminated on the basis of race; and to instruct all federal employment services that applicants not be screened because of race, creed, or color. The six-point program also called for executive orders forbidding defense contracts to any company that practiced racial discrimination in employment; and abolishing racial discrimination in the armed services and vocational and other training programs for defense workers and civil servants.[63]

Jonathan Daniels got a whiff of blackmail from a bit of information Randolph held on FDR's man in the State Department, Undersecretary Sumner Welles. Welles was among the administration officials representing Roosevelt at House Speaker William Bankhead's funeral in Alabama in September 1940, and on the return trip he drank heavily and propositioned a porter on the presidential train. Daniels said Randolph brought the story to the White House about Welles being "a sex pervert with predilection for Negro men. . . . There were certainly those who might have fabricated the story of homosexual acts between the austere, elegant Welles and menial blacks," he concluded, in a veiled reference to Randolph. For his part Roosevelt managed to cover up the incident for nearly three years until pressure from Secretary of State Cordell Hull and FBI Director Hoover finally forced him to request Welles's resignation.[64]

From the White House perspective Randolph's six-point program presented a no-win situation. With Great Britain near collapse and Nazis dominating the Continent in the pre–Pearl Harbor summer of 1941, large-scale demonstrations demanding an end to racial discrimination in defense jobs and segregation in the armed forces would undermine Roosevelt's preparedness campaign and boost the still-potent isolationists. On the other hand FDR reasoned that capitulation to Randolph's demands would undermine the attempt to make the United States an arsenal for democracy. To remove the racist props from American capitalism might have brought the whole economy crashing down at a time when it had to be mobilized for production. Even if the will could be summoned to do so, Undersecretary of War Robert M. Patterson added, the government lacked the ability to micromanage the employment policies of thousands of contractors.

Similarly, an abrupt end to segregation in the military would interfere with combat readiness. "We have not mingled white troops and negro troops in the same units," Patterson bluntly explained, because "such a mingling . . . would be impossible to put into operation." With the armed services also resting on racist props, every administration official agreed that now was not the time to knock those props out.[65]

So Roosevelt sent his wife to New York for what Stephen Early called "missionary work." Randolph recalled how Eleanor pleaded with him in Mayor Fiorello La Guardia's office. "'Phil, I may tell you that the President is disturbed. He believes that if you call this march . . . there's going to be bloodshed and death in Washington. . . . You carry a hundred thousand people there, nobody will be able to control them. You can't control them and nobody else.' She says, 'Now I want to appeal to you . . . I want to beg of you to call this march off.' And La Guardia says, 'Yes Phil, I'll tell you. This will be one of the greatest services you've ever given your country, and given the Negroes, too, for that matter.' He says, '*You are going to get Negroes slaughtered!* . . . It just can't come off without trouble.' And so I says, 'Well, I'll tell you Mrs. Roosevelt and Mayor La Guardia, we've gone a long way working on discretion. I've been to the Pacific Coast and back. Now, I can say to you that the only thing that Negroes are going to accept is jobs instead of a march, but they've got to have assurance of the jobs first.'"[66]

With Randolph refusing to budge, Eleanor Roosevelt and La Guardia worked on Walter White. "They took a ride in an automobile," Roy Wilkins said, "to try to persuade him to call off his support of Phil Randolph."[67] When White refused, the first lady and the New York mayor gave up. La Guardia told Anna Rosenberg that the White House ought to bring Randolph in and have "it out right then and there." Eleanor Roosevelt was in full agreement. For his part Randolph refused one last administration request to suspend his organizing work pending the proposed White House conference.[68]

While pressuring Randolph, Roosevelt called on the FBI for intelligence about movement strategies. Hoover's agents wiretapped March on Washington offices, recruited informants at the going rate of forty dollars a month, and generally spied on March organizers and allies anywhere they could be found. Randolph's success in keeping the movement free of leftist taint did not stop the FBI from advising the

White House "that the Communist Party will endeavor to convert the March into a Communist demonstration."[69] If few administration officials shared Hoover's obsession with (and fantasies about) communism, they viewed the March primarily as a security issue and welcomed any information that might provide an edge during negotiations with the troublesome Randolph. From the president and the first lady to Rosenberg and La Guardia, no administration official or New Deal friend objected to the FBI's methods in gathering such information or the underlying assumption that those who crusaded for racial justice in a manner deemed irresponsible were legitimate subjects of federal surveillance.

Randolph and White finally met with Roosevelt on June 18 in the Oval Office. The president, Randolph remembered, had his entire cabinet at the meeting because of the issue's magnitude. Roosevelt predicted "bloodshed and death" if the March proceeded, asking "what can we do to avoid this catastrophe?" When Randolph said the only way out lay in "an executive order guaranteeing Negroes jobs," FDR objected. "You issue an executive order here for your group and the Poles are going to call for one, and you're going to have this group and that group calling for one, and there'll be no end to it. Now I'm willing to see to it that these jobs are opened up and I think that we can do that, but I can't issue any executive order." Randolph held out. "I suggest that a part of this cabinet of mine go into the room with you and Walter White," Roosevelt responded, "and sit down to see if you can work something out."[70]

Randolph and White sat with an odd group that included Fiorello La Guardia, Aubrey Williams, Anna Rosenberg, labor leader Sidney Hillman, William S. Knudsen of the Office of Production Management, Secretary of War Henry Stimson, and Secretary of the Navy Frank Knox. "They wanted to do anything without issuing an executive order," Randolph said. "So I told them there's no use in my remaining here with you." He was back in New York, continuing to organize for the March, when the telephone call came. "They called me back and . . . presented me with the executive order," he said. Roy Wilkins recalled the moment. "A tall, courtly black man with Shakespearean diction and the stare of an eagle had looked the patrician Roosevelt in the eye—and made him back down."[71]

It was not a complete victory. On June 25, with the March on Washington barely a week away, Franklin Roosevelt acted on the recommendation of La Guardia, Williams, and Rosenberg and issued the first presidential directive on race since Reconstruction.[72] Executive Order 8802 prohibited discrimination in defense industries and established a Fair Employment Practice Committee (FEPC). FDR ignored the demand to desegregate the armed forces. "Secretary Knox was emphatic in his attitude that little, if anything, could be done in the Navy," La Guardia reminded Roosevelt. As if he needed reminding. On this issue the president was more emphatic than his secretary of the navy.[73]

The president's executive order offered enough for Randolph to cancel the March on Washington. But it was not a complete victory even on the issue of jobs. The administration did not head off the threatened demonstration at the expense of a divisive frontal assault on corporate hiring practices. For Roosevelt equal opportunity was a less important goal than the desire to "give Negroes a continuous forum" for blowing off steam (something FEPC might accomplish); or the perceived need to undercut Nazi propagandists who continued to zero in on racial discrimination in defense industries. In the words of the president's Negro question specialist, Jonathan Daniels, "our purpose was not the philanthropic purpose to uplift the blacks, but a wartime purpose to have unity between the races."[74]

Government surveillance continued unabated with the FBI filing a score of reports with the White House on Randolph and virtually all his contacts and sympathizers from North Dakota Senator William Langer to "'Mother Bloor' (alleged mother of Communism in the United States)."[75] On occasion administration officials more than matched the FBI's alarmism. Rotnem told Daniels, to cite one example, that a March on Washington pamphlet written by Dwight Macdonald, confiscated by police from a southern black, bordered on sedition. This surveillance often ranged beyond the question of Negro morale and the war effort to the strictly political realm. Randolph, J. Edgar Hoover reminded Harry Hopkins at the White House, "is said to have promulgated the idea of organizing members of the colored race throughout the country on a political basis, with relation to local, state and national candidates for office."[76]

Nor did FBI operatives limit their surveillance to Randolph and the March on Washington Movement. In summer 1942 they launched a nationwide survey of "foreign inspired agitation" in "colored neighborhoods." To find out "why particular Negroes or groups of Negroes . . . have evidenced sentiments for other 'dark races' (mainly Japanese) or by what forces they adopted in certain instances un-American ideologies," the FBI recruited informants and tapped the telephones of racial-advancement groups ranging from the pro-communist National Negro Congress to the anticommunist NAACP. Although Hoover's men had followed the NAACP since Roosevelt's first year in the White House, reporting on such things as the demand for more black representation in the alphabet agencies, they did not open a formal COMINFIL (communist infiltration) investigation. That came only in 1941 at the Navy's request after a protest against discrimination filed by "fifteen colored mess attendants." The FBI noted, even while spying on the NAACP, that Walter White was preferable to the "more aggressive Negro leaders who call the moderates 'handkerchief heads' or 'Uncle Toms.'"[77]

This surveillance continued after Randolph canceled the March on Washington because his issues (jobs and integration of the armed forces) remained constant and perplexing problems. On the question of integration the administration tried to finesse critics from all sides. Roosevelt told Office of War Information director Elmer Davis that public relations was "your No. 1 headache." The president was particularly upset with "the Army people" and their "dumb" policy on "the matter of information that Negro troops landing in Ireland are for 'service supply.' . . . In other words, it is the same old story of publicizing the fact during the [First] World War that the Negro troops were sent to France as 'labor battalions.'" Segregation may have soothed southern sensibilities, but it was continuing to interfere with Negro morale and thus the war effort in general. Davis promised to "neutralize the ill effect" of Army policy with the prompt release of "feature material about Negro combat troops."[78]

The mere presence of black soldiers abroad, whether combat troops or service supply, caused other problems. British officials complained in July 1942 about "the proportion of coloured people included in the U.S.A. troops being sent into this country." With race rioting possible, perhaps even likely, Prime Minister Winston Churchill wanted limits placed on African Americans in uniform. This prompted Harry Hopkins, then the head of the Lend-Lease program, to remark that "they are under the impression . . . we are planning to send about 100,000 over there." (At the time, 5,683 black soldiers were in Britain.) Hopkins patiently explained that Selective Service induction quotas dictated strict limits. African Americans in uniform could not possibly make up much more than their 10.6 percent quota in any given theater. The Roosevelt administration had to deal with criticism from civil rights groups for not using black soldiers enough, and complaints from its allies for using them at all.[79]

Additional problems arose when those soldiers returned home. The NAACP and the black press constantly complained about Negro Redistribution Centers which kept blacks away from "resort cities largely populated by whites." Of course, this was for their own good, as Secretary of War Stimson explained to FDR: Proximity to white civilians "might well subject the returning soldier to conditions unfavorable to his mental and physical rehabilitation." These veterans would thus be happier staying at segregated hotels "in the vicinity of large Negro populations" affording "the individual soldier an opportunity to be received and entertained by his own people." For the secretary of war and the president, Jim Crow remained an integral if far from perfect part of military strategy from Pearl Harbor to Hiroshima.[80]

With discrimination against African Americans and a dozen other racial and ethnic groups rampant, the question of home-front employment opportunity was equally troubling and persistent. Justice Department analysts tracked the problem in every city and every industry, and their summary of Los Angeles aircraft manufacturers' hiring practices was typical: "Douglas, Lockheed, Lockheed Vega, North American, Vultee, Northrup . . . Workers of Italian, German and Russian *extraction* not wanted. Vultee reported to hire only third generation Americans. North American prefers workers with 'American names.' Negroes, Mexicans, Orientals and Jews excluded. Citizenship mandatory. Army Air Corps Intelligence apparently direct or indirect supervisor of hiring."[81]

If Roosevelt established the Fair Employment Practice Committee to combat such discrimination and to serve as a safety valve, it functioned more in practice, much to the president's regret, as a lightning rod. State Department officials constantly complained that FEPC hearings provided grist for Axis propaganda, and FBI Director Hoover constantly reminded the White House that this latest alphabet agency provided a forum for Communists and "the Negro population in general"—especially "the younger negroes" and "the 'sporting type' negro."[82] War Manpower Commission chairman Paul V. McNutt also had to deal with the occasional radical idea emanating from FEPC staff members like Lucille McMillan. Speaking as "a white girl," McMillan argued that rampant employment discrimination justified draft exemption ("colored men and boys should not be compelled to fight and die in the Army and Navy"). Even Attorney General Francis Biddle, one of the administration's few civil rights advocates, advised the president to tone down FEPC. "Pressures arousing race emotions should be avoided," he said. "Results should be achieved by negotiation and persuasion locally, through men of local standing, with only occasional use of public hearings or application of sanctions."[83]

More typical than Biddle's qualified support was Victor Rotnem's invective. The Civil Rights Section chief, though a staunch advocate of black voting rights, considered FEPC a "political mistake from its inception," "political dynamite liable to explode at any moment" and do "infinite harm to the political interests of the Administration." It fed the "Southern rebellion" by catering to "the professional Negro," he reiterated. This view was a mainstream one. The Roosevelt White House, concluded the FEPC's historian, "opposed its creation, gave it lip service instead of support, used it callously to defuse black protest, and blocked it when political expediency so dictated."[84] Rotnem's reference to a southern rebellion largely explains the administration's hostility. Roosevelt created FEPC to keep order as the nation prepared for war, but the agency's very existence threatened the stability of the president's voting bloc.

Proposed hearings on the District of Columbia's Capital Transit Company, which refused to hire Negroes as platform workers or motormen, were especially troublesome. Virtually the entire White House staff was "a little perturbed," to use Marvin McIntyre's words. "[It] may be a case in which unfairness calls for action," Jonathan Daniels reminded Roosevelt. "[But] in a jumpy situation" it could "create

Southern fears that the government may be moving to end Jim Crow laws in transportation in the South under the guise of the war effort. It may also lift Negro hopes only to drop them again. . . . A civil rights *cause celebre* . . . might result in making more Negroes and more whites hostile toward the administration without, in fact, advancing the opportunities and rights of the Negroes." Sitting at Roosevelt's elbow, Daniels echoed Rotnem. The FEPC was little more than "a political instrument of Negro leaders who are now opposed to the President and the administration."[85]

Under Roosevelt's direction administration officials responded by pressuring FEPC to back off. Clarence Mitchell, who worked for the Office of Production Management and then FEPC before beginning his long service as the NAACP's Washington representative, remembered Daniels bringing civil rights people to the White House and telling them that their work interfered with the war effort. Daniels practically begged them to stop.[86] He later reminded Roosevelt that his true enemies remained "those who are undertaking to dictate the policies of this administration with regard to the Negro." The chief culprits were A. Philip Randolph, who with "the more radical Negro groups," Daniels claimed, "in large measure controls the President's Fair Employment Practice Committee"; and Walter White, who "[has] some sort of political deal . . . probably with Willkie." (These wild and demonstrably false conclusions, it should be remembered, came from FDR's race relations expert.) "Somebody must watch this business," Daniels concluded. Of course, somebody was watching. For Daniels and virtually every other administration official the FBI remained the principal data source on the politics of civil rights.[87]

Even when minimizing the Communist threat, the reports filed by J. Edgar Hoover's agents were numbing both in content and the oddity of their language. Black protests against FEPC cancellation of the southern railroad hearings inspired this speculation: "It appears to reflect the line of action of a continuing nature relative to the agitation among and by members of the Negro race in this country to remove *alleged* discrimination against them [emphasis added]." When the FBI looked beyond subversion its musings bordered on the absurd. "Militant demands by Negroes for a higher economic or social position have been regarded at times in some circles of the country as being inspired by anti-American sentiments," concluded the FBI bible on wartime racial conditions. "Yet, a number of inquiries have resulted in ascertaining such sentiments were expressed by Negroes as a result of ignorance or drunkenness."[88] Civil rights, in the bureau analysis, was the exclusive prerogative of Communists and Axis propagandists and Negro drunks and morons. If Eleanor Roosevelt served as her husband's civil rights conscience, Daniels and Hoover served as his guiding force for his actions.

While the FBI pushed on, the cancellation of FEPC's southern railroad hearings in January 1943 led Francis Biddle to again remind Roosevelt of "the seriousness of the Negro situation." Despite the little that FDR's government had done, he concluded, the white South was poised to fight back against "a supposed intention of government to intervene in every phase of race relationships." At the bottom, Biddle said, "the Klan is coming back to certain localities." At the top, he noted a move "on the Hill . . . to investigate the Fair Employment Practice Committee." Discontent among blacks further complicated things. "Politically I think the administration is losing the support of the Negro population," the attorney general added while offering a lonely recommendation that FEPC be reorganized and strengthened.[89] The real problem, as the president realized, was the widespread belief among white southerners and others on the far right that FEPC's issue (minority hiring) represented kowtowing to special interests. The Democratic party, according to Roosevelt's critics, was becoming a black man's party. Extremists asked, "What Man said to 'That' Woman/ 'You kiss the niggers/ I'll kiss the Jews/ We'll stay in the White House/ As long as we choose?'" [90]

Administration efforts to promote racial unity by placating the Democratic party's two constituencies most at odds with one another (blacks and southern whites) came crashing down with the riots of 1943. Particularly the bloody clash in Detroit where an influx of black southern migrants looking for jobs in the city's factories had led to crowded housing, recreational facilities, and public transportation. The results were predictable. Two days of guerrilla fighting left thirty people, black and white, dead. Above all else the lack of adequate housing lay behind the riots, and this was not a subject on which the New Deal had generally performed well. The lack of progress was no surprise given that the Federal Housing Authority (FHA) wrote into its own manual the basic real estate dictum that blacks in white neighborhoods depressed property values.[91]

Victor Rotnem, returning to the pose adopted against FEPC, called the Detroit riot an "outstanding example of Negro hoodlumism and wanton murder." In response to the NAACP demand that city police officers be investigated, he said the "police killings . . . probably, without exception, were warranted under the circumstances. . . . Negroes themselves would be in a sorry national plight if the truth of the Detroit riots were made clear to America. Maybe we should come forward with the exact facts, but given the problems of war I believe we are well advised not to."[92] Biddle agreed, proposing a series of reforms to contain or head off future rioting that included a troop deployment manual; draft deferments for city police officers; additional housing and recreational facilities construction; a federal race relations commission; and a prohibition against "Negro migrations into communities which cannot absorb them, either on account of their physical limitations or cultural background." This last item, NAACP activists argued, would simply bar blacks from defense factory jobs.[93]

Harold Ickes also recommended forming an all-white national commission on race relations. Such a commission, he reasoned, could preempt Martin Dies and his Special House Committee on Un-American Activities, who tended to equate New Deal reform with communism. (Dies had shown some interest in communist influences in riot-torn cities.) "You can't beat somebody with nobody," Ickes emphasized. The president rejected every proposal Ickes (and Biddle) offered, opting instead for what a Harlem columnist called an "ostrich policy."[94]

Roosevelt was aggressive only on the surveillance and countersubversion fronts. He directed Daniels and two Office of War Information staff, Philleo Nash and Ted Poston ("a very able colored man"), to set up a racial intelligence clearing house. This "White House team," as ever, relied on the FBI and its director to gather the requested "information as to these tensions and difficulties involving minority groups."[95] Hoover and Daniels both demonstrated an interest in the conservative view that traced all troubles to "the encouragement given Negroes by Mrs. Roosevelt." In Alabama, for example, the FBI launched an investigation of black domestic servants who supposedly joined "Eleanor Clubs" at the urging of "a strange white man and a large Negro organizer travelling in an automobile." Because the unrest here involved "white people who found difficulty in retaining their servants as a result of better opportunities offered by various Defense jobs," Hoover ordered his men to find out if female black domestics were really "demanding their own terms for working." He also wanted to know whether they were using the slogan, "A White Woman in the Kitchen by Christmas." This distinctly southern attitude also affected the white residents of FDR's adopted home of Warm Springs, Georgia. "She ruined every maid we ever had," a local merchant's wife said of the first lady.[96]

Here and elsewhere the FBI and its director gathered information on Eleanor Roosevelt and her civil rights activities real or imagined. "Edgar was not above relishing a story derogatory to an occupant of one of the seats of the mighty," Francis Biddle said.[97] But neither the attorney general nor the president would have been amused to find out the types of stories Hoover spread regarding the first lady; or that his agents had burglarized American Youth Congress offices to photograph her correspondence with Youth Congress leaders.[98]

When another round of stories regarding "Disappointing Clubs" surfaced, Daniels again sent the FBI to investigate. Eleanor Roosevelt had supposedly inspired the black domestics who belonged to these phantom clubs to "disappoint" their employers "for the express purpose of . . . antagonizing white people." The FBI then looked into "Pushing Clubs" whose black members supposedly went "about pushing white persons in public places . . . shadowed or escorted by a sufficient number of other colored people who protect them, subdue the resisting whites with force, promote a race riot if possible, and blame the white people for originating the clash." Harry Truman, among those who believed this absurdity, ordered daughter Margaret not to ride the Washington streetcar downtown on Thursdays because that was the day "they push people off." After extensive investigation the FBI admitted that no such pushing clubs existed. Mostly the rumors started at Washington luncheons and cocktail parties, spread, the bureau concluded, by such New Dealers as Supreme Court Justice William O. Douglas and Alaska Governor Ernest Gruening, among others. A liberal plot, in other words.[99]

Franklin Roosevelt was sensitive enough to the criticisms surrounding his wife's civil rights advocacy to take one other action in the Detroit riot's aftermath. Vice President Henry Wallace recalled a conversation with Garner Jackson of the Department of Agriculture: "I said, 'Mrs. Roosevelt's landing in New Zealand was a great surprise to me.' Pat replied, 'She did not want to go. She was ordered to go. The Negro situation was too hot.'" FDR merely told the first lady that a goodwill trip to the Pacific would be in order because New Zealand, being so far away, had been rather neglected.[100] By sending his wife out of the country for a few weeks, Roosevelt at least gained a brief respite from the ubiquitous Walter White—who still used the first lady to bombard the president with requests for action on every imaginable topic. White even wanted the White House to help convince Mme. Chiang Kai-Shek to address the NAACP annual meeting on "the national and global aspects of the color problem."[101]

Nagging concerns about the loyalty of black Americans persisted throughout the war years. Not only the FBI but agencies like the Office of War Information tended to lump reports on "Negro Organizations" with reports on "Communism" and "German, Italian, and Japanese" fifth columnists. Race influenced everything from the president's electoral prospects to the Manhattan project. "At Hanford, Washington, the first big reactors were being built for the production of plutonium," Jonathan Daniels recalled. "Nuclear detonation seemed threatened by a quarrel as to separate facilities not only for black and white workers but for Mexican workers as well, who were not welcomed in the white dormitories and resented their relegation to the quarters of the blacks. Production, not perfection, was the aim here and my memory is that separate provision was made for all three." At the dawn of the nuclear age segregation remained the presidency's best solution to racial problems.[102]

FDR's civil rights legacy remains ambiguous. Creation of FEPC and the Civil Rights Section were as important to the modern civil rights movement as A. Philip Randolph's threatened street demonstrations because these new bureaucracies legitimized for the first time since Reconstruction the idea that the government bore responsibility for closing the gap between the nation's democratic ideals and its white-over-black reality. In the wake of the New Deal's begrudging forward motion, however, bitterness prevailed on both sides. While the white South threatened revolt, civil rights activists saw their high hopes dashed as the administration undercut FEPC, kept the Civil Rights Section mired in lethargy, retreated from voting rights suits in the Jim Crow South, and stalled integration of the armed services. This last point was especially galling. Like everyone else during that good war, African Americans fought and died. Walter White lost a nephew, shot down over Hungary while returning from his fifty-seventh combat mission.[103]

Roosevelt had the right moral instincts but his political instincts told him to ignore racial dilemmas whenever possible, to split the difference between Walter White and Phil Randolph and Tom Connally and Jimmy Byrnes, to delegate authority to his experts (Daniels and J. Edgar Hoover), to send his wife out of the country when things got too hot. When the Julius Rosenwald Fund supported the call for a national commission on race relations, FEPC chairman Malcolm S. MacLean perfectly captured the president's position. "Such a commission appears . . . premature," he responded in Roosevelt's name. "There is a danger of such long-range planning becoming projects of wide influence in escape from the realities of war. I am not convinced that we can be realists about the war and planners for the future at this critical time." If civil rights activists saw opportunities during the war years, the president saw reasons for delaying justice till another day.[104]

Roosevelt had endless programs for helping victims of the Great Depression at home and Nazi oppression abroad, but on civil rights issues he ignored his conscience and did comparatively little to help African Americans. The president committed fully to nothing on this front, whether the NAACP's antilynching and voting rights campaigns or his own fair employment and fair housing bureaucracies. When finally opening the White House to the black press in his life's last year, he could only confess exasperation to the Negro Newspaper Publishers Association. The question asked by a black reporter had to do with segregation in the Army; the president's response could be applied to any race issue in that he concluded the problem was intractable not because of his administration's reluctance to confront it head on but because racism was too ingrained in too many Americans. "You know what kind of person it is," he said. "We all do. We don't have to do more than think of a great many people that we know. And it has become not a question of orders—they are repeated fairly often, I think, in all the camps of colored troops—it's a question of the personality of the individual. And we are up against it, absolutely up against it."[105] Like Theodore Roosevelt and Woodrow Wilson before him, FDR saw no way out.

Franklin Roosevelt's policy was one of escape, a flight from the endless nagging of Walter White and the horrors of lynching and rioting. Yet there was nowhere to flee. Even his beloved Warm Springs retreat, where he died on April 12, 1945, was not off limits. He visited Warm Springs to take treatment for his crippled legs, to dine on charcoal-broiled mallard at Cason Callaway's rustic log cabin, and to relax while Graham Jackson, a black man, played the accordion for him. He went to get away and to listen "to the darkies sing" while dressed like old plantation workers in overalls and bandannas or calico dresses and sun bonnets. Franklin ended up buying property and becoming a self-proclaimed adopted son of the cracker state; and Eleanor kept asking why Warm Springs had no facilities for black children. They could receive segregated treatment elsewhere, the president told his wife. "Tuskegee has a whole unit devoted to the care of Negro children suffering from infantile paralysis. Doc O'Connor can tell you all about it."[106]

: 4 :

COLD WARRIORS

Harry S. Truman came to the White House (1945–1953) poorly prepared to repair the Democratic party's racial rifts. Truly an accidental president, he was the product of a second Missouri Compromise which pushed Henry Wallace off the ticket in 1944 to the white South's delight and the dismay of Eleanor Roosevelt and other New Deal liberals. The latter championed Wallace as the heir apparent, and Franklin appeared at least vaguely sympathetic to that cause. He kept Vice President Truman in the dark, meeting with him only eight times—and five of those occurred during the campaign. None of this much bothered the southerners who looked to Truman at Roosevelt's death. "Everything is going to be all right," one senator predicted from the funeral train carrying FDR's body. "The new president knows how to handle the niggers." Civil rights advocates crossed their fingers and hoped that Truman's racial views would be more border state than uncompromising Dixie. They had no idea what to expect, as Roy Wilkins noted, from "an untested haberdasher from Klan country."[1]

Truman's background was surprisingly mixed. Born in rural Missouri twenty years after the Civil War, his grandfather had owned slaves and an uncle had served in the Confederate Army. His unreconstructed rebel mother still condemned Republicans as abolitionists. But as a Pendergast machine candidate Truman was dependent upon black votes, particularly in St. Louis and Kansas City, and never pandered to racist fears. As a United States senator, a genuine revulsion against Nazi racial atrocities led him to support antilynching legislation, the Fair Employment Practice Committee, and a petition to stop a filibuster against an anti–poll tax bill. As chair of the Special Committee to Investigate the National Defense Program he also demonstrated some interest in the problems of racial discrimination in war contracts and in the armed services generally. Still, Harry Truman knew where to draw the line. The Truman Committee, aide Harry Vaughan reportedly said, would accept "the Negro complaints, but did not intend to do anything about them; and if anybody thought the committee was going to help black bastards into $100-a-week jobs, they were sadly mistaken." Truman himself said that any Negro who tried to order a meal in his hometown of Independence "would be booted out" because management had the right to deny service to anyone.[2]

Senator Truman accepted separate-but-equal doctrines and often spoke out against "social equality" (still the day's great racial bugaboo). "The highest types of Negro leaders," he told the National Colored Democratic Association in 1940, "say quite frankly that they prefer the society of their own people." If he occasionally balanced such words with a call for "political equality," he had no timeline for that goal and never spoke with a sense of urgency or underlying moral commitment. "Regarding the negro problem," he wrote one constituent in 1942, "it is a most difficult problem to discuss because of its repercussions politically, and I would prefer not to discuss it with you until I have the chance to give it a great deal of thought, which I have been doing for the last ten years."[3]

Once in the White House, Truman could not afford such a leisurely pace.[4] Spurred on by mass production of the mechanical cotton picker and the sharecropper system's attendant demise, the great southern black migration to northern industrial centers accelerated in the immediate postwar years.[5] The black vote became increasingly important (something that no incumbent Democratic president or presidential candidate could ignore), and Truman had no lock on these new voters or the larger liberal voting block. Having inherited the Roosevelt administration's unresolved racial problems and little of the good will that the black voter held for Franklin and Eleanor, he worried about African Americans heading back to the Republican party reservation. He also worried about liberals organizing under the banner of Henry Wallace or some other convenient New Deal hero.

Truman knew what needed to be done. In fall 1945 he told James Byrnes, unabashed segregationist and then secretary of state, that "there were two persons he had to have on his political team, Secretary Wallace and Mrs. Eleanor Roosevelt—Mr. Wallace because of his influence with labor and Mrs. Roosevelt because of her influence with the Negro voters."[6] He appointed Eleanor to the U.S. delegation to the United Nations and kept Wallace on as secretary of commerce, but neither proved loyal members of the White House team. Mrs. Roosevelt was quick to criticize any deviation from the New Deal path, and Wallace opposed the administration's hard-line policy toward the Soviet Union.

Both the emerging Cold War and the United Nation's commitment to human rights and independence for the nonwhite nations of Africa and Asia placed America's civil rights movement in an entirely different and much accelerated context. When Byrnes would press Molotov on "Soviet high-handedness and ruthlessness in Eastern Europe," the Russian minister would needle him about the exclusion of blacks from voting booths in his home state of South Carolina.[7] The struggle for civil rights in this country got caught up in the global struggle against communism, and Truman himself got caught up in a political struggle with Wallace for the right to claim Franklin Roosevelt's mantle. Truman embraced the rhetoric of civil rights because this cause furthered the two things he cared about most—the prosecution of the Cold War and his own electoral prospects.

On April 17, 1945, five days after Roosevelt's death, a Negro Newspaper Publishers Association representative asked Truman where he stood "on the fair employment practice, the right to vote without being hampered by poll taxes, and all that." Truman passed the buck. "I will give you some advice," he said. "All you need to do is read the Senate record of one Harry S. Truman."[8] This was the new president's first press conference and his dodge was understandable, even predictable. Thereafter, Truman was invariably more forthright in rhetoric if rarely in action. "The strategy," White House aide Philleo Nash explained, "was to start with a bold measure and then temporize to pick up the right-wing forces. Simply stated, backtrack after the bang."[9]

The Fair Employment Practice Committee, created and funded as a temporary wartime agency, emerged as Truman's first civil rights test. Southern congressmen had been trying to kill the agency since its inception, and in 1945 the House Appropriations Committee deleted the funds Roosevelt had requested for its operation from the Wartime Agencies Appropriations Bill. After Senate Majority Leader Alben Barkley intervened FEPC received a token sum ($250,000) with the stipulation "that in no case shall this fund be available for expenditure beyond June 30, 1946." When Congress passed the Wartime Agencies Appropriations Bill, FEPC, lacking funds to operate effectively, could only limp along toward the day of its announced death. Having failed to reverse the House Appropriations Committee's decision, Truman started with a bang—announcing his support for a permanent FEPC in a letter to House Rules Committee Chairman Adolph Sabath.[10] That was as far as the president would go. He made no request for the existing FEPC's appropriation, sat and watched as a permanent FEPC bill remained locked up in the Rules Committee, and refused to meet with A. Philip Randolph or any other FEPC partisan.[11]

Truman backtracked for strictly political reasons. The Sabath letter, a White House analysis of constituent mail concluded, "had established [the president] as a liberal in the eyes of liberals. Prior to the letter, letter writers asked him to follow in President Roosevelt's footsteps. Afterward, they praised him for his independent and courageous stand." (Only nineteen of some 4,000 letters sent to the White House in June 1945 opposed FEPC.)[12] At the same time, Truman calmed southern Democrats by avoiding specific commitments. To keep his party's coalition whole the president appealed to both wings, preferring, in the manner of his predecessor, "the politics of stalemate to the politically unsound and politically unnecessary cause of equal justice for all." When he returned to FEPC in September, briefly mentioning his endorsement of a permanent agency in his twenty-one point message to Congress, he again refused to take any action that might antagonize white southerners.

This effort to cultivate a liberal image and thereby gain Roosevelt's New Deal mantle was thwarted by the White House's own actions. The most symbolic involved the refusal of the Daughters of the American Revolution to rent Constitution Hall to Hazel Scott, the pianist and wife of New York Congressman Adam Clayton Powell, Jr. When Bess Truman ignored her predecessor's example and attended a DAR tea given in her honor at the Sulgrave Club, Powell said "from now on there is only one First Lady, Mrs. Roosevelt; Mrs. Truman is the last."[13] Clearly, Bess Truman was no Eleanor Roosevelt. She was disinterested in civil rights, completely ignorant of the issues and people involved. When Eleanor Roosevelt's confidant, Mary McLeod Bethune, requested an audience, the president sent a curt note to White House aide David Niles. "Attached is a letter from Mary McLeod Bethune. Mrs. Truman wants to know whether or not she should see *these people* [emphasis added]." White House aides subsequently solicited FBI reports on both Bethune and Powell (who Truman called "that damn nigger preacher"). The former had been "selected to present the Negro problem," the bureau said, before the Washington Bookshop Forum, a supposedly "Communist-dominated organization."[14]

FBI Director J. Edgar Hoover also flooded the White House with sinister missives on the continuing FEPC fight. "Information received from a highly confidential and reliable source that an employee of the Committee on Fair Employment Practice has been in contact with Communist elements," one letter read. Hoover "thought the President . . . should know about the foregoing in view of the distinct possibility that a pressure campaign might be instigated by Communist elements in order to have this Committee kept in its present status." On another occasion he warned that Communists intent on influencing the FEPC debate had infiltrated the NAACP. Although the president and the FBI director had different agendas, they would soon find common ground, if only briefly, on the issue of a supposed Red menace at home.[15]

Whether or not such alarmist FBI reports influenced White House strategy in 1945–1946, Truman remained cautious. Washington's Capital Transit Company strike of November 1945 provides an example. After the president seized the company and ordered the Association of Street, Electric, Railway, and Motor Coach Employees back to work, FEPC chairman Malcolm Ross prepared a directive requiring Capital Transit "to cease and desist from practices and policies which have resulted in the denial of employment to Negroes." With no explanation other than an unspoken bow to the white South, Truman ordered Ross not to issue this directive. That prompted

FEPC member Charles Houston to resign in protest. "The failure of the Government to enforce democratic practices and to protect minorities in its own capital," he told the president, "makes its expressed concern for national minorities abroad somewhat specious, and its interference in the domestic affairs of other countries very premature."

Though Truman later embraced such logic in his prosecution of the Cold War, he adopted a narrow legalistic stance here. "The law," he reminded Houston (who happened to rank among the nation's most eminent attorneys, black or white), "requires that when the Government seizes a property under such circumstances it shall be operated under the terms and conditions of employment which were in effect at the time of possession. . . . The property was not seized for the purpose of enforcing the aims of the FEPC, laudable as these aims are, but to guarantee transportation for the citizens of Washington." Where Houston saw the Capital Transit strike as a possible opening for the federal government to step in and launch a frontal assault on the entire segregated southern transit system, the president intended to send a message to white southern Democrats that they need not worry about such things.[16]

Truman continued his mixed approach to FEPC. Five days before Christmas he issued Executive Order 9664 which effectively reduced the cash-starved committee to a fact-finding agency by taking away its power to issue "cease and desist" proclamations. In a radio address two weeks later and in his January 21 state of the union message he again called for a permanent FEPC. But in the weeks that followed he kept silent, with one minor exception (during a Senate filibuster against an FEPC bill), and he ignored those who asked him to rally support for cloture. Meanwhile FEPC ran out of money and expired. On June 28, 1946, Malcolm Ross and fellows submitted their resignations.[17]

Truman appeared to waffle less when meeting with a delegation representing an NAACP-sponsored National Emergency Committee Against Mob Violence. Walter White, the group's spokesman, recounted the details of a string of violent attacks for which no indictments on state or federal charges had been made. White began with Isaac Woodward, a black veteran who had been pulled off a bus while still in uniform, beaten, and finally blinded by the police chief in Batesburgh, South Carolina. In Columbia, Tennessee, Ku Klux Klansmen, police officers, and even National Guardsmen terrorized local blacks, shooting and killing two inside the town jail. Near Monroe, Georgia, Klan nightriders murdered Roger Malcolm and his wife and another black couple. Worrying about returning black veterans "getting out of their place," the Klan targeted Malcolm and the others because "one of the men had come back from the war a bad Negro." Truman listened to this litany for awhile and then rose from his chair, visibly shaken, and said, "My God! I had no idea it was as terrible as that! We've got to do something!"[18]

The president's response seemed to be deeply personal. "My very stomach turned over when I learned that Negro soldiers, just back from overseas, were being dumped out of army trucks in Mississippi and beaten," he later wrote daughter Margaret. "Whatever my inclinations as a native of Missouri might have been, as President I know this is bad. I shall fight to end evils like this." The meeting also forced painful memories of the South to the surface. "The Louisiana and Arkansas Railroad and the Southern Pacific Railroad had Negroes working as firemen in Louisiana and Texas," he recalled years later. "Their engines were coal burners, and the job was a terribly backbreaking one. When they went over to oil, and the firemen could wear white collars and clean overalls, the inhabitants of the states along these two roads used to shoot the Negro firemen as they went by. This and the incident of the sergeant and the assassination of the four Negroes in Georgia showed the lengths to which people would go."[19]

Truman had in fact known about the lynchings and beatings recounted by Walter White's group at the time they happened (February–July 1946). He remained silent through every one. Thus his my-God reaction to White's report was probably staged. He had already decided to create a special committee to investigate lynching and other civil rights abuses and recommend corrective action. He also timed the announcement to coincide with Henry Wallace's forced resignation from the cabinet on September 20 for criticizing the new Soviet policy. "I am very much in earnest on this thing," he told David Niles on the day Wallace left, "and I'd like very much to have you push it with everything you have." To drive his point home the president told Attorney General Tom Clark that he wanted "something similar to the Wickersham Commission on Prohibition." But this commitment did not extend to specific proposals and was motivated less by personal revulsion to rampant mob violence than the need to appease the New Deal faithful in the wake of Wallace's departure.[20]

On September 23, four days after meeting White's group and three days after forcing Wallace out, Truman met another delegation headed by Paul Robeson. This group, more militant (obnoxious, in the president's mind), represented some one thousand demonstrators who carried antilynching and we-want-Wallace-back banners. Robeson opened by promising to meet fire with fire. "If the government does not do something about lynching," he told the president in his passionate voice, "you can be sure that the Negroes will." When Robeson reminded the president that Secretary of State Byrnes supported Jim Crow in his native South Carolina, Truman nearly lost his temper. Surely the delegates would agree, the president said, that, domestic racial problems aside, the United States and its allies (notably Great Britain) represented the world's last hope for freedom. "The British empire is the greatest enslaver of human beings in the world," Robeson countered. From there the president sat stone faced as Robeson read a list of demands calling for a White House statement condemning lynching and introduction of civil rights legislation. The president refused to make any commitments beyond the committee that Niles and Clark were organizing.[21]

By Executive Order 9808 of December 5, 1946, Truman established the President's Committee on Civil Rights—a vehicle, in Niles's words, for "taking [Harry S. Truman] off the hot seat."[22] White House aides called it "Noah's Arc" because it included two of everything (blacks, women, Catholics, Jews, businessmen, southerners, labor leaders, college presidents). General Electric chief Charles E. Wilson served as chair. Other members were Sadie T. Alexander, a Philadelphia lawyer and National Urban League activist; CIO official James B. Carey; Dartmouth College president John S. Dickey; ACLU attorney Morris Ernst; Rabbi Roland G. Gittelsohn of Rockville, New York; University of North Carolina president Frank P. Graham; Rev. Francis J. Haas, bishop of Grand Rapids, Michigan, and former FEPC chair; Lever Brothers president Charles Luckman; Francis P. Matthews, vice-president of the National War Fund and a prominent Catholic layman; Franklin D. Roosevelt, Jr.; Rev. Henry Knox Sherrill, presiding bishop of the Episcopal Church; Boris Shiskin, an AFL economist and former FEPC member; Mrs. M. E. Tilley of Atlanta; and Phelps-Stokes Fund director Channing Tobias. Dartmouth political scientist Robert K. Carr served as executive secretary.

With such prominent liberals on board Truman could not hope to control the committee's investigations or recommendations. The White House nonetheless selected members based as much on their attitude toward the Cold War as anything else. The entire committee ended up taking a loyalty oath because, as Robert Carr put it, "it would be a rather nice symbolic gesture . . . to indicate, I suppose, that you are in complete sympathy toward the American ideals." One member, the ACLU's Morris Ernst, went even further by functioning as a quasi-official FBI informant. He offered "recommendations" at the bureau's request "for legislation requiring the registration of all private organizations whose activities affect civil rights and also to require publicity as to their financial backing and expenditures." Ernst was "interested," according to committee minutes, "in using the taxing and spending powers as means of forcing private and public organizations enjoying tax exemptions or government subsidies to avoid Jim Crow practices." Hoover's FBI, of course, was more interested in anti–Jim Crow practices.[23]

Cold War imperatives and the administration's concomitant attempt to keep the New Deal coalition whole had collided, and the Cold War came out on top. Truman had met with Robeson's group in September 1946 because the White House tried to distinguish, as Niles put it, "between a Negro [communist] front organization and other front organizations because the Negro press is an instrument we ought to use every chance we can. To get the President's name in the Negro press, whatever the circumstances, should be helpful." But by early 1947, a time when the Cold War began to heat up in earnest, the administration was no longer willing to court black radicals. Instead, the White House referred the troublesome Robeson to the House Committee on Un-American Activities.[24]

In the aftermath of his Truman Doctrine speech of March 12, 1947, and with Henry Wallace threatening a third-party run in the 1948 campaign, the president accepted Walter White's invitation to address an NAACP rally in front of the Lincoln Memorial. On June 29 Truman became the first American president to speak at an NAACP gathering.[25] A crowd of ten thousand listened and all four major radio networks carried the address to hundreds of thousands more while the State Department beamed the president's words abroad by short wave:

> Our national government must show the way. This is a difficult and complex undertaking. Federal laws and administrative machinery must be improved and expanded. We must provide the government with better tools to do the job. . . . Every man should have the right to a decent home, the right to an education, the right to adequate medical care, the right to a worthwhile job, the right to an equal share in making public decisions through the ballot, and the right to a fair trial in a fair court. We must insure that these rights—on equal terms—are enjoyed by every citizen.

Truman next placed the civil rights struggle squarely in the Cold War conflict between the United States and the Soviet Union.

> The support of desperate populations of battle ravaged countries must be won for the free way of life. We must have them as allies in our continuing struggle for the peaceful solution of the world's problems. They may surrender to the false security offered so temptingly by totalitarian regimes unless we can prove the superiority of democracy. Our case for democracy should be as strong as we can make it. It should rest on practical evidence that we have been able to put our own house in order.[26]

Turning to Walter White when finished, Truman said, "I mean every word of it. And I am going to prove that I do mean it."

By any standard, it was a remarkable speech. "An unequivocal pledge," Roy Wilkins concluded. "For the first time, the President was putting himself and the government where they should have been all along: at the head of the parade, not on the sidelines." But for all its rhetorical grandeur, the speech lacked concrete proposals.[27]

Many civil rights activists agreed with Truman's emphasis on the connection between the Cold War abroad and a ubiquitous racism at home. With the United States gearing up in freedom's name for a global crusade against communism, the struggle for racial justice found unexpected leverage.[28] How could the president fight for world freedom while the nation denied basic freedoms to its own nonwhite citizens? On a more practical level, if the Cold War is defined as a struggle between two rival empires (the United States and the Soviet Union) for the allegiance of the largely nonwhite third world and access to its resources, then America's racial baggage would prove a devastating handicap. Soviet propagandists realized this instinctively. For the next forty years tales of the racist atrocities African Americans endured would fill *Pravda's* pages.

The NAACP took advantage of this Cold War context to pressure the White House into moving beyond rhetoric. Walter White turned to the United Nations, enlisting W. E. B. Du Bois, Milton Konvitz, Earl B. Dickerson, and Rayford Logan to draft a petition of grievances—"a frank and earnest appeal to all the world for elemental justice against the treatment which the United States has visited upon us for three centuries." Holding that African-American demands for human rights were similar to those of the third world's colonized peoples, the petition called upon "the nations of the world to persuade this nation to be just to its own people." Although the United Nations Commission on Human Rights rejected a Soviet proposal calling for an investigation of the specific grievances, the NAACP petition received widespread publicity in the domestic and foreign press.[29]

More exposure of the nation's dismal racial situation followed on October 29, 1947, when the President's Committee on Civil Rights released its report. *To Secure These Rights*, as Truman later noted, "almost gave the Southerners hydrophobia" with its thirty-five sweeping recommendations and unqualified call for federal action on moral, economic, and diplomatic grounds. The most substantive recommendations called for creation of executive branch bureaucracies and congressional committees—specifically, a permanent civil rights division in the Justice Department, a permanent commission on civil rights, and a joint standing committee on civil rights in Congress. While praising *To Secure These Rights* as "an American charter of human freedom . . . a guide for action," the president made no commitment to implement the recommendations.[30]

Truman did embrace the report's call for federal action some three weeks later after reading a forty-three-page memorandum entitled "The Politics of 1948." This document, originally prepared by former Roosevelt "bird dog" James Rowe, who once said his "duties" were "to do, in effect, whatever [FDR] told me to do," outlined the battle plan that

Truman would follow in the coming election. The problem was that Truman hated Rowe and would not have read the memorandum had he known Rowe was the author. So Rowe sent the document to White House special counsel Clark Clifford, who reworked it (adding ten pages to Rowe's thirty-three) and then delivered it to the Oval Office. Clifford's revision went to Truman alone, and the president kept it handy in a desk drawer throughout the campaign.[31]

The issue in 1948 was clear. White House officials expected Henry Wallace to make a third-party charge (he declared in Chicago a month later, on December 29, on the newly formed Progressive party ticket), and with two of Franklin Roosevelt's former vice-presidents running the Democratic party's voting bloc would no doubt split. Conventional wisdom held that this would guarantee victory for the Republican party's likely nominee, Thomas E. Dewey. In this context, Clifford concluded, the president's only hope lay in the black vote. If Truman lost that vote in just a few "key states," Dewey would win.[32] Both Wallace and Dewey, moreover, could make a strong case for black support: Wallace through his New Deal lineage and more recent emergence as a civil rights champion; and Dewey through his record as governor of New York in securing a state FEPC and appointing blacks to office. Clifford predicted that the Republican platform would give Dewey an additional boost by calling for an antilynching bill, equal employment opportunity, abolition of the poll tax, and an end to segregation in the armed services. "The northern Negro," he said, "[has] under the tutelage of Walter White . . . become a cynical, hardboiled trader" and might "swing back to his traditional moorings—the Republican party."[33]

"The Administration would make a grave error if we permitted the Republicans to get away with this," Clifford told Truman. "It would appear to be sound strategy to have the President go as far as he feels he possibly could go in recommending measures to protect the rights of minority groups. This course of action would obviously cause difficulty with our Southern friends but that is the lesser of two evils." A lesser evil because of the lesser risk, in other words. "It is inconceivable," Clifford reasoned, "that any policies initiated by the Truman Administration no matter how 'liberal' could so alienate the South in the next year that it would revolt. . . . As always, the South can be considered safely Democratic. And in formulating national policy, it can be safely ignored. . . . The *only* pragmatic reason for conciliating the South in normal times is because of its tremendous strength in the Congress. Since the Congress is Republican and the Democratic President has, therefore, no real chance to get his own program approved by it, particularly in an election year, he has no real necessity for 'getting along' with the Southern conservatives. He *must*, however, get along with the Westerners and with labor."

If Truman could project a liberal enough image to get the black and labor vote and thus keep the New Deal coalition whole, in the Clifford/Rowe analysis, not only the South but the North could be ignored. By carrying the solid South and the West, the president could even afford to lose all "the 'big' states" (New York, Ohio, Pennsylvania, Illinois, New Jersey, Massachusetts) and still win. "That the Democratic Party is an unhappy alliance of Southern conservatives, Western progressives and Big City labor," Clifford reiterated, "is very trite, but it is also very true." The goal is to "lead enough members of these three misfit groups to the polls on the first Tuesday after the first Monday of November, 1948."

This campaign blueprint was somewhat contradictory, holding that the black vote was vital in several key northern states and then arguing that the North could be safely ignored. Clifford, eventually recognizing the contradiction, suggested the president "modify his stand on the civil rights issue" and thus run not so great "a risk in alienating the South."[34] Truman figured his man got it right the first time. Because Wallace represented the most pressing danger Truman simply had to cultivate a more liberal image or risk disintegration of the New Deal coalition. The problem was that the "ultra liberal" Wallace "appealed to the atavistic fear of all progressives—the fear of 'Wall Street.'" Truman was vulnerable here because too many of his appointments had Wall Street connections. (Harriman, Forrestal, Lovett, Draper, Saltzman, and McCloy, among others.) Clifford's original solution was appealing in its simplicity. If the president could display his New Deal credentials quickly and dramatically, he would not only keep the Democratic party's regular voters but insure the services of the nation's "artist[s] of propaganda." The right had the money, Clifford said. But the left had the pen.[35]

Henry Wallace's efforts to attract the black vote were particularly vexing. "Truman didn't need hints from us," Roy Wilkins recalled. "He could count. But the President did need help to keep Negroes from wandering off toward Wallace, who was travelling around the South that year with Paul Robeson." Although Robeson and Du Bois were virtually the only prominent African Americans to support Wallace, public opinion polls revealed solid black support for the Progressive party candidate. So Clifford advised Truman to Red-bait and isolate Wallace by persuading "prominent liberals and progressives—*and no one else*—to move publicly into the fray. They must point out that the core of the Wallace backing is made up of Communists and the fellow-travellers." Like every other suggestion in his memorandum, Clifford based this suggestion "solely on the politically advantageous course."[36]

Truman moved quickly on the civil rights and anticommunist fronts. He began with civil rights (because, in the words of one White House aide, "it can virtually assure the re-election of the President by cutting the ground out from under Wallace and gaining the enthusiastic support of the liberal and labor groups").[37] (Clifford was a bit off on labor as some unions supported civil rights while others were hostile to equal employment opportunity because they feared competition for jobs.) In a "properly staged" message to Congress on February 2, Truman called for legislation to outlaw lynching and the poll tax; strengthen existing civil rights law and otherwise protect the right to vote; and establish a civil rights division in the Justice Department, a joint congressional committee on civil rights, and a permanent FEPC.[38] "We appreciate the great loyalty our Party has had from the Southern States through the years," Democratic National Committee chair J. Howard McGrath told southern governors who objected to the president's proposals and warned of a "gestapo" if they became law.[39]

After a decent wait Truman retreated to the strategy adopted during the first days of the FEPC fight. This was what Philleo Nash called backtracking after the bang. In the months that followed the president "temporize[d] to pick up the right wing forces." He refused to send the omnibus civil rights bill to Congress, remained silent on all civil rights questions, and told McGrath and the Democratic National Committee that he favored adoption of the vague civil rights plank that FDR had run on in the last campaign.

Now ready to move on Clifford's second recommendation, Truman went after "Wallace and his Communists" in a St. Patrick's Day address in New York City. There would be no backtracking here. J. Edgar Hoover's agents had been investigating what they called Wallace's "Contacts with Negro Communist-Controlled Organizations and Individuals" since 1945, and after Clifford submitted his campaign memorandum Attorney General Tom C. Clark ordered an FBI probe of Wallace's "Soviet connections." Incorporating the highlights of the bureau's findings into his St. Patrick's Day address, the president continued to follow Clifford's advice thereafter by staying above the fray and allowing "prominent liberals" to lead the anticommunist charge.[40]

Americans for Democratic Action (ADA) opened "an offensive against Wallace" on the day after the St. Patrick's Day appearance. ADA officials were especially proud of their pamphlet, *Henry Wallace, the First Three Months*, which Francis Biddle, later national board chairman, praised as a Red-baiting masterpiece. "I think the best job on the Wallace movement was done by ADA," he said. "They did a pamphlet . . . that show[ed] the Commie tie-up right down the line." This "job" included paid advertisements in major urban newspapers listing Progressive party contributors and the groups on the attorney general's list of subversive organizations with which they were or had been associated. Because more than a few Communist party members and friends were active in the Progressive party, Wallace was vulnerable to such tactics.[41]

While Red-baiting Wallace and demonstrating a questionable posture on civil liberties, ADA came on strong for racial justice. Under the young Minneapolis mayor Hubert H. Humphrey, the organization pushed through what might be called, with some irony, a progressive civil rights plank that summer at the Democratic National Convention in Philadelphia. "If we had been mild," Humphrey said, "the Republicans might have seized the issue by our default. I felt that was ideologically absurd and politically stupid." "It was time," added another ADA activist, Joseph L. Rauh, Jr., "for the Democratic party to come out of the shadow of states' rights and into the broad sunshine of human rights." This was exactly what Clifford had counseled: Move left on civil rights for blacks and right on civil liberties for everyone.[42]

Truman held no lasting grudge against those who voted against ADA's civil rights plank and his own nomination. Only an occasional bitter remark surfaced. "They're no better than Fascists," he told the Gridiron Club chief. The president was more often empathic. "I would have done the same thing myself if I were in their place and came from their states," he remarked to Secretary of the Navy James V. Forrestal. When southern delegates bolted, following South Carolina Governor Strom Thurmond into a fourth party, the Dixiecrat party, Truman remained "chipper and in very good form," Forrestal concluded, absolutely confident that few white southern voters would desert the regular Democratic party on the first Tuesday in November.[43]

To solidify the liberal vote Truman nearly matched ADA's civil rights stance that summer by ordering an end to racial discrimination in federal employment and creating a fair employment board in the Civil Service Commission. This White House attack on discrimination in federal agencies also pushed forward the ongoing campaign against Jim Crow in the District of Columbia where "white" and "colored" signs still ruled city parks and recreation areas and practically everything else. Ralph Bunche, who lived in Washington during the war years while working for the Office of Strategic Services, told Dean Rusk about the family dog's death and his children's wish to bury it in the local pet cemetery—only to discover that one section of ground stood reserved for white folks' pets and another for black folks' pets. (Truman had sent Rusk to New York to persuade Bunche to accept the post of assistant secretary of state.) Progress here was slow and the president again backtracked after the initial bang. The Interior Department, not the White House, lead the charge (such as it was) to desegregate the nation's capital.[44]

To his credit Truman proved most aggressive on the most controversial front of all—segregation in the armed forces. Executive Order 9981 abolished the practice in the military and created the President's Committee on Equality of Treatment and Opportunity in the Armed Forces. And when progress toward that end dragged, as the Army clung to its ten-percent quota policy on black enlistments, Truman personally intervened with Secretary of the Army Gordon Gray. He ended up killing quotas and more. "I want this rounded out a little bit," he said. "Let's make it a Government proposition, as well as an Armed Services [proposition] . . . We might as well make a complete program out of it while we are at it, and not limit it to just one branch of the Government. That's what I have in mind all the way down the line. Not only that, I think that we've got to go further—not at this time, but later— and see that the state and local governments carry out the spirit of the laws which we hope to get on the books down here during this session of Congress."[45]

Truman pushed harder than his advisers thought wise. "[On] the National Guard problem," for example, Clifford proposed a states' rights strategy. "The solution," he said, "is to leave to the states the problem of determining whether their . . . units will be segregated or non-segregated."[46] Truman ignored Clifford's new-found caution and kept pushing on this and other fronts. In October he became the first American president to speak in Harlem, taking pride in his executive orders and for the first time since his February 2 message to Congress advocating the legislation proposed by the President's Committee on Civil Rights. After his surprising and razor-thin victory over Dewey in November (the black vote proved crucial in California, Illinois, and Ohio), he submitted legislation calling for a permanent FEPC and outlawing the poll tax and lynching. When a states' rights block in Congress stopped those initiatives, however, the courage Truman displayed when pressuring the army dissipated. The administration simply sent up its civil rights bills and let them die slow deaths.

Truman had again backtracked after the bang. Paul Robeson said the administration's civil rights program had "nothing to do with the background of terror, the atmosphere of horror in which most Negroes live. . . . Truman is with Dewey—words, only words: empty lies, vicious lies. Truman is with the Dixiecrats in deeds." Walter White blamed, in no particular order, "the Democratic Senators from outside the South [who] gave up and sold the civil rights program down the river"; "the Democratic party leaders [who] have turned tail . . . [and] practically announced they will ditch the civil rights program"; DNC chairman McGrath, who "since the election last November . . . has ducked and dodged any discussion of the civil rights program . . . refused to say what the Democratic party plans are . . . [and] never laid a card on the table"; and Truman himself, whose "surrender . . . [was] Appomattox in reverse. Apparently Strom Thurmond was elected last November so far as a half-century's fight for human rights is concerned."[47]

This exaggeration was not that far off. When Truman sent Congress another omnibus civil rights bill in 1950 virtually everyone in the White House knew it had little chance of passing and refused to waste energy on a lost cause. The president had launched an all-out fight for the Truman Doctrine, the Marshall Plan, and other Cold War legislation. But the energy he displayed there was noticeably absent in the civil rights fight. In the 1948 campaign Clark Clifford counseled the president to develop a liberal image and nothing more. If the administration's civil rights initiatives reflected a political agenda, the president's failure to follow through reflected a lack of personal commitment to the cause of equal justice for all.

Some progress was made nonetheless. The Truman administration's civil rights advocates and its allies ultimately had better luck in the courts than in Congress. Most notably in the Justice Department's friend-of-the-court briefs filed on behalf of black plaintiffs seeking to challenge racial restrictive covenants in housing and segregation in the public schools. In 1948 the Supreme Court held that agreements preventing minorities from owning real estate were unenforceable. Two years later, in *Sweatt* and *McLaurin*, the court chipped at segregation in public education, and those cases paved the way for the historic decision in *Brown v. Board of Education* (1954) declaring segregated educational facilities unequal and therefore unconstitutional. Truman himself, however, had little to say about these decisions, including *Brown*. Even years later, after segregationist thugs tried to prevent integration at Little Rock Central High School, he remained largely silent—though he did offer the incredible advice that "both sides" adopt "a common sense approach."[48]

From the FEPC fight's first days civil rights was at best a political sideshow. Cold War issues always occupied center stage at the White House, and when it came down to cases the demands of security always won out over racial justice. With an eye on the region's uranium mines, for example, the Truman administration quietly supported the Union of South Africa even after 1948 when it embraced apartheid.[49] Two years later, with the Cold War itself suddenly becoming hot in Korea, the administration further limited its modest interest in racial justice. There would be only one more initiative, a largely ineffective Committee on Government Contract Compliance.

Anticommunist ideology was strong enough to distract not only the president and his advisers but the most single-minded civil rights advocates as well. The NAACP embraced the administration's Cold War ethos as the Korean War raged, with Walter White taking a leadership post in the All-American Conference to Combat Communism; Thurgood Marshall briefing the White House on "the latest developments in the efforts of the Comrades to move in on our cases"; and Roy Wilkins proposing an in-house purge. "We do not want a witch hunt," he said, "but we want to clean out our organization." For assistance in this effort White and Wilkins went to the FBI just as the Truman White House had in dealing with Wallace, Robeson, and Du Bois.[50]

With Truman victorious in the 1948 election and black radicalism either co-opted or undercut by 1950 all that remained was the Cold War imperative to deny the Soviets a propaganda forum.[51] "The race problem," concluded the president's Psychological Strategy Board, "is distorted . . . by equalling a small number of Negro lynchings to the millions who are enslaved in Soviet labor camps. By adhering to the requirement that our hands be clean before we undertake propaganda, we tend to strike a defensive note in our discussion of race problems."[52] This is what McCarthyism was all about, and even the State Department and "Red" Dean Acheson, the main targets of the real McCarthyites, engaged in this sort of reasoning. If racism could not be eliminated in America, the image of American racism could be eliminated abroad. Hollywood films like No Way Out and Pinky, the State Department concluded, ought to be suppressed in favor of The Best Years of Our Lives, Father's Little Dividend, and other more wholesome fare.[53]

Whether or not Truman was truly committed to civil rights remains a contentious question. Those closest to him detected a moral pulse. "He meant absolutely everything he said in his well-known civil rights message of February 2nd, 1948," White House aide George M. Elsey said. "I don't think there was anything phoney about that at all. It wasn't a sham, it wasn't a pretense, it wasn't a lot of hot air just for political purposes." (Even the spirited Elsey stuck in an I-don't-think qualifier.)[54] Years later another White House aide, Stephen J. Spingarn, who drafted much of the president's civil rights legislation, became so incensed at New Left historian Barton Bernstein for knocking Truman's political opportunism that he tried to get Bernstein fired from Stanford University and drummed out of the profession.[55]

Spingarn was the exception, Elsey the rule. Jonathan Daniels, one of Franklin Roosevelt's six White House aides then briefly Truman's press secretary and finally author of *The Man from Independence* (1950), remembered a particularly telling comment: "While I was out there in Kansas City, [the president's sister, Mary Jane, said], 'Why, you know Harry feels the same way about the colored folks as I do,' meaning the conventional Missouri attitude." When asked if she used the words "colored folks," Daniels answered: "I wouldn't like to say what she said." (She said, "Harry is no more for nigger equality than any of us.") An ambivalent Roy Wilkins was probably closest to the mark. Having commended the president's "sheer personal courage" in January 1953, Wilkins backed off that unqualified praise in his memoir: "Anyone who mistook Harry Truman for a pint-sized [Theodore] Bilbo [the racist senator from Mississippi] was making a big mistake. . . . [But] anyone who expected Harry Truman to take us by the hand and lead us into Canaan was [equally] mistaken."[56]

Truman's principal civil rights accomplishment, White House appointments secretary Matthew J. Connelly concluded, was "the fact that he recognized it was there." The president himself said "the civil rights report and the civil rights program gave voice and expression to this great change of sentiment. . . . They are the trumpet blast outside the Walls of Jericho—the crumbling walls of prejudice."[57] Truman moved on civil rights because he had needs—a foreign policy need to abandon segregation; a political need to gain the African-American vote; and a domestic policy need to undercut black radicalism (Du Bois and Robeson were among the Cold War's most strident critics). If he did not rank civil rights a top priority, deferred too often to southern Democrats, and failed to rally public support for his initiatives in the manner in which he pushed the Truman Doctrine, Marshall Plan, and other security-state items, there is no doubt that he placed civil rights on the nation's political stage.

By desegregating the Army, addressing the NAACP, appointing the committee that compiled *To Secure These Rights*, and introducing civil rights legislation, Truman did more than Franklin Roosevelt or any other twentieth century president who came before him. More, too, than most who would come after. During his last months in the White House he watched in dismay as his party retreated from the 1948 civil rights platform and nominated Adlai E. Stevenson of Illinois, a liberal's liberal who nonetheless opposed compulsory FEPC for political reasons. For vice-president the Democrats chose John Sparkman, an Alabama segregationist. "I sometimes think the country might have been better off if I had turned out to be a pianist in a whorehouse," Truman was fond of saying off-the record.[58] Excepting McCarthyite sticks and stones, the president's civil rights travails inspired such self-deprecating comments as much as anything else.

Forty years after Truman left the White House, Clark Clifford reflected on the politics of the civil rights crusade. "Our most serious error was taking the South for granted," he said. "In recent years it has been the black vote that the Democrats have taken for granted, while white voters in the South have usually voted overwhelmingly Republican in Presidential campaigns. We did not realize how quickly Southern whites would abandon the President if he supported equal rights for all Americans."[59] Under Truman's successor the Republicans would begin to hammer out the new southern strategy that would eventually capture those voters. Like Clifford, GOP strategists saw the key to presidential elections in the (white) votes of the solid South and the West. To his credit the new Republican president refused to make this coalition whole by pushing racial politics past what even the most tough-minded cold warrior would consider the point of civility.

This is not to say Dwight D. Eisenhower (1953–1961) was a civil rights advocate. Preferring the late nineteenth century racial model to the mid-twentieth, Eisenhower had no personal or political interest in FEPC or any other "Federal compulsory thing." He was a voluntarist and habitually uncomfortable in black company. On those rare occasions where he addressed an African-American audience he would take off his glasses and ad lib, saying, "Now, you people have to be patient." Having spent forty years in a segregated Army, he told the Senate Armed Services Committee in 1948 that segregation should continue at the platoon level and below. He told "nigger jokes" to the men around him on the campaign trail and later in the White House, jokes picked up from his golfing friends at the Bobby Jones club in Augusta, Georgia.

Eisenhower outgrew none of these habits. After noting Roy Wilkins's stop in Illinois to meet with Adlai Stevenson and Averell Harriman, he invited the NAACP leader to drop by his suite at Manhattan's Commodore Hotel. "The atmosphere when I walked into his room couldn't have been more different from the one in Springfield," Wilkins remembered. "I could see right away that he knew very little about racial matters in the United States." Wilkins had questions about segregation in the District of Columbia, poll taxes, lynching, southern filibustering, even running mate Richard Nixon's civil rights voting record. After each question Eisenhower "turned to the squadron of aides at his side for the answers." Stevenson, in contrast, "put his feet up on his desk, sat back, and talked comfortably about black issues" for two hours. The stiff and befuddled Ike gave Wilkins fifteen minutes.[60]

Eisenhower and his men barely had more time for their only Negro "insider," E. Frederic Morrow. A graduate of Bowdoin College and Rutgers Law School, and resident of Hackensack, New Jersey, Morrow took leave from the TV Press Information Bureau at CBS to join the campaign at the recommendation of CBS president William Paley and Val J. Washington (who handled the black vote for the Republican National Committee). Morrow's principal responsibility at each campaign-train stop was to wander about black neighborhoods and get a feel for the common people. The consensus, he told Sherman Adams, who would go on to serve as White House chief of staff, was that the Republican party had little interest in African Americans. "Fear of loss of jobs gained under Democrats" motivated Negroes, not an abstract interest in civil rights. Adams and everybody else simply ignored the man and his advice.[61]

Segregated quarters on the campaign train provided another hint that Fred Morrow was little more than window dressing. "I had been one of the fortunate ones who had a bedroom to myself," he explained good naturedly. A bunkmate surfaced only on the final Boston-New York run. While Eisenhower and his wife and various campaign aides sang "Battle Hymn of the Republic," "You'll Never Walk Alone," "God Bless America," and the general's other favorites until 4:30 A.M.,

Morrow retreated to his berth and found Marty Snyder, Eisenhower's former mess sergeant, asleep in the upper. After the train pulled into New York, Morrow went to New Jersey to vote then headed back to the Commodore Hotel for the election watch and victory party. The police stopped him a block away. He never made it to the Commodore on election day.[62]

When Morrow finally got through to the Eisenhower campaign team Sherman Adams told him to come to Washington for a White House assignment. He resigned from CBS and made the move, then suddenly found himself indefinitely unemployed. There was no White House assignment or any other job. The administration would not even return his phone calls. "A very disturbing situation," Morrow recalled. "I had no communication, whatsoever, with the White House." He waited patiently, living off his savings and adjusting to the new environment. "Segregation was still de rigueur. . . . There was no place downtown that I could get a cup of coffee or a drink of water, unless I went all the way over to the Union Station." Adams's office finally called seventeen months after the election to offer interim work in the Commerce Department. Morrow eventually learned that another Eisenhower aide, Alabama native Wilton B. Persons, was responsible for the delay. Persons had threatened to lead the female clerks in a walk out if a black man came to the White House in a capacity other than butler.[63]

Selecting from "a list of qualified negroes" compiled by Val Washington, Eisenhower appointed a handful of other blacks—including Joseph Douglas at Health Education and Welfare, Scovel Richardson at the Parole Board, James Nabrit at the President's Committee on Government Contract Compliance, and Samuel Pierce and Ernest Wilkins at Labor. With Morrow and Washington this group formed an "Equality Committee," in the manner of FDR's black cabinet, that met informally to discuss "the Administration's approach to various Negro problems." Wilkins, sitting in for Secretary of Labor James P. Mitchell, had the good fortune to visit the regular Eisenhower cabinet. "The first time in American History," White House minority affairs specialist Maxwell M. Rabb noted, "that a Negro has attended a Cabinet meeting." Lois Lippman was another "first"—the first black woman to work in the White House office's secretarial pool. Otherwise the only blacks in sight were servants. "The President hardly knew we were there," recalled longtime White House domestic Lillian Rogers Parks, "and was definitely not friendly."[64]

With Cold War imperatives balancing personal preferences, Eisenhower and Secretary of State John Foster Dulles also pushed for Negro appointments "in embassy service in those countries where there is a large non-White population." A rampant McCarthyism in the State Department, however, made such appointments difficult. Otherwise enthusiastic about purging his shop of people who did not think right about communism, Dulles complained to Leonard Hall at the Republican National Committee about how it was impossible to get "colored people cleared by the FBI." Citing the case of "a Mr. Cyrus, who was an observer on the Caribbean Commission, and who was about to be taken off a plane," Dulles said "there was practically no negro . . . who could come through an FBI check lily white, because all of their organizations had been infiltrated at one time or another." Ralph Bunche, Nobel Prize recipient in 1950 for service as UN mediator in the Palestine dispute, was among those who failed to set the desired "lily white" clearance.

Dulles asked Hall, in the same odd words, "to take the problem up with the President or Sherman Adams . . . as they have been very particular about getting lily white clearance on everybody, but it is impossible to do this with negroes."[65] Because Bunche had listed Alger Hiss as a reference when he joined the United Nations staff, the FBI tried, among other things, to have him indicted on perjury charges for denying Communist party membership when testifying before the Senate Internal Security Subcommittee. If Eisenhower and Dulles complained about the inordinate influence of internal security bureaucrats, in the end they allowed Hoover's FBI free run at all black nominees. America fought the Cold War at home and abroad, and African Americans lost on both fronts.[66]

Eisenhower's civil rights policy extended no further than a few stray appointments who might entice Negroes to vote Republican. Problems of race and racism would be otherwise ignored—just as the president ignored black reporters at press conferences until the second term when Murray Kempton pointed this out in his newspaper column. Thereafter the White House press office planted an occasional "Administration question" with a friendly black reporter. The growing civil rights movement would of course prove considerably harder to ignore than Fred Morrow or the few less-than-friendly black faces at press conferences.[67]

Segregation in the schools led to Eisenhower's first civil rights crisis. Truman's Justice Department had filed a friend-of-the-court brief in December 1952 challenging the separate-but-equal doctrine, and six months later the Supreme Court "invited" Attorney General Herbert Brownell to submit arguments in *Brown v. Board of Education* and other pending cases. "Jesus," Deputy Attorney General William P. Rogers moaned, "do we really have to file a brief? Aren't we better off staying out of it?" That was not an option. With the Truman administration already on record as opposing segregation the new administration had to respond. Eisenhower saw the court's "invitation" for what it was (a command) and condemned it as a crude power play that interfered with his party's courtship of the white southern voter. "The rendering of 'opinion' by the Attorney General," he complained, constituted "an invasion of the duties, responsibilities and authority of the Supreme Court. . . . It seems to me that in this instance the Supreme Court has been guided by some motive that is not strictly functional." Even in the White House, he remained a nineteenth century man committed to the "functional" motives that lay behind *Plessy*. In practice, however, he adopted what he considered a posture of strict neutrality, telling Brownell to write a brief that took no position on segregation pro or con.[68]

At a July 20, 1953, luncheon, James Byrnes, then governor of South Carolina, warned Eisenhower of the risks inherent in the school desegregation cases. "The South no longer finds any great problem in dealing with adult Negroes," he explained. "They are frightened at putting the children together." Byrnes was "obviously afraid," Eisenhower concluded, "that I would be carried away by the hope of capturing the Negro vote in this country, and as a consequence take a stand on the question that would forever defeat any possibility of developing a real Republican or 'Opposition' Party in the South."[69] While the Supreme Court would likely hear *Brown* and other school desegregation cases, the president predicted that the justices would uphold segregation. Yet there would also be problems in that event because the schools were clearly not equal. "The task of establishing 'equal but separate' facilities will involve, I am told, extraordinary expenditures throughout all the southern states," he informed Byrnes. "Incidentally, I sometimes wonder just what officers of government would be charged with the responsibility for determining when facilities were exactly equal." This was the realm of "lawyers and historians," not politicians.

The school cases themselves, Eisenhower continued, "tended to becloud the original decision [*Plessy*] of 'equal but separate' facilities. One of these decisions, I am told, even held that a Negro in graduate school attending exactly the same classes as whites, but separated from them by some kind of railing, was held to be the victim of discrimination and could not be so separated from the white students."[70] Graduate school admission was the "one place" where Eisenhower "thought the South . . . wrong." He told HEW Secretary Oveta Culp Hobby, herself an ardent segregationist, "that the graduate schools of the recognized universities should establish disinterested boards to decide by examination . . . the eligibility for entry of all students." To separate black graduate students from whites within the classroom, the president had no objection to "some kind of railing." Anyone who objected to this Jim Crow prop was an "extremist."[71]

Eisenhower knew where he stood. On May 17, 1954, when the Supreme Court held in *Brown* that segregated public schools were inherently unequal and in violation of the Fourteenth Amendment, he privately condemned the decision as morally repugnant and politically confounding in that the South would view it as "a 'Republican' decision." He promised Governor Byrnes that the administration would not enforce school desegregation "with all deliberate speed," as required by a subsequent court decision. Instead the administration would "make haste slowly." When Attorney General Brownell presented the Justice Department's brief to the Supreme Court, the president added, he was "appearing as a lawyer, not as a member of the Eisenhower [team]." He reminded Brownell, in turn, that the issue "had never come before the cabinet," and again complained "that because of the Supreme Court's rulling [*sic*], the whole issue had been set back badly."[72]

With the courts and NAACP lawyers pulling the nation out of the nineteenth century, the president could only dream of *Plessy*'s tranquil world. If he spoke often of how laws and judicial edicts could not change the hearts and minds of white southerners, the truth is that this great man remained unmoved himself. Within the administration only Brownell and Dulles found *Brown* a blessing. Brownell, the cabinet's lone civil rights advocate, began planning a bill to protect black voting rights in the South—an initiative, Sherman Adams said, with some understatement, that created a "rift of opinion."[73] Dulles's enthusiasm was pragmatic. On the home front he was skeptical, agreeing with the president on "the impracticality of laws which deviated too far from accepted mores." Abroad he knew the court's decision would facilitate American foreign policy in the third world and provide a weapon in the global crusade against Soviet communism. So the Voice of America translated *Brown* into thirty-four languages and beamed it around the world—even as Dulles's CIA director brother, Allen, tracked W. E. B. Du Bois and other globe-trotting Cold War critics. The CIA noted, among other things, that the radical Pan African Congress was "the brainchild of [this] American Negro."[74]

Eisenhower remained disengaged as events escalated. With one minor exception the White House sat out the Montgomery bus boycott launched on December 5, 1955, when the seamstress Rosa Parks refused to give up her seat on a city bus to a white man. General Lewis B. Hershey, director of the National Selective Service system, blocked Montgomery draft board attempts to induct Montgomery Improvement Association attorney Fred Gray into the Army. That was the exception. Otherwise the administration merely observed as the boycott moved the civil rights movement from the courts into the streets, in the process catapulting Mrs. Parks's pastor into the national spotlight. When city authorities swore out arrest warrants for Martin Luther King, Jr., and other boycott organizers, the president simply mentioned "a state law about boycotts, and it is under that kind of thing that these people are being brought to trial."[75] When the boycott ended with the Supreme Court upholding a special three-judge panel's decision against segregation on intrastate buses, Eisenhower was crushed. "In some of these things," he said, "[I] was more of a 'States Righter' than the Supreme Court." The president believed that the decision was such a backward step that "even the so-called great liberals are going to have to take a second look at the whole thing."[76]

No White House action accompanied the desegregation fight at the University of Alabama either. After Autherine Lucy had enrolled under the watchful eyes of a racist mob and University officials subsequently suspended her ("for her safety"), Eisenhower promised to "avoid any interference with anybody else as long as that state, from its Governor on down, will do its best to straighten it out." While University authorities straightened things out in March 1956 by expelling Lucy, administration officials continued to sit dead still. They intervened only against their own civil rights advocates. When Frederic Morrow, who had finally moved to the White House from the Commerce Department, suggested direct discussions with black Alabama leaders, Sherman Adams squelched the idea. He cited a series of FBI reports supposedly documenting a "tremendous" Communist presence among the state's Negro leadership.[77]

Emmett Till's lynching was yet another nonevent for Eisenhower. Till, a fourteen-year-old Chicago boy, had gone to Money, Mississippi, to visit relatives and made the mistake of "whistling at a distaff white." He was beaten, shot, and dumped in the Tallahatchie River with a .45 caliber bullet in the crushed skull and a seventy-four pound cotton-gin fan tied around the neck. While a state court jury acquitted the woman's husband and half-brother of murder charges and a federal grand jury refused to issue indictments, Eisenhower ignored telegrams from Till's mother pleading for justice. The White House, like the FBI, seemed most interested in the Communist party's "agitation and protest over this . . . alleged murder." ("Alleged" was the director's word.) The NAACP, bureau officials added, also "seized upon this matter for exploitation purposes." Eisenhower took such reports seriously, alluding in his memoir to Communist infiltration of that organization. He also mentioned the Communist demand that he send federal troops to Mississippi to avenge Emmett Till. "[The president] saw the NAACP and other groups not as reform organizations," Brownell said, "but as political pressure groups."[78]

Viewing the Montgomery bus boycott, the University of Alabama desegregation crisis, and the Till lynching as internal security problems, Eisenhower continued to rely first and foremost on J. Edgar Hoover. Touting an FBI briefing on racial polarization as "an ideal matter" for "coordination" between the National Security Council and the cabinet, Maxwell Rabb arranged an appearance for March 9.[79] Hoover brought a briefing paper ("Racial Tension and Civil Rights") and various charts and graphs, including one depicting a tug of war between a Ku Klux Klan–led team and an NAACP-led team. Another chart focused on "Communist Party Tactics Affecting Racial Tension," particularly propaganda (the Till, Lucy, and Montgomery cases); infiltration (the NAACP); colonization (the textile industry); agitation (poll taxes, anti-lynching legislation, FEPC); and a "pressure campaign on government officials." On this last point, the director noted, Communist operatives proved clever enough to turn Chicago Mayor Richard Daley (however briefly) into an unwitting dupe.

"Current tensions," Hoover said, returning to his main line, represented a culture war. "Protection of racial purity is a rule of life ingrained deeply as the basic truth," a truth continually fed by "memories of Reconstruction," fears of "mixed education," and "the specter of racial intermarriages." White Citizens Councils, formed in *Brown's* wake and intended to exert economic pressure on NAACP members in the manner of the McCarthy-era blacklists, included, Hoover continued, "some of the leading citizens of the South." Bankers, lawyers, doctors, state legislators, and industrialists, among others. In contrast, Hoover claimed, the Ku Klux Klan was "pretty much defunct." On the other side the FBI director complained about "delicate situations . . . aggravated by some overzealous but ill-advised leaders of the NAACP and by the Communist Party, which seeks to . . . further the so-called class struggle. . . . The area of danger lies in friction between extremists on both sides ready with violence."[80]

With Brownell's civil rights proposals also scheduled for discussion at this March 9 cabinet meeting Hoover shifted to what he called the Communist party's "all out political mobilization." This ongoing campaign, the director said, might influence "the Negro people in the crucial Presidential election now at hand" and otherwise "alienate support which the Administration has previously secured from the South and border states." An NAACP-sponsored Leadership Conference on Civil Rights was particularly troublesome. "The Communist Party," Hoover warned, "planned to use this conference to embarrass the Administration by causing a rift between the Administration and Dixiecrats who have supported it, by forcing the Administration to take a stand on civil rights legislation with the present Congress. The Party hopes through a rift to affect the 1956 elections." Eisenhower's view of the South's troubles was nearly identical to Hoover's, and, excepting the attorney general, the entire cabinet considered the FBI director's conclusions "good starting points for any statements."[81]

Brownell followed Hoover with a report on civil rights legislation to empower the Justice Department to file civil suits in support of voting rights, to create a permanent civil rights commission, and to upgrade Justice's civil rights section to full division status. Administration officials found the proposals troublesome from top to bottom. Eisenhower worried that "this program would reopen the old constitutionality question concerning the anti–poll tax law." Secretary of Agriculture Ezra T. Benson wanted "to await a Republican Congress before submitting these measures." HEW chief Marion B. Folsom "thought that the recommendations might be limited to the establishment of a commission." "The President," he added, might "find occasion to speak clearly on the need for calmness and moderation," emphasizing "the complexity of the integration problem and its endangering of various HEW programs." Mutual Security Administrator Harold Stassen also "cited the great danger of moving too fast," recommending instead the creation of a special presidential assistant on civil rights.

Brownell pointed out "that the program would be recommended by the Justice Department, not by Presidential message." Congress, he added, would probably act on its own if the administration failed to submit civil rights legislation. (The FBI had already briefed the White House on Leadership Conference meetings with Senators Paul Douglas, Everett Dirksen, Herbert Lehman, Wayne Morse, Hubert Humphrey, and John Bricker.)[82] Eisenhower told Brownell to "work into his presentation the same atmosphere of calmness urged by Mr. Hoover" and to make "very clear the Administration's understanding of the complexities."[83] He did not consider the attorney general's proposals all that radical ("they look to me like amelioration"), but nonetheless warned Brownell not "to take the attitude that you are another Sumner." "People have a right to disagree with the Supreme Court decision," he reiterated. "[After all] the Supreme Court has disagreed with its own decision of 60 years standing."[84]

Eisenhower's hope for a more stable racial climate crashed three days after the March 9 cabinet meeting. Every congressman from the old Confederacy's eleven states and every southern senator excepting

Lyndon B. Johnson of Texas and Estes Kefauver and Albert Gore of Tennessee pledged to overturn *Brown*. Determined, as ever, to avoid a political confrontation, the president refused to comment at a press conference on any person's "right to confirm or not confirm" a court decision. He merely emphasized that the so-called Southern Manifesto's signers had promised to use "every legal means" in their quest and had not "talked nullification." (The Justice Department had actually sent the White House a Calhoun-ish study of "Interposition" and "Nullification.") This post-*Brown* refusal to choose sides provided comfort for the manifesto's signers and left a moral vacuum. "If Mr. Eisenhower had come through it would have changed a lot of things," said Supreme Court Justice Tom Clark, of all people.[85]

Eisenhower had no interest in using his office as a bully pulpit. What even such an unreconstructed Red hunter as Tom Clark wanted was a visible moral presence. What he got was a pathetic hidden-hand effort to enlist evangelist Billy Graham in a crusade to calm the white South by working "among denominational leaders." Of the "things" that "could properly be mentioned" in church pulpits, Eisenhower had few ideas beyond the election of "a few qualified Negroes to school boards" and a pet project calling for graduate school admission of Negroes "strictly on the basis of merit." Graham found the work difficult because Eisenhower refused to place himself and his office at the campaign's center; and conversely because of "rumors that Republican strategy will be to go all out in winning the Negro vote in the North regardless of the South's feelings." After a single White House meeting and a flurry of letters, Eisenhower lost interest in the Graham operation, again lamenting the "foolish extremists on both sides of the question who will never be won over to a sensible course of action."[86]

Billy Graham's reference to Republican strategy was revealing. One White House wing, led by Maxwell Rabb, urged Eisenhower to push for Negro votes in the 1956 campaign because it was the right thing to do morally and politically. If the president could bring back "the sheep which wandered away in 1932," Fred Morrow added, then the GOP could organize fiscal conservatives, white suburbanites, and blacks into a coalition broad enough to make the GOP a majority party.[87] Congressional liaison Bryce N. Harlow suggested that Eisenhower show his commitment here by abolishing segregation in the National Guard.

This would "remove a defense incongruity," highlight the administration's "shining armor in the field of civil rights," and "cascade salt into the racial sores festering the Democratic Party." "Our potential gains in the North," Harlow reasoned, "far outweigh any possible losses in the more or less solid South." In the manner of Clark Clifford, Rabb, Morrow, and Harlow proved willing to write off an entire section of the country.[88] Wilton Persons, who led the other White House wing, said the Republicans could only hope to crack the New Deal coalition by ignoring the black vote and going after the white South. The president had to prove that "we are the party of States Rights."[89]

Eisenhower tried to have it both ways. He made an appeal for the black vote while remaining committed to a hands-off civil rights policy that would not alienate white southerners. Not surprisingly, he had little hope of success on either front as he still worried that the white South saw *Brown* as a Republican decision and that African Americans remained deeply suspicious of his administration and party. On a day otherwise spent working on the acceptance speech for his second-term nomination, he met some sixty Negro Shriners and young black girls who had been awarded scholarships. When one girl announced in a loud voice, "I hope you win!," everyone smiled. After the Shriners and students left, however, the president said he "did not think the other members of the group liked that statement." A few days later, when the platform committee for the San Francisco convention drafted a plank crediting him for *Brown*, he ordered it removed.[90]

For all his caution Eisenhower was more aggressive on civil rights than his Democratic party opponent, Adlai Stevenson. He invited Morrow to sit in the presidential box to watch a World Series game between the Yankees and Dodgers at Brooklyn's Ebbets Field, and invited Adam Clayton Powell to the White House for a private meeting. When Powell walked out of that meeting the president had his endorsement for the re-election bid.[91] Stevenson, who so impressed Wilkins in 1952, spent most of 1956 in search of kind words from "responsible Negro leaders"—a difficult task as his only civil rights initiative was a proposal for a year-long "moratorium" on racial agitation. He gave his version of Eisenhower's standard line ("we cannot by the stroke of a pen reverse customs and traditions that are older than the Republic"), hoping to "remove this issue from the political arena and make possible its orderly resolution without the emotional coloration of a Presidential contest." Sick of "the clamor of the NAACP," Stevenson could not understand why Walter White and Roy Wilkins expected more from him than from the president. When the returns came in and Eisenhower received some 60 percent of the black vote, all he could do, like so many liberals before him, was throw up his hands. "I am quite bewildered about the Negroes," he said.[92]

Civil rights leaders themselves were a bit bewildered. For the first time since the New Deal, African Americans had voted Republican in substantial numbers. Yet Eisenhower remained ambivalent. When Martin Luther King, Roy Wilkins, and A. Philip Randolph organized a Prayer Pilgrimage for Freedom to pressure the president into condemning white racist violence, the administration panicked. Fearing this mass demonstration on *Brown*'s third anniversary would turn into an anti-Eisenhower rally, Maxwell Rabb and other White House aides not only turned to the FBI for intelligence but enlisted Adam Clayton Powell as a "mole" within the leadership group planning the event. Powell's mission was to contain the Prayer Pilgrimage. His motivation was financial. The White House had made "clandestine arrangements" to pay Powell for his support in the 1956 campaign and other services, defined broadly enough to include spying on King, Wilkins, and Randolph. Powell said he was merely part of the president's "team."[93]

Ironically, Wilkins also cooperated with the administration. He objected in principle to mass demonstrations, insisting that King speak about voting only and leave the immediate issue of school desegregation to the NAACP. Both Wilkins and Powell assured Rabb that this "would be no demonstration against the Administration," and it turned out to be, as one historian noted, "a mass supplication in support of the Administration's voting rights bill." As if to make a final check on things a military helicopter hovered briefly over the 30,000 people gathered at the steps of the Lincoln Memorial, appearing during Wilkins's speech and vanishing during Powell's speech. The timing of the helicopter's exit prompted private jokes about the congressman being Eisenhower's boy.[94]

In the end Wilkins's and Powell's cooperation did no good. While civil rights leaders planned the Prayer Pilgrimage, Eisenhower worked and golfed at the "little White House" in Newport, Rhode Island, looking forward to a two-week hunting vacation at Treasury Secretary George M. Humphrey's farm in Thomasville, Georgia. On his way out of a church service, where the sermon had called for civil rights legislation, he told the Navy chaplain what he told everyone: "You can't legislate morality." Martin Luther King's request for a meeting reached him in Georgia where he shot his first wild turkey and rode around in wicker carriages, a friend said, pulled by white mules and driven by "the old colored retainers." The president did not respond to King's telegram.[95]

Richard Nixon, who chaired the President's Committee on Government Contract Compliance, was more receptive. The vice-president had met King that March at independence ceremonies for a new west African nation. "I want you to come visit us down in Alabama," King said, "where we are seeking the same kind of freedom Ghana is celebrating." Nixon told King to stop by when he was in Washington and later scheduled a meeting for June 13 in the Formal Room of the U.S. Capitol. Seventy reporters waited outside for two hours while the two men discussed the politics of the administration's civil rights bill. Neither man answered questions when they came out, but a cautious King told Bayard Rustin in private that the movement may have found an ally. "Nixon has a genius for convincing one that he is sincere . . . he almost disarms you with his apparent sincerity." King paused for a moment, then added (somewhat prophetically): "If this man is not sincere, he is the most dangerous man in America."[96]

Nixon told Maxwell Rabb that he "was very much impressed with Reverend King and thinks the President would enjoy talking to him. He is not . . . a man who believes in violent and retaliatory pro-Negro actions, but sponsors an evolutionary but progressive march forward."[97] Eisenhower instead met with Georgia Senator Richard Russell, who convinced him to withdraw his support for Part III of Brownell's civil rights bill. (Part III empowered the attorney general to initiate civil suits to challenge school segregation and voting rights discrimination.) Russell said the bill was so "cunningly contrived" that the president did not understand its full scope. Eisenhower admitted as much, lamely explaining at a press conference that he was not a lawyer. He told Brownell that he did not "understand what any civil right meant—thought it varied from state to state"—and felt that the civil rights bill had "expanded to a form so general that it scares people to death."

Lacking White House support, the Senate eliminated the attorney general's authority to initiate civil suits from all areas except voting rights. "Administration capitulation to the South," Fred Morrow complained to Sherman Adams, "has resulted in a complete turnabout in feeling and attitude by Negro leadership."[98]

Eisenhower reversed field again later that month, opposing the efforts of Senator Russell and others to attach an amendment to the civil rights bill requiring a jury trial in all contempt cases. Clearly, no southern jury would convict a state official for violating a federal court order in a Negro voting rights case. No matter how sympathetic to the South on segregation, Eisenhower supported voting rights for all Americans regardless of race or creed. When Brownell mentioned the stark realities (only 7,000 of Mississippi's 900,000 blacks could vote), the president was shocked and dismayed. At a legislative leadership meeting he told the story of a white Mississippi law student who repeatedly failed the state bar exam. Finally the student's father asked the examiners for a look at the questions. "For goodness' sake," the father said when he saw them, "you gave him the Negro examination." The president had no sympathy for such trickeries.[99]

The proposed jury-trial amendment was open-ended. It not only left black voting rights in the hands of white southern juries but in theory jeopardized enforcement of antitrust, labor, and other federal laws. In negotiations with Senate Majority Leader Lyndon B. Johnson the White House got the amendment removed from all contempt cases but failed to eliminate jury trials in voting rights cases. At a few minutes past midnight on August 2 the Senate passed the amendment by a vote of 51–42. "The blackest of black days," Eisenhower's secretary, Ann Whitman, said. The president himself listed the jury-trial amendment among his most bitter defeats. "I wanted a much stronger Civil Rights bill in '57 than I could get," he noted ten years later when LBJ was in the White House. "But the Democrats, including Mr. Johnson, wouldn't let me have it."[100]

Even while siding with the movement Eisenhower had doubts about civil rights. "No single event has so disturbed the domestic scene in many years as did the Supreme Court's decision of 1954," he wrote a boyhood friend. "Laws are rarely effective unless they represent the will of the majority" and only then if implemented "with consideration for human feelings." *Plessy*, after all, made segregation "completely constitutional," giving it "a cloak of legality . . . in all its forms" and establishing an "ethical" precedent from which no one could "expect complete and instant reversal." Duty was thus painful: "To consider on the one hand the customs and fears of a great section of our population, and on the other the binding effect that Supreme Court decisions must have on all of us if our form of government is to survive." Later claims about the blackest of black days aside, Eisenhower considered his own civil rights legislation "too broad." He could only "hold to the basic purpose. There must be respect for the Constitution—which means the Supreme Court's interpretation of the Constitution—or we shall have chaos. We cannot possibly imagine a successful form of government in which every individual citizen would have the right to interpret the Constitution according to his own convictions, beliefs and prejudices."[101]

On September 9 Eisenhower signed the Civil Rights Act of 1957, the first civil rights legislation since Reconstruction. The law empowered the federal government to seek injunctions against obstruction or deprivation of voting rights, created a Civil Rights Commission, and upgraded the old Civil Rights Section to full division status in the Justice Department. "A victory," Lyndon Johnson had said, when submitting the bill to the White House, "for moderation and reasonableness among intelligent and patriotic people."[102]

Unfortunately, the chaos that President Eisenhower feared was already into its fifth day in Little Rock. Arkansas Governor Orval Faubus, in defiance of a federal court school desegregation order, had sent the National Guard to prevent nine black students from enrolling at previously all-white Central High School. A mob of white adults, parents and others, including Klansmen and neo-Nazis from across the South, gathered outside the school each morning to ensure that the guardsmen kept the students away. Because Faubus used state troops to oppose federal authority the Little Rock siege was perhaps the most serious constitutional crisis since the Civil War. "As close as you could get to an irreconcilable difference between the North and the South," Brownell said. It was also Eisenhower's worst nightmare. During the fight over the civil rights bill he had said he could not "imagine any set of circumstances that would ever induce me to send Federal troops . . . into any area to enforce the order of a federal court." Faubus had created exactly those circumstances.[103]

Little Rock created dilemmas for Eisenhower on every front. Regarding the president's habit of blaming "extremists on both sides," the NAACP's Thurgood Marshall asked if he meant "to equate lawless mobs with federal courts as 'extremists.'" John Foster Dulles told Brownell that "this situation was ruining our foreign policy," that its effects "in Asia and Africa will be worse for us than Hungary was for the Russians."[104] The crisis also threatened irreparable harm both to the office of the presidency and Republican electoral prospects. Neither federal judges nor civil rights advocates, Eisenhower told Sherman Adams, "take into consideration the seething in the south. . . . The whole U.S. thinks the President has a right to walk in and say 'disperse—we are going to have negroes in the high schools and so on.' That is not so." Given his silence on southern terror in the three years since *Brown*, Eisenhower was as much to blame for these dilemmas as anyone else. "[He] had done what he had done," Roy Wilkins said, "and the chickens had come home to roost in Little Rock."[105]

Eisenhower and Faubus met in Rhode Island on September 14 and tried to work things out. They spent twenty minutes alone in the president's tiny office at the Newport Naval Station, then moved to a larger office where Sherman Adams, Herbert Brownell, and Arkansas Congressman Brooks Hays joined them. Faubus thought Adams a competent if dispassionate man, Brownell a minor-league Sumner, and Eisenhower somewhat disengaged. "The President," he marvelled, "didn't know a thing about the situation." For their part Eisenhower and his men did not know what to make of Faubus. He was either a down-to-earth good old boy searching for a solution or a grandstanding politician. The meeting broke up with the president convinced that he had Faubus's pledge not to obstruct the court order. This surprised the governor. He expected the meeting to continue after lunch, but as the group walked outside Eisenhower "was already heading for the golf course."[106]

Upon returning to Arkansas, Faubus sinned by continuing to obstruct the court order and releasing to the press a fraudulent version of the president's Newport words. Eisenhower and his staff, never certain of the governor's cooperation in the first place, felt betrayed. When confronted with yet another ironclad contempt citation Faubus again negotiated with Adams and other White House aides, implying that he would comply with the court order simply by changing the National Guard's mandate. Instead of protecting Little Rock Central from nine black students, the Guard would protect the students from the white mob. This is what Brownell had been urging all along. When Faubus simply withdrew the Guard on September 23, however, Eisenhower exploded. While the president ranted behind closed doors the Little Rock mob beat up reporters, broke windows and doors, and nearly captured the nine students before the police evacuated them. After a few hours of integration Central High was again all white.

Eisenhower ordered federal troops into Little Rock the next morning. "Of all his acts in his eight years in the White House," Sherman Adams later wrote, this "was the most repugnant." The decision killed the president's dream of bringing white southerners to the Republican party. "The current administration," *U.S. News and World Report* publisher David Lawrence said, "is now dead in the South." Yet there was no choice. The president feared that the South might abolish their public schools, that the violence might spread. Brownell told Eisenhower that the crisis was comparable to the Whiskey Rebellion and only troops could crush it. One thousand soldiers from the 101st Airborne to be exact, and General Maxwell Taylor had them on the ground by nightfall. The black students were at their desks the next morning. But the situation remained so tense a week later, as Ann Whitman wrote at the White House, that Eisenhower "was not sure that he should play golf, though he wanted to and felt he should. After discussion by phone with Vice President, they both decided to go out to Burning Tree." Finally, on October 4, the crisis receded, pushed off the front pages by the Soviet Sputnik launch, the first man-made satellite.[107]

"There's no doubt," Brownell said, that Eisenhower looked at Little Rock "primarily not as a civil rights dispute. The basic problem that he was faced with as President there was the defiance of federal authority. He took the same action that they did in the early days of the country in Shay's Rebellion, Doar's Rebellion, and some of these other things." Texas Governor Allan Shivers, a hard-core states' righter, said "he wasn't going to let a governor of a state run over the President of the United States." "What Little Rock was to law in the United States," Eisenhower himself concluded, "Suez was to law among the nations: an example of the United States government's staking its majesty and its power on a principle of justice." For the president "order" was a "principle of justice," civil rights a mere "abstraction" that varied from state to state and city to city.[108]

Eisenhower's emphasis on order and not civil rights explains in part why even the civil rights establishment was reluctant to give the president any credit for sending troops to Little Rock. Roy Wilkins criticized Eisenhower for allowing the crisis to develop in the first place. "Firm words and resolute action by him and his Administration would have rallied public opinion in 1955 when there was ample evidence that things were going badly," Wilkins wrote. "The white people in the South who could be called moderate were begging for some encouragement from the Chief Executive. The wobbly liberal white opinion in the North that knew what was right but hesitated was looking to Washington for a word. The President kept silent. His administration wore kid gloves publicly and did nothing privately (that we know of) in the Roosevelt manner so that the White Citizens Councils, the ignoramuses, the fanatics, the Klan gangsters and every loose hoodlum in the South (and many in the North) felt they had a green light to do as they pleased." Eisenhower had simply "abdicated leadership in a great moral crisis," and Wilkins could not "help but believe that even Calvin Coolidge would not have turned in such a performance." He wrote these words five days before the president sent troops to Little Rock and held to them until his death twenty-four years later.[109]

Little Rock convinced a handful of White House aides that the president ought to repair the political damage by meeting with black leaders. Other than his visit with Wilkins during the 1952 campaign, Eisenhower had never met with any civil rights people, and even now it took a concerted staff effort to secure his agreement. After weeks of negotiation about whom to invite he finally sat down for forty-five minutes on June 23 with King, Wilkins, Randolph, and Lester Granger of the National Urban League. Daisy Bates of the Arkansas NAACP was notably absent; no White House aide recommended her presence because she was "too controversial."[110]

The civil rights delegation had stayed up the night before composing a nine-point agenda which Randolph read to an unimpressed and "quite stiff" president. When Randolph "said we all respected his courage and integrity," commending "him for what he had done at Little Rock," the president brightened. "That's laying it on," Wilkins thought, trying to keep a straight face. When King suggested a White House conference on civil rights, Eisenhower said "there may be some value to your idea . . . But I don't think anything much would really come of [it]." After King and the others left White House staff noted that the president was "extremely dismayed to hear that after five and a half years of effort and action in this field these gentlemen were saying that bitterness on the part of the Negro people was at its height. He wondered if further constructive action in this field would not only result in more bitterness."

Other reactions varied. White House aide Rocco C. Siciliano, the driving force behind the White House meeting, saw it as "an unqualified success—even if success in this area is built on sand." King and Wilkins went on to criticize Eisenhower repeatedly and harshly for refusing "to make a strong positive statement morally condemning segregation." More bitterness, in the president's view. In the aftermath Sherman Adams again turned away Daisy Bates, refusing her request to bring by the students who had integrated Little Rock Central. About the only thing everyone agreed on was that Eisenhower hated sitting in the same room with Negroes. This president had only those forty-five minutes for American citizens of color in his eight White House years.[111]

If anything Eisenhower kept an even lower civil rights profile after that solitary White House meeting. When Mississippi Governor J. P. Coleman protested the FBI's investigation of the Mack Charles Parker lynching, the president merely reminded Coleman of the damage done by such incidents to the American image abroad. He saw no need for antilynching legislation. "At last," one Mississippi newspaper editor rejoiced, "we find a Yankee who publicly admits that much of this equality propaganda is so much baloney." That low profile extended, as ever, to Eisenhower's lone black adviser. In January 1959, nearly four years since his initial appointment, Frederic Morrow finally received an official White House commission as administrative officer for special projects. The president did not attend the ceremony.[112]

Eisenhower kept to this low profile so faithfully during his last White House year that he tried to ignore the sit-in movement begun in February 1960 at a Greensboro Woolworth's lunch counter by four black students from North Carolina A & T College. When a reporter asked if he considered the "Gandhi-like" sit-ins "manifestations of moral courage," the president refused to endorse the students' tactics. He did express a sympathy "with the efforts of any group to enjoy the rights guaranteed by the Constitution." (This was a kinder view than that of former President Truman, who dismissed the sit-ins as Communist inspired and advised "the Negro . . . [to] behave himself.") Of this last year's other major event, the Civil Rights Act of 1960, Eisenhower remained lukewarm. He refused to push for "spectacular stuff" and, after signing the legislation, enforced it, constitutional scholar Alexander Bickel noted, "with about the vigor and imagination displayed by William McKinley in enforcing the Sherman Antitrust Act."[113]

Of Eisenhower and racism, Frederic Morrow said "he just could not bring himself to come to grips with the thing." Administration officials followed the president's lead and continued to treat Morrow himself like a second class citizen from the day he came to the White House to the day he left. Women entered and exited his office in pairs so as not to raise the issue of sexual misconduct; and he could not get a secretary until a Catholic woman from Massachusetts volunteered. With a tear in her eye she cited obligations of her faith. "One of your greatest assets," Nixon told Morrow in the midst of this debilitating harassment, "is the fact that you do not resent being a Negro, and you do not use your color as an excuse for any misfortune you may encounter." When Eisenhower loaned Morrow to the Nixon campaign in 1960 he was rarely seen with the candidate, always traveling at the rear of the train or motorcade. He took it for a while then went back to Washington and worried about finding private-sector employment. Eisenhower pulled him aside at the White House Christmas party to say he had called his Wall Street and college friends and no one would hire a black.

"Literally, out on my ear," Morrow said. "I was the only member of the staff for whom the President could not find a job." It took three years to land a position with the Bank of America International at the recommendation of former Treasury Secretary Robert B. Anderson. The former president never lifted a finger.[114]

According to a Gallup poll in the *Washington Post,* a nagging criticism of Eisenhower's leadership was that he "encourages segregation" (a
finding that was largely the result of the president's waffling on *Brown*).
"This is, of course, outrageous," Maxwell Rabb said. "We have an extraordinary record in this field," a record that included the first civil
rights legislation in eighty years; the end of Jim Crow in the federal civil
service (by the middle of the second term all the white- and colored-
only signs had been removed from the Post Office, the last bastion of
Wilsonian segregation); and the elimination of *de jure* segregation in
the District of Columbia. Eisenhower even called in Louis B. Mayer
and associates. "They were all told to please help clean up the theaters,"
Rabb continued. "[But] these movie magnates didn't own the theaters.
There was a consent decree problem, and they mentioned it to the
President, and said, 'We're not supposed to have anything to do with
the theaters. Production is our thing.'" Eisenhower told them not to
worry about the antitrust problem, promising to "wink at that one."[115]

If Rabb erred in calling the administration's record "extraordinary,"
progress, no matter how fitful, was made. And progress was the key. Eisenhower told Attorney General William Rogers, Brownell's successor,
to "avoid predictions that the law (integration) will necessarily be permanent. . . . A satisfactory integration plan did not necessarily, in my
view, contemplate complete success in a matter of five or ten years."
Thirty or forty or even a hundred years would be acceptable. If any
progress was shown, the president reiterated, then "the time element for
completion becomes unimportant." The problem was that Eisenhower
was not certain that the nation was marching forward or even that it
should. "The entire situation distresses me profoundly," he told *Atlanta
Constitution* publisher Ralph McGill. "There doesn't seem to be any solution in sight—for the simple reason that not even the principles of
political and economic equality will be accepted in some of our
states."[116]

With *Brown,* Little Rock, Montgomery, and the sit-ins behind him,
Eisenhower knew that his call for patience had fallen on deaf ears. He
left the White House, like so many predecessors, bewildered and largely
unmoved by the call for racial justice. "The worst enemies of the civil
rights thing have been a great group or section of the Democratic Party,
and yet most of our negroes go and vote Democratic," he said. "It's a

strange thing."[117] He came to the White House comfortable in the nigger-story world of his Georgia golfing buddies and in retirement was just as comfortable spreading apartheid propaganda to Augusta National chairman Clifford Roberts. "Dear Clif," the former president wrote. "We hear so much mis-information about South Africa, I thought you might like to read this letter from the Ambassador of that nation."[118] For all his talk about progress and the need to obey the land's law, he remained a nineteenth century man to the end—utterly convinced that his nation had been blessed by *Plessy* and cursed by *Brown.*

: 5 :

TOUGH GUY

John F. Kennedy's values and opinions on racial issues were grounded in the nineteenth century. *Profiles in Courage*, the Pulitzer Prize–winning book completed in 1955 while he recovered from surgery, took a neo-Wilsonian slant on Reconstruction. Dismissing Thaddeus Stevens ("crippled, fanatical") and Charles Sumner ("the South's most implacable enemy"), Kennedy condemned the era as "a black nightmare . . . nourished by Federal bayonets."[1] Eight years later, however, he led a nation poised on the brink of a second Reconstruction. He used the moral authority of the White House to condemn racism in all its forms and the executive authority of his office to attack discrimination in voting, federal civil service, public facilities, private-sector employment, and housing. And he introduced the most important civil rights legislation in a century. By the time the assassin's bullet took this young president's life, *de jure* segregation was reeling under the civil rights movement's righteous force and the federal government's legal force.[2]

To his credit Kennedy acted. And his instincts, as Father Theodore Hesburgh of the Civil Rights Commission once said of Kennedy's brother, Robert, were usually "on the side of the angels."[3] But this angel followed more often than he led, just as he followed the canons of Reconstruction historiography in his book. Reform was orchestrated primarily by the civil rights movement and not the Oval Office. The

189

president's general strategy was to slow or otherwise contain the struggle for racial justice. Largely unmoved by the domestic morality play that the civil rights movement became during his White House years (1961–1963), he made decisions based on a cold political calculation and with a contempt for anyone, whether a movement activist or someone on the periphery of the administration itself, who claimed the race issue transcended partisan politics. "[He] was, in the end," admitted former aide and Camelot myth-maker Arthur M. Schlesinger, Jr., "a realist disguised as a romantic."[4]

Kennedy thought he discovered the secret of America's race-based politics early on, a secret that would forever preclude the need for a second Reconstruction. Or even what an aide during the 1952 run for the Senate called "a clear-cut, strong position on civil rights." Robert F. Kennedy revealed this secret after the assassination and in the process explained why his brother considered racial justice no more than a peripheral issue: "Those running for office in the Democratic party looked to just three or four people who would then deliver the Negro vote. And you never had to say you were going to do anything. . . . It was mostly just recognition of them. And it was much easier if you were a Democratic politician running for office. You could receive the vote quite easily. So there was never anywhere where we'd have to get certain civil rights legislation passed or fight for them. That was never an issue in Massachusetts." John Kennedy held to these rules throughout his Senate watch and greater part of his thousand White House days.[5]

Presidential aspirations and the attendant need for both African-American and white-southern votes made this no easy task. The first glitch came when Kennedy sided with Lyndon Johnson on the jury-trial amendment to the Civil Rights Bill of 1957. (The amendment provided jury trials in voting rights cases, and in the South that meant that all-white juries would hear complaints against registrars who denied blacks the right to register and vote.) John sent Robert "into the Confederacy" to remind white people that he had voted right here and remained committed to the Reconstruction lines in *Profiles in Courage*. He also met Roy Wilkins in the Senate restaurant for ninety futile minutes trying to explain why his vote was in the movement's best interest.

Wilkins went on during the 1958 reelection campaign to speak against Kennedy in Massachusetts, prompting JFK to complain: "You came to Pittsfield to say that my record . . . did not deserve the support of Negro voters." These voters, Wilkins responded, wanted more than "quibbling support" from a politician intent on an "apparent entente cordiale" with "Eastland, et al., of Dixie." Because Wilkins was among the "three or four people" who could deliver the black vote, Kennedy had to appease him—which he did, mostly through follow-up fluff letters. "Another one running for President, I thought to myself—and forgot about it," Wilkins wrote after receiving one such letter.[6]

Lingering bitterness convinced Kennedy that his team needed a better entree to black America. His choice pleased no one. The pragmatic Robert Kennedy considered Belford V. and Marjorie M. Lawson, two K Street lawyers with a summer place at Martha's Vineyard, mere "socialites." Civil rights activists knew nothing of the couple. The Lawsons' appeal centered on their skin color, amiability, and connections to the national black fraternity Alpha Phi Alpha. "I guess we have three hundred chapters," Belford said. "Being president, I had access to these. Thirty-five thousand men. . . . When I spelled this all out to Kennedy, he got interested." Belford contributed little more than that list, remaining focused on his law practice. "I couldn't afford the time," he explained.[7] Perhaps his most substantive contribution was the arrangement of a brunch for *Ebony* and *Jet* publisher John Johnson at Kennedy's Georgetown home. While baby Caroline sat in a high chair at the table, JFK complained about his coverage in Johnson's magazines and asked what it would take to get fair treatment. An ambassadorship? Patronage for a friend? Johnson mentioned the Kennedy family patriarch's involvement in the liquor business. Perhaps Joseph P. Kennedy could arrange for advertising dollars. Considering this too direct, the son instead had Henry Ford II tell Johnson that the Ford Motor Company would buy ad space in *Jet*.[8]

Simeon Booker, one of Johnson's reporters, said Kennedy cultivated "a certain image among the Negroes, making statements here and there, but realizing the Negro wasn't part of the technical machinery of the primary, the Convention. . . . I think intentionally he just steered away from making any overall approach toward Negroes. His strategy was to just keep in with Negroes he considered powerful or who could help him."[9] Victory in the West Virginia primary, however, briefly called this line into question. Senator Robert Byrd, a former Klansman, had backed Hubert Humphrey, but JFK carried the black vote and won. "This proved to me that it's absolutely fatal to have southern support," Kennedy told Arthur Schlesinger. "I don't want to go screwing around with all those southern bastards." Sticking to this tack until the convention, he had reporters from the Negro Press Club out to Georgetown and met Thurgood Marshall in his Senate office.[10]

Kennedy also walked into Harry Belafonte's West End Avenue apartment in New York to ask how baseball great Jackie Robinson could be for Nixon. (Robinson had refused to have his picture taken with JFK at an NAACP dinner.) Belafonte was surprised, as movement chronicler Taylor Branch noted, by Kennedy's recognition that Robinson was a major political problem; his assumption that he would win the nomination; his brashness in barging in to ask an enormous favor. (He wanted Belafonte to organize black celebrities for the campaign.) Belafonte told him to see Martin Luther King. "What can he do?," the candidate asked. "Forget me," Belafonte responded. "Forget Jackie Robinson and everybody else. . . . If you can join the cause of King, and be counselled by him, then you'll have an alliance that will make the difference."[11]

A month before the Democratic National Convention, Kennedy met King for ninety minutes in Joseph Kennedy's New York apartment. Other than the Lawsons, King concluded, JFK "didn't know too many Negroes personally." Yet the candidate somehow managed to convince King that he had, to use King's words, "a long intellectual commitment" lacking only "the emotional commitment . . . [of] one who had been right-out active." King walked out committed to Kennedy. "I just felt that his basic bent would have to be right," he explained. "He was at least surrounded by good people [notably Harris Wofford, the first white to attend Howard University Law School since the 1910s, and Chester Bowles, chair of the Democratic Convention's platform committee]. I didn't see the same people, or the same type of people, surrounding Nixon."

King's confidence in Kennedy seemed well placed. JFK endorsed the sit-in movement a few days later, telling several African diplomats that "it is in the American tradition to stand up for one's rights—even if the new way to stand up for one's rights is to sit down." A week after that meeting he made another (futile) play for Jackie Robinson's support. Robinson walked out still carrying Nixon's banner.[12]

Another key endorsement came easier. "Up in Harlem," Kennedy brother-in-law Sargent Shriver said, "the guy who worked for Adam Clayton Powell, was a guy named Ray Jones. . . . We never actually handed any money to Adam." Louis Martin, a presidential campaign veteran since 1944 and for twelve years editor of the *Chicago Defender*, handled the Kennedy cash. Via radiophone from a yacht in the Mediterranean, the vacationing Powell instructed Jones to open the bidding at $300,000 for mobilizing his (nonexistent) nationwide organization for bringing out the black vote. Martin bought ten endorsement speeches but refused Jones's request for the $50,000 up front. Earlier, in a crude blackmail attempt, Powell had informed the Kennedy campaign that he was on call for a southern tour—a bluff that Robert Kennedy had called. The Kennedys were not about to pay this man or his agent in advance. They sent in another brother-in-law, Steve Smith, who gave the money to New York Mayor Robert Wagner. The mayor/middleman then passed it on to Powell in $5,000 chunks after each speech.[13] The congressman stayed out of the South and on the payroll. "One Saturday," Martin remembered, "he was in the gymnasium of the House of Representatives. I gave it [$5,000] to him inside a book. We always took the position that when we gave Adam money, we were paying for the speeches."[14]

The Kennedys also figured they could buy another leading black politician, Congressman William Dawson of Chicago. "What you did was you brought Bill Dawson up and gave him a big office," Shriver said. "And . . . 'walking around money.'" Working with Shriver and Wofford out of the K Street building that served in effect as the campaign's civil rights headquarters (safely segregated from the main campaign office on Connecticut Avenue), Dawson, a protégé of Oscar DePriest, immediately complained about the quality of his space. He also complained about the Shriver/Wofford push to call their unnamed section the "Office of Civil Rights." Those words would insult "our good Southern friends," Dawson reasoned. More hard-headed campaign powers, like Colorado attorney and former football star Byron "Whizzer" White, also worried about offending white southerners. Acting on the advice of Louis Martin, who joined the campaign to provide "G2 on what was happening in the black community," Shriver and Wofford handled Dawson by building him better digs (nicknamed

"Uncle Tom's Cabin") and then ignoring him (except for ceremonial occasions). They also got to keep the words "civil rights" in their office name. Such concessions, however, were cosmetic. When it came time to staff the Justice Department and its Civil Rights Division, RFK listened to the man who stood with Dawson. "A high percentage of those who were selected," he said, "were recommended by Byron White."[15]

From RFK and Whizzer White to Sargent Shriver and Harris Wofford, about the only thing agreed upon unanimously was that the campaign ought to distance itself from Belford and Marjorie Lawson. The dismissal occurred on the eve of the convention when Robert Kennedy learned that Belford had once represented Jimmy Hoffa's Teamsters. The meetings with King and Belafonte had also convinced John Kennedy that he "didn't know much about Negroes and Negro issues," and the Lawsons were not much help there. "He suddenly realized," Wofford said, that "they were . . . just two people that weren't located anywhere and they sort of attached themselves to Kennedy and they were his two Negro advisors and it was making him look silly." Though Marjorie stayed active on the fringe and later received an appointment to the District of Columbia's juvenile court bench, the Lawsons' relationship largely remained what it had always been—a social relationship. Belford asked for such things as "a letter of endorsement for our son to Groton." On the subject of parties and dinners JFK would ask the Lawsons to "get some Negroes to come." The couple last saw him the day before he left for Dallas. They sat next to Charles DeGaulle and Haile Selassie at the funeral.[16]

With the Hoffa connection a mere rumor Simeon Booker called the Lawson dismissal "the number one item of gossip in the Negro political world because nobody could figure out how Belford, who had been with Kennedy for four years, would be dismissed as his top Negro." Speculation soon hardened into a belief that Kennedy was trying to appease the white South.[17] JFK further enraged civil rights activists at the Los Angeles convention by naming Lyndon Johnson as his running mate. "He hit the ceiling!," Thurgood Marshall said, recalling Roy Wilkins's reaction. "He bounced off the ceiling." Kennedy met early the next morning with 250 equally upset black delegates at the Shrine Auditorium. "They were cold as fish" (Shriver's assessment), and when the candidate spoke they booed until the NAACP's Clarence Mitchell shouted for silence. Booker said it was "an off-the-record sort of thing" with Kennedy promising to "do this and that." The campaign had no illusions. "We're in trouble with Negroes," RFK admitted.[18]

John Kennedy looked to Shriver and Wofford for advice ("What do I need to know, who do I need to see?"), and Shriver and Wofford looked to Louis Martin. "You've got to go after the Negro newspapers," Martin advised. "They lynched Sparkman and Kefauver as Southern-ers, and they'll lynch Lyndon Johnson the same way if you don't do something about it." Martin also realized, "as an old newspaperman," that "those papers aren't going to do a damn thing for you unless you pay us some money." (The Kennedys had understood this since the John Johnson brunch.) Here the only problem was $49,000 in unpaid bills that the Democratic party owed various black newspapers for ad-vertising space in the previous campaign. By getting that debt repaid Martin fixed himself in the Kennedy mind as the closest thing to a pragmatist (that is, someone with "balls") in the campaign's civil rights section. This was a pleasant surprise since his initial appointment dis-appointed the Kennedys. "I was particularly concerned to organize the black preachers, because of the Catholic issue," Martin recalled. "[But] when Bobby heard I was on the staff and he was told I was a Catholic, he said, 'You mean you got a son of a bitch in here who is a black Catholic? That's the last thing we need.'"

The Kennedys and their inner circle treated the others in the civil rights circle as objects of scorn. They called Shriver a "Boy Scout," the "house Communist," the "too-liberal in-law." Wofford was even worse. "He didn't have nearly the judgment that Louie Martin did," Robert Kennedy said. "Of course, he's not Negro . . . rather in some areas a slight madman." The campaign kept Shriver and Wofford on because they were the only ones with contacts. "[Because they] knew these people [Negroes]," RFK continued, "much better than any of *us* knew them." Shriver was also indispensable in his home state of Illinois where JFK needed every black and white vote he could get.[19]

John Kennedy locked up the Negro vote in Illinois and elsewhere with two gestures. First, he said that federally assisted housing could be "desegregated by the stroke of a presidential pen," implying that he would issue an executive order if elected. This signaled a reversal of the Eisenhower insistence that no federal law, regulation, or court decision could overcome historic patterns of segregation. The second gesture, a telephone call from the candidate to a pregnant Coretta Scott King as her husband sat in a Reidsville, Georgia, jail, nearly cost Shriver, Wofford, and other civil rights section "bomb throwers" their jobs. "Bobby Kennedy landed on me like a ton of bricks," Shriver said. "He scorched my ass." Then he settled down and saw the prize. When Georgia Governor Ernest Vandiver mentioned that a jailed King could hurt JFK's chances of carrying the state in November, Robert Kennedy made his own call from a New York phone booth to the judge who had denied bail. The call secured King's release.[20]

John Kennedy's people pushed forward while the Nixon campaign hesitated. Shriver and Wofford distributed to black churches North and South two million copies of a pamphlet entitled "'No comment' Nixon versus a Candidate with a Heart, Senator Kennedy." Frederic Morrow had suggested that Nixon send a telegram to Mrs. King, too, but the Republican candidate's senior "staff figuratively threw daggers at me, telling me this was a stupid move." Another black campaign aide, John C. Calhoun of Fulton County, Georgia, also urged Nixon to respond. "He knows King," Calhoun pleaded. "Kennedy doesn't know him. He ought to make some kind of statement." "The vice president got your message," a Republican National Committee official responded. "He says he knows he is going to loose some Negro votes. But he is going to gain some white votes too. He is going to sit it out."

Nixon was reeling from running mate Henry Cabot Lodge, Jr.,'s recent pledge at a Harlem rally that a Republican administration would appoint a Negro to the cabinet. (Lodge had not discussed this with Nixon or campaign advisers beforehand.) Now making his own play for white votes, Kennedy called Lodge's gesture "racism at its worst" and promised to consider "qualifications" and not the "color" of prospective nominees. Kennedy played the race issue both ways against Nixon. In white areas his campaign circulated what the Fair Campaign Practice Committee called a "flier displaying three photographs of Nixon in various poses of affection and affinity with Negroes." (Nixon's family was especially bitter about this flier.)[21] In black areas the Kennedy campaign circulated the restrictive-housing covenant which Nixon had signed for his Washington home. Because the Supreme Court had already struck down such covenants the FBI had a half-baked excuse to open an election-law case and assign a handful of special agents to investigate. The team included G. Gordon Liddy. "We were never able to solve that case," the future plumber said, "but it did serve as my introduction to political hardball."[22]

Nixon lost all the way around. He failed to take the southern states he concentrated on (South Carolina, Georgia, and Alabama), and lost enough black votes in the North to suffer defeat in Michigan and Illinois. Afterward he remembered "one of the exceedingly rare occasions" where his chauffeur of eight years, John Wardlaw, spoke. "Mr. Vice President, I can't tell you how sick I am about the way my people voted in the election. You know I had been talking to all of my friends. They were all for you. But when Mr. Robert Kennedy called the judge to get Dr. King out of jail—well, they just all turned to him."[23]

John and Robert Kennedy's dramatic gestures, nonetheless, had much in common with Nixon's obvious caution. They intended to do just enough to secure Negro votes and no more. "It was mostly just recognition of them," Robert Kennedy had said. "You could receive the vote quite easily." The Kennedys understood what a black Chicagoan told campaign chronicler Theodore White. "Mister, they could put a dog at the head of that ticket and if they called him Democratic I'd vote for him." So the Kennedys backed off actual commitments for action. In response to a campaign-trail question to both candidates about whether they would refuse to use segregated facilities or take part in segregated affairs as president, Shriver and Wofford prepared "an affirmative answer" but held it up and then buried it when it became clear that Nixon would not reply. JFK approached racial issues systematically only when the people of color in question were thousands of miles away. His campaign speeches included 479 references to Africa—a perfect way to attack the Eisenhower administration for its policy of neglect and appeal to African Americans without alienating whites.[24]

Kennedy won the election because he straddled the racial fence and Richard Nixon lost because he did the same thing but less skillfully. At the Republican National Convention in Chicago, Nixon made a deal with New York Governor Nelson Rockefeller to beef up the party's civil rights plank—a decision that Barry Goldwater called "immoral politics," "the Munich of the Republican party." "It lay in Nixon's power to reorient the Republican Party toward an axis of Northern-Southern conservatives," Theodore White wrote. "[He] made his choice, I believe, more out of conscience than out of strategy," and "succeeded, in the end, in alienating Northern Negro *and* Southern white, losing both along with the election." This could be seen even at the convention. When Fred Morrow gave a speech about racial progress, noting how a man whose grandfather was a slave had risen to the rank of presidential aide, the television networks cut away to avoid offending southern viewers.

Trying to have it both ways, Nixon came across as neither the white man's candidate nor the black man's. Theodore White credited him for refusing to risk "America's domestic peace" by organizing the South "generally out of racial fear," by abandoning "all seeking of Negro votes in the North," by forming "a new and triple alliance between the Midwest farm belt, the racists of the Old South and those political forces in the Northern suburbs that more and more seek to exclude Negroes from their neighborhoods and segregate them in the old core cities." Nixon held in *Six Crises* that he "would follow the same course of action if I had the decision to make again." In his second run for the White House, however, he would pursue the divisive racial politics that White commended him for avoiding in his first run.[25]

John Kennedy would have no part of the latest Republican southern strategy (which White called a trade-off: "Let us give the Northern Negro vote to the Democrats, and we shall take the Old South for ourselves").[26] He intended to keep the votes of both by ignoring racial issues whenever possible and making the occasional symbolic gestures whenever necessary. Unfortunately, race kept intruding. Kennedy dropped his first choice for secretary of state, Arkansas Senator J. William Fulbright, after Roy Wilkins reminded him that Fulbright had signed the Southern Manifesto. Racial politics even influenced his brother's appointment. Abraham Ribicoff was the first choice for attorney general, RFK admitted. "[But the president-elect] didn't think a Jew should be putting Negro children in Protestant schools in the South . . . at the instruction of a Catholic."[27] An opportunity for a symbolic gesture arose at the inaugural parade when the all-white Coast Guard contingent passed the reviewing stand. That evening JFK ordered the commandant to "get some Negroes." "And this is the most important day in a man's life," Roy Wilkins marveled, finally forgetting the jury-trial amendment. "Who else would do that except John Fitzgerald Kennedy?"[28]

Once in the White House, Kennedy had no civil rights program other than what ADA activist Joseph Rauh called a play on the New Deal idea of "spend and spend and elect and elect." Only here it was "'appoint and appoint and elect and elect' theory. It was 'appoint Negroes . . . but stay away from Congress.'" "It got to be a kind of sub rosa joke around Washington even among Negroes," Wilkins said, "that Kennedy was so hot on the Department heads, the Cabinet officers, and Agency heads that everyone was scrambling around to find himself a Negro in order to keep the President off his neck."[29] JFK did talk about the "hiring of Negroes" at the first cabinet meeting (in the manner of his telephone call to the Coast Guard commandant), but for all the fanfare the "effort to recruit outstanding Negroes" met "only limited success." The result, a White House aide explained, of "the scarcity of qualified top-level candidates" and "indifference of certain department and agency heads." If black employment in the upper civil service ranks increased 88 percent by Kennedy's last five months in office, the numbers remained at the level of tokenism. Still, there was little disappointment at the top. The goal of the entire exercise, the president noted, was merely to "indicate my interest and put the matter on ice for awhile."[30]

No executive agency or department pushed harder on the affirmative-action front than State. "The biggest single burden we carry on our backs in our foreign relations in the 1960's," Dean Rusk concluded, "is the problem of racial discrimination here at home." To recruit blacks for the foreign service Rusk worked with the Urban League and publisher John Johnson who agreed to run a *Jet* article on employment opportunities. State also created a special protocol service section to help nonwhite diplomats cope. "Once a newly arrived black ambassador came to my office and asked me with some trepidation," Rusk remembered, "'Where can I get a haircut?' It pained me to tell him I didn't know." Victories came, though slowly—in part because many career officers resisted (hardly surprising given the department's enduring McCarthyite legacy); and in part because many problems were beyond Rusk's or any other well-intentioned person's control. Particularly vexing were the Jim Crow practices of the roadside establishments on

Maryland's Route 40, where segregationists continually humiliated and sometimes beat up African diplomats.[31]

Kennedy delegated most civil rights responsibilities to the largely un-interested attorney general. "I did not lie awake at night worrying about the problems of Negroes," RFK conceded. That blunt style created problems. "[John Kennedy] had a grace and a charm and above all an intelligence on this thing that immediately invited you in to commune with him on it, so to speak," Roy Wilkins said. "I never got the impres-sion that you were communing with Robert Kennedy."[32] In practice, however, this difference between the brothers blurred. When pens marked "one stroke of the pen" flooded the White House mail room (to remind the president of his promise to desegregate public housing), JFK simply flashed a (graceful and charming) grin and ordered, "Send them to Wofford!" There would be no stroke until after the 1962 elec-tions "because of the political implications" on both sides of the Mason-Dixon line, the attorney general later explained. "A good number of liberal Congressmen—I remember, from Michigan, for in-stance—were opposed to issuing it." The Kennedys did not think "the country could have been moved" so they did nothing.[33]

The bold stroke-of-the-pen rhetoric remained a throw-away cam-paign line until November 20, 1962. Even then, the promise was only partially fulfilled with an executive order that excluded existing housing and applied only to new construction owned or financed directly by the federal government. Theodore Sorensen said the president waited this long in hope of ensuring passage of his Urban Affairs Bill, which pro-posed the creation of a new cabinet department out of the Housing and Home Finance Agency. JFK intended to name Robert Weaver secretary, Sorensen added, making him the first African-American cabinet member. From the president on down, in other words, the adminis-tration assumed an executive order fulfilling the campaign promise would antagonize moderate southern congressmen whose votes were needed for the Urban Affairs Bill. Only when the House Rules Com-mittee killed the bill (that is, when he had nothing to lose) did Kennedy issue his watered-down executive order.[34]

Civil rights leaders wanted more than executive orders. They wanted legislation and considered the administration's announcement that it would not go that route tantamount, in Wilkins's words, "to telling the opposition, for example—in football analogy—that you weren't going to use the forward pass." For the Kennedys, their endless games of touch on Hyannis Port grass aside, this was a nondecision. "I never even thought or suggested or even had a very serious conversation—or any conversation that I can remember about sending civil rights legislation up," RFK admitted. "And there wasn't anybody who was calling for civil rights legislation that could really give any leadership in getting it through." So the White House remained silent when Senator Joseph Clark and Representative Emanuel Celler introduced civil rights legislation, and also when Vice President Johnson pushed for a change in Rule 22 making it harder for southern Democrats to filibuster against any such legislation.[35]

That wall of silence smothered Shriver, Wofford, and Martin, who accepted the no-legislation strategy provided that John Kennedy launch a program of aggressive executive action. All they got while waiting out the Urban Affairs Bill was an order in March establishing the President's Committee on Equal Employment Opportunity. The White House civil rights circle simply could not get their "cause within the moral framework of the guys who are in power." Theodore Sorensen and other "hardnose Pauls . . . were not anti-Negro," Martin concluded, "[but] they were always counting noses, you know, they wanted to know where were you—what's your army like? . . . I couldn't get anywhere unless I showed the politics of it." "Success required selectivity," Sorensen explained. "To provoke a bitter national controversy without achieving any gains would divide the American people at a time when the international scene required maximum attention."

Martin did his best. He sent endless memoranda to Sorensen about the "two Democratic Parties" above and below the Mason-Dixon line and the dangers inherent in the president's reliance on a few prominent African Americans to deliver the vote. "Negro leaders are quite expendable," he warned, "because the pressure for social changes comes from the bottom in Negro life." Nor did Martin and other White House aides with civil rights interests get anywhere when screaming "the politics of it" (that is, by emphasizing what they saw as the political advantages in an aggressive civil rights program). They could do little more than sit around Arthur Schlesinger's Georgetown living room and complain about "the president's excessive caution." What they considered to be his obsession with moving so slowly on civil rights that white southern voters would not be unduly upset.[36]

Kennedy cultivated those civil rights activists deemed "reasonable" and "responsible" even as he brushed them off. Before meeting with sixty-five NAACP leaders, the president took Roy Wilkins, Arthur Spingarn, and Stephen Gill Spottswood upstairs to his study for a private conversation. On the way back they met Jacqueline Kennedy in a corridor. The first lady had grit and grime on her face, having rummaged in the White House basement and attic. "I heard her say 'I've found the Lincoln china,'" Wilkins remembered. "And the President kept saying I'd like to introduce you . . . and he reached over and brushed the smudge off her cheek and we went down to the meeting." Spottswood talked for five minutes about the need for legislation, then Kennedy spoke briefly. Then it was over. "Everyone went out of there absolutely charmed by the manner in which they had been turned down," Wilkins continued. "He wasn't a man to give up easily," always willing to pat "a head" and never willing to "bind up a joint."[37]

Kennedy's only initiative, other than the minority hiring push and the single executive order on housing, was a voter-registration campaign modeled after the (very) modest trailblazing of the Eisenhower administration's last six months. The Civil Rights Acts of 1957 and 1960 provided for injunctive relief against any person, "acting under color of law or otherwise," involved in racial discrimination regarding registration or voting itself through threats, intimidation, or any other form of coercion. By July 1960 the Justice Department's Civil Rights Division had moved forward with voter discrimination suits in Georgia, Alabama, and Louisiana. The Kennedys incorrectly reasoned that the voter-registration campaign posed little risk of inciting a white southern reaction ("backlash"). "This was the area in which we had the greatest authority," RFK said, "and if we were going to do anything on civil rights, we should do it in that field where we had the authority."

Voter registration also held the promise that the pace of the civil rights movement could be slowed. Managed. Moving "Negro by Negro" the Kennedy administration could push the movement away from volatile boycotts and sit-ins and toward the more stately order of legal briefs presented by men in vested suits to white men in black robes—an effort that lasted for all of John Kennedy's White House tenure. "We're trying to figure out what we can do," the president told Louisiana Governor James H. Davis two years after launching the voter registration drive, "to put this stuff in the courts and get it off the street."[38]

At the same time, a few White House and Justice Department aides hoped that increased black voting rolls might transform the Democratic party in the South into a more liberal, multiracial party. "Voting rights was the most natural way to move," Nashville newspaperman John Seigenthaler, then an RFK aide, said. "If Negroes were voting in places like Mississippi . . . people like Jim Eastland wouldn't be so fresh."[39] The Kennedys themselves had no illusions about liberalizing white southern politics and for that matter got along fine with Senator Eastland just as he was.

The push for voting rights in the South had a final theoretical advantage in that the president could remain uninvolved. John Kennedy defined voter registration strictly as a law-enforcement issue and delegated it to the attorney general's shop. In so doing the Kennedys figured (incorrectly, once again) that they had a reserve of political capital. "All the southerners were very much in favor of my being Attorney General," RFK claimed, citing his staff work on the Hoffa-chasing Senate Rackets Committee. "Because I had been investigating labor unions. They didn't like labor unions much." He would discover that they liked the Justice Department's civil rights lawyers even less.[40]

An overriding desire to move slowly without upsetting white southerners surfaced in the appointment of Burke Marshall to head the Civil Rights Division. "The fellow who should naturally have been appointed was Harris Wofford," Robert Kennedy reasoned. "I was reluctant to appoint him because he was so committed on civil rights emotionally, and what I wanted was a tough lawyer who could look at things objectively. . . . I didn't want to have someone in the Civil Rights Division who was not dealing with facts but was dealing from emotion and who wasn't going to give what was in the best interests of President Kennedy—what he was trying to accomplish for the country—but advice which the particular individual felt was in the best interest of a Negro or a group of Negroes or a group of those who were interested in civil rights. I wanted advice and ideas from somebody who had the same interests and motivation that I did." The Kennedys categorized

"Negroes" as a special interest and lumped them with other "interests" ranging from organized labor to Standard Oil and Du Pont.[41]

This view brought the attorney general to Marshall, a partner with Wofford at Covington and Burling, Dean Acheson's blue-chip Washington firm, and a respected corporate lawyer whose clients happened to include Standard Oil and the Du Ponts. When he came in for an interview he assumed it was for a post in the Antitrust Division. The assistant attorney generalship for civil rights was perhaps the only job in America, as many newspaper columnists later pointed out, where the principal qualification was lack of experience. Meanwhile, Wofford ended up in the White House as the president's civil rights adviser. This appointment seems ironic at first glance given RFK's view ("a slight madman"), but Wofford got that post precisely because it was one where he could not act. He never got JFK's ear either and after a year left in frustration for the Peace Corps. "Africa is in my blood," he wrote in his resignation letter, holding that he could do more good tackling "the larger problem of our integration in this new world."[42]

If Robert Kennedy and Burke Marshall began with the same civil rights interests and motivations (none), by the time they were through both were involved, as White House aide Kenneth O'Donnell later said of the attorney general, "up to [their] eyeballs."[43] Simply put, the civil rights movement forced that involvement. The immersion began on March 19 when Kennedy and Marshall met with Civil Rights Division line lawyers, including John Doar, a Wisconsin native and Eisenhower holdover, to map out voter-registration strategy. Kennedy made the policy; Marshall thought it out; Doar put it to work. By the time RFK quit to run for the Senate in August 1964, Marshall, Doar, and their fellows had filed fifty-seven voting rights suits including one in Senator Eastland's Sunflower County and twenty-nine other actions in Mississippi. Through it all the attorney general took a hands-on approach. "He'd come down, walk into your office, sit on your desk and start asking what you were working on," division attorney David Norman said. "You never knew when he would come in."[44] Yet the entire campaign was essentially a stall, an effort to obstruct the more ambitious strategies of civil right movement activists.

The goal was to inch forward "Negro by Negro," and the Kennedy administration intended to fight off anyone, whether within the government or without, who urged a faster pace. This included the Civil Rights Commission, established by the Civil Rights Act of 1957 and empowered to hold hearings and investigate allegations "that certain citizens of the United States are being deprived of their right to vote." The commission had ventured into the South only once, when President Eisenhower personally intervened after Maxwell Air Force Base in Montgomery, Alabama, refused to house commission members and staff. That president could not dictate rental practices to motel owners, but he had no such inhibitions when dealing with Air Force officers and the housing they controlled at Maxwell. The new president failed to match his predecessor's gesture. Kennedy practically made Eisenhower look like a "civil rights extremist" by promising only to keep the commission from returning to the South.

"Two or three times we decided to hold a Mississippi hearing," Father Hesburgh said, "and were called off because of political considerations because a good man was running for governor and if we'd had a hearing, we'd throw the election the other way. Well, it went the other way anyway." JFK joked about it, telling Hesburgh and the commission's other members to chose a less controversial locale. "I understand there's some problems in Alaska," he would offer. Eventually the commission recommended that the White House withhold federal funds from Mississippi, prompting the president to present himself as protector of the white South against the "draconian" commission.[45]

Robert Kennedy saw the Civil Rights Commission as an unwelcome federal instrument guaranteed to invoke southern memories of Reconstruction. Hearings in Mississippi and other hot spots would create "an emotional demand" for civil rights legislation and thus collide with the administration's no-legislation agenda. "I didn't have any great feeling that they were accomplishing anything of a positive nature," RFK said. "It was almost like the old House Un-American Activities Committee investigating Communism." The commission had simultaneously invaded the Justice Department's domain. "Doing what we were really doing," the attorney general complained. "Voting." Staff director Berl Bernhard said he "had never seen anyone so angry at the commission as Robert Kennedy—not even [Alabama Governors] John Patterson or George Wallace." The attorney general had the dual goals of protecting his turf and containing the civil rights movements and its allies.[46]

The House Committee on Un-American Activities reference was ironic because Robert Kennedy sided with an even more powerful security pillar, the FBI, when the Civil Rights Commission requested access to voting rights and police brutality files. The Civil Rights Act of 1960 granted the "Attorney General or his representative" authority to photograph voter registration records, and the FBI received the assignment—proceeding lethargically but proceeding nonetheless and eventually accumulating a tremendous database. "My inclination was to defer to the Department because they could take remedial action," Berl Bernhard said. "Then we'd want to get the factual basis from the Department and they wouldn't let us see the Bureau reports. . . . Justice would come in and we'd have a big meeting with Seigenthaler, Doar, Bob, Burke and me. There'd be lots of give and take. But in the end, we'd lose out." Bernhard concluded that segregationists, including HUAC members, had better luck. "I knew that Mr. Eastland, Mr. Thurmond, and the rest of them did not have the investigating capacity to get the facts that they had. . . . I knew that they got them from somewhere, from the Civil Rights Division or the Bureau." Kennedy's people just shrugged. "They were very chary. They would say, 'We've got material from the FBI, we can't let you see it.'"[47]

FBI officials provided substantive information to the Civil Rights Commission only on alleged Communist infiltration of the civil rights movement. J. Edgar Hoover assigned a liaison agent, Bernhard noted, and "he gave me specific documents. I got one or two direct from Mr. Hoover saying, 'You might be interested to see some of the activities of your friend, Dr. Martin Luther King.' That kind of thing. I got one on Roy Wilkins." King was of course a particular target. He not only "cavorted with people who were of doubtful loyalty to the United States," the FBI warned, but was a "sexually perverted . . . switch hitter" prone to "orgies with more than one woman." Bureau agents also provided "name checks on witnesses" to prevent "people who were just out-and-out Communists from testifying," and security reports on applicants for commission employment. "Throwbacks to the McCarthy era," thought William L. Taylor, Jr., the commission's White House liaison. In Robert Kennedy's opinion, nonetheless, it was the Civil Rights Commission that resembled HUAC.[48]

While defending Mississippi and other hard-core states from the Civil Rights Commission, John Kennedy appointed five segregationist judges to the federal bench. This was a balancing act—another counterweight to offset the phone call to Coretta King, the limited push for affirmative action in federal hiring, and the voting litigation campaign. The appointment of James Eastland's old college roommate, Harold Cox, who referred to African Americans as "niggers" and "chimpanzees," was the worst of the lot. Robert Kennedy removed Thurgood Marshall from consideration, in contrast, in deference to "the people at the New York Bar" who called the NAACP giant "just a one-client lawyer" and "basically second-rate." "The Wall Street lawyers would look down on that," Burke Marshall explained.

When Roy Wilkins complained about the quality of the judicial appointments ("[it] bodes ill for any litigation not keyed to the mores of 1861"), Robert Kennedy ignored him. Instead he turned to Eastland—a man, Lyndon Johnson once said, who "could be standing right in the middle of the worst Mississippi flood ever known, and he'd say the niggers caused it, helped out by the Communists." "A vicious little fat toad," agreed longtime civil rights activist and Johnson family friend Virginia Durr. "He used to invite people over for the weekend and tell them to 'pick out a nigger girl and a horse!' That was his way of showing hospitality." Yet the attorney general found Eastland's advice "very helpful" and the man himself "much more pleasant to deal with . . . than many of the so-called liberals in the House Judiciary Committee or in other parts of Congress or the Senate." "The White House was beginning to look like a dude ranch," Roy Wilkins charged, "with James O. Eastland as the general manager." David Norman said "Eisenhower appointed liberal judges and then decided not to enforce the law. Kennedy decided to enforce the law and then appointed backward judges. Either way the net result is the same—zero."[49]

Following Justice Charles E. Whittaker's resignation the Kennedys briefly considered a black man, William Hastie, for the Supreme Court. (Truman had appointed Hastie in 1949 to a Circuit Court seat, the first African American to hold that position.) The White House decided against it after RFK talked with Earl Warren. "[The chief justice] was violently opposed," the attorney general noted, since Hastie was "not a liberal, and he'll be opposed to all the measures that we are interested in." Robert Kennedy said he shared Warren's view (though his admitted preference for Senator Eastland over the Judiciary Committee's liberals hardly supports the claim). "I thought it would mean so much overseas and abroad that we had a Negro on the Supreme Court," he lamented. "It could do all kinds of good for the country. . . . We came that close. And then finally there was a conflict. . . . I think a lot of people in the White House were opposed to having a Negro."[50]

Hastie failed at every stop. He was apparently too black for the president, supposedly too conservative for the chief justice and the attorney general, and certainly too tainted for the internal security people. In a preliminary background check forwarded to Robert Kennedy's desk, Hoover's FBI hooked Hastie to ten allegedly subversive organizations. In the midst of this opposition John Kennedy asked Clark Clifford if he had a "personal interest" in a Supreme Court seat. Having advised against Hastie because "his qualifications were shaky," Clifford said he had no such interest and instead suggested constitutional scholar Paul Freund of Harvard. Passing over Freund (in part because Felix Frankfurter was still on the Supreme Court and thus the "Jewish seat" was filled), the president settled on Byron White.[51]

Ultimately, the White House lost both ways. John Kennedy designed the something-for-everyone approach to placate both the Democratic party's northern liberal wing and southern states' rights wing. He offered voting rights litigation and affirmative action initiatives to one wing, the appointment of segregationist judges and a rejection of the Civil Rights Commission's legislative agenda to the other wing. Only no one was placated. While liberals attacked the administration for moving too slowly and with too much deference to states' rights, the specter of blacks voting in the deep South fueled the so-called white backlash the Kennedys had feared. This last development was something that neither Kennedy had predicted and never fully appreciated. If anything they anticipated the opposite.

"Did you ever discuss with the President the political implications . . . of an increase of Negro voting in the South?," *New York Times* columnist Anthony Lewis asked RFK after his brother's death. "The obvious possibility of a transformation of the Democratic party into a more liberal, multiracial party in the South?" "No, I didn't,"

Kennedy responded flatly. "I thought, practically—which I said to Burke at the time—that if I were a Republican, that's the area that I would emphasize. And I'd be a moderate in the South if I were a Republican. Because I thought that the Democratic leadership in the South was traditionally opposed to civil rights." "You didn't anticipate the way it has actually turned out—at least in 1964—with the Republican party becoming a racist, white party in the South," Lewis prompted. "No," RFK reiterated. "I would have gone the opposite direction."

At most the attorney general discussed the potential of the new black southern voter with the president "in passing," concluding after the fact and after his brother's assassination that for every vote gained two were probably lost among white southerners because "we were alienating so many people."[52] The Kennedys saw no political gain in pushing too hard for voting rights for southern blacks. They also had no moral commitment to the cause. By their own account they pursued voting rights as the least objectional and least intrusive course of action. If it had not been for the pressure brought by the civil rights movement, in all probability the Kennedys would not have moved at all.

John and Robert Kennedy tried to limit any possible alienation of the white southern voter by throwing another bone to the segregationists. In this case they refused to protect the young voter registration workers who went into the black belt from Ku Klux Klan and local law-enforcement brutality. "We abandoned the solution, really, of trying to give people protection," RFK said in defending the administration's states' rights stand here. "We ran through that a dozen times over the period of a thousand days. . . . We were resisting that all of the time, except where we had some legal basis and the situation warranted it. We were always struggling with that."[53]

In practice this did not slow the white South's alienation and drift toward the Republican party. Southerners blamed the Kennedys (Robert especially) for "sending in" the voter registration workers in the first place (in the manner in which they later blamed him for "organizing" the Freedom Rides), and it made no difference that the administration gave Klansmen and sheriffs free run at the young people who canvassed the delta and the sharecroppers who gathered the courage to come to their county courthouses. "Headin' your flock out of the

chains and fetters of Egypt," as Fanny Lou Hamer of Mississippi's Sunflower County said. "Taken' them yourself to register—tomorra—in
Indianola." Administration policy made such journeys more rather
than less life threatening.[54]

With many civil rights workers in the deep South nearly as alienated as the resistance, the circle squared. This was particularly true
within the Student Nonviolent Coordinating Committee (SNCC—
pronounced "snick"). Of Robert Moses, who quit his job teaching
mathematics at the prestigious Horace Mann High School in New York
to work in the poverty and danger of Mississippi, Burke Marshall told
the attorney general that after three years of the no-protection policy he
was a "radical and embittered young man."

"Is he now?," RFK asked.

"Yes."

"He always was?"

"He's gotten more so."

"Is he bitter against us?"

"He's bitter against the government," Marshall continued. "It isn't
personal. With a lot of them, it gets to be personal."[55]

Civil rights movement activists' disillusionment with the Democrats
damaged the party even if it led not to a Republican exodus but the
later radicalism of the New Left and black power movements. To appreciate how far this radicalism went and how quickly this happened,
it should be remembered that SNCC activists were surprisingly conventional in their politics through the sit-ins of Eisenhower's last year.
If blacks had equal educational opportunity, Fisk student Diane Nash
offered, they could make a more dramatic contribution to the global
struggle against communism: "Maybe someday a Negro will invent one
of our missiles." By the end of the Kennedy years Nash and other
SNCC members, including John Lewis (later elected to Congress from
Georgia), identified the government in Washington as the enemy and
not the one in Moscow.[56]

Violence against voter registration workers and the faint rumblings
of white backlash aside, the Kennedys were confident that things were
under control. They would keep to the minority hiring and voter-
registration ruts, form the oddest of alliances with the Hoovers and
Eastlands to contain the Civil Rights Commission, and otherwise ap-

pease the white South with judicial appointments. But in the administration's fourth month the civil rights movement came roaring along the highway on Greyhound and Trailways buses, Freedom Riders who pulled the Kennedys' Oval and Justice Department offices in their wake. For nearly all of the president's remaining 900 days, reform was initiated by the movement and not the White House. JFK himself would remain, as ever, disengaged, content to delegate authority to the crack crew that his brother (and Byron White) had assembled. The administration reacted more than acted, coming down on the movement's side in eight cases out of ten but always hedging its bets and harboring bitterness toward the civil rights activists who were causing so many problems.

Technically, the Kennedys knew about the Freedom Rides beforehand. James Farmer, national director of the Congress of Racial Equality (CORE), sent a press release to the White House. He also invited Simeon Booker to accompany the riders, and this *Jet* reporter, who had been a Nieman fellow at Harvard with RFK's press secretary Edwin O. Guthman, alerted both the attorney general's office and the FBI. But the White House filed and forgot Farmer's press release in the excitement of the president's preparation for his Paris (DeGaulle) and Vienna (Khrushchev) meetings. For its part the Justice Department ignored Booker's tip, too—largely because Marshall was battling the mumps in his Washington apartment. With Doar and other line lawyers in the Civil Rights Division remaining focused on their voter-registration work, no administration official gave more than a minute's thought to the Freedom Ride.

James Farmer had been thinking about the Freedom Ride for fourteen years. In 1947 a CORE and Fellowship of Reconciliation crew had organized a mostly uneventful Journey of Reconciliation on buses and trains in the upper South to test a limited and largely ignored Supreme Court ruling (*Morgan v. Virginia*) against segregation in interstate transportation. The new Freedom Ride, inspired by a more recent if still limited and ineffectual Supreme Court decision against segregated transportation (*Boynton v. Virginia*), would venture into the deep South from Washington, D.C., to Jackson, Mississippi.[57] Farmer hoped to provoke "an international crisis" that would bring Cold War America's fundamental contradiction to the world's attention. "We were counting

on the bigots of the South to do our work for us," he said. The Freedom Riders would "fill up the jails, as Gandhi did in India," with a
jail-no-bail strategy designed to move the struggle for racial justice onto
the high moral ground of global politics. Roy Wilkins thought it "a desperately brave, reckless strategy, one that made those touch-football
games played by the Kennedys look like macho patty-cake."[58]

A domestic crisis was the last thing President Kennedy wanted. Seven
blacks and six whites left Washington on May 4, and as they headed on
a Greyhound and a Trailways for the Alabama state line Robert Kennedy gave his maiden civil rights address at the University of Georgia.
Like Farmer, RFK located the struggle for racial justice within the larger
struggle against communism abroad, saying that disrespect for the law
would "hurt our country in the eyes of the world."[59] He returned to
Washington still oblivious to the Freedom Riders and their initial
troubles—arrests at bus stations in Charlotte, North Carolina, and
Winnsboro, South Carolina, and an assault in Rock Hill, South Carolina. These were only the first of a series of incidents that would bring
the United States into disrepute in every third world nation.

The Freedom Riders sparked the crisis that James Farmer wanted and
the Kennedys dreaded in a few short hours on Mother's Day (May 14)
when the Greyhound arrived in Anniston, Alabama, sixty miles from
Birmingham. An angry mob quickly surrounded the bus, smashing windows and pounding away until police arrived. When the bus pulled out
dozens of rioters pursued in cars. They overtook the Greyhound and
forced it off the road with shotguns and a homemade bomb tossed
through a window. Eight rioters boarded the second bus (the Trailways)
when it pulled into Anniston, Alabama, within an hour and beat up two
white Freedom Riders. When that bus arrived at the Birmingham terminal fifty minutes later a wave of Ku Klux Klansmen carrying baseball
bats, chains, and lead pipes appeared. Birmingham police had promised
the Klan twenty free minutes to break heads, and those thugs did exactly
that before the bloodied riders made their way to Rev. Fred Shuttlesworth's home. Back in Anniston the mob lay siege to the hospital
where the wounded riders had fled. Nearly everyone predicted that the
violence would continue because Diane Nash and ten other SNCC sit-
in veterans at Nashville's Fisk University pledged to come down, board
the Montgomery bus, and continue the Freedom Ride.

Failing to appreciate the seriousness of the Anniston and Birmingham incidents, Kennedy administration officials were not among those who shared such fears. "These things [civil rights demonstrations] were seen as a pain in the ass" and nothing more than that, Nicholas deB. Katzenbach said. Robert Kennedy, after learning of the bus burning in his morning paper, saw no need to call JFK. "I wouldn't call or talk to him just to be gabby about what was going on in the South," he explained. "The President's brother . . . didn't really seem to understand," Roy Wilkins concluded after a meeting that afternoon. "The Administration's first reaction to the rides was that they were a destructive form of grandstanding that could only embarrass President Kennedy at his summit meeting with Khrushchev two weeks hence." When Harris Wofford briefed the president on the Freedom Riders' plans to continue their journey, he received a startling order. "Tell them to call it off!" "I don't think anybody's going to stop them right now," Wofford responded. Yet the president persisted in his effort to obstruct the civil rights movement.[60]

The Kennedys next turned to John Seigenthaler, the former Nashville newspaperman and now a Justice Department official, in the hope that his Nashville contacts might include someone capable of convincing SNCC to back off. When Simeon Booker telephoned Justice from Shuttlesworth's home, Seigenthaler relayed yet another naive request given the horde of newspaper reporters descending on Birmingham: The administration wanted the press to downplay the story. "I think what they were trying to do was to hold down the Negro enthusiasm and determination," Booker concluded. "It seemed to me any time they would say don't do something, they just made five people where one had been before."[61]

When the seriousness of the situation dawned on them, and when they realized they could not call off the rides or the press, the Kennedys tried to defuse the situation by stopping the violence. And they remained convinced that Birmingham would not escalate into another Little Rock because the Alabama governor was in their corner. "I had this long relationship with John Patterson," RFK said. "He was our great pal in the South." What the Kennedys wanted from Patterson and what the Freedom Riders needed was protection for their continuing trip to Montgomery and then Jackson. Yet this pal would not even return the attorney general's phone calls—an affront, Marshall said, that "was shocking to the Kennedys." Patterson instead issued a warning: "The State of Alabama can't guarantee the safety of fools."[62]

Robert Kennedy received no more cooperation from J. Edgar Hoover. The FBI had known about the Birmingham Klan's plans for the Freedom Riders weeks in advance and had actually facilitated the violence by passing details of the riders' itinerary to Police Commissioner Eugene "Bull" Connor and Sergeant Thomas H. Cook. Bureau officials did this knowing full well that Cook relayed everything to his fellow Klansmen. Hoover's main interest was not to protect the Freedom Riders but the FBI's Klan informant on the scene, Gary Thomas Rowe, who kept his cover by participating in the bus station beatings. Rather than force Hoover to change bureau policy of disseminating information to local police regardless of Ku Klux Klan infiltration, the attorney general helped the FBI keep secret its role in the violence. He also kept secret the request from his office for bureau file checks to see if any Freedom Rider had subversive or criminal associations.[63]

Robert Kennedy and Burke Marshall, now shed of the mumps, finally came to the White House where they found a pajama-clad president sitting behind a breakfast tray. All three believed that the federal government lacked authority to protect Freedom Riders or any other civil rights demonstrator short of sending in troops or federal marshals—solutions that smacked of Little Rock. When the president asked about an injunction to prevent the Klan from interfering with interstate travel and to force local police to protect interstate travelers, Marshall told him there was no real precedent. All he could think of was the late nineteenth century Sherman Antitrust Act case against socialist Eugene V. Debs and the American Railway Union. Ultimately, the trio decided to rely on John Patterson and J. Edgar Hoover to protect the Freedom Riders on their journey's next stage. The president ended the meeting by walking off to get dressed, leaving behind his untouched breakfast.[64]

When Patterson finally returned one of Robert Kennedy's telephone calls, he agreed to give the Kennedy administration half of what it wanted. The Alabama governor somehow convinced Bull Connor to protect the Freedom Riders as they waited at the Greyhound terminal for the Montgomery bus. The wait was a long one because Greyhound could not locate a driver, a development that prompted Robert Kennedy to suggest a "cooling off" period. That remark prompted James Farmer to remind the attorney general that Negroes "had been cooling off for 100 years." RFK then ordered Hoover to assign an FBI agent to drive the bus, prompting the director to remind him that the bureau's special agents were investigators and not chauffeurs. The attorney general understood the irony in that comment as the only black special agents were chauffeurs or servants whose duties included driving prominent Americans around. He knew that Eisenhower received such special FBI favors. He also knew that the FBI chauffeured his own father during his travels outside the Boston area. With Hoover threatening to resign, Kennedy got tough with a bus company superintendent, suggesting that the man get in touch "with Mr. Greyhound" and find a driver.[65]

That remark became part of Robert Kennedy's tough-guy lore. RFK, however, quickly regretted it because the bus company superintendent quoted the attorney general's exact words to the press: "We've gone to a lot of trouble to make it possible for these people to move, and now it's all falling down because you don't have a driver." Opportunistic southern politicians took those words to mean that the Justice Department had convinced CORE to launch the Freedom Ride in the first place. "That was damaging," the attorney general said. "I never recovered from it."[66]

Robert Kennedy's man in Birmingham, John Seigenthaler, would have a recovery of a different kind. At 8:30 A.M. on Saturday, May 20, the Freedom Riders' Greyhound pulled onto the highway for the two-hour ride to the state capital, surrounded by police cars. A helicopter buzzed overhead. "An armed escort," Fred Shuttlesworth marveled, "to take a bunch of niggers to a bus station so they can break these silly old laws." Back in Washington it looked like Patterson was keeping his word. So the attorney general went for a horseback ride in the Virginia hills then on to an FBI baseball game while the president relaxed at his Middleburg retreat. Meanwhile, the Freedom Riders' police escort melted away as the Greyhound entered Montgomery. Now it looked like the Alabama governor was giving his Klan constituents half of what they wanted. When the Freedom Riders stepped off the bus at the Montgomery terminal another white mob appeared, bigger and more bloodthirsty than the Birmingham mob. John Doar watched from across the street and phoned in a report to the attorney general: "The passengers are coming off. . . . There are no cops. It's terrible." Seigenthaler, who, like Doar, had been waiting for the bus at the terminal, came to the aide of two young female Freedom Riders and was savagely beaten by Klansmen. When RFK got through to him at the hospital, he said, dryly, that what Seigenthaler had done "was very helpful for the Negro vote, and that I appreciated [it]."[67]

The Kennedys appreciated little else. "He was fed up with John Patterson," Robert Kennedy said of his brother. "He was fed up with the way they handled it in Alabama. He was fed up with the Freedom Riders who went down there afterwards when it didn't do any good to go down there." Obsessed with crisis management and the management of impressions, the Kennedys now had what even they recognized as a major disaster that could yet degenerate into another Little Rock if not handled properly. Still, the president continued to focus almost exclusively on preparations for his summit with Khrushchev; thus he dismissed Harris Wofford's recommendation that he meet with a Freedom Rider delegation. "It would be better . . . to see them for ten or fifteen minutes," Wofford had said, "than to wait until they launch fasts in jail or encampments outside the White House." With the president largely uninvolved and Wofford completely unheard, both symbolic and strategic management remained in the attorney general's hands.[68]

Robert Kennedy sent a squad of FBI agents and 500 U.S. marshals to Montgomery with Byron White in command. Reinforced by Alabama Public Safety Director Floyd Mann's troopers and the Alabama National Guard, the marshals held off another mob that evening at Rev. Ralph Abernathy's First Baptist Church where Martin Luther King, dozens of Freedom Riders, and some 1,500 blacks had gathered for a rally. With the government's help the movement won the battle of the First Baptist Church and the riders moved on, without noticeable incident, to Jackson. There was no violence in Jackson either—because city and state police made mass arrests of the Freedom Riders and shipped dozens to the state penitentiary at Parchman. RFK also had the FBI run another round of file checks on all those arrested in search of criminal or communist activities. "I think you could play it a more demagogic way," he reflected, "but you know, that never entered in the conversations during any of these periods of time, at least between me and my brother."[69]

RFK also asked the Interstate Commerce Commission to draft regulations prohibiting discrimination in interstate travel, and the ICC did so in September—much to the chagrin of the white South and Republican party alike.[70] "The Freedom Riders' saga," Robert Kennedy's press secretary, Ed Guthman, said, "left members of Bob's staff with a new sense of *esprit de corps*, heightened respect for Bob's leadership and confidence in the Department's ability to act effectively under heavy pressure."[71] This was the result not only of the ICC order (a truly "spectacular achievement"), but the deal cut with Senator Eastland to insure against a Mississippi rerun of the Birmingham and Montgomery violence and further escalation of the crisis. The attorney general saved the Freedom Riders from a beating in Jackson by allowing them to be arrested and imprisoned instead. This was an extraordinary balancing act.

Year one of the New Frontier ended with that Kennedy balance firmly in place. On behalf of integration, the Justice Department secured the ICC order and the indictment of nine men for their role in the Anniston bus burning; intervened on the right side in nearly a dozen school desegregation suits; hired some forty black attorneys; successfully recommended the appointment of two black United States attorneys and two district court judges; filed fourteen voting-rights suits and opened "active investigations or negotiations" with registrars in sixty-one southern counties.[72] But weighing in on the other side, on behalf of segregation (or at least segregationist votes) the administration nominated racist judges; stuck to its no-arrest/no-protection policy for more routine violence against civil rights workers; repeated the "no civil rights legislation" promise; continued to cut deals with the segregationist Senator Eastland and frustrate the Civil Rights Commission; and unleashed the FBI (as if Hoover needed unleashing) on the civil rights movement as a whole.

The Kennedys considered that first year a good one because a Little Rock–size crisis had been averted and the prospects of white southerners defecting in large numbers to the Republican party still seemed remote. This changed for the worse in year two. When a black twenty-nine-year-old Air Force veteran named James Meredith attempted to enroll at the University of Mississippi in Oxford, the Kennedys finally got a crisis to match Little Rock. The Ole Miss controversy began, as had Little Rock's, with the federal courts—specifically, a Fifth Circuit Court of Appeals request that the government enforce its order that Meredith be admitted. The Kennedys responded, as Eisenhower had in Arkansas, more for the sake of order than racial justice.

John and Robert Kennedy saw enemies on both sides. For the segregationists, the enemy was best symbolized by Mississippi Governor Ross Barnett, a grandstanding segregationist whom the attorney general described "as genuinely loony." ("[Bob] told me," Arthur Schlesinger remembered, that the governor "had been hit on the head by an airplane propeller last summer and had never been the same.")[73] The Kennedy administration did not find a likeable symbol in James Meredith either. "I was in Mississippi with 'I' James Meredith," RFK's assistant deputy attorney general, Joseph Dolan, recalled. "That's what we used to call him because he was always, 'I, I, I.'" Meredith first sent an admission application to Ole Miss in January 1961, inspired by the November elections. (He said that he probably would not have filed the application had Nixon won.) After the court order came down and the White House decided to enforce it, the attorney general concluded that he was dealing with another genuine nut.

"Did the President ever talk to James Meredith, on the phone or otherwise?," Anthony Lewis asked Kennedy and Marshall:

RFK: No.

LEWIS: A character, eh?

RFK: Oh, a real character.

MARSHALL: The gold Thunderbird. That was one of the great crises of the administration.

LEWIS: He wanted a gold Thunderbird?

RFK: He bought one. . . . Didn't you know that?

LEWIS: No. . . .

RFK: Boy, that's all we needed . . . to have him arrive on the campus with a gold Thunderbird.

LEWIS: That would have been wonderful.

RFK: These are momentous matters for the Attorney General.[74]

Levity aside, the decision to send troops to Oxford was measured. Administration officials acted decisively if in stages, first sending Justice

Department lawyers (and a football coach, Johnny Vaught), then marshals, finally troops. RFK called this "the apparent anomaly"—that is, the administration's refusal to violate principles of federalism one time but not the next.[75] When it became clear that intervention was inevitable the administration sent Nicholas Katzenbach, bracing him with more tough-guy humor. "Hey Nick," Robert Kennedy said. "I said, 'Yeah.' He said, 'Don't worry. . . . if you get shot, 'cause the President needs a moral issue.'" Because John Kennedy had been critical of Eisenhower's Little Rock intervention, Katzenbach explained, "the psychological block that both of them had came out of the campaign, which was understandable enough, which was that they weren't going to use troops in the South."

So the administration escalated the federal presence from Katzenbach to the marshals and finally soldiers, always focusing less on racial justice than the looming public-relations nightmare. To minimize the first significant federal presence RFK said the president ordered the marshals "not to fire under any conditions. . . . With the exception of James Meredith. They could fire to protect his life. That was understood. The ones who were protecting him—they could. The ones who were just protecting themselves couldn't."[76]

Given this strategy, Meredith himself was particularly galling. The man who wanted to arrive in a gold T-bird had managed to miss most of the chaos. "I went to sleep," he admitted. "I was not really aware of what was happening that night on campus . . . until they came in the morning to get me to go to register, and the car the marshals drove me in had all the windows shot out."[77] Meredith constantly disappointed the Kennedys. Once enrolled he threatened to drop out and thus raised the specter of yet another public-relations nightmare. John Kennedy, prepared to "read the riot act to Meredith" if he continued to talk about dropping out, spoke out against the "national shame of racial inequality" only when relatively certain that Meredith would stick to his end of the bargain.[78]

With the Bay of Pigs disaster and the Cuban missile crisis, Robert Kennedy ranked Ole Miss among the administration's "crunch" issues. "I think we were very lucky to get out of it. . . . Public relations-wise as well, I mean. . . . The idea that we got through the evening," when an armed mob surrounded the federal force at the University's administration building (the Lyceum), "without the marshals being killed and without Meredith being killed was a miracle. . . . That's what [my brother] was torn with that night. I mean, we could just visualize another great disaster, like the Bay of Pigs."[79]

When it was over the Kennedy administration patted itself on the back. "This was a battle that *had* to be won," Howard P. Jones, ambassador to Indonesia, told Robert Kennedy. "What might have been a severe set-back to our prestige in Asia and Africa was turned into a gain." "I hope you will continue your policy of 'keep moving but move slowly,'" Theodore Sorensen advised the president. "In contrast to your predecessor, you are demonstrating how many graduated steps there are between inaction and troops." JFK himself, his brother remembered, said he would "never believe a book on Reconstruction again. . . . He said that they can say these things about what the marshals did and what we were doing at this period of time—and believe it. They must have been doing the same thing a hundred years ago."[80] If John Kennedy had finally abandoned the view outlined in *Profiles in Courage*, his assessment of the civil rights movement had scarcely changed. The main lesson learned in Oxford was that black protest had to be contained and managed since it could not be stopped. Katzenbach later said that Burke Marshall's primary mission was to "keep in close touch with Negro groups in an effort to channel and control their activities," and that mission appealed to the administration as a whole.[81]

Movement strategy, in contrast, was to force the Kennedys to take sides, and with the spring 1963 Birmingham demonstrations it appeared that Martin Luther King and other civil rights leaders had finally forced the administration to join the struggle for racial justice without qualification. When the Birmingham campaign began on April 3 neither the White House nor the Justice Department gave the mass demonstrations their full attention. Things began to change nine days later when city police arrested King, Abernathy, Shuttlesworth, and eight others. On April 26 the courts found all eleven civil rights leaders guilty of criminal contempt. Things changed even more dramatically the first week of May after King put school children on the front lines and Police Commissioner Bull Connor rose to the bait. Connor attacked with nightsticks, police dogs, high-pressure fire hoses, and, after finally calming down, mass arrests. Scattered rock throwing by Negro bystanders aside, the television news footage was numbing. Battered by monitor guns, which forced water from two fire hoses through a single tripod-mounted nozzle, children flew through the air like rag dolls.

With the footage also providing a boon to propagandists abroad from Moscow to Baghdad ("a veritable barrage of broadcasting to foreign audiences," the State Department complained), President Kennedy said simply: "It's bad for us in the world." Administration officials also marveled at what they considered the stupidity of both sides. "The civil rights movement should thank God for Bull Connor," Sorensen said. "He's helped it as much as Abraham Lincoln." Meanwhile, the attorney general offered the flip estimate that ninety percent of the civil rights demonstrators had no idea what they were demonstrating about.[82]

If the thought of bringing brutality charges against Connor's cops never entered their minds, the Kennedys considered all other "alternatives in Birmingham." This included the submission of legislation limiting the right to demonstrate.[83] JFK rejected that draconian option and instead sent his brother and Burke Marshall to Montgomery to see Governor George Wallace. This failed miserably. "It was out of Kafka," Marshall said. "The attorney general and I got there in an FBI car. The steps of the state capitol were lined with police with very fat stomachs, so we had to go single file. The governor turned on his tape recorder; the attorney general made his speech. It went downhill from there. It was not a conversation; it was an event." Marshall remained on point nonetheless, stopping next in Birmingham where he unsuccessfully pressured King to stop the demonstrations.[84]

Meanwhile, John Kennedy had cabinet heads telephone chain store executives to pressure them into abolishing segregation in their Birmingham outlets. (He placed a few calls himself.) Robert Kennedy moved beyond the peacemaker and mediator role by raising bail for the demonstrators (without discriminating against the great mass who supposedly had no idea why they were in the streets in the first place). Working through national labor leaders George Meany, Walter Reuther, and David McDonald, he rounded up several hundred thousand dollars. "A matter of slush funds and satchels," Taylor Branch wrote. An exercise similar in methods if not goals to the things that the attorney general, when in pursuit of Jimmy Hoffa, had criticized the Teamsters for doing.[85]

By May 10 the administration's mediation and other efforts had led to a biracial agreement between Birmingham's black and white civic leaders to desegregate public accommodations, increase job opportunities, and free those demonstrators who remained incarcerated. That night, however, fanatics threw bombs at Martin Luther King's motel room and the home of King's younger brother, A. D. King. Rioting rocked the city's black neighborhoods the next day. "The group that has gotten out of hand has not been the white people," Robert Kennedy told his brother. "It's been the Negroes by and large." The president speculated (however briefly) that George Wallace might have been right in his outlandish charge that the bombs were thrown by "Negro extremists" who, knowing the Klan would be blamed, hoped to bring Birmingham to a boil. "It could be Black Muslims," JFK offered. RFK's simple response ("I doubt it") ended that Oval Office fantasy.[86]

Things were so tense in Birmingham a week later that John Kennedy talked peace with Governor Wallace on a helicopter between Huntsville and Muscle Shoals. (The president was in the area to celebrate TVA's thirtieth anniversary.) Wallace had known Kennedy since a 1956 handshake at the Democratic National Convention, but he was no New Frontier partisan. He compared liberals to Hitler's Nazis and warned Alabama's good people about how the Kennedy crowd's "international racism . . . seeks to persecute the international white minority." The two men got along scarcely better on the helicopter. When the president asked why southern whites would hire Negro servants but objected to Negro clerks at downtown department stores, the governor said demonstration leaders were fakers. King and Shuttlesworth were the worst, riding "around town in big Cadillacs smoking expensive cigars" and competing to see "who could go to bed with the most nigger women." Kennedy stressed the economics of the situation, the "absolutely impossible reputation throughout the country and the world" that Birmingham had acquired. "Its industries would leave," he said, unless some progress was made. Wallace responded with another attack on King. When the helicopter landed the president and the governor continued this useless conversation in a Muscle Shoals men's room. While Kennedy fixed his hair, Wallace ranted.[87]

The administration faced other crises as the Birmingham drama played out. Six days after JFK met with Wallace, Robert Kennedy and Burke Marshall met in Joseph Kennedy's New York apartment with Jerome Smith, a young CORE field worker and Freedom Rider who had been beaten and jailed repeatedly, and several friends of novelist James Baldwin, who had made *Time* magazine's May 17 cover and a recent breakfast date at RFK's Hickory Hill home. Among others, Baldwin's friends included playwright Lorraine Hansberry, psychologist Kenneth B. Clark, singers Harry Belafonte and Lena Horne, and actor Rip Torn. If the subject of discussion was supposed to be Birmingham (and more generally the administration's civil rights agenda), policy was the last thing Baldwin and friends had in mind. The meeting turned into a brutal and mostly one-sided encounter session. When Baldwin suggested that the president personally escort black students into the University of Alabama, where another integration crisis was brewing, Kennedy laughed aloud. "He didn't get the point at all," Baldwin said. "We just broke out into hysterical laughter [ourselves] . . . the laughter of desperation." Smith established the tone when he said that being in the same room with Kennedy made him feel like throwing up.[88]

"Bobby took it personally," Baldwin recalled. "And he turned away from him. That was a mistake because he turned toward us. We were the reasonable, responsible, mature representatives of the black community. Lorraine Hansberry said, 'You've got a great many very, very accomplished people in this room, Mr. Attorney General. But the only man who should be listened to is that man over there.'" "Then they all started sort of competing with each other in attacking us, the President, the federal government, and the whole system of government in addition to the United States," Marshall said a year later. The primary message that Kennedy heard was "that the way to deal with the problem is to start arming the young Negroes and sending them into the streets—which I didn't think was a very satisfactory solution, because, as I explained to them, there are more white people than Negroes. And although it might be bloody, I thought that the white people would do better."

If Marshall looked into the possibility of prosecuting Jerome Smith's assailants under civil rights statutes, the overall Justice Department response to the Baldwin meeting was neither gracious nor sympathetic. Robert Kennedy called Baldwin a "nut" in a conversation with J. Edgar Hoover; and after Robert P. Mills of General Artists Corporation sent Marshall the names of everyone who had come to the Kennedy patriarch's apartment, the attorney general had the FBI run name checks in search of derogatory information. "Burke," he wrote when moving here, "you have swell friends."[89]

To explain the behavior of Baldwin's artistic group, Kennedy reasoned that they had "complexes about the fact that they've been so successful. I mean, that they've done so well and this poor boy [Jerome Smith] had been beaten by the police. Others had been beaten, and they hadn't been beaten." Nightstick envy, in other words. "Like Kenneth Clark," Marshall added. The attorney general passed on more psycho-babble to his brother, even noting that guilt drove several participants as they had white wives. Overall, he added on a less emotional level, the Negro community was becoming increasingly like Baldwin's gang—"mad," "antagonistic," "tough to deal with." He also predicted the virtual disappearance of the moderate black leader. "They can't be moderate because all their competitors are not moderate."[90]

While reading the FBI dossiers on Baldwin et al., Robert Kennedy sent Nicholas Katzenbach to handle the latest integration crisis at the University of Alabama. George Wallace (like Ross Barnett at Ole Miss) had pledged to stand in his schoolhouse door to bar the admission of two black students, Vivian Malone and James A. Hood. "I told Bobby, 'Why bother?,'" Katzenbach recalled. "'The court's ordered them registered. That's good enough.' And Bobby, I think, made the right decision. He said, 'Look, it's too dangerous a situation, and I don't know what that man'll do if he's crossed. He wants his show; you're gonna have to give him his show.'" When Katzenbach handed Wallace a proclamation from the president commanding him to cease and desist his unlawful obstruction of a federal court order, the governor did not budge. Luckily he withdrew after a second confrontation later that day.[91]

There would be no Ole Miss rerun. The earlier crisis had demonstrated that the Kennedy White House would send troops if pushed far enough, and the Alabama governor had sense enough not to push much while the Birmingham stink remained in the air. "Wallace concluded not because of us but for his own reasons, his own political reasons," Burke Marshall reasoned, "that it would be bad to have a riot. . . . So he went through a performance. . . . He just wanted to be on television standing in the door." Saying he understood "Wallace's position politically," RFK moved quickly to help the University of Alabama get grant money to increase police coverage on the newly integrated campus.[92]

On the same day that George Wallace had his show (June 11, 1963), John Kennedy made a seemingly extemporaneous decision to reverse his no-legislation tack. (There was, of course, nothing extemporaneous about this decision; the movement, and the segregationist resistance, had forced the president to act.) In a televised address that evening Kennedy promised, in language that largely avoided words like "'mediation' or 'conciliation' or other Uncle Tom[isms]," to introduce civil rights legislation. (The Justice Department had been working on a bill since February.) "This is a land of the free except for the Negro," the president said, promising that the administration would face this "moral crisis" head on. Shortly after midnight the depth of the crisis was further demonstrated by the assassination of Mississippi NAACP leader Medgar Evers in the driveway of his Jackson home.

"Christ, you know, it's like they shoot this guy in Mississippi," the president complained to House Speaker Carl Albert about how civil rights had overwhelmed the entire New Frontier. "I mean, it's just in everything. I mean, this has become everything." Looking, as ever, for balance of some sort, the president did not attend the Evers burial service eight days later in Arlington Cemetery. Instead he sent a limousine for the widow and two oldest children. The family received a White House tour and PT–109 souvenirs.[93]

For his part Robert Kennedy ducked any responsibility for not protecting Evers, who had received several death threats before the June 12 shooting. The attorney general told the press that the government had no authority to protect Evers or anyone else. Such responsibilities, he said, rested with the state of Mississippi.[94]

While Evers's assassination was a nightmare for the Kennedys, it did give the administration new insight into the fissures within the civil rights movement itself. When Martin Luther King and Mordecai Johnson of the Gandhi Society announced the formation of a Medgar Evers Memorial Fund, Roy Wilkins exploded. "Can you imagine it? Medgar was an NAACP man all the way, and King comes in and tries to take the money." "I had never seen my uncle so incensed," Roger Wilkins recalled. "Really pissed." RFK noted, simply: "Roy Wilkins hates Martin Luther King." Knowledge of such divisions, the Kennedys figured, might prove useful in the effort to play off one movement wing against another in order to minimize the political risks inherent in the position outlined in the president's June 11 address.[95]

With Birmingham still a hot spot and the Kennedy brothers still stung by the personal affronts of the John Pattersons and Ross Barnetts (which called their "toughness" into question), the administration saw the civil rights bill as a way to take the pressure off. White House staff, Justice Department officials, and the president himself, moreover, predicted that riots like those that swept Birmingham's black neighborhoods following the childrens' march would be duplicated on a grander scale if something were not done. "It's going to be up North," John Kennedy said. "This isn't any more just a southern matter."[96] At the same time, according to Sorensen, JFK believed that "too much attention . . . could accelerate demands and expectations more rapidly than they could be fulfilled, and thereby increase tensions during a long, hot summer."[97] In other words the president had to take a stand (and to his credit he made the choice for racial justice). But it was more posture than stand. Although he had framed the issue in moral terms in his June 12 address, Kennedy was still trying to slow the movement. He remained more worried about how many white votes his stance would cost him than the possibility of enacting even the modest Civil Rights Bill of 1963.

While joking about how "the civil rights legislation should be called 'Bull Connor's Bill,'" the Kennedys made certain that neither the Evers assassination nor any other post-Birmingham event would push them into moving too fast. "What we can do to help," John Kennedy said, "but without getting us too far out front." He thought Harry Truman erred gravely, for example, "by prematurely throwing FEPC at the Congress" (Robert Kennedy's words). So the employment discrimination provisions of the Civil Rights Bill of 1963 were exceptionally vague and moderate in the extreme. To a lesser degree, the same could be said of the bill's other provisions regarding equal access to public accommodations and a stronger role for the Justice Department in initiating or joining desegregation suits. This approach eventually diluted the initial wave of liberal support. "He sent up such an inane package of legislation," the ADA's Joseph Rauh complained, "as to make the civil rights movement feel that it wasn't worth going for." Berl Bernhard of the Civil Rights Commission warned the White House that the bill was "wrong" since nobody favored it, nobody understood it, and nobody was willing to explain why it was necessary.[98]

Such carping fed the Kennedys' bitterness toward the movement and its allies. When Anthony Lewis asked Robert Kennedy if he spoke with his brother about the "excruciating frustration about liberalism," RFK said it proved "what my father said about businessmen. . . . They're sons of bitches. The people who are selfish are interested in their own singular course of action and do not take into consideration the needs or requirements of others or what can ultimately be accomplished. . . . I thought that an awful lot of them, as I said at the time, were in love with death. . . . It why they like Adlai Stevenson. . . . He never quite arrives there; he never quite accomplishes anything. That's a terrible way of putting it, but I think that they like it much better to have a cause than to have a course of action that's been successful."[99]

Complaints about liberals, whether they supported the Civil Rights Bill of 1963 or not, extended across the spectrum from Martin Luther King to Lyndon Johnson. King's leadership, Robert Kennedy concluded, "was constructive, I think." That, however faint, was far more praise than Johnson got. The attorney general dismissed the vice-president as an enemy of the Kennedy program. "He was opposed to the civil rights bill. He was opposed to sending up any legislation." "What he thought should be done," Marshall explained in greater detail, "was simply stick to the economic aspect of it [meaning antipoverty programs], not civil rights legislation as such. . . . He went back to his own experiences—his Youth whatever-it-was in the '30 [National Youth Administration] . . . how they'd created so many jobs. . . . [He] also sent Hobart [Taylor] over to see me. Hobart came over to see me and said that you couldn't do anything without more education. The Negroes had to be educated." Even here the attorney general dismissed the vice-president as an incompetent fraud. According to Secretary of Labor Willard Wirtz, in fall 1963 two thirds of the companies holding government contracts employed no Negroes, and RFK blamed that dismal fact on LBJ, chair of the President's Committee on Equal Employment Opportunity.[100]

Robert Kennedy's bitterness about real and imagined liberal opponents of the administration's civil rights bill extended to Taylor, who served as Johnson's chief aide on equal employment matters. "His man Hobart Taylor," Robert Kennedy fumed, "whom I have contempt for, because I thought he was ineffectual and also in my judgment, he was an Uncle Tom." (For his part Taylor considered the attorney general "a doer," "a fine American in my book.") Kennedy's view of the vice-president was even more candid. On the night before the assassination he said the president told "Jackie . . . [that] Lyndon Johnson was incapable of telling the truth." After Dallas he called LBJ "the intruder," a man who stained the memory of "our President [who] was a gentleman and a human being. . . . This man is not. . . . He's mean, bitter, vicious—an animal in many ways. . . . Very difficult" to get along with "unless you want to kiss his behind all the time." In contrast to Taylor's graciousness, LBJ had an equally harsh attitude toward Kennedy.[101]

Comments about Johnson's opposition to the civil rights bill aside, the Kennedys objected principally to the vice-president's ambitious and adventuresome approach. In the week before John Kennedy's dramatic television address, LBJ bombarded anyone within earshot on the politics of civil rights—and he had an opinion about everything, even the now-despised James Baldwin. Baldwin's point, he told Sorensen, was straightforward: "I don't want to marry your daughter, I want to get you off my back." Norbert A. Schlei of the Justice Department's office of legal counsel reported back to RFK on one such monologue. Johnson wanted the president to call in Republican leaders and Negro leaders, "get together the three living ex-presidents," and then "make a major speech in each of the main southern states" telling whites "that he might have occasion at any time to order Negro citizens of this nation to die in a foxhole in some foreign jungle for this flag (at this point the Vice President grasped the flag beside his desk), and yet on their way to die for this country those Negro citizens would not be able to go into a public lunch room in the State of Mississippi to have a cup of coffee."

Arthur Schlesinger offered a similar if more modest suggestion, advising the Kennedys to find a leading southern senator who could play the role of Michigan Senator Arthur Vandenberg "in the isolationist fight." Get Lister Hill "to do a Vandenberg," he said. (Vandenberg, a Republican, had organized bipartisan support in Congress for the

Truman Doctrine and the Marshall Plan.) The difference was that the Kennedys were polite when dismissing Schlesinger.[102]

Johnson kept to it nonetheless, moving on to question the timing of the civil rights bill (and implicitly the Kennedys' political acumen).[103] Wait until "the President's tax program was enacted or defeated," he told Sorensen. "We haven't passed anything. I think he ought to make them pass some of this stuff before he throws this thing out. This is just what the Republican Party [wants]. . . . They're sitting back giggling."[104] But the vice-president was wrong in assuming that the Kennedys were fully committed to moving their civil rights legislation through Congress. "What about the President?," Anthony Lewis asked Robert Kennedy. "Did he really think that there was a chance?"

> RFK: I don't think that we ever discussed it, particularly.
> LEWIS: It wasn't a big thing to him? It wasn't like the labor legislation?
> RFK: No.

That was it. A simple no. "The President himself," RFK realized, "was not always rejoicing in the fact that we were doing it. As I said, he would ask me every four days, 'Do you think we did the right thing by sending the legislation up? Look at the trouble it's got us in [with white southerners].' But always in a semi-jocular way."[105]

President Kennedy was astute enough to realize that meaningful civil rights reform could cost him votes in the next election. Lost votes were among the things the Kennedys discussed constantly, and to mitigate the damage Robert Kennedy even offered to resign the attorney generalship. It never came to that. "[The president] felt that it was impossible to do," RFK noted, "because it would make it look as if we were running away from it. It became that much of a factor, that much of a problem. Everything I did before then, up to '62, was focused on *me*. And *he* wasn't such a bad fellow [in the South]. By 1963 it was focused on both of *us*. And that caused problems, politically, as we got ready for the election in 1964." In addition to the white South, the Kennedys worried that the civil rights issue would also cost votes "even in the suburbs" and "the big cities in the North." RFK remembered a construction worker standing on a girder high above the New York concrete and shouting down, "Hey, Bobby, don't forget about the Irish and the Italians!"[106]

So the Kennedys adopted the less-than-grand strategy of sitting and waiting. By sending up the civil rights bill and then doing little to insure its passage, they pursued a variation on Truman's backtracking-after-the-bang strategy. The brothers mostly counted on luck to see them through. "We didn't know at that time who was going to be the opponent [in 1964]," RFK said. "The one [the president] was most concerned about was [George] Romney . . . He'd be so difficult to soak. . . . Such an evangelist would have been more difficult to run against. He was always for God . . . [and] against big government and big labor—everything that appealed. So he would have some appeal in the South and some appeal in the North."

The Kennedys preferred to run against the Republican party's cowboy or yankee candidates. "[The president] thought that, if he was running against Goldwater," RFK continued, "[civil rights] wasn't going to be a problem. If he was going to run against Rockefeller, it was going to be less of a problem, too, because Rockefeller would have to take the same position. It wasn't going to hurt that much. If he was going to run against Goldwater, he'd pick up so many other votes to offset the losses in this area. And then we all felt—we had worked with Goldwater—we just knew he was not a very smart man. He's just going to destroy himself. [The president] was concerned that he would destroy himself too early and not get the nomination."[107]

While waiting for Goldwater, the Kennedys enlisted the FBI in a two-front strategy to minimize the political risks raised by the introduction of the civil rights bill. Acting on bureau reports suggesting that two of Martin Luther King's advisors were secret Communists (Jack O'Dell and Stanley Levison), the attorney general authorized wiretaps on King's home and office telephones.[108] This was yet another example of how the Kennedys hedged their bets. The decision to tap King was itself the subject of little debate. Having encouraged bureau surveillance of the civil rights movement since the Freedom Rides, it was an easy decision for the administration to extend that surveillance to the movement's heart by tapping and bugging its most visible leader.

Kennedy also sent John Seigenthaler and Burke Marshall to convince King to break all ties with O'Dell and Levison. When that failed the president met King at the White House and took him outside for a private walk in the Rose Garden. ("I guess Hoover must be bugging him too," King later speculated.) "They're communists," JFK said. "You've got to get rid of them." This had a faint, family-tree echo. Twenty years earlier Kennedy's father offered to mobilize his "many Jewish friends in the moving picture industry" and help the FBI ferret out Hollywood Reds.[109]

Years later, when asked to explain the wiretap and interference in SCLC personnel matters, Burke Marshall, Arthur Schlesinger, and other administration officials overstated President Kennedy's commitment to civil rights. Marshall said nothing could be left to chance since the president's "whole stake, politically and historically in a way, rode on that [civil rights] bill." Arthur Schlesinger was equally adamant that the administration had to resolve the Communist issue. "The Kennedys went bail for the movement," he argued, and if the FBI's reports turned out to be true the movement's ship and the administration's ship would sink together. RFK himself told Ed Guthman that he approved the wiretap because "he felt that if he did not do it, Mr. Hoover would move to impede or block the passage of the Civil Rights Bill . . . and that he felt that he might as well settle the matter as to whether [Levison] did have the influence . . . that the FBI contended." In an earlier comment, offered shortly before the electronic surveillance was authorized, the president best captured the spirit of this explanation: "The trouble with King is everybody thinks he's our boy."[110]

"We never wanted to get very close to [Martin Luther King]," Robert Kennedy babbled to Anthony Lewis in surreal detail. "Just because of these contacts and connections that he had, which we felt were damaging to the civil rights movement. And because we were so intimately involved in the struggle for civil rights, it also damaged us." Of Stanley Levison's sinister nature, Kennedy and Burke Marshall were absolutely convinced.

MARSHALL: A secret member of the Communist party.
RFK: A high official.
MARSHALL: Well, at that time, all that I knew was that he was a secret member.
RFK: Later on, he became a member of the Executive Board.

MARSHALL: Made a member of the Executive Committee, secretly, of the Communist party.

RFK: So he was quite a big figure.

MARSHALL: He was a very important figure in the Communist party. . . .

RFK: It's very unhealthy to have an association with a person who is elected to the Executive Board of the Communist party. . . .

MARSHALL: And to continue it after warning.

RFK: Continuing it. That in itself was bad.[111]

Neither Kennedy nor Marshall appreciated King's response to their repeated warnings. "He's just got some other side to him," RFK concluded. "He sort of laughs about a lot of these things, makes fun of it." Marshall thought King refused to fire Levison because "he was just probably weak about it." (Anthony Lewis had a more dramatic response, gasping "My God!" when told that King had continued to phone up Levison even after the Rose Garden walk.) King sinned by asking to see the proof—something that the administration had never bothered to ask of J. Edgar Hoover for the simple reason that they had no more than a passing interest in such things. The Kennedys were primarily interested in wiretapping the civil rights movement's most visible leader because that tap promised a gold mine of useful political information, and "communism" provided the most convenient excuse to place the tap. "King," as the president noted, "is so hot these days." Simple as that. One taps a hot phone, not a cold one.[112]

Robert Kennedy had no conflict with Hoover here. A year before introducing the civil rights bill he offered advice for "those on both extremes of this [Communist] question." "Leave the job to the expert," he said, adding that "Mr. Hoover is my expert." The director had his uses indeed. His bureau could carry out night raids on the administration's behalf and report back on virtually anything (including such things, in RFK's words, as which "Senators had Negro girlfriends"). The bureau could also be blamed when things got ugly (as they did years later when the King wiretap surfaced during Muhammad Ali's draft-evasion trial), and quickly disciplined at the first hint of unilateralism.

To prove that the FBI was under his control, Robert Kennedy cited Hoover's dissemination of a derogatory report on King to the Army.

"The Army hated Negroes," Nicholas Katzenbach complained. "It's practically like sending it to the *Washington Post.* "[So] I called up Hoover," Kennedy bragged. "I said that, of course, we had the legislation up . . . that I was concerned about this [Communist] matter as he was or anybody was, but that we wanted to obtain the passage of legislation. And we didn't want to lose, to fail in the passage of legislation by a document that gave only one side. He said, 'I think it should be recalled.' So I said, 'Fine.' " The report was recalled, but the wiretaps remained (loyally) in place (as did Hoover himself, in RFK's blissful view).[113]

"Hoover served our interests," the attorney general believed. "It was a danger that we could control, that we were on top of, that we could deal with at the appropriate time. That's the way we looked at it. In the interests of the administration and in the interests of the country, it was well that we had control over it. There wasn't anything he could do. We were giving him direction. And there wasn't anybody he could go to or anything he could do with the information or the material. So it was fine. He served out interests." Kennedy approved the King taps, in other words, because they served the administration's interest.[114]

Because the White House wanted to plug into the movement's center, the King wiretap had to do with politics and not communism or the FBI director's thinly veiled blackmail threats centered on the president's extramarital affairs. Hoover's bureau hoped to define how and with what information the civil rights movement would be understood by a national audience. Administration officials shared that goal and formed an alliance—with the Kennedy tough-guy image creating the delusion that things were under their control. Hoover had an additional goal that neither John nor Robert Kennedy fully appreciated: To define how and with what information the movement would be understood by the presidency and other particular constituencies in the Department of Justice and Congress. The wonder in all this, as historian Garry Wills noted, "is that King retained his faith in a country whose best leaders thwarted and plotted against him, while lower officials like Bull Connor threatened his life."[115]

So while Martin Luther King planned the March on Washington to pressure Congress to pass the administration's civil rights bill, the White House looked for subversives there, too. "We kept track of the people who were Communists and who might get involved in it around the country," Robert Kennedy said. "Whether they were included or excluded." Another problem involved the specter of a largely or even all-black march which John Kennedy feared would lose votes on the hill and increase the chances of violence. "Most white people," Burke Marshall divined, "[think] that you can't possibly have several thousand or a hundred thousand Negroes without having a riot." The project as a whole made the administration, in presidential aide Ralph Dungan's words, "remember when the rioters in Birmingham were going down the street and we'd say, 'When is this all going away?' As if it were a snowstorm. That was the feeling with the March on Washington."

To foster a white presence, the president called on UAW chief Walter Reuther to join King's march. To counter any possible violence, he relied on the FBI for intelligence and placed the Army on alert. On August 28 the March took place without incident, closing with some 200,000 Americans, black and white, gathered around the Lincoln Memorial on the mall to hear King's "I Have a Dream" speech. "He's damn good," the president told his aides at the White House while watching the speech on television.[116]

The Kennedys were more interested in another scheduled March on Washington speaker, SNCC's John Lewis. A draft of his speech called on the movement to oppose "the Administration's civil rights bill" because "there's not one thing in the bill that will protect our people from police brutality." Lewis's speech also contained an embarrassing reminder ("the party of Kennedy is also the party of Eastland") and raised a troubling question: "Which side is the federal government on?" The specific reference was to Albany, Georgia, where SNCC had been engaged since October 1961 in a citywide campaign of civil disobedience. Lewis was particularly upset with the indictment of nine Albany activists on federal charges (three for conspiring to obstruct justice and six for perjury), a case with roots in a jury verdict in favor of the brutal Baker County sheriff. One juror owned a store in Albany, and movement activists picketed it—to force him to change his segregated hiring practices, they said. Looking for a bone to throw the white South, the administration saw it differently. Robert Kennedy himself announced the indictments, and in the privacy of his Oval Office the president denounced SNCC: "They're sons of bitches."[117]

To avoid the embarrassment of John Lewis's speech, Burke Marshall talked to Walter Reuther, and Reuther, among others, including Washington's Archbishop Patrick O'Boyle and Martin Luther King, convinced Lewis to tone it down. Marshall remembered getting "hold of the edited speech" and delivering it "down to the Lincoln Memorial—right through all the marchers—in the sidecar of a police motorcycle." Some would have preferred the original version. As King delivered his great lines, one black man kept shouting, "Fuck that dream, Martin. Now, goddamit, NOW!" Malcolm X called the demonstration the "Farce on Washington," claiming, in the language of the times, that the Kennedys ("the K.K.K.," with Edward being the third "K"), had co-opted the March.[118]

Later that day March leaders met John Kennedy in the White House. While the president emphasized the importance of black parents encouraging their children to study hard in school (like "the Jewish community"), A. Philip Randolph called for JFK to lead a nationwide civil rights crusade. Kennedy made no commitment here but did agree to follow up on King's suggestion to enlist Dwight Eisenhower's support. He even made a joke about how Ike was a Democrat when he goes to church. Unfortunately, little came of the Eisenhower contact either. Rev. Eugene Carson Blake of the National Council of Churches approached the former president at Kennedy's direction and reported back that he seemed "pretty cold." "It's a great temptation to the Republicans," JFK mused in response, "to think they're never going to get very far with Negroes anyway so they might as well play the white game in the South."[119]

Two weeks after the March on Washington a dynamite bomb signaled the New Frontier's last civil rights crisis. The September 15 explosion rocked Birmingham's Sixteenth Street Baptist Church, killing four African-American girls ages eleven to fourteen. The administration's response was tepid. Beyond statements expressing moral outrage, the president's only substantive act, in the manner of an early action at Ole Miss (when he called on Johnny Vaught), was to send another football coach to Birmingham as a peacemaker. (When West Point's Earl Blaik came to the White House, as Garry Wills observed, "JFK talked football with him.") Otherwise the president relied on the FBI to bring the guilty parties to justice. With little success the bureau looked into "all angles," including Georgia Senator Richard Russell's suggestion "that Negroes might have perpetrated this incident in order to keep emotions at a fever pitch." This paralleled the president's own brief thoughts about Black Muslim responsibility for the earlier Birmingham bombings.

Failing to break the Sixteenth Street case, Hoover had Courtney Evans, his liaison with Robert Kennedy, explain that "the integration groups" were frustrating the FBI's investigation. "I had the Attorney General's complete attention, and there is no question he heard what I said," Evans later briefed the director. "Nevertheless, he only remarked 'Yeah' and immediately followed by [changing the subject and] saying, 'I think Senator McClellan is interrupting Valachi too much in his testimony'" (a reference to the televised revelations of the well-known organized crime informant). The FBI kept investigating the Sixteenth Street bombing, and when John Kennedy died in Dallas two months later the bureau's wiretaps and bugs recorded the celebrations of Birmingham's Klansmen and neo-Nazis.[120]

John and Robert Kennedy remained civil rights minimalists for the whole thousand days, holding as best they could to the basic rules learned in the Massachusetts politics of the 1940s and 1950s: Cultivate the handful of people who could deliver the black vote, make an occasional symbolic gesture, never risk any political capital on behalf of anyone's civil rights. To the extent that the Kennedys pushed the envelope on minority hiring, voting rights, federal housing, and combating segregationist violence, they did so because the civil rights movement forced their hand. Even Arthur Schlesinger conceded that the brothers were at best "abstractly in favor of equal opportunity. But it took presidential politics to involve them with the movement; and then the prospect of responsibility to make them think intensively about the problem."

Still, the Kennedys, determined not to offend their white constituents of the South and North, did not take a step forward without plotting a step back. They kept to this tack to the very end. In the week before Dallas the president was still complaining about the real enemies of his civil rights legislation: "The extreme liberals who are gonna end up with no bill at all." After Dallas, Robert Kennedy said the president and his administration had been committed to only one black-side political goal: "To retain the confidence of the Negro population in their government and in the white majority."[121]

"John Kennedy lived in a different world," Roy Wilkins concluded, charitably. "On weekends he went sailing and that sort of thing. . . . I think he was still learning about this matter up to the day he died."[122] "I had the impression," Anthony Lewis mused, even more charitably, in a question to Robert Kennedy, "that the President tended to think of these racial matters not in terms of the law, as some of us do. In fact, he may have been impatient with the limitations of the law. . . . How did he think of it? Did he think of it in terms of children? In terms of the future? Where did he think we were going? Did he philosophize a bit?" The answer that came back was a simple one once again, beautiful and chilling in its clarity: "No, no."

A double this time and it shook Anthony Lewis, who no doubt agreed with King's assessment: "No President can be great, or even fit for office, if he attempts to accommodate to injustice to maintain his political balance."[123] So Lewis begged Kennedy to say there was something in the heart, something more in the soul than a "traditional bloc-vote affair."

> LEWIS: Was there anything during the campaign that you think brought you or your brother face to face with the actual situation . . . of the Negro in the South?
>
> RFK: No.
>
> LEWIS: This terrible helplessness?
>
> RFK: No. . . .
>
> LEWIS: Yes, but there were some rather acute incidents of killings and beatings . . .
>
> RFK: But when you asked me: 'Did you ever talk about it or concentrate on it?'—well, we didn't do it. And we didn't do it after he became President and I became Attorney General, either.
>
> LEWIS: I didn't ask you whether you talked. I asked you whether you became aware of the rather special horror of life for the Negro in the South.
>
> RFK: No.[124]

: 6 :

BRAVE KNIGHT

After Dallas "the usurper" pursued racial reform with a passion that betrayed his image in the North as "a Southern cracker" ("that's all he is," Malcolm X charged) and fed his image in the South as a traitor to white supremacy. All agreed on one thing: Lyndon Baines Johnson played politics to win. "His style," South Carolina Senator Strom Thurmond, a rabid segregationist, concluded, "was to gain all the power." "If you know anything about that guy at all," SNCC's John Lewis noted on the other side, "he's a wheeler dealer out of this world. He believes in . . . pushing people all the way." This was tempered only by what Clarence Mitchell of the NAACP's Washington office called "an arithmetic type of consideration." "Very often," Mitchell remembered, "he said to me when he was in the Senate, 'Clarence, you can get anything that you have the votes to get. How many votes do you have?'"[1]

Only the Kennedys disagreed with such assessments. They had seen Johnson as a sentimental "peasant" on civil rights issues, a man with irrational fears ("that Rockefeller was going to try to out-Negro our administration just like he out-Negroed Averell Harriman"); and obsessions (over such inconsequential things as whether daughter Lynda should stay at an all-white University of Texas dormitory). Lee White, White House civil rights adviser, said LBJ was "super or hyper-

239

sensitive—to the little symbols." So the Kennedys mocked his boyhood stories of hiding in the cellar as his father, Sam Ealy Johnson, Jr., sat up one night on the porch, with a shotgun in his lap, waiting for the Klan to make good a death threat. And they ridiculed his memories as the New Deal's man in Texas, director of the state's National Youth Administration—though he was tough enough to resist Mary McLeod Bethune's call to appoint Negroes to supervisory positions. He established an all-black advisory committee instead.[2]

Because their perspectives were so different, the Kennedys cut Johnson out. "They would send [him] abroad and he'd come back with all these reports or some silly incident with a camel driver and all of that," Nicholas Katzenbach said. "They really didn't think much of it and, you know, would be somewhat critical of it." Roy Wilkins, in contrast, found this style "somehow sincere." When going through a photograph portfolio from an African trip, Wilkins remembered Johnson saying, "You know, in Senegal, when I looked in the eyes of the mothers there they had the same look as the people in Texas. The mothers in Texas. . . . All mothers want the best for their children. And the mothers in Senegal were no different from the white mothers in Texas." Still, Wilkins had doubts. "With Johnson," he cautioned, "you never quite knew if he was out to lift your heart or your wallet."[3]

Johnson had a vision (another mark of an un-tough guy) and a Cold War fascination with the presidency that gave him the confidence to assume willpower and arithmetic skills alone could remake the nation and the world. When vice-president, he practically begged Kennedy to exert "moral" and "Christian" leadership in the civil rights struggle—to use "this aura, this thing, this halo around the President." Convinced that the White House was the perfect vehicle for the all-out liberalism of his Great Society (of which racial justice was merely one of many goals), Johnson would show the surviving Kennedy what a real reformer could do. And what he could do for America he could do for the world. Civil rights legislation and other war-on-poverty elements coexisted in LBJ's mind with a blind faith in military power. "We've had the leadership of the world because we took the air away from Hitler," he said, and to keep it the nation could not sit on its "fanny and let the British and the French build mach 2.2." What social scientists cum federal bureaucrats would do in the nation's ghettoes bomber pilots would do abroad. LBJ (1963–1969) would make the world safe from want, fear, and Communist tyranny, owing as much or more to Wilson than FDR (his much-cited inspiration).[4]

Johnson started fast. He spoke on the telephone or met in the days and weeks following the assassination with the so-called big six civil rights leaders—Wilkins, King, Randolph, Young, Lewis, and Farmer. Roy Wilkins was in first on November 29, and the new president slid his chair within an inch of the NAACP man's knees. "He wanted to talk about the Civil Rights Bill," Wilkins noted. "He said the outcome, the very future of the country, depended on how we all handled ourselves over the next few months." Martin Luther King came in four days later and received the same treatment. "Martin used to say that when you went to see President Kennedy," Andrew Young noted, "he listened for an hour and asked questions. When you went to see Lyndon Johnson, *he* talked for an hour." James Farmer got ninety minutes (with the president making telephone calls the entire time), complete with a story of how Lady Bird once asked the family's black servants to take the family dog with them when driving back to Texas from Washington. When the servants explained that it was trouble enough traveling through the South without a dog, Johnson said it "almost brought me to tears." Farmer called the story "a little corny, but touching."[5]

Over the next four years Johnson would award presidential freedom medals to Wilkins, Randolph, and Young (but not King, who had no hope of passing the FBI file check), and appoint Robert Weaver secretary of Housing and Urban Development. Weaver learned of the honor when summoned to the White House one morning and told to come in through the back door. Upstairs he found LBJ in bed and in his pajamas. Whitney Young, moreover, nearly received the directorship of the Office of Economic Opportunity and was seriously considered for a cabinet post. Thurgood Marshall served as solicitor general before the president nominated him to the Supreme Court. Here Johnson overruled the FBI. In response, according to Patrick J. Buchanan, then with the *St. Louis Globe-Democrat*, Hoover crept surreptitiously to the press to spread more dirt and gossip. Marshall, in the director's view (and apparently that of at least one sitting justice), was "just a 'dumb Negro.'" But LBJ held out and Marshall got his seat.[6]

Two months after Dallas, on January 17, Johnson had Wilkins, King, Young, and Farmer in again to secure their support for his ambitious war-on-poverty initiative. More interested in the southern white vote than the black vote (because he had a surer lock on the latter), John Kennedy had envisioned poverty programs as a way to transcend the race issue. "The war on poverty was in no sense a help-the-blacks program," Adam Yarmolinsky, one of Kennedy's people, explained. "We felt it would do very little for the blacks. . . . Color it Appalachian if you are going to color it anything at all." Johnson pushed beyond this, aiming at the North's urban poverty and for once seeing eye to eye (more or less) with a suddenly maturing Robert Kennedy. "Civil rights is just a narrow part of unemployment," RFK realized. "You could pass a law to permit a Negro to eat at a Howard Johnson's Restaurant or stay at the Hilton Hotel. But you can't pass a law that gives him enough money to permit him to eat at that restaurant or stay at that hotel. I think that's basically the problem of the Negro in the North, and that's why I think it's more difficult."[7]

Johnson stood RFK's construction on its head. "You know, in reality these are civil rights bills," he told newspaper columnist and former U.S. Information Agency director Carl Rowan, referring to the war-on-poverty package. "But of course, we aren't going to call them that."[8] His antipoverty strategy incorporated virtually every form of direct and indirect assistance imaginable from education and training to nutritional advice for pregnant women and medical care for all indigent souls. Along with these programs came a bureaucratic army to administer the grants and food stamps and so forth. Johnson put Kennedy brother-in-law and former Peace Corps head Sargent Shriver in charge of the Office of Economic Opportunity, with responsibility for the whole program. The poverty empire included, among other new bureaucracies, the Job Corps, Neighborhood Youth Corps, VISTA, Head Start, Upward Bound, and the extremely controversial Community Action which assumed a mandate to secure the poor's "maximum feasible participation."

While gearing up for the war on poverty Johnson pushed through his own beefed-up version of the Kennedy civil rights legislation. A minute after the Civil Rights Bill of 1964 passed in the House, Clarence Mitchell and Joe Rauh were standing in a corridor congratulating themselves. Rauh picked up a pay telephone ringing nearby and heard LBJ's voice urging them to get on with the business of pushing the bill through the Senate. "No lobbyist could outdo Lyndon Johnson," Roy Wilkins marveled. "He even knew how to raise you on the pay phones." The president got Everett Dirksen to organize Republican support in the Senate, and for the first time in history that body voted to end a civil rights filibuster. New York Senator Jacob Javits credited Dirksen "even more" than Johnson for that achievement, but Burke Marshall knew that the Illinois Republican was little more than the president's bipartisan front. "It was more of making him appear important than his real importance," Marshall said. The triumph, insofar as government officials can take credit, was Johnson's.[9]

The legislation's sweeping provisions guaranteed both the right to vote and access to all public accommodations. To enforce these rights, the new law authorized the federal government to sue to desegregate public facilities and schools and to cut off funds to any state that tolerated discrimination in the administration of federal programs. A single statute all but destroyed Jim Crow. In the eyes of many white Americans it completed the second Reconstruction. Of course not everyone was pleased. Anticipating affirmative-action and other interest-group furor, Richard Russell condemned the delegation of "plenary powers to bureaucrats to enable them to create a horde of special benefits for a selected group of citizens in defiance of our exalted Jeffersonian doctrine of equal rights to all and special privileges to none." LBJ never blinked. "Dick, you've got to get out of my way," he warned the Georgia senator. "I'm going to run over you." When asked by a group of southern politicians at the LBJ Ranch not to set firm guidelines for implementing the legislation, he said, "Nigger, nigger, nigger—that's all I hear. You might as well stop, because we're going ahead."[10]

Other white Americans, more extreme than the politicians at the LBJ Ranch, pledged outright resistance to what Russell and his "little group of constitutionalists" called the new law's "evils and vices." Twelve days before the president signed the Civil Rights Act of 1964, three young civil rights workers in Neshoba County, Mississippi, learned firsthand the depth of this extremism. Michael Schwerner and Andrew Goodman (New York Jews) and James Chaney (an "upitty" local black) made a particularly loathsome crew in the Klan view. All three were part of the Freedom Summer voter registration project put together by SNCC and other civil rights groups under an umbrella structure (the Council of Federated Organizations). They had driven a CORE station wagon from Meridian to Longview to investigate the burning of the Mt. Zion Church and on the return trip were arrested for speeding and jailed in the small burg of Philadelphia. Released at 10:00 P.M., according to the sheriff's office, they were last seen driving out of town.

Earlier, Robert Moses and other Freedom Summer organizers had tried to arrange a meeting with Johnson to ask for federal protection from the expected racist terror in Mississippi. But Robert Kennedy had already briefed the president on SNCC, concentrating on the group's solicitation of legal assistance from the National Lawyers Guild (a well-known "Communist front," in the day's mainstream political jargon) and apparent desire to incite the very violence that they had demanded protection from. "Some of them are more interested in forcing federal action in connection with street demonstrations than anything else," the attorney general said. With LBJ sharing this view of SNCC, Moses's letter went unanswered. This was in sharp contrast to the president's interest in the more moderate civil rights leadership. "Johnson was on the phone constantly," Roy Wilkins noted. "During one of those calls, he dropped whatever issue it was that preoccupied him, practically in mid-sentence, and said, 'I'm always calling you. Why don't you call *me* more often.'"[11]

Though President Johnson kept to a negative view of SNCC after the three civil rights workers disappeared, he was unable to avoid that troublesome group. "Congressman Bill Ryan [D.,N.Y.] called me," Lee White recalled, "so I . . . say, 'Mr. President, Bill Ryan's calling on behalf of the parents . . . they really want to see you.'" "*What for?*," LBJ asked. "Well, they just want the world to know and they want to be reassured that you're doing everything you can to find those kids." "This is June," the president responded. "Every goddamn time somebody's going to be missing, I got to meet with all those parents." "He sort of said, 'No,'" White continued. "I said, 'Well, it's not a case of whether we're gonna invite them. I have to go back and tell Ryan no . . . The *Herald-Tribune* is going to have an article saying the president refuses to see the parents of the missing civil rights workers.'" At first this just made Johnson angry. Then he settled down and agreed to see Schwerner's and Goodman's parents. "And while they were all there," White added, "J. Edgar Hoover called and said we found the station wagon."[12]

After that the search for Schwerner, Chaney, and Goodman fully engaged the president. He sent former CIA Director Allen Dulles to Mississippi as his special emissary and ordered Hoover to go to the state personally and open a new FBI field office in Jackson. "Edgar," the president said, "I want you to put people after the Klan and study it from one county to the next. I want the FBI to have the best intelligence system possible to check on the activities of these people." (This order by-passed Attorney General Robert Kennedy, who learned about Hoover's Mississippi trip in his morning newspaper.) Given the director's preferences, however, the FBI displayed less interest in the Klan than the civil rights volunteers who signed up for Freedom Summer and the National Lawyers Guild attorneys who helped out. Among other initiatives bureau agents wiretapped the telephone of Schwerner's father. Since Hoover sent the White House highlights from such surveillances from time to time, Johnson was at least vaguely aware of this preference for spying on the civil rights movement. He nonetheless responded warmly when the director returned from Mississippi. "I find it a great solace to lean on an old friend, such as you," he wrote in a short note, "in handling such delicate assignments."[13]

Johnson knew that television newsman Walter Cronkite erred when describing the search for the still-missing civil rights workers as "the focus of the whole country's concern." For some in the North as well as the South it was good riddance. While watching FBI agents drag the Pearl River in an unsuccessful search for the bodies of Michael Schwerner, James Chaney, and Andrew Goodman, a Neshoba County farmer called out, "Hold a welfare check over the water. That'll get that nigger to the surface."[14] The administration realized that the public mind had already identified war on poverty and attendant welfare programs as Negro programs, a point driven home by George Wallace's strong showing in the 1964 Wisconsin and Indiana Democratic presidential primaries. The Alabama governor received more than 30 percent of the vote in those states and swept several white working-class precincts ordinarily considered liberal strongholds. White southern resentment of the Civil Rights Act of 1964, combined with midwestern ethnic voter resentment of Great Society handouts, seemed capable, in the near future, of building a new white coalition. Martin Luther King predicted on CBS television's "Face the Nation" that the Republican party might yet fulfill Theodore Roosevelt's dream of being the "white man's party."

This "backlash" against a perceived White House tilt toward blacks at white expense led to an assault on the Great Society as "un-American" (in the manner in which the 1930s' right attacked New Deal reform). According to this argument Negroes had no incentive to study, work, save. They were simply given welfare cash, food stamps, jobs, scholarships, medical care, affirmative-action promises, access to lawyers, even their own special law. White folks, on the other hand, got nothing from Washington and just to get by had to work fingers to the bone. "The only contact" poor white trash had with the federal government, as a North Carolina Klansman said, was with IRS auditors or FBI wiremen. "You have to be black to get a welfare check," another segregationist complained. "Uncle Sam won't help poor nigger-hating me."[15] With Malthusian logic the hard right predicted that this new Great Society "permissiveness" would inevitably lead to higher birth rates, crime, idleness, and a general disrespect for (white) authority and the nation's (white) institutions.

"America's real majority is suffering from a minority complex of neglect," Johnson realized, with the white middle feeling "forgotten, at the second table," and thus emerging as "the real foes of Negro rights, foreign aid, etc." Only his "powerful conviction that an attack on poverty was right and necessary," the president explained, "blotted out any fears that this program was a political landmine."[16]

Backlash theorists received a boost on July 18, sixteen days after Johnson signed the Civil Rights Act of 1964, when race rioting broke out in New York. When more riots followed a week later in upstate Rochester many conservative Republicans argued that the violence confirmed the predictions about Great Society permissiveness and the lax law enforcement policies of elite reformers who saw the roots of crime in poverty. This was profoundly distressing for the administration but hardly surprising. White House staff constantly reminded Johnson that summer riots were possible in virtually any northern city. Eric Goldman, the Princeton historian who succeeded Schlesinger as White

House academic in residence, said "the breakaway from the established organizations of the more irresponsible Negroes" increased the likli-hood of major rioting. After consulting with other intellectuals, including Margaret Mead, Goldman urged Johnson "to help the estab-lished Negro leaders, who may well be losing control of the civil rights movement, to re-establish control and keep the movement going in its legitimate direction."[17]

To further this goal, the president, who practically lived on the tele-phone, increased the frequency of his calls to the "responsible" civil rights leaders. For the irresponsible ones the administration authorized more FBI surveillance, including a wiretap (under Robert Kennedy's signature) on Malcolm X's phone.[18] With the King wiretaps still in place every base seemed to be covered. The government aimed its most intrusive weapons at both the prince of nonviolence and the prince of violence.

White House headaches remained nonetheless. Rioting continued (notably in three New Jersey cities, a predominantly Negro Chicago suburb, and Philadelphia, Pennsylvania); and so did the search for Schwerner, Chaney, and Goodman in Philadelphia, Mississippi. After paying $30,000 to an informant for a tip, the FBI finally located the re-mains on August 4 under thirty feet of Mississippi mud. When the bureau telephoned the White House to say that two "WBs" (white bodies) and one "BB" (black body) had been found, the president interrupted a National Security Council meeting to take the call. SNCC and CORE also made good their pledge not to honor a White House call for a moratorium against civil rights demonstrations, choosing a particularly troublesome spot—Atlantic City, where the Democratic National Convention had come to nominate the party's candidates for president and vice-president. Michael Schwerner's widow, older brother, and mother and father were on the boardwalk, a Mississippi newspaperman wrote, among Negroes milling about and "singing 'freedom songs' that sounded like African war chants."[19]

Johnson's number-one concern in Atlantic City was that the dele-gates would draft Robert Kennedy by acclamation for the ticket's number-two spot. It made no difference that Kennedy would not run with the president under any circumstances. RFK had already an-nounced (two days before the convention opened) that he would resign the attorney generalship and seek the party's nomination for senator from New York. With a revised image of Johnson, moreover, the vice-presidency was especially unappealing. "I've seen . . . what he could do and what he has done in the last three months," he explained. "The fact is that he's able to eat people up, even people who are considered rather strong figures. I mean, as I say, Mac Bundy or Bob McNamara: There's nothing left of them." Apparently, the president was now seen as too tough for the toughest Kennedy. RFK's attitude toward a vice-presidential nomination, however, had no effect on LBJ's obsession.[20]

A second and ultimately more troublesome Atlantic City problem involved the predominantly black Mississippi Freedom Democratic party (MFDP) and its challenge to the state's regular delegation. Charging that the all-white slate did not represent blacks, the freedom delegates intended to present their case to the Credentials Committee—a prospect that threatened the president's dream of a harmonious, celebratory convention. If they won their case, the administration reasoned, the results would be disastrous. Even among delegates from more moderate southern states the attitude seemed to be, as MFDP attorney Joe Rauh paraphrased, "If you let those black buggers on the floor we will have to walk out." The last thing the White House wanted was a replay of the 1948 convention where Strom Thurmond led a Dixiecrat exodus.[21]

To head off any move to dislodge Mississippi's all-white slate or to name Robert Kennedy as the party's vice-presidential candidate (no matter how remote a possibility that was), Johnson (literally) wired the Atlantic City convention. J. Edgar Hoover, who had his own fantasies about Kennedy ("[he] blames me for his not being selected to run for Vice President with President Johnson"), supplied the resources. Cartha DeLoach, who one presidential aide described as "a good old boy, a friend of Eastland's," handled the details.[22] The FBI assistant director assembled a special squad of twenty-seven agents, one radio maintenance technician, and two stenographers. They wiretapped everyone in sight. While Martin Luther King testified before the Credentials Committee, two FBI men tapped the phones in his Claridge House Hotel rooms. (Nearly caught in the act, they "had to get out before they could get mike coverage.") Other taps and bugs covered the Gem Motel, where the MFDP had set-up its headquarters, and the basement of the

Union Baptist Temple Church, where the freedom delegates held strategy meetings. One bureau agent even got press credentials through NBC News and roamed the convention floor. "Our 'reporter,'" De-Loach bragged, "was so successful, in fact, that [name deleted] was giving him 'off the record information' for background purposes, which he requested our 'reporter' not to print."[23]

These sources provided a wealth of information which the FBI relayed "minute by minute" to Walter Jenkins and Bill Moyers at the White House. Moyers supplemented bureau sources with at least one informant of his own, Robert Spike of the National Council of Churches. "A good friend," he told Johnson. "One of these quiet, anonymous, little guys who devotes his life to causes like this. He is a very responsible, non-crusading type . . . [who] has the confidence of the Negro groups working in Mississippi."[24]

The president used the information gathered in his own inimitable fashion. "Johnson was paranoid, absolutely paranoid," Joe Rauh said, recalling the strong-arm techniques. "Whenever I did anything that Johnson didn't like I got two phone calls. . . . He figured if he got Hubert Humphrey, who was my friend and political ally, and Walter Reuther, who was my number one client, to call, he would get his way. So I heard from Walter. 'Joe, you just elected Goldwater.' He hangs up, the phone rings, and the girls in our office were rather funny by this time. They would say, 'It's the other one.'" Rauh picked up the phone and heard Humphrey's voice ("Joe, boy, the president's on a rampage"). Years later Rauh learned from newsman Sandy Van Oaker that the FBI "had tapped my wire in Atlantic City."[25]

Electronic surveillance, informants, and his own political skills gave Johnson a huge edge at the convention. His proposed compromise, which Rauh accepted, merely gave the MFDP two "special" seats. The Freedom delegates and their SNCC allies considered this more sell out than compromise and blamed everyone from Johnson to Rauh. They even blamed Martin Luther King who had told Lee White that he hoped "that some compromise might be developed which would hold down any southern white resentment and still keep the Negro moral[e] from a disastrous decline." The president was more interested in white morale. King swallowed the thing because he viewed the Republican party's presidential candidate, Barry Goldwater, "as a threat to the

Nation and recognized that, wittingly or unwittingly, he would attempt to capitalize on the white backlash." Jenkins and Moyers celebrated after the convention closed by exchanging congratulatory notes with the FBI men who had helped lock the White House deal.[26]

"'Law and order' became a major thrust of Senator Goldwater's campaign," Johnson wrote in his memoir. "I shared the growing concern about violence, but I believed the real danger, far more profound than violence and far more perilous, was the increasing alienation of the black citizens from American society."[27] Yet Johnson contributed to this alienation in Atlantic City. The Civil Rights Act of 1964 and the war on poverty notwithstanding, the Mississippi freedom-delegate compromise proved that the Democratic party would not break all ties with segregationist southerners. With Goldwater's nomination, in contrast, the Republicans made a more significant break with their own pro–civil rights, eastern-establishment wing (the Rockefeller wing).

That Goldwater would exploit the breakdown of law and order with what Wilkins called "sophistry and antebellum oratory" came as no surprise. In *The Conscience of a Conservative*, a book that became the New Right bible, Goldwater stood squarely for states' rights. "I am therefore not impressed," he wrote (Faubus style) on the subject of *Brown*, "that the Supreme Court's decision on school integration is the law of the land." His message was clear ("In your heart, you know he's white"), and he used the opportunities presented by the riots shamelessly. "Violence in our streets," journalist Richard Rovere wrote, was his "number-two issue. It came hard on the heels of 'the wall of shame in Berlin, [and] the sands of shame at the Bay of Pigs, [and] the slow death of freedom in Laos." Running mate William E. Miller of New York even welcomed a Ku Klux Klan endorsement, saying "Senator Goldwater and I will accept the support of any American citizen who believes in us, our platform and our posture." With Republican National Committee chair Dean Burch echoing this view ("we're not in the business of turning away votes"), it took a Gettysburg meeting with Eisenhower and Nixon to convince Goldwater to repudiate Klan support.[28]

Johnson responded on every front to the problems magnified by the riots ("Goldwater rallies," as they were called in Democratic circles). He began by asking the big six leaders to halt all civil rights demonstrations until after the November elections. Wilkins, King, Young, and Randolph did so after much debate, ultimately deciding that another wave of demonstrations might help Goldwater's candidacy. When SNCC's John Lewis and CORE's James Farmer flatly refused to join the moratorium, the president (in Lee White's words) made "every effort" to persuade them "to encourage their followers to hold their demonstrations to specific objectives and . . . prevent them from becoming leaderless riots with attendant looting and violence."[29] Goldwater himself was surprisingly easy to handle. After a single White House meeting both candidates pledged to keep race out of the campaign. "If we attacked each other," Goldwater explained, "the country would be divided into different camps and we could witness bloodshed." Sensitive to the charge hurled "again and again . . . that I was a racist," he stuck to his word even in the campaign's last desperate days when fringe advisor F. Clifton White produced a documentary film intended to exacerbate white fears of black urban violence. Goldwater condemned the film and ordered it suppressed.[30]

Johnson also worked to get J. Edgar Hoover's endorsement. The logic here was straightforward: If the nation's top cop said the president was tough enough, who could criticize the administration for being soft on law and order? Originally, LBJ wanted a White House conference on law enforcement with the bureau slotted to "mastermind" the project. He rejected that idea on the advice of staff. "It might become a forum for civil rights discussions," Myer Feldman said, "something we do not need at the present time."[31] The president instead had Hoover release to the press an FBI report on the riots—a report that Thomas E. Dewey, a decidedly anti-Goldwater Republican, had secretly supervised. (Dewey's name surely would have leaked as the report's author if the director's name alone had failed to do the job.) The report abandoned Hoover's right-wing orthodoxy to endorse the war on poverty, emphasizing social and economic factors and not bleeding-heart judges or subversive conspirators. "[It] cleared the civil rights movement completely," as Wilkins noted. "After the F.B.I. report there was no excuse for race to be drawn into the campaign." Leaving nothing to chance, Johnson even threw Hoover a bone by expanding the bureau's riot control training for state and local police. It was in its entirety a classic example of a master politician at work.[32]

President Johnson carried every state in November except Gold-water's Arizona and five in the deep South, and northern Democrats picked up thirty-seven House seats to assure a liberal/progressive majority for the first time since the New Deal ground to a halt in 1938. But LBJ would have lost Arkansas, Florida, Tennessee, and Virginia save for the black vote. Texas was the only southern state in which he carried the white vote by a clear majority. King's prediction about the Republican party evolving into a white man's party was coming true even in the midst of a Democratic runaway.

A month after the election Johnson watched as King received the Nobel Peace Prize. He also watched (and tacitly supported) the FBI war against King that had now moved into high gear. Always in the habit of reading tidbits from the bureau's tap and bug transcripts, the president was on occasion a voyeur and always a politician looking for an edge. Typical of the information picked up was a conversation between King and his wife (which Hoover paraphrased for Moyers) noting "the absence of congratulations from 'high Government officials' on the occasion of King's winning the Nobel Peace Prize." LBJ, they concluded, felt even a nod of acknowledgement would fuel the dreaded white backlash. So he would keep King at arm's length hereafter.[33]

According to Bill Moyers the opposite was true. "[Johnson] was very concerned," he explained years later. "He didn't want to have a southern racist Senator produce something [about King] that would be politically embarrassing to the President and to the civil rights movement. We had lots of conversations about that." Moyers himself became Hoover's conduit for endless reports about such things as King's "personal conduct." If any dirt turned up, in other words, the White House wanted first crack—either to neutralize it or to use it to the president's advantage. There is no evidence that Johnson appreciated the irony of "embracing" King and then relying for "protection" on the FBI director—a man who considered the dreamer "a burr head," "a tom cat," "a colossal fraud," an "evil, vicious . . . dissolute, abnormal moral imbecile" with an equally "filthy" and "fraudulent" personal and public life. There is also no evidence that Johnson appreciated the irony of the bureau listening in on at least one, and perhaps several dozen, telephone conversations between King and the president himself.[34]

Johnson continued to work with King. On February 9 the two men met at the White House to discuss possible voting rights legislation. This was just a week since King and some three thousand demonstrators were arrested during the Selma voting drive. Selma, a former slave-market town on the Alabama River, turned especially violent a month later on Sunday, March 7, when mounted police beat back marchers on the Edmund Pettus Bridge—Bloody Sunday, the single most brutal repression of any civil rights demonstration. Two days later segregationist toughs assaulted Rev. James Reeb, a Boston Unitarian, and on March 11 Reeb died. Unlike the earlier killing of a young black man, Jimmy Lee Jackson, by a state trooper, Reeb's murder attracted national attention.

Selma presented both problems and opportunities for the White House. Obviously if the situation continued to deteriorate Johnson would have to send troops, a prospect that he dreaded given the slim chance that George Wallace would request assistance. (Even J. Edgar Hoover considered the Alabama governor to be "psycho-neurotic.") Simultaneously the bloody spectacle of segregationist terror pushed "white backlash" into a temporary retreat as the civil rights movement acquired more political capital during the Selma voting drive than during any other event since the Birmingham demonstrations. However great the risks, Selma presented Johnson an opportunity to introduce voting rights legislation (the main area not covered by the Civil Rights Act of 1964) and finish the Second Reconstruction.[35]

Johnson moved quickly after Rev. Reeb's death. He met with Wallace in the Oval Office, getting close enough to rub the man's nose and give him the full treatment. "If I hadn't left when I did," the governor recalled, "he'd have had me coming out *for* civil rights." Yet Wallace made no commitment to restore order in Selma or to request federal assistance in doing so.[36] The president then moved on to the new attorney general, Nicholas Katzenbach, telling him "to write the goddamnedest toughest voting rights act that you can devise." Katzenbach, already at work on a bill, did exactly that—with one approved exception. There would be no expansion of federal jurisdiction to combat violence and other crimes against civil rights workers. No protection, in other words. Not even the modest approach that Katzenbach himself favored. "If we submit legislation along the lines which I believe both appropriate and useful," he later explained, "we will not satisfy any of the civil rights groups who want much more." Combined with the prospect of a "run-away" House Judiciary Committee inclined to give the movement all it wanted and more, this "would then run the danger of making the Administration the target of civil rights criticism without any compensating political advantage."[37]

When announcing his voting rights bill on March 15 to a joint session of Congress, Johnson placed Selma alongside Lexington and Concord and Appomattox as turning points "in man's unending search for freedom." "There is no Negro problem," he said in what proved to be his greatest speech. "There is no Southern problem. There is no Northern problem. There is only an American problem." Roy Wilkins called this historic address "the godamnedest commitment to the civil-rights cause I had ever heard."[38]

A week later, more violence in Selma underscored the need for the proposed legislation (and the item that Katzenbach had left out). On March 21, after State troopers turned back two earlier attempts including the Bloody Sunday spectacle, King led three hundred civil rights workers and volunteers out on the roads for a fifty-four mile march to the state capitol. This time soldiers and National Guardsmen provided protection, the result of Secretary of Defense Robert McNamara's personal appeal. He told the president that his daughter, Margaret, a graduate student at Washington University in St. Louis, was among the demonstrators. "I thought he [LBJ] was going to tear the telephone off the wall," McNamara said when recalling the incident. "I finally persuaded him to do it [federalize the Alabama National Guard]. I told him I know that he loved Margy and he was surely right in calling out the Guard because it protected her on the march."[39]

Not even troops could protect everyone, however, as yet another murder demonstrated the local resistance to outside interference. Viola Liuzzo, a red-haired Detroit housewife and mother of five, had come to Selma as a civil rights volunteer and spent her last day, March 25, shuttling Selma-Montgomery marchers back to their homes in her car. On the day's final trip on Highway 80 near Lowndes County's Big Bear Swamp, twenty-five miles from the Edmund Pettus Bridge, four armed Klansmen sped past in another car and opened fire. With blood spurting from her temple, Liuzzo died instantly. The car crashed into the ditch and the only passenger, a nineteen-year-old black barber named Leroy Moton, hitchhiked into town for help.

Johnson ordered the FBI to "find the perpetrators of this heinous crime," to "do everything possible around the clock." He telephoned bureau headquarters twice and Hoover himself two or three times in the middle of the night and again at 6:00 A.M. By 8:00 A.M. the case had already been solved. The president announced the arrests later that morning on nationwide television flanked by his FBI director and attorney general. On its face it was a remarkable accomplishment, sullied only by the embarrassing presence of an FBI informant, Gary Thomas Rowe, in the murder car; and Hoover's erroneous missives. "On the woman's body," he told Johnson, "we found numerous needle marks indicating she had been taking dope although we can't say that definitely because she is dead." He also told Katzenbach that Mrs. Liuzzo "was sitting very, very close to the Negro in the car . . . it had the appearance of a necking party." The administration ignored such nonsense and instead pressed the FBI to go after the Ku Klux Klan.[40]

In the manner of the Kennedys, Johnson thought he had Hoover's FBI under control. But the director had his own agenda. "White citizens are primarily decent, but frightened for their lives," he told a group of newspaper editors in an off-the-record session three weeks after Liuzzo's murder. "The colored people are quite ignorant, mostly uneducated, and I doubt if they would seek an education if they had an opportunity. Many who have the right to register [to vote] seldom do register."[41] The FBI stood with the practitioners of the new backlash politics—with the frightened people in what Hoover called "white ghettoes" and their racist nightmares about an American Mau Mau, declining property values, and black schoolchildren enrolling in their neighborhood schools. The irony is that the president, as he lost whatever control over the FBI he once had, turned more and more to Hoover for help on virtually every racial problem that arose.

Johnson lost control of everything. He began summer 1965 with a major address at Howard University calling for a "move beyond opportunity to achievement." Two months later, on August 6, he signed the Voting Rights Act of 1965, providing for registration by federal examiners in any state or county where fewer than fifty percent of the adults were registered to vote. Things deteriorated quickly and dramatically from there. Johnson's ability to manipulate movement symbols (including the we-shall-overcome refrain) disappeared, and he spent the remainder of his presidency entirely on the defensive. Reduced to reacting, that is, to the new law-and-order cant of racism's latest synthesis. Urban rioting had followed the Civil Rights Act of 1964 by sixteen days. Now the Watts riot in Los Angeles followed the Voting Rights Act of 1965 by five days, giving yet another boost to the cause-and-effect reasoning of the Great Society's critics.

The problem of what White House press secretary George Reedy condemned as the degeneration of "the Negro masses . . . into savagery" was compounded by the outbursts of a new type of activist. "Breaking, screaming, bleeding, laughing," wrote Eldridge Cleaver, who would go on to join the Black Panthers. "Smashing the windows of the white man's store, throwing bricks they wished were bombs, leaping whirling like a cyclone through the white man's Mind, past his backlash, through the night streets." Watts was the first major race riot since World War II and the first major riot to be televised, so there was absolutely no way it would race past anyone's backlash.[42]

"How is it possible," the president asked, "after all we've accomplished? How could it be? Is the world topsy turvy?" LBJ could not even understand, in EEOC chair Clifford Alexander's words, "why blacks were not turning around every ten seconds and saying, 'Thank you, Mr. President.'" So how could he understand the rage of Watts? "He just wouldn't accept it," Joseph Califano remembered. "He refused to look at the cables from Los Angeles describing the situation. . . . I tried to reach him a dozen times. We needed decisions from him. But he simply wouldn't respond." When the president finally moved he demonstrated a bitter conspiratorial bent. "It simply wasn't fair for a few irresponsible agitators to spoil it for me and for all the rest of the Negroes, who are basically peace-loving and nice," he said. "A few hoodlums sparked by outside agitators who moved around from city to city making trouble. Spoiling all the progress I've made in these last few years." Combined with the pressures of Vietnam and the emerging antiwar movement on the homefront, this odd combination of paranoia and megalomania would dominate LBJ's last three years in the White House.[43]

It surfaced everywhere and in virtually every corner of the administration. In response to Watts, Johnson called a White House conference on civil rights and then had the FBI run name checks on the proposed invitees in search of derogatory personal or political information. He also had Hoover brief Democratic National Committee officials on the alleged plans of certain "elements" to disrupt the conference. Louis Martin, then DNC deputy chair for minorities, was especially interested in "the sources of revenue which enable these bomb throwers to carry out their programs." He found the FBI director "very warm," "cordial," and "anxious to cooperate." A more serious problem involved the negative FBI dossier on Bayard Rustin, former Communist and a homosexual to boot. Most troubling was Rustin's suggestion that the conference not focus, as the White House intended, on the controversial report, prepared by Daniel Patrick Moynihan, then assistant secretary of labor, on the Negro family's "tangle of pathology." Rustin wanted to concentrate on jobs and housing not illegitimate births, female heads of households, and welfare dependency.

Johnson thought the former would fuel white backlash while the latter might deflect it. But the Moynihan report created such an uproar that Rustin won out even with all the FBI material stacked against him. The administration could do little more than side with Moynihan in spirit. When a troublesome critic of Moynihan's "tangle of pathology" angle, Robert Spike of the National Council of Churches (and Bill Moyers's source in Atlantic City), was found "dead in a motel room, naked, killed by his partner, his homosexual partner," White House aide Harry McPherson said, simply: "Great man to understand the problems of the Negro family!"[44]

The wave of rioting that the Johnson White House expected in 1966 never came. That relatively peaceful summer witnessed serious disturbances only in Cleveland (four killed and fifty injured) and Chicago (where a white mob stoned Martin Luther King and other marchers). Backlash politics, nonetheless, continued unabated. In California, where "the racial backlash . . . is not latent but immediate, vocal and strong," the administration closely monitored a master manipulator of white resentment. "[Governor Ronald Reagan] is an attractive, plausible, persuasive 'good guy' whose synthetic packaging is not apparent," Fred Dutton advised Moyers. "He is a 'natural' not only in the TV era but for the emerging cultural, psychological wave-lengths to which much of the country is attuned." Administration officials had no idea what to do about Reagan ("just pretend that [his] speeches do not exist," George Reedy advised); or about anything else, including the possibility of more violence in Watts. "The federal government's pipe line . . . is crowded with projects," Dutton noted, "but . . . there are still no really visible results besides press releases."[45]

Two nonriot events in June helped politicians like Reagan get their message across. First, during the "march against fear" begun by James Meredith in Memphis, SNCC's Stokely Carmichael repeatedly used the words "black power"—a slogan hyped by the press and guaranteed to provoke a reaction. Even King and Wilkins condemned it as mindless posturing. The second event, the Supreme Court's decision in *Miranda* (requiring police officers to inform suspects of their constitutional rights), confirmed for some the charge that liberal judges and bureaucrats cared more for criminal rights than victim rights. Reflecting on that decision, FBI Director Hoover told Senator Birch Bayh that "you have an intense demoralizing situation where they [Negroes] cry 'police brutality' on the slightest provocation and the newspapers serve no useful purpose in printing the picture, such as in civil rights cases particularly, of a Negro on the ground with officers above. . . . That does not show the picture of his having assaulted the officers and in order to protect themselves they had to subdue him."

White House political strategists worried that much of white middle America stood with the officers above and their nightsticks (called "niggersticks" in Watts), and not the Negro on the ground. In September, public opinion polls and Mike Wallace's CBS report on "Black Power, White Backlash" further confirmed these fears.[46]

With the November mid-term elections approaching, the White House and the Justice Department began a dialogue on the question of how to keep backlash from "spreading to the white middle-class from the white lower-class." "The housing thing" was a particular problem given the widespread belief that LBJ's reformers intended to "move a lot of Negroes into the tree-lined streets of suburbia." If the administration pushed housing initiatives too hard, it might prove "fatal at the polls." Any civil rights measure would no doubt be doomed by the "feeling among members of Congress of too much bending over backwards to help Negroes."[47] McPherson and Katzenbach, the braintrust on these problems, advised the president to exert his "leadership" of the civil rights issue and attempt to limit black protest in all forms from peaceful marches and demonstrations to Watts-type outbreaks.

"The Negro problem will be reflected in white backlash this November," McPherson told Johnson. "We can reduce some of that backlash if Negro leaders speak out for order, for respect for the rights of others." The president faced a dilemma nonetheless. "If you do nothing to exercise your leadership," McPherson continued, "you will be damned by the Negroes, who will turn increasingly to extremist leaders, and by the whites, who will still identify you as the Negroes' protector. The pressure will grow for you to silence the protests, and to take vigorous action to 'bring the Negro into line.' At an earlier stage in history this might have worked. But the Negro is not about to return to subservience now." Because Johnson's stock would rise and fall with the movement's, the only way out lay in presidential action.

It was hardly surprising, given this logic, that McPherson's only specific proposal for "action" was a recommendation to bring a dozen black leaders to the White House for a discussion "on where the civil rights movement should go now." McPherson's most novel idea was to include several "young militants." Randolph was in his seventies and Wilkins in his sixties, he reminded the president, and "even Whitney Young and Martin Luther King have been around so long that they seem 'old school.' . . . The young on the streets will not always respond to advice from middle-aged and elderly men in their vested suits and regimental stripes. Our lines of communication to the movement run generally (and from the White House, only) to the older Negro establishment. We have very few contacts with younger Negro leaders. We must develop these contacts." This was not all that dramatic a suggestion. The Rap Browns and Stokely Carmichaels would not be coming. By "young leaders" McPherson meant "those who believe in the American system." "It is up to the established Negro leaders," he added in yet another qualification that gutted the basic idea, "to identify these young men and women and to bring them along."[48]

Even this was too much for Katzenbach. "[Since] we are not going to reach these people" under any circumstances, he recommended instead the creation of "a militant but peaceful organization of young people which could successfully compete with SNCC. I think this is worth discussing with Roy Wilkins, Dr. King and others, informally and quietly. But to launch it at the White House would be to kill it before it was born." The brain trusters did agreed that "the civil rights movement is obviously a mess" and that "white people are scared and sore and the consensus behind improvement of the Negro condition is running out—has run out." On a minor item Katzenbach and McPherson also agreed on the need to "take the curse of 'President's boy' off Whitney and Roy." "You can criticize me," LBJ told Wilkins shortly thereafter. "You can hit me a little bit."

President Johnson acted here, Louis Martin explained, "because [he] was worried about Wilkins' posture with his own people." He was aware of his predecessor's habit, moreover, of making the same offer to the other side. During the Jackson demonstrations, for example, John Kennedy asked his staff to get "the stud duck down there" on the telephone, and when they did JFK gave Mayor Allen C. Thompson "full permission to denounce me in public as long as you don't in private."[49]

Martin Luther King scarcely fit into Lyndon Johnson's equations. While Katzenbach and McPherson worried about damaging King's stature ("the president does not strengthen [his] leadership . . . when [he is] made to appear . . . [a White House] apologist"), the dreaded Carmichael offered a more thoughtful view. "Martin Luther King is going through an agonizing reappraisal," he said on Mike Wallace's CBS backlash special. "He doesn't belong to the decadent aristocratic colonials of the civil rights movement." In Chicago six months later, on March 25, 1967, King showed that Carmichael was close to the truth by leading an anti–Vietnam War demonstration. Ten days after that, in New York, he called on all young American men, black and white, to boycott the war by declaring themselves conscientious objectors.

Johnson was crushed by King's criticism. In February the president had ignored the advice of staff and introduced additional civil rights legislation with an open-housing provision—and housing was King's key issue in his attempt to bring the civil rights movement North. Still, the break came as no great surprise. At the president's specific request the FBI had been tracking King's "position . . . relative to Vietnam" since 1965 with a view to "any hard Communist Party line tying to-

gether Vietnam and the civil rights movement." King had commended
Robert Kennedy's stance on Vietnam and "contemporary colonial revo-
lutions" generally, and the SCLC board was on record as opposing "the
immorality and tragic absurdity of our position."[50] Until the end Johnson hoped he could keep King in line. On March 24 he told his staff to
"ask Louis Martin why he hasn't brought him in. He's cancelled two en-
gagements with me, and I don't understand why."

When King marched against the war in Chicago the next day, President Johnson had his answer. But the break was not complete until
King's New York statements appeared in the press. "Quite an item,"
former ADA chief and latest White House intellectual-in-residence
John Roche told Johnson. "To me it indicates that King—in desperate
search of a constituency—has thrown in with the commies. . . . The
Communist-oriented 'peace' types have played him (and his driving
wife) like trout."[51]

King was only one of many to speak out against the president's war.
While old-line civil rights leaders like Roy Wilkins supported the administration ("we kept the N.A.A.C.P. from losing itself in the peace
movement"), Carmichael et al. offered both flip comments ("war is for
the birds, Lynda Bird and Lady Bird") and more serious analyses of
western colonialism. "[Blacks] are asked to die for the System in Vietnam," Eldridge Cleaver wrote. "In Watts they are killed by it. . . . Why
not die right here in Babylon fighting for a better life, like the Viet
Cong?" King's own rhetoric had moved left with a recent call for "a
radical redistribution of economic and political power" and emphasis
on the connection between racism and poverty in a nation that acted
as if it were "God's military agent on earth." "King was the person we
were most upset about," Roche said, with some understatement.
"Martin was spectacular. The problem with Martin going off with the
Hanoi Hawks . . . This disturbed us profoundly."

No longer the harmless dreamer of black children and white children
holding hands on a hillside, the King of 1967 had no interest "in being
integrated into *this* value structure." It was one thing to challenge the
authority and values of Bull Connor and the city of Birmingham, quite
another to challenge the authority and values of Lyndon Johnson and
the United States. But that is exactly what King and the others proposed as the movement's next project. The president saw this as both a

personal betrayal and a fratricidal rejection of the entire Great Society idea. "You know the difference between cannibals and liberals?," he asked the ever loyal Wilkins and Young. "Cannibals eat only their enemies."[52]

King also issued a warning to the White House on the other front, predicting that summer rioting would visit at least ten cities. The administration expected violence, but was unprepared for its scope and intensity. Rioting hit Boston, Tampa, and Cincinnati in June, and on July 12 Newark exploded in violence that left twenty-three dead, over 700 injured, and more than 1,000 persons arrested in six days of arson and pitched street battles. The century's worst riot opened in Detroit on July 23 and culminated in forty-three deaths and some five thousand homes burned to the ground amid 1,500 separate fires. In Cambridge, Maryland, rioters destroyed nearly twenty buildings in an outbreak following a speech by SNCC's Rap Brown. (Brown called on young black men to "burn this town down.") Neighborhoods in nearly 150 other cities experienced disorders, too, from minor disturbances to widespread looting and sniping.

Predictably this led to what Vice President Hubert Humphrey called "extremely hostile racial attitudes" among a "shockingly large number of Americans." The typical white man, Roche told Johnson, "is afraid, and more significantly, his womenfolk are afraid." Other White House advisers warned the president that he "might get 'backlashed'" by this angry white male vote in November. "The American voter today," pollster Dick Scammon agreed, "is un-young," "un-black," and "un-poor." So "campaign strategy should be carefully aimed at the white, middle-aged, middle class voters—the people . . . who bowl regularly." Because Scammon touted Reagan and not Nixon ("a born loser") as "the only Republican who can really sweep the 'fearful white' vote," Johnson had Humphrey look into the possibility that the California governor would get the nomination. The vice-president quit after hearing what Barry Goldwater had told the hard right's latest hero: "Reagan shouldn't kid himself into believing that he could beat Johnson. . . . The same little old ladies in tennis shoes that used to cheer and clap for him did the same thing for Bob Taft and Tom Dewey. In other words, don't be fooled by the enthusiastic response of a handful of hard-core conservative Republicans."[53]

The administration was of a single mind on only one riot-related question—the decision to get Republican Michigan Governor George Romney's invitation to move troops into Detroit. This was also the only area where Johnson was in his usual form. "The President . . . whacked the hell out of Romney, mentioning him ten or fifteen times," recalled Mayor Jerome P. Cavanagh, who watched the televised announcement with the governor himself. "Really the traditional Johnson overkill. . . . Romney couldn't handle the situation, 'He has requested help, it's beyond his control.' He was really killing him. When the TV set went off . . . Romney just stood up and walked around in circles, just mad as hell."[54]

Otherwise Johnson was in anything but top form as his administration split in both its response to the riots and dwindling political prospects. Harry McPherson, Louis Martin, and Clifford Alexander, the most articulate advocates of what could be called the traditional liberal approach, urged the president (once again) to meet with "a large group of responsible Negro leaders." But this troika had no idea what to discuss at such a meeting ("we really don't have an immediate program to put to them"), and admitted that the political risks were enormous in the event such a meeting actually convened. "Some of the 'liberal' press," McPherson noted, "would be sure to point out that these people have not much more contact with, or power of persuasion over the terrorists, than the NAM [National Association of Manufacturers]."[55]

McPherson, Martin, and Alexander even worried about what "Rap Brown, Carmichael, Karenga and company" might think of the invitees. "To the Black Power crowd, these people are Uncle Toms (and some of them are quite conservative defenders of the status quo)," McPherson continued. "But to the Communists, Roosevelt was a fascist, because he wanted to preserve a voluntary way of life in America. I don't think we should let the Carmichael crowd deter us by their scorn of men like these." A more serious problem was that any White House "meeting would be sure to dwell on social needs and programs; but what the country wants to hear about is how to bring the riots under control." McPherson argued that there was no choice. "While these men may not have much sway with the terrorists, they do represent whatever Negro leadership there is. . . . As in a period of labor strife the White House talks to representatives of labor and industry, in a racial revolt we should talk to responsible representatives of the Negro community."[56]

Rather than call this conclave, Johnson sent his three liberals on a New York ghetto tour. "Harlem looks like Calcutta," McPherson, a self-described "neo-Malthusian," reported back. "[And] Bedford-Stuyvesant . . . is the home of what Marx called the 'lumpen-proletariat,'" an "incredibly depressing" cityscape with "every tenth car—as in Harlem—a Cadillac Eldorado, Buick Riviera, or Chrysler, double-parked before a busted decaying house." He offered a few political impressions ("I am coming to believe that 95% of the Negro leaders in this country are West Indian"), but mostly stories of the sort that the Kennedys had ridiculed Johnson for telling. "A statue, in the park of a public housing project, of Lincoln—seated, with his hand around the shoulder of a Negro boy," he wrote. "There is a lot of modern playground equipment in the park, but when we were there, the kids weren't playing on the equipment; they were climbing all over the statue. It almost seemed as if they were trying to lift Lincoln's other hand and put it on *their* shoulders. The statue's bronze is worn to a light brown by thousands of children's hands. It is the statue of a father—a powerful figure for kids without one at home."[57]

Much to Johnson's dismay empathetic liberals scored their most enduring intellectual (if not practical) triumph through the National Commission on the Causes and Prevention of Violence (the Kerner Commission, after its chair, Illinois Governor Otto Kerner). LBJ used commissions much like he used the telephone or the Oval Office chairs that could be pulled in tight for knee-to-knee conversations. It was part of the way he governed. Twenty-eight commissions in all and some 134 secret task forces made up what one scholar called "a tour de force of presidential advisement."[58] Unfortunately, Johnson lost control of this particular enterprise. The Kerner Commission's final report, released in February, concluded that the nation was "moving toward two societies, one black, one white—separate and unequal." To reverse the "deepening racial trend," the commission called for a massive and sustained "commitment to national action" and recommended sweeping reforms in the areas of employment, education, welfare, housing, news reporting, and law enforcement. "Discrimination and segregation have long permeated much of American life," the report concluded. "They now threaten the future of every American."[59]

After four years of Great Society reform, including the war on poverty and the civil rights legislation of 1964 and 1965, such conclusions infuriated Johnson. The Kerner Commission had ignored "the Marshall Plan we already have," he groaned, and by proposing expensive new programs allowed Congress "to run away from" the things already in place. "That was the problem," he reiterated. "Money." Since the money was not there, McPherson explained, "it intensified arguments about the war, raised impossible demands, and implicitly diminished the significance of what was already done." The commission was an even bigger disaster from the standpoint of backlash politics. Since its report identified white racism as "the proximate cause of the riots," McPherson continued, "it provoked the deepest resentment among white workers whose unions had helped to pass the laws of the Great Society. The charge against white racism was true—but so was the bitterness of white families, who lived and worked among blacks, when they were told that they were responsible for the sacking of the cities. . . . The commission had weakened the liberal bloc by charging part of it with crimes against the other. 'That's what I've been trying to tell you,' Johnson said. 'There aren't that many of us that we can afford to set some of us against the rest of us.'"[60]

In practice the president ignored the Kerner Commission. He refused to receive its members when their work was done, ignoring McPherson's warning ("certainly there will be little public acceptance of future Presidential commissions as even temporary palliatives in meeting national problems, if we are silent on this one"). LBJ held out, even refusing to sign the thank-you letters to individual commission members that McPherson had prepared. "I just can't," he said. "I'd be a hypocrite. And I don't even want it let known that they got this far . . . otherwise somebody will leak that I wouldn't sign them. Just file them—or get rid of them."[61]

While the Kerner Commission went about its work Johnson worried about the conservatives in Congress and elsewhere who supported the rival investigations of Arkansas Senator John McClellan's Permanent Subcommittee on Investigations (PERM)—the same subcommittee that Joseph McCarthy had once chaired. Promising to emphasize "law enforcement rather than the social causes underlying the disorders," McClellan received the complete if often covert cooperation of Hoover's FBI and police departments across the country. Sixty-three officers from state and local police Red squads testified, including a sergeant from the Chicago Police Department's intelligence unit who assured the subcommittee that "the Communist threat does exist."

Administration officials had no illusions about the real purpose of what would turn into a three-year, twenty-five part investigation into the breakdown of law and order that had occurred on Johnson's watch. "Senator McClellan," as James Gaither put it plainly to Joseph Califano, "is conducting a nationwide investigation of the OEO [Office of Economic Opportunity] involvement in the riots." Maine Senator Edmund Muskie's staff concluded that PERM threatened "the future of poverty and urban development programs" and even "the attitudes of many white Americans with respect to the 20 million Negroes who were not involved in the riots."[62]

Rioting by persons who received OEO funds directly or indirectly was a false issue. Of the 30,565 employees of the various antipoverty agencies, only six full-time staff, nine summer employees, and one VISTA volunteer were arrested during the urban disturbances. These sixteen cases led to a single loitering conviction and fifty-dollar fine in Cincinnati (where former Republican Mayor Charles P. Taft's firm filed an appeal). If anything OEO was a stabilizing force in the riots. In Detroit 160 VISTA volunteers helped in every way imaginable after the fires stopped burning, from removing rubble to rebuilding homes and businesses. In Newark dozens more filled in for teachers who fled the public schools. In New York and Tampa, Neighborhood Youth Corps enrollees put on white helmets and helped police patrol hot spots.

OEO even supplied the best intelligence on the riots while they were happening. The inspector general's office, general counsel Donald M. Baker said, "had guys crawling around on their bellies in the middle of the Newark riot, for God's sake, as to what was going on and who was doing what." "Our Community Action workers were . . . drawn out of the same people who were rioting," Sargent Shriver added. "They understood what was going on far better than the FBI or anybody. . . . We had two or three thousand spies in there. . . . We were like combat troops, we were like Green Berets."[63]

The Office of Economic Opportunity had been under a congressional microscope from day one. "Lyndon Johnson told us we could not spend any money before election day 1964 under the OEO legislation," Shriver remembered. "On the 20th of January, Congress established an investigation committee to inspect OEO and find out what we were doing wrong. That is the fastest creation of an inspection division by Congress in the history of the United States. [We] hadn't even started, so to speak, and Congress was already investigating what was wrong. That's a psychic phenomena. If Congress appropriates $5 billion to build an airplane, they don't create a month later a huge commission to find out what's the matter with the airplane in the Defense Department. That doesn't happen. . . . But in the case of OEO, it did happen."

Whenever something was found it always made the newspapers. "Some Job Corp kid gets drunk," Baker complained, "or an employee of a sub-contractor training organization, in some town in West Virginia, left that job and came to Washington and raped a girl. You know what the headline was in the good, liberal, intelligent, careful *Washington Post*? 'OEO Employee Rapes Girl.' And that was sort of the way it always was."[64]

Even without substance the charge that poverty workers incited the riots stuck. "Because we were in there with the people—in with the revolutionaries," Shriver said, "some of the blame came off on us." There was more to it than that. That few poverty workers were arrested and only one convicted of any riot-related crime slowed no hard-line critic. From the White House to the lowest judge in the criminal courts, liberals controlled the system, the right argued, and were more interested in giving grants to thugs than throwing them in jail. "[Even] snipers . . . working as teams" and "using two-way radios" were merely slapped "on the wrist and release[d]," Dwight Eisenhower charged. (The former president, who offered no evidence for this fantastic charge, said he preferred the riot-control techniques favored by Moscow's "Red Square" commissars.) And for every unqualified OEO success story, like that of heavyweight boxer and Job Corps graduate George Foreman (who would go on to wave the American flag after winning a gold medal at the Mexico City Olympics), there was an embarrassing incident like the West Virginia rapist.

FBI officials (who collected such things for the McClellan subcommittee) alerted the White House to one of the senator's favorites: "Transportation of H. Rap Brown . . . in an automobile leased to an antipoverty agency receiving funds from the Office of Economic Opportunity." Johnson understood how the middle class would react to news that the Harlem group in question, Haryou-ACT, received at least some money from OEO, from their war-on-poverty taxes. One way or another Great Society largess had not only provided a revolving door of justice for snipers and riot instigators but a rental car for the burn-baby-burn man himself.[65]

Since the war on poverty's first months the administration had received the steadiest stream of complaints about OEO using federal funds to instruct the poor in any number of controversial areas. These ranged from birth control to sit-in tactics and other forms of direct-action protest. If family planning lay dormant (for the time being), the protest lessons posed immediate dangers because they enraged even those who had voted for the Great Society in the first place. "Congressmen who supported CAP [Community Action Program] in the belief that it was a management tool, or a way to get money to the poor quickly," McPherson told Johnson, "have found CAPs in their districts organizing protests against their own mayors. They are sore as hell, justifiably."[66] Under the leadership of a Democratic president, in other words, a Democratic Congress had subsidized the creation of rival political organizations in the nation's overwhelmingly Democratic big cities.

This was compounded by Johnson's habit of ignoring "regular political leadership" in those cities in favor of "coordination with the so-called Big Six civil rights leaders." Hobart Taylor had been warning the president of problems on this front for three years to no avail. The White House found time to do little else but ask the FBI for name checks on "[Negro] elected officials" in the North's troubled cities.[67]

Lyndon Johnson did not need an explanation of "the *political implications*" which former FDR bird dog James Rowe and numerous other Democratic party strategists felt compelled to give. "Johnson was genuine in his concern for the poor and the blacks," Don Baker said, "a concern that rooted in his days teaching Chicano kids, seeing the hard time of the Texas hill country, and working with the New Deal. After he became president, he really undertook to do something. But he understood as well as anyone how the old sonofabitches over in the Senate can take advantage of bad publicity and do a lot of damage to programs. At the same time, he never quite approved of Community Action and never really approved the participation of the poor. He talked to Sarge about it. He was never sure we were doing the right thing in OEO." The riots hardened those doubts.[68]

The riots also hardened Johnson's soul. He embraced McClellan's notion that subversives and criminals had instigated the riots, and "having earned recognition as the country's preeminent civil libertarian" now seemed oddly determined "to become its chief of police" (McPherson's words). Desperately trying to hold the Democratic party's voting bloc together, the president dismissed the ghetto riots as the product of Marxist-Leninists, Trotskyites, Maoists. And he did so while trying to contain the growing conservative critique of his administration's policies. Edwin Willis, the Louisiana Democrat who chaired HUAC, reminded him of how effective old Republican party tactics might be in the present. "Just like some years ago the Republicans made a dent in the Democratic column on the false issue that Democrats were 'soft' on Communism, so I regret to say that in my opinion they will try to portray Democrats in general, and you in particular, as being 'soft' on law enforcement and respect for law and order."

Johnson had even less luck in countering such charges than Truman had twenty years earlier. (At least Truman won his election.) LBJ claimed the Community Action "red hots" and other left-wing critics of the Great Society (and Vietnam) were all revolutionaries or plain criminals. McClellan subcommittee supporters like Richard Nixon, who had experience with this sort of thing (having used the Alger Hiss case to discredit New Deal reform), said the revolutionaries and street thugs were all children of the Great Society. The radicals and Nixon had one thing in common: They were all critics of liberal reform.[69]

The president's descent into his own defensive version of law and order began with a push to convince the Justice Department and latest attorney general, Ramsey Clark, to arrest the most visible rabble rousers, Rap Brown and Stokely Carmichael. The FBI picked up Brown for inciting the Cambridge riot, taking the trouble (in Hoover's words) to have "a Negro Agent participate in the arrest." But there was nothing on which to base a warrant for Carmichael's arrest. "Johnson despised us at Justice," Roger Wilkins, then director of the Community Relations Service, remembered. "Because we wouldn't put Stokely Carmichael in jail." At the White House, John Roche came up with a bizarre alternate plan to neutralize him by planting "a rumor that Stokely is really white."[70]

Johnson himself attempted to resuscitate the McCarthy-era apparatus—particularly the Subversive Activities Control Board and the House Committee on Un-American Activities. He practically begged Cartha DeLoach, the usually accommodating FBI assistant director, to convince HUAC to subpoena Carmichael and CORE's Floyd McKissick. DeLoach declined. Since this committee's day had come and gone, he told the president, "hearings on McKissick and Carmichael might react to their advantage rather than hurting them." When LBJ suggested a leak to columnist Drew Pearson instead, DeLoach said he "doubted Person would print derogatory information concerning these characters." In this last case the president had included Martin Luther King's name.[71]

While proving more receptive to McClellan's OEO probe and otherwise pursuing its own agenda, the FBI also fed Johnson's paranoia by reminding him of the links between the civil rights and peace movements. King and "comrades," DeLoach began one Oval Office briefing, "had realized that there was more financial gain and more publicity in being in anti-Vietnam activities than in heading up civil rights drives. . . . The general public is gradually beginning to realize that the civil rights activities of these men have been phoney since the start."[72] The bureau supplemented this with a report, rushed to the White House at LBJ's request, detailing the linkage between the two movements. Hoover emphasized the Communist party's "massive effort to create a united front in opposition to United States military presence in Vietnam" and parallel efforts "to exploit racial issues and to create the chaos upon which communism flourishes."

"Vietnam," the FBI director's men concluded, "has racial overtones." In the months to come, then, bureau agents closely tracked not only Brown and Carmichael but the antiwar candidate for the Democratic party's presedential nomination, Eugene McCarthy, and his contacts with black activists. Interesting items, no matter how conspiratorial or misleading, were sent immediately to the White House and put to use. "You tend to view everything in terms of whether it hurts your Administration, your President and that sort of thing," McPherson explained. "Or helps. You look at almost nothing from the point of view of whether it's true or not." "The life of the White House is the life of a court," George Reedy agreed with a different twist. "The most important, and least examined, problem of the presidency is that of maintaining contact with reality."[73]

That attitude certainly dominated Johnson's last year in the White House. Following the antiwar movement's explosion in the wake of North Vietnam's Tet offensive and in anticipation of more summer ghetto rioting, the president gave the FBI free run even as he decided not to seek a second term. The bureau supplied most of the information for Attorney General Ramsey Clark's surveillance-state creation, the Interdivisional Intelligence Unit (IDIU). "A secret intelligence unit," Joseph Califano told LBJ, with an interest in "advance planning for summer riots" and "investigating Black Nationalist groups." Clark ordered Hoover to "use the maximum available resources, investigative and intelligence, to collect and report all facts bearing upon the question as to whether there has been or is a scheme or conspiracy by any group of whatever size, effectiveness or affiliation, to plan, promote, or aggravate riot activity." This included the development and expansion of "sources or informants in black nationalist organizations, SNCC and other less publicized groups." Even John Roche called it a "lunatic operation" that gave internal-security bureaucrats "an open-hunting license." Clark noted, simply, that "events outran leadership throughout the period that I was at Justice."[74]

While IDIU staff analyzed the FBI material for the purpose of predicting summer riots (what Johnson called "an advance warning system"), the bureau analyzed the same material for its own purposes. Hoover intended to put that data to use in a special counterintelligence program (COINTELPRO) designed "to expose, disrupt, misdirect, discredit, or otherwise neutralize the activities of black nationalist, hate-type organizations and groupings, their leadership, spokesmen, membership, and supporters." Targeting was indiscriminate, ranging from Black Panthers (Newton and Seale) to Baptist preachers (King and Abernathy). It included, as a COINTELPRO supervisor later admitted, "organizations that you might not today characterize as black nationalist but which were in fact primarily black."

Without President Johnson's direct knowledge, FBI agents carried out thousands of *ultra vires* and felonious dirty tricks against hundreds of activists. Any African American who could be seen or heard, in the bureau view, was part of a conspiracy to create "a real 'Mau Mau' in America." FBI officials had perhaps an even greater interest in audience than target. The overall intent was "to eliminate the facade of civil rights and show the American public the true revolutionary plans and spirit of the Black Nationalist movement and its leaders." The FBI director was thus among those who did the most damage to the president's civil rights legacy. Trusting Hoover until the end, Johnson never understood this.[75]

When Martin Luther King was assassinated on April 4, race rioting again shook the nation. The worst hit Washington. "Only two months after Tet," Clark Clifford, then secretary of defense, said. "It seemed as if we were experiencing our own national uprising. As I drove from my house to the Pentagon the morning after Dr. King's death, I could see the smoke rising from the inner city, only ten blocks from the White House." For the president, it was as if the Great Society itself had gone up in flames.[76]

While Johnson met, as ever, with Wilkins and Young, Senator Robert Kennedy "insisted," in the ever-snooping FBI's words, "upon holding a rally in the midst of one of the Negro ghetto areas in Indianapolis." Kennedy had come out against the Vietnam War and for the past year had battled the twin dragons of militarism and poverty—the result, in part, of what Marian Wright Edelman of the Child Development Group of Mississippi called "*a sort of epiphany.*" Wright remembered Kennedy with a baby on a delta shack's mud floor. "The baby was filthy, and it had a swollen, bloated belly, and Bobby sat there trying and trying to get that baby to respond, and he couldn't. It was one of the most moving things I've ever seen. You could see him get a sense of rage." If any white politician could walk safely in a black ghetto on the night King died, it was Robert Kennedy. He had now stolen the mantle Johnson coveted most. "How could it be?," the president repeated, now deep into his own permanent rage. "After all *I've* done."[77]

Another affront came with the Southern Christian Leadership Conference's decision to go ahead with the project King had been working on at the time of his death. The Poor People's Campaign, Andrew

Young explained, represented the politics of "symbolism," "a deliberate concentration of poverty and all its problems" in Resurrection City, the plywood and canvas encampment built near the Lincoln Memorial to house some 3,000 campaign participants. Congressman George Bush was among the few elected officials to tour the place. Another was Vice President Hubert Humphrey who also participated in the campaign's Solidarity Day march from the Washington Monument to the Lincoln Memorial. Most other government people, including the president, seemed most interested in the possibility of additional rioting and the apparent rise in street crime in and around the encampment. Bush, who had chatted amiably with Resurrection City residents, later reported back to his Texas constituents that he had told Ralph Abernathy and other organizers to tear the place down. For Johnson, Resurrection City was a reminder that he was no closer to winning the war on poverty (or crime) than the one in Vietnam.[78]

Law and order dominated the administration's agenda. White House staff devoted a great deal of time during summer 1968 to such things as making sure that state and local police had access, through the Defense Department, to tear gas supplies and other "nonlethal weapons." Even the Justice Department's Civil Rights Division focused on police functions. "With a corresponding curtailment," Assistant Attorney General Stephen Pollak said, "of our . . . [civil rights] enforcement programs." Hard-liners had won on every front, and liberals were on the run everywhere. The McClellan/Hoover version of the Omnibus Crime Control and Safe Streets Bill, legislation that Johnson reluctantly signed, included wiretapping provisions, McPherson complained, that could "turn any given town or state into a little soviet. All that is needed is the will of the D.A. and permissiveness on the part of the judge." Criminals seemed to be even more omnipresent. At the White House signing of an executive order on crime, a thief nipped Senator McClellan's hat in the presence of the attorney general and the heads of the FBI, Secret Service, Bureau of Narcotics, and Bureau of Drug Abuse Control. Rather than veto the distasteful omnibus legislation, Johnson vetoed Califano's suggestion that he give McClellan one of his Stetsons and then leak the hat-thief story to the press.[79]

The other major riot of 1968 occurred not at Resurrection City (which District police closed on June 24) but in Chicago, where the

Democrats gathered to nominate their presidential candidate. It was Chicago police and not ghetto blacks or New Left kids who launched that riot. In the convention hall, the ghosts of Atlantic City roamed. Nominee Hubert Humphrey requested, among other things, an FBI "team" of the sort that had once helped Johnson.[80] In Martin Luther King's absence the bureau continued to tap his widow. And when the Loyal Democrats of Mississippi successfully challenged the seating of the regular all-white delegation (the Atlantic City deal forbade racial discrimination in the selection process beginning with the Chicago convention), the bureau had five informants seated on the floor as delegates or alternate delegates. Hoover was better represented than Humphrey himself. "The Humphrey crowd again wanted a compromise," Joe Rauh said. "They wanted to put five [all-white] regulars on the delegation. . . . [But] we got the whole thing." More than he knew, in fact.[81]

Law and order in Chicago and throughout the country was a winning issue for the Nixon crowd. Everyone understood that the words themselves were the new code words for racism. "You can forget about the Vietnam war as an issue," an NBC pollster told a White House aide. "Race is the dominant issue without any question." The Nixon voter and as well those who tilted toward third-party candidate George Wallace were "really riled up at the violence caused by Negroes and in protest to the Government giving them too much." "More vitriolic mail in greater quantity," Califano confirmed, "had arrived at the Johnson White House on civil rights issues than on the Vietnam War." The 1960s had protestors of every stripe, and more common than the anti-war marchers and demonstrators were the white Catholics of Chicago's working- and middle-class neighborhoods and suburbs who put black buttons in the collection box whenever the parish priest gave a sermon that had something good to say about civil rights.

In his last months the president simply heard too many such stories from advisers who could only tell him to get tough on "well fed demagogues who speak for the 'poor.' " Or draft dodgers. Or Communists. Or "race-exploiters, and political outs who want to get in." There was no one left to encourage "the hidden reserve of decent people." Only the hidden reserve was being overshadowed by a visible resentment. And Nixon, who shared that resentment, could express it far better than Johnson. In spite of everything, LBJ retained too much of the liberal's soul. In the bitter retirement of the LBJ Ranch (where he took up chain smoking cigarettes again in what family and friends considered a pathetic attempt to pull death closer), he sympathized with the white South in one breath ("remember the Negroes in Reconstruction who got elected to Congress and then ran into the chamber with bare feet and white women"); and in the next with those blacks who set his cities ablaze ("God knows how little we've really moved on this issue, despite all the fanfare. As I see it, I've moved the Negro from D+ to C-. He's still nowhere. He knows it. And that's why he's out in the streets. Hell, I'd be there too").[82]

Ten years after Lyndon Johnson gave way to Richard Nixon an American Civil Liberties Union poll rated LBJ the "best civil libertarian president." He got nineteen points because of the Civil Rights Acts of 1964 and 1968, the Voting Rights Act of 1965, the Jury Selection and Service Act of 1968, and the executive order creating EEOC. Nixon got zero because of Watergate.[83] This ranking discounted the community surveillance aimed at everyday black people during Johnson's later White House tenure and as well the wiretaps and counterintelligence actions aimed at black leadership. It also overlooked a fundamental contradiction in pitting LBJ (best) against Nixon (worst). White House interest in spying on African Americans was greater under Johnson than Nixon because the Democratic party had a greater need to know what was happening. The Democratic electorate was black and white, the Republican electorate just white. The ACLU polled mostly white liberals—the enemies Nixon got into trouble for spying on. No one held the sin of spying on black people against either chief executive.

"You need to have been there at the time," Harry McPherson said in trying to explain the degeneration of Johnson's Great Society vision into the seedy reality of a surveillance state:

> Students are burning the American flag in the streets, campuses are turned into trash-America scenes, the faculties are united in celebrating Marxism, Maoism, the most benighted kind of left-wing radicalism. So you look for the money. You look for where money and support might be coming from just to help generate these views. Anti-American. You're in a war with a communist country and anytime anybody would suggest to you that

there's got to be foreign money and influence involved—malign, adversarial money and influence—it would be hard to turn it down right away. . . . [Johnson understood] that conditions are horrible in poor America, that people have a sense of outrage and all that. . . . [He tried] to ameliorate that with education and civil rights and he got race riots thrown in his face. Well, why should the response in the poorest of all poor areas be violence, unless it was being subsidized by your enemies? You do something for your children, you really give them time and attention and special counselling and you care for them and you really make a life as good as you possibly can, and they are venomous little bastards towards you and you wonder, 'How can this be? Someone has put them up against me.' . . . We felt both ways. We felt astonished and not a little bit enraged.[84]

In the end rage won out.

Race riots and Vietnam and his own paranoia destroyed Lyndon Johnson's dream of national and even global consensus. To speak of this president's triumph and tragedy is no cliché. Johnson once told Roy Wilkins, while still vice-president, that all mothers want the same things for their children. But he never quite understood that no mother, black or white, wanted her son to fight and die in a Southeast Asia jungle for a reason that the president himself could not articulate. "I've seen these kids all my life," he told his cabinet two months before Tet. "I've been with these poor children everywhere. I know that you can do better by them than the NYA or the Job Corps. Defense Department can do the job best. Go to it."[85]

For all the glory of the Second Reconstruction and the Great Society's new alphabet soup of war-on-poverty agencies, the president, worn out by the riots and militants, ended up in an odd place. His cabinet remark suggested that the Army, Navy, Air Force, and Marines could best help blacks and not OEO and Head Start. This could be interpreted as confirming what the militants had been saying, unfairly, all along—namely, that African Americans were viewed as nothing more than cannon fodder for the president's war in Vietnam. That cabinet remark, in fact, was merely the last progressive's version of TR's "ugh," the way this commander-in-chief declared himself too tired and too much at wit's end in dealing with problems along the color line.

: 7 :

DEMOGRAPHER

Richard Nixon (1969–1974) learned all he needed to know about race on the hard pines at Whittier College. His coach, former University of Southern California all-American Wallace ("Chief") Newman, taught the lesson. "I went out for football, basketball, baseball, and track, and never made a letter," Nixon wrote in his thousand-page memoir. "But I learned more about life from sitting on the bench with Chief Newman that I did getting 'As' in philosophy courses. . . . He never asked for re-spect because he was an American Indian. The fact that he was one of the best players of his time at USC earned our respect. He treated the two fine black players on our squad exactly the same as the white ones. . . . *No one was entitled to better treatment because he happened to be black. There was never a hint of racism on that team* [emphasis added]." Nixon had brought together the two timeless touchstones of the nation's political morality (its treatment of Negroes and Indians) and turned them over. Black and Native v. white, in sport metaphor, was "two against one" and therefore unfair. Chief Newman's lesson was not that reverse discrimination was the American dilemma's only evil, but that was the lesson learned by the attentive scrub.[1]

When Nixon moved on to study law at Duke, he discovered that not all blacks were as fortunate as the two on the Whittier squad. Rarely venturing beyond the classrooms and library, Nixon remained oblivious to Jim Crow and other unpleasant southern realities until he and a friend happened to be downtown one afternoon when the to-bacco plant workers changed shifts. "Pouring out of the factory doors like smoke from a furnace came thousands of blacks on their way home after work. They walked down one side of the street and we walked down the other. No one really seemed to think of them as individuals. They were just a mass. . . . Disraeli saw two nations, the rich and the poor, in nineteenth-century England. That day in Durham, North Carolina, I for the first time saw two nations, black and white, in twentieth-century America." What, if anything, could be done about this was a question that never crossed his mind—at the time or decades later. In his first White House year Nixon noted in amazement that "black students [had] seized the administration building at Duke and demanded a nongraded black education program and money for a black student union."[2]

Upon entering politics after the war Nixon still had no interest in acting on the greater evil—whether the largely phantom problem of re-verse discrimination (Whittier) or the reality of white over black (Durham). He mostly tried to avoid race altogether, only occasionally succumbing to temptations and acting in a dishonorable way. Not con-tent merely to Red-bait Jerry Voorhis in the 1946 race for the House, he made something of his opponent's staunch support for the Fair Em-ployment Practice Committee. Still, avoidance of racial issues was the chosen tack. These issues proved increasingly difficult to avoid, how-ever, as he rode Hiss-case glory up from the House Committee on Un-American Activities. During a 1950 Senate campaign stop, for ex-ample, he walked into an Oakland gym and an unexpected black audience. They might as well have been card-carrying Communists. "He saw it and cursed like a pirate," sometime adviser Adela St. Johns recalled, then went on somehow to make "a very good speech."

Later, when looking to balance his commie-bashing chores as Eisen-hower's vice-president (and hatchet man), Nixon surprised everyone by emerging as the administration's most progressive civil rights advocate after Herbert Brownell. His work on behalf of equal employment op-portunity as chair of the President's Committee on Government Contracts earned Martin Luther King's qualified praise and an hono-rary membership in a California NAACP chapter. (Nixon thought so little of the Contracts Committee assignment that it earned only one line in the thick memoir.) During the 1960 campaign he tried and failed to make peace both with his party's pro-civil rights Rockefeller wing and states' rights Goldwater wing. With neither avoidance of racial issues nor moderation on civil rights demands getting him anywhere, all that remained was the more radical choice between what he called "the extremists of both races."[3]

Nixon allowed a hint of racial moderation to surface only twice during the second run for the White House. Given what he had in mind for the campaign it took a certain amount of weird courage to ignore staff advice in April 1968 and go to Atlanta after Martin Luther King's assassination. Determined to pay his respects to King's family, he met the four children at the Auburn Avenue house and saw Coretta Scott King in her room. "I was moved by her poise and serenity," he said. Two days later he again ignored staff advice and returned to Atlanta for the funeral.[4] The second surfacing of what might be called racial moderation involved Nixon's promotion of "black capitalism." He promised, without offering any specific plans, to increase the number of black-owned businesses if elected.

Otherwise Nixon followed the advice of his advisers and courted the white majority, blending the seemingly contradictory Whittier and Duke lessons and making them the heart of a divisive, bean-counting message. He did so not necessarily because he was racist himself per se (although there is some sad evidence of that), but because he saw political fortune in the simple fact that there were more white people than black. He understood that resentment was *the* engine of American politics at a time when many doubted the myth of an ever-expanding middle class. Racism equaled opportunity in his calculus, a way to smash the New Deal coalition and realign the American political landscape now and forever to the Republican party's advantage. To turn a minority party into a majority party, he called upon the alchemy of race and the status-anxieties of people like himself.

Finally choosing between a policy of tackling racial problems head on (as he tried to do when chairing the Contracts Committee) or exploiting them for partisan purposes, Nixon became the white man's champion against the special pleadings and privileges of the blacks. It was a transparent attempt to pit the two nations he had first seen at

Durham's tobacco-factory gates against one another. If Lyndon Johnson began with a dream of healing racial divisions, Nixon ended with a dream of making those divisions permanent.

Social mobility remained at the heart of the Republican message in Nixon's time as it did in Lincoln's time. Race blocked the ladder up for the great white middle in the manner that the slave power had blocked the ladder up for the common people in the decades before Fort Sumter. Echoing Barry Goldwater's failed southern strategy of 1964, Nixon redefined liberalism as an elitist ideology that called for casting whites out of the middle class to make room for blacks. He also condemned liberalism's reform spirit for tolerating such threats to the middle class as riots, drugs, illegitimate births, welfare fraud, street crime, homosexual conduct, moral anarchy, and USA bashing. All subsidized, naturally, by the white middle's tax dollars. The liberal establishment thus became the new enemy of Nixon's divisive campaigning, replacing the corporate elite that had been the traditional target of populist politics. Ironically, the people Nixon claimed to speak for had something in common with the young blacks and students tearing up the cities and campuses. They all felt alienated, absolutely and utterly convinced that "the system" was impervious to their needs.[5]

Nixon took his cues from another racial alchemist, the true believer George Wallace, and his assaults on the courts, pointyheads, and bureaucrats with their bicycles, briefcases, and umbrellas. "They've looked down their noses at the average man on the street too long," the Alabama governor said during his second and suddenly serious third-party run for the presidency:

> They've looked at the bus driver, the truck driver, the beautician, the fireman, the policeman, and the steelworker, the plumber, and the communication worker, and the oil worker and the little businessman and they say, 'We've gotta write a guideline, We've gotta tell you when to get up in the morning, We've gotta tell you when to go to bed at night.' And we gonna tell both national parties the average man on the street in Tennessee and Alabama and California don't need anybody to write him a guideline to tell him when to get up.

Race was at the bottom of this message. "He can use all the other issues—law and order, running your own schools, protecting property rights—and never mention race," a fellow Alabama politician said. "But people will know he's telling them, 'A nigger's trying to get your job, trying to move into your neighborhood.' What Wallace is doing is talking to them in a kind of shorthand, a kind of code."[6]

Nixon spoke the same stilted code where "bloc vote" meant "black vote" and "neighborhood schools" meant "all-white schools." "Hard-core unemployed," "welfare cheats" and "laggards," and "muggers" and "rapists" and assorted other "street punks" meant black people generally. "The ideas expressed by George Wallace are the ideas a great many Republicans espouse," as Nixon's campaign coordinator in the South, Howard ("Bo") Callaway, plainly put it.[7]

Launching a frontal assault on "the general tone of American society and the growth of permissiveness," Nixon had an answer to the decade's basic paradox: Why had ghetto riots and a rise in crime, welfare dependency, illegitimacy, drug abuse, and joblessness followed the Great Society's civil rights revolution and expanded social-service entitlements? His answer was a simple one: There were no structural problems of race or class, only "excesses" caused by "the malaise of affluence" and bleeding heart liberalism. "Many political figures in this country have promised too much with the passage of each new piece of social and civil-rights legislation," he warned. "It is both wrong and dangerous to make promises that cannot be fulfilled, or to raise hopes that come to nothing." That was the campaign's basic theme. Black expectations had risen and now had to be pushed down.

"Ours is becoming a lawless society," Nixon said with Johnson still in the White House. "Permissiveness," "indulgence," and "sympathy for the past grievances of those who have become criminals" produced "the doctrine that when a law is broken, society, not the criminal, is to blame." "Violence must be suppressed," he continued, especially the violence of "the poor, the ignorant, and the irresponsible." These were the "new criminals," blacks and students who learned from liberals in high places that "each individual should determine what laws are good and what laws are bad." Nixon promised law and order, and many expected the coming crackdown to go beyond the poor, the ignorant, and the irresponsible to the government's social engineers. "When you pay your income taxes after you figure them all out, pay an additional five hundred dollars," LBJ advised Joseph Califano on his last night in the

White House. "It's not enough for Nixon to win. He's going to have to put some people in jail."[8]

Nixon's first campaign priority was to neutralize the remnants of racial moderation within the Republican party. The prevailing political winds combined with the self-destruction of the civil rights faction's leader to make the task relatively easy. During the Miami convention the *Miami Herald* ran an ad laid out like a memorandum from "Black America" to the delegates expressing disgust at Nixon's record. William F. Buckley, Jr., recovering from a broken collarbone in a yachting accident but well enough to be in town for a debate with Gore Vidal, said that the ad's "Black America" was one white man—Nelson Rockefeller. When Rockefeller laughed off a reporter's follow-up ("we ought to recognize that Mr. Buckley had an unfortunate fall on the boat"), Buckley "beamed at the [television] set, 'You'll be sorry, Governor.'" He confirmed that Rockefeller's staff supplied the money and names for the ad without bothering to request permission. Louis Armstrong, Lionel Hampton, Charles Evers, Marian Anderson, and other "signers" protested the fraudulent use of their names.[9]

With Rockefeller reeling Nixon turned to the Goldwater wing's candidate, Ronald Reagan, and his effort to steal the Republican nomination. To prevent a midnight run of southern delegates, Nixon met with those delegates and promised a go-slow approach on civil rights. His pledges, secretly tape recorded by the *Miami Herald*, included opposition to federal open-housing legislation, court-ordered busing, and virtually any other racial-justice initiative that might arise. "The first civil right," Nixon added, was "to be free from domestic violence," and on this front he also pledged to put "real men" on the courts and into the vice-presidency and attorney generalship. Unlike Democratic candidate Hubert Humphrey, this candidate had no interest in "satisfying some professional civil rights group." By the time Nixon took the podium for his acceptance speech on "Forgotten Americans," the police had killed three blacks while Liberty City burned across Biscayne Bay.[10]

The importance of the Miami convention's southern delegates cannot be overstated. Goldwater had run well in the South in 1964, and convention rules apportioned delegate votes to the states according to their performance in the last election. Given the bonus votes to the five southern states that had gone for Goldwater, plus Texas, one border state (Maryland), and Goldwater's Arizona, the numbers added up to 414 of the 667 votes needed to nominate. The candidate could count and knew what had to be done for his own good if not the nation's. "Here was the birth of the Southern strategy," wrote columnists Rowland Evans and Robert Novak, "conceived in necessity" and "gradually taking on the trappings of grand political doctrine under the guidance of John Mitchell."[11]

Nixon shaped his southern strategy with George Wallace in mind as much as those Miami delegates—for the obvious reason that the governor's American Independent party candidacy might split the right-of-center vote and hand the election to the Democrats. Nixon's solution at the convention and in the campaign that followed, as countless observers noted, was an unqualified appeal to the Wallace voter. In the manner in which Truman had flaunted his New Deal credentials to counter Henry Wallace twenty years earlier, Nixon flaunted his law-and-order credentials to counter George Wallace. The difference was that Truman compared himself to FDR while Nixon compared himself to an Alabama politician already on record as promising never to be out-niggered in any campaign for any office. Nixon did not blame Wallace for being Wallace and putting the campaign in the gutter; he merely resented the man for forcing him to share it. He wanted the gutter all to himself.

Nixon knew where the votes were and understood both the numbers and history. Despite his party's success from Lincoln to Hoover (interrupted only by Cleveland and Wilson), the Republicans had never been a true national party. From the Roosevelt administration forward this became painfully obvious. The Democrats began each election with a lock on the South and thus had no need to win a majority in the rest of the country. The Republicans had to win big outside the South and as a result usually concentrated on the large electoral blocs in the East. Beginning with the Dixiecrats in 1948, however, the solid South started to crumble—a process accelerated not only by the race issue but the erosion of blind rebel loyalty through such homogenizing forces, among others, as suburbanization and industrialization. Unable to compete with Democrats in the traditional centers of urban liberalism, Goldwater and then Nixon ignored the Northeast.

This southern strategy remained oddly true to Republican roots. The party had come to power in 1860 without the South and would come to power again in 1968 more or less without another region of the country. (Nixon took New Hampshire, Vermont, New Jersey, and Delaware.) In addition, Nixon intended, as Lincoln had, to use patronage and other federal largess (defense contracts and construction funds) to build a southern GOP.[12]

Nixon relied on South Carolina Senator Strom Thurmond, the former Democrat and Dixiecrat and now Republican whom Evans and Nowak called the candidate's "great Southern vassal." He also worked with Mississippi Senators James Eastland and John Stennis and virtually every other segregationist politician of stature regardless of party affiliation. "The Southern white leaders, as the detached and analytical Nixon was able to see, were not bigoted 'segs,'" *New York Times* writer Tom Wicker concluded with unbelievable charity. "They were honorable men, victims of history, confronting a problem that most Americans did not have to face." For his part Nixon did not mind the label. He later blamed "Goldwater's rhetoric. . . . Republicans had always been tagged as reactionary, but after his campaign we were portrayed as reckless and racist." There was no virtue, political or otherwise, in recklessness. Political virtue lay only in the new coded racism, and during his own campaign Nixon cultivated a whiter-than-the-other-guy image consciously and consistently.[13]

Nixon's men always denied the charge of racism with a wink. Harry S. Dent, the Thurmond protégé and self-described "full-bred southern white boy" from John C. Calhoun County who walked point for the candidate on this issue, said "the national press could never understand that for most Southerners in the Republican Southern strategy movement, the motivation was not racial." It was strictly political. Nixon could not hope to capture the black vote, Dent continued, so he "was virtually forced—as he would say—'to hunt where the ducks are.'" Again, numbers, not race, ruled. "Nobody is being written out, the South is only being written in," Dent told Nixon, who responded: "Exactly right *theme*." "The fact is," Dent concluded, mistaking the obvious for irony, that "the Democratic party is the one with the racial problem. It swings between love and hate for the Wallecites."[14]

Nixon took Dent's advice, spending no time or money trying to get black votes in the South or anywhere else. Nor did he spend time and money reminding white voters of the Democratic party's history of peaceful coexistence with racism (the love side of its relationship with Wallace backers). On the other hand the Nixon campaign spent a great deal of time and money getting out another reminder—namely, that the Democrats swung between love for and infatuation with blacks. "Substantial Negro support is not necessary to national Republican victory," announced Kevin Phillips, campaign manager John Mitchell's expert on ethnic voting patterns. "The GOP can build a winning coalition without Negro votes. Indeed, *Negro-Democratic mutual identification* was a major source of Democratic loss—and Republican or American Independent Party profit—in many sections of the country [emphasis added]."

Campaign funds were best spent getting out the message that the Democrats were "a black party" (just as the Republicans had been labeled a black party in the South during Reconstruction). Once the message took, Phillips predicted, "white Democrats will desert their party in droves." Supremely confident, he even called George Wallace a plus "in the long run" because "people will ease their way into the Republican party by way of the American Independents. . . . We'll get two thirds to three fourths of the Wallace vote in nineteen seventy two." (If Nixon had been this serene he might have spared himself Watergate.) Only one thing tried Phillips's confidence. "There will be no landslide this year," he said. "No charisma. The only mystique that can be built around Nixon is a mystique of the non-mystique."[15]

Bronx Irish and educated at Colgate and Harvard Law, Phillips used his racial analysis to divide and conquer. Even after the election, he argued, "abandonment of civil rights enforcement would be self-defeating" because "maintenance of Negro voting rights in Dixie, far from being contrary to GOP interests, is essential if southern conservatives are to be pressured into switching to the Republican Party." Even with a change of administration, moreover, the Democrats would still be blamed for any pro-Negro policies that might be necessary to prevent a possible uprising in the nation's ghettos. "[With] the *national* Democratic Party . . . becoming the Negro party through most of the

South," Phillips predicted that the GOP would be able to work freely not only among that region's whites but among Northern suburbanites and Catholics alienated by "liberalism's upscale transformation . . . into a cultural and intellectual elite" of "well-paid professionals pontificating from remote comfort." Pontificating, that is, on behalf of black people and at the expense of white people.[16]

Just as Dent had called the southern strategy a "movement," Phillips saw the pieces as part of a larger whole. "The clamor in the past has been from the urban or rural proletariat," he said. "But now 'populism' is of the middle class, which feels exploited by the Establishment. Almost everyone in the productive segment of society considers himself middle-class now, and resents the exploitation of society's producers. This is not a movement *in favor of* laissez faire or any ideology; it is *opposed* to welfare and the Establishment." This new populism elevated "certain rules of exclusion." In New York, for example, Phillips held that no candidate could "get the Jews *and* the Catholics." On the national level "the same kind of basic decision has to be made. . . . Who needs Manhattan when we can get the electoral votes of eleven Southern states? Put those together with the Farm Belt and the Rocky Mountains, and we don't need the big cities. We don't even want them. Sure, Hubert will carry Riverside Drive in November. La-de-dah. What will he do in Oklahoma?" "The whole secret of politics," Phillips reiterated, "[is] knowing who hates who." With every campaign sage agreed that whites hated blacks, that is where the candidate and his men went duck hunting. Who needed the black vote when you can get the white vote.[17]

Having promised the Miami delegates a vice-president they would like, Nixon delivered someone who understood Kevin Phillips's secret. Spiro T. Agnew, the Maryland governor with the wrap-around hair and tube suits, was exactly what Garry Wills said he was—Nixon's Nixon. Where the old Nixon had Red-baited Democrats for Eisenhower-era Republicans, Agnew baited blacks and kids—proving himself a crude specialist in the art of "positive polarization." "It is time to rip away the rhetoric and to divide on authentic lines," he announced after the election. "When the President said 'bring us together' he meant the functioning, contributing portions of the American citizenry." If those portions made up a majority, they included only the white and the silent—the people who slapped on the "Spiro Is My Hero" bumper stickers that Bo Callaway distributed. "Dividing the American people has been my main contribution to the national political scene," the governor explained. "I not only plead guilty to this charge, but I am somewhat flattered by it." As Dent later put it to the boss, "The Southerners like him, and he gets through to them very effectively" because his main polarization chore pit white against black. "*Good*," Nixon responded.[18]

Agnew rose in ten years from the vice-presidency of the Kiwanis Club to the vice-presidency of the United States. The Cambridge riot on the Eastern Shore over the Choptank River provided an early opportunity to show his hard-line credentials by bringing in the National Guard. In the aftermath Agnew got in the habit of playing over and over again for reporters and other office visitors a police tape of Rap Brown's incendiary pre-riot speech. If he knew few Maryland blacks personally beyond Rev. Robert Newbold and Dr. Gilbert Ware, he knew a great deal about the militants thanks to the intelligence reports supplied by state police chief and former FBI man Robert Lally. More recognition came with his fiscal year 1969 budget which incited protest marches by welfare mothers in Baltimore. (Paul Sarbanes called it the "East Coast version of the Ronald Reagan budget.") When some 250 Bowie State students marched on the state house and asked to meet with Agnew, he ordered Lally to arrest them and close that all-black school.

Agnew caught Nixon's eye after racial disturbances hit Baltimore. He identified the city's moderate civil rights leadership as the source of all evil, focusing for some unknown reason on an earlier meeting at the Emmanuel Christian Community Church. The moderates were concerned about the rising militancy of people like Robert Moore, a SNCC red-hot who had opened an office in February and ran about condemning the city's war on crime as a war on the black man. State Senator Parren Mitchell and others came to the meeting hoping to cool things down and present a united black front, but the affair quickly degenerated into a name calling contest between "extremists" and "Uncle Toms." From there Agnew seized on Stokely Carmichael's appearance in Baltimore on April 3, the day before King's assassination, finding the visit especially sinister even though Carmichael apparently did little more than meet with friends at a bar. Finally, on April 11, two days after King's funeral and after the riots had been contained, Agnew called for a meeting with "responsible Negroes" at the State Office Building. Of the hundred who showed up none expected what the conspiracy-prone governor delivered.

"We did not know the cameras would be there, turning this into a show," State Senator Verda Welcome said. "We thought it was meant as a meeting of reconciliation." That was the last thing Agnew had in mind. "I did not request your presence to bid for peace with the public dollar," he began, then went right for this roomful of moderate blacks. "But when white leaders openly complimented you for your objective, courageous action [in criticizing SNCC's burn-baby-burn rhetoric] you immediately encountered a storm of censure from parts of the Negro community. . . . *And you* ran." At that eighty of the hundred walked out. "Nobody calls me a coward," fumed Parren Mitchell, head of the city's poverty program. "I had gone forty-eight hours without sleep, walking streets at war, trying to calm them." Agnew, still rolling, aimed the other barrel at those who stayed. "You met in secret with that demagogue [SNCC's Robert Moore] . . . and you agreed that you would not openly criticize any black spokesman, regardless of the content of his remarks."

With the room down to a handful of blacks, Agnew laid out his conspiracy theory. "The looting and rioting which has engulfed our city during the past several days did not occur by chance. It is no mere coincidence that a national disciple of violence, Mr. Stokely Carmichael, was observed meeting with local black-power advocates and known criminals in Baltimore on April 3, 1968, three days before the riots began." If Agnew had thought this "conspiracy" through, he might have realized that it could be true only if Carmichael and King's murderer were in cahoots. The assassination on April 4 sparked the riots, not Carmichael's preriot beers in a city bar.

"That reckless incredible statement of April 11 made Agnew Vice-President," Garry Wills concluded. In the aftermath of the State Office Building meeting, when someone asked the governor, "What if everybody had walked out?," he replied: "I would simply have been faced with a situation where I would have to find other Negro leaders." This was truly someone who could be Nixon's Nixon. Later, in the heat of the presidential race, Wills asked Nixon if he could reach blacks and bring peace back to the cities. "Well, you have to be conceited to be in this business, and this will sound conceited," he responded. "But I think I could do it as well as any man. I'm very good at one-to-one relationships." The last man in America who could have brought peace to the cities was Spiro Agnew, and that was who Nixon chose because the last thing he wanted was peace between the races. The southern strategy demanded not peace but resentment.[19]

Nixon had his urban expert, someone to go South with Harry Dent and Bo Callaway and stay out of Baltimore's segregated neighborhoods and every other American ghetto (because "once you've seen one slum, you've seen them all"). Someone to hammer the rioters' liberal benefactors who did not understand the civilizing effects of such things as police brutality. "In my judgement," Agnew later told John Ehrlichman at the White House, "nothing makes the average American any angrier than to see the pained, self-righteous expressions of a Muskie or a Percy as they attach like leeches to the nearest Negro funeral procession." When Ehrlichman passed this up, Nixon said, simply, "I agree." Yet Nixon treated Agnew with the same contempt that he himself had experienced at Eisenhower's hand. After the election returns came in he asked Ehrlichman and H. R. Haldeman: "How much did Agnew hurt us?"[20]

For their own reasons everyone from the civil rights community to both the outgoing and incoming administrations expected the worst.[21] It was in the cities where the changing administrations expected trouble. When Nixon's men arrived in the White House they received a stack of blank executive orders from LBJ's people declaring martial law. All they needed to do was fill in date and name of city. Even those who were not quite so pessimistic on the matter of future riots managed to put a chilling twist on things. "That cycle's over," Kevin Phillips said. "If there are any more [riots], we might have to choose a key city, bring in the troops, and just cream 'em. That will settle it." Having promised law and order, the new president would deliver (in Malcolm X's words) by any means necessary.[22]

Vice President Spiro Agnew, FBI Director J. Edgar Hoover, Attorney General John Mitchell, and National Security Adviser Henry Kissinger rounded out Nixon's Negro question experts. Mitchell had his pet projects (e.g., using "computer power" to bring Department of Justice "operations into this Century"), but was most interested in image projection. "There existed in fact," as Edward Jay Epstein noted, "a curious coincidence of interests between the Nixon strategists, who wanted to depict a *hard-line* attorney general, and their political opponents, who wanted to depict a *repressive* attorney general. Journalistic attacks . . . which emphasized the dramatic differences between Attorneys General Ramsey Clark and John Mitchell in their administration of justice, played willy-nilly into the bête-noire strategy by heightening the repressive image of the new attorney general." When Jeffery Donfeld, assistant to Egil ("Bud") Krogh at the White House, worried about the repressive charge, Krogh told him, "Don't you think those guys know what they're saying!" "They weren't trying to correct [it]," Donfeld finally realized. "It was all a matter of perspective . . . a tough image was exactly what they wanted."[23]

Given that the days of respectable racism were over, the Nixon administration walked a thin line here. White House and Justice Department rhetoric on civil rights held that discrimination was morally, legally, and socially wrong and had to be "substantially eliminated if we are to survive as a nation of free and independent people." Yet Mitchell, the man who spoke those words, told a group of civil-rights workers concerned about the new "repressive" image that they had nothing to fear: "You will be better advised to watch what we do instead of what we say." "In the Administration's plans," Jonathan Schell wrote, "the words would deceive the civil-rights workers, and the actions would deceive the Southern segregationists, and in the process the political onus for integration would shift from the executive branch of government to the legislative and judicial branches."[24]

John Mitchell got along especially well with Nixon's other top-cop Negro question expert. In contrast to Ramsey Clark ("a jellyfish . . . a softie"), FBI Director J. Edgar Hoover considered his new boss an "honest, sincere and very human man. . . . There has never been an attorney general for whom I've had higher regard." Patricia Collins, a Justice Department lawyer who worked under fourteen attorneys general, said "they were the same kind, actually. Hoover was a Republican from beginning to end."[25] Mitchell and Nixon were both fond of telephoning Hoover and rambling about law and order—an almost comic series of ruminations on sex, drugs, and rock and roll. In Nixon's case these topics included "jigs." The director recorded his conversations with the president from time to time, later dictating summaries in memorandum form, and the more serious concerned such things as the need to put a "real man" on the Supreme Court, reform the prison system ("country clubs"), and apply the death penalty to an ever-expanding assortment of crimes. "The President said," according to one of Hoover's accounts, that "[I should] stir up this thing on capital punishment . . . and if I see they are not doing something, to let him know as he is going to ride herd."[26]

On occasion Nixon shared his national security adviser's wisdom on such things as draft resistance with the FBI director. Again, Hoover's account: "He said Dr. Kissinger was in today and told him he was concerned because if it gets going in this country, we might have some sort of breakout in Viet Nam. The President said if that happens, that is what brings down governments, for example, the Russian revolution as I would recall, when the troops turned on their commanders." National Security Council staff member William Watts had in fact warned Kissinger that the White House plan to escalate the Vietnam War (the so-called November plan) might lead to a "black and ghetto population" uprising at home. Combined with the ever-present problem of college students protesting the war, Watts said, "the Administration would probably be faced with handling domestic dissension as brutally as it administered the November plan."[27]

Nixon and Kissinger cared as little about racial justice abroad as Hoover and Mitchell did at home. When not on the phone with the director discussing Pentagon "employees who are still McNamara people and express a very definite Kennedy philosophy," Kissinger pursued what he and the president called the "tar baby" option (which accepted the permanence of white rule in southern Africa). He also cheered on William Buckley's and then Daniel Patrick Moynihan's ritual defiance of the United Nations. Newspaper columnist Chuck Stone called Moynihan "the apostle of 'benign neglect' for blacks and contempt for all Third World countries." (Moynihan had called the UN a "theater of the absurd.") Kissinger's ego was big enough, in any event, to produce a jealous fit over the excellent press coverage given to Secretary of State William Rogers's African trip. A phone call from

Nixon calmed him down: "Henry, let's leave the niggers to Bill and we'll take care of the rest of the world."[28]

Those remarks were no aberration. Once in Key Biscayne, home to one black (the island's "garden man"), Kissinger and staff worked on a draft of the first presidential message to Congress on foreign policy while Nixon was at play with Bebe Rebozo and Robert Abplanalp on Rebozo's yellow houseboat. When telephoning ship-to-shore for an update, Nixon told Kissinger to "make sure there's something in it for the jigs." A minute later he asked again: "Henry . . . *is* there something in it for the jigs?" Kissinger assured him that there was. The president constantly used the words "nigger" and "jigaboo" in his phone calls; and if Kissinger constantly complained about such pejoratives to his staff he tolerated much the same thing in his West Basement office at the White House. Roger Morris, the NSC aide who came up helping Walt Rostow and the Kennedys on African affairs, remembered the response at the rare staff meetings that dealt with such things. "[Alexander] Haig would begin to beat his hands on the table, as if he was pounding a tom-tom. It was all very manly—a locker-room mentality. Haig would make Tarzan jokes." And everyone would laugh. "You couldn't find . . . subjects less important [to Kissinger]," Morris complained, "and more the object of ridicule."[29]

Andrew Young, later the Carter administration's UN ambassador, said a flaw "in Henry Kissinger's equation was that he couldn't understand something that W. E. B. Du Bois wrote in 1903: That the problem of the 20th Century is the problem of the color line." That a German Jew would ignore or even condone racism ("one of the most powerful dynamics in the world") was troubling but hardly surprising or unprecedented. Young continued, comparing Ralph Bunche to Kissinger: "A lot of his energy went into not being black and trying to assimilate. I think that the horrors of racism in Kissinger's childhood were so terrible that in order to function, he had to put it behind him. Otherwise, he would have been so bitter and filled with hate that he never could have done anything else." So Kissinger just sat at the table in the White House basement, laughing with everyone else as Haig pounded the table top and told his Tarzan jokes.[30]

Martin Luther King's memory brought Nixon's Negro question experts together. Agnew, Mitchell, and Kissinger all received a steady stream of derogatory FBI material from Hoover on the slain civil rights leader's "highly immoral personal behavior." Nearly a dozen others in and around the Oval Office were on this mailing list, too, including the immensely unpopular Haldeman and Ehrlichman. ("The Germans," as Harry Dent and other southern strategists referred to them.) Nevertheless the bureau's mailing list was hardly broad enough and the material itself never quite sufficient to satisfy the administration's appetite. File envy at lower levels of the White House was so rampant that Hoover filed a grievance. All the requests for dossiers, in his view, amounted to harassment of the FBI. When Egil Krogh put in his request for the dirt on King, the director scribbled an angry order: "Tell [him] they already have it."

Hoover was more accommodating when dealing with the men at the top. To supplement the written reports and weekly *FBI Racial Digest* sent to the White House, he occasionally briefed Nixon personally. "[King's] basic problem was he liked white girls," Ehrlichman recalled. "I do remember Hoover parading a good bit of very persuasive evidence." The bureau was on guard against everything. When Postmaster General Winton Blount came under some pressure to issue a King commemorative stamp, he turned to Hoover and received a dossier. In response to the larger campaign to have Congress declare King's birthday a national holiday, Kissinger received an even thicker dossier "in order that [he] can bring it to the President's personal attention."[31]

Nixon and Mitchell approved the continuation of the wiretap on Stanley Levison because Levison still advised Coretta Scott King, Ralph Abernathy, and other Southern Christian Leadership Conference figures. Hoover offered the attorney general the following example of the tap's value on the southern strategy front: "The installation provided data regarding a contact between Andrew Young . . . and Levison in which they discussed the sending of a team to Columbia, South Carolina, to organize against the scheduled visit to that city of President Nixon." Levison also suggested that Mrs. King, when requesting a White House meeting to discuss "a proposed memorial center commemorating Martin Luther King, Jr.," take the line "that it is not a question of asking . . . for a favor but rather that the Federal Government owes it to the Negro." (Kissinger was also alerted here.) This latest of the many Levison taps dating to 1954 continued until the original

King wiretaps surfaced at Muhammad Ali's draft evasion trial. Hoover subsequently pulled the surveillance, he told Mitchell, because "information has been sparse and nonpertinent."[32]

Nixon kept Coretta King at arm's length. Arthur Burns and Leonard Garment recommended that the president stop in Atlanta on his way for a Florida rest and meet with Mrs. King on Good Friday, but Patrick Buchanan reminded him that it would send the wrong message to his white constituency. "It would outrage many, many people who believe Dr. King was a fraud and a demagogue, and perhaps worse. Dr. King *is one of the most divisive men in contemporary American history*—some believe him a Messiah, others consider him the devil incarnate." In either case, Buchanan reiterated, King had "background"—"if we can believe our friends in the Bureau." With Haldeman and Ehrlichman also against a visit with Mrs. King, the president listened to his staff this time (in contrast to his decision to pay his respects following the assassination). He skipped Atlanta and went directly to Key Biscayne for his vacation.[33]

Nixon's fourth Negro question expert, Spiro Agnew, was the most aggressive in soliciting FBI material. Concerned about the continuing push for a national holiday, he asked Hoover to supply "the details" regarding Martin Luther King. "The Vice President said he would like to be thoroughly conversant with all of that," the director noted when promising to send over "the highlights" within "the next 24 to 48 hours," "because if the crisis comes where we need to throw it, he will." The two men also commiserated on Kent State, where the FBI had been called in to determine whether the Ohio National Guard had abused the civil rights of thirteen white students by killing four and wounding nine. "Six of one and half a dozen of another," Hoover told Agnew, "as you can't say it is proper to shoot, but we found at Kent that they were throwing 7 pound rocks at the soldiers and they hit one Guardsman in the back and knocked him down. There is just so much a human being can stand." The bureau's own investigation failed to substantiate this and was critical of the Guardsmen who fired.[34]

In another wild knee-jerk reaction Hoover told Agnew that "sniper fire on the troops" provoked the Mississippi State Police fusillade at a Jackson State dormitory that killed two students and wounded twelve. Both men sided with the police, who described the victims as "nigger

gals" and "nigger males"; the Hinds Country grand jurors who exoner-
ated the troopers; and a Kennedy judge, Harold Cox, who said students
participating in civil disorders "must expect to be injured or killed."
Such notions, Nixon's own Commission on Campus Unrest concluded,
"may reflect the views of many Americans today." No one understood
this better than the men in the White House. When the commission
condemned the shootings as "an unreasonable, unjustified overreaction"
to chants ("Pig! Pig! Pig!") and obscenities ("Motherfucker"), the vice-
president dismissed the report as "pablum for the permissivists."[35]

Agnew was particularly aggressive in requesting FBI assistance in
"destroying Ralph Abernathy's credibility." With racial disturbances in
Georgia coming hard on the heels of the Jackson State killings, the vice-
president was enraged by the SCLC leader's "inflammatory
pronouncements" and immediately phoned up Hoover—who agreed
that Abernathy was "one of the worst." Again, the director best captured the rambling logic behind the request:

> He said in view of what went on in Augusta and other places it is
> important to have information . . . [documenting] the involvement of
> these people, what information we have, whether fleeing from looting
> or what is going on. . . . He saw a picture about Augusta showing some
> of the Negroes jumping out of store windows with loot and booty and
> fleeing and you never hear anything about that [from the media]. He
> said whatever I can give him that can ameliorate some of the impact;
> that he understands some of these things are wrong and we are probably
> going to find some of the [police] shootings showed too much force,
> but nonetheless . . . [they never show] what happened before—why did
> they shoot at them—not just because they felt like killing people.

Agnew ended his strange monologue by again asking for every possible
assistance in destroying Abernathy's credibility. "I would be glad to,"
the FBI director responded.[36]

This was all part of Nixon's southern strategy, what Agnew aide Kent
Crane called a mission to go below the Mason-Dixon line and "put the
red flag up on" Abernathy and other "characters." Here and elsewhere,
Crane told one of the director's assistants, the FBI material was destined
for the vice-president's "big speeches in the South." Hoover, in turn,
was Agnew's number one fan. "The President can't say some of the

things the Vice President can," he told Crane. "I think the Vice President today is one of the most popular figures in the country largely because he spoke out and named names. . . . Mr. Crane commented that 'you two' are birds of a feather, and I said I was glad to be in that company." The FBI director, after all, had been a southern strategist for nearly all of his half century of civil service.[37]

With his Negro question experts in place and an eye on the 1972 re-election campaign, Nixon moved through the first term in a predictable manner. His appeals to the Wallace voter included a call for no-bail and preventive detention legislation in the District of Columbia, and those "reforms" eventually became part of the White House crime-control package on the grounds that if all federal courts applied them defendants who would otherwise be out committing crimes could be kept in jail. Because it began with the District, heavily black and crime ridden, no one had any illusions about the message or the intent. "One more way of making second-class citizens," Tom Wicker concluded. "One more way of reacting punitively to the victims of conditions that breed and even encourage crime and violence, rather than of launching any real or effective attack upon those conditions." Whitney Young emphasized the racist precedent for the proposals: the World War II internment of Japanese-Americans.[38]

From preventive detention Nixon moved against two of the civil rights movement's greatest victories, *Brown* and the Voting Rights Act of 1965. To avoid a southern filibuster original supporters of the voting rights bill had agreed to limit its life to five years—long enough, it was hoped, to provide southern blacks a grip that could not be loosened. Because the law applied only to particular counties in seven deep-South states, Mitchell announced that he could not "support what amounts to regional legislation." The administration lost that fight when Congress extended the Voting Rights Act. On the matter of *Brown* both the Justice Department and HEW petitioned the federal courts for further delay in desegregating Mississippi's thirty-three school districts. When the Supreme Court rejected the idea in *Alexander v. Holmes County* and ordered desegregation to proceed "at once," the White House saw a small victory nonetheless because the onus for immediate integration and its consequences now clearly lay with the courts. This fit Dent's southern strategy perfectly. "We should insure that whatever blame emanates from the South is placed elsewhere," he told the president, "than on the back of this Administration."[39]

Activist judges sympathetic to black demands made a perfect target. They were of the Establishment from whom Nixon had promised the white middle protection, and it was victory enough to show the president doing battle with them over *Brown* and the Voting Rights Act. "[He] had moved to undercut the two main pillars of the civil-rights movement," as Jonathan Schell observed, "but in a manner that would predictably fail." That was the goal all along. The president wanted *manageable* division and bitterness between the races, not the chaos that would have followed unqualified success on such explosive fronts. "The racial issue was both a problem and an opportunity," Ehrlichman explained. "[If] the President . . . [had an] interest in trying to keep the Negroes and the white South happy" (Dent's words), the overriding goal was not to placate Negroes in order to avoid domestic violence but to show white America North and South where he stood on the crunch issues of jobs, housing, crime, schools (Ehrlichman's point).[40]

While the voting rights battle came and went, school desegregation emerged as the administration's most important and enduring (anti-) civil rights crusade. Nixon knew this would be so early on. HEW had established "guidelines" in 1966 to enforce desegregation under the Civil Rights Act of 1964, with the threat to cut federal education funds under the Primary and Secondary Education Act of 1965 providing a compliance incentive. By election day 1968 Nixon's people already felt "sandbagged." Dozens of desegregation suits from the Kennedy and Johnson years had finally worked their way through the system, and during the transition period several southern school districts ignored federal orders to desegregate (stalling in the hope that the orders would be withdrawn after the inauguration). Nixon's first month in office, however, brought disappointment to those school districts as HEW and the Civil Rights Division kept on as if Lyndon Johnson still sat in the White House. "A new Administration couldn't turn things around here even if it wanted to," one division attorney noted. "The self-perpetuating mechanism of the law makes any basic change unlikely." Division chief Jerris Leonard, a member of the all-white Order of the

Eagles back in his home state of Wisconsin, filed nine new desegregation suits (all approved by John Mitchell).

By mid-February 1969 the new South's new Republicans had seen enough. Enraged party chairs from the Old Confederacy's eleven states met in Atlanta, of all places (when last in Atlanta a hundred years ago the Republicans "burned it down," noted a rising Jimmy Carter), and they unanimously accused the new president of the United States of betraying the region that had put him in office. "I asked why they (Southern Chairmen) can't see the President and hold a news conference at the White House like Roy Wilkins," Dent reported. "They say 'we supported him and Wilkins fought him.'" With "southern fever running high" and "'Tricky Dick' editorials" appearing in the region's newspapers, Dent stressed school desegregation as the most pressing issue. Strong enough, perhaps, to spark a second southern revolt in another four years. Unless convinced "that this will not be a wild Administration on the subject of guideline implementation," Dent reiterated, all eleven states represented at the Atlanta meeting might cast their votes in 1972 for George Wallace.[41]

Nixon and Mitchell got the point. Ignoring Dent's bizarre suggestion for taking the mind of the South off the schools and putting it on the president as cop (he wanted Mitchell to nail "a character like Stokely Carmichael"), they embarked instead on a dual strategy of dumping some school desegregation suits and weakening others. They also brought Jerris Leonard around. "The South," the former Wisconsin congressman had said, "I'm so goddamn tired of hearing about the South. When is somebody going to start worrying about the North? That's where the votes are." Mitchell took "corrective action" (at Nixon's direction), and after that Leonard supported the southern strategy. "Like a good German," one of his line lawyers complained. The attorney general made it clear, moreover, that more was at stake than the Wallace vote below the Mason-Dixon line. With the courts leaning toward "forced busing" as the method to achieve integration, the schools might prove more explosive in cities like Leonard's Milwaukee than in the South.

As the Nixon administration's principal political organizing tool, race knew no regional boundaries in John Mitchell's Justice Department or anywhere else. "The fantastic part," recalled a former Johnson administration official, "is that it would never occur to a man like Mitchell that this made him as much a racist as the worst of them. He'd be indignant as hell at such a suggestion. As he sees things, if something is good politics, it's good. He's so out of touch that he doesn't call us 'blacks' or 'Negroes'—he calls us 'colored people.'" That did not trouble Nixon. The southern strategy demanded an attorney general who could count votes and be in touch with the white majority North and South.[42]

Nixon's policies against desegregation, one Democrat on the House Judiciary Committee complained, represented "the most blatantly racist appeal to George Wallace's constituency since George Wallace's campaign for the Presidency."[43] If Nixon expected opposition from "special interests" (i.e., "professional Negroes" in the civil rights groups and "professional liberals" in Congress), he was a bit surprised by the reaction from within his own shop. Divisions between a desegregation compliance faction and a noncompliance faction were deep, with one of Nixon's few personal friends, HEW Secretary Robert H. Finch, leading the compliance charge. Although Mitchell convinced Finch to support the petition asking for a delay in the desegregation of Mississippi's thirty-three school districts, the HEW chief would prove harder to discipline than Jerris Leonard. The Civil Rights Division (if not Leonard himself) remained a sore spot. Sixty-five of its seventy-four line lawyers signed a protest memorandum to Mitchell charging that the Mississippi deal was a pay back to John Stennis (who led the administration's ABM treaty fight in the Senate). Getting no response, they sent a second memorandum to the press. The president initially demanded the resignation of every attorney who criticized his desegregation priorities, but settled for a more modest purge.[44]

Nixon wanted to manage school desegregation and other civil rights enforcement matters, not grind them to a complete halt. Total noncompliance would raise security problems by increasing the risk to domestic peace and political problems by contradicting Kevin Phillips's wisdom. "Abandonment of civil rights enforcement would be self-defeating," the who-hates-who expert had said. "If southern conservatives are to be pressured into switching to the Republican Party" some degree of enforcement was "essential." The key was to present the enforcement bureaucracy not as part of the administration but as part of the Establishment that Nixon had campaigned against. Finally, some degree of civil rights enforcement was inevitable because the law was crystal clear. Mitchell admitted that southern school districts had to be held to the Johnson administration's deadlines unless they had "bona fide educational and administrative problems."

Nixon's men could only offer loopholes and general statements of sympathy. "It is not our purpose here to lay down a single arbitrary date by which the desegregation process should be completed in all districts," read a joint statement by Mitchell and an unenthused Finch that went through a dozen drafts before Nixon approved it. "Or to lay down a single arbitrary system by which it should be achieved." Journalist Richard Harris called this "an open invitation to segregationists to do their worst."[45]

With little tolerance for selective law enforcement or other Nixon administration strategies, the federal courts threatened to gum things up. Mitchell and Finch had explained the White House decision not to enforce Title VI of the Civil Rights Act of 1964 (requiring the government to terminate federal funds to school districts or other recipients practicing discrimination) by reference to the law's elastic language. A district judge and a unanimous court of appeals disagreed in *Adams v. Richardson,* holding that the language was clear and mandatory and ordering the administration to execute the law. Once again, however, the president found a small victory in defeat. The onus remained on the courts and establishment judges determined to act on their supposedly problack prejudices. Hereafter the Nixon policy would be to funnel everything through the courts where Kennedy and Johnson judges could be blamed for any "bad" decision and not administration appointees or worse yet the president himself. This had the further advantage of slowing the process in its entirety. The courts were leisurely enough without a deliberate Justice Department effort to slow them even more.[46]

Selective and minimalist enforcement of school desegregation orders supplemented the stall strategy. Dent told Haldeman and Ehrlichman that "the full dose can be had" only in districts "where the percentage of Negroes is not high. In others, freedom of choice should be permitted where they are trying and the population ratio is a problem." When criticism from civil rights groups and other liberals continued and a few administration officials responded defensively, emphasizing the suits that were moving forward, Nixon exploded. "Our people have got to quit bragging about school desegregation. We do what the law requires—nothing more. This is politics, and I'm the judge of the politics of schools; believe me, all this bragging doesn't help. It doesn't cool the blacks. . . . They must not—they *will* not—be sucked into praising 'our great record.'"

Nixon showed the level of his commitment by placing Agnew in charge of a titular cabinet committee on school desegregation (with staff assistance provided by HEW general counsel and extreme hardliner Robert Mardian). "I told them," the president wrote in the memoir, "first of all I want everyone, but especially the Negro leaders, to know that our motto around here is 'I care.'" He could not have chosen anyone who cared less than Agnew and Mardian. The I-care motto was much like the bring-us-together-again campaign slogan. Both meant exactly the opposite.[47] "I wonder what Mr. Nixon will say to Mr. Wilkins and myself," Medgar Evers's brother Charles asked, "when the young Negroes tell us, 'I told you it wouldn't work. I told you that the American way of legislation won't work for black people.'" The president probably would have said that was the point: To stop it from working. Nixon found positive results in the *Savannah News* and other southern newspapers that stopped running "Tricky Dick" pieces in favor of stories with headlines like "Desegregation Deadlines Won't Be Enforced." When Dent showed him this one he wrote a two-word reply. "Excellent job." Charles Evers's question never crossed his desk. It probably never crossed his mind either.[48]

Nixon kept focused on the school desegregation battle, knowing that even minimal enforcement would be greeted in some quarters with disdain and further that today's headlines could change overnight. In response to a South Carolina story predicting (again) that he would lose the South unless he stopped HEW and the Civil Rights Division and federal judges from wrecking the schools, the president turned to Haldeman and Ehrlichman. "What is our answer to this? . . . Can't we do or say something to bring some sense into the dialogue?—I just disagree completely with the Courts naive stupidity—& think we have a duty to explore ways to mitigate it." "I was determined," he later explained, "that the many young liberal lawyers . . . [not] run wild through the South enforcing compliance with extreme or punitive requirements they had formulated in Washington."

The palace guard responded by reading the riot act to department heads, repeating the president's instruction for the umpteenth time: "Nothing more is to be done in the South beyond what the law requires." At that the departments were told not to open offices on site and instead work out of the District (or if absolutely necessary motel rooms) and otherwise keep "the lowest possible profile." Ehrlichman got his orders from the top: "Ride herd" on Justice's Civil Rights Division, HEW and other agencies ("vigilante squads") that took the law too seriously.[49]

Nixon's hands-on approach again led to personal involvement in the purge of civil rights advocates. Horace Bohanan, a black man with Civil Service protection, was an early target. As acting regional director of the Office of Civil Rights in Atlanta, Bohanan kept the NAACP posted and displayed other tendencies "to go off on his own." When Stanley Pottinger got him out of the civil rights field (by arranging a job change to the Maritime Commission in the Commerce Department), Nixon had a typically brief response: "Excellent job." Enthusiastic civil rights lawyers in the Justice Department, like Texas-based Joseph Rich, were ordered back to Washington and fired. "In line with your instructions . . . over the telephone," as the White House counsel's office assured the president. "Good" was the only response. Having entered politics in 1946 on McCarthyism's rising tide, Nixon found this the most familiar and natural way to handle personnel problems in the executive branch.[50]

With no Alger Hiss to out Nixon settled for the biggest available fish—Leon Panetta, director of HEW's Office of Civil Rights. When Robert Finch brought in Panetta and other liberals (including CORE's James Farmer, who embraced Nixon's campaign line about "black capitalism"), Mitchell insisted that such appointments be balanced by more tough-minded men like L. Patrick Gray, who served as Finch's assistant; and Mardian, who had once played high-school baseball with Jackie Robinson back home in Pasadena but whose service as the Goldwater campaign's western chair better reflected his politics. Forever in the habit of telling people to "ride herd," Nixon quickly discovered that even Gray and Mardian could not do it here. North Carolina Senator Sam Ervin complained that the president said he "was in favor of neighborhood schools . . . But his man Friday, his secretary of health, education, and welfare, came down and insisted that Congress should defeat these proposals. . . . I would say Mr. Nixon tried to work both sides of the street." George Wallace, echoing Ervin, said the southern strategy "has been all talk." Nixon responded by ordering his staff to "get a 'hot group' on this" and "give me a plan," reminding everyone (as if they needed reminding) that "I am not interested in the professional civil rights position on it."[51]

HEW (and what Agnew called its "continual surfacing of radical left ideas") became a lightning rod for southern discontent. And Leon Panetta, as Ehrlichman explained, "became a symbol for Richard Nixon of all that was wrong." The White House acted accordingly. "The President knew Leon Panetta's travel plans before Panetta's wife did, thanks to Bryce Harlow's Congressional pipelines," Ehrlichman continued. "More than once I was given instructions to 'tell Finch to keep that goddamned Panetta out of Atlanta' or some other Congressman's district." Nixon understood the symbolism. "In these race matters," he said, "one strong action is better than a lot of words. Firing Panetta is worth dozens of speeches and statements about integrating the schools." Ever loyal (in his own way) to his friend (Finch), the president initially suggested as Panetta's replacement William Casey (who would go on to greater adventures in the Reagan campaign and the CIA). "He's smart, strong and tough. We need such a person for Bob Finch's sake," Nixon said. Friendship was not enough, however, as Finch resigned less than two years into the job.[52]

In much the same manner in which he had forced Panetta's resignation (and also EEOC chair Clifford Alexander's), Nixon drove Father Theodore Hesburgh from the Civil Rights Commission chair by criticizing the way he waffled on the busing issue.[53] Busing had emerged as the most divisive and therefore the most useful school desegregation issue for the president. It was also the specific issue that led to Panetta's ouster. Inspired by Alexander Bickel's *New Republic* article arguing that busing was self-defeating, Nixon drew a line in the sand. "I have decided to reverse this process. We will take heat from the professional civil righter—but education comes first. I want Panetta's resignation on my desk Monday (as a starter)." "This is *my decision*," he reminded his staff. "If there are those in the Administration who disagree they can resign." Ehrlichman complained that one of those who disagreed, HUD Secretary George Romney, constantly babbled about "suburban integration." But Romney had more staying power than Finch (lasting the entire first term), and the president could only issue a meek order: "Stop this one."[54]

Nixon knew Romney had a point. Behind the school desegregation problem and busing lay perhaps the most intractable problem of all, segregated housing (which the president called a "natural outgrowth of economic and social patterns within individual communities and neighborhoods"). White House staff advised him to avoid housing altogether and stick with busing, but even here the counsel's office warned about the dangers of "overkill" because the president's position appeared "contrived." "Any help it would be to us in the South," Edward Morgan said, "would be so marginal as to be out-weighed by the risk to you nationally." Nixon remained his own judge of "the politics of schools." "There are no votes in . . . desegregation," he told Ehrlichman. "It's a Washington issue. The NAACP would say my rhetoric was poor even if I gave the Sermon on the Mount." With votes for the taking in his antibusing posture, he kept hitting this "new evil" and other methods of "compulsory racial balancing"—using code words like "forced integration" so often that his own Labor Department complained. "The Federal Courts were ordering the busing of white kids and black kids," Ehrlichman explained. "And Richard Nixon wanted every one of their parents to know that he opposed it."[55]

"What we need now is not just speaking out against busing," Nixon told Congress. "We need action to stop it." "The president pressed full court on bussing," one White House aide said, moving beyond rhetoric to a game plan that included a moratorium. "Whether Congress passed the bussing moratorium was not as important as that the American people understood that Richard Nixon opposed busing as much as they did," Ehrlichman again elaborated, for emphasis. Charles Colson pointed out a potential problem nonetheless: White southern backlash was possible because busing had already begun in that region and thus the South might conclude that the moratorium would only stop busing in the

North. Nixon then suggested a constitutional amendment outlawing busing forever and told Ehrlichman to "put some of your boys on this."

When analyst Dick Scammon suggested that some of those boys were "'embarrassed' to be strongly pushing this issue because it 'runs against the mainstream of Georgetown thought,'" the president gave Ehrlichman another order. "Tell *all* to quit paying attention to the N.Y. Times [Washington] Post-Georgetown clique." In theory an amendment was "the way to put the issue in clearest focus," but in practice Nixon knew it was pie in the sky. Noise, in any event, was more important than action.[56] The busing game plan's purpose was electoral, its full-court press aimed squarely at the Democrats. "We still need someone to put Muskie and Kennedy on the spot as to whether they are for or against busing," Haldeman said. "It is very important not to let them get a free ride on this." That someone turned out to be Michigan Congressman Gerald Ford who received a mass of antibusing material from the president's men which he used against Kennedy, Muskie, and their party in speeches on the House floor and in press releases. Reporting from Ford's home state, Scammon told Colson that this was a "more important issue to the Democratic primary voter than either inflation or unemployment"—with "one in three Wallace voters vot[ing] for him *solely* because of the busing issue."

Recognizing that "busing is only a code word for the real issue, which is black/white relations," White House demographers hoped to exploit it politically during the 1972 reelection campaign "wherever large numbers of lower middle class whites live in close proximity to blacks." Scammon nonetheless believed the administration was too timid. With ten major school systems of at least 75,000 students each under court-ordered busing, he suggested applying the full-court press in "critical cities across the nation" and complained to Colson about what he called a "restrained posture on our part on the busing issue. . . . We do not appear to be exploiting it the way we did law and order, for example, and yet this issue is demonstrably voter motivational." When the president read Colson's summary of Scammon's argument, he asked, simply, "Why?" His agreement with Scammon's analysis aside, it would be hard to imagine the administration being more aggressive on this issue than it already was.[57]

"Presidents are necessarily political animals," Sam Ervin said, and the truth of this was best seen in Nixon's use of the Supreme Court in pursuit of the antibusing mission. Dent had recommended as much ("at least, let's go *now* with a Supreme Court Justice"), though the boss hardly needed encouragement. Getting "the courts changed" was not only a favorite topic of conversation with FBI Director Hoover but also with Chief Justice Warren Burger. Nixon and Burger frequently spoke about pending cases. "Especially civil-rights cases," Ehrlichman admitted. "Nixon was hung up about busing. . . . He took advice from Burger. I was with Mitchell and Nixon when they discussed Burger's advice." "In effect," he continued, the chief justice was "predicting how the Court was *going* to go." The president knew which way to go when Justice Abe Fortas resigned. "What they really want to do is appoint someone like Judge Cox," Burke Marshall concluded from the safety of Yale Law School, referring to Cox's racist reputation. "But they can't be identified that way."[58]

Marshall was only half right. The White House did, in fact, want to identify the nomination that way and thus sent up South Carolina's Clement F. Haynesworth, Jr. Hoover's FBI, when conducting the background check, ignored Haynesworth's segregationist baggage (notably Fourth Circuit Court of Appeals votes against key civil-rights cases) and instead sent a glowing report: "Judge Haynesworth is generally regarded as the foremost jurist in the area, is considered very conservative, and is well disposed toward law enforcement. He is definitely in favor of law and order. . . . Judge Haynesworth has a slight lisp but is considered to have a brilliant mind." Roy Wilkins had a predictably different view. He called the nomination "grotesque." As Marshall had said, the president and his men wanted someone as grotesque as Harold Cox.[59]

Harry Dent led the separate "full-court press" on the Haynesworth nomination with help from Kevin Phillips—who contacted "contributors who are important to uncommitted Senators." Georgia Pacific Plywood Corporation, to cite one example Dent gave Haldeman, was "working on all target Senators." With Haynesworth also having problems with organized labor, Phillips moved beyond civil rights to leak derogatory information on the nominee's opponents. This included publicizing Indiana Senator Birch Bayh's "union contributions to show his 'conflict.'" (This was brazen given Haynesworth's stock

holdings in companies affected by his Fourth Circuit decisions.) Haldeman's enthusiasm aside ("Damn good job! Glad someone is off his heels
& running!"), neither Phillips nor any other southern-strategy wizard
had any luck. With the nomination mobilizing both the civil rights
movement and organized labor, the Senate turned it down.[60]

Never one to give up, Nixon told Dent to "find a good federal judge
further South and further to the right." The southern strategy team
came up with a perfect revenge nominee, Florida's G. Harrold Carswell.
"[He] made Haynesworth look like Learned Hand," Bayh said. "They
think he's a boob, a dummy," one of Nixon's own White House aides,
Bryce Harlow, later admitted. "And what counter is there to that? He
is." Hoover and Mitchell, in contrast, were ecstatic. "He is a good
man," the FBI director told his (ostensible) boss. "The Attorney
General said he thought they had been around him pretty well and
with his age, he should have a long tenure with the right kind of approach on the Supreme Court." When running the background check,
the homophobic FBI missed Carswell's homosexuality (learning of it
only in 1976 after he pleaded no contest to a "battery" charge arising
from an incident in a shopping mall men's room). Adept at going back
forty years to document Communist-front affiliations, the bureau also
missed or overlooked everything in Carswell's segregationist past from
a 1948 white-supremacy speech that ran in his hometown newspaper
to his involvement in the conversion of a Tallahassee public golf course
(under court order to desegregate) into a private club.[61]

Nixon's floor leader in the Senate was especially enraged at the
NAACP's Clarence Mitchell and Marian Edelman of the Children's
Defense Fund, who led the successful fight to block the Carswell nomination. (Wright uncovered the golf club item, not the FBI.) When the
nomination died with Maine's Margaret Chase Smith "offer[ing] a very
testy no" and the gallery bursting into applause, Richard Russell
ordered the spectators cleared. After the sergeants-at-arms swept
through, Roy Wilkins remembered, only one person remained seated
in the gallery—Clarence Mitchell.[62]

Nixon's rage surpassed Russell's. He had the FBI give dossier dirt to
Gerald Ford on the liberal's darling Supreme Court justice, William O.
Douglas, regarding a complex pornography issue, and otherwise prom-
ised to hang tough on the next nomination. When the president put

up Minnesota's Harry Blackmun, he told his staff to get "somebody like [Senator Roman] Hruska . . . [to] praise the nomination as being that of a man who has the same philosophy on the Constitution as Haynesworth and Carswell. This line must be gotten out, not only by Hruska, but must be of the highest priority with our whole Congressional and PR staff. The attempt of the liberals will be to find shades of difference between Blackmun and Haynesworth and Carswell. As a matter of fact, Blackmun is to the right of both . . . on law and order and perhaps slightly to their left, but very slightly to the left only in the field of civil rights. I know the argument will be made that we ought to give the liberals a chance to save face, but there are much higher stakes—my pledge to name strict constructionists to the Court and the inevitable charge that I was forced to back down by the Senate and name a liberal or even a quasi-liberal."[63]

With the Senate worn out Blackmun easily won confirmation. So did the next two nominees: Lewis Powell, a distinguished if decidedly conservative Virginia attorney (to replace Hugo Black); and William Rehnquist of Phoenix (by way of Milwaukee), a trenchant critic of Warren Court activism whose civil-rights views were scarcely better than Haynesworth's or Carswell's. Although administration ideologues like Pat Buchanan still dreamed of "the Big Rock" (i.e., "the Southern Strict Constructionist") or at least a little rock ("an ethnic Catholic . . . Holy Name Society Daily Communicant"), most of them settled for what they got.[64]

Buchanan, the former newspaperman and now White House speech writer whose clear and colorful "idea" memoranda always found their way to Nixon's desk, was among those unwilling to settle. The Supreme Court nomination process had nothing to do with abstract things like justice and integrity and everything to do with politics. It also had no down side. "If the Southerner is impeccable, it is a bitterly divisive issue for Democratic candidates. . . . Either they kick their black friends in the teeth, or they kick the South in the teeth," Buchanan practically squealed. "De facto . . . divisive." "The race issue" was a "dividing line," a wedge with which to pry apart "the old Roosevelt Coalition" and set one member group against another. In his own way Buchanan was one of Nixon's most accomplished tricksters. Not a White House plumber exactly (because he fixed no leaks), but of the Liddy/Hunt mentality. A plumber who used typewriter keys and not lock picks or silly CIA-manufactured disguises to advance the cause of what he called God, country, and "suburban conservatism."[65]

A Soviet military paper said Buchanan's rising star in the White House reflected the "growth and consolidation [of the Ku Klux Klan]." "Shame!," Nixon told Buchanan upon reading this item. "You didn't tell me!"[66] Unfortunately the Soviets were not that far off. When not writing speeches for the president, Buchanan pursued a semi-covert mission (the same mission Kevin Phillips had pursued) "to champion the cause of the Blacks within the Democratic party; elevate their complaints of 'being taken for granted.'" (His words.) As long as "white America" believed that the Democrats lacked "the moral courage ever to say no to the NAACP" and otherwise "kow-towed" to "black political leadership," Buchanan was doing his job. He had range—briefing Julie Nixon Eisenhower on "the Butch Brigade" (the women's movement was a bigger "pain in the butt than the black chauvinists"); and no sense of shame. He also suggested that "Julie should have herself thoroughly briefed on what the Administration has done for blacks. . . . [Her] posture in this area should be one of deep sympathy for the aspirations of blacks, pride in her father's record, and disagreement with the conventional wisdom, which is false, that her father and his Administration are antiblack." The conventional wisdom was not only true but Buchanan himself had been brought in to spread it.[67]

Like many of the previous century's slaveowners, Buchanan should have known somewhere in his soul that his mission was morally questionable. He had covered the March on Washington for the *St. Louis Globe-Democrat*, standing just a few feet from King and later ranking the "Dream" speech among "the most memorable addresses in American history." From Washington he went to Birmingham's Sixteenth Street Baptist Church then on to the Freedom Ride battleground in Anniston. The following summer he covered the Schwerner-Chaney-Goodman disappearance in Philadelphia, Mississippi. "In retrospect," he said, "the civil-rights movement was liberalism's finest hour. The liberals paid a heavy price for having championed civil rights in the '50s and early '60s, for preaching and advancing the idea of equality and justice under law." Again, that was exactly why Nixon brought him in—to make sure the Democrats kept paying the price and that "the curtain" stayed dropped "on the Second Reconstruction." "Men of the right were long ago dismissed as racists," he explained. "There is no reason why they should not, openly and unapologetically, champion public opposition to the 'second generation' of civil rights demands." No reason, in other words, not to wear their racism on their sleeves.[68]

At best Buchanan merely crusaded against "the un-wisdom of Government's massive intrusion to change the racial topography of the nation."[69] At worst he rivaled "the young bloods of the South," the "sons of planters" from a hundred years before who scared even Sherman. "War suits them," the general wrote, "and the rascals are brave, fine riders, bold to rashness and dangerous subjects in every sense. They care not a sou for niggers, land, or anything. They hate Yankees *per se*, and don't bother their brains about the past, present, or future." Buchanan differed by plotting the present and future. In "school integration and neighborhood integration" he saw the opportunity to manufacture a constitutional crisis and "cement a New Majority" with a "throw of the dice" that risked a new if less bloody civil war. "This would really tear up the pea patch . . . and cut the Democratic Party and country in half," he told Nixon (in a memorandum that remained his blueprint twenty years later when making a run at George Bush for the Republican nomination.) "My view is that we would have far the larger half."

Buchanan's assumption was that mixing "the races" could only lead to "wrong and contra-productive" political alignments. To counter court-ordered busing and other perceived evils he urged the president to make a "historic decision" to defy the judiciary and the legislature, thereby "bringing a constitutional end to the national pressure to integrate races in housing and schooling." His only real concern was that Nixon, Mitchell, Haldeman, and Ehrlichman all lacked the courage of his convictions. Buchanan could do little more than submit his scheme, outline the ways a national schism could "be exploited to the benefit of the President," and state the obvious fact about implementation: "That is not my decision [to make]." Nixon did not object to manufacturing a phony constitutional crisis to mark a permanent division between a ruling-class GOP "us" and a nonwhite "them." But he did not share this twentieth-century fire-eater's dream of glory in tearing up the pea patch and otherwise cutting the country in half.[70]

When the school wars pushed beyond the primary and secondary levels to the universities, Nixon generally listened less to the Buchanans and performed more honorably. Still, he tended to muddle things. After a White House reception for student government leaders, for example, he pressed Haldeman on defense grants and other "funds for the teachers and students" at the Negro colleges to build up science departments, upgrade faculty, improve teaching skills, and otherwise develop excellence. When Arthur Burns objected on the grounds that the administration did not know enough about the black colleges to know what they needed or did not need, Nixon pushed on. "Be heavy-handed to get it through the board of NSF," he told Ehrlichman. "Don't let colleges down drain bec[ause] they are black." "Well, its a good thing," he said after discovering that federal scholarship programs for blacks did exist. "They're just down out of the trees." He could not help putting a southern-strategy twist on everything touched.[71]

The president also had something for the South's all-white private colleges: A promise that they would not lose their tax exemptions. "The IRS shouldn't try to make cases or force the issue," he told Ehrlichman. "I don't want the IRS rushing around. Let the policy be that if blacks apply to those schools they can be admitted."[72] This was in marked contrast to the administration's policy regarding black activists. Arthur Burns had met with IRS Commissioner Randolph Thrower in June 1969 to convey the president's interest in rooting out the use of "tax-exempt funds to support activist groups engaged in stimulating riots both on the campus and within our inner cities." In response the IRS established a Special Service Staff that opened dossiers on the Great Society's Head Start program; the U.S. Civil Rights Commission; fifty National Urban League chapters; a black congressman from Detroit, Charles Diggs (and presumably all other black elected officials); the Ford Foundation (because of its racial-justice grants); and more generally "persons associated with or 'disassociated' with various racially oriented groups." None of this satisfied the president. "Dominated by Democrats," in his view, the IRS would not go as far as he thought necessary.[73]

Hoover's FBI disappointed Nixon less, proving more than eager to lead the charge against the black groups on the IRS list and virtually every other politically active individual and organization in the country. Nixon took a hands-on approach to the principal target, the Oakland-based Black Panther party founded by Huey Newton and Bobby Seale. The president pressured the FBI to forward intelligence on the Panthers, and Hoover obliged (sending Agnew, among other things, "colorful" materials "in a briefing book form" about the Panthers' off-the-pig rhetoric and shootouts with police officers). Agnew's aide, Kent Crane, told the director that the vice-president "wants to be able to let them have it" and was especially interested in "graphic incidents that could be used as examples, which Governor Ronald Reagan has done a beautiful job with." Nixon, like Agnew, hoped to use the FBI material to publicize the Panthers' nihilist strain, its beyond-Mao rhetoric about "Babylon" and race war. This was relatively easy to do, especially after the formation of a separate faction headed by Eldridge Cleaver from exile in Algiers. Cleaver followed up the best-seller *Soul on Ice* by publishing assassination lists topped by Nixon and Kissinger.[74]

While making the case that the Panthers were nothing more than a collection of crackpots and thugs, the White House set out to smash the party's wholly legitimate service mission (which included everything from a free breakfast program for ghetto children to adult literacy workshops). Haldeman spread the word among top staff: "The President feels it is extremely important that Mitchell et al. get the word out to Congress and other leaders on what the Black Panthers actually stand for. He was concerned by the recent report that most blacks support the Black Panthers, and feels that this could only be the case if the blacks were not aware of what the Panthers were really trying to do." "Black Panthers," Ehrlichman wrote in his notepad during an Oval Office meeting. "Not a polit pty," "get pub word out," "expose them," "kill." The last word was particularly chilling given the death of Chicago Panther Fred Hampton during a police raid. A prime FBI counterintelligence target, Hampton was shot before dawn as he slept in his bed. "Completely neutralized," in bureauspeak. An FBI informant who helped with preraid logistics got a $300 bonus.[75]

Nixon hoped the Panther campaign would also discredit the party's liberal backers ranging from Marlon Brando to Leonard Bernstein and even Mrs. W. Vincent Astor. "K note?!," the president alerted his national security adviser. "The complete decadence of the American 'upper' class intellectual *elite*." Others joined in the fun. Daniel Patrick Moynihan, White House intellectual-in-residence, circulated a "directive" after learning that Newton had purged a Boston Panther for being a "cultural nationalist opportunist": "Effective immediately, Mr. Chico Neblett and his renegade crew are not to be considered for appointments, invitations, emoluments or honors by the Administration."[76]

Such jokes should not obscure the grim focus. Nixon's memoir included a section on the Huston plan (named in honor of White House aide Tom Charles Huston), which created, however briefly, the police-state structure that figured so prominently in the congressional impeachment debate. He opened that memoir section by putting the knife in once more. Newton and Seale, he wrote, had founded the Panthers "while working for the Office of Economic Opportunity." The president's signature authorizing the Huston plan's wholesale mail openings, burglaries, warrantless electronic surveillance, and other "clearly illegal" (Huston's words) investigative techniques was thus fully justified because the Panthers were not only "affiliated with North Korean" and "Arab terrorists" but the Democratic party. This pushed Kevin Phillips's idea of "Negro-Democratic mutual identification" far enough to suit even Pat Buchanan.[77]

In rhetoric if not always in action the Nixon White House matched the ferocity of the campaign against the Panthers and their breakfast programs and day-care and adult-literacy centers with an assault on the government's own "serve-the-people" programs. Nixon's memoir reference to OEO and Huey Newton in the same sentence was tame compared to the internal references that floated in the White House. Gutting welfare, Buchanan told Mitchell and Haldeman, "might well be considered philistine or worse by the media, but would seem to be good politics." By substituting a war on the poor for LBJ's war on poverty the administration "could divide it [the Roosevelt coalition] between the loafing classes (welfare, students) and the working classes" and thus "force Democrats to choose between the[m]." By aiming at OEO and other Great Society agencies ("the Pleasure Island of the Welfare State—that wholly owned and operated subsidiary of liberalism—that has destroyed the moral fiber of America's black poor"), Buchanan again had the urge to roll the dice: "[It] requires really the kind of go-for-broke decision that we may or may not feel is either necessary or justified by our comparatively good field position."[78]

Nixon did not need Buchanan's encouragement on this issue. "[He] got into a deep discussion of welfare . . . with E[hrlichman] and me," Haldeman wrote in his diary, "[and] emphasized that you have to face the fact that the *whole* problem is really the blacks. The key is to devise a system that recognizes this while not appearing to." Nixon was in the White House barely a month before telling Bob Finch that he wanted a "complete shake-up" of OEO and programs like Head Start. When the HEW chief instead requested increased funds for Head Start and other pre-school programs, Nixon countered with a freeze and a suggestion to change OEO's name. "As long as the Community Action Program remains the mainstay of OEO," Arthur Burns said when advising against the latter, "the organization is likely to be troublesome to you. With its present name, the Democrats will at least share the blame." The president took the advice and then came back with another suggestion on the nomenclature front. "We must above all change the name *of the Job Corps.*" Not yet fully engaged, he backed off that idea, too.[79]

From there the White House launched another "full-court press" with Buchanan monitoring poverty and other grant applicants and recipients in the manner of a HUAC name checker. These included Ossie Davis, Buchanan complained to Ehrlichman. "The old fellow traveller has landed the drug office's contract to produce the anti-drug film. . . . Is there not something we can do to take this considerable patronage away from a fellow, one of whose characteristics is 100 percent opposition to Richard Nixon and the political goals which he pursues?" While waiting to "dis-establish" OEO, Buchanan suggested shifting poverty grants from the black and Spanish-speaking communities to "poor Jewish and Italian neighborhoods." "The handout programs," he said, should ignore "fashionable minorities" and go with the minorities the president had a chance with at the ballot box. Of OEO's cadre of social workers and assorted other bureaucrats who reviewed and dispensed the grants, Nixon himself wanted "immediate action on these characters." He turned to Burns for a "game plan" and got it the next day (March 24, 1969). Forget the name change stuff, Burns said. Instead he advised the president to "dismantle OEO."[80]

Nixon's people chipped away at OEO nearly every day until the president's resignation. "Model Cities—flush it," Ehrlichman wrote on his Oval Office note pad. "OEO—legal services. Sally Payton [a black lawyer on the White House staff]—tell her to screw it up. . . . Flush Model Cities and Great Society. It's failed. Do it, don't say it." To do the heavy lifting Charles Colson nominated thirty-two-year-old movement conservative Howard Phillips. "The President needs politically astute loyalists throughout the government," Colson explained. "But he needs them most in old line liberal agencies that are going to take the most heat. It is essential that we name a [permanent] director to OEO who is willing to be a human bomb and walking target. Howie Phillips wants to kill the agency and has a loyal staff capable of doing it. He does not want a job, he wants to do a job." With the president preoccupied by the unfolding Watergate scandal, however, Phillips never got congressional confirmation and remained acting director.[81]

When White House budget writers for fiscal year 1974 omitted all funds for OEO programs, Phillips started to dismantle the agency—arguing that Nixon's budget message superseded congressional authorization. The courts disagreed in a hardly startling finding that the executive budget was "nothing more than a proposal to the Congress for the Congress to act upon as it may please."[82] Nixon shifted gears, finding enough non-Watergate time to order a systematic collection of "horrible examples" of OEO waste, fraud, and abuse that could be "well scattered among the Congress and among our surrogates." "Put one of our brighter people on this job," he told Ehrlichman. "[This] will do far more good than [the] tons of lofty rhetoric which we are spewing out." Nixon, like Agnew, admired Reagan, an expert in the "'Horror Stories' package." So he ordered "all Presidential Spokesmen . . . to use one or two horror stories per speech." The administration ultimately produced a dozen Watergate horrors for every OEO item. Even the agency's most controversial program outlasted Phillips, Agnew, and everyone else commissioned to slay it. Ten years after Nixon left the White House there were some 900 Community Action agencies scattered across the United States.[83]

While fighting for "neighborhood schools" and against Black Panthers and poverty bureaucrats, Nixon occasionally pursued policies that seemingly contradicted the southern strategy. The man who bagged Alger Hiss showed a soft spot when W. E. B. Du Bois's widow wanted to come home to the United States to die. "Her husband was really a great man who only very late in life became a kind of bitter Stalinist," Moynihan advised. "E[hrlichman]—," Nixon responded, "sounds like a good case for 'clemency'? Ask Mitchell & give me recommendation." The administration's welfare reform proposals, moreover, were not all draconian. In fact the family assistance plan, with emphasis on guaranteed income rather than guaranteed services, was innovative. "No President in history has come near to proposing anything like [it]," Moynihan said with less than total exaggeration. With Nixon being Nixon, however, even this was something of a dirty trick at bottom. He told Haldeman "to be sure its killed by Democrats and that we make a big play for it, but don't let it pass, can't afford it."[84]

Before the 1970 elections and again in 1972 the White House made several (very) modest attempts to get a few black votes without the bonds of "promises" and "hokey rhetoric about equality." When Nixon had himself photographed with the thirty-five highest ranking African Americans in government, the Republican National Committee put the shot on a campaign pamphlet entitled "The Black Silent Majority." (When James Farmer, one of the thirty-five, saw it, he laughed aloud.) Nixon even had his staff float anecdotes about how "RN" (he liked to use third person) would walk "on Fifth Avenue or Park during trips to New York as Vice President" and "sometimes stop to have his shoes shined by one of the Negro teenagers along the Avenue—less for the shine's sake than for the boy's." A good shine always earned a five-dollar tip.

Moynihan (not Phillips or Buchanan) had Nixon's ear here and had convinced him (in Ken Khachigian's words) that there was "no reason for us to kiss off the Black vote." "Negro businessmen—bankers—Elks etc." could be reached without jeopardizing the southern strategy. "Let's pull this," the president said. "If we don't alienate them like Goldwater did, we should get about twenty percent." Nixon plotted white against black and black against black, too (a rising black middle versus a falling black bottom), but at least for a few seconds of his White House time paid some attention to voters of color.[85]

Nixon also met occasionally with those black leaders "who are favorably inclined toward the Administration and not militants or opponents." (*Ebony* publisher John Johnson was a particular favorite.) On rare occasions these meetings included White House enemies like Roy Wilkins, whose mention of Charles Hamilton's article on "the silent Black majority" prompted the president to order a summary of the piece prepared for his nightly reading. This courtship failed. So did the pursuit of Whitney Young. "Can you believe [it]?," Moynihan asked Nixon in July 1970. "The Today Show has had a full week of black 'leaders' denouncing us, including the National Urban League." "I think this ends Whitney Young," the president told Ehrlichman before turning to Haldeman with an order: "Can't some of our people who help finance the Urban League hit him?—See if we can't get someone on this."[86]

From the beginning Nixon had his doubts about Whitney Young's ambition—specifically, the possibility that he might be tempted "to go all the way to get King's mantle."[87] He had even more doubts about Ralph Abernathy, who succeeded King as head of the Southern Christian Leadership Conference. Agreeing with the Agnew/Hoover assessment ("he is one of the worst"), the president nonetheless accepted Moynihan's advice and arranged a meeting in the Roosevelt Room at the White House. This was a surprising decision since he rarely even met with the few African Americans on staff. "Bob Brown, the President's 'liaison with the black community,'" Ehrlichman said, "was not included in most of the President's meetings; Nixon found it hard to talk freely with Brown around. Brown, of course, was black." For a soul-searching "talk about problems and viewpoints of a responsible intelligent Negro," the president sent for Dwight Chapin's secretary, Harriet Elan. "Kept saying to me," Haldeman wrote in his diary after Elan left, "there's really no adequate solution and nothing we can do in the short haul to settle this, it will have to take one hundred years, but people don't want to wait."[88]

The Abernathy meeting started poorly then deteriorated. After a Poor People's Campaign delegation of Marian Wright Edelman, Andrew Young, and Jesse Jackson arrived late (keeping most of the cabinet waiting), Rev. Abernathy opened by reading an entire nine-page statement demanding new poverty and job programs. Nixon listened, mumbled, and finally stood silent for a few minutes with his arms folded stiffly before fleeing (saying a Vietnam matter needed attention). Agnew took over for the next twenty minutes, then he left—leaving Moynihan to preside for two hours. Most galling was Abernathy's response after things broke up. He walked out of the Roosevelt Room "angrier than I had been in a long time. . . . I could not contain my disappointment when reporters outside asked me how the meeting had gone." Upon hearing Abernathy's comments about "economic double-talk," Moynihan burst into the Oval Office. "After the way you and the rest of us listened," he told Nixon, "and indicated our sincere desire to find solutions to the problems, he goes into the press room and pisses on the President of the United States." After that Nixon would refer derisively to "that Moynihan meeting" (the memory faded only with Watergate). Such affronts demonstrated what the president described as the "futility of trying to be considerate of these people—they have to show off for their constituency."[89]

No matter how poorly such racial-justice forays tended to go, the Nixon White House continued its episodic policy of "reaching out" to black America. Since this contradicted conventional southern-strategy wisdom many commentators have emphasized what the historian Hugh Davis Graham called the president's "lack of any coherent and internally consistent ideology. . . . Little interested in the substance of domestic policy beyond its political repercussions, Richard Nixon was free to tailor his policies on civil rights to maximize their political payoff." The pursuit of "contradictory policies for short-term tactical gains," in other words.[90] Yet there was an idea holding everything up, something more than policy incoherence as policy—something hidden in what Ehrlichman and other Oval Office advisers called the "zig-zag."[91]

Nixon's attempt to fold an apparent policy incoherence into the southern strategy had a clear if multilayered motivation. Victory in 1968 had presented a Lincolnesque problem, Richard Harris noted, given the campaign's law-and-order slant. "How could the winner keep the pledges he had made to those who had elected him, and thereby maintain his power base, and at the same time do what was necessary to preserve the Union?"[92] Where Buchanan saw glory and victory for "the presidential party" in race riots and a nation torn in half, Nixon saw horror and defeat. Lacking the courage of Buchanan's convictions, he would not roll Buchanan's dice but instead throw the occasional bone to the blacks and liberals in order to preserve the peace and the Union. This was what Ehrlichman called racial-justice "zigs" to accompany southern-strategy "zags."

Still, southern strategy ruled and demanded an underlying if hidden consistency. No matter how limited, Nixon's courting of black America (or at least "the silent black majority") was intended to force the Democrats to pay even more attention to civil rights—to prevent the one bloc from the Roosevelt coalition that had not yet splintered from doing so. This in turn fed the southern-strategy goal of hyping "Negro-Democratic mutual identification." Civil rights issues were so ingrained in the public mind as Democratic party priorities, Kevin Phillips had also said, it made little difference if a Republican administration pushed a few such initiatives. The Democrats would be blamed.

At the same time the handful of things the Nixon administration accomplished or proposed served as wedges to further split the Roosevelt coalition's other pieces. The basic goal was to pit different segments against one another (notably, blacks versus organized labor), in hope of creating chaos within that coalition and breaking off the white working class vote (what the president's men called "the ethnic vote"). This would complete the process begun in 1968 and bring labor into the Republican column. What FDR had done in 1932, Nixon would reverse in 1972.

"Our welfare reform effort has been a good zig," Ehrlichman told the president, to cite one example. "Without damage to the Social Issue, with promise of blue-collar support." The administration designed its welfare package in the precise hope that it would get the support of organized labor and the opposition of the civil rights groups. Nixon thought it would float provided there was enough "emphasis on work requirement." On the larger "Social Issue," Ehrlichman saw political fortune in "some neo-conservative initiatives deliberately designed to furnish some zigs to go with our conservative zags in the same way we have included Moynihans with our Dents (rather than trying to recruit only those non-existent middle-of-the-roaders). . . . We will try to co-opt the opposition's issues . . . if the political cost is not too great. But we will not blur your [the president's] position on crime, youth, values or race."[93]

Nixon even embraced affirmative action as a neo-conservative zig. A contracting program known as "8-A" set aside fixed percentages of federal contracts for minority-owned businesses; the Department of Commerce set up an Office of Minority Business Enterprise to help such businesses secure government contracts; and the so-called Philadelphia Plan increased black access to union jobs in the construction industry. Nixon took a special interest in the latter, having made a 1968 campaign stop in Philadelphia's ghetto (the only ghetto visited), and considered it perhaps his shrewdest political move. George Shultz, who pulled the Philadelphia Plan from the ashes of the late Johnson years, handled the details. "I had, as secretary of labor," Shultz said, "broken, with a sledge-hammer called the Philadelphia Plan, the quota system (zero) in the skilled construction trades." None of this stopped Nixon from campaigning against affirmative action, which had begun informally under Kennedy and formally under Johnson, as a Democratic party evil. Later, when accepting his party's nomination for a second term at the Miami convention, Nixon called quotas "totally alien to the American traditions. . . . This Nation proudly calls itself the United States of America. Let us reject a philosophy that would make us the divided people of America."[94]

The purpose of 8-A and the other programs, nonetheless, was exactly that—to divide the American people. On its face the Philadelphia Plan was the most ambitious and straightforward of the administration's affirmative action proposals because it required construction companies doing business with the federal government to set "goals and timetables" for minority hiring and promotion. It also set specific "ranges" for plumbers, pipefitters, and other craft jobs, with a 5–8 percent hiring goal in 1970 and 22–26 percent within four years. In November 1969 the plan began with six construction unions working on a federally funded hospital. From there it extended to trade unions in New York, Pittsburgh, Seattle, Los Angeles, St. Louis, San Francisco, Boston, Chicago, and Detroit. The government wrote goals and timetable mechanisms into federal procurement and contracting in 1970, affecting thousands of businesses and potentially a third of the nation's entire work force. "This thing is about as popular as a crab in a whorehouse," Everett Dirsksen, who died in September 1969, had told the president before all this started. "You will split your own party if you insist on pursuing it."[95]

Nixon figured the Philadelphia Plan would merely split the Demo-cratic party between its ties to blacks and labor, and in the process give the GOP a better chance of winning a larger percentage of the labor vote. "George Meany hit the roof," the president remembered, "charg-ing that the Administration was making the unions a whipping boy and trying to score 'brownie points' with civil rights groups." "While anti-labor and pro-black," Ehrlichman reported to the Oval Office, the Philadelphia Plan "drove a wedge between the Democrats and labor which has stretched the membrane. The Plan itself is not widely under-stood in non-labor circles, in my view. Labor understands it and hates it." "OK," was the president's response.

"Nixon thought that Secretary of Labor George Shultz had shown great style in constructing a political dilemma for the labor union lead-ers and the civil rights groups," Ehrlichman later elaborated. "Before long, the AFL-CIO and the NAACP were locked in combat over one of the passionate issues of the day and the Nixon Administration was located in the sweet and reasonable middle. . . . After that, Shultz was just naturally invited in to help out with school desegregation."[96]

In a sense the Philadelphia Plan was little more than an extension of an earlier Nixon campaign initiative. Michael W. McMinoway, a campaign operative who had infiltrated the Hubert Humphrey headquarters in Philadelphia, sabotaged the call cards of the telephone bank he supervised in a conscious attempt to pit working-class whites against inner-city blacks. "The cards were so placed," McMinoway said, "that anyone calling them could not distinguish between a Negro call sheet or a union call sheet. The call sheet is the speech read to the person called."[97] For his trouble McMinoway got twenty minutes of fame as one of Watergate's tiniest villains. Shultz got the school-desegregation duty and ten years later the secretary of state slot in the Reagan cabinet.

No matter how many zigs and zags, Nixon never pushed civil rights issues too far regardless of their underlying political purpose. Overall policy remained what Moynihan called, in his famous January 1970 memorandum, "benign neglect." "The subject [of race] has been too talked about," he wrote. "The forum has been too much taken over to hysterics, paranoids, and boodlers on all sides. . . . Greater attention to Indians, Mexican Americans and Puerto Ricans would be useful."

Nixon agreed. When the furor over the memorandum hit, Moynihan offered to resign. "Of course, I refused his offer," the president said. Because, as he told Ehrlichman (the Abernathy meeting aside), he found Moynihan "so stimulating."

Nixon kept to "benign neglect" so faithfully that even when asking Leonard Garment for "proposals for the *inclusion* of various minorities in our political planning," he nixed virtually everything involving African Americans—except an occasional dinner with black editors and publishers, breakfast with Sammy Davis, Jr., at Camp David, or a White House birthday party for Duke Ellington. (The president wanted to invite "all the jazz greats" to the latter—"like Guy Lombardo.") The 1972 reelection campaign had no real interest in the black vote other than using it as a club against the Democratic candidate, South Dakota Senator George McGovern. Campaign strategists worried about how Irish, Italian, Polish, and dozens of other ethnics would vote along with the groups Moynihan mentioned, but failed to even include African Americans on their list of "important demographic groups." The president expressed more interest, as ever, in southern-strategy symbolism, telling Alexander Haig to look into the possibility of a federally funded memorial for the Civil War's Confederate soldiers. A statue of Robert E. Lee or whatever. "[It] could have a dramatic effect," the president said, "in healing some of the wounds in the South that still exist."[98]

Nothing could chase Nixon's demons. He remained obsessed with numbers, with how he would do at the polls and whether he could carry his party on his coattails (something even Eisenhower could not do). Charles Colson fed this obsession with an analysis of the 1970 congressional elections. "*Except in the urban Northeast, we did not succeed in making the public believe that Democratic, Liberal permissiveness was the cause of violence and crime. . . .* We didn't sell the point that violence and disorder in our society are caused directly by the rhetoric, softness, and catering to the dissidents [blacks and students] which the Democrats have engaged in. We just didn't make the connection in the mind of the average voter." Except in the urban Northeast! But wasn't that the area of the country written off by the southern strategy?[99]

During the 1972 reelection campaign Nixon's obsession worsened. Again concerned that George Wallace might split the right-of-center vote, the president decided to recruit American Independent party (AIP) members in key states, and his men did so in particularly imaginative ways. Robert J. Walters, a California businessman and former Wallace supporter, came up with the most bizarre plan on this front. Meeting with Jeb Stuart Magruder for drinks at the Beverly Hills Hotel's Polo Lounge, Walters asked for $10,000 in Republican campaign funds to hire "canvassers" who would target AIP members. With campaign manager John Mitchell's approval, the money channeled through Lyn Nofziger, then communications director for the Republican National Committee, and another California businessman, John Lindsey. "Seemed like the bargain of the year," Magruder said, apparently unaware that half the money went to Joseph Tommassi, the head of the Nazi party in Southern California, who put twenty of his fellows on the payroll as canvassers. Magruder's mind boggled "at the thought of Nazis trying to convert Wallecites to Republicanism."[100]

When Arthur Bremer shot Wallace during a Milwaukee stop Nixon's men simply shifted gears. They tried to plant Muskie and McGovern campaign literature in Bremer's apartment (the police got there first), and then circulated "rumors" (in Colson's words) "that there were political motivations in the killing, to wit: Bremer had ties with Kennedy or McGovern political operations, that obviously there could be a conspiracy and immediate danger to others." Wallace, in contrast, later sent a note and flowers when Nixon fell ill at San Clemente. "I felt compassion for him when he was down," the former Alabama governor explained. "Perhaps more than before I was shot, I have come to appreciate the quality of mercy." Wallace could change, but not Nixon.[101]

With the Wallace threat thus diminished Nixon turned to Maine's Edmund Muskie. Of all the Democrats competing for their party's nomination the president believed the centrist Muskie could mount the most credible challenge in the November elections. Thus, Muskie had to be destroyed. Nixon wanted to run against McGovern, considering him the liberal's version of Barry Goldwater. Among other things the Republicans published a pamphlet by the bogus "Citizens for a Liberal Alternative" that accused Muskie of telling "Black Americans that there is no room for them in his politics. Blacks are the backbone of the Democratic party, and Mr. Muskie told them to go to hell. This is Muskie's way of playing on Southern Strategy. We don't want a racist to represent Democrats in 1972." The impetus here was Muskie's remark to community leaders in Watts that the time was probably not right for a black vice-presidential candidate. This also inspired dirty-trick specialist Donald Segretti to place the following add in a college newspaper: "Wanted. Sincere gentleman seeks running mate. White preferred but natural sense of rhythm no obstacle. Contact E. Muskie." "Senator Muskie," another ad asked, "would you accept a Jewish running mate?"[102]

While Segretti handled such minor-league chores, Pat Buchanan worked on his latest big-league project: "*Black Vice President* bumper stickers calling for black Presidential and especially Vice Presidential candidates should be spread out in the ghettoes of the country. Also, anti-Muskie stickers. We should do what is within our power to have a black nominated for Number Two at least at the Democratic National Convention." Buchanan wanted "to promote, assist and fund a Fourth Party candidacy of the Left Democrats and/or the Black Democrats." "Nothing . . . can so advance the President's chances for reelection," he said. "Not a trip to China, not four-and-a-half percent unemployment—as a realistic black . . . campaign." He settled for New York Congresswoman Shirley Chisholm's half-baked run and Mitchell's subsequent approval of a suggestion offered by another southern strategist "to take whatever steps are necessary to have [Chisholm] . . . on the ballot in all critical states." From Buchanan and Mitchell to the lowest CREEP operative, everyone in the reelection campaign tried to split every imaginable voting bloc.[103]

When Muskie failed to get the nomination Nixon turned in delight to George McGovern and running mate Sargent Shriver. Although racial issues were never central to McGovern's run (the main issue was of course Vietnam), his stance proved attractive enough to inspire seven Civil Rights Division lawyers to resign and join his campaign staff. Attractive enough as well to give Nixon dozens of opportunities to publicize such things as McGovern's "$1000 baby bonus for welfare recipients." "One of the factors that brought Goldwater down to such a shattering defeat in 1964," the president told Mitchell, "was the success of the media in tying him to ultra-right-wing supporters like H. L. Hunt. . . . While we will not have the media cooperation in a similar effort directed against McGovern, at least we can try to develop a tactic to the extent that it will sail. . . . This must be carefully done but nailing him to his left-wing supporters and forcing him either to repudiate them or to accept their support is essential. . . . A top priority objective." He suggested starting with McGovern's "ties" to Angela Davis. No administration official considered it relevant that there were no such ties.[104]

Racial hooks were not hard to find given the administration's "Radical Chic" and "Assault Book materials" already on hand. "It is fair to say he [McGovern] would cut off all assistance to our NATO ally Greece," Buchanan noted in a memorandum on integration and race, "but consider giving military aide to the black guerrillas in Southern Africa." Buchanan also found "it legitimate to charge McGovern with wanting to use federal coercion to integrate the suburbs, with favoring 'racial balance' in the nation's public schools, with believing that bussing is an 'essential' tool to accomplish the job." Agnew should dog the Democrat's trail in blue-collar America and remind voters that Nixon favored "retaining the integrity and value of ethnic neighborhoods." Southern members of Congress, Buchanan continued, "should be shown the specifics of the Black Caucus program which McGovern has endorsed 'in toto' . . . [They] will have to repudiate McGovern or force McGovern to repudiate these proposals—or take hemlock." Then, "when McGovern backs off some of these Black radical schemes, as back off he must—we should continue to hang them around his neck—and then mail his recantation to the black media."[105]

Other campaign powers matched Buchanan's aggression. Robert Mardian had a plan, to cite one especially bizarre example, to "neutralize a portion of the Black voters which cannot be won over. This neutralization will be attempted through a process of neutralizing Black leaders." Mardian had an endless array of dirty tricks in mind. What, if anything, came of this "neutralization" scheme remains unknown even though virtually everything attempted on this and every other racial front attracted the interest of the Watergate investigating committees.[106]

Nixon's demons stayed on after he took 61 percent of the popular vote and crushed McGovern (who took only Maine, the District of Columbia, and the votes of hard-core antiwar activists and liberals, the poor and the blacks). Even as the disaster that would cost him the presidency loomed on the horizon, Nixon remained focused on what he described in the third person as "RN's Southern Strategy, his opposition to busing, his appointments to the Supreme Court, his standing firm on the patriotic theme, his opposition to expanded welfare programs, his support of the work ethic."[107] Yet he worried the voters would find him out, discover that even on law-and-order matters his real men at Justice were at times scarcely tougher than Ramsey Clark. There were no race riots to match Watts, Newark, or Detroit during Nixon's five years in office, but street crime and murder rates continued unabated—even the murder of police officers in New York City and elsewhere for which various black militant organizations were only too happy to take credit. Such killings produced only impotent ravings at the White House.

Immediately after the election, on November 3, black sailors on the aircraft carrier *Constellation*, just back from the Gulf of Tonkin, staged a protest—pumping fists into the air for their own pride and the benefit of news cameramen. What Nixon saw on TV that evening was a "mutinous" challenge to his authority as commander-in-chief. He made two angry phone calls to Kissinger, who then called Admiral Elmo R. Zumwalt, chief of Naval Operations. "[He] all but shrieked at me," the admiral said. "Opponents of integration had been fulminating about how 'permissiveness'—an obvious buzz word for 'integration'—was about to destroy the Navy." Kissinger then relayed Nixon's order that the sailors be dishonorably discharged on the spot. "What seemed to me," Zumwalt concluded, "a preemptory, angry, illegal order" given the Uniform Code of Military Justice requiring a general court-martial. Besides, the offense was not that serious. The conversation with Kissinger, nonetheless, continued "on a note of unreality."

Nixon next had his national security adviser order Secretary of Defense Melvin Laird to dismiss Zumwalt for insubordination. "[Laird] told Kissinger," the admiral later learned, "that if Kissinger wanted me fired he should try firing me himself." Ultimately, Haldeman complained at the White House, Zumwalt kept his post and the black sailors got "active shore stations with Coca-Colas and ice cream." The president was "terribly displeased" with Zumwalt but hardly surprised. "You know," he told his chief of staff, "he's a McNamara man."[108]

The unraveling Watergate scandals fueled such bitterness and consumed the president's last days. Nixon saw no irony whatsoever, as G. Gordon Liddy did, in the master plumber's jail-cell cohabitant. "I met my first Black Muslim," Liddy said while waiting to be sentenced, "since my days in the FBI." Nixon's southern strategists were of no use here. The president told Haldeman "to have [Harry] Dent get a candidate fielded and going against Sam Ervin, to give him some trouble in his district, to slow him down a little on his Watergate activities." Instead the scandal stretched far enough to nip Dent. Indicted for violating a campaign-practice law by disposing funds from an illegally organized political committee, Dent said his guilty plea and sentence (one month's probation) were comparable to "a high-class moving violation." A traffic-ticket, in other words.[109]

While Nixon prepared his last State of the Union address, Stanley Scott, Vice President Gerald Ford's black aide, went to Pat Buchanan, of all people, with a request for a few positive lines about African Americans. "Blacks and other minorities—with few exceptions," Scott argued, "have been silent on the Watergate controversy."[110] The request, like Nixon himself, was dumped.

"Nixon's got to come by the black community one of these days," Andrew Young assumed while waiting for the second term to start. Two years later, he knew he had guessed wrong about Nixon (and Gerald Ford as well). "They were racists not in the aggressive sense," Young concluded, "but in that they had no understanding of the problems of colored people anywhere."[111] Whether racist to the bone or not, Nixon certainly tilted in that direction. "Like the flat, dark side of the moon," Ehrlichman said. "There were subliminal racial messages in a lot of Nixon's campaigning." Something "subtler than code words. It was, 'I am on your side. I am going to deal with it in a way you'll approve of.' I know he saw Johnson's embrace of blacks as an opportunity. He exploited it." Nixon told Ehrlichman that the Great Society's programs were a waste on every level, that at best "America's blacks could only marginally benefit . . . because blacks were *genetically inferior* to whites." Scarcely fit for any task, in other words. The president also complained habitually to Ehrlichman and Haldeman about the too many black waiters at the White House.[112]

A reasonable person might conclude that Nixon's record on racial justice and other liberal causes remains something of an enigma (at least if Ehrlichman's forthright explanation of the zig-zag approach is discounted). The distinguished historian Herbert Parmet described the president as (almost) the second coming of Martin Luther King: "It would do a great injustice to deny [his] intellectual and spiritual commitment to racial equality." This echoed Pat Buchanan: "With the lone exception of Lyndon Johnson's, no Administration so consciously tilted policy toward black America as did Richard Nixon's." Buchanan dug out facts to support this, going on and on as if he were a Great Society publicist. "U.S. aid to black colleges more than doubled . . . More school integration was achieved in four years that in the previous fifteen since *Brown*," and so forth. Nixon's years also witnessed the Environmental Protection Act, the Occupational Safety and Health Act, the Comprehensive Employment and Training Act, and a price freeze when the economy went sour. Abroad the president normalized relations with China and pursued detente with the Soviet Union. Zigs and zags indeed.[113]

On civil rights matters Nixon had his own explanation for the apparent enigma. "I was walking a fine line between the instant integrationists and the segregation-forever extremists," he wrote in the memoir. "As a Republican and a moderate conservative I had a better chance of achieving an accommodation between the races than a Democrat or a liberal who was publicly committed to one particular cause."[114] There is no arrogance in that statement; it is simply untrue. Nixon was always arrogant in his attitude toward the exercise of power but never arrogant about his intentions. "It is quite obvious," he told Congress from retirement, "that there are certain inherently governmental actions which if undertaken by *the sovereign* in protection of the interests of the nation's security are lawful but which if undertaken by private persons are not [emphasis added]."[115] This was true whether those actions were intended to topple Salvator Allende in Chile or Huey Newton in Oakland or even Martin Luther King in the nation's memory.

Rehabilitation of his civil rights record demanded obfuscation and outright lies. "The Republican Party must have no room for racism," Nixon's memoirs say. "The Deep South had to be virtually conceded to George Wallace. I could not match him there without compromising on the civil rights issue, which I would not do."[116] A few lines in a book, however, could not wipe away Nixon's blue-ink scribble on thousands of southern-policy documents or the spectacle of his operatives using Nazis to recruit Wallace voters. Watch what we do and not what we say, John Mitchell had quipped. Or vice versa. There was truth in none of it. "Our position is to withhold information and to cover up," Nixon told Ehrlichman and press secretary Ron Ziegler during Watergate's darkest hour. "This is totally true—you could say this is totally untrue."[117] With indifference to racial justice rivaling indifference to truth, Nixon's southern strategy was particularly unfortunate for the nation and its citizens regardless of their color.

Richard Nixon held to the lesson learned on Chief Newman's Whittier bench. In a second memoir he indirectly admitted a second cue taken from another surprising source: "We sometimes forget that FDR was a master of invective. His most useful enemies were all members of the upper class, as was he. He attacked these 'princes of privilege' and 'economic royalists' with relish. Some criticize him for cynically instigating class warfare. But during the Depression, the nation was deeply divided between the haves and the have nots. Since there were more of the latter, he became their champion and profited politically from doing so. This enabled him to get and keep power. What he did with that power is a matter for an entirely separate debate."[118]

Nixon forgot to mention that he, too, was a master of invective; that his most useful enemies were not the traditional populist enemies (economic royalists) but the new populism's enemies (blacks); that he attacked these new princes of affirmative action privilege with relish; that some criticized him for cynically instigating racial conflict (if not racial warfare); that during his watch the nation was deeply divided between black and white; that since there were more of the latter he became their champion and profited politically from doing so. The simple counting skills required on this last point enabled Nixon to get power if not keep it (the southern strategy did not consider Frank Wills, the black watchman at the Watergate apartment and office complex who noticed something suspicious and brought the police into CREEP's lap). What he did with that power on the racial front, as on the Watergate front, was a disgrace. An entirely separate disgrace.

: 8 :

ACCIDENTALS

Richard Nixon's resignation left everything, including an exploding busing crisis in Boston, to a poorly prepared Gerald Ford (1974–1977). LBJ had joked, cruelly, about Ford having played football too long without a helmet and ending up "so dumb he can't walk and chew gum at the same time." In fact Ford had a good sense of right and wrong early on. Even on the football field. When his University of Michigan team played Georgia Tech in Atlanta and black teammate Willis Ward was not allowed to dress, Ford called his stepfather for advice. The man told him to do whatever the coach said. Ford then went to Ward, who said, "'You owe it to the team.'" To play, that is. "That Saturday we hit like never before and beat Georgia Tech 9–2," Ford remembered. Unquestionably the best athlete to make the White House and possibly the toughest man physically, that epitomized Gerry Ford: student-athlete (or politician) who agonized and then made the easy choice. Do what the coach says. On race this translated to what the columnist Chuck Stone called Ford's "buck and wing litany of 'some of my best friends are black.'"[1]

Ford had a mixed civil rights record as a Michigan congressman. NAACP activists blamed him for leading the fight in the House against open housing in 1966 and again in 1968, for siding with the real-estate

331

lobby and Republicans representing suburban constituents. Clarence
Mitchell said he was in cahoots with Strom Thurmond, a criticism that
stung no matter how exaggerated. Ford supported housing reform only
after King's assassination, voting on April 11, 1968, for the bill that
became the Civil Rights Act of 1968. Although he supported the
Nixon administration's antibusing campaign, he spoke out (at Massachusetts Senator Edward Brooke's urging) against Agnew's extreme
law-and-order cant because the words were code for repression of
blacks. (He preferred the term "order with justice under law.") By the
time he replaced Agnew, who turned out to be a crook, Ford was aware
of the president's own shortcomings. "The Nixon Administration had
closed the door to minorities," he noted, simply. "Particularly blacks."
But he took the job anyway, just like at Georgia Tech. He would work
that much harder to do the right thing.[2]

Vice President Ford held regular meetings with black leaders, saying:
"I wanted these groups to know that I could be—and really wanted to
be—point man for them in their dealings with the government." But
when he submitted "recommendations for follow-through to officials
in the West Wing of the White House," nothing happened. "There was
no follow-through; the people there didn't care." When Martin Luther
King's mother was murdered while playing the organ at Ebenezer Baptist Church, Ford volunteered to represent the administration at the
funeral. Stanley Scott took the offer to the West Wing where Alexander Haig rejected it. "Instead, the Praetorians contrived that the Vice
President must fly to Loring, Maine, to welcome Nixon home from
Moscow at almost the same hour," another Ford aide explained. Ford's
wife Betty took it on herself to go to Atlanta where she saw Daddy
King at the family home and sat in the church for the funeral. "I can
remember only two white people," she said. "One was Jimmy Carter
and the other was me."[3]

Loyalty to Nixon had brought Ford to the vice-presidency in the first
place and on the big issues he remained true. He had stuck up for the
president in Congress, defending the administration's "stance" on both
Watergate and "social issues." Ford's press secretary and Michigan
friend Jerald F. terHorst said the latter included Nixon's image "as
something less than a friend of minorities." Ford stood by Nixon after
the resignation, too, most spectacularly with the presidential pardon.

That act was the most controversial of his administration and it sparked a wave of protest, including one by terHorst (who resigned his position). Nixon misjudged everyone during the Watergate daze except Ford.[4]

President Ford ocassionally broke with southern-strategy doctrine nonetheless. He met with Jesse Jackson and other black leaders and (eventually) ignored Dixie clamor and simply asked Congress for another five-year extension of the Voting Rights Act. (Initially he suggested that the law be applied nationwide and ended up confusing and enraging every side in what Edward Kennedy called an incompetent attempt "to have it all ways.")[5] Ford also sought out black audiences, though his efforts bordered on the absurd. John J. Casserly, assigned to write a speech for North Carolina Central University's fiftieth anniversary celebration, received orders to produce ten minutes of jokes. Enlisting the support of John Calhoun, Ford's second black aide, Casserly won permission to prepare a more suitable address for this "solemn and historic occasion." Still, there could be no sharp edges. Casserly said Ford's senior staff removed everything of substance from another speech for the National Baptist Convention—including references to slavery; Martin Luther King ("because he and Dr. Jackson, the Baptist leader, didn't always agree"); blacks in the military; and even "quality education."[6]

Other than the Watergate pardon, Ford proved his loyalty best in the continuing school war—as the censored reference to "quality education" suggested. This was in line with his own inclinations and those of his cabinet. On the matter of the colleges HEW Secretary Caspar Weinberger advised against any use of quotas or goals in the faculty-hiring or student-admission process. Such things, he feared, would impose "terribly burdensome requirements." Treasury Secretary William Simon joined the defense by arguing that the Civil Rights Commission erred in criticizing the IRS for not going after all-white private colleges. Based on his reading of Title VI of the Civil Rights Act of 1964, the federal tax system could not (and should not) be used to enforce any civil rights law. This avoided a sticky problem, Simon added, as some 18,000 private schools operated in the United States from preschool through graduate school and more than 12,000 of these were church-related.[7]

Ford mostly limited his personal involvement in the school wars to the busing issue. He was always on the alert to condemn the courts for interfering with what he considered the natural order of things. "It was not based on racism per se, at least in his own mind," an aide explained. "He was a product of neighborhood schools in Grand Rapids, and he thought that was a very positive experience that all American children should have." Besides flights of antibusing rhetoric for mass consumption, Ford had the Justice Department look for "a proper record in a case that would justify . . . a proceeding before the Supreme Court to see if the court would review its decision in the Brown case and the several that followed thereafter." He apparently misspoke himself here and later announced that he supported *Brown v. Board of Education.* Yet he continued to trace the busing controversy to *Brown* and to note that "nobody in the executive branch can change that judgment." The president also ordered a study to document busing's harmful effects (for use in argument before the courts) and submitted legislation to Congress restricting the judiciary's use of "radical remedies" when addressing the problem of segregation in the schools. He said the purpose of the School Desegregation Standards and Assistance Bill was to protect "community control of schools."[8]

In all of this Ford found himself, as his staff put it, between a rock and a hard place. Constant White House reminders that the president "respectfully disagreed" with court-ordered busing upset the civil rights groups and inspired embarrassing questions. When Roy Wilkins challenged Ford to name one instance where federal judges had gone too far in ordering busing, White House staff had no answer. They collected a few lame examples only after telephoning Harvard neo-con Nathan Glazer for help and digging through the files for days. All this prompted the administration to sever its "dialogue" with the bothersome Wilkins and other NAACP voices. At the same time the president's rhetoric had led to rising expectations among the antibusing people—a development that had political consequences. More and more voters were asking themselves, as another White House aide noted: If busing was so bad, why wasn't Ford stopping it?[9]

That was what Louise Day Hicks and ROAR (Restore Our Alienated Rights) wanted to know in Boston, where the busing controversy had erupted in violence. Ford ended this dialogue before it began by refusing the requests of Massachusetts Senators Brooke and Kennedy to meet with Hicks and her (very) white delegation. Ford could not possibly satisfy them, as presidential aide Richard Parsons put it, and could not possibly learn anything from them. Parsons instead met with a fifteen-person ROAR delegation in Boston. That meeting confirmed his original judgment. Busing was indeed a mess, and Mrs. Hicks's rantings about "rich people in the suburbs," like Spiro Agnew's laments about "limousine liberals," were not far off base. "The plain people of the city" paid the price of busing, Hicks said: "The workingman and woman, the rent payer, the home owner, the law-abiding, tax-paying, decent-living, hard-working, forgotten American." Upscale suburbs remained effectively segregated, and the city's "wealthy practitioners of 'compassion'" tended not to send their children to public schools at all.[10]

Like the decision to suit up against Georgia Tech, there was an easy choice: To speak out against busing. And Ford took it. In the process he acted as if both sides (symbolized by Roy Wilkins and Louise Day Hicks) were unclean. He stood in the end pretty much where Wilkins said: "I thought that he had jumped to the forefront of the mob. . . . He was leading the way against the courts and the Fourteenth Amendment, the *Brown* decision and black children. The way he undermined us was a craven retreat and a capitulation to the lawlessness and ignorance of the people who were fanning the race issue."[11] Nixon had already marked the spot on the southern-strategy map, and, with an "X" at the mob's head, Ford stepped forward and hit the mark. He rode out the Watergate president's second term but not his civil rights legacy.

In 1976 it took Watergate *and* a southern candidate with a lock on the white Christian evangelical vote to push out the presidential party. James Earl Carter of Georgia ran 2.1 percentage points better than Ford in the popular vote and took the electoral college by only a slightly more comfortable margin (297–240). The Republicans did well in the white South even with a vice-presidential candidate, Nelson Rockefeller, who had as much civil rights baggage as any white politician outside Lyndon Johnson. Ignoring advice that he dump Rockefeller, Ford calculated that Watergate had temporarily turned Nixon's southern strategy inside out and thus given the neck-and-neck nature of this race the black vote would be crucial. The magnitude of Nixon's disgrace was such that a few anti–southern strategy advisers actually suggested that Ford "try to characterize Carter's campaign as a mirror image of Nixon's '68 and '72 campaigns" and Carter himself as driven by the same demons (personal ambition, an obsession with secrecy, etc.).[12]

None of this meant that Ford would lead the first presidential party play for the African-American vote since Eisenhower. "Most blacks were unlikely to vote for me no matter what I did," he realized. Campaign pressures ultimately led to a modest southern strategy revival—what White House aide Mike Duval called a program to "*neutralize the anti-Ford feeling among blacks*" and otherwise "discourage active black opposition on election day." This was done in a convoluted manner. The president pondered a ghetto visit in search of "anecdotal" material for the campaign's great debate, thinking of Bedford-Stuyvesant first because that was the location of the Development and Service Corporation started by Robert Kennedy to improve job opportunities and living conditions in central Brooklyn. "*It may result in some pro-Ford comments from the Kennedy crowd,*" Duval noted. "This is a Kennedy project and they certainly have every motive to oppose Carter." Any criticism by Edward Kennedy of Carter's liberal credentials could only help Ford's play to keep the black vote home.[13]

Obviously it did not work. If Carter ran soft in his own region (getting 36% of southern white voters earning more than $20,000 a year), African-American votes North and South proved the margin of victory in twelve states. That vote came primarily because Carter was a Democrat. What Ford feared most (a strong black turnout) came because Carter established his civil rights credentials in *Why Not the Best?*, a memoir/campaign broadside that provided an almost mythic account of his willingness to befriend blacks and otherwise do the right thing during Georgia's Jim Crow days. Endorsements from Daddy King, Coretta Scott King, and Andrew Young also helped, as did Carter's talent for speaking in black Baptist churches. The candidate always seemed more comfortable with "Yes, suh" and "Amen, brother" than polite applause. Wife Rosalynn carried much of the load here by campaigning in the nation's African-American neighborhoods accompanied most of the time only by another white woman and a driver. The sight of a white southern lady listening to black troubles, eating in black restaurants, and sleeping overnight in black hotels probably did as much to get out the vote as the King family endorsements.[14]

"The descendants of black slaves united," Chuck Stone observed with something less than celebratory spirit, "to provide the balance of power for a Georgia redneck's election as the 39th President of the United States." Stone labeled Carter "at best a cautious integrationist, at worst a subcutaneous segregationist."[15] Carter saw himself as a spokesman for a New South that would march toward the twenty-first century without the burden of white over black at all costs. He proposed substituting a politics of racial empathy for a politics of racial division. Chuck Stone's redneck liked to quote Reinhold Niebuhr, Bob Dylan, and Dylan Thomas and sometimes spoke in the psycho-babble of those who had no other holy grail to search out than their true selves and inner feelings. The only Bubba-like things about him were the accent, place of birth, refusal to abandon "Jimmy" for "James."

From Stone and others who adopted a wait-and-see attitude, Jimmy Carter asked for trust. Roy Wilkins remembered one such request that arrived in the post during the primaries and began with the fawning, "As a longtime admirer of yours . . ." "I looked at that neat, earnest handwriting and shook my head," Wilkins said. "There was always something of the prize schoolboy about Jimmy Carter, but it was hard not to like him."[16] Everyone wanted to believe. "John Kennedy read about racism and poverty in a sociology class at Harvard," Andrew Young said, "but Jimmy Carter lived it."

Carter remained true, electorally and otherwise, to the two images of himself that he lived and built: That of a Joan Baez red-dirt Georgia farm boy from Plains, located in the west end of Sumter County and part of the Mississippi-Alabama-Georgia black belt; and that of the Annapolis graduate and card-carrying nuclear engineer. Unlike Nixon and Ford, whose growing-up associations stretched no further than football fields, Carter spoke of a childhood in the predominantly black hamlet of Archery, Georgia. In a community of twenty-five families only the Carters and one other were white. "We grew up alike," Young added. "I grew up in New Orleans in a white neighborhood playing with white kids but going to schools with only black kids. Jimmy Carter grew up surrounded by black playmates but went to schools with only white kids."[17]

"All my playmates were black," Carter wrote in *Why Not the Best*. "We hunted, fished, explored, worked and slept together," spent summer nights "on the banks of Choctawhatchee and Kinchafoonee creeks, catching and cooking catfish and eels when the water was rising from heavy rains. . . . We ran, swam, rode horses, drove wagons and floated on rafts together. We misbehaved together and shared the same punishments. We built and lived in the same tree houses and played cards and ate at the same table. But we never went to the same Church or school." They never quite played as equals either. Jimmy's sister, Ruth Carter Stapleton, said the black kids were conditioned to let their white playmate win at everything.

In adolescence, even besting black friends was not permitted by Jim Crow norms. "I was literally a grown man," Carter noted, "before I was thrown into social situations in which I routinely met and talked with black men and women on an equal basis." The only sustained non-white presence in Carter's childhood and adolescence resulted from the work schedule of his mother, Miss Lillian, a registered nurse. Annie Mae Jones, one of the African-American women who raised him, said Miss Lillian "nursed day and night." So black women cooked meals for Jimmy and the other Carter children, got them off to school, met them at day's end.[18]

What the young Carter had in common with Nixon and Ford was a profound interracial experience through sports. The difference was that he merely observed while Nixon participated (if only from the Whittier bench) and Ford anchored the Michigan line. In *Why Not the Best*, Carter used one of the greatest moments in sports history to make a point about how race divided the South and his own family. "All our black neighbors came to see Daddy when the second Joe Louis–Max Schmeling fight was to take place," he wrote. "We propped the radio up in the open window of our house, and we and our visitors sat and stood under a large mulberry tree nearby." The fight ended quickly. "There was no sound from anyone in the yard, except a polite, 'Thank you, Mr. Earl,' offered to my father," Carter continued. "Then, our several dozen visitors filed across the dirt road, across the railroad track, and quietly entered a house about a hundred yards away out in the field. At that point, pandemonium broke loose inside that house, as our black neighbors shouted and yelled in celebration of the Louis victory."

In contrast the elder Carter "was deeply disappointed in the outcome." It made no difference that Hitler promoted Schmeling (however unfairly) as an Aryan champion. All Mr. Earl saw was a great white hope.[19]

Grown up the son took a different tack. Carter refused to join the White Citizens Council when it organized in Plains after *Brown*, holding out even when threatened with a boycott of the family peanut business. "But the boycott failed to materialize," Rosalynn Carter remembered, "with one or two minor exceptions—one being my cousin, who never came back to our office again." When the Citizens Council tried another approach, offering to pick up the five-dollar dues for the Carters, Jimmy and Rosalynn instead bought shoes for the children of a poverty-stricken black farmer who lived nearby. The segregationists steamed but again did nothing but mumble about peanut boycotts. The Carters's courage, however, had little effect on the town's white families. Plains changed slowly if at all. In fact, Rosalynn remembered with disgust that the owner of the local tavern had passed out free beer in celebration of Martin Luther King's assassination. Georgia realities were hard to change and even harder to escape. So certain compromises were probably inevitable. When Jimmy ran for governor in 1970 some said he conducted a racist campaign. Others said it was merely populist and noted that Carter ordered King's portrait hung in the state capitol once in office.[20]

Carter also sent mixed messages during the 1976 push for the White House. The most controversial were his remarks about busing and use of the phrase "ethnic purity" to describe white-ethnic enclaves and neighborhood schools. The remark, originally reported on April 2 by *New York Daily News* political correspondent Sam Roberts, was buried on page 134 (paragraph sixteen). Primaries in New York and Wisconsin came and went before CBS News picked it up, and correspondent Ed Bradley, then traveling with the campaign team, asked Carter about it in Indianapolis. Follow-up questions in South Bend and Pittsburgh led to additional warnings from the candidate about "alien groups" and "black intrusion." "Interjecting into [a community] a member of another race" or "a diametrically opposite kind of family" or a "different kind of person" threatened what Carter called the admirable value of "ethnic purity." "We had a little bit of a cultural problem," Hamilton

Jordan, Carter's chief aide, said. Aryan culture, in Andrew Young's view. "[It was] a disaster for the campaign. I don't think he understood how loaded it is with Hitlerian connotations."[21]

The phrase, stark by any definition, sparked a debate about the candidate's intent. Most commentators saw it (and especially the details that followed on black intrusion) as a reflection of Carter's stubbornness. Rather than admit error or obfuscate, Carter tried to talk his way out and only got in deeper. Others saw the remark as measured. With George Wallace on the way out of the race and with primaries coming up in Pennsylvania and Michigan, Morris Udall said Carter had an eye on the white-ethnic vote in those states. The Ford campaign shared this view. Ethel Allen, a black surgeon in Philadelphia who chaired the president's campaign in that city, called the ethnic-purity statement a "brilliant" political move "calculated . . . . to get the Wallace vote in Texas, Missouri and Georgia, and it's paying off handsomely. It made him an instant household word, and it didn't antagonize the Ku Klux Klan, and White Citizens Council, or the American Nazi Party. . . . He didn't lose points with blacks because blacks can forgive a man who's religious sooner than they can forgive a man who's not close to God. That's why they didn't turn off when they saw the pictures of Daddy King embracing him like they did when they saw Sammy Davis, Jr., hugging Nixon."[22]

Carter had also undercut busing (the Ford campaign's trump issue) and practically invited the president to say something unkind about "ethnic purity." Ford took the bait, scribbling out notes for a question and answer session with the press: "That's not a phrase I would use to describe any of my policies. 1) Always *believed in* diversity. 2) Govt's obligation to make certain all constitutional rights are fully protected. 3) At same time each of us, within constitutional and legal limitations, have inalienable rights and freedom." Carter was no traditional liberal on busing or anything else and that made him a difficult target. "There is some resemblance between the Carter and Ford positions," David Gergen noted at the White House, "because they both favor community-based efforts to defuse the issue of busing." The only real difference was that Carter did not support a constitutional amendment. Ford's people concluded here and elsewhere that it would be difficult to "hang the liberal program" on this moderate or otherwise "nail him" as a Kennedy/Humphrey/McGovern clone.[23]

Even an apparently unqualified civil rights embrace was not what it seemed. Speech writer Patrick Anderson cobbled King's "I Have a Dream" words with Robert Kennedy's remarks on the night King died, and Carter's reading on June 1 at the dedication of a new wing for the Martin Luther King Hospital in Los Angeles rivaled in passion the original inspirations. Unfortunately, the Carter/Anderson refrain ("But the dream lives on") struck the press bus gang as corny. When the reporters later surrounded Anderson and began singing "We Shall Overcome," the speech writer could not believe "they were making fun of my finest moment." Carter himself was more tough minded than the press suspected. The single line deleted from Anderson's final draft was a critical reference to George Wallace.[24]

Carter's only other mixed campaign message on the racial front barely caused a ripple beyond Jesse Jackson and the other black leaders who came to the Democratic National Convention in New York. Jackson, upset because Carter did not even consider Los Angeles Mayor Tom Bradley for the ticket's number-two spot, met with the Carter team at the nominee's temporary office on the Americana Hotel's twenty-first floor. The meeting came to nothing. When Carter, the ultimate outsider, explained that he picked Minnesota's Walter Mondale because he needed a Washington insider, Jackson said no one really expected him to choose Bradley but the sight of a black man stepping off an airplane in Plains, Georgia, would have done wonders for African-American morale. Carter saw no good in such a charade and was stunned by Jackson's reasoning. Likewise, Jackson could not fathom this peanut farmer.[25]

Carter remained an enigma once in the Oval Office. "One hears over and over again," Roger Wilkins complained, "that black access to the White House . . . is more limited than it has been since the days of Franklin Roosevelt. Even Nixon had John Ehrlichman who, until they drew the wagons around the White House, was said to be sympathetic and eager to learn." Carter's initial appointments, excepting Andrew Young (United Nations), Patricia Harris (HUD), and Eleanor Holmes Norton (EEOC), deepened these suspicions. The president "ignored the largest pool of seasoned black governmental talent the country had ever developed," Wilkins continued. "Those people who cut their teeth on government during the Kennedy-Johnson years and came to wield responsibility on a national level." More disturbing was the choice for attorney general, Griffin Bell, who belonged to two segregated Atlanta men's clubs (Capital City and the Piedmont Driving Club) and, as a legal adviser in the 1950s to Georgia Governor Ernest Vandiver, had tried to block school desegregation. An attorney who criticized Bell's selection, Joe Rauh, found himself in an honored position. "The only person on my enemies list," Carter told HEW secretary Joseph Califano.[26]

This was nothing much to criticize. Carter had been a racial radical by Plains standards and remained one by the Washington standards of the Nixon/Ford years. More progressive appointments included Norton's fellow SNCC veteran John Lewis as associate director of Action (where he joined Mary King, another SNCC veteran and Action's deputy director); Wade McCree, a black appeals court judge, as solicitor general; and Drew Days from the NAACP Legal Defense and Education Fund as assistant attorney general for civil rights. Since FBI harassment had been an issue during the campaign (Coretta King said the bureau "treated the civil rights movement as if it were an alien enemy attack on the United States"), Carter even considered (however briefly) appointing a black man to the directorship. The only name that surfaced, however, was William Lucas—a former special agent with a conservative bent. When Lucas ran (unsuccessfully) for governor of Michigan on the Republican ticket nine years later, he made the evils of affirmative action a campaign centerpiece.[27]

Carter moved beyond appointments eleven months into the term by announcing a civil rights reform/reorganization plan ("a comprehensive series of measures to consolidate and to streamline the enforcement of equal employment laws in our country"). He then brought Louis Martin into the White House to work on "special programs and policies that are of interest to Black Americans." The main focus, however, was on what Gerald Rafshoon, the president's so-called secretary of symbolism, called "the discipline of themes." Carter visited Ebenezer Baptist Church to celebrate King's birthday (and to receive the Martin Luther King, Jr., Nonviolent Peace Prize); videotaped messages to the Black Athletes Hall of Fame, among other African-American groups;

plotted photo opportunities when scheduling tennis time with Bill Cosby; and sent a plane carrying Andrew Young, Vernon Jordan, Patt Derian, and Hodding Carter III to Fanny Lou Hamer's funeral in Mississippi.[28] None of this much impressed those civil rights leaders who wanted more than symbols and a discipline of themes.

The Carter administration responded to any unkind word with a Nixonian siege mentality. "You were on television criticizing our [urban] policy at the same time it was announced—I personally doubt you even read it," White House chief of staff Hamilton Jordan complained to Vernon Jordan in April 1978. "I am not aware of a positive thing you have said about the President since he has been in office." Vernon Jordan found the other Jordan's words "a regrettable exercise in hypersensitivity, reflecting a defensiveness that's simply not called for."[29] Whereas Adlai Stevenson once expected black gratitude (because he was not Eisenhower), Carter expected the same because he was not Nixon. He never quite understood that civil rights leadership expected much more out of his administration in the first place.

With equal opportunity for jobs and scholarships and the accompanying "quota" dilemmas emerging as Carter's most pressing headache, nowhere was the organized civil rights community's disappointment more apparent than on the contentious question of affirmative action. If the president intended to avoid what one White House aide called the "high profile approach" favored by the Ford administration on its crunch civil rights issue (busing), he was successful.[30] Whereas Ford looked for federal court cases in which to intervene and otherwise shout his opposition to busing, when Carter stumbled upon a major affirmative action case he tried to manage and otherwise tone down rising divisions about "preferential treatment" for African Americans and other minorities. His efforts had the opposite effect and ultimately fed the reconstituted southern strategies of Ronald Reagan and other presidential hopefuls who were willing (as a Reagan aide once put it) "to settle for the white vote."[31]

Allan P. Bakke, an unsuccessful applicant to the Medical School at the University of California at Davis, brought affirmative action into Carter's lap by challenging a special minority admissions program that accepted minority students for admission with lower test scores and lesser qualifications than his own. Administration involvement came in an odd way. Normally the Supreme Court would request the Justice Department's participation in a case the magnitude of *Regents of the University of California v. Bakke.*[32] When the Warren Court "invited" Attorney General Herbert Brownell to submit a brief in *Brown,* for example, Eisenhower understood that it was really a "command." But there would be no invitation/command in *Bakke* (the result of the court's desire to prevent a replay of the previous administration's opportunism on busing). Carter's people entered the case not at the invitation of Supreme Court justices but at the behest of University of California officials who met with HEW's Joseph Califano and then various Justice Department attorneys to ask for a brief on their institution's behalf. This meant a brief for affirmative action and "set aside" quotas for minority applicants.

Carter hoped to land in the comfortable middle and thereby appease all contending groups. The problem was that no contending group shared his definition of a middle where affirmative action programs were constitutional but rigid quota systems were unconstitutional. This issue, as Pat Buchanan would say, was *de facto* divisive. Some found it ridiculous that an affluent white in his thirties who worked as an engineer like Allan Bakke could claim to be a victim of "reverse" or any other sort of discrimination. Legal scholar Derrick Bell pointed out that "many special preferences" already existed at colleges and professional schools benefiting "directly to applicants who are faculty, alumni, or donor offspring, and indirectly to those fortunate enough to be born into upper income homes where quality schools and upper social class environment increase the likelihood of top grades and test scores." In Bell's view the problem was that "the advocates of 'merit' have managed to transfer the burden of justification from the preferences that favor the white elite to the preferences forged by minorities in order partially to correct the bias which results from the socioeconomic preferences."[33]

The affirmative action arguments of Derrick Bell and other advocates proved a hard sell to the general electorate. White middle America saw the issue as cut and dried. Because Bakke had "merit" (higher test scores than successful minority applicants) but did not get his medical school seat, he was a classic victim of reverse discrimination. The whole notion of merit could not be dismissed in Bell's easy manner. For millions of white families merit was their only connection to the American dream. The belief that hard work would be rewarded was as old as the Republic. It had been challenged before, most notably and some said ironically by slavery. (Lincoln opposed slavery first and foremost, re-member, because it interfered with "the right to rise.") Social mobility now stood challenged by arbitrary guardians at the University of Cali-fornia and elsewhere. In this view affirmative action discriminated against those white men not fortunate enough to have been born into upper-income homes where they could attend quality schools and grow up in an upper social class environment. What the "populist" Nixon had understood was that most white people resented both the old "spe-cial preferences" for the rich and the new ones for blacks. Carter never quite understood that Allan Bakke was speaking for Nixon's silent and forgotten majority.

If Carter's presidency disintegrated with the economic riddle of "stagflation" and the Iranian hostage crisis, the process began with *Bakke* and the president's awkward attempt to support affirmative action while condemning quotas. After making the decision to inter-vene, the administration lobbied every conceivable interest group from the Jewish organizations to the National Lawyers Guild. (The latter, in its McCarthy-era heyday, had nearly made the attorney general's list of subversive organizations.) Every administration official had an opinion on the proper course, too, and few in the White House or the cabinet departments were hesitant to leak their wisdom to the press. Joseph Califano, at the center of the controversy from his HEW desk, com-plained that "the political struggles and infighting . . . over the *Bakke* brief were front-page news in the nation's major papers." The result was chaos in the Oval Office and a feeding frenzy in the media. When the NAACP board met in New York to discuss the case, for example, Carter's staff tracked the reporters and camera crews "swarming around the Board waiting for them to issue acrimonious statements." At issue here was what White House aide Bunny Mitchell called "our alleged (and previously published) position."[34]

Califano was among the administration's most aggressive affirmative action advocates, and his service in the Johnson White House provided a standard by which to judge Carter's commitment to racial justice. Nothing measured up. "I thought about the sea-change from Johnson's Justice Department," he said. "The Justice Department's *Bakke* brief would set civil rights back a generation." He told the president that the brief (or at least its current draft) represented "pernicious social policy" and that "race-sensitive programs are not 'presumptively unconstitutional,' as that brief asserts." Califano's blunder came during an interview with a *New York Times* reporter when he used the forbidden word (quota) and thereafter "was never able to shake the 'quota' stamp."[35]

Carter exercised scarcely more control over the *Bakke* intervention than Califano as he wavered between an aggressive approach and an attempt to disassociate himself from the case entirely. White House aides had pressured Justice to include a "strongly" argued section leaving no doubt about the president's basic belief "that racial quotas were unconstitutional." But the brief's final draft (of some dozen attempts) upset the president because it contained only "one relatively mild anti-quota sentence." While one presidential aide, Stuart Eizenstat, worried about "backlash" from the Jewish groups (among others), Hamilton Jordan was nearly alone in urging Carter to cut his losses. *Bakke* raised racial justice issues in such a "muddled and confused" way that it represented the worst possible "opportunity for us to state the political philosophy of this Administration. . . . Neither you nor I have been able to understand the legalisms in this case. How can we expect illiterate and disadvantaged people to understand." Bakke's attorney called the brief a "desperate" attempt "to find some trap doors in the record" that might "magically open, and through them the government's political problems will magically disappear."

Hamilton Jordan knew that both the white majority and African-American minority would only care about which side the administration came down on. "*We are going to suffer the worst of both worlds,*" he concluded. "*We are going to be held politically responsible for our involvement in a brief that we have had little or no involvement in.* Despite your instructions that Stu and Bob 'jump into the drafting,' the people at Justice have not allowed them to participate. This has created something of an institutional problem." It created an additional political problem, too, as it seemed to suggest that Carter could not control his own people. While Griffin Bell complained that "everyone in the nation was trying to help us write the brief," Califano countered (his earlier complaints about press leaks aside) that this was how "it should be." In either case the president was included among those whose help was turned away.[36]

The irony is that the Supreme Court came close to giving the administration what it wanted. Its decision, handed down in 1978, held that affirmative action in university admissions was not unconstitutional in principle but that use of numerical quotas in this particular case was unconstitutional. Carter wanted middle of the road, and the *Bakke* decision was reasonably near the yellow line. Unfortunately, the court's decision settled nothing. The president's performance, as Hamilton Jordan predicted, led the civil rights groups to question his commitment to racial justice. For the white majority and especially those millions not fortunate enough to be wealthy, the president's performance led to a loss of faith in his commitment to merit and other equal opportunity doctrine. The president ended up alienating black and white alike. Worst of both worlds indeed.

Jimmy Carter, the good old boy from Plains, Georgia, lost his tenuous hold on the white southern voter before any of those voters had heard the word "stagflation" or the name "Khomeini." Not even such a dramatic White House gesture as the forced resignation of UN ambassador Andrew Young would get those voters back. Young had endeared himself to Carter during the 1976 primaries and general election by working black communities and civil rights, antiwar, and labor groups. In the course of his own successful run for a House seat, he campaigned for his fellow Georgian in some twenty-seven states and fifty-one cities. Young was also a natural choice for the UN post. Carter's human rights crusade, fed by what National Security Adviser Zbigniew Brzezinski called a "deep religious commitment to freedom and racial justice," recognized a relationship between African Americans and the world's nonwhite peoples. The president needed someone who could speak credibly to the Third World on human rights and convey his "genuine determination on majority rule in Africa."[37]

Few Americans had more direct experience with human rights abuses and majority rule issues than Andrew Young. He had been Martin Luther King's number-two man (after Ralph Abernathy) during all those years of battle against southern sheriffs, Klansmen, voting registrars, and FBI agents. Four years after J. Edgar Hoover's death, the supposedly reformed bureau tried to sabotage Young's run for

Congress. Other intelligence community bureaucracies demonstrated an interest after Young won election. "In the freshman orientation . . . one of the things you are told," he noted, "is that there are seven agencies that keep files on private lives of Congressmen." All this gave Young more credibility with the Third World than any diplomat in American history (Ralph Bunche included).[38]

Young's goal in the United Nations (putting America on "the right side of the moral issues of the world") was admirable; his methods more questionable. Critics said he practiced "Open Mouth Diplomacy." Young called Cuba a more-or-less stabilizing influence in Angola; dismissed Britain, Sweden, and Russia as racist nations; labeled former Presidents Nixon and Ford racist to the bone; championed the cause of "political prisoners" (poor blacks, apparently) in this country; blamed the America bashing so common at the UN by reference to white racist attitudes and other Eurocentric sins; and had nice things to say about the Palestine Liberation Organization (PLO). No conventional diplomat, Young was a thoughtful and intelligent man who made detailed and articulate cases for all of the above thoughts. Predictably, the press skipped the nuances and went with naked caricature instead, and that was all the public and the president's congressional opponents saw. "Ambassador Andrew Young and his 'Manson family' at the United Nations in New York," Barry Goldwater roared. "Young's people were leftovers from the hippie generation. They were what some of us called 'looney tunes.'" Goldwater picked up this "intelligence" during a casual conversation with a CIA agent.[39]

The Israeli lobby, hardly amateurs in the game of racial politics or intelligence community manipulation, forced Young's resignation following his unauthorized conference on July 26, 1979, with Zehdi Terzi, the PLO's chief UN representative. When Menachim Begin's government protested, Young explained that the meeting, held at the UN, was accidental. Begin blew that cover story (something he could do since Israeli spies kept watch on Terzi and probably Young, too), forcing Young to backtrack and admit the PLO contact was prearranged.[40] His future was grim given Carter's success that past September in bringing Begin and Egypt's Anwar Sadat together to sign a "Framework for Peace in the Middle East." The president believed that posterity would remember him primarily for that document and especially the

Camp David accords finalized that March during a trip to the Middle East. Begin knew what buttons to push on the Andrew Young matter.

"I was in the room when he fired Andy Young," Griffin Bell remembered. "It was terrible to have him talk to Andy the way he did about meeting with the PLO. President Carter was big on using the word 'disgrace,' and he accused Andy Young of bringing disgrace on him." Yet there was no bitterness. "A mountain was made of a molehill," Carter later explained. The whole thing could have been avoided had "[Andy] informed the Secretary of State more fully about the controversial meeting." For his part Young continued to support the president. But this had little impact on Carter's dwindling support among African-American voters. It also made no difference that a black man, Donald McHenry, replaced Young at the UN. "Andy is clearly the titular leader of blacks in the country today," one White House aide said. "The loss is deep, profound, and serious." This is what Gerald Ford wanted in 1976 (a "hostile" and "low ebb" climate in the black community that would minimize voter turn out). With Jesse Jackson and others reminding their constituents that "the Klan didn't move on Andy," Young's firing cost Carter black votes while earning no white votes.[41]

Carter reached out for those black votes in the 1980 campaign. While Louis Martin organized mailing lists containing the names of "key blacks," the reelection team sought every endorsement it could get (even that of Nation of Islam leader Elijah Muhammad's son, Wallace D. Muhammad).[42] The president, sadly famous for what Elizabeth Drew called an "inability to talk to all manner of groups in a way that reaches them," also returned to the only place he seemed to be successful—the black Baptist churches. Up front at the Olivet Institutional Baptist Church on Cleveland's east side or any other church, Carter would bounce feet wide apart and sing out "Glory, glory, hallelujah!" with the congregation while "Rafshoon's crew" crouched and weaved silently "among the members of the choir, filming the President and his audience." Chuck Stone had called this "the mystique of the evangelical umbilical chord that still binds the black experience to a Southern gestalt. . . . [Carter] 'preached' and appeared to feel at home. This rapport was communicated in waves among friends and relatives of blacks who were exposed to him in these chitlin convocations." Stone wrote that after the first campaign and held to it during the second.[43]

Ronald Reagan, the Republican nominee, took an entirely different approach. "I believe in states' rights," he said while opening his campaign at the Neshoba County Fair in Philadelphia, Mississippi. The men who murdered Schwerner, Chaney, and Goodman sixteen summers earlier believed in states' rights, too, and there was no mistaking Reagan's intent. Reagan had calculated (correctly on both fronts) that the symbolism would be understood in the South and ignored in the North. Jesse Jackson learned as much seven years later when invited to speak at Harvard Law School. He asked the handful of students attending a private dinner before the speech if they knew where Reagan had opened the campaign. No one had even heard of Philadelphia, Mississippi. "So if the brightest of you don't uncover these signals," Jackson asked, "who will?"[44]

Even those who pretended that southern strategy had come and gone with Nixon were forced to admit that Reagan brought it back with a vengeance. The Ku Klux Klan had already endorsed Reagan, and it took the Republican candidate a week to reject that endorsement and three weeks to do so formally in an August 22 press release. (One Klan newspaper said the Republican platform "reads as if it were written by a Klansman.") Stung by criticism that he secretly welcomed Ku Klux Klan support, Reagan tried to lay the charge to rest during a September speech at the Michigan State Fair in Detroit. A heckler in a Carter mask triggered this line: "[I am] happy to be here where you are dealing at first hand with economic policies that have been committed, and he's opening his campaign down in the city [Tuscumbia, Alabama] that give birth to and is the parent body of the Ku Klux Klan." (The Klan was actually founded in Pulaski, Tennessee.) Reagan's diversion from southern strategy doctrine was brief. He righted himself immediately here (in contrast to the delay in repudiating Klan support) by sending letters of apology to Alabama's governor and Tuscumbia's mayor.[45]

Carter swung back hard (too hard, in the conventional wisdom). On the way in to Tuscumbia from the airport, he reminded reporters, the campaign entourage passed dozens of Klansmen in full-bed-sheet splendor carrying "Reagan for President" signs. From the pulpit of King's Ebenezer Baptist Church in Atlanta, Carter next called Reagan, in effect, a racist: "You've seen in this campaign the stirrings of hate and the rebirth of code words like 'states rights' in a speech in Mississippi, in a campaign reference to the Ku Klux Klan relating to the South."[46] The Republican response was predictable. "Ugly little insinuations," vice-presidential nominee George Bush said. Especially "ill suited" because Carter's opponent in the 1970 gubernatorial race in Georgia accused *him* of running a racist campaign.

Media reaction to the Tuscumbia and Ebenezer remarks, in contrast, was quite surprising. Of the Neshoba County Fair remark ("I believe in states' rights"), *New York Times* columnist Anthony Lewis said Reagan was either courting the racist vote or simply unaware of the symbolism. In other words Reagan got the benefit of the doubt. When Carter backed off the charge of racism at a press conference, in contrast, Lewis called the retreat a "hand-wringing hypocrisy worthy of Uriah Heep." "There is a mean streak in Carter the campaigner," he added, "and there always has been."[47]

This from a newspaper that had already reported matter of factly on the Republican party's direct appeals for the racist vote. These items included Reagan tales about standing in a grocery check-out line behind a "strapping young buck" who used food stamps to purchase T-bone steaks and booze or cigarettes with the change.[48] (Only in the South did Reagan use "buck," once a common slave-auction term for males— "wenches" for females.) There would be no debate in the press or anywhere else, however, about the nature of such appeals. George Bush understood the issue best and constantly hammered a simple theme: "I'm appalled at the ugly, *mean* little remark Jimmy Carter made [emphasis added]." The result was a media debate not about whether Reagan was racist to the bone but about just how *mean* Jimmy Carter was. Even the president's own people blamed him. "Rafshoon was right," Hamilton Jordan concluded. "It was the old Carter hyperbole. Jimmy Carter's tendency toward overstatement sometimes got him in trouble."[49]

Carter again skirted the racism charge at a fund-raising dinner in Chicago on October 6, accusing the other candidate of practicing a segmented politics predicated upon dividing black from white, Jew from Christian, North from South, rural from urban. Given what Reagan said in Neshoba and elsewhere (and what he would do over the next eight years), the president's charge appears in hindsight closer to understatement. Ironically, Reagan was practicing exactly what he had condemned during his movie star days. He spoke out on a Los Angeles radio program in 1946, part of a series entitled "It's Happening Here," against the wave of KKK lynchings in Georgia and other southern states. "A capably organized systematic campaign of fascist violence," he said, carried out by "the kind of crackpots who know that 'divide' comes before 'conquer.'"[50]

Carter had no better luck on any other racial front. His staff compiled a thick "book" of Reagan remarks on the assumption, in Stuart Eizenstat's words, that "the most effective way" to attack the Republican nominee "is simply by quoting him." "What makes the case against Reagan compelling," another White House aide reasoned, "is the procession of one simplistic or unrealistic statement after another."[51] So the campaign did exactly that, quoting Reagan on (among other topics included in the book):

The restrictive housing covenant he signed in 1941 ("I never read the deed and wouldn't have known how to interpret the legal technology there");

Brown ("there was nothing that said there had to be—while it said you could not enforce segregation, it did not say that you had to force integration");

Hearts and minds ("you can pass a law, but you don't change the heart of the individual who is discriminating now");

The Civil Rights Act of 1964 ("bad . . . legislation . . . [that] went beyond and infringed on the individual rights of citizens");

The Voting Rights Act of 1965 ("humiliating to the South");

The Roosevelt coalition ("the Negro has delivered himself to those who have no other interest than to create a federal plantation");

Busing ("it isn't a racial issue");

Affirmative action ("reverse discrimination");

The riots following King's assassination ("if the Negroes don't cool it, Martin Luther King will have died in vain");

The Attica prison riot ("if civilization is to survive, we can never buy peace through appeasement").

Carter's men ought to have followed the advice of Sam Popkin of Cambridge Survey Research. "If we try to nail him," Popkin told Eizenstat, "we'll look silly and desperate for no one looks good chasing a butterfly." Long before the media dubbed Reagan the Teflon president,

Carter's people called him the Muhammad Ali of American politics. The president must have felt like Sonny Liston.[52]

By quoting Reagan at every opportunity the Carter campaign helped the rival campaign spread its southern strategy message. Joseph Califano, like Popkin, thought Carter would have been better off leaving Reagan's message to Reagan and instead adopting a more positive approach. "Speaking out on civil rights was not his style," Califano lamented. "It was nevertheless remarkable that a Democratic President could go through almost all of his term without delivering a fervent, ringing, major public address on civil rights (until his campaign attempt to brand Ronald Reagan as a racist). It was more extraordinary that this could happen with a President who placed such emphasis on human rights abroad. . . . Carter dealt with civil rights issues when he had to, but he did not reach out with the kind of public energy and passion I thought was needed, after the setbacks of the Nixon years, to lead the nation or to break new ground."[53]

Carter's excursions into the politics of race from *Bakke* forward only piled more troubles on top of the hostage crisis and the stagflation mess that was the American economy. Initial delight at the Republican nomination of Reagan ("it seemed inconceivable that he would be acceptable as President when his positions were exposed clearly to the public") turned to despair. Jimmy and Rosalynn brooded over Christopher Lasch's (malaise-laden) *Culture of Narcissism* and other books that focused more specifically on the travails of prior Oval Office occupants (Lincoln and Truman especially). After Reagan's landslide the Carter men and women who cared about racial justice, like Louis Martin, could only commiserate with Coretta King on their adversary's main message: "That the general public perceives the so-called 'social programs' of the Administration as essentially government handouts to Black Americans." Some five weeks after the election Martin sent Mrs. King data indicating "that the chief beneficiaries of these programs are not Blacks." The Carter people had the facts all right, but they were unable to use them effectively.[54]

Jimmy Carter was not only vilified by conservatives as a champion of the blacks and an enemy of the white tax-paying middle. He was also vilified in liberal circles both as a selective human rights crusader (given his harsh policy on Haiti's "economic migrants" compared to the greetings extended the Cubans who arrived on the Mariel boat-lift); and an ersatz Republican with an "'austere' budget" that exacerbated what Martin called "the defeatism in the highly charged Black communities." He was vilified as well in the Democratic party's corridors of power. "The DNC is virtually a foreign power in the White House," Gerald Rafshoon said in the administration's first year. In four years, the president failed to win over the party or Washington's insider culture (excepting the few minutes he spent jitterbugging with Rosalynn on the Gridiron Club stage). Carter was reduced to calling Reagan's civil rights record "embarrassing for our nation" and "a disgrace to the White House."[55]

No one called Jimmy Carter mean here. Although he would reestablish himself as a community activist and problem-solving diplomat in the years to come, no one paid much attention to anything he said at all at the dawn of Reagan's America.

: 9 :

QUOTA KINGS

"A lot of lies are told about people who go into politics," Nancy Reagan said, "but the only one that ever got Ronnie steamed up was the occasional allegation that he was a bigot."[1] The charge was more than occasional and controversial only when Jimmy Carter hurled it during the campaign. Of all the predictions made about the Reagan (1981–1989) administration (including speculation that this White House would have a resident astrologer), the notion of an imminent assault on the civil rights gains of the 1960s was perhaps the most common. It was also borne out by the first term's end. David Norman, an assistant attorney general for civil rights under Nixon, noted "the emergence of an unspoken doubt about *Brown*'s premise." Hodding Carter called Ronald Reagan part Wallace and part Nixon and a more effective southern strategist than both put together. Pundits who debated Carter's meanness suddenly took the new president's "friendly racism" as a given. The *New York Times* reported on the mutual hatred between Reagan and blacks, and the *Wall Street Journal* commented on the forceful move "to alter the course of civil-rights enforcement."[2] Through it all Reagan presented himself as the sort of color-blind person Martin Luther King dreamed about during the March on Washington.

Reagan answered charges of racism and bigotry with anecdotes dating to his boyhood in Dixon, Illinois. He even crusaded (in his own

355

way), he claimed, against the Ku Klux Klan. When D. W. Griffith's *Birth of a Nation* came to the Dixon movie theater after the war, thirteen-year-old Ronald Wilson Reagan (he was four years old when the film originally opened) pleaded with his father for permission to see it. "The Klan's the Klan, and a sheet's a sheet," Jack Reagan told his son. "And any man who wears one over his head is a bum. And I want no more words on the subject." "My brother and I," Reagan remembered, "were the only kids not to see it." They went to the library instead. When more wholesome fare arrived in Dixon the family also crusaded in their own way against the theater's segregated seating. "My brother's best friend was black," Reagan recalled, "and when they went to the movies, Neil sat with him in the balcony."

Jack and Nelle Reagan raised their sons right, encouraging both boys, Ronald Reagan also recalled, "to bring home our black playmates, to consider them equals, and to respect the religious views of our friends, whatever they were." Tolerance exacted a price. Reagan not only missed an "early film classic" but believed that his father paid for his unbigoted nature with his life. Jack Reagan, on the road as a shoe salesman, once checked into a small-town hotel and then immediately checked out upon discovering Jews were not allowed. "I'm a Catholic," he told the clerk, "and if it's come to the point where you won't take Jews, you won't take me either." Reagan remembered his father as someone who "rebelled against the universe" and thus was not surprised to learn that he spent that night in his car during a blizzard. "He contracted near-pneumonia," the son said, "and a short time later had the first heart attack of the several that led to his death."³

These were family stories told repeatedly by the entire clan. Reagan mined the sports world in the Nixon/Ford manner for more personal stuff, managing to up Gerald Ford ("some of my best friends are black") with a claim that his best friend was black. "We bled together down there in the center of the line," he said of William Franklin Burghardt, a fellow "sixty-minute man" on the Eureka College football team. "I remember one day we met a team with no colored boys on its roster. This always made a difference." The opposition kept up a barrage of racist epitaphs interrupted only by cheap shots at Burghardt's knees. Burghardt hung in the entire hour and his silent courage won over everyone. Near the game's end the instigator on the other team stuck out his hand, telling Burghardt, "You're the whitest man I ever knew." Later, in the locker room, Reagan said "we had to cut Burky's pants to get them over his swollen knee." The following season (Reagan's senior year and Burghardt's sophomore year), the Eureka team spent a night in Dixon on the way to a game. When the local hotel refused to put up "our two colored boys—Burky and a reserve tackle named Jim Rattan," Reagan took them home for the night. "Nelle and Jack didn't even blink," he boasted.[4]

After graduating from Eureka, Reagan found the setting for a final athletic-field homily. "On the air as a sports announcer years and years ago," he noted during the run for the Republican nomination in 1980, "[I] was editorializing against the gentlemen's agreement that kept blacks from playing organized baseball." Now he was offering to "weigh my fight against bigotry and prejudice against that of the most ardent civil rights advocate, because I was doing it when there was no civil rights fight."[5] Reagan failed to note that his latest civil rights tale was some forty years old. In the more recent past he could only point to his record as California's governor (1966–1971). Of Reagan's 3,709 appointments to state jobs, however, the Carter campaign counted only nine blacks. Perhaps remembering that Burghardt's grandfather and uncle had worked as barbers, one of these appointments was to the state board responsible for licensing and regulating that industry.[6]

Over the years, Reagan repeated the Dixon and ball-field experiences so often that they appeared scripted. This was particularly true whenever he spoke to African Americans, and White House staff actually named the president's individual tales ("the Jackie Robinson story," the "Burky story," etc.). Reagan found it inconceivable that anyone would label him racist and equally inconceivable that the Black Panthers and other nationalists who plagued him in California could include anyone "who ever participated in athletics on a team that numbered among its personnel both Negroes and whites."

This is not to say that Reagan spoke often to African Americans either before entering the White House or after. One rare moment occurred during the 1966 gubernatorial primary after his opponent, former San Francisco Mayor George Christopher, called him a right-wing fanatic. When both candidates appeared before the state convention of the National Negro Republican Assembly and Christopher made an issue of Reagan's opposition to the Civil Rights Act of 1964, Reagan exploded. "I resent the implication that there is any bigotry in my nature," he told the Negro Republicans. "Don't anyone ever imply that—in this or any other group." He then fled with tears in his eyes (some said), and with a promise of revenge against Christopher. ("I'll get that S.O.B.") Then he calmed down and came back into the hall to shake hands and tell the Dixon and ball-field stories.[7]

Once in the White House, Reagan made episodic appearances before African-American audiences at a Chicago high school, Tuskegee University, the NAACP, and a Maryland home after the *Washington Post* reported a cross burning and other terrorism launched against a black family by white neighbors. "Needless to say," Reagan said of the latter appearance, "this fine family had no further harassment." After a concerted staff effort convinced him to omit the Jackie Robinson story from his address to the NAACP's annual convention, Reagan instead mentioned a black soldier in Vietnam who saved his (white) buddies by throwing himself on a live hand grenade. The soldier's last words were, "You have to care." The president's words to the NAACP delegates warned of "a new kind of bondage" fostered by welfare programs and other government handouts. His reception was chilly. The message seemed to be, "I don't care."[8]

President Reagan had little time for black people either in general or in the particular case. He would not even meet the only prominent civil rights leader who took a clear position against the welfare system and campaigned for the Reagan-Bush ticket to boot. Ralph Abernathy, holding high hopes for the Republican promise of jobs for poor people, did see Reagan in a Southfield, Michigan, hotel during the Republican National Convention.[9] After the election, however, Abernathy could not get through to the White House troika of Meese, Baker, and Deaver. So he asked Gerald Ford to pitch his welfare reform ideas. Telephoning Meese from his Palm Beach office while Abernathy sat on the other side of the desk, Ford got nowhere. "It was a bad time to call," Meese said, as the Pope had just been shot. Finally, in 1983, George Bush got back to Abernathy. Scheduled to give a speech commemorating Martin Luther King's birthday, the vice-president wanted a photo opportunity. Abernathy came to Washington with his wife (paying his own way) and flew back to Atlanta with Bush so the television cameras could get them stepping off the plane together. Bush, like Meese, never got back on the welfare reform matter. In 1984 no one at the White House was surprised (or for that matter upset) when Abernathy campaigned against Reagan and for Jesse Jackson.[10]

Reagan would occasionally contact those African Americans who questioned his commitment to racial justice. Roger Wilkins, for one, received a telephone call after writing a critical newspaper column. The president relayed the Jack Reagan and Burky stories, but they failed to change Wilkins's mind. "Any fair reading of that column would reveal that I had called him an ignorant bigot," Wilkins later explained, "and any fair reading of my mind would reveal that this is exactly what I think." A more serious sounding of the racism charge came when Supreme Court Justice Thurgood Marshall told a TV reporter that Reagan was "the worst in the White House since Herbert Hoover." "I literally told him my life story," the president said concerning the subsequent meeting with Marshall held in the family quarters upstairs at the White House. Reagan brought out all the big guns, including the Jackie Robinson story, and concluded, blissfully, after Marshall shook hands and left: "That night, I think I made a friend." If anything Marshall walked out of the White House even more convinced that he had pegged the president right in the first place.[11]

Reagan objected to the so-called civil rights establishment on both philosophical and political grounds. While announcing his support for racial justice and condemning the degeneration of the civil rights movement into mere interest group politics, he saw political fortune in continuing Nixon's southern strategy of pitting white Americans against the "special interests" and pleadings of African Americans. So with black unemployment at 14 percent on the day he took office and the black poverty rate at 36 percent some eighteen months into the first term, the president called the inner-city homeless, in effect, campers. "One problem that we've had . . . is the people who are sleeping on the grates," he noted on *Good Morning America*. "The homeless, who are homeless, you might say, by choice." When Marian Wright Edelman accused "Mr. Reagan" of coming in and trying "to repeal or weaken everything, every single federal children's program and every program protecting the poor," the president quipped: "In the war on poverty, poverty won."[12]

While Edwin Meese echoed this line with his claims that Scrooge got bad press and that soup kitchens were reappearing everywhere "because the food is free," Reagan remained on point. His favorite story (the Chicago welfare queen story), told to congressional and foreign leaders alike, inflated with each telling to the point where the woman in question, Linda Taylor, had "eighty names, thirty addresses, twelve Social Security cards." This helped her collect "veterans' benefits on four non-existing deceased husbands" and other welfare-state funds to produce a tax-free income of over $150,000. (Taylor had been convicted in 1977 for fraud and perjury involving $8,000 in public aid checks.) There was no mistaking the president's attempt to put a black face on such abuses. The term itself, "welfare queen," is of course linked in the popular culture with race.

Like Nixon, Reagan spoke in code. He advocated both racial justice and a rollback of the civil rights movement's achievements, including any government program smacking of welfare. "I don't think people are entitled to services," budget director David Stockman explained. "I don't believe that there is any entitlement, any basic right to legal services or any other kind of services. . . . I don't accept that equality is a moral principle."[13] Reagan's rhetoric held that the pursuit of racial justice ought to be a moral imperative and not an interest group issue. His practice gave free reign to a budget cutter who said the pursuit of racial justice wasn't a moral issue either.

David Stockman had sat on the New Left's fringes during high school and college in his home state of Michigan. Looking back from his OMB desk he said the antiwar protestors and blacks "reminded me of the reason Gary Cooper had given the House Committee on Un-American Activities for being opposed to communism: 'From what I hear about it, I don't like it because it isn't on the level.'" He also remembered his brother Steve hearing Stokely Carmichael, in a tirade against "white devils," work the crowd "so [well] . . . that one word and Steve would have been an ex–white devil." Stockman thus led the nation's charge from a war on poverty to Reagan's war on welfare.[14]

Their goals did not stop Reagan administration officials from borrowing much of the rhetoric and symbolism of both civil rights and black power. From the president on down the Reagan people jettisoned the Nixon era's southern strategy language and instead referred to their own "movement." A "Reagan revolution" elastic enough to appropriate Martin Luther King's memory and what Edwin Meese and others called King's constitutionally correct advocacy of a color-blind society where the color of one's skin truly did not matter.[15] The words themselves, "color blind," were simply new code for an assault on affirmative action, and there was no mistaking the president's appeal to the voting block that mattered most (white males). "If you happen to belong to an ethnic group not recognized by the federal government as entitled to special treatment," he said, "you are the victim of reverse discrimination."[16]

Reagan enlisted King's memory for his fight against the civil rights movement's gains most dramatically in 1983 when he reversed his long-standing opposition to a national holiday in the dreamer's name. He did so only after it became clear that Congress would pass a bill with or without his support; and at that could not resist a crack when asked about North Carolina Senator Jesse Helms's unearthing of the old charge that King had Communist sympathies. "Well," the president said in reference to the FBI's sealed wiretap and microphone surveillance recordings, "we'll know in about thirty-five years, won't we."[17]

This was southern strategy by any other name because it rested on a systematic attempt to exploit the racial conflicts plaguing the Democratic party. Nixon, by bringing the white South to the Republican party, had begun the process of bringing the entire white working- and middle-classes over. The latest Republican strategists vowed to complete that process by continuing to play "the race card" advocated by Kevin Phillips and other southern strategists from the 1968 campaign. It largely consisted of heavy-handed claims that the Democrats catered to blacks, in the process demanding that white middle America pay taxes to support programs to help welfare queens and street criminals.

"[It's] like having an elephant in the room," one long-time New York liberal said. "Democrats have black people, and the Republicans don't. . . . All they have to do is say to the Democrats, 'Jesse Jackson is with you.'" The Democrats could not counter by saying, "Well, Pat Robertson is with you . . . [because] evangelicals are [not] committing robberies in Flatbush every day." Republicans spread the message that both crime and welfare had a black face in Reagan's America, and that strategy pushed "urban populists" in the North toward the GOP. With northern white ethnics and white southerners emerging as the swing votes of American politics, as William Schneider of the American Enterprise Institute noted, George Wallace met Archie Bunker.[18]

While appropriating and distorting King's reference to a color-blind society, the Reagan administration also turned inside out the civil rights movement's effort to make race what Thomas Byrne Edsall called "a straightforward, morally unambiguous force in American politics." The movement wanted to move racism onto the nation's main political stage where it could be fought honorably and destroyed once and for all. Reagan, in contrast, wanted to move non–color blind remedies like affirmative action onto the nation's main political stage where they could be fought honorably and destroyed. If the Democratic party from Kennedy to Carter had been a vehicle for a policy that mixed social experiment with middle-class guilt, Reagan would complete Nixon's work and make the Republican party a vehicle for those whites who resented the welfare state. If the liberal solution to past racial injustices not only asked working-class and middle-income whites to support black programs with their tax dollars but to offer public atonements, Reagan's message was that racial injustice no longer existed and any past injustices were not at issue. The issue was African Americans' behavior and self-destructive values (crime, drugs, teenage pregnancy, laziness, etc.).

The Reagan administration's biggest and most systematic push was against affirmative action. Assistant Attorney General for Civil Rights William Bradford Reynolds, who led the charge here, quickly emerged as the president's point man in the divisive politics of racial backlash. Educated at Exeter, Yale, and Vanderbilt, Reynolds came from a wealthy Delaware family (his mother was a Du Pont) and came up as a corporate lawyer in the Washington, D.C., firm of Shaw, Pittman, Potts, and Trowbridge. Government experience was limited to work with former Solicitor General Erwin Griswold. He had no civil rights experience at all when taking charge of the Civil Rights Division's 170 attorneys, 243 clerks and secretaries, and $18.2 million budget, and no hesitation in pinpointing affirmative action as the root cause of white America's pain. No hesitation in announcing a prescription either: "No longer are the federal laws in this area regarded as the special province of discrete groups."

Reynolds promised to pursue the Civil Rights Division's new mission "with unshakable resolve and a variety of innovative steps to bring the Nation's civil rights policies into line with the better angels of its nature." This meant fighting "the battle of racial quotas, minority set-asides, and forced busing"; championing "*individual* opportunity" versus "*group* entitlements"; and questioning "the efficacy, wisdom, and indeed, in some cases, the legality, of various sputtering and often ineffective remedial programs . . . which the civil rights 'establishment' has advocated." Reynolds presented himself in the Reagan/Meese manner as Dr. King's color-blind heir. "We are all—each of us—a minority in this country," he announced. "A minority of one." The only people blocking King's dream were the blacks themselves and their liberal benefactors from the 1960s who seemed bent on creating "a racially ordered society similar to that approved by the *Plessy* Court in 1896." Archie Bunker had not only met George Wallace in this skewed world; Bull Connor had met Martin Luther King.[19]

Reynolds's style grated even those who agreed with most of his line. "I emphasized the sinister tendency toward a bureaucratic-collectivist state implicit in government-imposed racial and gender preferences," Solicitor General Charles Fried recalled. Yet Reynolds dismissed Fried as a "fancy-pants neocon." Reynolds didn't say much during Justice Department staff meetings, Fried complained, "but what he did say dripped with scorn and was rich in spoken or implicit accusations of apostasy and unmanly cowardice." (This from a man who was always threatening, like a little kid, to go tell "the AG".) When Fried once deviated from the line (by noting that quotas and preferences might be necessary "as a last resort to bring proven discriminators into line"), he recalled "the chilling way Reynolds made his points: the cold stare, the tense, high-pitched, but quiet voice speaking between clenched teeth. . . . After a conversation with him, you needed a stiff drink."[20]

Reagan rewarded Reynolds's loyalty by nominating him to the post of deputy attorney general. When the Senate turned back that nomination Meese named Reynolds his counselor—effectively giving him the job, as *Washington Post* reporter Juan Williams noted, that the Republican-controlled Senate said he could not have. With Meese immobilized by scandal (Iran-Contra, Wedtech) and personal tragedy (his grandson's death), Reynolds practically ran the Justice Department from mid–1987 on. If his official title gave him a limited role, he was, as Fried lamented, ubiquitous. This meant that Reynolds handled what Meese called Reagan's main charge: "The President was adamant that we crack down on hate crime, discrimination, and organized bigotry." Whether Meese or Reynolds ran things, Justice stood exactly where it had under John Mitchell and his dictum (watch what we do and not what we say).[21]

"Under Mr. Reynolds, the civil rights division has changed sides," Nicholas Katzenbach charged. "Rights for Americans seems to him to mean rights for white males."[22] On affirmative action this meant Carter policy without the angst—a policy that one constitutional scholar called "a preconceived ideological result in search of . . . the conveniently created theory that . . . quota relief is beyond the scope of a court's equitable remedial authority." In practice it meant a drive "to reopen fifty-one settled cases" and promised to deliver more relief from affirmative action rules and regulations than even corporate America wanted.

Drew Days, Carter's assistant attorney general for civil rights, pointed out that an all-out assault on affirmative action would simply result in "more lawsuits, more court orders, more disputes over implementation, in sum, more labor unrest, at a time when the energies of business should be devoted to increasing productivity and providing jobs for America's unemployed." The *Wall Street Journal* reminded its readers that many businesses were reluctant to scrap minority hiring goals and timetables because such things reduced vulnerability to discrimination suits. "No segment of our business is run without setting goals and having timetables," Union Carbide's Charles Blake said. "Affirmative action is just another management-by-objectives program." Nonetheless, Reagan remained convinced that government programs to ensure that corporations hired a diversified work force were both a terrible burden on those corporations and a formula for Republican electoral success.[23]

While Reagan offered corporate America cash (through tax-rate cuts, depreciation allowances, etc.), he offered the rest of white America little more than antiblack rhetoric and Meese/Reynolds sideshow campaigns that did nothing to stop the slide of working- and middle-class living standards. The president found his specific constituency here among small business and white families in the cities and suburbs. In its most extreme form this constituency organized into such groups as SPONGE (The Society for the Prevention of Niggers Getting Everything) based in Booklyn's Canarsie section. If carried out in the name of equal opportunity and color blindness, the assault on reverse discrimination remained tuned to white anxieties. The administration's 1986 budget proposal called affirmative action goals, timetables, and quotas "a tax on the employment of white males." Meese condemned "counting by race" as "a form of racism" and even quotaless affirmative action as "nothing short of a legal, moral and constitutional tragedy." "As a white man," Secretary of the Interior James Watt added, "I will be very hesitant to allow a black doctor to operate on me because I will always have the feeling that he may have been carried by the quota system." Reynolds said that such policies were "pro-black" and therefore antiwhite and racist.[24]

Charles Fried came closest to offering a civilized opposition to affirmative action. "Preferences were irrelevant to the deplorable plight of the black underclass," the solicitor general noted with some accuracy. "Preferences tend to help the black middle class and the most ambitious and ablest poor blacks—people who would not in any event sink into the ghettos of despair." That was about it. Fried generally carried on like a good soldier despite his caveats about the Reynolds style. He saw American history as "three centuries of slavery and another hundred years of apartheid" that had given way in a single decade to an equally pernicious quota system that had "dangerously aggrandize[d] government." So he used his office to sharpen "the rather smeary focus" of civil rights law and enlisted in the crusade against quotas and preferences (which he condemned as the "gut commitment uniting the attitudes and principles of left-collectivism"). The term color blindness itself, Fried explained, came not from Dr. King but Justice Harlan's dissent in *Plessy*. "Aside from the white-supremacist caveats," he said, Harlan "offered a pretty good slogan for this part of the Reagan Revolution."[25]

Where the economic interests of poor people and the working- and lower-classes once held the Roosevelt coalition together, race was the wedge that Reagan's people used to split that coalition. Pundits called these voters from the white working-class suburbs "Reagan Democrats." The Democrats themselves called them "defectors." In either case there

was no doubt that race incited the exodus and overrode economic interests. This could be seen most clearly in a study of Macomb County
defectors financed by the Michigan Democratic party a few months
after the 1984 election. Once a Democratic party bedrock on the edges
of Detroit but suffering in the late 1970s and early 1980s the full force
of the automobile industry blow out, Macomb's residents, the study revealed, now seemed united only by a "distaste for blacks."

Stanley Greenberg, head of the Analysis Group that conducted the
Macomb County voter survey, said "blacks constitute the explanation
for their vulnerability and for almost everything that has gone wrong
in their lives; not being black is what constitutes being middle class; not
living with blacks is what makes a neighborhood a decent place to live.
These sentiments have important implications for Democrats, as virtually all progressive symbols and themes have been redefined in racial
and pejorative themes. . . . The special status of blacks is perceived by
almost all of these individuals as a serious obstacle to their personal advancement. Indeed, discrimination against whites has become a
well-assimilated and ready explanation for their status, vulnerability,
and failures." "Ronald Reagan's image," Greenberg added, almost gra-
tuitously, "formed against this backdrop."[26]

That was the purpose all along. If Reagan's spoken promise was to
get the government off the backs of the American people, his unspoken
promise was to get the "niggers" off the backs of the white middle and
working classes who had lost control over their schools and neighborhoods while paying taxes to support busing, Medicaid, public housing,
assorted welfare programs, and civil rights enforcement lawyers at every
level of government. Reagan despised consensus. He saw hope in a
nation divided between tax payers and tax recipients, advocates of meri-
tocracy and advocates of race preference, those who worshipped the
private sector and those who worshipped the public sector, disciples of
the work ethic and disciples of the welfare dime. A division, in other
words, between the white people who bore the cost of the Democratic
party's "rights revolution" and the nonwhite beneficiaries of liberal
interventionist policies.[27]

The president and his men advanced this polarized politics in rhetoric and action. While slashing data collection and analysis budgets for
all federal civil rights agencies, the administration recruited few blacks

for positions on any level. A notable exception was Samuel R. Pierce, Jr. ("Silent Sam"), named secretary of housing and urban development but unknown to the president (who once greeted him as "Mr. Mayor"). Pierce had been the FBI's "messiah designate" to replace Martin Luther King seventeen years earlier, and would go on in the 1980s to preside over the monstrous HUD scandals. For speech writers the administration recruited from the *Dartmouth Review*—an unofficial Dartmouth College publication that had called a black music professor, William Coles, "a cross between a welfare queen and a bathroom attendant." Reagan got a *Review* alum himself. So did Vice President Bush and Secretary of Education William Bennett. Bennett's find, Keeney Jones, liked to quote "black students" on Ivy League rigors. "Dese boys be sayin' that we be comin' here to Dartmut an' not takin' the classics. You know, Homa." Dinesh D'Souza, another *Review* alum hired as a White House policy analyst, would go on to some fame as the RC (Republican-correct) author of a bestseller on the PC debate.[28]

Judicial nominations followed the same pattern. Edwin Meese pushed Lino A. Graglia of Texas for the Fifth Circuit Court of Appeals even though Graglia was reportedly in the habit of referring to black children as pickaninnies. Another Meese favorite, Jefferson B. Sessions III, unwound by telling racist jokes and taking potshots at the NAACP ("un-American," "Communist-inspired"). He also called a white civil rights lawyer "a disgrace to his race" and said he thought the Ku Klux Klan was "OK until I learned they smoked pot." When the Sessions nomination suffered the same fate as the Graglia nomination, Meese blamed "liberal organizations" and called his man "the unfortunate victim of people . . . willing to smear anyone in order to advance their agenda." Of the 160 appointments to the federal courts made in Reagan's first term, most were better than the failed Graglia and Sessions only by degree. Two African Americans made it to the federal bench, a negative record only Eisenhower had surpassed in recent history. The general appointed none.[29]

For the Supreme Court, Reagan offered Sandra Day O'Connor (after Justice Potter Stewart retired) and then a series of divisive nominations. Justice William Rehnquist, named to replace Chief Justice Warren Burger when he retired in May 1986, had done a tour as assistant attorney general for the office of legal counsel in the Nixon

Justice Department where he proved to be an advocate of wiretapping and other aggressive surveillance techniques employed in the name of internal security. When serving as a clerk in 1952 and 1953 for Justice Robert Jackson, Rehnquist wrote a memorandum, titled "A Random Thought on the Segregation Cases," arguing that *Plessy* "was right and should be affirmed." After moving on to Phoenix he participated in an organized campaign to intimidate minority voters by challenging their eligibility; repeatedly criticized efforts to desegregate the city's public schools; and attacked a proposed public accommodations ordinance because it "summarily does away with the historic right of the owner of a drug store, lunch counter, or theatre to choose his own customers." On the last point Rehnquist found it "impossible to justify the sacrifice of even a portion of our historic individual freedom for a purpose such as this." He got the chief justiceship because of such views and not in spite of them.[30]

Reagan got to put two more men on the Supreme Court: Anthony Kennedy and the extremely conservative Antonin Scalia. The Leadership Conference on Civil Rights and its executive director Ralph Neas (white, male, Catholic, and Republican) led a coalition of racial justice and labor groups against the most controversial nominee of all, Robert Bork. When that battle culminated in a Senate vote of October 23, 1987, not to confirm, Bork blamed "the 60s generation and its left-liberal culture [which] commands much of the institutional high ground in our society. Until recently, one of its major strongholds was the Supreme Court of the United States." In fact the Senate rejected Bork because he represented (too starkly) the entire Reagan/Meese constitutional agenda and thus alienated Americans of all colors on too many fronts. A prolific writer, he had left a wide paper trail on the idea that the nation should return to the "original intent" of the men who wrote the United States Constitution. He not only advocated the elimination of affirmative action and the dilution of standards with respect to racial discrimination, but wanted to abolish procedural protections for criminal defendants (*Miranda*); ease the separation between church and state; crush "New Left" longhairs who "remain cultural revolutionaries"; reduce citizen access to the courts; overturn a woman's right to an abortion (*Roe v. Wade*); and otherwise return to the Founders' gender- and race-dominated world.

For black Americans the campaign against Bork rivaled in significance the campaign against Judge Parker during the Herbert Hoover years. For President Reagan and Attorney General Meese, however, the bitterness of the Bork defeat was tempered. The nomination had forced the Democratic party to "play up" its civil rights advocacy and thus drove home the gut Republican message about one party being a haven for blacks and the other a haven for whites. And from the Bork-less Supreme Court on down the Reagan White House pretty much turned around the federal judiciary anyway. Justice Thurgood Marshall, the friend Reagan never made, actually called on Congress to "send a message to the [Supreme] Court—that the hypertechnical language games played by the court in its interpretations of civil rights enactments are simply not accurate ways to read Congress' broad intent."[31]

Administration officials went beyond their anti–affirmative action and judicial nominations' strategies to oppose extension of the Voting Rights Act of 1965. Meese and Reynolds made the usual argument that the law discriminated against the South, but were oddly silent when Congress amended the law in 1982 to allow Justice Department intervention to correct instances where racial minorities had "less opportunity than other members of the electorate to participate in the political process and to elect representatives of their choice." Nor did the Republican National Committee object to racial gerrymandering. Creation of strong black majorities in local voting districts would lead to extremism, the attorney general apparently reasoned, because candidates for office would have no need to appeal for white votes. Elected officials from majority-black districts would increasingly act as a group—thus making racial divisions more visible and increasing the numbers of districts that were almost exclusively white and therefore "Republican prone." From the black caucuses on Texas school boards to the Congressional Black Caucus in Washington, D.C., this Justice Department welcomed token black electoral success because it reduced Democratic votes outside the black districts and otherwise facilitated the us-against-them message.[32]

The Reagan administration took yet another familiar line by going after housing and school integration. In the president's first year Justice Department attorneys filed no cases under the Fair Housing Act of 1968. In 1982 they filed two. (Under Nixon, Ford, and Carter, the department averaged thirty-two cases a year.)[33] Reynolds spoke with his usual bluntness on the schools: "We are not going to compel children who don't choose to have an integrated education to have one." So in a Charleston County, South Carolina, case, Reynolds referred to black parents as "those bastards" and vowed to block their participation by making them "jump through every hoop." He tried to kill a St. Louis busing program even though it was voluntary, used magnate schools, and promised overall improvements in the city's public schools. In Charlotte, North Carolina, a city where busing enjoyed a rare success, Reagan himself made a speech against the evils of moving children out of their neighborhoods. When visiting a black high school in Chicago, the president made the point that the entire issue was bogus: "[I was] under the impression that the problem of segregated schools had been settled."[34]

This notion (that most if not all racial problems surrounding the schools had been settled) led Reagan to call for the abolition of the Department of Education. Secretary of Education Terrel H. Bell, who called his department "Reagan's *Titanic*," was certainly no liberal on civil rights or any other aspect of his duties; but even he was appalled (as Charles Fried had been) by the general tone of the assault on the schools. With the rate of black high school graduates going to college dropping from 34 percent to 26 percent by the first term's end (the result of the administration's cuts in federal financial aid to students), the Justice Department redoubled its efforts, Bell said, "to weaken civil rights enforcement in the nation's colleges and schools." Mid-level staff at the White House and OMB, Bell added, favored "sick humor and racist clichés" featuring "Martin Lucifer Coon" and "sand niggers" (Arabs). When Bell tried to fight Reynolds's "intent . . . to find gaps in the law through which he could avoid taking what I thought was necessary and desirable enforcement action," senior White House staff pegged him as a traitor. Ed Meese, who favored neckties dotted with the profile of free-market god Adam Smith, liked to joke about how Bell had tiny hammers and sickles on his ties.[35]

Reynolds moved on to the colleges in pursuit of the Reagan administration's most spectacular crusade—the battle to grant a tax exemption to Bob Jones University of Greenville, South Carolina. This grew out of a 1980 Republican platform plank promising to "halt the unconsti-

tutional regulatory vendetta launched by Mr. Carter's IRS commissioner against independent schools," and Mississippi Congressman
(later Senator) Trent Lott's letter to Reagan in 1981 reminding him of
the plank. With the case heading for the Supreme Court, Lott asked
the president to take Bob Jones's side. "I think we should," Reagan
wrote in the margin of Lott's letter. Biographer Lou Cannon concluded
that the president assumed this was a clear-cut religious freedom issue
since Bob Jones cited the Bible as the basis for its rules prohibiting students from engaging in such things as interracial dating and marriage.
The president, in other words, "was so cut off from the counsel of black
Americans that he sometimes did not even realize he was offending
them." So the Justice Department, which had stood with the IRS, now
switched sides and stood with Bob Jones.[36]

Charles Fried called the White House crusade on Bob Jones's behalf
a perfect example of a "suicidal" tendency to push forward in support
of "blatantly racist if somewhat nutty practices." "If nothing else" this
demonstrated "a complete miscalculation of the civil-rights community's strength and determination." The president was more in tune
with the strength and determination of the white Christian
community. He wavered only briefly after Thaddeus Garrett, Jr., a
Methodist minister, told him about a sermon making the rounds of the
black churches: A woman saved the life of a wounded serpent and was
bitten for her reward. "Reagan is that snake," the preachers were saying,
and their congregations were responding with choruses of "Amens." A
"horrified" Reagan stuck with Bob Jones nonetheless—though he
modified his position. It was now morally right to deny tax exemptions
even to Christian schools that discriminate, but morally wrong to do
so by regulatory fiat. If members of Congress wanted this done, in
other words, then they had to pass legislation.

In 1983 eight of nine Supreme Court justices ruled against Bob
Jones University and the Reagan administration in a decision that Attorney General William French Smith called "essentially sociological."
With Chief Justice Rehnquist dissenting, the court agreed that the IRS
had authority to deny tax exemptions even without a specific law granting such authority. Joel Selig said the whole affair "was akin to an
unmasking: The administration had aligned itself as a willing partner
of unalloyed racism." Reagan, ever the optimist, saw victory somehow

in this resounding Supreme Court defeat. "[I] prevented the IRS from determining national social policy all by itself," he said.[37]

Reagan achieved a more certain victory in a follow-up crusade against the U.S. Civil Rights Commission, a harsh critic of the Bob Jones affair. Hoping to gut the commission or turn it into an administration appendage, he began by firing Chairman Arthur Flemming and Commissioner Stephen Horn (both Republicans) and appointing a new chair (Clarence Pendleton, Jr.) and staff director (Linda Chavez Gersten). Two other fired commissioners, Mary Frances Berry and Blandina Cardenas Ramirez, sued the president in federal district court and won reinstatement. With the House threatening to take authority to appoint commissioners away from the president (because he had abused it), the Republican-controlled Senate pushed through a compromise. Congress now named half the commission with no required presidential involvement and the president named the other half with no Senate advice and consent. Appointments by Senate Republicans and Reagan's own appointments gave the White House its majority.[38]

The new Civil Rights Commission appointees were a strange mix bound together by opposition to quotas and anything else smacking of affirmative action. Mary Louise Smith and Morris B. Abram were the best of the lot. Smith, former national chair of the Republican party, proved a pleasant surprise to the organized civil rights community and demonstrated little of the expected partisanship. Abram, former president of Brandeis University, criticized the civil rights movement, much like Charles Fried, in a largely civilized manner. The struggle for racial justice, he said, had "turned away from its original principled campaign for equal justice under law to engage in an open contest for social and economic benefits conferred on the basis of race or other classifications previously thought to be invidious." Where Reynolds and Meese praised Martin Luther King for color blindness, Abram praised the movement's first generation as "fair shakers"—in contrast to the second generation's "social engineers" and their preoccupation "with equality of *results*" and desire to allocate "social goods by race." In Bork-like language, Abram called on the movement to return to its founders' "original intent."[39]

If Morris Abram and Mary Louise Smith were the best the Reagan administration offered black America, the new Civil Rights Commission chair was the worst. Clarence Pendleton, brought in from California where he headed the San Diego Urban League, seemed most interested in baiting affirmative action advocates. "I say to America's black leadership open the plantation gates and let us out!," he noted in a typical outburst. "We refuse to be led into another political Jonestown as we were led during the presidential campaign. No more Kool-Aid, Jesse [Jackson], Vernon [Jordan], and Ben [Hooks]! We want to be free." While dispensing such wisdom Pendleton had to deal with his own Jonestown—mini-scandals involving expense-account padding and rumors of how he allowed two white businessmen to use the San Diego Urban League as a front to qualify for special preference and thus secure government contracts. Through it all the press referred to him as an "administration spokesperson," and this in turn lead to a constant headache for White House press secretary Larry Speakes. A native Mississippian who had worked as Senator Eastland's press secretary and in Nixon's White House press office, Speakes was used to controversy but not the sort Pendleton generated.

Had the White House gotten everything it wanted things would have been worse. Pendleton was probably better than Rev. Edward Hill, a black fundamentalist and friend of Jerry Falwell's Moral Majority who reportedly turned down an offer to chair the Civil Rights Commission. Another black minister, B. Sam Hart of Philadelphia, nearly made it onto the commission before his nomination evaporated amid a time-warp monologue about Communists and homosexuals in government. Elsewhere the administration tried to appoint a borderline neo-Nazi to the Iowa Advisory Commission on Civil Rights. This nominee had written for the racist Liberty Lobby publication *Spotlight* and received funding for antibusing work from the equally racist Pioneer Fund. The latter had been established in the 1930s by the American Eugenics Society.[40]

From the anti–affirmative action crusade to the gutting of the Civil Rights Commission, the Reagan administration's policy of favoring white men over minorities helped the president achieve a remarkable success against Walter Mondale in the 1984 elections. Every identifiable white ethnic group voted Republican to give Reagan 66 percent of the total white vote. Conversely, 89 percent of African Americans voted against the president. Reagan, a brilliant politician by any standard, had the uncanny ability to disassociate himself from his own policies and authority. "He can pull it off," Reagan-Bush campaign strategist Stuart Spencer said. "In 1970 he pulled it off. He ran against the fucking government he was running. I mean, he believes he's above it all."[41] On racial matters, however, the president had no intent or need to disassociate himself from his policies or otherwise stand above it all. His message went out clear and true and without much debate from any quarter. There was a media uproar only about the "racially polarizing" effect of Jesse Jackson's bid for the Democratic party nomination. The hot issue was Jackson's reference to New York as "hymietown" and relationship with Nation of Islam hatemonger Louis Farrakhan.[42]

Jesse Jackson's issue was voter registration, and on that issue the Republican National Committee launched what it called a "ballot-integrity" counterdrive to keep the black vote down. The Reagan White House also enlisted the FBI to crush Jackson's Rainbow Coalition in Alabama where civil rights activists concentrated on elderly shut-ins and workers holding jobs outside their home counties. By 1982 the voter registration drive had led to black majorities on commissions and school boards in five counties, and in 1984 Jackson received more than 70 percent of the Alabama black belt vote in the presidential primaries. That autumn some fifty FBI agents visited the homes or job sites of nearly a thousand newly registered voters and then shipped busloads under armed guard to Mobile where they were questioned by a grand jury. Other blacks were taken to Birmingham where they were fingerprinted and photographed. FBI initiatives included "electronic" coverage of a Perry County get-out-the-vote meeting and a Greene County raid on the offices of Booker T. Cooke, Jr.

This culminated at a cost of $2 million in the indictment of eight civil rights activists on 210 counts of vote fraud. Five were acquitted, two plead guilty to misdemeanor charges to avoid trial, and one (Albert King of Perry County) was convicted on four counts. That lone conviction was reversed on appeal. The affair as a whole inspired the rise of a liberal grass-roots organization, the Alabama New South Coalition, that played a role in retiring Alabama's Republican senator, Jeremiah Denton; blocking the federal judgeship for Jefferson Sessions (the U.S. attorney in Mobile who had helped prosecute the case); and stopping the Bork nomination.[43]

But the FBI's campaign did not end with their assault on the get-out-the-vote movement. They also targeted black elected officials. "It's like post-Reconstruction after the Civil War, when all Blacks were driven from office," Alabama State Senator Hank Sanders said. With one-third of the state's African-American elected officials under investigation or indictment by the end of Reagan's second term, Sanders charge struck the black community as no great exaggeration. Rumors of another FBI effort called "*Fruhmenschen*" (primitive man) fed a growing paranoia. This sting operation supposedly targeted elected and appointed black officials in metropolitan areas throughout the United States on the grounds, according to a former bureau informant, that they were "intellectually and socially incapable of governing." That informant revealed this (alleged) *Fruhmenschen* program in an affidavit regarding the case of Reginald Eaves, a black county commissioner in Atlanta, who had been recently convicted in a bribery case. No matter how sketchy the evidence (the program probably was no more than an "unofficial" creation of bureau agents in Atlanta), many prominent blacks took it as a hard fact. Mervyn Dymally and the Congressional Black Caucus believed it. So did the NAACP's Benjamin Hooks and Birmingham Mayor Richard Arrington.[44]

With the president's last years in office increasingly filled with the Iran-Contra scandal, the administration had little time to break new ground on the racial front or any other front. Yet South Africa ranked among the few subjects that could hold the president's attention at National Security Council meetings. Reagan praised Botha's Pretoria government for "eliminat[ing] the segregation that we once had in our own country, the type of thing where hotels and restaurants and places of entertainment and so forth were segregated—that has all been eliminated." He was convinced that even South African police violence had no racial aspects because several of the police officers slaughtering blacks were themselves black.[45]

Otherwise, Reagan kept to familiar terrain and found enough non-scandal and non–South Africa time to re-fight the battle of Bob Jones University. In *Grove City v. Bell* (1984) the Supreme Court limited anti-discrimination sanctions to the specific program or programs that discriminated and not the entire institution. Thus if a university's chemistry department had discriminated then that department would be ineligible for federal funds but the university as a whole would remain eligible. When Congress undid *Grove City* with the Civil Rights Restoration Bill of 1988, Reagan vetoed it, claiming that it would "vastly and unjustly expand the power of the federal government over the decisions and affairs of private organizations." He then submitted a new bill, the Civil Rights Protection Bill of 1988, which also overturned *Grove City* but exempted from the sexual discrimination provisions all educational institutions "closely identified with religious organizations." Even the White House press office recognized that as a public-relations gimmick. Meanwhile, Congress overrode the veto and made the Civil Rights Restoration Act of 1988 the law of the land.[46]

"It is a new America, Ronald Reagan's America," Hodding Carter said, "and at times it smells a lot like the old Mississippi. . . . The Reagan Presidency has given new hope to America's bigots and renewed legitimacy to the sly slogans of white supremacy. If it is not precisely a return to the time of Redemption . . . it is not because the President and his men have not tried."[47] Yet it was an odd redemption. With the administration unable to roll back voting rights laws and enforcement strategies, even the old-line segregationists were forced to recognize the power of the new voters. George Wallace's populism found enough room for blacks to earn an honorary degree from Tuskegee while James Eastland gave the NAACP a $500 check shortly before his death and Strom Thurmond sent his child to an integrated school. At the same time the new racism that roared up was less distinctly southern and more distinctly national. The Anti-Defamation League counted sixty-seven racist and anti-Semitic hate groups in the country by 1988 ranging from the Klan to Identity Church and Posse Comitatus cults.

Up was down and down was up in Reagan's America. "We want what I think Martin Luther King asked for . . . a color-blind society," the president said (while his aides made their "Martin Lucifer Coon" jokes in private). The color-blind reference completely ignored the civil rights movement's radicalism and Dr. King's own call for an economic restructuring of American society. "Proportionally," the president also claimed, "blacks benefited more than any other racial group from our economic policies." Obviously, during his White House years they benefited least by any definition—including the most numbing measure of all: For the first time in a century, according to the National

Center for Health Studies, life expectancy for black Americans dropped while life expectancy for white Americans rose.

"The myth about myself that has always bothered me most," Reagan later wrote in the memoir (echoing Nancy), "is that I am a bigot who somehow surreptitiously condones racial prejudice. . . . Whatever the reasons for the myth that I'm a racist, I blow my top every time I hear it." Yet that was the idea all long. Reagan's politics demanded that he be seen in this light, and the opinion polls showed that he was. Seventy percent of African Americans considered him to be prejudiced.[48]

That black America did not "think well" of him merely reflected "what their leaders were telling them," Reagan told White House chief of staff Donald Regan. This sort of leader would never acknowledge what the president described as his own grand achievement in making the nation a true color-blind society "because it might reveal then that there's no longer a need for that [civil rights leader's] particular organization."[49] This reduced anyone who struggled against racial injustice to no more than a spoke with a vested interest in a bureaucratic wheel that turned only to perpetuate racism. Reagan got it exactly upside-down, as ever. The president himself and his own Republican party were the ones with the vested interest in white over black.

From his first White House day to his last, Reagan's pro-civil rights policies extended no further than "Burky stories." At the March 26, 1988, Gridiron dinner, the Reagans sat with the club's first black president, Carl Rowan. Only Nancy was on the program this evening, not Ronald (at a prior dinner he did a soft-shoe routine in a black and silver sombrero to the tune and time of "Mañana Is Soon Enough for Me"). So the president of the United States was relaxed enough and had time enough to keep up a private monologue with Rowan on one point: "Me on this business of racism." Rowan, busy enough as the evening's master of ceremonies, could scarcely follow Reagan at times but somehow managed to get the gist. "I tried hard to win friendship among blacks," the president rambled. "But I couldn't do it. I talked to black leaders after my election in 1980, and they went out and criticized me in horrible ways. . . . They attacked me at the outset, so I said to hell with 'em." When Nancy Reagan left the table for her song and skit on the Gridiron stage, Reagan nodded at her and said "she wanted me to tell you that we are not the enemies of poor and black people." He gave up with another nod, at Colin Powell, this time, and final pearl: "Now there is one of the smartest black men I ever knew."

Two months passed before Reagan invited Rowan to the White House for lunch and hit him with all barrels (the Burky, Jack Reagan, and Jackie Robinson stories). "I had a feeling often that you didn't have the straight thing on me and racism and so forth," the president opened. Another monologue followed. "I just sipped soup as he went on and on," Rowan remembered, "about how Meese and Reynolds were powerful foes of racial discrimination."[50] In this world the Klansmen in the Griffith film that Reagan did not see as a kid in Dixon or the Waffen SS he praised at Bitburg for their "opposition" to Hitler could fit that category, too. Powerful foes of discrimination every one.[51]

Ronald Reagan retired no more color blind than when he first began the push for the White House. From the New Hampshire primary in 1976 he telephoned Nancy at a GOP dinner in Chicago and told her about the state's beautiful white snow. Later, when briefing the well-heeled guests, Nancy said she told Ronald that she wished he could be with her in Chicago "to see all these beautiful white people." Michael Deaver, no friend of Nancy Reagan during the White House tenure, called the remark a slip.[52] But it was less the sort of slip an honest and principled color-blind person could make, more the sort a cynical and vote-counting color-blind person would make. And it troubled Nancy Reagan's husband not at all.

Reagan's vice-president and the Republican presidential nominee in 1988, George Bush (1989–1993), ran a campaign so implicitly racist that it appeared suited to a prior century. Bush's symbols were quota queens *and* Negro rapists, and his maturation as a practitioner of racial politics represented the last flop in a series of flip-flops dating to his senior year at Yale (1948) when he chaired the campus drive for the United Negro College Fund. Bush came out of the Republican party's wing of racial liberalism embodied by his father, Senator Prescott Bush, Jr., who served, three years after his son's Yale duties, as Connecticut chair for the Negro College Fund. When Bush moved to Texas, drilled oil, got rich, and decided to enter politics, he stuck with the Yankee Republicans and otherwise challenged the Sun Belt's conventional racial wisdom—telling a Houston newspaper reporter in 1963 that he did

"not think the Republican Party should be a rallying place for segregationists." In June of that year, as chair of the Harris County Republican
party, he established an organization of black Republicans (the Republican Alliance), opened an office near an all-black college (Texas
Southern), placed party funds in a black-owned bank, and sponsored
"a black girls' softball team."

Those were the flips. The first flop came two weeks after the March
on Washington. "I believe in the finest concept of States' rights," Bush
said when announcing his candidacy for the United States Senate.
With the opponent (incumbent Democratic Senator Ralph Yarborough) having voted for Kennedy's Civil Rights Bill of 1963 as a
member of the Commerce Committee, Bush decided to organize his
campaign around opposition to that bill. The Civil Rights Act of 1964
made an even bigger target, and here he focused on the fair employment and public accommodations sections (calling them "unconstitutional"). In the language of the day Texas politicians were either
racists by conviction or convenience—and Bush fit the latter category
best. It did not help him much at the polls, however, as Yarborough got
56 percent of the total vote and some 97 percent of the black vote.[53]

Flip-flops continued. When running successfully for the House
in 1966 Bush first opposed then supported the Open Housing Bill.
This failed to impress minority voters. When counting the returns, the
congressman-elect had only that one regret ("being swamped in the
black precincts"), which he found "both puzzling and frustrating."
Ultimately, he found it was the majority voters who were more appreci-
ative of his "courageous" stand on open housing. When first explaining
his vote to his white constituents in the Memorial-West section of his
district, he was practically booed off the stage. Then he made the point
that blacks were fighting and dying in Vietnam, and gradually the cat-
calls died down. When the speech ended the audience gave their new
congressman a standing ovation. "All the ugliness that had gone before
seemed to wash away," Bush said, "and I sensed that something special
had happened. . . . More than twenty years later I can truthfully say
that nothing I've experienced in public life, before or since, has measured up to the feeling I had when I went home that night."[54]

Bush also appeared to support affirmative action in 1970 when
making another try for Ralph Yarborough's Senate seat. Yarborough,

taking labor's side, angered Texas blacks by opposing Nixon's Philadelphia plan. Bush saw an opportunity here to split the labor/black coalition so he embraced the Philadelphia plan—briefly winning a reputation in the Nixon White House as a heavy (southern strategy) hitter and in the process retiring Yarborough (who lost the Democratic primary to Lloyd Bentsen). When Bush lost the general election to Bentsen, who got more than 90 percent of the black vote, the Nixon men reversed their opinion and now labeled him a wimp. "Bush was convinced that he had the election won provided no one rocked the boat," Charles Colson told the president. "He refused to allow us to use some very derogatory information about Bentsen."

Refusing to run a negative campaign was not a mistake Bush would repeat during his runs on the Reagan ticket or his own run for the White House. Still, the occasional flip-flop remained. If committed by 1980 without qualification to a politics of attack and racial exclusion, he did suffer brief lapses in 1988 (when he invited Coretta King into the family box at the Republican National Convention) and more significantly in 1991 (when he signed civil rights legislation that he had previously condemned as a "quota bill").[55]

When Bentsen ran with Michael Dukakis against Bush and Indiana's Dan Quayle in 1988, it was a mere coincidence (however symbolic) that the two Texans were facing off again. Bush attacked to a degree that would have made the Chuck Colson of 1970 proud, relying on what even the mainstream press called the "sleazy gutter politics" of media adviser Roger Ailes and especially campaign manager Lee Atwater. A South Carolina baby boomer, horror-film buff, and musician who played backup in high school for Percy Sledge and would go on to play blues on Letterman, Atwater was also a legendary frat-house party guy who "made it cool to be a Republican." "'Animal House,'" one commentator noted, "was not a movie for Lee Atwater; it was autobiography." An elitist prone to disparaging the public ("people's capacity to focus on politics is about the depth . . . of their thumbnail"), Atwater described his one true love as "a young man's game" full of "high motherfuckin' stress" and dominated by the "great minds" like that of his hero, Richard Nixon. He reminded some of Huey Long, others of Spiro Agnew. Nixon once told him that Reagan needed a "nut-cutter" like Agnew to do the dirty work, and he plotted to be Bush's Agnew.[56]

A Strom Thurmond and Harry Dent protégé, Atwater considered Nixon's southern strategy in 1968 "a model campaign . . . a blueprint for everything I've done in the South since then." When polling for South Carolina Congressman Floyd Spence, this included ringing up white voters and telling them that the other candidate, Tom Turnipseed, belonged to the NAACP (he did not). "I'm not going to respond to that guy," Atwater said when dismissing Turnipseed's complaint. The "great political mind" behind such Watergate-style dirty tricks divided the South into three main voting blocks—country clubbers, blacks, and populists who resented the country clubbers' wealth and the blacks' color. Thus their votes were up for grabs. This block was "the trump card in the game of politics," Atwater said. Since the Republican party had the country club vote already, race was the only wedge issue of much use in further splitting the populist vote from its traditional Democratic moorings.[57]

Bush signed up Atwater because he was the latest in a line of South Carolina masters of this wedge issue and the first boomer recognized as such. If Reagan had begun the process of moving the politics of race across generational lines, Bush wanted to finish it and considered Atwater the perfect man to handle the details. Atwater exceeded the vice-president's wildest expectations and in the end earned the unprecedented distinction of making what Jesse Jackson called "psycho-sexual fears" the campaign's dominant issue. "There is no stronger metaphor for racial hatred in our country than the black man raping the white woman," grumbled Susan Estrich, campaign manager for Democratic presidential candidate Michael Dukakis. (Estrich, a rape survivor herself, remembered the first question the police asked her after the attack: "Was he a crow?") "If you were going to run a campaign of fear and smear and appeal to racial hatred," she said, "you could not have picked a better case to use than this."[58]

That case, involving escaped black convict William J. Horton, Jr., began with a name change. Atwater called him "Willie" (a name Horton never went by), hoping to get more racial mileage, and managed to make his subject so infamous by that *nom de guerre* that newspaper reporters would argue with their editors that no one would know who they were writing about if they used Horton's proper name. Before becoming a Bush campaign symbol Horton had committed a robbery in which a seventeen-year-old boy, Joseph Fournier, had been stabbed to death. Massachusetts prosecutors never proved who wielded the knife (Horton or one of his two accomplices), but they did not have to as commonwealth law held that a person party to a felony resulting in murder was guilty of murder even if he had not committed the act itself. Though convicted of first-degree murder in 1974 Horton was eligible for a prison "furlough" program, and by April 1987 he had taken nine such furloughs without incident. This time, however, he did not come back. Eventually arrested in Maryland behind the wheel of a car belonging to Clifford Barnes, he was charged with kidnapping Barnes and assaulting him—and also kidnapping and raping Barnes's fiancee, Angela Miller.[59]

Atwater made sure that Dukakis, as governor of Massachusetts, got the blame for Horton's latest crimes. It made no difference that furlough programs were common in many states or even that furloughed convicts had committed two murders while Ronald Reagan was governor of California. "A police officer and a schoolteacher, no less," Susan Estrich said. There was no political damage here. "Reagan [merely] decried the killings, expressed anger and sympathy and regret—and continued the furlough program," Estrich marveled. It also made no difference that the federal government regularly furloughed prisoners or that one furloughed drug dealer raped and murdered a woman the same year that Horton went on his spree.

Dukakis, unlike Reagan, proved vulnerable because Atwater's operatives successfully exploited the Democratic party's reputation for being soft on crime and problack. Bush himself compared Clint Eastwood ("go ahead, make my day") with Dukakis ("go ahead, have a nice weekend"). "Neither the Iran-Contra scandal nor Noriega," Elizabeth Drew explained, "presented the kind of immediate threat to the voters that Willie Horton had." Haynes Johnson, the *Washington Post* reporter who won a Pulitzer for his coverage of Selma, called the Horton gambit "the single most powerful political device of the campaign." It represented "the other side of the flag issue, the dark and dangerous side." This strategy was so successful that even Atwater professed amazement. "There's an endless fascination with Willie Horton," he complained when it was all over (and with Horton's name forever linked with his own).[60]

Willie Horton's story surfaced slowly. Robert James Bidinotto, a free-lance writer, did some preliminary research in November 1987, approached *Reader's Digest* in December, and signed a contract for a piece a month later. Furlough stories were already underway by Susan Forrest and other reporters at the Lawrence, Massachusetts, *Eagle-Tribune* (a decidedly anti-Dukakis paper). Forrest and her colleagues focused on five cases with the first page-one story about a former state trooper who received a furlough. A seemingly more horrendous tale of a white cop who had gone bad and killed a friend over insurance money was not what Atwater et al. had in mind. Horton, the black face among the five cases, had the only face of much use in this latest game of racial politics. The *Eagle-Tribune* had also pushed the race angle but failed to develop the story into an effective weapon against Dukakis—in part because its 250 published Horton items included false charges claiming the rape victim was pregnant and the murder victim had his genitals cut off. During the primaries Lawrence reporters crossed into the equally saturated New Hampshire market to ask Dukakis about Horton, but to no noticeable effect.

The *Eagle-Tribune* exposé, for which the paper got a Pulitzer, was more accurate about Dukakis's deeds than Horton's, reminding its readers that the governor not only supported the furlough program but had once pocket-vetoed a bill to ban furloughs for first-degree mur-derers. The articles also resulted in Dukakis's decision to place an administrative freeze on furloughs for first-degree murderers and later to sign legislation banning such furloughs. "I try to listen, I try to learn," he explained. From there, however, his problems multiplied. In April the *Wall Street Journal* published an op-ed piece ("Dukakis's 'Murder' Record Is a Crime") by an *Eagle-Tribune* editorial writer; and Al Gore, among the Democrats competing in the primaries, mentioned Horton in a candidate debate. "Al," Dukakis responded, "the difference between you and me is that I have run a criminal justice system and you haven't." Jim Pinkerton, a Bush campaign "opposition research" operative, actually stumbled onto the Horton story when reviewing the debate transcript.[61]

Pinkerton took the item to another "opposition research" guy, Andrew H. Card, Jr., and Card, who ended up in the White House as John Sununu's deputy, took it to Atwater. In May, Charles R. Black, Jr., became the first prominent Republican to suggest using the prison furlough issue against Dukakis. Card also kept in touch with Bidinotto, still at work on the *Reader's Digest* piece. A former Massachusetts state legislator who had tried (and failed) to get the Republican nomination for governor in 1982, this "fellow with a political instinct" (Card's description) denied that the Bush campaign had encouraged his article. Bidinotto had other Republican ties (two years before their marriage his wife had run as a party candidate for the Massachusetts legislature), and so did *Reader's Digest* executive editor Kenneth Y. Tomlinson (Voice of America director from 1982 to 1984). When Bidinotto's piece appeared on June 2 the Republican National Committee sent a copy to all delegates at the Republican National Convention. "Every woman in this country," a Bush strategist boasted to Elizabeth Drew, "will know what Willie Horton looks like before this election is over."[62]

Atwater repeated that boast over and over, and to make sure it came true he went to work when the *Reader's Digest* piece came out. "Willie Horton," he told a Republican Unity meeting, "will [soon] be a household name." A month later, on July 9, he alerted Republican leaders in Atlanta to a Jesse Jackson sighting "in the driveway of his [Dukakis's] home" and then offered this speculation: "Maybe he will put this Willie Horton on the ticket after all is said and done." That same day Atwater told the press about "a fellow named Willie Horton who for all I know may end up being Dukakis's running mate." At the time, Bush was down eighteen points to the Massachusetts governor in the polls.

"There is no better issue to use against a liberal than crime," noted Daniel L. Casey, the American Conservative Union's executive director. Yet Casey, like Atwater, chose not to focus on the murder committted by the furloughed white cop, only on the rape by the black man. So Casey wrote an "excellent background paper" that made its way to Sandy McPherson of the Conservative Victory Committee, an "independent expenditure" group that produced a television commercial featuring Horton's grotesque mug shot alternating with a photograph of Dukakis. ("I looked like a zombie," Horton admitted. "They chose the perfect picture for the ads. I looked incredibly wicked.") With the National Security Political Action Committee supplementing this "saturation-level PAC campaign," a racist momentum built with no official or unofficial Bush campaign operative ever having to mention that the specimen was black. "You started reporters looking into the Horton case on their own," Roger Simon wrote, "and that would produce more stories in print and on TV. And both media liked pictures. Mention Willie Horton's name and you got Willie Horton's picture on TV." The mug shot became so ubiquitous, joked former NBC president Robert Mulholland, that "I'm expecting any day now to see Willie Horton endorse a line of jeans."[63]

By the time the regular Bush campaign ran its own television spot featuring black and white cons heading to prison through a turnstile gate and then heading back toward middle-America's living room, Willie Horton was already firmly established in the public mind. The official ad did not mention Horton. It merely emphasized "revolving door" justice and implied (falsely) that Dukakis had sent 268 first-degree murderers out on "weekend passes" to rape, kidnap, and kill. Direct mail from state headquarters continued to hammer this point. Daniel Fleming, chair of the Maryland Republican party, sent a fund-raising letter warning of the "Dukakis/Willie Horton Team." "Is this your pro-family team for 1988?," he asked. "You, your spouse, your children and your friends can have a visit from someone like Willie Horton if Mike Dukakis becomes president." Connecticut voters got yellow "Get Out of Jail" cards (like those used in the board game "Monopoly"); and New York voters got a flier featuring Horton's mug shot courtesy of Victory '88 (organized by state and national Republican party officials). Illinois voters got a virtually identical package.[64]

This momentum was particularly hard to stop after some of Willie Horton's victims began holding press conferences. These included Clifford Barnes, who said Massachusetts officials treated him like "an acceptable statistic," and Donna Fournier Cuomo, whose brother had been stabbed to death (either by Horton or an accomplice). The Committee for the Presidency, another PAC, raised some $2 million to finance the tours and buy victim ads in the newspapers and on local TV. Meanwhile, Republican staffers contacted Horton in an unsuccessful effort to get him to endorse Dukakis. Everything else worked. The official and unofficial Bush campaigns took a frightening black face from the cable channels to the networks, in the process creating what presidential campaign scholar Kathleen Hall Jamieson called "a coherent narrative" about race. This narrative had anything but a subliminal message. "Dukakis's negatives with white voters are so high," one (official) Bush aide said, "as to be insuperable."

George Bush jumped in with relish. An initial and quite cautious use of Horton's name came in a June 22 speech to the National Sheriffs Association in Louisville. Then, in a Xenia, Ohio, speech, the vice-president discussed the "notorious Willie Horton" in what the *New York Times* called "vivid" detail. At a Medina, Ohio, rally, he labeled Dukakis a "furlough king" who specialized in "Club Med" vacations for murders and rapists. On those initially rare occasions when someone raised the charge of racism, Bush's assistant press secretary, Kristin Clark Taylor, a black woman, would remind them that her boss had not sent Horton "out galavanting around on a weekend party pass." Besides, she added, in a reference to the Democratic primaries, "your man Gore was the first on the scene."[65]

Dukakis remained oddly silent through most of this. He responded occasionally by citing dry statistics; more often not at all. The most bizarre and damaging example of this limp strategy came during the second debate when CNN anchor Bernard Shaw asked, "Governor, if Kitty Dukakis were raped and murdered, would you favor an irrevocable death penalty for the killer?" Shaw got back only a bland monotone: "No, I don't, Bernard. And I think you know I've opposed the death penalty during all my life. I don't see any evidence that it's a deterrent, and I think there are better ways . . ." He never recovered from this bloodless response. "Willie Horton was now stalking Dukakis on the stage," Sidney Blumental wrote. "And Horton was not only terrorizing him; he had 'raped and murdered' his wife. The fact that the question was posed by a black man, Bernard Shaw, the CNN anchor, subliminally heightened the effect."[66]

A strategy reevaluation came only in the three weeks before the election. In an October 8 speech at Bates College in Maine, Dukakis accused Bush of "exploiting a human tragedy for your own political ends." He reminded everyone that his younger brother, Stelian, had been killed by a hit-and-run driver in 1973 and that his father had been the victim of an assault and robbery. "So I don't need any lectures from Mr. Bush on crime fighting or on the sensitivity or compassion we must extend to the victims of crimes." Then, on October 19, Dukakis held a Horton mug-shot flier over his head and called it garbage. Two days later he approved a television spot featuring Angel Medrano, a convicted heroin dealer "furloughed" from a federal prison. While Vice President Bush led a "war on drugs," the ad said, Medrano raped and murdered Patsy Pedrin, a pregnant mother of two. Bush hit back immediately and hard, accusing the Dukakis campaign of racism against Hispanics—an accusation that confirmed, for some, a feeling that both campaigns had now met in the gutter.[67]

Dukakis had his own doubts about the Angel Medrano ad. The Sawyer/Miller Group in New York went through twenty or thirty versions of a TV commercial to counter the Bush/Atwater soft-on-crime message before producing one that the governor approved. Inexplicably the Dukakis campaign held it until October 21. By then the damage had already been done. "At some point," as a media consultant put it, "one side or the other owns the imagery." In the end Dukakis's counters and complaints had no more impact that Willie Horton's own pathetic words. "He may be just a cheap political opportunist," Horton said of Bush after the election, "but I can't help but question his moral judgment." Even Atwater claimed the high ground. "Our campaign made no TV commercials about Willie Horton," he said, "and Dukakis used a Hispanic in a furlough ad in Texas." If technically true, this was a hollow claim. The official Bush campaign participated in the debate about the unofficial Bush campaign's use of name and photograph on the narrow question of whether to show Willie Horton with or without a knife in his hand. Roger Ailes said that was the only real issue.[68]

"The Democratic Party has been assaulted on the crime issue," Susan Estrich explained, "and we have behaved as timid and frightened victims, afraid that we have done something wrong." In the campaign's last month the Dukakis strategy boiled down to a charge of racism against the Republicans, a charge that simply did not stick. "The average voter just didn't go for the Democratic, liberal-guilt mindset," as one conservative commentator noted. "They just plain don't feel guilty for being scared of black criminals. . . . They didn't understand why it was racist to talk about reality." Estrich realized that "Democrats are seen as the party of blacks" even though "the Republicans never attack us for that explicitly. But everytime we are attacked as the party of the poor and the party that is soft on crime, there lurks, I think, that subtle hint of our 'blackness'—and with it, an appeal to those who want no part of it."

Bush strategists knew that white Americans wanted no part of the African Americans who accounted for 62 percent of all robbery arrests, 50 percent of all rape and murder arrests, and almost 30 percent of all burglary arrests; or a culture that not only glorified the murder of police officers but whites in general. Rapper Ice Cube, among others, urged urban America's angry young black men to take their guns out to the suburbs, invade homes, and otherwise terrorize the Caucasians who lived there.

Dukakis remained silent for the three months it took Lee Atwater to make Willie Horton his running mate for a variety of reasons. He remembered what happened when Jimmy Carter called Reagan a racist. "Whites might be put off," other and supposedly more seasoned campaign advisers counseled Estrich, "if we 'whine' about racism." In all probability, however, Dukakis remained silent because he wanted to disassociate his candidacy from his party's reputation. He remained silent for the same reason that he failed to mention Schwerner, Chaney, and Goodman on August 4 when speaking at the Neshoba County Fair—a silence that Marian Wright Edelman called the campaign's most disgraceful moment. More disgraceful even than what Bush and Atwater had done.

"Willie Horton, Crime 'n' Commies, Furloughs, Flags, and Read My Lips!," Richard Ben Cramer observed. "It was ugly, brainless . . . and Bush knew he had to keep it up to the end—not just blood-roar, but the full measure, till the cup was dry, till he, too, was brainless. The system demanded totality." The system demanded totality of Dukakis, too; but he resisted to the end and never did find an Atwater who could make Angel Medrano fly.[69]

The post-Horton Atwater somehow managed to get himself invited to speak at Ebenezer in celebration of Martin Luther King's birthday. "I was too young to appreciate the significance of his life, the bravery of his work," he told the congregation. "But I know now. I know *now* that Martin Luther King, Jr., is a towering giant in our history. . . . I share his dream of a united America and a brotherhood of man." Back in his Washington office an editorial cartoon hung on the wall showing Atwater walking off with a diploma from "Willie Horton University."

Atwater managed a more surprising feat by getting himself appointed to Howard University's board of trustees, and was "stunned and saddened" when the Howard students who occupied the administration building in protest accused him of having masterminded "the most racist strategy in a national presidential campaign in the 20th century." Always one to get the last lick, Atwater said he resigned from the Howard board only to prevent an outbreak of violence—implying that African Americans could not protest without degenerating into savagery.[70]

During an early morning jog in Houston's Memorial Park, Bush rewarded Atwater by offering him the Republican National Committee chair. "Just as Nixon could go to China," the president said, "I think it'd be terrific if you, a young guy from the South, could be the guy who could break the old minority voting pattern. I'm convinced that you're the perfect guy to embark on an outreach program to blacks and other minorities." Bush got 10 percent of the black vote in 1988, Atwater told the *Wall Street Journal*, and if he could double that in 1992 the GOP would "become the majority party through the millennium." Buckley's *National Review* echoed this new line: "Any Republican who can capture 20 percent of the black vote, while holding the GOP base, won't even have to campaign in 1992: The election will be his."[71]

Hardly as radical a goal as it seemed. The strategy, merely a variation of a standard politics of division, intended to slice off what might be called the black Yuppie vote. "Affirmative action has worked," Atwater explained. "We've got a larger black middle class—and that's good for us, because we are the party of the middle class. . . . We are looking to attract the baby-boom blacks, the more educated, more open-minded blacks." His motivation was cynical. Atwater not only wanted to sanitize his own past but to make the Democrats waste time and money defending their most faithful voting block. This supplemented rather than contradicted Atwater's prime message that the Democrats were becoming more and more a black party, and it largely explained why Bush and Attorney General Richard Thornburgh proved willing to meet with Jesse Jackson while Democratic party leaders treated Jackson as a pariah. Even White House counsel C. Boyden Gray, a race-first man first among the president's race-first men, had something nice to say— lumping Jackson with Bush as the "only two modern-day politicians who can make instant rapport with the disabled."

Simultaneously, the Atwater/Bush strategy of seeking the "more open-minded blacks" would placate moderate and liberal Republicans troubled by racial polarization. "That the program simultaneously addresses the party Chairman's major public relations problem only adds to its charm," as one political commentator noted. "Atwater's biggest problem is that he and Willie Horton became household names together." He had to shake the racist label, in other words, and tried to do so by telling outright lies. "We were just trying to campaign solely against that criminal furlough program, and Willie Horton was one of the worst examples of a criminal who was turned loose," he claimed. "In retrospect, I'm sorry he was black. Now, looking back, we should have used a white guy." Neither the Howard students nor anyone else bought this, and Atwater died (victim of what protégé Mary Matalin called "a galloping grade-four brain tumor") with his name known in too many households as the racist who made Willie Horton famous. The worst kind of racist at that because he was no true believer.[72]

Lee Atwater knew right from wrong here and probably took no comfort from the Gridiron Club spectacle of a Dukakis impersonator moving Elvis-style through the notes and bars of "Jail House Rock." Bush and Vice President Dan Quayle, in contrast, roared with delight at the lyrics:

> I said, Hey, Willie, I will set you free
> Come on and do the furlough rock with me.[73]

Atwater had put his man in the White House and otherwise made it so big that he inspired the Gridiron Club's featured number that evening. By the Washington standards of Republicans and Democrats alike, Willie Horton had made Lee Atwater the ultimate insider.

Bush followed the Horton symbolism with a crime bill that proposed $1.4 million in new spending for judges and prosecutors and only $150,000 for public defenders. "More executions, more prisons, more hardware," editorial writers for *The Nation* groaned. All part of Bush's pandering to his "'white nationalist' constituency." Congress passed the legislation, but it had no impact on crime rates or the rise in interracial violence symbolized by, among other disturbing events, New York's Crown Heights riots, the Howard Beach and Bensonhurst murders, and the rape of the Central Park jogger. No chief executive could stop crime. But this president set the moral tone of the crime issue with Willie Horton, and his message was that crime was less a problem than it was an electoral opportunity. With murder the leading cause of death among black males between the ages of 15 and 24, Bush captured 70 percent of the white male vote in the South and 66 percent of the overall white male vote by leading with an image of a black rapist and a white victim.[74]

To supplement the image of white women at risk, President Bush continued to push the Reagan message of white males as the nation's most oppressed group. He did this by continuing the quota wars and otherwise exploiting white male fears of affirmative action. Administration strategists understood the forces that social scientists Paul Sniderman and Thomas Piazza later documented: "Prejudice is part of the politics of race, but a larger part is politics itself. . . . Today there is a politics to issues of race. Racial policies themselves—the specific goals they are intended to serve, and the particular means by which they propose to accomplish those goals—define significantly the structure of conflict over race. . . . The conventional wisdom is that opposition to affirmative action is driven by racism. . . . [But] apparent cause and effect can be reversed: dislike of affirmative action can engender dislike of blacks. . . . At the deepest level . . . racial politics owes its shape not to beliefs or stereotypes distinctively about blacks but to the broader set of convictions about fairness and fair play that make up the American creed."[75]

The Supreme Court gave the Bush campaign against affirmative action a boost in 1989 with six decisions eroding minority employment rights. Most notable was *Wards Cove Packing Company v. Atonio* which forced plaintiffs in discrimination suits to prove a negative (that employers had no business justification for a discriminatory practice). When Senator Edward Kennedy introduced remedial civil rights legislation in response, Bush labeled it a "quota bill" and ran with the issue for nearly all of his remaining three years in office. "To talk quotas will be the polite way to talk race and class," *Newsweek* magazine predicted. "With a recession deepening the resentments of white swing voters, quotas will be the hot-button issue of the 1992 presidential race . . . [and] could easily degenerate into the politics of rage. . . . By attacking quotas George Bush will be able to say to those Republocrats he must keep to stay in the White House, in essence: if you don't get a job, promotion or a place in the freshman class, blame the Democrats. They are the ones mugging the middle class and giving the spoils to their minority friends."[76]

Bush's quota wars involved a complicated backdrop and skirmishes that did not always involve the White House directly. The president himself ignored straightforward civil rights issues and saw only a way to win elections by exploiting what everyone now agreed were divisive and explosive racial tensions. "The word 'quota' is Bush's answer for everything," United Mine Workers President Richard Trumka said at the National Rainbow Coalition Conference. "If you ask the President how he feels about the fact that he just spent billions of dollars on a war that killed 150,000 people and the Kurds and Shiite Moslems are living in misery and Saddam Hussein is back in power, he just says, 'I will veto any quota bill the Democrats send me.'"

At the same time the quota wars were conducted as arcane lawyer-led fights about the meaning of such legalisms as "disparate impact" and "business necessity." "[We're] dancing on the head of a pin," one civil rights lawyer said. A movement with a lame and overly bureaucratized slogan ("The burden of proof in antidiscrimination lawsuits should be on the employer!") and not the fiery lines of the past ("*Justice. Equality. Jobs.*"), could hardly start what *The Nation* called "a prairie fire of enthusiasm in this country." Many civil rights activists moved off the streets and into a world of guidelines and standards and regulation and debates about precise wordings and lawsuits over the placement of commas and semi-colons. It was indeed "a long slide since the brave days."

While civil rights advocates no longer sounded their old calls, the president did not mind borrowing their legacy. "Black and white," the president said at West Point, "the great civil-rights leaders of the fifties and sixties deplored intolerance, demanded equality of opportunity and equality under the law." An opportunistic advocacy of color blindness ruled this administration just as it had the last. As ever, opportunity and equality under law meant opportunity and equality for whites only.[77]

Quota wars heated up in October 1990 when Bush vetoed the Kennedy bill. A month later North Carolina Senator Jesse Helms used the quota issue in a reelection campaign TV ad that showed a white man's hand crumbling a job-rejection letter with a white voice over ("You needed that job and you were the best qualified, but they had to give it to a minority because of a racial quota"). The ad also included a logo about Helms's black opponent ("Harvey Gantt supports Ted Kennedy's racial quota law"). Pete Wilson had used the quota issue in his successful race for governor of California, and in Louisiana the neo-Klansman/Nazi David Duke got more than 60 percent of the white vote in a failed attempt to win a Senate seat. "'The quota issue is radioactive,'" a House Democratic aide told Elizabeth Drew. "The result has been nothing less than panic in the Democratic ranks. A lot of members are asking why their leaders are putting them through the agony of having to vote on the civil-rights bill again this year." It made no difference, as political analyst Joe Klein pointed out, that Kennedy's proposal was "a rather minor piece of legislation that will probably do more for lawyers than for minorities." "When the President says it's a quota bill," Vice President Dan Quayle chipped in, "it's a quota bill, notwithstanding what Ted Kennedy may say about it."[78]

In December a most unlikely administration source entered the quota wars by announcing that college scholarship set-asides for blacks were unconstitutional. Michael Williams, a thirty-seven-year-old African-American lawyer and the Department of Education's assistant secretary for civil rights, acted in the wake of the National Football League's decision to boycott Arizona (in protest of the state's refusal to recognize the Martin Luther King holiday), and Fiesta Bowl organizers' attempts to repair the damage by offering $200,000 in minority scholarships to the Universities of Louisville and Alabama (whose football teams would meet in Tempe on January 1). Williams told those officials that their offer violated the Civil Rights Act of 1964, which prohibited discrimination by schools that receive federal aid. Williams apparently made this ruling on his own as Bush claimed that he learned of it only in his morning newspaper. Whether that was true or not, Williams's announcement fit all too nicely into the president's so-called New Paradigm. A rollback of liberal social policies like affirmative action would prove that Bush had what he was so often accused of lacking ("the vision thing"). Further, these rollbacks could be accomplished with no taxes of any kind (new or old). Domestic policy on the cheap, in other words.

William Bennett, former NEH secretary and "drug czar" and then Republican National Committee chair, dropped another bombshell that same month by challenging the Democrats to a national debate on affirmative action. Bennett, who along with Bush had campaigned for Jesse Helms, described the senator's quota ad ("they had to give it to a minority") as perfectly legitimate. In a *Bakke*-inspired book co-authored in 1979 (*Counting by Race*), Bennett had also argued that quotas "perpetuate the legacy of slavery." *Newsweek* called him "a pit bull with a brain," and *Time* said his appointment reflected Bush's willingness "to exploit atavistic emotions to gain votes." Fortunately, Bennett was not nearly as tough as he sounded. He quit the Republican National Committee almost immediately, citing the job's headaches and his own need to earn outside income on the lecture circuit.[79]

While Bennett blasted the Democrats, Senator Kennedy tried to negotiate a compromise with White House chief of staff John Sununu. It was not an easy task. Several of the business and conservative groups that Sununu approached for advice immediately turned around and announced they had prevented the president's man from "caving." That was a stretch. When Sununu warned of "ghosts" in Kennedy's bill, he meant the specter of quotas. Boyden Gray, counsel to the president and Bush's longtime friend, complicated things by suggesting that any proposed civil rights legislation allow employers to plead "legitimate community or customer relationship efforts" to avoid hiring or promoting minorities. Obviously this was a Jim Crow loophole. "Even people within the Administration were horrified," Elizabeth Drew said. Those officials rejected Gray's proposal but were not horrified enough to support a legitimate compromise. Sununu and Gray remained in charge, leading a White House charge to pressure business leaders then negotiating with congressional Democrats. Those talks collapsed when Robert Allen, AT&T chair and head of the Business Roundtable (a coalition of some 200 top CEOs), succumbed to White House pressure and pulled out of the talks. Sununu and Gray had worked the phones here, telling Allen and other Roundtable leaders that the discussions were "inconvenient."

Ultimately, a compromise was reached in Congress which even Utah Senator Orin Hatch said he could live with. When the legislation got to the White House, however, Bush called it a quota bill and vetoed it—with the Senate subsequently falling one vote short of the two-thirds needed to override. The president, preoccupied with the Persian Gulf mobilization and a budget/taxes crisis, found time to play more color-blind games. "Each time the bill's sponsors made a concession to pick up the votes of waverers the Administration, like Lucy, moved the ball," Drew added. "No matter what changes were made, the Administration designated the Democrats' bill a 'quota bill.' Even when the bill's sponsors added language specifically making quotas illegal."[80]

Bush explained his stance in a series of speeches in May and early June. At the University of Michigan he attacked "the notion of political correctness" and "multiculturalism." Advocates of such un-Americanisms were "political extremists" bent on roaming "the land, abusing the privilege of free speech, setting citizens against one another on the basis of their class or race." "Congressional leaders," the president told the graduating class at the FBI National Academy in Quantico, Virginia, "again want to pass a bill that would lead employers to adopt hiring quotas and unfair job practices." At West Point he promised to "destroy the racial mistrust that threatens our national well-being as much as violence or drugs or poverty. . . . We must think of ourselves not as colors or numbers . . . [and] cast off now the politics of division." All this from as cynical and mean-spirited a practitioner of racial politics as ever occupied the Oval Office.[81]

Bush made what he probably considered his shrewdest move in fall 1991 by taking Boyden Gray's advice and nominating Clarence Thomas for Thurgood Marshall's Supreme Court seat. A sharecropper's grandson from Pin Point, Georgia, who attended Catholic boarding school in Savannah, Holy Cross College in Worchester, Massachusetts, and then Yale where he specialized in tax and corporate law, the forty-three-year-old Thomas was in many ways a classic success story. "Horatio Alger in Blackface," said *Harper's* editor Lewis Lapham. Yet Thomas was more the product of affirmative action and the patronage of two Republican presidents. "The most sponsored black man in American history," Jesse Jackson concluded. William Bradford Reynolds held, with considerably more charity (a rare trait in that man), that Thomas represented "the epitome of the right kind of affirmative action."

Named chair of the Equal Employment Opportunity Commission by Reagan and a federal judge by Bush, Thomas, widely regarded as a "house black," got Reynolds's endorsement precisely because he opposed quotas and even the most benign forms of affirmative action. His reforms at EEOC included a blanket rejection of class action lawsuits, and, having once confided to a friend that he idolized *Star Wars* villain "Darth Vader," he was equally loyal to the Reagan revolution's emperors. He objected only to Republican efforts to minimize black voter turnout and his party's general view of blacks "as an interest group not worth going after."

Thomas's nomination to the Supreme Court was only the most extreme example of the favored Republican practice of moving up right-thinking blacks. It could be seen in Reagan's appointment of Clarence Pendleton to head the Civil Rights Commission and Bush's earlier failed attempt to name ex–FBI agent William Lucas assistant attorney general for civil rights. Lapham called the latest nomination "puppet theater" with Thomas "dancing in the strings once occupied by Willie Horton. . . . The President apparently thinks that he can play at racial politics as if it were a game of horseshoes."

When Bush appointed Thomas to the United States Court of Appeals for the District of Columbia, arguably the most important appellate tribunal after the Supreme Court, the civil rights community voiced no significant protest. The latest nomination, in contrast, sparked a wave of protest that rivaled the mobilization against Bork. Thomas, however, sounded more like Pendleton than Bork. All that movement leaders ever did was "bitch, bitch, bitch, moan and whine," he said on a number of occasions before Bush put up the nomination. In the process, Thomas added, movement leaders had created a "cult mentality" that had "hypnotized black Americans into a mindless political trance."[82]

Having learned from Bork's experience, both the White House and Thomas attacked in their own way. Bush's men helped white fundamentalists set up fronts to secure the nomination (African-American Freedom Alliance and Coalition for the Restoration of the Black Family and Society). Thomas maintained during the confirmation hearings that he had no constitutional philosophy at all. He explained away controversial statements by claiming that he was merely pandering to his audiences and had not even read the cant that he had endorsed. Because this black Reaganite was constantly invited to speak before conservative groups (especially the evangelical associations of the religious right), there were dozens of these endorsements—including a call for the Supreme Court to overturn *Roe v. Wade* and a condemnation of his own sister as a welfare lout. (He claimed to have driven all night from Washington to Georgia to apologize, but Emma Mae did not recall the visit.) Even Chief Justice William Rehnquist got tagged: "We can no longer rely on conservative figures to advance our cause."[83]

Anita Hill, a black University of Oklahoma Law School professor, raised the most serious threat to the nomination with the charge that Thomas had sexually harassed her when she worked as his assistant at the Department of Education and EEOC. One might think, given where Thomas was heading, that his civil rights performance in those jobs might be deemed as important as the harassment charge. He had, after all, displayed a contempt for the judicial branch of government in general while running EEOC. Hauled into court by women and minority plaintiffs, who asked that he be held in contempt for refusing to investigate discrimination complaints, Thomas admitted a contempt for the judicial class:

Q. But you're going ahead and violating these time frames. . . . You're violating them in compliance reviews on all occasions, practically, and you're violating them on complaints most of the time, or half the time; isn't that true.

A. That's right.

Q. So aren't you in effect substituting your own judgement as to what the policy should be for what the court order requires? The court requires you to comply with this 90 day period; isn't that true?

A. That's right.

Q. And you have not imposed a deadline; is that correct?

A. I have not imposed a deadline.

Q. And meanwhile, you are violating a court order rather grievously, aren't you?

A. Yes.[84]

Anita Hill's charges overwhelmed this issue and other questions in the nominee's past. She cited details ranging from pubic hairs on Coke cans to the exploits of such porno-film stars as "Long Dong Silver," and Thomas denied the point-by-point recital with a "bitch-set-me-up" ferocity. With help from Republican allies in the Senate, he moved on to cast himself as an "uppity black" victim of "a high-tech lynching" carried out by the Judiciary Committee's fourteen (white) man crew— a strategy that scarcely pleased the administration even though it worked. "What's most ironic, and sad, about the whole situation is that Clarence Thomas, in his fight to save his good name, played the 'victim card,'" Dan Quayle later wrote. "He was appealing to the kind of race-consciousness he'd spent most of his professional life trying to move people away from."[85] It made no difference that Thomas was anything but an uppity black or that his accuser was a black woman. He played the race card to secure his seat on the court. "These are charges that play into racist, bigoted stereotypes," he told the assembled senators. "It is a message that you will be lynched, destroyed, caricatured by a committee of the U.S. Senate rather than hung from a tree."

This was of course the first lynching in history arising from a black man coming too close to a black woman and ending with the victim sitting on the United States Supreme Court. (Bork had also used lynch-mob imagery, less successfully, in defense of his nomination.) Before Thomas got life tenure on the land's highest bench, NAACP executive director Benjamin Hooks had called the Supreme Court decisions that inspired all the "quota" bills in the first place a "legal lynching of black America's hope." Hooks was closer to the mark with that imagery than Thomas (or Bork), and things were expected to worsen with the latest arrival on the court. Thomas remained a bitter politicized ideologue. "It was spiritual warfare," his (white) wife, Virginia Lamp Thomas, told *People* magazine after the Anita Hill hearings. "Good versus evil." Satan's devils included the civil rights and women's groups, senators and their aides, and the print and television media (especially National Public Radio, which helped break the charges).

"He doesn't owe any of the groups who opposed him anything," Mrs. Thomas added, and her husband's first years on the court would prove that the justice agreed with his wife. "He ain't evolving," as one Thomas critic put it. Though Thomas failed to ask a single question during the ninety-nine oral arguments of the Supreme Court's 1993–1994 term, he quickly emerged as an ultraconservative icon ranking with Oliver North, Jesse Helms, and Rush Limbaugh. (He officiated, in his own home, at Limbaugh's wedding.) Bush wanted to make the court an arm of the presidency and guarantee that its justices would uphold the state against its citizens. He picked Clarence Thomas because this black man shared those basic goals and otherwise furthered the cause of racial polarization.[86]

In the end George Bush and Boyden Gray were too clever for their own good as the president ended up where he had started. The flip-flops of his Texas years returned, marking, some said, a return to a more reasonable posture. Others said it merely confirmed the one name (wimp) that had somehow always stuck to this president. Bush reversed himself on the "quota" bill and signed the Civil Rights Act of 1991 into law—a minor piece of legislation that restored some of the rights removed by the Rehnquist court. Gray called it a victory over the "demonically quota-oriented crowd," announcing, "We won, they capitulated." Patrick Buchanan and everyone else knew it was the same old bill that Bush had vetoed before and thus represented "pre-emptive surrender":

> With the Thomas victory, the GOP had the Democrats divided, defeated, on the run. How sweet it was! With a chance to turn victory over Kennedy & Co. into rout, Mr. Bush rushed out to cut a deal, and give back his ill-gotten gains. Unable to believe their good luck, Mr. Kennedy and Mr. Mitchell are now mocking the man who made it possible. Is there a clinical term to describe a terror of winning?[87]

Bush's reasons for reversing field and signing the Civil Rights Act of 1991 were complex. With even Republican senators like John Danforth, Thomas's mentor, accusing him of playing "race politics," Bush lacked the stomach to organize the reelection campaign around (anti–) civil rights issues. Things would just not let up here. Nearly simultaneous to the Thomas nomination, other storms erupted over the Department of Labor's use of "race norming" in the evaluation of the General Aptitude Test Battery; and the administration's announcement that high school diplomas ought to be required even for janitorial jobs. Bush was even being criticized for his lack of commitment to educational opportunity by his own advisory board on the Historically Black Colleges and Universities. This was particularly debilitating, White House aide Charles Kolb noted, because criticism here cut back to Bush's Yale days and his father's work with the United Negro College Fund.[88]

In addition the president discovered, as Lincoln had, that he needed the black poor to fight. Service in Kuwait and Iraq, Garry Wills noted, was of the sort that required repayment. It was also of some importance that Colin Powell, the Joint Chiefs of Staff's first black chair, made no great secret of his disgust at the prior campaign's race-baiting.[89] Anita Hill's charges, hurled into this suffocating atmosphere, had further upped the ante by raising the specter of a "sexual backlash" against the administration. If approval of the civil rights legislation was a way to mitigate this new threat as well, many commentators argued that Bush would have to run a Horton-esque campaign anyway. With communism dead, post–Desert Storm foreign policy a bust, abortion a losing issue, and the economy stumbling through a double-dip recession, what non–southern strategy choice was there but to appeal to white male fears and resentments? With his popularity plummeting, however, the president was less willing to "hang tough."

Probably the most important reason Bush backed off involved former Klansman David Duke's electoral success in Louisiana (and threatened campaign for the Republican party's presidential nomination). Because Duke had co-opted Bush's images and code ("quotas," "affirmative action," "welfare," "urban crime," "heritage"), he forced the chief executive who gave the nation Clarence Thomas, all those Willie Horton ads, and two-plus years of sound-bite whining about Teddy Kennedy's "quota bill" to look in the mirror. Bush saw a hooded Duke staring back and blinked.

With anti-Semitism on the march in France, Germany, Russia, and virtually every Eastern European nation, David Duke symbolized something that even George Bush could not ignore. Duke, who favored Baby Ruth candy bars for breakfast and *Mein Kampf* for inspiration, looked at Reagan and Bush and saw a natural home for himself in the Republican party. He ran on the GOP ticket and won a place in Louisiana's November 1991 gubernatorial run-off with a straightforward pitch: In a state hit hard by plummeting oil prices and the Bush recession, he traced the loss of white jobs to a non-white and/or Semitic "them." "Horses," he said, "contributed more to the building of American civilization than blacks." Such rhetoric, from a former vacuum-cleaner salesman who in his college days paraded around the LSU campus in a storm-trooper uniform complete with swastika, took the president's quota wars a bit too far. Still, it was not an illogical extension. Duke, in the words of Senator Paul Tsongas, a Democratic presidential hopeful, was merely "the son of George Bush."[90]

"Duke," said Frank Greer, a consultant to Arkansas Governor Bill Clinton, "blows another Willie Horton gambit out—entirely." Pat Buchanan was among the few who disagreed with this assessment. Buchanan, like Duke, also entered the presidential race with an America-first campaign that prescribed prayer in the schools and much corrective social surgery. Affirmative action would be cut out first, followed by welfare, foreign aid, third-world immigrants, and anything manufactured abroad. Otherwise Buchanan remained stuck, in effect, in Nixon's White House. He continued to see the Republican party's future solely in terms of racial politics, and that was precisely his gripe against Bush: The president had lost his nerve while racial politics played out in Louisiana. Buchanan resented Bush for folding the party's race cards (much like the Laffer-curve quacks never forgave Reagan for folding his supply-side cards in the early 1980s). So he made a run for Bush's nomination, going to Louisiana and managing (Wallace style) to out-hate even David Duke.

Bush's people made a few half-hearted attempts to reconstitute a southern strategy in the months before the election. Boyden Gray, for one, suggested flushing every affirmative action program and regulation in every federal agency and department. And Marlin Fitzwater blamed the spring riots in Los Angeles on the welfare-state handouts of LBJ's Great Society. When that balloon failed to float Fitzwater backed off by claiming that he had misspoken (hardly the sort of error he was known for making.) The reason for the retreat was clear. "Simply put," Kevin Phillips wrote, "liberalism circa 1992 had been out of power too long to be an effective straw man and conservatives had been in power too long to shift responsibility."[91] It should also be noted that the cause-and-effect reasoning that Republicans had applied to the 1960s' riots led to no backlash in the latest riot's aftermath.

Los Angeles exploded because a Simi Valley jury acquitted the police officers who beat a black man, Rodney King, an assault immortalized by a citizen's camcorder and played repeatedly in endless gruesome detail on the evening news. In the riot's midst there would also be footage taken by a TV news helicopter of a white truck driver, Reginald

Denny, being dragged from his truck at the corner of Florence and Normandie Avenues and beaten by young blacks wielding a tire iron, brick, and fire extinguisher. (The difference was that no police officer helped Rodney King while black citizens intervened to save Reginald Denny's life.) In all the violence left fifty-four dead, some 2,000 injured, and more than $1 billion in property damage. With some 3,500 Latinos arrested and 650 whites, this riot was also interracial—a drive-by, la-la land *intifada* set to rap music. Looting spread to the affluent parts of West LA and the San Gabriel Valley.

"I thought of Lincoln," Barbara Bush said. "Imagine being President when your country is at war with itself. How awful." "George went to California," she added. "The thing that really bothered him was what happened to the Koreans. Over 2,000 small businesses owned by the Koreans were burned. Could some in the black community be racists?"[92]

With references to the "profoundly racist" Great Society programs (Alexander Haig's words) falling flat and the president's initial response to the Simi Valley verdict falling even flatter ("the court system has worked"), the administration sent in troops trained to deal with third-world hot spots.[93] These included Army and Marine veterans of Panama and Desert Storm respectively. Bush also appointed William Webster, former FBI and CIA director, to head up an official inquiry into police performance in Los Angeles, and facilitated the post–Cold War reassignment of hundreds of federal agents from foreign counter-intelligence work to jobs gathering data on big-city street gangs. The military solution was perhaps best symbolized by Los Angeles Police Chief Daryl Gates, the most visible and by far the Rodney King affair's most controversial figure, who walked city streets in a flak jacket. Gates had made an ad for Bush in the 1988 campaign, and Bush in turn had called Gates "an American hero." In the end, however, the president recognized that there was more to this riot than law and order. He distanced himself from Gates and spoke of a "weed and seed" program designed to remove the criminal element and plant such things as drug-treatment centers.

Patrick Buchanan, again emboldened by a presidential retreat, spoke at Jerry Falwell's Liberty College about "evil exultant and triumphant" and the use of force as the only possible response, in either the short or long run, to the LA violence. Buchanan made this last point by recalling his Connecticut Avenue view of General Norman Schwarzkopf's victory parade:

> This is what it must have been like reviewing the Roman legions as they marched in triumph after yet another victory in Gaul or Spain. The analogy holds. As America's imperial troops guard frontiers all over the world, our own frontiers are open, and the barbarian is inside the gates. And you do not deal with the Vandals and Visigoths who are pillaging your cities by expanding the Head Start and food stamp programs.

Buchanan not only dreamed of the presidency for himself but conversion of the nation's Cold War military might for use against the internal (nonwhite) enemy. He made the point again when speaking at the Republican National Convention in Houston's Astrodome, glorifying the 18th Cavalry troops who "took *our* city back block by block." Brave words, considering, among other things, that the 165-person Republican National Committee had only three black members. All represented the U.S. Virgin Islands.[94]

"There is a saying in Washington," Michael Deaver wrote, "that the left and the right meet behind your back." His specific reference was to "the 'Jim Jones wing' of the Republican party, those willing to prove their loyalty by drinking the spiked Kool-Aid." Reagan controlled that wing while president, but even Reagan could not control Buchanan and his ilk in Houston. With Phyllis Schlafly, Pat Robertson, and Pat Boone, Buchanan, as Garry Wills noted, defined the campaign's meaning and proved strong enough to push the former president himself out of prime-time network coverage.[95] If Reagan failed to keep the GOP from disintegrating into its own civil wars, how could anyone expect Bush to succeed? Houston made the Republicans look like their inclusive big-tent approach to politics meant an exclusive evangelical revivalist tent. The flamboyant "cultural conservatives" had not only pushed Reagan aside in Houston; they pushed aside the larger Republican voting bloc of more secular, economic-issue conservatives.

Bush knew that Buchanan's Republicans did not speak for the white middle's God and country and were as responsible for his dismal electoral chances as the sour economy. For twelve years Reagan and Bush had cynically exploited patriotic rites (notably the flag and the

Pledge of Allegiance) and offered little more than racial, religious, and nationalist extremism to those with incomes too short to worry much about capital gains tax cuts. By summer 1992 the real evangelicals had practically captured the Republican party, and for that Bush had only himself and his predecessor to blame. He ought to be commended only for refusing to push himself all the way down to Buchanan's level. Then again, he probably would have sunk that low had he figured there were votes enough there to secure another four years as commander-in-chief.

This president lacked his predecessor's cheerful-salesman gift for denying the obvious. The Caesar of Desert Storm did not think it remained morning in America in the twelfth year of the Reagan revolution, and he campaigned like a man who knew he had fallen far and had no chance. Even communism's collapse on his watch proved of little comfort as it gave rise not to Reagan cheer but the pessimism of a beleaguered if still predominantly white nation in a largely nonwhite world that looked increasingly bewildering without the stability of a bipolar myth. Trouble with "the vision thing" led only to a less-than-catchy campaign slogan (the New Paradigm) pitting Republican values (empowerment, responsibility) against Democratic policies (racial quotas, cultural permissiveness). Bush's other initiative elevated congressional paralysis to the level of policy objective. The Reagan revolution's most enduring accomplishment, as the pundits reminded the voters, was to make the government broke, announce that the government intended to stay that way, and thus preclude the things that even Bush saw fit to talk about in his 1990 state of the union address (child care for working women, homes for the homeless, drug-free kids and neighborhoods, a clean environment, an absolute commitment to education).

In 1988 Bush had come out swinging, tying his Democratic opponent not only to "Willie" Horton but to a "criminal lobby" (the ACLU) that supposedly cared more about a furloughed black con than the white woman that con had raped. He supplemented this by hyping the death penalty, the Pledge of Allegiance, school prayer, and "democracy" in Kuwait as the sole national issues worth his or any other citizen's attention. The pundits smelled blood now, and when they looked at Bush they deemed him capable only of refining the prior strategy. What the president called a New Paradigm in 1992 others called a "KKK campaign" (Kuwait, Krime, Kuotas) that crashed and burned when he got too cute and put up Clarence Thomas's name for the Supreme Court. When that happened Bush had no ground under him. He could only question his Democratic rivals' patriotism in a spasm of "bozo" (Clinton) and "ozone man" (Gore) name calling. "This guy," the president said of the straightlaced Gore, "is so far off in the environmental extreme, we'll be up to our neck in owls. . . . This guy's crazy. He's way out. Far out, man." There was also an especially pathetic plea to recall battlefield glory others would deny him: "They said I was inarticulate and could not lead."[96]

After four years in the White House about the only thing one could say for certain about this president was that he hated quotas and liked capital gains tax cuts. Without the former he could scarcely sell the latter to an electorate that had finally begun to understand what the Reagan revolution was about (however fleeting that understanding was). The rich were getting richer while the poor got poorer and the middle class stagnated, and the unremitting racial politics of the past twelve years had been constructed as a distraction to hide these facts. Even Kevin Phillips, the Nixon expert on ethnic voting patterns, said that Reagan and Bush had betrayed the tenets of right-wing populism by giving too much to the economic royalists. It was as much a southern strategy sin to use the government's tax, debt, and budgetary and regulatory policies in favor of the rich as it was to use those government tools in favor of the blacks.[97]

That Bush and the presidential party's atavistic appeal to white nationalism collapsed in 1992 was no great comfort to the Democrats. Since Nixon in 1968 candidates who attracted virtually no black votes captured the presidency in four of six elections. One of those Democratic victories was a fluke. Without Watergate there would have been no Carter presidency, and even at that Jimmy Carter might not have made it had he been running against someone tougher and shrewder than Gerald Ford. The monster Reagan recession of 1981–1982 and then the Reagan revolution scandals (Iran-Contra, S&L, etc.) propped up the nonpresidential party. So did Bush's utter incompetence—best reflected in his bulldog pursuit of a capital gains tax cut and only a capital gains tax cut in the midst of an election eve double-dip recession.

Republicans nonetheless remained convinced, in then House whip Newt Gingrich's words, that their rivals were the enemies of "normal Americans" and fast "becoming an aberrant party." "Partisan competition for the votes of black Americans has been absent for over a generation, and its absence has corrupted both parties," Thomas Edsall concluded in his study of race, rights, and taxes in modern America.[98] With no sign that Bush's defeat inspired the GOP to reevaluate southern strategy tenets, that corruption will likely remain for some time. If a two-party political system where one party has staked all on white over black is hardly new to American history, it is no more in the national interest today than it had been in Jackson's or Lincoln's time.

There is also no sign that any of this much troubled George Bush other than the sting of losing an election to a "bozo." If he pondered nothing upon retiring to his Texas home in that downtown Houston hotel, he might have been better served as a citizen and human being had he recalled a family trip some thirty-five years earlier. While Bush and oldest son traveled from Texas to Maine by air, Barbara Bush drove Jeb, Neil, and baby Marvin because the family's black help, Otha Fitzgerald (later Taylor) and Julia May Cooper, were afraid to fly. Mrs. Bush recalled no racial incidents along the way, but the help remembered a hotel manager who said Negroes could not stay. Bush got the man on the telephone and convinced him to put up everyone. "I don't know what Mr. Bush did," Mrs. Taylor recalled. "I guess he did the same thing he did over there in the Persian Gulf." To prevent future problems Barbara Bush bought Otha and Julia May uniforms, having heard that black women dressed as proper southern maids had less trouble on the road. This proved not to be the case, especially on the return trip from the rented Pierce house on the rocks past St. Anne's Church on Kennebunkport's Ocean Avenue. Even Mrs. Bush admitted the drive back was a nightmare with the group forced into a side-of-the-road Jim Crow diet of 7-Eleven fare.

"You know," Barbara Bush later explained, "Little Rock happened in the middle of the trip so it polarized people. It was disgusting."[99] To get to the White House, and in trying to stay there, George Bush fanned those same disgusting flames.

RECTORS AND SOULJAS

"Where I come from we know about race-baiting," Arkansas Governor Bill Clinton said when declaring for the presidency at the Old State House in Little Rock and promising not to let "them" get away with a campaign predicated upon "the politics of division." He backed up that boast during the primaries and general election, deflecting George Bush's suddenly half-hearted southern strategy with a little race-baiting of his own. Victory came in November not simply because Clinton followed his own blockhead advice ("it's the economy, stupid") with a reminder to all voters that giving the incumbent four more years would be "like hiring General Sherman for fire commissioner in Georgia."[1] He understood that racial tensions and resentments had an economic base and that no presidential candidate could succeed by allowing (Dukakis style) an opponent to control a campaign's racial symbols. Where Bush made Willie Horton famous while pursuing the votes of the white middle, Clinton, in a manner nearly as opportunistic as anything Lee Atwater had ever done, would make another black murderer and a gangsta rapper famous in pursuit of those same votes.

Unlike his predecessors dating to Nixon, Clinton's experiences went deeper than ballfield stories about black teammates or the generic claim that "some of my best friends are black." When his widowed mother went to New Orleans for nursing school, one-year-old Bill stayed with her parents at the general store they ran, and Eldridge and Edith Cassidy, racial liberals by Louisiana standards, began teaching him right from wrong. Even before the crisis at Little Rock Central, Clinton's mother remembered her son, still short of his teenage years, telling her that segregation was a sin. While civil rights movement activists marched and organized in the 1960s he quietly told classmates at Hot Springs High School that he admired Martin Luther King. It took some courage for a white southern teen to do that in those days. His grandparents' lessons and the movement for racial justice itself so affected Clinton that there is no reason to doubt the later claim in the famous letter to Colonel Eugene House regarding his draft status and Vietnam. "A war I opposed and despised," he wrote, "with a depth of feeling I had reserved solely for racism in America."

Clinton acted on those feelings upon leaving Arkansas for college. While at Georgetown he watched Washington burn from his dormitory roof after King's assassination and then did volunteer work for the Red Cross in the hottest spots while wearing gloves, hat, and scarf to hide his skin color. (All white volunteers were required to cover up). "Driving my car with a big red cross on it down into the inner city to the churches," he remembered, "where the people who were burned out of their homes were huddled in church basements waiting for food." Carolyn Staley, a next-door neighbor from Little Rock who had come up for a visit, went with him, and later that night, back at the dorm, she heard him whispering snippets from Dr. King's "I Have a Dream" speech. He could recite the whole thing by heart.

Clinton entered Yale Law School in 1971 and in his second year roomed with William Thaddeus Coleman III, son of Nixon's transportation secretary and one of ten blacks in the 125-student class. When those ten students established a black table in the cafeteria Clinton was the only white to violate "the unspoken taboo" and plop himself down. Glares and mutterings about "honkies" greeted him at first, but he kept eating and gabbing and coming back day after day until it got to the point where even the most militant militant would ask about his whereabouts on those few occasions when he missed a regularly scheduled meal. In Yale's classrooms law instructors ranged from First Amendment scholar Thomas Emerson to Robert Bork—with the former encouraging community service. So Clinton did volunteer work for a downtown New Haven lawyer this time, investigating open-housing and other civil rights cases. "I wound up going into tenements where people were shooting up heroin, doing stuff like that," he said. "I mean, I had some interesting jobs."

Classmate and future wife Hillary Rodham had an even more interesting job. With even Yale President Kingman Brewster, Jr., questioning "the ability of black revolutionaries to achieve a fair trial anywhere in the United States," Rodham organized shifts from among the students in Emerson's class to monitor the New Haven prosecution of Bobby Seale and several local Panthers on an assortment of charges arising from the torture/murder of suspected police informant Alex Rackley. Rodham's duties included trips to the Panther's Connecticut headquarters where she caught the eye of the FBI.[2]

Neither Clinton continued such community services or kept such company when they moved into electoral politics. Five years after Yale, in 1978, when Bill and Hillary were preparing to dance at Robinson Auditorium in downtown Little Rock, they invited no Black Panther, needless to say, to the governor's inaugural ball. But Governor Clinton did invite Orval Faubus, a predecessor who knew something about race-baiting, too. Having come up when Nixon's southern strategy was all the rage and then observing the new masters, Reagan and Bush, Clinton would seem determined, while plotting his own White House run, to split the difference between a Seale and a Faubus. Whenever forced to chose, however, he tilted toward the latter. If he understood the poverty and despair of the black underclass, he understood as well what he called, after the Los Angeles riots, the "fears" of whites who "have been scared for so long that they have fled to the suburbs of America to places like Simi Valley" (home of the jurors who acquitted the policemen who beat Rodney King and home as well to the Ronald Reagan presidential library).

Other than appearances in black churches, where he was at home, like Jimmy Carter, and a spot on Arsenio Hall's television show, where he was cool enough, like Lee Atwater, to play sax in shades, Clinton emphasized race as a nonissue from the primaries forward. He kept black advisers in the background, made no promises, accepted the nomination at a Democratic National Convention that had two hundred fewer black delegates than in 1988, and timed his rare appearances at black events so that they would be too late for the evening news or overshadowed by other events. His book, *Putting People First,* co-authored with vice-presidential nominee Al Gore, was as thin on civil rights as the platform these New Democrats ran on. Race rated less space in a Civil Rights chapter than sexual preference or physical disability and did not make the thirty-one "crucial issues" listed and addressed in alphabetical order from Agriculture to Women. The candidates pledged only to "oppose racial quotas."

Clinton's heralded bus tours to middle America featured white faces on the speaker's platform and in the crowds, and his mention of "welfare reform" (a legitimate issue) mixed race, class, and a touch of social Darwinism with a "two years and out" formulation designed to limit benefits and force "welfare mothers" into low-wage jobs. "Welfare is part of the racial inoculation system," one anonymous Democrat said, and the party's candidate was simply playing to the code—that is, he was trying to protect himself from the party's reputation for providing never-ending handouts.[3]

On March 2, the day before the Georgia, Maryland, and Colorado primaries, Clinton distanced himself from the Democratic party's image of being soft on black criminals. He did so at the Stone Mountain Correctional facility by posing for photographers, alongside Georgia Senator Sam Nunn, with a formation of mostly black convicts providing the backdrop. "Two white men and forty blacks prisoners, what's he saying?," asked California's Jerry Brown, another primary candidate. "He's saying we got 'em under control, folks, don't worry." Jesse Jackson called it a moderately more civilized "version of the Willie Horton situation." Two weeks later, on the day after the Illinois and Michigan primaries, Clinton again showed he was a different type of Democrat by golfing nine holes, accompanied by a television camera crew, at a segregated Little Rock country club. Campaign manager James Carville called this last event a gaff that the team could have avoided had "somebody close to the body [Clinton]" checked out the country club beforehand. "We got cocky and we got sloppy," Carville explained. "A lapse in concentration. You wish it didn't happen, but it's hardly the S&L crisis." Denials aside, there was nothing unintentional about that round of golf.[4]

On the crime issue, Dukakis's weakest point, Clinton's pose with Nunn was extra insurance. The governor had already arranged to mark his position on criminals with what *Nation* columnist Christopher Hitchens called "photo-op executions in Arkansas's jails."[5] The most opportunistic of these occurred during the New Hampshire primary with the campaign reeling from the Gennifer Flowers tabloid allegations. The subject here was Rickey Ray Rector, a forty-five-year-old African American who had killed a police officer eleven years earlier and now sat on death row in Arkansas, waiting, in a windowless cell in Cummins Prison, for the executioner to administer his sentence by lethal injection. Confronted with the decision of whether to allow the execution to take place, Clinton told Jesse Jackson that he was "praying about it" and then left New Hampshire Thursday evening, January 23, for the governor's mansion in Little Rock. Rector's date was Friday.

Given Rickey Ray Rector's crime (cop killer) and condition (brain damaged), the case provided an effective if hideous opportunity for Clinton, as Marshall Frady has shown in chilling detail, to demonstrate that he was not Dukakis. Rector, a high school dropout, had murdered a man at a dance in Conway, a small town in Faulkner County, and after avoiding capture for three days consented to his family's plea that he surrender. It was agreed that Robert W. Martin, a Conway policeman who had known Rector since he was a child, would make the arrest. At the appointed hour Martin entered the home of Rector's mother and spoke to her briefly in the parlor. When Rector suddenly appeared in an adjoining bedroom's doorway, Martin said, simply, "Hi, Rickey, how you doin?," got a "Hi, Mr. Bob" in return, and then turned to continue his conversation with Mrs. Rector. He never saw Rector pull the .38 pistol from underneath his shirt. Two shots hit the jaw and neck.

Rector walked out back in a daze, continuing past a neighbor's yard before stopping beside a berry bush and putting the gun to his temple. The blast and subsequent surgery took three inches from the front of his brain, and bullet and bone fragments damaged the right temporal lobe. Rector's suicide attempt left him, in effect, with a frontal lobotomy and the understanding of a young child. Not unlike the Jack Nicholson character in *One Flew Over the Cookoo's Nest* after his lobotomy, the surgeon said.

This happened in March 1981, some five months after Clinton lost his bid for a second term as governor of Arkansas. Having commuted nearly seventy sentences in his first term, including the life sentences of thirty-eight first-degree murderers, Clinton had been vulnerable to the GOP's soft-on-crime refrain. One murderer, a seventy-three-year-old man, had killed again during a robbery attempt within a year of his release. After winning back the governor's chair in 1982 Clinton began setting execution dates (seventy for twenty-four death-row inmates over the ten-year road to the New Hampshire primary). "Poor ole Rickey Rector's timing just happened to be real bad," a defense attorney said. When prison officials mailed Rector's belongings to his sister, Stella, they included a letter:

Dear Mr. Rector,

After careful review of the information provided, your request for executive clemency has been denied.

Sincerely,

Bill Clinton.

The governor needed to prove something and used Rector to do it. "He had someone put to death who had only part of a brain," political analyst David Garth said. "You can't find them any tougher than that."[6]

While waiting for Rector to die (there was an hour delay while the execution crew searched for a serviceable vein), Clinton and his advisers concentrated on the Gennifer Flowers flap. The next day, Saturday, Clinton flew out of Little Rock for campaign appearances in Washington, D.C., which included a forum sponsored by Jesse Jackson's National Rainbow Coalition. Even here most questions were about Flowers. Clinton and his wife taped a *60 Minutes* interview on Flowers's charges Sunday and then flew back to Little Rock to watch the program in the governor's mansion. In one weekend the candidate used television and the executioner's needle to deal with the "character" issue on two fronts. Charges of infidelity would return, but it would never again be credibly whispered that this New Democrat had compassion for the criminal element rather than that element's victims.

Clinton learned from his own electoral difficulties in 1980 and as well Dukakis's difficulties in 1988, offering the Rickey Ray Rector execution as a preemptive strike against any Horton-ish schemes the Bush campaign may have been plotting. He also studied the difficulties encountered by the other recently failed Democrat, Walter Mondale, and concluded that the biggest mistake of his campaign involved the "handling" of Jesse Jackson. Carville estimated that Mondale's campaign manager "had something like seventy-three meetings with Jackson in 1984. I wasn't sure I was up to it."[7] Convinced that Mondale should have broken cleanly with Jackson (because he was seen as heavy political baggage among white voters), Clinton looked for opportunities to distance himself. When chairing the Democratic Leadership Council in May 1991, for example, he supported the decision to bar Jackson from speaking at the group's Cleveland meeting. Then, when sitting at a microphone during the primaries, he exploded when misinformed that Jackson had endorsed Iowa's Tom Harkin and was campaigning for him in South Carolina. "I thought the mike was dead," he explained.

Since neither the intentional nor unintentional shot completely achieved the desired result, Clinton moved again on June 13 at the Sheraton Washington Hotel when speaking before a summit conference of Jackson's Rainbow Coalition. Sister Souljah (Lisa Williamson), a rapper invited to attend a youth workshop, had spoken at the conference the previous night, and her post–Los Angeles riot comments had caused a minor stir—fitting in nicely with the major stir created by better-known rapper Ice–T and Time-Warner's release of his heavy-metal "Cop Killer." "I mean if black people kill black people every day," Sister Souljah suggested to a *Washington Post* reporter, "why not have a week and kill white people?" With Jackson sitting at his left in a Sheraton auditorium, Clinton blasted the Rainbow's rapper-in-residence. "If you took the words 'white' and 'black' and reversed them, you might think David Duke was giving that speech." Having sat through the remarks staring stonily ahead, Jackson suffered yet another public indignity later that day. To avoid the problems Mondale encountered and otherwise "shut down" any speculation along this line, Clinton told Jackson, and then the press, that he would not be the Democratic party's vice-presidential candidate.

Criticism of a black rapper before a largely black audience was part of Clinton's "counter-scheduling" strategy. To make sure the message got out the campaign counted on Jackson's ego. And Jackson rose slowly to the bait. He told the initial wave of reporters that Clinton had caught him off guard. "I don't know what his intention was. I was totally surprised. . . . I don't know why he used this platform to address those issues. . . I was really stunned and amazed." The second wave of reporters heard calm criticism of the candidate's "very bad judgment" and a lame defense of Sister Souljah (she had been "misunderstood"). Eventually, Jackson got Clinton's message right. "This had strictly to do with insulting our audience," he told the third wave of reporters (and every subsequent wave throughout the summer). "He was actually talking to the TV audience. He was not talking to the people who were there. He was using the people who were there as a platform to spread his message . . . purely to appeal to conservative whites by containing Jackson and isolating Jackson."

Several reporters covering the campaign concluded that the affair invigorated Clinton ("as his prospects brightened a bit, so did [his] gloomy countenance"). All the candidate had to do was sit back and let Jackson do the heavy lifting. An occasional poke kept the prey at full roar. "I bragged on the Rainbow Coalition and its programs," Clinton told reporters in Little Rock. "I criticized divisive language by Sister Souljah. If Jesse Jackson wants to align himself with that now and claim that's the way he felt, then that's his business." "The attempt to align me with her is an attempt to malign me with her," Jackson responded. And round and round it went. By keeping at Clinton's bait Jackson spread the man's message. Even when Jackson took DNC chair Ron Brown's advice and called a truce, Clinton stayed on message. At the National Baptist Convention on September 10 he squirmed away from Jackson's attempt for a photo-op of the two men, hands clasped and raised high in the air. "There wasn't going to be a picture of Bill Clinton and Jesse Jackson arm in arm on the front page of *The New York Times*," the campaign manager noted. Or anywhere else.

Denying that the Sister Souljah assault was calculated, the always spinning James Carville admitted that the campaign wanted to bait a prominent African American. Earlier, for example, he suggested that Clinton endorse Chicago Congressman Gus Savage's opponent since

Savage was "prone to making bigoted and anti-Semitic remarks." Carville also admitted that this "big story" was a winner. What Clinton got out of the Sister Souljah affair were votes, particularly the votes of the so-called Reagan Democrats like the North Philadelphia electrician who said "the day he told off that fucking Jackson is the day he got [mine]."[8]

Bush campaign director (and later Carville's wife) Mary Matalin had a predictably different take. "Trust me, you *never* get that lucky in politics," she wrote in their co-authored book on the race for the White House. "Everyone in politics understood their continuing need to assuage Jackson, still a phenomenal force in their party, while simultaneously backing away from him. . . . We thought it [the Souljah assault] was a stroke of genius. Clinton was running as a so-called New Democrat while the Democratic party had previously been captive to minority extremists, mostly identified with the leadership of Jackson. . . . We wondered from the beginning how they were going to deal with the Jesse Jackson factor, and they did it all in one fell swoop. Not only did they not kowtow to him, they publicly humiliated him. I don't know how that travelled in the electorate, but in political circles the Clintonistas got a lot of points for courage and for staying in the mainstream. It was a particularly creative coup."[9]

Clinton risked little in alienating black voters who could only turn to George Bush (completely unlikely) or Ross Perot (highly unlikely). America's first welfare billionaire (with a fortune made processing Medicare and Medicaid claims for Texas, California, and nine other states), Perot had also met with Jackson and other National Rainbow Coalition leaders in a more straightforward attempt to get black votes. Those audiences squirmed as they listened to such pet Perot recollections as his days as the first Texarkana paperboy brave enough to make deliveries in the black section (on horseback, no less). Such claims passed without incident until July 10, 1992, when Perot addressed the NAACP national convention in Nashville. The audience failed to appreciate his Eisenhower-ish choice of words ("you people") or the story of how his father paid his old black sharecroppers. "Son," the senior Perot told young Ross, "these are people too, and they have to live." Pursuit of African-American and all other votes ended that day with Perot coming across as the patronizing son of Depression-era Texas. Or

worse. "This sound bite," he complained to CNN president Tom Johnson, "has made me sound like David Duke." Five days later he dropped
out of the race.[10]

The best that can be said for Clinton is that he took African Americans and their votes for granted. The worst is that he baited their
best-known leader to further his tooth-and-nail fight with Bush for the
vote of white America—which stood virtually deadlocked two months
before the election (43 percent to 44 percent). He lost some ground
there (because of Perot's suddenly on-again candidacy), but still managed thirty-nine percent of the white vote to Bush's forty and Perot's
twenty. In effect, Rector, Souljah, and other efforts at racial inoculation
allowed this New Democrat to distance himself enough from "lingering liberal fundamentalism" to split the white vote. (He took the North
and Bush the South.) Black votes accounted for 8 percent of total
turnout on election day (down from 10 percent in 1988) and 15 percent of Clinton's vote (compared to 20 percent of Dukakis's vote).
Those largely ignored voters provided the margin of victory in Illinois,
Michigan, Ohio, and New Jersey.

Once in the White House, Clinton pursued a balancing act on matters of race largely patterned after the civil rights approach of his hero,
John Kennedy. The difference was that he did not take a "no legislation" pledge. On the conservative side, Clinton tried to establish a
Perot-tough stance on the deficit and a part–Dan Quayle/part–Jerry
Fallwell line on social programs and "family values." So he promised to
"end welfare as we know it," rejected "race-specific" solutions to the
problem of urban poverty, and continued the Bush policy on Haitian
refugees until a Congressional Black Caucus protest and Randall
Robinson's hunger strike forced a reversal. On crime, Clinton proposed
capital punishment for an ever expanding list of federal violations,
"three strikes and out" (mandatory life sentences for repeat offenders),
funds for 100,000 new police officers across the nation, and the constant message of "personal responsibility."

This last was reserved exclusively for black audiences, including the
president's November 1993 address at Memphis's Mason Temple
Church of God in Christ—site of Martin Luther King's last sermon.
He asked the gathering of black ministers what Dr. King, if he were still
alive, would say about the "great crisis of the spirit that is gripping

America today," and then, like a carnival medium, told them: "I did not live and die to see the American family destroyed. I did not live and die to see thirteen-year-old boys get automatic weapons. . . . I did not live and die to see young people destroy their lives with drugs." To plug his crime bill Clinton also went to a particularly violent public housing project, Chicago's Robert Taylor Homes, and posed for photographers with the automatic weapons cache seized in sweeps of the units.[11]

While establishing his conservative credentials on certain issues, Clinton came across as a Great Society liberal on others (education, job training, health care). He even put funding for midnight basketball and drug treatment centers into the crime bill (prompting the conservative Republican charge that such "crime prevention" money merely disguised increased spending on urban social programs). The president looked most like an old Democrat when making appointments. He promised and largely delivered a race- and gender-balanced cabinet that would "look like America," and of the forty-eight judges appointed in his first year, including Ruth Bader Ginsburg to the Supreme Court, eighteen were female. Fourteen were black. Thirty-eight percent of the president's first-year nominees were white males compared to 98 percent of Reagan's first-year nominees.

Still, as historian Gerald Horne noted, "the administration's rainbow of hues is not . . . matched by a rainbow of views." Commerce Secretary Ron Brown, whose resumé included service as a lobbyist for "Baby Doc" Duvalier, the Haitian dictator, can hardly be called a voice for the black masses. Another black appointee, Energy Secretary Hazel O'Leary, had worked for energy monopolies with little concern for consumers of any color or the environment generally. Horne called this "a superficial multiculturalism," and Clinton's critics in Little Rock said the substitution of patronage for policy echoed his approach as governor. It should also be noted that Clinton tended to bail out on those nominees who promised something more than the superficial. When Johnnetta Cole, president of Atlanta's Spellman College and apparent first choice for secretary of education, found herself the victim of a red-baiting campaign, the president took her off his short list.[12]

President Clinton bailed out most spectacularly on Lani Guinier, his choice for assistant attorney general for civil rights. Guinier had grown up in New York, daughter of a black father and white mother and self-described "child of Queens" who attended Yale Law School with Bill Clinton and Hillary Rodham, worked in the Civil Rights Division during the Carter administration, and served as an assistant counsel with the NAACP Legal Defense Fund. Friendship with the Clintons aside (they attended her 1986 wedding on Martha's Vineyard), she was a relatively obscure University of Pennsylvania law professor when the president put her name up. Her equally obscure published writings made the nomination controversial.

Those articles in law reviews and other scholarly journals focused on the notion of "cumulative voting," "super majorities," and other methods to ensure minority representation. Guinier's results-oriented analysis of voting rights law included dozens of red-flag statements (for example, empowerment for people of color should result in "roughly equal outcomes, not merely an apparently fair process"), making her a perfect specimen for those still plotting revenge for the hard time Robert Bork received. On April 30, 1993, the *Wall Street Journal* dubbed Guinier a "Quota Queen," and the attorney who set up the attack, Clint Bolick, explained that the president "has not had to expend any political capital on the issue of quotas and with her we believe we could inflict a heavy political cost."

Since the nomination was already out Clinton had two obvious choices, withdraw it or fight for it. He did neither in large part because another Justice Department nominee, Webster Hubbell (for associate attorney general), was in trouble and the president's men wanted to get him through first. (At the time Hubbell's principal problem was his membership in the same all-white Little Rock country club that Clinton had visited during the campaign). The president remained silent on Guinier until May 11 at the annual dinner of the Leadership Conference on Civil Rights when he said the Senate "ought to be able to put up with a little controversy in the cause of civil rights and go on and confirm her." That soft endorsement was all she would get. The president simply left the nomination hanging, and in the interim began hearing criticism from Jewish groups worried about Guinier's position on quotas (even though her mother was Jewish) and several Democratic members of the Senate Judiciary Committee.

Being both what the media liked to call an FOB (friend of Bill) and FOH (friend of Hillary), Guinier went to see Hillary Rodham Clinton in the West Wing of the White House. The first lady passed by in a corridor, entourage in tow, and without slowing said, "Hi, Kiddo." When someone managed to stop her and blurt out that Guinier was there to "strategize" on the nomination, she said "I'm 30 minutes late to a lunch" and resumed walking. The reason for the snub was obvious. Both the president and first lady wanted Guinier to resign, and when she refused (insisting on a "hearing") they took it as disloyalty. A presidential nomination was a privilege but this nominee seemed to take it as a right, in the process showing an independent streak that would not serve the administration well.

Now Bill Clinton finally got around to reading Guinier's controversial law journal articles, and when finished telephoned Vernon Jordan from the Oval Office. "This is some shit we're in," he said. "Get yourself over here." (The president wanted to "strategize" on how to dump his nominee and simultaneously minimize the political fallout from the civil rights groups that supported Guinier without qualification.) "He *had* to read her articles after she chose not to get out," a White House aide told Elizabeth Drew. "He had to find a way to assassinate her." Clinton called Guinier in on June 3 and quizzed her for an hour about her scholarship. Guinier left thinking the nomination would still go forward, but the president telephoned her hotel room shortly before nine that evening to say that the nomination had been withdrawn. She thanked him for the call and hung up. Then the president called back. "Did you hang up on me?," the angry voice demanded. She did not hear again from either Clinton until December when two identical, machine-signed White House Christmas cards arrived in the mail.

After that June 3rd meeting and telephone call, Clinton, with a tear rolling down his cheek, told the press that Guinier's writings "clearly lend themselves to interpretations" (meaning "quotas") and contained "anti-democratic" ideas that were "difficult to defend." Upon hearing this Guinier felt "like a four-inch tall Alice in Wonderland," a character "in this odd world of 'real life' . . . [where] misrepresentation had become reality. . . . My 'dis-appoint' meant that the Government had not changed sides—not yet. The polarization around issues of race had created a leadership and policy vacuum into which no one dared step." The president campaigned here against his own nominee, using her fate to prove that he could be counted on to get tough with "special interests"—even when the special interest advocate in question was a personal friend.

That last fact explained the contradiction (a tough guy with a tear), and that was what most troubled Clinton's closest aides. "Injured friend or no," as Drew summarized this view, "a commanding President shouldn't come undone over a fourth-rank Cabinet department position." No one should have expected this president to fight for Guinier as Bush had fought for Clarence Thomas. Clinton displayed little courage on behalf of his nominee, even when contrasted with the fierce cynicism and opportunism masquerading as courage that Bush had displayed in standing by his man.

In the end there would be no appeasing of critics from either left or right. Clinton next sent up John Payton, a District of Columbia attorney, and his major qualification for the post of assistant attorney general for civil rights seemed to be a total lack of legal experience regarding voting rights. When Payton withdrew (after admitting that he had not voted in the last District election), Clinton sent up Deval Patrick, partner in a prestigious Boston firm who had also worked with the NAACP Legal Defense Fund. Without missing a beat the *Wall Street Journal* dubbed Patrick a "stealth Guinier" and the less restrained began pronouncing his first name as "Devil." He has also proved somewhat devilish to Clinton himself, having refused to appear with the president in Atlanta in January 1995 after learning that the president would not mention civil rights when speaking in Martin Luther King's birthplace.[13]

It is a sad commentary on where we stand as a nation 130 years after slavery, thirty years beyond Jim Crow, and twenty-five years since Nixon played his piano at the Gridiron Club that our current chief executive, arguably the least prejudiced of the forty-one men who preceded him, sees fit to include a racial calculus in politics and policy. Bill Clinton calculated that he could not win in 1992 unless he used Sister Souljah to bait Jesse Jackson, put a black chain gang in a crime control ad, golfed at a segregated club with a TV camera crew in tow, and allowed that search for a serviceable vein in Rickey Ray Rector's arm. He calculated as well that he could not win reelection in 1996 unless he continued to send signals that the administration would stand fast against the Lani Guiniers and other advocates of "special interests."

And after the Democratic party's disastrous showing in the 1994 elections (taking only 35 percent of the southern white vote and 34 percent of the white Protestant vote in House races), Clinton adjusted his calculus once more. Now the president located the only hope for a second term in running not as a New Democrat but as a "Newt Democrat," in deference to the new House speaker, Georgia's Newt Gingrich, and his decidedly unsocial "Contract With America."

These are bleak times even for the social contract that our Founders pondered. Since 1970 the middle-class share of per-capita income has dropped nine points to 48.2 percent and that class appears determined to blame its fall on the poor and working poor who lost twenty points during the same period. There are also signs that Mr. Clinton's party may go the way of the Whigs. "The New Deal era is over," lamented Al From, executive director of the Democratic Leadership Council. "It was a great ideology while it lasted—it was the ideology that built the middle class—but the policies that built the middle class can no longer earn their support." This was particularly true on the other side of the Mason-Dixon line. Republicans won nineteen House seats from the South in 1994, for the first time since 1872 giving the GOP a majority among southern congressmen.[14] Those partial to Whig imagery err only in their assessment of their party's long-term prospects. Republican calls for capital gains tax cuts, prison construction, welfare reform, and other war-on-the-blacks initiatives will not hold the middle-class for long because these coded clauses in the Contract With America address anxieties and not the source of middle-class pain.

Affirmative action remains the principal symbol for those anxieties, and for the 1996 elections all signs point to the final battle of the quota wars. A few Justice Department officials and White House aides have urged Clinton to cut back if not eliminate the government's commitment to affirmative action, and the president did in fact order a review of all federal affirmative action policies and guidelines. "Are they all working?," the president explained in a speech at the California Democratic party convention in Sacramento. "Are they all fair? Has there been any kind of reverse discrimination?"[15] Clinton also had his chief of staff, Leon Panetta (of all people), make the rounds on Capitol Hill to see what fellow Democrats would do if the administration signaled its support for California's so-called Civil Rights Initiative. (Nixon fired

Panetta, remember, for being too aggressive on busing). Having colored the 1994 elections with Proposition 187, a ballot initiative that denied basic social services to illegal immigrants and otherwise carpet bombed those Americans and especially their children, California's latest offering would forbid the use of ethnicity or gender "as a criterion for either discrimination against, or granting preferential treatment to, any individual or group." The only question is whether this initiative will go on the primary ballot (March) or the general-election ballot (November).

With an eye on the White House, the national Republican party has been pouring money into California with the stipulation that the anti–affirmative action initiative's sponsors work toward a general election ballot appearance and thus ensure that Clinton's reelection will be held hostage to this issue. "Obviously," complained Will Marshall, another Democratic Leadership Council executive, "a lot of Republicans look at affirmative action as the ultimate wedge issue." These men include such Nixon-era holdovers as Patrick Buchanan, who sees a "Holy War" as the GOP's (and his own) best chance to capture the presidency, and William Bennett, still a key GOP strategist who somehow manages with a straight face to counsel Buchanan and everyone else seeking the nomination not to let the cause degenerate "into mean-spirited racial crap."[16] One thing is certain: The nation's forty-second chief executive will have a tougher time putting the California initiative to sleep than the nation's first chief executive had in putting that Quaker memorial to sleep.

Meanwhile, the Supreme Court has continued to erode federal affirmative action programs and policies—most notably in its June 1995 decision in *Adarand Constructors v. Pena*. A month later, following completion of the five-month White House review, Clinton promised to comply with that ruling. He rejected the advice of those race-first aides, however, and reaffirmed his commitment to affirmative action sans quotas, reverse discrimination, and preferences for the unqualified. Clinton also promised to terminate any affirmative action program that had attained its goal. Without missing a beat, Senator Robert Dole and other candidates for the Republican nomination responded, in effect, by calling the president a quota king and lackey of Jesse Jackson.

The politics of race is less dishonorable today than it was two hundred years ago when Washington commiserated with Lafayette on the evils of slavery and then conspired alone to do nothing to stop it. In our time we merely have candidate Bill Clinton commiserating with the ghosts of Richard Nixon's law-and-order crew and then doing nothing to stop the execution of a brain-damaged black man, and then President Bill Clinton trying to figure out how he might in the odd case get to Speaker Gingrich's right on matters of race. If the southern strategists of the 1980s made Willie Horton as fitting an image for the Republicans as the elephant, Clinton campaigned and to some extent governed as if he were conspiring to replace the Democratic donkey with the image of Rickey Ray Rector.

That the forty-second president could also quote from memory the lines of Dr. King's "I Have a Dream" speech is a smaller though no more comforting irony than that of our Founders who knew slavery was wrong and yet lived with it and wrote that contradiction into our nation's basic documents. Too many presidents of the far past devoted too much energy to protecting slavery and then Jim Crow, and too many presidents of the more recent past have devoted too much energy to ensuring that the nation's politics remains organized along racial fault lines. Since 1968 presidential elections have been influenced and sometimes dominated by such things as Nixon's southern strategy, Ford's opportunism on busing, Carter's words on behalf of ethnic purity, Reagan's color-blind war on the civil rights movement's achievements, Bush's black rapist, and Clinton's Rectors and Souljahs.

Lincoln and Johnson helped change the Constitution for the better on slavery and Jim Crow, but the politics that came out of the Constitution and its articles on slavery are still stuck in a racial rut. With few exceptions, the deeds and dreams of our presidents, and the choices they made and did not make on matters of race, deepened that rut. When Richard Nixon played his piano at the Gridiron Club in 1970 the performance symbolized more than the incredible and arguably racist insensitivity of a single chief executive. Nixon's piano, as much as anything else, symbolized the presidency and the politics of race backwards and forwards in history—from the day Washington brooded about the Quaker memorial to the day Clinton's Republican opponents set out to make affirmative action the centerpiece of the next campaign.

NOTES

Bones and Tambo

1. Prayer breakfasts, a regular routine in the Nixon White House, had a political and not a spiritual utility. Personally, according to his chief of staff, the president considered the events "total torture at best." H. R. Haldeman, *The Haldeman Diaries: Inside the Nixon White House* (New York: G. P. Putnam's Sons, 1994), 241.

2. Hedrick Smith, *The Power Game: How Washington Works* (New York: Random House, 1988), 392.

3. Harold Brayman, *The President Speaks Off-the-Record: From Grover Cleveland to Gerald Ford* (Princeton, N.J.: Dow Jones Books, 1976), 318–19, 399. In 1975 the Gridiron took its first woman, Helen Thomas, chief White House correspondent for United Press International.

4. Arthur Wallace Dunn, *Gridiron Nights* (New York: Frederick A. Stokes Co., 1915), 80–81, 149. In 1972 the Gridiron elected its first African-American member, Carl T. Rowan of the Publishers-Hall Syndicate.

5. Brayman, *The President Speaks*, 51.

6. Ibid., 766–67, 772, 774–75.

7. Roger Wilkins, *A Man's Life* (New York: Simon and Schuster, 1982), 275–82. For the Nixon/Agnew piano duet, see also Brayman, *The President Speaks*, 11–13, 278–79; Haldeman, *Diaries*, 138. With Meg Greenfield, deputy editor of the *Washington Post's* editorial page,

promising to give him whatever space he needed, Wilkins wrote it all up ("A Black at the Gridiron Club"). Before publishing on March 26, 1970, he checked with Tom Wicker, who got him into the dinner in the first place, to see if he would mind. "Hell no," Wicker responded. "Help yourself. We sure deserve whatever you dish out." This being America, what Wilkins dished out in that emotional piece lead to a call from Ben Bradlee, an interview with *Post* publisher Katherine Graham at her Georgetown mansion, and a job with the newspaper. Gridiron loyalists, in contrast, offered a blackball. "The only way you'll ever come back," a club member told Wilkins, "is feet first."

8. Thomas Byrne Edsall and Mary D. Edsall, *Chain Reaction: The Impact of Race, Rights, and Taxes on American Politics* (New York: Norton, 1991).

9. Quoted in Robert W. Johannsen, *Lincoln, the South, and Slavery: The Political Dimension* (Baton Rouge: Louisiana State University Press, 1991), 97; Michael Kammen, *A Machine That Would Go of Itself: The Constitution in American Culture* (New York: St. Martin's Press, 1994), 101. See also Donald L. Robinson, *Slavery in the Structure of American Politics, 1765–1820* (New York: Harcourt Brace Jovanovich, 1971); Paul Finkelman, *An Imperfect Union: Slavery, Federalism, and Comity* (Chapel Hill: University of North Carolina Press, 1981); Gary B. Nash, *Race and Revolution* (Madison, Wis.: Madison House, 1990); John P. Kaminski, ed., *A Necessary Evil? Slavery and the Debate Over the Constitution* (Madison, Wis.: Madison House, 1995). For the persistence of racial assumptions in the constitutional/legal order, see Mary Frances Berry, *Black Resistance, White Law: A History of Constitutional Racism in America* (rev. ed.; New York: Allen Lane/Penguin, 1994); Paul Finkelman, ed., *Race, Law, and American History, 1700–1900: The African-American Experience*, 11 vols. (New York: Garland, 1992), and *Slavery and the Law* (Madison, Wis.: Madison House, 1995); Mark Tushnet, *The American Law of Slavery, 1810–1860* (Princeton, N.J.: Princeton University Press, 1981); Derrick A. Bell, Jr., *Race, Racism, and American Law* (Boston: Little, Brown, 1973).

10. Edmund S. Morgan, *American Slavery, American Freedom: The Ordeal of Colonial Virginia* (New York: Norton, 1975), 328, 330–31; C. Vann Woodward, *The Strange Career of Jim Crow*, 2d rev. ed. (New York: Oxford University Press, 1966). Carl Degler, *Neither Black Nor White: Slavery and Race Relations in Brazil and the United States* (New York: Macmillan, 1971), also demonstrates that there was nothing inevitable or natural about racism among poor and lower-class whites.

Chapter 1. Owners

1. Washington to Lafayette, April 5, 1783, in John C. Fitzpatrick, ed., *The Writings of George Washington*, 39 vols. (Washington, D.C.: Government Printing Office, 1931–1944), 26: 300; Lafayette to Washington, Feb. 5, 1783, ibid.; James Thomas Flexner, *George Washington*, 4 vols. (Boston: Little, Brown, 1967–1972), 4: *Anguish and Farewell, 1793–1799*, 119.

2. Washington to Lafayette, May 19, 1786, in Walter H. Mazyck, *George Washington and the Negro* (Washington, D.C.: Associated Publishers, 1932), 94; Washington to John Fr. Mercer, Sept. 9, 1786, ibid., 101.

3. Robert V. Remini, *Henry Clay: Statesman for the Union* (New York: Norton, 1991), 27. See also Herbert Aptheker, *Anti-Racism in U.S. History: The First Two Hundred Years* (Westport, Conn.: Greenwood, 1992).

4. Flexner, *Anguish and Farewell*, 447. For "abject slaves," see Paul K. Longmore, *The Invention of George Washington* (Berkeley: University of California Press, 1988), p. 135.

5. Matthew T. Mellon, *Early American Views on Negro Slavery* (reprint ed.; New York: Bergman Publishers, 1969), 73, 75; Douglas Southall Freeman, *George Washington: A Biography*, 7 vols. (New York: Charles Scribner's Sons, 1948–1957), 6: *Patriot and President*, 308.

6. Winthrop D. Jordan, *White Over Black: American Attitudes Toward the Negro, 1550–1812* (New York: Norton, 1977), 319.

7. Washington to David Stuart, March 27, 1790, quoted in Mazyck, *George Washington*, p. 117; Stanley M. Elkins and Eric McKitrick, *The Age of Federalism* (New York: Oxford University Press, 1993), 151–52. See also Jordan, *White Over Black*, 325; Flexner, *Anguish and Farewell*, 122; Mellon, *Early American Views*, 70–72.

8. Washington to Tobias Lear, May 6, 1794, in Fitzpatrick, ed., *George Washington Papers*, 33: 358; Flexner, *Anguish and Farewell*, 125. For Washington's interest in indentured servants, see Worthington Chauncey Ford, ed., *Washington as an Employer and Importer of Labor* (reprint ed.; New York: Burt Franklin, 1971), 47–73.

9. Eugene D. Genovese, *Roll, Jordan, Roll: The World the Slaves Made* (New York: Vintage Books ed., 1976), 308.

10. Mellon, *Early American Views*, 73.

11. Flexner, *Anguish and Farewell*, 432, 437.

12. Jordan, *White Over Black*, 353; Genovese, *Roll, Jordan, Roll*, 10.

13. Flexner, *Anguish and Farewell*, 444; Mazyck, *George Washington*, 19–20, 43–47; John Hope Franklin, *From Slavery to Freedom* (New York: Vintage ed., 1969), 132–33, 135.

14. Frederick M. Binder, *The Color Problem in Early National America* (The Hague: Mouton and Co., 1968), 16–17; John R. Howe, Jr., "John Adams's Views of Slavery," *Journal of Negro History* 49(July 1964): 201.

15. Adams to James Warren, July 7, 1777, in Robert J. Taylor, ed., *Papers of John Adams*, Series III (Cambridge, Mass.: Harvard University Press, 1977–), 5: 242; John E. Ferling, *John Adams: A Life* (Knoxville: University of Tennessee Press, 1992), 173.

16. Taylor, ed., *Papers of John Adams*, 3: 390n; Ferling, *John Adams*, 172.

17. Page Smith, *John Adams*, 2 vols. (Garden City, N.Y.: Doubleday, 1962), 2: 759; Binder, *Color Problem*, 18–19; Adams to George Churchman and Jacob Lindley, Jan. 24, 1801, in Charles Francis Adams, ed., *The Works of John Adams*, 10 vols. (Boston: Little, Brown, 1856), 9: 92–93.

18. John Chester Miller, *The Wolf by the Ears: Thomas Jefferson and Slavery* (New York: Free Press, 1977), 130.

19. William Seale, *The President's House*, 2 vols. (Washington, D.C.: White House Historical Association, 1986), 1: 101; Kathryn Allamong Jacob, *Capital Elites: High Society in Washington, D.C., after the Civil War* (Washington, D.C.: Smithsonian Institution Press, 1995), 38.

20. Franklin, *From Slavery to Freedom*, 129–30; William D. Richardson, "Thomas Jefferson and Race: The Declaration and *Notes on the State of Virginia*," *Polity* 16(Spring 1984): 447–66; Sidney Kaplan, "The 'Domestic Insurrections' of the Declaration of Independence," *Journal of Negro History* 61(July 1976): 243–53.

21. Quoted in Mazyck, *George Washington*, 58. Slavery was more widespread in the North than Jefferson suggested. By 1790 one-fifth of New York City's white families owned slaves. Merchants owned slaves. So did artisans. Shane White, *"Somewhat More Independent": The End of Slavery in New York City, 1770–1810* (Athens: University of Georgia Press, 1991).

22. Quoted in Miller, *Wolf by the Ears*, 263.

23. Russell B. Nye, *Fettered Freedom: Civil Liberties and the Slavery Controversy, 1830–1860* (Urbana: University of Illinois Press ed., 1972), 226–27.

24. Jordan, *White Over Black*, 321–22; Charles A. Miller, *Jefferson and Nature* (Baltimore: Johns Hopkins University Press, 1988), 67–68.

25. Jefferson to Monroe, June 17, 1785, in Julian Boyd, ed., *The Papers of Thomas Jefferson* (Princeton, N.J.: Princeton University Press, 1950–), 8: 229. In 1769, as a freshman legislator in the Virginia House of Burgesses, Jefferson claimed to have supported a bill allowing private manumission. A year later he represented Samuel Howell, a mulatto suing for his freedom. Howell was bound out and not a slave. Paul Fin-

kelman, "Jefferson and Slavery: 'Treason Against the Hopes of the World,'" in *Jeffersonian Legacies*, ed. Peter S. Onuf (Charlottesville: University Press of Virginia, 1993), 188–89.

26. Thomas Jefferson, *Notes on the State of Virginia* (reprint ed.; New York: Harper and Row, 1964), 132–34. See also David Grimsted, "Anglo-American Racism and Phillis Wheatley's 'Sable Veil,' 'Length'ned Chain,' and 'Knitted Heart,'" in *Women in the Age of the American Revolution*, ed. Ronald Hoffman and Peter J. Albert (Charlottesville: University Press of Virginia, 1989), 418.

27. Jordan, *White Over Black*, 481.

28. Ibid., 502–04.

29. Quoted in Grimsted, "Anglo-American Racism," 428–29.

30. Jefferson to Brissot de Warville, Feb. 11, 1788, in Boyd, ed., *Papers of Thomas Jefferson*, 12: 578.

31. Miller, *Wolf by the Ears*, 143, 145, 234–42.

32. Ibid., 132–41; Jordan, *White Over Black*, 378–96; Michael Zuckerman, *Almost Chosen People: Oblique Biographies in the American Grain* (Berkeley: University of California Press, 1993), 175–218.

33. Jefferson to Edward Bancroft, Jan. 26, 1788, in Boyd, ed., *Papers of Thomas Jefferson*, 14: 492–94; Jefferson to Thomas Mann Randolph, Feb. 4, 1790, ibid., 16: 154; Grimsted, "Anglo-American Racism," 415–16; Jordan, *White Over Black*, 431–32; Miller, *Wolf by the Ears*, 108.

34. Barbara McEwan, *Thomas Jefferson: Farmer* (Jefferson, N.C.: McFarland, 1991), 146–47; Lucia C. Stanton, "'Those Who Labor For My Happiness': Thomas Jefferson and His Slaves," in Onuf, ed., *Jeffersonian Legacies*, 148–49.

35. Joseph J. Ellis, *Passionate Sage: The Character and Legacy of John Adams* (New York: Norton, 1993), 115–16; Jordan, *White Over Black*, 465; Dumas Malone, *Jefferson and His Time*, 6 vols. (Boston: Little, Brown, 1948–1981), 6: *The Sage of Monticello*, 513–14.

36. Malone, *Jefferson and His Time*, 5: *Jefferson the President, Second Term*, 543.

37. Miller, *Wolf by the Ears*, 131, 145.

38. Malone, *Jefferson the President, Second Term*, 542.

39. Nash, *Race and Revolution*, 16–17; Miller, *Wolf by the Ears*, 1.

40. Willard S. Randall, *Thomas Jefferson: A Life* (New York: Henry Holt, 1993), 593.

41. "James Madison's Attitude Toward the Negro," *Journal of Negro History* 6(Jan. 1921): 82; Drew R. McCoy, *The Last of the Fathers: James Madison and the Republican Legacy* (New York: Cambridge University Press, 1989), 257.

42. Robert A. Rutland, *James Madison: The Founding Father* (New York: Macmillan, 1987), 239; Jordan, *White Over Black*, 303–04, 323.

43. Binder, *Color Problem*, 126–27; Genovese, *Roll, Jordan, Roll*, 155; Franklin, *From Slavery to Freedom*, 170.

44. Mellon, *Early American Views*, 131–32; Miller, *Wolf by the Ears*, 146.

45. Mellon, *Early American Views*, 133–37.

46. Merrill D. Peterson, ed., *The Founding Fathers: James Madison—A Biography in His Own Words* (New York: Newsweek/Harper and Row, 1974), 378; Paul Jennings, *A Colored Man's Reminiscences of James Madison* (Brooklyn, N.Y.: G. C. Beadle, 1865), iii–iv, 14–15.

47. John F. Marszalek, "Battle for Freedom: Gabriel's Insurrection," *Negro History Bulletin* 39(No. 3, 1976): 540; W. P. Cresson, *James Monroe* (Chapel Hill: University of North Carolina Press, 1946), 340; Jordan, *White Over Black*, 394.

48. Harry Ammon, *James Monroe: The Quest for National Identity* (New York: McGraw-Hill, 1971), 451, 458.

49. Binder, *Color Problem*, 69; Miller, *Wolf by the Ears*, 221–33, 241.

50. Jordan, *White Over Black*, 546–47.

51. Adams to Jefferson, Feb. 3, 1821, in Lester J. Cappon, ed., *The Adams-Jefferson Letters*, 2 vols. (Chapel Hill: University of North Carolina Press, 1959), 2: 571–72; Ellis, *Passionate Sage*, 138.

52. Howe, "John Adams's Views," 202–05.

53. Binder, *Color Problem*, 29.

54. Alexander Saxton, *The Rise and Fall of the White Republic* (New York: Verso, 1990), 35–36, 38. See also William E. Weeks, *John Quincy Adams and American Global Empire* (Lexington: University Press of Kentucky, 1992).

55. Robert V. Remini, *The Legacy of Andrew Jackson* (Baton Rouge: Louisiana State University Press, 1988), 89; Leonard L. Richards, "The Jacksonians and Slavery," in *Antislavery Reconsidered: New Perspectives on the Abolitionists*, ed. Lewis Perry and Michael Fellman (Baton Rouge: Louisiana State University Press, 1979), 99–118.

56. Jackson to Andrew J. Donelson, April 1820, in John Spencer Bassett, ed., *Correspondence of Andrew Jackson*, 7 vols. (Washington, D.C.: Carnegie Institution of Washington, 1926–1935), 3: 21; Robert V. Remini, *Andrew Jackson and the Course of American Empire, 1767–1821* (New York: Harper and Row, 1977), 391.

57. Jackson to John Quincy Adams, May 1 and 21, 1821, and Jackson to John C. Calhoun, May 22, 1821, in Bassett, ed., *Correspondence of Andrew Jackson*, 3: 57–58.

58. Jackson to William B. Lewis, May 4, 1833, ibid., 5: 74; Genovese, *Roll, Jordan, Roll*, 88.

59. Jackson to John Coffee, April 9, 1833, in Bassett, ed., *Correspondence of Andrew Jackson*, 5: 56.

60. Jackson to Amos Kendall, Aug. 9, 1835, ibid., 5: 360; Nye, *Fettered Freedom*, 74; Arthur M. Schlesinger, Jr., *The Age of Jackson* (Boston: Little, Brown, 1945), 425.

61. Nye, *Fettered Freedom*, 48.

62. Ibid., 13, 45–46, 48, 51; Saxton, *Rise and Fall of the White Republic*, 88.

63. Binder, *Color Problem*, 126.

64. Donald B. Cole, *Martin Van Buren and the American Political System* (Princeton, N.J.: Princeton University Press, 1984), 272; Remini, *Legacy of Andrew Jackson*, 105.

65. *Colored American*, March 11, 1837; Major L. Wilson, *The Presidency of Martin Van Buren* (Lawrence: University Press of Kansas, 1984), 19, 41. Van Buren intended to "refashion the party system as a major tool for resolving the looming crisis over slavery," offering a "theory of party as a way of calming the recurring slavery controversy." J. David Greenstone, *The Lincoln Persuasion: Remaking American Liberalism* (Princeton, N.J.: Princeton University Press, 1993), 172.

66. Wilson, *Van Buren*, 16, 201.

67. Daniel Webster to Edward Everett, Jan. 29, 1842, in Kenneth E. Shewmaker, ed., *The Papers of Daniel Webster—Diplomatic Papers* (Hanover: University Press of New Hampshire, 1983), 179–80. Twenty years later Arthur Tappan, treasurer of the American Missionary Society, opened a Sunday school for free blacks in the former president's home.

68. Carl Sferrazza Anthony, *First Ladies* (New York: Morrow, 1990), 134; Polk to Silas Wright, Jr., Feb. 9, 1844, in Wayne Cutler and James P. Cooper, Jr., eds., *Correspondence of James K. Polk* (Nashville: Vanderbilt University Press, 1969–), 7: 59–62.

69. Schlesinger, *Age of Jackson*, 452.

70. Ibid.

71. Elbert B. Smith, *The Presidencies of Zachary Taylor and Millard Fillmore* (Lawrence: University Press of Kansas, 1988), 40; Seale, *President's House*, 1: 282.

72. A few conspiracists thought the slave power poisoned Taylor, the owner who stood, in a manner, against the further spread of slavery into the territories; and their heirs dug up his body 141 years later on the bizarre hunch of a Classic scholar. Poison may have been a political tool in ancient Greece and Rome, but not in Taylor's America. Pathologists found no trace in the president's hair or bones. *Newsweek*, July 1, 1991, pp. 64–66.

73. See David M. Potter, *The Impending Crisis, 1848–1861* (New York: Harper and Row, 1976); Holman Hamilton, *Prologue to Conflict: The*

Crisis and Compromise of 1850 (Lexington: University of Kentucky Press, 1964).

74. Robert J. Rayback, *Biography of a President: Millard Fillmore* (Buffalo: Henry Stewart, Inc., 1959), 252, 368–69.

75. Roy F. Nichols, *Franklin Pierce* (Philadelphia: University of Pennsylvania Press, 1958), 102, 210, 211. See also Robert E. May, *The Southern Dream of a Caribbean Empire, 1854–1861* (Baton Rouge: Louisiana State University Press, 1973).

76. David Donald, *Charles Sumner and the Coming of the Civil War* (New York: Knopf, 1960), 282–311.

77. Larry Gara, *The Presidency of Franklin Pierce* (Lawrence: University Press of Kansas, 1991), 117. See also James A. Rawley, *Race & Politics: "Bleeding Kansas" and the Coming of the Civil War* (Philadelphia: J. B. Lippincott Company, 1969).

78. For Republican party ideology, see Eric Foner, *Free Soil, Free Labor, Free Men* (New York: Oxford University Press, 1970).

79. Henry Adams, *The Education of Henry Adams* (reprint ed.; New York: Modern Library, 1931), 48.

80. *Dred Scott v. Sanford*, 19 Howard 393 (1857); Kenneth M. Stampp, *America in 1857: A Nation on the Brink* (New York: Oxford University Press, 1990), 92. See also Donald E. Fehrenbacher, *Slavery Law and Politics: The Dred Scott Case in Historical Perspective* (New York: Oxford University Press, 1981); Walter Ehrlich, *They Have No Rights: Dred Scott's Struggle for Freedom* (Westport, Conn.: Greenwood, 1979).

81. James Buchanan, *Mr. Buchanan's Administration on the Eve of the Rebellion* (New York: D. Appleton and Company, 1886), 9–20, 57–66; U. S. Grant, *Personal Memoirs of U. S. Grant* (reprint ed.; New York: World, 1952), 108.

82. Genovese, *Roll, Jordan, Roll,* 273; David Donald, *Lincoln Reconsidered* (New York: Knopf, 1956), 147.

83. Lawanda Cox, "Lincoln and Black Freedom," in *The Historian's Lincoln,* ed. Gabor S. Boritt (Urbana: University of Illinois Press, 1988), 187–88. See also Cox's *Lincoln and Black Freedom* (Columbia: University of South Carolina Press, 1981); Garry Wills, *Lincoln at Gettysburg: The Words That Remade America* (New York: Simon and Schuster, 1992).

84. Roy P. Basler, ed., *The Collected Works of Abraham Lincoln,* 8 vols. (New Brunswick, N.J.: Rutgers University Press, 1953–1955), 2: 256, 3: 145–46; David Zarefsky, *The Complete Lincoln-Douglas Debates of 1858,* ed. Paul M. Angle (Chicago: University of Chicago Press, 1991), 140–41. See also David Zarefsky, *Lincoln, Douglas, and Slavery* (Chicago: University of Chicago Press, 1990).

85. Donald, *Lincoln Reconsidered*, 19, 20, 131–33; Nye, *Fettered Freedom*, 18.

86. Foner, *Free Soil*, 72.

87. Ibid., 12, 30; Jonathan A. Glickstein, *Concepts of Free Labor in Antebellum America* (New Haven, Conn.: Yale University Press, 1991), 209.

88. Foner, *Free Soil*, 16, 30.

89. See Eugene H. Berwanger, *The Frontier Against Slavery: Western Anti Negro Prejudice and the Slavery Extension Controversy* (Urbana: University of Illinois Press, 1967); V. Jacque Voegeli, *Free But Not Equal: The Midwest and the Negro during the Civil War* (Chicago: University of Chicago Press, 1967).

90. Voegeli, *Free But Not Equal*, 45.

91. Basler, ed., *Collected Works of Abraham Lincoln*, 5: 535; Forrest G. Wood, *Black Scare: The Racist Response to Emancipation and Reconstruction* (Berkeley: University of California Press, 1970), 20; Foner, *Free Soil*, 273.

92. Genovese, *Roll, Jordan, Roll*, 438; Boritt, ed., *Historian's Lincoln*, 197–98. In March 1860 Lincoln had compared slavery to a rattlesnake on the prairie. Unlike Tubman, however, he saw no simple solution. "I take a stake and kill him. Everybody would applaud the act and say I did right. But suppose the snake was in a bed where children were sleeping. . . . By meddling with him here, I would do more hurt than good. Slavery is like that. We dare not strike at it where it is." Basler, ed., *Collected Works of Abraham Lincoln*, 4: 5.

93. Basler, ed., *Collected Works of Abraham Lincoln*, 5: 370–75; James M. McPherson, *Battle Cry of Freedom: The Civil War Era* (New York: Oxford University Press, 1988), 506–09; David W. Blight, *Frederick Douglass' Civil War* (Baton Rouge: Louisiana State University Press, 1989), 139, 122–47; William S. McFeely, *Frederick Douglass* (New York: Norton, 1991), 229–30, 232–35.

94. McFeely, *Frederick Douglass*, 229–30.

95. McPherson, *Battle Cry of Freedom*, 565.

96. Ibid., 789–90; Wood, *Black Scare*, 60; Basler, ed., *Collected Works of Abraham Lincoln*, 7: 508; Iver Bernstein, *The New York City Draft Riots* (New York: Oxford University Press, 1990), passim.

97. Mark E. Neely, *The Last Best Hope of Earth: Abraham Lincoln and the Promise of America* (Cambridge, Mass.: Harvard University Press, 1993), 182.

98. In 1964, to cite one example, White Citizens Councils placed ads in the *Washington Post* and elsewhere, under the heading "Lincoln's Hopes for the Negro—In His Own Words," praising the archsegregationist and

colonizer of the Douglas debates. Merrill D. Peterson, *Lincoln in American Memory* (New York: Oxford University Press, 1994), 358.

99. Leon F. Litwack, *Been In the Storm Too Long: The Aftermath of Slavery* (New York: Knopf, 1979), 527, 529, 531.

100. By far the best biography of Johnson is Hans L. Trefouse, *Andrew Johnson* (New York: Norton, 1989).

101. Hans L. Trefouse, *Impeachment of a President: Andrew Johnson, the Blacks, and Reconstruction* (Knoxville: University of Tennessee Press, 1975), 5, 15; W. E. B. Du Bois, *Black Reconstruction* (New York: Russell and Russell, 1935), 296–300; David W. Bowen, *Andrew Johnson and the Negro* (Knoxville: University of Tennessee Press, 1989), 1–6.

102. LeRoy P. Graf and Ralph W. Haskins, eds., *The Papers of Andrew Johnson* (Knoxville: University of Tennessee Press, 1967–), 3: 326.

103. Wood, *Black Scare*, 93; Du Bois, *Black Reconstruction*, 258; Bowen, *Andrew Johnson and the Negro*, 151.

104. McFeely, *Grant*, 279, 281, 283, 289.

105. Ibid., 72–73, 238–39.

106. Ibid., 277, 375–79; John Y. Simon, ed., *The Personal Memoirs of Julia Dent Grant* (New York: G. P. Putnam's Sons, 1975), 34; Grant, *Memoirs*, 109.

107. Du Bois, *Black Reconstruction*, 708. For the era generally, see Eric Foner, *Reconstruction: America's Unfinished Revolution, 1863–1877* (New York: Harper and Row, 1988).

108. DuBois, *Black Reconstruction*, 30.

109. C. Vann Woodward, *Reunion and Reaction: The Compromise of 1877 and the End of Reconstruction* (rev. ed.; Boston: Little, Brown, 1966), 24; Stanley P. Hirshon, *Farewell to the Bloody Shirt: Northern Republicans and the Southern Negro, 1877–93* (Bloomington: Indiana University Press, 1962), 25.

110. Woodward, *Reunion and Reaction*, 24; George Sinkler, *The Racial Attitudes of American Presidents: From Abraham Lincoln to Theodore Roosevelt* (Garden City, N.Y.: Doubleday, 1971), 163.

111. Franklin, *From Slavery to Freedom*, 384; Rayford W. Logan, *The Betrayal of the Negro: From Rutherford B. Hayes to Woodrow Wilson* (rev. ed.; New York: Collier, 1965), 23–47; Hirshon, *Farewell to the Bloody Shirt*, 59.

112. McFeely, *Frederick Douglass*, 289; Woodward, *Reunion*, 214–15.

113. Foner, *Reconstruction*, 583–85.

114. Justus D. Doenecke, *The Presidencies of James Garfield and Chester Arthur* (Lawrence: University Press of Kansas, 1981), 47; Sinkler, *Racial Attitudes*, 202, 205; Logan, *Betrayal*, 49.

115. Logan, *Betrayal*, 54; Margaret Leech and Harry J. Brown, *The Garfield Orbit* (New York: Harper and Row, 1978), 164.

116. Hirshon, *Farewell,* 118; Doenecke, *Presidencies of Garfield and Arthur,* 48. Garfield had reverted to the doubts that plagued him as a young lawyer, doubts that he frequently expressed in conversations with Jeremiah Black, attorney general (1857–1860) and secretary of state (1860–1861) in Buchanan's cabinet. "Perhaps Judge Black's view of the want of 'set' in the Negro character may have something in it," he reasoned, "and that they will be found untempered mortar in the national temple." Harry J. Brown and Frederick D. Williams, eds., *The Diary of James A. Garfield,* 4 vols. (East Lansing: Michigan State University Press, 1967–1981), 2: 169, 184–85.

117. August F. Meier, *Negro Thought in America, 1880–1915* (Ann Arbor: University of Michigan Press, 1963), 22, 27; Hirshon, *Farewell,* 99, 107; Logan, *Betrayal,* 55–57.

118. *The Civil Rights Cases,* 109 U.S. 1 (1883); McFeely, *Frederick Douglass,* 314.

119. Thomas C. Reeves, *Gentleman Boss: The Life of Chester Alan Arthur* (New York: Knopf, 1975), 14–16, 312.

120. Richard E. Welch, Jr., *The Presidency of Grover Cleveland* (Lawrence: University Press of Kansas, 1988), 67; Logan, *Betrayal,* 61.

121. *Plessy v. Ferguson,* 163 U.S. 537 (1898); *Brown v. Board of Education of Topeka,* 349 U.S. 294 (1955); Welch, *Presidency of Cleveland,* 65, 67–68; C. Vann Woodward, *The Origins of the New South, 1877–1913* (Baton Rouge: Louisiana State University Press, 1951), 218.

122. Booker T. Washington, *Up From Slavery* (reprint ed.; New York: Bantam, 1963), 160–61.

123. For a useful survey of the struggle to bring black rights under the Constitution's protections, see Donald G. Nieman, *Promises to Keep: African-Americans and the Constitutional Order, 1776 to the Present* (New York: Oxford University Press, 1991).

124. Meier, *Negro Thought,* 22; Logan, *Betrayal,* 62–87; Franklin, *From Slavery to Freedom,* 339.

125. Logan, *Betrayal,* 85–86; Woodward, *Origins of the New South,* 220; Hirshon, *Farewell,* 182; Harry J. Sievers, *Benjamin Harrison: From the Civil War to the White House, 1865–1888* (New York: University Publishers, 1959), 361.

126. Lewis J. Gould, *The Presidency of William McKinley* (Lawrence: University Press of Kansas, 1980), 154; Joel Williamson, *The Crucible of Race* (New York: Oxford University Press, 1984), 342, 344–45.

127. Gould, *Presidency of William McKinley,* 28.

128. Ibid., 158; Franklin, *From Slavery to Freedom,* 416.

129. Gould, *Presidency of McKinley,* 156, 158.

Chapter 2. Progressives

1. Samuel P. Hays, *The Response to Industrialism* (Chicago: University of Chicago Press, 1957); Robert H. Wiebe, *The Search for Order: 1877–1920* (New York: Hill and Wang, 1966); Richard Hofstadter, *The Age of Reform* (New York: Knopf, 1955).

2. For surveys of the Progressive Era, see William L. O'Neill, *The Progressive Years* (New York: Harper and Row, 1975); Arthur S. Link and Richard L. McCormick, *Progressivism* (Arlington Heights, Ill.: Harlan Davidson, 1983). See also John M. Blum, *The Progressive Presidents* (New York: Norton, 1980); John Milton Cooper, Jr., *The Warrior and the Priest* (Cambridge, Mass.: Harvard University Press, 1983). For a critical interpretation, see Gabriel Kolko, *The Triumph of Conservatism* (New York: Free Press, 1963).

3. Richard Hofstadter, *Social Darwinism in American Thought* (Boston: Beacon ed., 1955), 175; Louis R. Harlan, *Booker T. Washington*, 2 vols. (New York: Oxford University Press, 1972–1986), 1: *The Making of a Black Leader, 1856–1901*, 312.

4. Willard B. Gatewood, Jr., *Black Americans and the White Man's Burden, 1898–1903* (Urbana: University of Illinois Press, 1975), 306–07. For a survey of the colonization panacea into the twentieth century, see Elliott P. Skinner, *African Americans and U.S. Policy Toward Africa, 1850–1924* (Washington, D.C.: Howard University Press, 1992), 21–57.

5. George Sinkler, *The Racial Attitudes of American Presidents: From Abraham Lincoln to Theodore Roosevelt* (Garden City, N.Y.: Doubleday, 1971), 318; Hofstadter, *Social Darwinism*, 188–89, 195; Seth M. Scheiner, "President Theodore Roosevelt and the Negro, 1901–1908," *Journal of Negro History* 47(July 1962): 170; Stephen R. Fox, *The Guardian of Boston: William Monroe Trotter* (New York: Atheneum, 1970), 150.

6. Thomas G. Dyer, *Theodore Roosevelt and the Idea of Race* (Baton Rouge: Louisiana State University Press, 1980), 95; Leon F. Litwack, "Trouble in Mind: The Bicentennial and the Afro-American Experience," *Journal of American History* 74(Sept. 1987): 333.

7. David McCullough, *Mornings on Horseback* (New York: Simon and Schuster, 1981), 45.

8. Gatewood, *Black Americans*, 203, 243.

9. Fox, *Guardian*, 21; Sinkler, *Racial Attitudes*, 342.

10. Fox, *Guardian*, 147–48; Roosevelt to Booker T. Washington, Nov. 10, 1900, Special Corr.—Roosevelt, Box 75, Booker T. Washington Papers,

Library of Congress, Washington, D.C.; Roosevelt to Washington, Dec. 25, 1906, and Feb. 16, 1907, Personal Corr.—Roosevelt, Box 17, ibid.; Roosevelt to Edwin W. Sims, March 20, 1908, Personal Corr.—Roosevelt, Box 17, ibid.

11. August Meier, *Negro Thought in America, 1880–1915* (Ann Arbor: University of Michigan Press, 1963), 218; Roosevelt to Washington, Dec. 28, 1904, Oct. 12 and 16, 1905, Personal Corr.—Roosevelt, Box 17, Washington Papers.

12. Nathan Miller, *Theodore Roosevelt: A Life* (New York: Morrow, 1992), 362; John Hope Franklin, *From Slavery to Freedom* (New York: Vintage ed., 1969), 434; Scheiner, "Theodore Roosevelt," 171; Roosevelt to Washington, Sept. 14, 1901, Personal Corr.—Roosevelt, Box 17, Washington Papers.

13. Arthur Wallace Dunn, *Gridiron Nights* (New York: Frederick A. Stokes Co., 1915), 118–19; Harlan, *Making of a Black Leader*, 317.

14. Joel Williamson, *The Crucible of Race* (New York: Oxford University Press, 1984), 350; Willard B. Gatewood, Jr., *Theodore Roosevelt and the Art of Controversy* (Baton Rouge: Louisiana State University Press, 1970), 36–37.

15. Scheiner, "Theodore Roosevelt," 171, 177; Gatewood, *Theodore Roosevelt*, 32–61; William Seale, *The President's House*, 2 vols. (Washington, D.C.: White House Historical Association, 1986), 2: 708–10; Elting E. Morison, ed., *The Letters of Theodore Roosevelt*, 8 vols. (Cambridge, Mass.: Harvard University Press, 1951–1954), 3: 184.

16. Richard B. Sherman, *The Republican Party and Black America: From McKinley to Hoover, 1896–1933* (Charlottesville: University Press of Virginia, 1973), 43; Gatewood, *Theodore Roosevelt*, 62–89; Fox, *Guardian*, 149; Neil R. McMillen, *Dark Journey: Black Mississippians in the Age of Jim Crow* (Urbana: University of Illinois Press, 1989), 61–62; Williamson, *Crucible of Race*, 352.

17. Gatewood, *Theodore Roosevelt*, 90–134; Williamson, *Crucible of Race*, 351–52; Fox, *Guardian*, 148; Sherman, *The Republican Party*, 40; Roosevelt to Washington, March 4, 1903, Personal Corr.—Roosevelt, Box 17, Washington Papers.

18. Roosevelt to Albion Winegar Tourgée, in Morison, ed., *Letters of Theodore Roosevelt*, 3: 190; Fox, *Guardian*, 150.

19. Williamson, *Crucible of Race*, 346, 349; Scheiner, "Theodore Roosevelt," 172–73, 177–80; C. Vann Woodward, *Origins of the New South, 1877–1913* (Baton Rouge: Louisiana State University Press, 1951), 463; Henry F. Pringle, *Theodore Roosevelt* (rev. ed.; New York: Harcourt, Brace and World, 1956), 161, 242.

20. Roosevelt to Washington, June 17, 1904, Personal Corr.—Roosevelt, Box 17, Washington Papers; Scheiner, "Theodore Roosevelt," 172–73.

21. Roosevelt to Winfield Taylor Durbin, Aug. 6, 1908, in Morison, ed., *Letters of Theodore Roosevelt*, 3: 540–41; Dunn, *Gridiron Nights*, 136; Meier, *Negro Thought*, 164; Scheiner, "Theodore Roosevelt," 180–81; Fox, *Guardian*, 165; Sinkler, *Racial Attitudes*, 345–46, 355.

22. Fox, *Guardian*, 150; Sinkler, *Racial Attitudes*, 343–44. For the battle against peonage, see Pete Daniel, *The Shadow of Slavery: Peonage in the South, 1901–1969* (Urbana: University of Illinois Press, 1972).

23. Fox, *Guardian*, 151–53; Franklin, *From Slavery to Freedom*, 442; Pringle, *Theodore Roosevelt*, 322–27.

24. Williamson, *Crucible of Race*, 354–55.

25. Harold Brayman, *The President Speaks Off-the-Record: From Grover Cleveland to Gerald Ford* (Princeton, N.J.: Dow Jones Books, 1976), 48–55; Dunn, *Gridiron Club*, 176–90; Miller, *Theodore Roosevelt*, 467–69.

26. Emma Lou Thornbrough, "The Brownsville Episode and the Negro Vote," *Mississippi Valley Historical Review* 44(Dec. 1957): 476.

27. John D. Weaver, *The Brownsville Raid* (New York: Norton, 1970), 145–278, passim. See also Ann J. Lane, *The Brownsville Affair* (Port Washington, N.Y.: Kennikat Press, 1971).

28. Gatewood, *Black Americans*, 280; Fox, *Guardian*, 151, 155.

29. Taft to Washington, May 28 and July 19, 1908, Personal Corr.—Taft, Box 19, Washington Papers.

30. Taft to Washington, June 5, 1908, Box 19, ibid.; Fox, *Guardian*, 159–60; Williamson, *Crucible of Race*, 355.

31. *New York Times*, March 5, 1909; Memo, re Authority of the United States to Protect Negroes, March 31, 1910, No. OG 3057, Record Group 65, Bureau of Investigation Files, National Archives, Washington, D.C.; McMillen, *Dark Journey*, 62; Williamson, *Crucible of Race*, 357, 360; Dunn, *Gridiron Nights*, 226; Sherman, *The Republican Party*, 88.

32. McMillen, *Dark Journey*, 62; Judith Icke Anderson, *William Howard Taft: An Intimate History* (New York: Norton, 1981), 72; William Garrott Brown to Charles D. Norton, Oct. 13, 1910, Series 6, No. 83, William Howard Taft Papers, Library of Congress; Charles H. Eliot to Taft, July 25, 1910, ibid.; Eliot to Norton, Aug. 2, 1910, ibid.; Francis C. Caffey to Norton, Aug. 18, 1910, ibid.

33. Brown to Norton, Oct. 13, 1910, Series 6, No. 83, Taft Papers. The Gridiron Club spoofed the southern tours, too. "The Taft Georgia Minstrels (white)" sang, to the tune of "Marching Through Georgia" and in

reference to the president's girth, "Eating Through Georgia." Dunn, *Gridiron Nights*, 217.

34. Washington to Norton, Nov. 25, 1910, Series 6, No. 83, Taft Papers. See also the newspaper clippings in Series 5, No. 466, ibid.

35. Williamson, *Crucible of Race*, 358, 362–63; Arnold Rampersad, *The Life of Langston Hughes*, 2 vols. (New York: Oxford University Press, 1986–1988), 1: 13.

36. Franklin, *From Slavery to Freedom*, 453; George E. Mowry, "The South and the Progressive Lily White Party of 1912," *Journal of Southern History* 6(May 1940): 240.

37. Mowry, "South," 238–39; Arthur S. Link, ed., "Correspondence Relating to the Progressive Party's 'Lily White' Policy in 1912," *Journal of Southern History* 10(Nov. 1944): 481.

38. "Extract from Mr. Roosevelt's Speech at the Chicago Coliseum on the Negro Question," Aug. 6, 1912, Series 3A, Vol. 68, Theodore Roosevelt Papers, Library of Congress.

39. Roosevelt to Julian Harris, Aug. 1, 1912, ibid.

40. Ibid.

41. Mowry, "South," 239, 246; Roosevelt to Tourgée, Nov. 8, 1901, in Morison, ed., *Letters of Theodore Roosevelt*, 3: 190.

42. David H. Burton, *The Learned Presidency* (Rutherford, N.J.: Fairleigh Dickinson University Press, 1988), 138.

43. Woodrow Wilson, "The Reconstruction of the Southern States," *Atlantic Monthly*, Jan. 1901, p. 6. See also Wilson's textbook, *A History of the American People*, 5 vols. (New York: Harper, 1902).

44. In 1948 Princeton awarded its first undergraduate degree to a black student.

45. From the diary of Mary Yates, July 31 [1908], in Arthur S. Link, ed., *The Papers of Woodrow Wilson*, 69 vols. (Princeton, N.J.: Princeton University Press, 1966–1993), 18: 386.

46. Ronald W. Walters, *Black Presidential Politics in America* (Albany: State University of New York Press, 1988), 11; Meier, *Negro Thought*, 187; Nancy J. Weiss, "The Negro and the New Freedom: Fighting Wilsonian Segregation," *Political Science Quarterly* 84(March 1969): 61–62; Henry Blumenthal, "Woodrow Wilson and the Race Question," *Journal of Negro History* 48(Jan. 1963): 4–5.

47. Kathleen Long Wolgemuth, "Woodrow Wilson's Appointment Policy and the Negro," *Journal of Southern History* 24(Nov. 1958): 458–59, 461, 467; Fox, *Guardian*, 170; Lillian Rogers Parks, *My Thirty Years Backstairs at the White House* (New York: Fleet Publishing, 1961), 131.

48. James Weldon Johnson, *Along This Way* (New York: Viking, 1933), 306.

49. August Meier and Elliott Rudwick, "The Rise of Segregation in the Federal Bureaucracy, 1900–1930," *Phylon* 28(June 1967): 178–79.

50. Weiss, "The Negro and the New Freedom," 61–62.

51. Ibid., 61–79; Meier and Rudwick, "Rise of Segregation," 178–84; Arthur S. Link, *Wilson*, 5 vols. (Princeton, N.J.: Princeton University Press, 1947–1965), 2: *The New Freedom*, 248.

52. Williamson, *Crucible of Race*, 366–67; Wolgemuth, "Wilson," 462–63.

53. Wilson to Thomas Dixon, July 29, 1913, Series 4, No. 152, Woodrow Wilson Papers, Library of Congress.

54. Nancy Weiss, *Farewell to the Party of Lincoln: Black Politics in the Age of FDR* (Princeton, N.J.: Princeton University Press, 1983), 20.

55. Wilson to Oswald Garrison Villard, July 23, 1913, Series 4, No. 152A, Wilson Papers; Blumenthal, "Wilson," 9.

56. Villard to Wilson, Aug. 15, 1913, Series 4, No. 152A, Wilson Papers; Wilson to Villard, Aug. 21, 1913, ibid.

57. Wilson to Villard, Sept. 22, 1913, ibid.

58. Wilson to Villard, Oct. 2, 1913, ibid.; Oswald Garrison Villard, *Fighting Years* (New York: Harcourt, Brace, 1939), 10.

59. Christine A. Lunardini, "Standing Firm: William Monroe Trotter's Meetings With Woodrow Wilson, 1913–1914," *Journal of Negro History* 64(Summer 1979): 246–50; Fox, *Guardian*, 173–74.

60. Lunardini, "Standing," 256–62.

61. *Washington Herald*, Nov. 16, 1914; *Washington Post*, Nov. 16, 1914.

62. Wilson to Dixon, July 29, 1913, Series 4, No. 152, Wilson Papers; Dixon to Wilson, July 27, 1913, ibid.

63. The quotation appears in many different places and in many different forms. If there is some debate about Wilson's exact words, the substance of what he said always comes through.

64. Link, *New Freedom*, 253; John Hope Franklin, *Race and History: Selected Essays, 1938–1988* (Baton Rouge: Louisiana State University Press, 1989), 17; Fox, *Guardian*, 189.

66. Wilson to Tumulty, n.d. [ca. March 5, 1918], ibid.

67. Elliott Rudwick, *Race Riot at East St. Louis* (New York: Atheneum, 1972), 8, 41–57, passim.

68. William English Walling to Wilson, July 3, 1917, Series 4, No. 152, Wilson Papers; Wilson to Tumulty, n.d. [ca. July 4, 1917], ibid. See also Thomas Gregory to Wilson, July 27, 1917, No. 186835-54, Record Group 60, Dept. of Justice Files, National Archives.

70. Memo, re Racial Disturbances 1917–1919, Aug. 3, 1943, Civil Rights—Race Riots, Box 5, Eleanor Bontecou Papers, Harry S. Truman Library, Independence, Mo. Several locales avoided riots only because Army troops were nearby. Dwight David Eisenhower, fresh from West

Point, remembered "difficulties" in Columbus, Georgia, where the mayor appealed for help and Eisenhower "had a little parade with tanks." Memo, re Telephone Briefing by Andrew J. Goodpaster, July 25, 1967, Goodpaster-Wheeler Briefings (1), Post-Pres./Gettysburg, Dwight D. Eisenhower Papers, Dwight D. Eisenhower Presidential Library, Abilene, Kan. For the disturbances generally, see William M. Tuttle, Jr., *Race Riot: Chicago in the Red Summer of 1919* (New York: Atheneum, 1970); Richard J. Cortner, *A Mob Intent on Death: The NAACP and the Arkansas Riot Cases* (Middleton, Conn.: Wesleyan University Press, 1988); Arthur I. Waskow, *From Race Riot to Sit-In: 1919 and the 1960s* (Garden City, N.Y.: Doubleday, 1966).

71. Johnson, *Along This Way*, 323–25.

72. Baker to Wilson, July 1, 1918, Series 4, No. 152, Wilson Papers; Emory Morris, William Brigham, and Trotter to Wilson, March 5, 1918, Series 4, No. 543, ibid.

73. Wilson to George Creel, June 18, 1918, Series 4, No. 152, ibid.; Creel to Wilson, June 17 and July 5, 1918, ibid.

74. See *Federal Surveillance of Afro-Americans (1917–1925): The First World War, the Red Scare, and the Garvey Movement* (microfilm; Frederick, My.: University Publications of America, 1987).

75. Clinton Rossiter, *The American Presidency* (rev. ed.; New York: New American Library, 1960), 99.

76. See Skinner, *African Americans and U.S. Policy Toward Africa*, 381–422.

77. Richard B. Sherman, "The Harding Administration and the Negro: An Opportunity Lost," *Journal of Negro History* 49(July 1964): 153.

78. Johnson, *Along This Way*, 357–60.

79. Robert K. Murray, *The Harding Era: Warren G. Harding and His Administration* (Minneapolis: University of Minnesota Press, 1969), 401; Sherman, "Harding," 155; Eugene P. Trani and David L. Wilson, *The Presidency of Warren G. Harding* (Lawrence: University Press of Kansas, 1977), 102–03.

80. James Weldon Johnson to George B. Christian, March 28, 1921, No. 93, Warren G. Harding Papers, Ohio Historical Society, Marion. The Library of Congress has a microfilm edition of Harding's papers.

81. John T. Adams to Harding, Sept. 28, 1921, No. 93, ibid.; Murray, *Harding Era*, 399–400.

82. Murray, *Harding Era*, 398–402.

83. Francis Russell, *The Shadow of Blooming Grove: Warren G. Harding in His Times* (New York: McGraw-Hill, 1968), 26, 372, 403–05, 413–15.

84. June 28, 1924.

85. Donald R. McCoy, *Calvin Coolidge: The Quiet President* (New York: Macmillan, 1967), 257, 328. For White House mail on the Klan issue,

see Series 1, Case File No. 28, Calvin Coolidge Papers, Library of Congress.

86. C. B. Slemp to C. O. Sherrill, May 2, 1923, Series 1, No. 93, Coolidge Papers; memo, re Segregation in the Departments, n.d. [ca. Oct. 1924], ibid.

87. Hoover to Hill, March 13, 1928, Commerce Dept.—Census Bureau/Colored Clerks, Commerce Papers, Herbert Hoover Papers, Herbert Hoover Library, West Branch, Iowa; *Washington Eagle*, April 6, 1928.

88. Slemp to Frederick C. Hicks, July 31, 1924, Series 1, No. 93, Coolidge Papers.

89. A. Philip Randolph Oral History, Jan. 14, 1969, p. 54, Ralph J. Bunche Oral History Collection, Moorland-Spingarn Research Center, Howard University, Washington, D.C.; Roy Talbert, Jr., *Negative Intelligence: The Army and the American Left, 1917–1941* (Jackson: University Press of Mississippi, 1991), 118.

90. John Sargent to Coolidge, Nov. 12, 1927, in Robert A. Hill, ed., *The Marcus Garvey and Universal Negro Improvement Association Papers*, 7 vols. (Los Angeles and Berkeley: University of California Press, 1983–1991), 6: 607.

91. Walter White, *A Man Called White* (reprint ed.; New York: Arno Press/New York Times, 1969), 81; Hoover to Robert Moton, May 24, 1927, Robert Moton, Commerce Papers, Hoover Papers.

92. Lawrence Richey to George Akerson, June 9, 1927, Miss. Valley Flood—Negroes, Commerce Papers, Hoover Papers; Richey to James J. Davis, June 10, 1927, Miss. Valley Flood—Negroes, Commerce Papers, ibid.; Hoover to Arthur Capper, May 13, 1927, Miss. Valley Flood—Negroes, Commerce Papers, ibid.; Hoover to Arthur Kellogg, July 13, 1927, Robert Moton, Commerce Papers, ibid.; White, *A Man Called White*, 81.

93. Neil R. McMillen, "Perry W. Howard: Boss of Black-and-Tan Republicanism in Mississippi, 1924–1960," *Journal of Southern History* 48(May 1982): 207–24; E. E. Conroy to J. Edgar Hoover, July 21, 1928, Perry Howard File, No. 72-40-1, Dept. of Justice Files. See also Samuel O'Dell, "Blacks, the Democratic Party, and the Presidential Election of 1928," *Phylon* 48(Spring 1987): 3–4.

94. After the Mississippi flood Hoover tried to convince the Julius Rosenwald Fund to support a "project for organizing a corporation looking toward the colonization and the eventual farm ownership of Negroes in the Mississippi Valley." Mary and Eugene Booze played a prominent role in this, but the Rosenwald Fund declined to participate and the project never received seed money. When the Great Depression hit, Hoover again tried and largely failed to find a way to help the farmers

of the Boozes's all-black Mound Bayou community. Edwin R. Embree to Hoover, March 1, 1928, Negroes—Plan to Make Good Farm Land in South Available, Commerce Papers, Hoover Papers; Mabel Walker Willebrandt to Walter Newton, Aug. 23, 1929, States File—Miss./Justice, Pres. Papers, ibid. For the Justice Department official, see Dorothy M. Brown, *Mabel Walker Willebrandt: A Study of Power, Loyalty, and Law* (Knoxville: University of Tennessee Press, 1984).

95. O'Dell, "Blacks," 10.
96. White, *A Man Called White*, 99–101.
97. Douglas B. Craig, *After Wilson: The Struggle for the Democratic Party, 1920–1934* (Chapel Hill: University of North Carolina Press, 1992), 174–75.
98. White, *A Man Called White*, 101.
99. Akerson to Theodore Bilbo, Oct. 19, 1928, Campaign of 1928—Commerce Dept./Segregation, Special Collections-Misrepresentations, Hoover Papers; Richey to J. W. Summer, Oct. 13, 1928, ibid.; Harold N. Graves to Thomas B. Love, Oct. 5, 1928, ibid.
100. Hoover to Robert McCormick, March 30, 1929, Subject File—RNC/Colored Voters, Pres. Papers, ibid.; *Chicago Tribune*, March 28, 1929.
101. David Burner, *Herbert Hoover: A Public Life* (New York: Knopf, 1978), 215; George H. Nash, *The Life of Herbert Hoover* (New York: Norton, 1983–), 1: *The Engineer, 1874–1914*, 505.
102. Memo re Diplomatic Dinners, n.d. [ca. 1929], Subject File—Colored Question, Pres. Papers, Hoover Papers; Richard N. Smith, *An Uncommon Man: The Triumph of Herbert Hoover* (New York: Simon and Schuster, 1984), 111–12; Franklin, *From Slavery to Freedom*, 526.
103. Eugene Kinckle Jones to Richey, July 25, 1932, Negro Matters, President's Personal File, Hoover Papers; Hoover to Jones, April 1, 1929, ibid.
104. Johnson to Hoover, May 24, 1929, Secretary's File—NAACP, Pres. Papers, Hoover Papers.
105. Roy Wilkins, with Tom Mathews, *Standing Fast* (New York: Penguin ed., 1984), 91–92; White, *A Man Called White*, 104–15; Kenneth Goings, *The NAACP Comes of Age: The Defeat of Judge John J. Parker* (Bloomington: Indiana University Press, 1990).
106. Carl G. Bachmann to Newton, Aug. 21, 1930, Subject File—Colored Question, Pres. Papers, Hoover Papers; Hamilton Fish to Bachmann, Aug. 18, 1930, Subject File—Colored Question, Pres. Papers, ibid.
107. J. Edgar Hoover to Newton, April 25, 1930 (see also the accompanying Bureau of Investigation "blind" memo—that is, a memo typed on plain white paper without identifying letterhead), Subject File—Judiciary/Supreme Court—Parker Endorsements, Pres. Papers, ibid.; J. Edgar

Hoover to Charles P. Sisson, April 19, 1930, Subject File—Colored Question, Pres. Papers, ibid.; J. Edgar Hoover to Newton, Sept. 5, 1930, No. 61-3176-7, FBI-NAACP File, J. Edgar Hoover FBI Building, Washington, D.C.

108. Bureau of Investigation "blind" memo, n.d. [ca. April 25, 1930], Subject File—Judiciary/Supreme Court—Parker Endorsements, Pres. Papers, Hoover Papers.

109. Summary of J. Edgar Hoover letter, Jan. 7, 1930, Cabinet Offices—Justice, Pres. Papers, ibid.; J. Edgar Hoover to John D. Mitchell, Sept. 12, 1931, Secretary's File, Moorhead, H.—Moss, A., Pres. Papers, ibid.; Rhea Whitley to Director, Sept. 12, 1931, no. 62-258891-1, FBI-Moorish Science Temple of America File.

110. See Kenneth O'Reilly, *"Racial Matters": The FBI's Secret File on Black America, 1960–1972* (New York: Free Press, 1989). Chapter I surveys the Bureau's first five decades.

111. Wilkins, *Standing Fast*, 92, 93, 98.

112. White, *A Man Called White*, 114; Wilkins, *Standing Fast*, 92. For the "reservation" quotation, see James A. Cobb to Newton, July 9, 1932, Subject File—Colored Question, Pres. Papers, Hoover Papers. Cobb was a Washington, D.C., municipal court judge and an ardent Republican.

113. Ray L. Wilbur to Hoover, Oct. 20, 1930, Subject File—Colored Question, Pres. Papers, Hoover Papers.

114. Hoover to Mary McLeod Bethune, Feb. 28, 1931, Personal File—Mary McLeod Bethune, Pres. Papers, ibid.; Weiss, *Farewell*, 25–26.

115. Hoover to Mitchell, Aug. 16, 1931, Cabinet Offices—Justice/Corr., Pres. Papers, Hoover Papers; L. B. Reed to J. Edgar Hoover, June 15, 1930, David E. Henderson File, Hoover Library; J. Edgar Hoover to Sisson, June 14 and 17, 1930, ibid.; Bureau of Investigation Rept., June 13, 1930, ibid; Sisson to David E. Henderson, Oct. 22, 1931, ibid.; Roy St. Lewis to Henderson, March 14, 1933, ibid.

116. Notes, re Theodore Roosevelt, Jr., telephone calls, June 22, 1931, Secretary's File—NAACP, Pres. Papers, ibid.; Hoover to Joel E. Spingarn, June 23, 1931, Personal File—NAACP, Pres. Papers, ibid.

117. Francis E. Rivers to Newton, Nov. 1, 1932, Subject File—RNC/Colored Voters, Pres. Papers, ibid.; F. H. Payne to Lawrence Richey, Oct. 25, 1932, Subject File—Gold Star Mothers, Pres. Papers, ibid.

118. Akerson to White, Oct. 21, 1930, Subject File—Colored Question, Pres. Papers, ibid.; White to Hoover, Oct. 3 and Dec. 13, 1930, ibid.

119. Hoover to Mitchell, Dec. 31, 1931, Subject File—Colored Question, Pres. Papers, ibid.

Chapter 3. New Dealers

1. William E. Leuchtenberg, *Franklin D. Roosevelt and the New Deal* (New York: Harper and Row, 1963); Paul Conkin, *The New Deal* (New York: Crowell, 1967); Arthur M. Schlesinger, Jr., *The Coming of the New Deal* (Boston: Houghton Mifflin, 1959) and *The Politics of Upheaval* (New York: Houghton Mifflin, 1960); Richard H. Pells, *Radical Visions and American Dreams* (New York: Harper and Row, 1973); Otis L. Graham, Jr., *An Encore for Reform: The Old Progressives and the New Deal* (New York: Oxford University Press, 1967).

2. Nancy J. Weiss, *Farewell to the Party of Lincoln: Black Politics in the Age of FDR* (Princeton, N.J.: Princeton University Press, 1983).

3. Roy Wilkins, with Tom Mathews, *Standing Fast* (New York: Penguin ed., 1984), 18, 127; Joseph P. Lash, *Dealers and Dreamers: A New Look at the New Deal* (Garden City, N.Y.: Doubleday, 1988), 103.

4. Weiss, *Farewell*, 19–20; Geoffrey C. Ward, *A First-Class Temperament: The Emergence of Franklin Roosevelt* (New York: Harper and Row, 1989), 173–74n, 447–48, 766–67; Blanche Wiesen Cook, *Eleanor Roosevelt, 1884–1933* (New York: Viking, 1992), 134–38, 250–51.

5. Ward, *First-Class Temperament*, 459–60. For the Elaine riot, see Richard Cortner, *A Mob Intent on Death* (Middleton, Conn.: Wesleyan University Press, 1988).

6. Walter White, *A Man Called White* (reprint ed.; New York: Arno Press/New York Times, 1969), 139.

7. Walter White to Roosevelt, Sept. 28, 1932, NAACP, PPF1336, Franklin D. Roosevelt Papers, Franklin D. Roosevelt Library, Hyde Park, N.Y.; Arthur R. Forbush to Marguerite LeHand, Oct. 15, 1932, ibid. Forbush, a DNC official, passed on Howe's comment.

8. Weiss, *Farewell*, 34–35; Lash, *Dealers and Dreamers*, 416; Leuchtenberg, *Franklin D. Roosevelt*, 186.

9. Lash, *Dealers and Dreamers*, 415–16; Weiss, *Farewell*, 35–36, 56, 119. See also Jordan A. Schwarz, *The New Dealers: Power Politics in the Age of Roosevelt* (New York: Knopf, 1993). Schwarz's subjects are notable in their near total disinterest in civil rights.

10. John B. Kirby, *Black Americans in the Roosevelt Era* (Knoxville: University of Tennessee Press, 1980), 109, 131, 147.

11. Weiss, *Farewell*, 136–56; B. Joyce Ross, "Mary McLeod Bethune and the National Youth Administration," *Journal of Negro History* 60 (Jan. 1975): 1–28; Robert C. Weaver Oral History, Nov. 19, 1968, pp. 4–5, Lyndon B. Johnson Library, Austin, Texas.

12. Weiss, *Farewell*, 51; Leuchtenberg, *Franklin D. Roosevelt*, 185; J. L. Nicholson to Charles F. Roos, June 12, 1934, Negro Workers, Box 7, Leon Henderson Papers, Roosevelt Library.

13. Roosevelt to Robert Fechner, Jan. 15 and Sept. 26, 1936, Colored Matters, OF93, FDR Papers; Leuchtenberg, *Franklin D. Roosevelt*, 85. See also Nancy L. Grant, *TVA and Black Americans: Planning for the Status Quo* (Philadelphia: Temple University Press, 1990).

14. Alfred B. Rollins, Jr., *Roosevelt and Howe* (New York: Knopf, 1962), 269; John Hope Franklin, *From Slavery to Freedom* (New York: Vintage ed., 1969), 529; Weiss, *Farewell*, 59, 296.

15. Louis Howe to James J. Hoey, Nov. 15, 1933, Scottsboro, OF532, FDR Papers; Harvard Sitkoff, *A New Deal for Blacks* (New York: Oxford University Press, 1978), 43. For the case, see Dan T. Carter, *Scottsboro: A Tragedy of the American South* (Baton Rouge: Louisiana State University Press, 1969); James Goodman, *Stories of Scottsboro* (New York: Pantheon, 1994).

16. Memo, re Meeting with the President, July 21, 1943, FDR, Box 2, Biddle Papers; Patrick S. Washburn, *A Question of Sedition: The Federal Government's Investigation of the Black Press during World War II* (New York: Oxford University Press, 1986), 201.

17. James A. Farley to Howe, Dec. 19, 1934, Colored Matters, OF93, FDR Papers; Joseph L. Johnson to Howe, July 6, 1933, ibid.; Johnson to Howe, Dec. 7, 1934, Negroes, Box 86, Louis Howe Papers, Roosevelt Library.

18. Lillian Rogers Parks, *The Roosevelts* (Englewood Cliffs, N.J.: Prentice Hall, 1981), 32–33; Wilkins, *Standing Fast*, 128; Robert H. Ferrell, *Harry S. Truman: A Life* (Columbia: University of Missouri Press, 1994), 292.

19. Jonathan Daniels Oral History, Nov. 16, 1973, p. 7, Eleanor Roosevelt Oral History Project, Roosevelt Library.

20. George Wolfskill and John A. Hudson, *All But the People: Franklin D. Roosevelt and His Critics, 1933–1939* (New York: Macmillan, 1969), 91; Wilkins, *Standing Fast*, 131; Eleanor Roosevelt to Walter White, Sept. 10, 1935, Corr.—White 1935, Box 1362, Eleanor Roosevelt Papers (hereafter ER Papers), Roosevelt Library.

21. Weiss, *Farewell*, 40–42, 252–53; William H. Harris, *The Harder We Run* (New York: Oxford University Press, 1982), 49.

22. C. R. Smith Oral History, Feb. 6, 1978, p. 18, Eleanor Roosevelt Oral History Project.

23. White to Roosevelt, June 9, 1933, NAACP 1933–35, OF2538, FDR Papers; Stephen Early to White, June 12, 1933, NAACP 1933–35, OF2538, ibid.; Roosevelt to White, June 22, 1934, NAACP, PPF1336,

ibid.; Early to Charles Michelson, June 21, 1935, NAACP, PPF1336, ibid.; Michelson to Early, June 22, 1935, NAACP, PPF1336, ibid.; Roosevelt to White, June 22, 1935, NAACP, PPF1336, ibid.

24. Arthur B. Spingarn to J. Edgar Hoover, Sept. 15, 1943, no. 61-3176-150, FBI-NAACP File, J. Edgar Hoover FBI Building, Washington, D.C.; T. J. Starke to Louis B. Nichols, Sept. 23, 1943, no. 100-382824-X1, FBI–Walter White File.

25. See the undated notation in Anti-Lynching Bills, Box 67, Howe Papers. For the antilynching crusade, see Robert L. Zangrando, *The NAACP Crusade Against Lynching, 1909–1950* (Philadelphia: Temple University Press, 1980).

26. White, *A Man Called White*, 166.

27. Ibid., 168; Eleanor Roosevelt to White, May 2, 1934, Corr.—White 1934, Box 1325, ER Papers.

28. White to Eleanor Roosevelt, May 14, 1934, Corr.—White 1934, Box 1325, ibid.; White, *A Man Called White*, 168–69.

29. James R. McGovern, *Anatomy of a Lynching: The Killing of Claude Neal* (Baton Rouge: Louisiana University Press, 1982), 115–39.

30. Eleanor Roosevelt to White, Nov. 23, 1934, Corr.—White 1934, Box 1325, ER Papers; Wilkins, *Standing Fast*, 132; Weiss, *Farewell*, 109.

31. Marvin McIntyre to Malvina Scheider, March 14, 1935, Corr.—White 1935, Box 1362, ER Papers; Early to Scheider, Aug. 5, 1935, ibid.; Eleanor Roosevelt to Early, Aug. 8, 1935, NAACP, PPF1336, FDR Papers.

32. Lash, *Dealers and Dreamers*, 421; Sitkoff, *New Deal for Blacks*, 43.

33. Eleanor Roosevelt to White, n.d. [ca. March 5, 1935], Corr.—White 1935, Box 1362, ER Papers; Sitkoff, *New Deal for Blacks*, 287–88.

34. Roosevelt to Eleanor Roosevelt, March 9, 1936, Corr.—White, Box 1411, ER Papers; Eleanor Roosevelt to White, March 19, 1936, ibid.

35. Homer Cummings to Roosevelt, Jan. 27, 1937, Lynching, OF93-A, FDR Papers; Cummings to Roosevelt, Feb. 11, 1937, Justice 1933–37, PSF, ibid.

36. Cummings to Roosevelt, June 8, 1937, Lynching, OF93-A, ibid.; Roosevelt to Robert Wagner, June 10, 1937, Lynching, OF93-A, ibid.; Gilbert C. Fite, *Richard B. Russell, Jr.: Senator from Georgia* (Chapel Hill: University of North Carolina Press, 1991), 169.

37. Sitkoff, *New Deal for Blacks*, 326–27.

38. Robert K. Carr, *Federal Protection of Civil Rights: Quest for a Sword* (Ithaca, N.Y.: Cornell University Press, 1947).

39. Dominic J. Capeci, Jr., "The Lynching of Cleo Wright: Federal Protection of Constitutional Rights during World War II," *Journal of American History* 72(March 1986): 859–87.

40. Memo, re meeting with the President, Nov. 17, 1942, FDR, Box 2, Francis Biddle Papers, Roosevelt Library.

41. Francis Biddle to James Rowe, Nov. 23, 1942, Negroes, Box 38, James Rowe Papers, Roosevelt Library. For Houston, see Genna Rae McNeil, *Groundwork: Charles Hamilton Houston and the Struggle for Civil Rights* (Philadelphia: Temple University Press, 1983).

42. Victor Rotnem to Wendell Berge, July 23, 1942, Civil Rights—Fair Employment, Box 1, Biddle Papers.

43. Roosevelt to Biddle, Nov. 17, 1942, FDR Folder, Box 2, ibid.; memo, re Meeting with Roosevelt, Nov. 17, 1942, ibid.

44. Thurgood Marshall to Morris Ernst, Oct. 20, 1943, Justice Dept. 1938–44, PSF, FDR Papers.

45. Charles Fahy to Biddle, Oct. 29, 1943, Justice Dept. 1938–44, PSF, ibid.; Biddle to Roosevelt, Oct. 30, 1943, ibid.

46. Daniels to Roosevelt, Sept. 28, 1944, Colored Matters, OF93, ibid.

47. John B. O'Brien, Jr., to Rotnem, n.d. [ca. Aug. 7, 1943], Civil Rights/Fair Employment, Box 1, Biddle Papers. See also Johnpeter Horst Grill and Robert L. Jenkins, "The Nazis and the American South in the 1930s: A Mirror Image?," *Journal of Southern History* 58(Nov. 1992): 667–94; Stefan Kuhl, *The Nazi Connection: Eugenics, American Racism, and German National Socialism* (New York: Oxford University Press, 1994).

48. Rotnem to Wendell Berge, July 23, 1942, Civil Rights/Fair Employment, Box 1, Biddle Papers; Hoover to SAC Boston, April 28, 1942, no. 61-3176-24X, FBI-NAACP File. Nearly everyone believed that Axis propagandists hammered away at America's race relations problems, but OWI's own analysis concluded that this was rarely the case. Of some 8,000 Axis short-wave radio broadcasts in the six months after Pearl Harbor, Berlin mentioned African Americans a mere thirteen times, Rome seven, and Tokyo five. "Axis Propaganda on the Status of the Negro in American Society," May 9, 1942, Negroes—Enemy Propaganda, Philleo Nash Files, Box 54, Harry S. Truman Papers, Harry S. Truman Library, Independence, Mo.

49. Eugene Katz to Gardner Cowles, Jr., Feb. 8, 1943, Alpha—Minorities Memo, OWI Files, Box 18, Philleo Nash Papers, Truman Library; Washburn, *Question of Sedition*, 8, passim; White, *A Man Called White*, 207.

50. Elmer Irey to Henry Morgenthau, Jr., Aug. 7, 1941, Conf. Repts. About People 1941, Henry Morgenthau, Jr., Papers, Roosevelt Library; Intelligence Unit Report, July 31, 1941, ibid.

51. Roosevelt to Eleanor Roosevelt, Sept. 26, 1941, Walter White, Box 1626, ER Papers.

52. James M. Burns, *Roosevelt: The Soldier of Freedom* (New York: Harcourt Brace Jovanovich, 1970), 266, 472; Godfrey Hodgson, *The Colonel: The Life and Wars of Henry Stimson, 1867–1950* (New York: Knopf, 1990), 249–50; Early to Edwin P. Watson, Sept. 19, 1940, NAACP, OF2538, FDR Papers; Henry Stimson to Roosevelt, Aug. 20, 1940, Corr.—White 1940, Box 1584, ER Papers.

53. Memo, re Conference at the White House, Sept. 27, 1940, Corr.— White 1940, Box 1584, ER Papers.

54. Rowe to Roosevelt, Oct. 23, 1940, Negroes, Box 23, Rowe Papers; Sitkoff, *New Deal for Blacks*, 306–07.

55. White, *A Man Called White*, 198–99; James F. Byrnes, *All in One Lifetime* (New York: Harper and Brothers, 1958), 228, 230. Byrnes's name also surfaced in 1944. Eleanor Roosevelt to White, Aug. 3, 1944, Walter White, Box 1751, ER Papers.

56. White, *A Man Called White*, 199. White later worked with Willkie in an attempt to have the motion-picture industry portray blacks in a more favorable light.

57. Biddle to Rowe, Oct. 21, 1940, NAACP, OF2538, FDR Papers; White to Jacob Billikopf, Oct. 9, 1940, ibid.

58. Rowe to Roosevelt, Oct. 23, 1940, Negroes, Box 23, Rowe Papers.

59. Memo, re Negroes, Oct. 25, 1940, ibid.; Rowe to Roosevelt, Oct. 31, 1940, ibid.

60. A. Philip Randolph Oral History, Jan. 14, 1969, p. 60, Ralph J. Bunche Oral History Collection, Moorland-Spingarn Research Center, Howard University, Washington, D.C. See also Herbert Garfinkle, *When Negroes March* (Glenco, Ill.: Free Press, 1959).

61. Randolph Oral History, 59–61.

62. Ibid., 59; Roy Wilkins Oral History, May 5, 1970, p. 85, Bunche Collection.

63. Memo, re Proposals of the Negro March-On-Washington Committee, n.d. [ca. June 16, 1941], Marches on Washington, OF391, FDR Papers.

64. Jonathan Daniels, *White House Witness, 1942–1945* (Garden City, N.Y.: Doubleday, 1975), 192–93.

65. Robert Patterson to Watson, June 3, 1941, Marches on Washington, OF391, FDR Papers.

66. Early to Wayne Coy, June 6, 1941, ibid.; Randolph Oral History, 63.

67. Wilkins Oral History, 86; Wilkins, *Standing Fast*, 180.

68. Randolph to Roosevelt, June 16, 1941, Marches on Washington, OF391, FDR Papers; Watson to Roosevelt, June 14, 1941, ibid. Rosenberg phoned Watson at the White House.

69. Hoover to Watson, June 19, 1941, FBI Rept. 835, OF 10-B, Box 13, Roosevelt Papers; memo, re Randolph, June 18, 1941, ibid.

70. Randolph Oral History, 64–65. See also White, *A Man Called White*, 190–92.

71. Randolph Oral History, 65–66; Wilkins, *Standing Fast*, 180.

72. FDR also started something of a tradition. See Ruth P. Morgan, *The President and Civil Rights: Policy-Making by Executive Order* (New York: St. Martin's Press, 1970).

73. Fiorello La Guardia to Roosevelt, June 19, 1941, Negro—Negro March on Washington, Box 3, Aubrey Williams Papers, Roosevelt Library.

74. Coy to Early, June 12, 1941, Marches on Washington, OF391, FDR Papers; Lawrence M. C. Smith to Lowell Mellett, Dec. 4, 1941, Special War Policies Unit, Box 3, Lowell Mellett Papers, Roosevelt Library; Daniels Oral History, 11.

75. Most of these are filed in the numbered FBI reports, OF 10-B (Boxes 13–18), FDR Papers; FBI Repts. Misc., Box 151, Harry Hopkins Papers, Roosevelt Library.

76. Rotnem to Daniels, Aug. 7, 1943, Office of Production Management, FEPC—Justice, OF4245–G, FDR Papers; Hoover to Harry Hopkins, Sept. 15, 1943, FBI Repts. Misc., Box 151, Hopkins Papers.

77. Washington Field Office Rept., March 11, 1941, no. 61-3176-15, FBI-NAACP File; [deleted] to Melvin H. Purvis, July 4, 1943, no. 61-3176-9, ibid.; "Survey of Racial Conditions in the United States," n.d. [ca. Sept. 1943], 1–10, 424, passim, in OF 10-B, FDR Papers.

78. Roosevelt to Elmer Davis, June 17, 1942, Colored Matters, OF93, FDR Papers; Davis to Roosevelt, June 19, 1942, ibid.

79. EEB to Martin (Office of the War Cabinet), July 21, 1942, Colored Troops, Box 136, Hopkins Papers; Harry Hopkins to George C. Marshall, Aug. 19, 1942, ibid.; Marshall to Hopkins, Aug. 21, 1942, ibid.; Hopkins to Sir Ronald Campbell, Aug. 22, 1942, ibid.

80. Stimson to Roosevelt, Sept. 20, 1944, Segregation, OF93-B, FDR Papers.

81. J. W. Innes to Organizations and Propaganda Analysis Section, Nov. 17, 1941, Special War Policies Unit, Box 3, Mellett Papers.

82. Hoover to Watson, Aug. 3, 1943, no. 2377, FBI, OF10-B, FDR Papers.

83. Lucille McMillan to Paul V. McNutt, Jan. 18, 1943, Colored Matters, OF93, FDR Papers; Biddle to Roosevelt, Jan. 29, 1943, Civil Rights—Fair Employment, Box 1, Biddle Papers.

84. Merl E. Reed, *Seedtime for the Modern Civil Rights Movement: The President's Committee on Fair Employment Practice, 1941–1946* (Baton

Rouge: Louisiana State University Press, 1991), 99–101, 345. See also Louis Ruchames, *Race, Jobs, and Politics: The Story of FEPC* (New York: Columbia University Press, 1953).

85. McIntyre to Roosevelt, Nov. 25, 1942, Colored Matters, OF93, FDR Papers; Daniels to Roosevelt, Nov. 24, 1942, ibid.

86. Daniels to Roosevelt, Nov. 24, 1942, ibid.; Clarence Mitchell Oral History, Dec. 11, 1968, pp. 36–37, Bunche Collection.

87. Daniels to McIntyre, Dec. 14, 1942, Office of Production Management, FEPC—Justice Dept., OF4245-G, FDR Papers; McIntyre to Roosevelt, Dec. 22, 1942, ibid.

88. "Survey of Racial Conditions," 419; Hoover to Hopkins, Jan. 29, 1943, FBI Repts. Misc., Box 151, Hopkins Papers.

89. Biddle to Roosevelt, Jan. 29, 1943, Civil Rights—Fair Employment, Box 1, Biddle Papers; Biddle to Roosevelt, Feb. 4, 1943, FDR, Box 2, ibid.

90. Memo, re Meeting with Roosevelt, Jan. 14, 1944, FDR, Box 2, Biddle Papers.

91. Sitkoff, *New Deal for Blacks*, 50.

92. Rotnem to Biddle, Aug. 9, 1943, Office of Production Management, FEPC—Justice Dept., OF4245-G, FDR Papers.

93. Biddle to Roosevelt, July 15, 1943, ibid.; Roosevelt to Biddle, Aug. 16, 1943, Detroit Riots, OF93-C, ibid.; Biddle to Roosevelt, July 15, 1943, Detroit Riots, Box 2, Biddle Papers.

94. Harold Ickes to Roosevelt, July 1, 1943, Office of Production Management, FEPC—Interior Dept., OF4245-G, FDR Papers; Roosevelt to Daniels, Aug. 11, 1943, ibid.; Dominic J. Capeci, Jr., *The Harlem Riot of 1943* (Philadelphia: Temple University Press, 1977), 148.

95. Daniels to Biddle, July 28, 1943, Office of Production Management, FEPC—Justice Dept., OF4245-G, FDR Papers; Jonathan Daniels Oral History, Oct. 4–5, 1963, p. 30, Truman Library.

96. Theo Lippman, Jr., *The Squire of Warm Springs: F.D.R. in Georgia, 1924–1945* (Chicago: Playboy Press, 1977), 91; D. Milton Ladd to FBI Director, Sept. 11, 1942, FBI File 62-116758; Ladd to Edward Tamm, Oct. 21, 1942, ibid.; Richmond Field Office Rept., Jan. 26, 1943, no. 62-25889-9, FBI–Moorish Science Temple of America File; Hoover to SAC Louisville, Aug. 5, 1943, no. 66-6200-44-12, FBI–Civil Rights Policy File. Eleanor Roosevelt, who also wanted to know if these clubs really existed, requested and received several FBI reports.

97. Francis Biddle, *In Brief Authority* (Garden City, N.Y.: Doubleday, 1962), 259.

98. See the documents in the American Youth Congress Folder, J. Edgar Hoover Official and Confidential FBI Files.

99. Hoover to Daniels, Dec. 23, 1943, and March 10, 11, and 31, 1944, Office of Production Management, OF4245-G, FDR Papers; memo, re Disappointing Club, n.d., ibid.; William C. Berman, *The Politics of Civil Rights in the Truman Administration* (Columbus: Ohio State University Press, 1970), 20. Truman later denied having made the remark.

100. John Morton Blum, ed., *The Price of Vision: The Diary of Henry A. Wallace, 1942–1946* (Boston: Houghton Mifflin, 1973), 243; Eleanor Roosevelt, *The Autobiography of Eleanor Roosevelt* (New York: Harper and Brothers, 1961), 253.

101. White to Eleanor Roosevelt, Dec. 5, 1942, Walter White, Box 1668, ER Papers.

102. Daniels, *White House Witness*, 205.

103. White, *A Man Called White*, 268.

104. Roosevelt to Edwin R. Embree, March 13, 1942, Colored Matters, OF93, FDR Papers; Malcolm S. MacLean, March 13, 1942, ibid.

105. Burns, *Roosevelt: Soldier of Freedom*, 472.

106. Lippman, *Squire of Warm Springs*, 227; Roosevelt to Eleanor Roosevelt, Jan. 31, 1944, Colored Matters, OF93, FDR Papers; Roosevelt to Daniels, Feb. 7, 1944, ibid. Ray Sprigle, the Pittsburgh reporter who broke the story of Hugo Black's past membership in the Ku Klux Klan, thought he saw another scandal in FDR's purchase of some 1,200 surrounding acres of mountain farmland because the nonprofit Georgia Warm Springs Foundation held title. Hoover to Hopkins, Oct. 16, 1942, FBI Repts. Misc., Box 151, Hopkins Papers.

Chapter 4. Cold Warriors

1. Roy Wilkins, *Standing Fast* (New York: Penguin ed., 1984), 192.

2. William C. Berman, *The Politics of Civil Rights in the Truman Administration* (Columbus: Ohio State University Press, 1970), 15, 19.

3. Truman to Rudolph J. Schwenger, Dec. 16, 1942, Negroes, Senatorial File, Harry S. Truman Papers, Harry S. Truman Library, Independence, Mo.; *Congressional Record*, 76th Cong., 3d sess., 1940, vol. 86, pp. A5367–69.

4. Donald R. McCoy and Richard T. Ruetten, *Quest and Response: Minority Rights and the Truman Administration* (Lawrence: University Press of Kansas, 1973); Berman, *Politics of Civil Rights*; Barton J. Bernstein, "The Ambiguous Legacy: The Truman Administration and Civil Rights," in *Politics and Policies of the Truman Administration*, ed. Barton J. Bernstein (Chicago: Quadrangle, 1970), 269–314.

5. Nicholas Lehmann, *The Promised Land* (New York: Knopf, 1991), 1–7.

6. James F. Byrnes, *All in One Lifetime* (New York: Harper and Brothers, 1958), 373.

7. Richard Kluger, *Simple Justice* (New York: Knopf, 1976), 421; John Hope Franklin, *From Slavery to Freedom* (New York: Vintage ed., 1969), 645–46. See also Mark Solomon, "Black Critics of Colonialism and the Cold War," in *Cold War Critics: Alternatives to American Foreign Policy in the Truman Years*, ed. Thomas G. Patterson (Chicago: Quadrangle, 1971), 205–39.

8. *Public Papers of the Presidents of the United States: Harry S. Truman, 1945* (Washington, D.C.: Government Printing Office, 1961), 10–11.

9. Quoted in Bernstein, "Ambiguous Legacy," 286.

10. Truman to Adolph Sabath, June 5, 1945, OF40, Truman Papers; Louis Ruchames, *Race, Jobs and Politics: The Story of FEPC* (New York: Columbia University Press, 1953), 122–35; Will Maslow, "FEPC—A Case History in Parliamentary Maneuver," *University of Chicago Law Review* 13(April 1946): 407–45. See also Louis Kesselman, *The Social Politics of FEPC* (Chapel Hill: University of North Carolina Press, 1948).

11. A. Philip Randolph to Truman, Aug. 31 and Sept. 30, 1945, OF40, Truman Papers; Matthew Connelly to Randolph, Sept. 4, 6, and 10, and Oct. 16, 1945, OF40, ibid.; Randolph to Connelly, Oct. 10 and 19, 1945, OF40, ibid.

12. Analysis of Presidential Mail on FEPC, n.d. [ca. June 25, 1945], OF40, ibid.

13. Adam Clayton Powell to Truman, Oct. 1, 1945, OF93, Truman Papers; Truman to Powell, Oct. 12, 1945, OF40, ibid.; Adam Clayton Powell, Jr., *Adam by Adam* (New York: Dial Press, 1971), 79.

14. Wil Haygood, *King of the Cats: The Life and Times of Adam Clayton Powell, Jr.* (Boston: Houghton Mifflin, 1993), 129; memo, re Mary McLeod Bethune, Dec. 20, 1946, FBI B, PSF, Truman Papers; Truman to David K. Niles, Sept. 30, 1946, Civil Rights—Negro Affairs, Box 26, David K. Niles Papers, Truman Library. Truman already had reason to be miffed because Powell, who always demanded cash for services rendered, had threatened the White House. "I campaigned for Mr. Roosevelt," the congressman reminded Niles, "with the understanding that there would be an allocation of funds to my paper for advertising and that my personal secretary, Mr. Joseph Ford, would receive a job." Because payment had not been received Powell was "preparing to campaign against the administration." Powell to Niles, June 7, 1945, ibid.

15. J. Edgar Hoover to Harry Vaughan, Dec. 3, 1945, FBI J, PSF, Truman Papers; Hoover to Vaughan, Jan. 11, 1946, FBI Personal, ibid.; Hoover to Vaughan, Jan. 17, 1946, FBI Communist Data, ibid.

16. Charles Houston to Truman, Dec. 3, 1945, OF40, ibid.; Truman to Houston, Dec. 17, 1945, OF40, ibid.; Berman, *Politics of Civil Rights*, 29–30.

17. Berman, *Politics of Civil Rights*, 32–35; Bernstein, "Ambiguous Legacy," 274. See also Malcolm Ross's memoir, *All Manner of Men* (New York: Reynal and Hitchcock, 1948).

18. Walter White, *A Man Called White* (reprint ed.; New York: Arno Press/New York Times, 1969), 330–31; Berman, *Politics of Civil Rights*, 44–47.

19. Margaret Truman, *Harry S. Truman* (New York: Morrow, 1972), 392; Truman to Stephen J. Spingarn, Oct. 18, 1956, Civil Rights—Truman Administration Correspondence, Stephen J. Spingarn Files, Truman Papers.

20. Truman to Niles, Sept. 20, 1946, Civil Rights—Negro Affairs, Box 26, Niles Papers; Truman to Tom C. Clark, Sept. 20, 1946, ibid.

21. *Chicago Tribune*, Sept. 24, 1946; *New York Times*, Sept. 25, 1946.

22. Niles to Matthew Connelly, Feb. 19, 1947, OF596-A, Truman Papers.

23. Minutes of Civil Rights Committee Meetings, Feb. 5 and 6, and May 1, 1947, Philleo Nash Files, Truman Papers. For Ernst's relationship with the FBI, see the voluminous Morris Ernst Folder, J. Edgar Hoover Official & Confidential FBI Files, J. Edgar Hoover FBI Building, Washington, D.C.

24. Niles to William Hassett, Jan. 17, 1946, PPF30, Truman Papers; Hoover to File, n.d. [ca. May 17, 1947], no. 100-12304-79, FBI-Paul Robeson File.

25. See Eleanor Roosevelt's moving account in her "My Day" newspaper column, July 2, 1947, in NAACP Speech, Box 17, George Elsey Papers, Truman Library.

26. Truman, *Public Papers 1947*, 311–13.

27. White, *A Man Called White*, 330–31; Wilkins, *Standing Fast*, 199.

28. Policy makers have often been aware of (if not always sensitive to) global questions of race and racism. See Alexander DeConde, *Ethnicity, Race, and American Foreign Policy* (Boston: Northwestern University Press, 1992).

29. Berman, *Politics of Civil Rights*, 65–66.

30. Truman, *Public Papers 1947*, 480; Robert H. Ferrell, *Harry S. Truman: A Life* (Columbia: University of Missouri Press, 1994), 295; President's Committee on Civil Rights, *To Secure These Rights* (Washington, D.C.: Government Printing Office, 1947; reprint ed., New York: Simon and Schuster, 1947). For Truman's comment to Wilson, Luckman, and Carr, see Minutes of the Civil Rights Committee, June 30, 1947, Nash Files, Truman Papers.

31. Confidential Memo for the President, Nov. 19, 1947, Box 16, Clark Clifford Papers, Truman Library; James H. Rowe, Jr., Oral History, Sept. 30, 1969, pp. 3, 26–28, ibid.; Clark Clifford, *Counsel to the President* (New York: Random House, 1991), 191–94.

32. On this point see also Henry Lee Moon, *Balance of Power: The Negro Vote* (Garden City, N.Y.: Doubleday, 1948). Moon was the NAACP's chief publicist. Walter White sent a copy of the book to Truman with a note: "You will enjoy and profit from this."

33. Clifford memo; Bernstein, "Ambiguous Legacy," 287–88.

34. Clark Clifford Oral History, Feb. 14, 1973, p. 232, Truman Library.

35. Clifford memo.

36. Ibid.; Wilkins, *Standing Fast,* 200; Martin Bauml Duberman, *Paul Robeson* (New York: Knopf, 1988), 325–27.

37. Memo for Clark Clifford, n.d., in Feb. 2, 1948, Civil Rights Message, Box 20, Elsey Papers.

38. Truman, *Public Papers 1948,* 122; Clifford, *Counsel,* 204.

39. Gilbert C. Fite, *Richard B. Russell, Jr.: Senator from Georgia* (Chapel Hill: University of North Carolina Press, 1991), 231; press release, Democratic National Committee, Feb. 23, 1948, Governors Conference, Box 26, J. Howard McGrath Papers, Truman Library.

40. *Des Moines Register,* Sept. 4, 1983; diary entries, March 17 and 18, 1948, Eben Ayers Papers, Truman Library. For FBI letters to the White House on Wallace, see Hoover to Vaughan, Oct. 23, 1946, June 25, July 31, Aug. 18, and Dec. 19, 1947, and Jan. 27, 1948, FBI W, PSF, Truman Papers; Hoover to Vaughan, Jan. 19 and 27, and March 16, 1948, FBI Communist Data, PSF, ibid.; Hoover to George Allen, Sept. 20 and 25, 1946, and March 18, 1947, FBI Communist Data, PSF, ibid.; Hoover to Vaughan, March 3, 1948, FBI S, PSF, ibid.; Hoover to Vaughan, March 11, 1948, FBI Personal, PSF, ibid.; Hoover to Vaughan, April 3, 1947, FBI P, PSF, ibid.; Hoover to Allen, Sept. 20, 1946, FBI Argentina, PSF, ibid.; Hoover to Allen, Sept. 23, 1946, FBI N, PSF, ibid.; Hoover to Tom Clark, Feb. 12, 1948, Justice Dept. (1), CF, ibid.

41. Executive Committee Minutes, March 18, 1948, Series 2, Box 36, Americans for Democratic Action Papers, State Historical Society of Wisconsin, Madison. Biddle is quoted in U.S., House, Select Committee on Lobbying, *Hearings on Lobbying, Direct and Indirect,* pt. 6, *Americans for Democratic Action,* 81st Cong., 2d sess., 1950, p. 12.

42. Hubert H. Humphrey, *The Education of a Public Man* (Garden City, N.Y.: Doubleday, 1976), 111; Joseph L. Rauh, Jr., Oral History, Jan. 31, 1978, pp. 25–26, Eleanor Roosevelt Oral History Project, Franklin D. Roosevelt Library, Hyde Park, N.Y.

43. Walter Millis, ed., *The Forrestal Diaries* (New York: Viking, 1951), 458; Harold Brayman, *The President Speaks Off-the-Record: From Grover Cleveland to Gerald Ford* (Princeton, N.J.: Dow Jones Books, 1976), 454.

44. Steven J. Diner, "From Jim Crow to Home Rule," *Wilsonian Quarterly* 13(New Year's 1989): 92; Brian Urquhart, *Ralph Bunche: An American Life* (New York: Norton, 1993), 109.

45. Transcript, re Meeting with the President, Jan. 12, 1949, Box 2, President's Committee on the Equality of Treatment and Opportunity in the Armed Forces Papers, Truman Library; Richard M. Dalfiume, *Desegregation of the U.S. Armed Forces: Fighting on Two Fronts, 1939–1953* (Columbia: University of Missouri Press, 1969); President's Committee on Equality of Treatment and Opportunity in the Armed Forces, *Freedom to Serve* (Washington, D.C.: Government Printing Office, 1950).

46. Clifford to Truman, April 19, 1948, Segregation in Armed Forces, Box 16, Clifford Papers.

47. Walter White to All NAACP Branch Presidents, Feb. 21, 1949, Walter White, Box 60, McGrath Papers; White to McGrath, March 15, 1949, ibid.; Duberman, *Paul Robeson*, 334.

48. *New York Times*, Nov. 16, 1957; *Shelley v. Kraemer*, 334 U.S. 1 (1948); *Sweatt v. Painter*, 399 U.S. 629 (1950); *McLaurin v. Oklahoma Board of Regents*, 339 U.S. 637 (1950).

49. See Thomas Borstelmann, *Apartheid's Reluctant Uncle: The United States and Southern Africa in the Early Cold War Years* (New York: Oxford University Press, 1993).

50. Roy Wilkins to White, July 21, 1950, Communism, Box 22, Roy Wilkins Papers, Library of Congress, Washington, D.C.; Thurgood Marshall to Spingarn, June 16, 1950, Civil Rights—Thurgood Marshall, Spingarn Files, Truman Papers.

51. Mary L. Dudziak, "Civil Rights as Cold War Imperative," *Stanford Law Review* 41(Nov. 1988): 80–93.

52. Staff Meetings, June 27, 1952, SMOF, Psychological Strategy Board Files, Truman Papers.

53. See the State Department documents in Communism/Anti-Communist Propaganda Films, Series 7, Box 8, Alexander Wiley Papers, State Historical Society of Wisconsin.

54. George M. Elsey Oral History, July 10, 1970, p. 450, Truman Library.

55. See the voluminous correspondence in Misc. Documents—Civil Rights, Box 68, Stephen J. Spingarn Papers, Truman Library.

56. Jonathan Daniels Oral History, Oct. 4–5, 1963, p. 137, Truman Library; David McCullough, *Truman* (New York: Simon and Schuster, 1992), 588; Ferrell, *Truman*, 296; Wilkins, *Standing Fast*, 192, 203.

57. Matthew J. Connelly Oral History, Aug. 21, 1968, p. 439, Truman Library; Bernstein, "Ambiguous Legacy," 302.

58. Brayman, *The President Speaks*, 454.

59. Clark Clifford, "The Truman Years," *New Yorker*, April 11, 1991, p. 60.

60. Wilkins, *Standing Fast*, 212; memo, re Items for Eisenhower Interview, Aug. 26, 1952, Wilkins Papers.

61. E. Frederic Morrow Oral History, Jan. 31, 1968, p. 14, Dwight D. Eisenhower Library, Abilene, Kan.; press release, Oct. 2, 1952, Aboard the Eisenhower Train, Box 1, E. Frederic Morrow Papers, Eisenhower Library; Morrow to Sherman Adams, Sept. 20, 1952, ibid.; E. Frederic Morrow, *Forty Years a Guinea Pig* (New York: Pilgrim Press, 1980), 86, 89–90.

62. Morrow to File, n.d. [ca. Nov. 2, 1952], Aboard the Eisenhower Campaign Train, Box 1, Morrow Papers.

63. Morrow Oral History, 2–4, 62; Morrow, *Forty Years*, 92, and *Black Man in the White House* (New York: Coward-McCann, 1963), 11–13.

64. Lillian Rogers Parks, *My Thirty Years Backstairs at the White House* (New York: Fleet Publishing, 1961), 313; telephone message, Herbert Brownell to Sherman Adams, Jan. 3, 1953, OF 142-A, WHCF, Dwight D. Eisenhower Papers, Eisenhower Library; Maxwell M. Rabb to Adams, June 20, 1956, OF138-A–6, WHCF, ibid.; Rabb to Eisenhower, Aug. 16, 1954, Whitman File (Diary), ibid.; Dwight D. Eisenhower, *Waging Peace, 1956–1961: The White House Years* (Garden City, N.Y.: Doubleday, 1965), 149.

65. Memo, re Appointment with Adam Clayton Powell, May 11, 1955, Whitman File (Diary), Eisenhower Papers; memo, re Telephone Conversation with Leonard Hall, May 6, 1953, Telephone Calls Series, Box 7, John Foster Dulles Papers, Eisenhower Library. See also Michael L. Krenn, "'Outstanding Negroes' and 'Appropriate Countries': Some Facts, Figures, and Thoughts on Black U.S. Ambassadors, 1949–1988," *Diplomatic History* 14(Winter 1990): 131–41.

66. Charles P. Henry, "Civil Rights and National Security: The Case of Ralph Bunche," in *Ralph Bunche: The Man and His Times*, ed. Benjamin Rivlin (New York: Holmes and Meier, 1990), 50–60; Alan H. Belmont to Leland V. Boardman, Feb. 15, 1956, no. 61-3176-1241, FBI-NAACP File.

67. Morrow to James Hagerty, April 29, 1957, Civil Rights—Office Memoranda, E. Frederic Morrow Files, Eisenhower Papers.

68. Memorandum for the Record, Aug. 19, 1953, Brownell 1952–54 (6), Whitman File (Administration), Eisenhower Papers; Herbert Brownell, *Advising Ike* (Lawrence: University Press of Kansas, 1993), 190; Robert

F. Burk, *The Eisenhower Administration and Black Civil Rights* (Knoxville: University of Tennessee Press, 1984), 134.

69. Diary entry, July 24, 1953, Whitman File (Diary), Eisenhower Papers.

70. Eisenhower to James F. Byrnes, Dec. 1, 1953, Byrnes (1), Whitman File (Names), ibid.

71. Diary entry, March 21, 1956, Whitman File (Diary), ibid.

72. Diary entries, March 21 and Aug. 19, 1956, Whitman File (Diary), ibid.; Robert Griffith, "Dwight D. Eisenhower and the Corporate Commonwealth," *American Historical Review* 87(Feb. 1982): 116.

73. Sherman Adams, *Firsthand Report: The Story of the Eisenhower Administration* (New York: Harper and Brothers, 1961), 338.

74. Gerald Horne, *Black & Red: W. E. B. Du Bois and the Afro-American Response to the Cold War, 1944–1963* (Albany: State University of New York Press, 1986), 187; Cabinet meeting minutes, March 23, 1956, Whitman File (Cabinet), Eisenhower Papers.

75. Burk, *Eisenhower Administration*, 160; Taylor Branch, *Parting the Waters: America in the King Years, 1954–63* (New York: Simon and Schuster, 1988), 192n.

76. Diary entry, Nov. 14, 1956, Whitman File (Diary), Eisenhower Papers.

77. Burk, *Eisenhower Administration*, 84.

78. Eisenhower, *Waging Peace*, 152; Brownell, *Advising Ike*, 194; Belmont to Boardman, Sept. 26, 1955, no. 62–31615–941, FBI–Walter Winchell File; Director to Attorney General, Jan. 3, 1956, no. 61–3176-not recorded, FBI-NAACP File; Hoover to Dillon Anderson, Jan. 3, 1956, no. 61–3176-not recorded, ibid.

79. Maxwell M. Rabb to Dillon Anderson, Jan. 17, 1956, FBI L-N (3), Office of the Special Assistant for National Security Affairs, Eisenhower Papers.

80. "Racial Tensions and Civil Rights," March 1, 1956, Minutes of Cabinet Meeting, March 9, 1956, Whitman File (Cabinet), Eisenhower Papers.

81. Rabb to Brownell, March 9, 1956, Whitman File (Cabinet), ibid.

82. U.S., Senate, Select Committee to Study Governmental Operations with Respect to Intelligence Activities, *Final Report*, Book II, *Intelligence Activities and the Rights of Americans*, 94th Cong., 2d sess., 1976, pp. 51, 180. See also Hoover's letters to Dillon Anderson, in FBI L-N, Office of the Special Assistant for National Security Affairs, Eisenhower Papers.

83. Cabinet meeting minutes, March 9, 1956, Whitman File (Cabinet), Eisenhower Papers.

84. Rabb to Brownell, March 9, 1956, Whitman File (Cabinet), ibid.

85. Burk, *Eisenhower Administration*, 161–62. Clark is quoted in Kluger, *Simple Justice*, 950. For the Justice Department study, see J. Lee

Rankin to William J. Barba, Feb. 16, 1956, Integration Problems, Henry Roemer McPhee, Jr., Files, Eisenhower Papers; Barba to Gerald D. Morgan, Feb. 8, 1956, Integration Problems, McPhee Files, ibid.

86. Diary entry, March 20, 1956, Whitman File (Diary), Eisenhower Papers; Eisenhower to Billy Graham, March 22 and 30, 1956, Whitman File (Name), ibid.; Graham to Eisenhower, March 27 and June 4, 1956, Whitman File (Name), ibid.

87. Morrow to Rabb, Jan. 5, 1956, Civil Rights—Official Memoranda, Morrow Files, ibid.; Rabb to Adams, March 1, 1956, Civil Rights (3), Gerald Morgan Files, ibid.

88. Bryce N. Harlow to Adams, Dec. 1, 1955, Racial Affairs, WHCF, CF, ibid.

89. Diary entry, Nov. 13, 1956, Whitman File (Diary), ibid.

90. Diary entry, Aug. 20, 1956, Whitman File (Diary), ibid.; Brownell, *Advising Ike*, 197.

91. Morrow, *Black Man*, 67; Branch, *Parting the Waters*, 191.

92. Walter Johnson, ed., *The Papers of Adlai E. Stevenson*, 8 vols. (Boston: Little, Brown, 1972–1979), 6: 66–67, 73; Branch, *Parting the Waters*, 192.

93. Powell, *Adam*, 95–101; Herbert S. Parmet, *Eisenhower and the American Crusades* (New York: Macmillan, 1972), 506–07. See also the correspondence in Powell Alpha File and OF142-A–1, WHCF, Eisenhower Papers. For Powell's relationship with the administration in general, see Charles V. Hamilton, *Adam Clayton Powell, Jr.* (New York: Atheneum, 1991), 199–223, 266–81.

94. Branch, *Parting the Waters*, 216–17; Rabb to Jack Toner, May 16, 1957, GF124-A–1, WHCF, Eisenhower Papers.

95. Branch, *Parting the Waters*, 213.

96. Ibid., 218–19; David J. Garrow, *Bearing the Cross: Martin Luther King, Jr., and the Southern Christian Leadership Conference* (New York: Morrow, 1986), 119.

97. Quoted in Rabb to Adams, June 24, 1957, OF142-A, WHCF, Eisenhower Papers.

98. Phone call, July 3, 1957, Diary, ibid.; Morrow to Adams, July 12, 1957, Civil Rights Bill, Morrow Files, ibid.

99. Legislative leadership meeting, July 30, 1957, Whitman File (Diary), ibid.

100. Diary entry, Aug. 2, 1957, ibid.; Burk, *Eisenhower Administration*, 172; Dwight D. Eisenhower Oral History, July 13, 1967, p. 28, Eisenhower Library. For LBJ's role, see Robert Dallek, *Lone Star Rising* (New York: Oxford University Press, 1991), 517–28.

101. Eisenhower to Everett E. Hazlett, July 22, 1957, Diary, Eisenhower Papers.

102. Quoted in Bryce Harlow to Eisenhower, Aug. 27, 1957, Whitman File (Diary), ibid.

103. Burk, *Eisenhower Administration*, 173; Henry Hampton and Steve Fayer, *Voices of Freedom: An Oral History of the Civil Rights Movement* (New York: Bantam, 1990), 47.

104. Thurgood Marshall to Eisenhower, Sept. 6, 1957, Group IIIA, Box 113, NAACP Papers, Library of Congress; telephone call, Sept. 24, 1957, Box 7, Telephone Calls Series, Dulles Papers. See also the USIA report, "Public Reactions to Little Rock in Major World Capitals," Oct. 29, 1957, in Little Rock, Morrow Files, Eisenhower Papers.

105. Telephone call, Sept. 11, 1957, Diary, Eisenhower Papers; Wilkins, *Standing Fast*, 252.

106. Notes, re Faubus visit, Oct. 8, 1957, Whitman File (Diary), Eisenhower Papers; Orval Faubus Oral History, Aug. 18, 1971, pp. 41, 52–53, Eisenhower Library

107. Adams, *Firsthand Report*, 355; Louis B. Nichols to Clyde Tolson, Oct. 16, 1957, no. 94-4-3169-62, FBI-David Lawrence File; telephone calls, Sept. 20 and 24, 1957, Diary, Eisenhower Papers; diary entry, Oct. 2, 1957, Whitman File (Diary), ibid.

108. Herbert Brownell Oral History, Jan. 31, 1968, pp. 214–15, Eisenhower Library; Allan Shivers Oral History, Dec. 23, 1969, p. 49, ibid.; Eisenhower, *Waging Peace*, 175. Neither the Cold War analogy nor the law-and-order analogy held up. Truman's secretary of state, Dean Acheson, said "the lessons of Little Rock" lay squarely on the shoulders of "a weak President who fiddles along ineffectually until a personal affront drives him to unexpectedly drastic action. A Little Rock with Moscow and the SAC in the place of paratroopers could blow us all apart." Acheson to Truman, Oct. 8, 1957, Acheson-Truman Corr., Box 166, Dean Acheson Papers, Truman Library.

109. Wilkins to Powell, Sept. 19, 1957, Group IIIA, Box 113, NAACP Papers; Wilkins, *Standing Fast*, 251.

110. Val J. Washington to Adams, Oct. 16, 1957, OF 142-A, Eisenhower Papers.

111. Rocco C. Siciliano to File, June 24, 1958, Diary, ibid.; Siciliano to Eisenhower, June 25, 1958, Diary, ibid.; Morrow to Adams, Aug. 21, 1958, Civil Rights—Official Memoranda, Morrow Files, ibid.; Wilkins, *Standing Fast*, 255–56; Garrow, *Bearing the Cross*, 107, 119.

112. Morrow, *Black Man*, 199; Howard Smead, *Blood Justice: The Lynching of Mack Charles Parker* (New York: Oxford University Press, 1986), 121, 169.

113. Clayborne Carson, *In Struggle: SNCC and the Black Awakening of the 1960s* (Cambridge, Mass.: Harvard University Press, 1981), 14; Burk, *Eisenhower Administration*, 198; Arthur M. Schlesinger, Jr., *Robert Kennedy and His Times* (Boston: Houghton Mifflin/Book Club ed., 1978), 303; Morrow Oral History, 23; Truman to Edward M. Turner and Arthur L. Johnson, March 24, 1960, General 1960, Post-Pres. Speech File, Truman Papers. For the legislation, see Daniel C. Berman, *A Bill Becomes a Law* (New York: Macmillan, 1962).

114. Milton S. Katz, "E. Frederic Morrow and Civil Rights in the Eisenhower Administration," *Phylon* 42(June 1981): 143; Morrow, *Forty Years*, 2, 4, 186; Morrow Oral History, 8, 41.

115. Rabb to Governor Pyle, Aug. 8, 1955, OF142-A-4, Eisenhower Papers; "Advances in the Field of Equal Opportunity During the Eisenhower Administration," n.d. [ca. January 1960], Civil Rights (2), Gerald Morgan Files, ibid.; Siciliano to Gerald Morgan, Dec. 18, 1955, Civil Rights (1), Morgan Files, ibid.; Maxwell Rabb Oral History, Oct. 6, 1970, p. 32, Eisenhower Library.

116. Memo for the Record, Aug. 22, 1958, Rogers 1958 (3), Whitman File (Administration), Eisenhower Papers; Eisenhower to Ralph McGill, Sept. 3, 1958, OF142-A-5, ibid.

117. Eisenhower Oral History, 31.

118. See the note scribbled on H. L. T. Tawell to Eisenhower, Nov. 15, 1966, Clifford Roberts, 1963–66 (1), Post-Pres. (Special Names), Eisenhower Papers.

Chapter 5. Tough Guy

1. John F. Kennedy, *Profiles in Courage* (New York: Harper and Row, 1956), 131, 152–53, 161.

2. Carl M. Brauer, *John F. Kennedy and the Second Reconstruction* (New York: Columbia University Press, 1977).

3. Theodore Hesburgh Oral History, March 27, 1966, p. 21, John F. Kennedy Library, Boston, Mass.

4. Edwin O. Guthman and Jeffrey Shulman, eds., *Robert Kennedy: In His Own Words* (New York: Bantam, 1988), xv. The editors reprint Anthony Lewis's interviews with Robert Kennedy and Burke Marshall (New York/Dec. 4, 1964, and McLean, Va./Dec. 6 and 22, 1964) located in the Kennedy Library. For the reader's convenience all citations will be to the published volume.

5. Ibid., 67–68; Joshua A. Guberman to John F. Kennedy et al., n.d. [ca. Fall 1952], Issues and Speeches—Civil Rights, Pre-Pres. Campaign Files, John F. Kennedy Papers, Kennedy Library.

6. Roy Wilkins Oral History, April 1, 1969, p. 3, Lyndon B. Johnson Library, Austin, Tex.; John Kennedy to Roy Wilkins, May 6, June 6, and July 18, 1958, Group IIIA, Box A176, NAACP Papers, Library of Congress, Washington, D.C.; Wilkins to John Kennedy, May 29, 1958, ibid.; Arthur M. Schlesinger, Jr., *Robert Kennedy and His Times* (book club ed.; Boston: Houghton Mifflin, 1978), 224; Roy Wilkins, with Tom Mathews, *Standing Fast* (New York: Penguin ed., 1984), 264.

7. Belford V. Lawson Oral History, Jan. 11, 1966, pp. 1–2, 7, Kennedy Library; Simeon Booker Oral History, April 24, 1967, pp. 1–2, ibid.

8. Lawson Oral History, 5; John H. Johnson, with Lerone Bennett, Jr., *Succeeding Against the Odds* (New York: Warner Books, 1989), 270–71.

9. Booker Oral History, 2.

10. Ibid., 1; Schlesinger, *Robert Kennedy*, 225; Thurgood Marshall Oral History, April 7, 1964, p. 1, Kennedy Library; Lawson Oral History, 4, 8.

11. Taylor Branch, *Parting the Waters: America in the King Years, 1954–63* (New York: Simon and Schuster, 1988), 306–08.

12. Ibid., 314; Martin Luther King, Jr., Oral History, March 9, 1964, pp. 1, 3, 6, Kennedy Library.

13. Guthman, ed., *Robert Kennedy*, 72; Anthony K. Shriver, "Kennedy's Call to King: Six Perspectives," 18, Oral History Collection, Kennedy Library; Branch, *Parting the Waters*, 343; Nicholas Lemann, *The Promised Land* (New York: Knopf, 1991), 114.

14. Wil Haygood, *King of the Cats: The Life and Times of Adam Clayton Powell, Jr.* (Boston: Houghton Mifflin, 1993), 272.

15. Guthman, ed., *Robert Kennedy*, 47; Shriver, "Kennedy's Call," 16; Branch, *Parting the Waters*, 341–43; Louis Martin Oral History, March 25, 1970, p. 5, Ralph J. Bunche Oral History Collection, Moorland-Spingarn Research Center, Howard University, Washington, D.C. The Kennedy campaign overestimated Dawson's influence in the first place. William J. Grimshaw, *Bitter Fruit: Black Politics and the Chicago Machine, 1931–1991* (Chicago: University of Chicago Press, 1992), x–xi, 81–86.

16. Lawson Oral History, 3, 12, 21. Wofford is quoted in Shriver, "Kennedy's Call," 81–82.

17. Booker Oral History, 6.

18. Ibid., 7; Thurgood Marshall Oral History, 9; Branch, *Parting the Waters*, 317; Shriver, "Kennedy's Call," 37, 82; Harris Wofford, *Of Kennedys and Kings* (New York: Farrar, Straus and Giroux, 1980), 47.

19. Branch, *Parting the Waters*, 342; Lemann, *Promised Land*, 114; Guthman, ed., *Robert Kennedy*, 72, 78. Martin is quoted in Gerald S. Strober and Deborah H. Strober, *"Let Us Begin Anew": An Oral History of the Kennedy Presidency* (New York: HarperCollins, 1993), 26, 43.

20. Lemann, *Promised Land*, 115; Shriver, "Kennedy's Call," 33.

21. E. Frederic Morrow Oral History, Feb. 23, 1977, p. 8, Dwight D. Eisenhower Library, Abilene, Ka.; John C. Calhoun Oral History, May 23, 1968, p. 57, Bunche Collection; Branch, *Parting the Waters*, 346–47; Richard M. Nixon, *Six Crises* (New York: Pocket Books ed., 1962), 350–51, 362–63, 377–78; Julie Nixon Eisenhower, *Pat Nixon* (New York: Simon and Schuster, 1986), 193.

22. G. Gordon Liddy, *Will* (New York: St. Martin's Press, 1980), 88–89.

23. Nixon, *Six Crises*, 435.

24. Theodore H. White, *The Making of the President 1960* (New York: Atheneum, 1961), 354; Harris Wofford to John Kennedy, Dec. 30, 1960, Political—1960 Campaign, Pre-Admin., Box 52, Robert F. Kennedy Papers, Kennedy Library; Richard D. Mahoney, *JFK: Ordeal in Africa* (New York: Oxford University Press, 1983), 30–31.

25. White, *Making of the President 1960*, 203–04, 360; Nixon, *Six Crises*, 325, 350; Branch, *Parting the Waters*, 321.

26. White, *Making of the President 1960*, 203.

27. Wilkins to John Kennedy, Nov. 17, 1960, Group IIIA, Box 176, NAACP Papers; Guthman, ed., *Robert Kennedy*, 42, 74.

28. Theodore Hesburgh Oral History, 4; Wilkins Oral History, 6.

29. Joseph L. Rauh, Jr., Oral History, Dec. 23, 1965, p. 106, Kennedy Library; Wilkins Oral History, 7.

30. Ralph A. Dungan to John Kennedy, March 4, 1963, Subjects—Civil Rights General, Pres. Office File, JFK Papers; notes, dictated by the President, Feb. 8, 1961, Staff Memoranda—Sorensen, Pres. Office File, ibid.; Guthman, ed., *Robert Kennedy*, 53; Brauer, *John F. Kennedy*, 319.

31. Memo, re Contributions of the Department of State to Progress in Civil Rights, n.d. [ca. Nov. 1, 1961], Civil Rights Progress File, WHSF—Harris Wofford, JFK Papers; Frederick Dutton to John Kennedy, Nov. 3, 1961, HU2/St20, WHCF—Subject Files, ibid.; Herman Pollock to Wofford, n.d. [ca. Dec. 1, 1961], HU2/St20, WHCF—Subject Files, ibid.; Dean Rusk, *As I Saw It* (New York: Norton, 1990), 581–83.

32. Wilkins Oral History, 14; Victor S. Navasky, *Kennedy Justice* (New York: Atheneum, 1971), 97.

33. Guthman, ed., *Robert Kennedy*, 154–55; Wofford, *Kennedys and Kings*, 124.

34. Theodore C. Sorensen, *Kennedy* (New York: Harper and Row, 1965), 481–82.

35. Wilkins Oral History, 4; Guthman, ed., *Robert Kennedy*, 149.

36. Martin Oral History, 25, 27; Richard Goodwin, *Remembering America* (Boston: Little, Brown, 1988), 311; Louis Martin to Theodore

Sorensen, May 10, 1961, Subject—Civil Rights, Box 30, Theodore Sorensen Papers, Kennedy Library; Sorensen, *Kennedy*, 476.

37. Wilkins Oral History, 11; Wilkins to Wofford, April 5, 1961, Alpha—Roy Wilkins, WHSF—Harris Wofford, JFK Papers.

38. Guthman, ed., *Robert Kennedy*, 102; telephone conversation, JFK and James H. Davis, June 3, 1963, Item 21A, Pres. Recordings (Logs and Transcripts), Pres. Office File, JFK Papers.

39. Interview (phone), John Seigenthaler, Jan. 16, 1987.

40. Guthman, ed., *Robert Kennedy*, 77.

41. Ibid., 57, 78–79.

42. Wofford to John Kennedy, March 7, 1962, Staff Memoranda—Wofford, Pres. Office File, JFK Papers.

43. Quoted in Ovid Demaris, *The Director: An Oral Biography of J. Edgar Hoover* (New York: Harper's Magazine Press, 1975), 186.

44. Interview, David Norman, Nov. 19, 1975, Box 1, Scott J. Rafferty Papers, Kennedy Library.

45. Theodore Hesburgh, with Jerry Reedy, *God, Country, Notre Dame* (Garden City, N.Y.: Doubleday, 1990), 193; Hesburgh Oral History, 11; interview, William L. Taylor, July 18, 1986, Washington, D.C.; Berl Bernhard Oral History, June 17, 1968, p. 32, Kennedy Library. See also Foster Rhea Dulles, *The Civil Rights Commission: 1957–1965* (East Lansing: Michigan State University Press, 1968).

46. Wofford, *Kennedys and Kings*, 161; interview, Berl Bernhard, July 23, 1986, Washington, D.C; Guthman, ed., *Robert Kennedy*, 77–78.

47. Navasky, *Kennedy Justice*, 110; Bernhard interview.

48. Bernhard and Taylor interviews; Bernhard Oral History, 52.

49. Virginia Durr Oral History, March 1, 1975, p. 37, Lyndon B. Johnson Library, Austin, Tex.; Norman interview; Wilkins, *Standing Fast*, 284; Guthman, ed., *Robert Kennedy*, 72; Wilkins to John Kennedy, June 22, 1961, Group IIIA, Box 176, NAACP Papers; Burke Marshall Oral History, Jan. 19–20, 1970, p. 18, Kennedy Library. LBJ is quoted in Schlesinger, *Robert Kennedy*, 244.

50. Guthman, ed., *Robert Kennedy*, 115–16.

51. Ibid.; Clark Clifford, *Counsel to the President* (New York: Random House, 1991), 374–75; FBI Director to Attorney General, April 2, 1962, no. 100–392452-not recorded, FBI–Stanley Levison File, J. Edgar Hoover FBI Building, Washington, D.C.

52. Guthman, ed., *Robert Kennedy*, 105–06.

53. Ibid., 173.

54. Quoted in Kenneth O'Reilly, *"Racial Matters:" The FBI's Secret File on Black America, 1960–1972* (New York: Free Press, 1989), 1. For

Hamer's story, see Kay Mills, *This Little Light of Mine* (New York: Dutton, 1993).

55. Guthman, ed., *Robert Kennedy*, 196–97. See also Eric R. Burner, *And Gently He Shall Lead Them: Robert Parris Moses and Civil Rights in Mississippi* (New York: New York University Press, 1994).

56. Clayborne Carson, *In Struggle: SNCC and the Black Awakening of the 1960s* (Cambridge, Mass.: Harvard University Press, 1981), 13; Wofford, *Kennedys and Kings*, 181.

57. 328 U.S. 373 (1946); 364 U.S. 454 (1960).

58. Howell Raines, *My Soul Is Rested: Movement Days in the Deep South Remembered* (New York: G. P. Putnam's Sons, 1977), 109–10; Wilkins, *Standing Fast*, 283. See also August Meier and Elliott Rudwick, "The First Freedom Ride," *Phylon* 30(Fall 1969): 213–22.

59. Branch, *Parting the Waters*, 414.

60. Guthman, ed., *Robert Kennedy*, 82–83; Wilkins, *Standing Fast*, 283. Katzenbach is quoted in Strober, *Let Us Begin Anew*, 294.

61. Booker Oral History, 22.

62. Guthman, ed., *Robert Kennedy*, 91; Wofford, *Kennedys and Kings*, 153; Strober, *Let Us Begin Anew*, 301.

63. Clement L. McGowan to Alex Rosen, May 18, 1961, no. 100-225892-268, FBI-CORE File.

64. Marshall Oral History, 7; Guthman, ed., *Robert Kennedy*, 99; Branch, *Parting the Waters*, 433.

65. For Hoover's account, see Milton A. Jones to Cartha D. DeLoach, Dec. 2, 1964, no. 77-68662-126, FBI–Don Whitehead File; Hoover to Clyde Tolson, John P. Mohr, and DeLoach, Dec. 8, 1964, no. 94-4-3169-127, FBI-David Lawrence File.

66. Guthman, ed., *Robert Kennedy*, 93.

67. Ibid., 87. Shuttlesworth and Doar are quoted in Wofford, *Kennedys and Kings*, 153, 154.

68. Carson, *In Struggle*, 38; Guthman, ed., *Robert Kennedy*, 101.

69. Guthman, ed., *Robert Kennedy*, 101–102.

70. "It's a political issue with them [the GOP], as far as I can make out," Marshall speculated, "because Franklin Roosevelt put so much legislation on the commerce clause that they just never forgot it." Burke Marshall Oral History, 5.

71. Edwin O. Guthman, *We Band of Brothers* (New York: Harper and Row, 1971), 176.

72. Justice Dept. Press Release, Dec. 29, 1961, Subjects—Civil Rights General, Pres. Office File, JFK Papers.

73. Guthman, ed., *Robert Kennedy*, 159; Schlesinger, *Robert Kennedy*, 331.

74. Guthman, ed., *Robert Kennedy*, 195–96; Strober, *Let Us Begin Anew*, 303.

75. Burke Marshall, *Federalism and Civil Rights*, foreword by Robert F. Kennedy (New York: Columbia University Press, 1964), vii.

76. Guthman, ed., *Robert Kennedy*, 160, 162; Nicholas deB. Katzenbach Oral History, Nov. 16, 1964, p. 17, Kennedy Library. For "don't worry," see Raines, *My Soul Is Rested*, 339.

77. Strober, *Let Us Begin Anew*, 307.

78. *Public Papers of the Presidents of the United States: John F. Kennedy, 1963* (Washington, D.C.: Government Printing Office, 1964), 221–30; James Silver to Arthur M. Schlesinger, Jr., Jan. 16 and 23, 1963, Subject—Mississippi, WH15, Arthur M. Schlesinger, Jr., Papers, Kennedy Library; Silver to Schlesinger, Jan. 7, 1962, ibid.; Schlesinger to Robert Kennedy, Jan. 9, 17, and 26, 1963, ibid.

79. White House meeting, Sept. 30, 1962, Audiotape 26A1, Int. of the Univ. of Miss., Pres. Recordings (Transcripts), Pres. Office File, JFK Papers; Guthman, ed., *Robert Kennedy*, 165–66, 422–23.

80. Guthman, ed., *Robert Kennedy*, 161; Sorensen to John Kennedy, Sept. 28, 1962, Subjects—Civil Rights/Mississippi, Pres. Office File, JFK Papers. Jones is quoted in Schlesinger, *Robert Kennedy*, 340.

81. Katzenbach to Robert Kennedy, June 29, 1963, Civil Rights Legislation, Attorney General's Corr. File, Box 1, RFK Papers. The effort was not productive. "The Freedom Rides made it clear . . . that events could not be controlled, managed, or timed," Marshall said many years later. "So in that sense, things were out of control." Strober, *Let Us Begin Anew*, 299.

82. White House meetings, May 21 and June 1, 1963, Audiotapes 88.6 and 90.3, Civil Rights 1963, Pres. Recordings, Pres. Office File, JFK Papers; Sorensen to John Kennedy, May 7, 1963, Staff Memoranda—Sorensen, Pres. Office File, ibid.; Wilkins, *Standing Fast*, 291; Sorensen, *Kennedy*, 489. For the commissioner, see William A. Nunnelley, *Bull Connor* (Tuscaloosa: University of Alabama Press, 1991).

83. Sorensen to John Kennedy, May 7, 1963, Staff Memoranda—Sorensen, Pres. Office File, JFK Papers; White House meeting, May 20, 1963, Audiotape 88.4, Civil Rights 1963, Pres. Recordings, Pres. Office File, ibid.

84. Strober, *Let Us Begin Anew*, 289.

85. Branch, *Parting the Waters*, 788–89.

86. White House meeting, May 12, 1963, Audiotape 86.2, Civil Rights 1963, Pres. Recordings, Pres. Office File, JFK Papers.

87. Pierre Salinger memo, re Summary of Conversation, May 8, 1963, Subjects—Civil Rights/Alabama, Pres. Office File, ibid.; George Wallace, *Stand Up For America* (Garden City, N.Y.: Doubleday, 1976), 75, 77.

88. Interview (phone), Kenneth B. Clark, April 8, 1987. See also the newspaper clippings in FBI-James Baldwin File (100-108763-A).

89. Theodore R. Newman, Jr., to Burke Marshall, May 28, 1962, Subject File—Committee of Inquiry, Box 31, Burke Marshall Papers; Ralph P. Mills to Marshall, June 7, 1963, Special Corr.—Attorney General, Box 8, ibid.; Clarence Jones to Editor, *New York Times*, June 7, 1963, Special Corr.—Attorney General, Box 8, ibid.; [name deleted] to Alex Rosen, Sept. 24 and 29, 1963, no. 62–108763–3 and –5, FBI–Baldwin File. In the aftermath of the Baldwin meeting, Robert Kennedy was amazed that "Lorraine Hansberry's friends," with "her last play . . . a failure," would send "me a telegram to help save her play." With no hesitation he wrote the plug, and the Hansberry partisans ran it in the *New York Times*. Guthman, ed., *Robert Kennedy*, 226.

90. White House meeting, May 20, 1963, Audiotape 88.4, Civil Rights 1963, Pres. Recordings, Pres. Office File, JFK Papers; Richard Reeves, *President Kennedy: Profile of Power* (New York: Simon and Schuster, 1993), 506; Guthman, ed., *Robert Kennedy*, 199, 225; *New York Post*, May 28, 1963; Navasky, *Kennedy Justice*, 112–15; Schlesinger, *Robert Kennedy*, 344–48; Wofford, *Kennedys and Kings*, 224. "I think Bobby also sensed that most of the blacks were on the make themselves," Louis Martin added. "They were looking for a place in the sun. He was thinking of them like the Boston Irish in the old days—like Honey Fitz—they were always scrambling." Strober, *Let Us Begin Anew*, 291.

91. Raines, *My Soul Is Rested*, 342. See also E. Culpepper Clark, *The Schoolhouse Door: Segregation's Last Stand at the University of Alabama* (New York: Oxford University Press, 1993).

92. Burke Marshall Oral History, Feb. 27, 1980, p. 17, Bunche Collection; Guthman, ed., *Robert Kennedy*, 211; Burke Marshall to Robert Kennedy, June 26, 1963, Univ. of Alabama, Attorney General's Corr. File, Box 10, RFK Papers.

93. Telephone conversation, JFK and Carl Albert, June 12, 1963, Item 22A2, Pres. Recordings (Logs and Transcripts), Pres. Office File, JFK Papers; Wilkins, *Standing Fast*, 290; Branch, *Parting the Waters*, 833; Chuck Daly to Lawrence F. O'Brien, June 14, 1963, Subject—Civil Rights, Box 30, Sorensen Papers. Evers's murderer was finally convicted in 1994 and sentenced to life in prison.

94. For the FBI's approving analysis of RFK's position, see Jones to DeLoach, June 24, 1963, no. 77–51387–406, FBI–Robert F. Kennedy File.

95. White House meeting, May 20, 1963, Audiotape 88.4, Civil Rights 1963, Pres. Recordings, Pres. Office File, JFK Papers; Roger Wilkins, *A Man's Life* (New York: Simon and Schuster, 1982), 290. Wilkins was at the breaking point even before King arrived on the scene. Bayard Rustin

said A. Philip Randolph "refuses to raise money. He always jokes and says, 'Well, you can raise the money. Don't worry.' Which means that we often left Roy Wilkins holding the bill." Bayard Rustin Oral History, June 17, 1969, p. 5, Johnson Library.

96. Telephone conversation, JFK and Davis, June 3, 1963, Item 21A, Pres. Recordings (Logs and Transcripts), Pres. Office File, JFK Papers. Harris Wofford sounded the alarm even before the inauguration. Wofford to John Kennedy, Dec. 30, 1960, Political—1960 Campaign, Pre-Administration, Box 52, RFK Papers.

97. Sorensen, *Kennedy*, 503.

98. Bernhard and William L. Taylor to Lee White, Feb. 21, 1963, Subject—Civil Rights, Box 30, Sorensen Papers; White House meeting, June 1, 1963, Audiotape 90.3, Civil Rights 1963, Pres. Recordings, Pres. Office File, JFK Papers; Rauh Oral History, 107; Schlesinger, *Robert Kennedy*, 361; Guthman, ed., *Robert Kennedy*, 171.

99. Guthman, ed., *Robert Kennedy*, 203–05.

100. Ibid., 23, 150–54, 177–78; Schlesinger, *Robert Kennedy*, 350.

101. Guthman, ed., *Robert Kennedy*, 46, 151–52, 411, 417; Hobart Taylor, Jr., Oral History, Jan. 6, 1969, p. 18, Johnson Library.

102. Schlesinger to Robert Kennedy, July 1, 1963, Depts. and Agencies—Justice, Pres. Office File, JFK Papers; Norbert A. Schlei to Kennedy, June 4, 1963, Civil Rights Legislation, Attorney General's Corr. File, Box 11, RFK Papers; dictaphone recording, June 3, 1963, Subject—Civil Rights, Box 30, Sorensen Papers.

103. Roy Wilkins shared this view. "For all his talk about the art of the possible, he didn't really know what was possible and what wasn't in Congress." *Standing Fast*, 296.

104. Telephone conversation, LBJ and Sorensen, June 3, 1963, Subject—Civil Rights, Box 30, Sorensen Papers.

105. Guthman, ed., *Robert Kennedy*, 176, 179, 202.

106. Ibid., 75–76; Guthman, *We Band of Brothers*, 222–23.

107. Guthman, ed., *Robert Kennedy*, 76, 392.

108. See the documents in the June Mail Folder, FBI–J. Edgar Hoover Official and Confidential File.

109. SAC Boston to FBI Director, Dec. 27, 1943, Joseph P. Kennedy Folder, FBI–Hoover Official and Confidential File. For the rose garden walk, see Schlesinger, *Robert Kennedy*, 372.

110. White House meeting, May 20, 1963, Audiotape 88.4, Civil Rights 1963, Pres. Recordings, Pres. Office File, JFK Papers; Schlesinger, *Robert Kennedy*, 373; Burke Marshall Oral History, 22. For Guthman, see U.S., Congress, Senate, Select Committee to Study Governmental Operations with Respect to Intelligence Activities, *Final Report*, Book

III, *Supplementary Detailed Staff Reports on Intelligence Activities and the Rights of Americans*, 94th Cong., 2d sess., 1976, p. 92.

111. Guthman, ed., *Robert Kennedy*, 141–43, 146.

112. Ibid., 143; White House meeting, May 20, 1963, Audiotape 88.4, Civil Rights 1963, Pres. Recordings, Pres. Office File, JFK Papers.

113. Guthman, ed., *Robert Kennedy*, 130, 146; *Time*, Aug. 17, 1962, pp. 118–19 (for Hoover as "my expert"); Katzenbach Oral History, 61.

114. Guthman, ed., *Robert Kennedy*, 134.

115. Garry Wills, "The Kennedys in the King Years," *New York Review of Books*, Nov. 10, 1988, p. 16.

116. Branch, *Parting the Waters*, 883; Guthman, ed., *Robert Kennedy*, 226–28; Strober, *Let Us Begin Anew*, 309; Schlesinger, *Robert Kennedy*, 364–65.

117. White House meeting, Sept. 23, 1963, Audiotape 113.1, Civil Rights 1963, Pres. Recordings, Pres. Office File, JFK Papers; O'Reilly, *Racial Matters*, 115–21.

118. Guthman, ed., *Robert Kennedy*, 228–29; Schlesinger, *Robert Kennedy*, 365–66; David J. Garrow, *Bearing the Cross* (New York: Morrow, 1986), 282–83.

119. White House meetings, Aug. 28 and Sept. 30, 1963, Audiotapes 108.2 and 113.2, Civil Rights 1963, Pres. Recordings, Pres. Office File, JFK Papers.

120. DeLoach to Mohr, Sept. 20, 1963, no. 157-1025-144, FBI-BAP-BOMB File; Courtney Evans to Alan H. Belmont, Sept. 30, 1963, no. 157-1025-337, ibid.; Birmingham Field Office Rept., Dec. 1, 1963, no. 157-1025-725, ibid.; Wills, "Kennedys in the King Years," 14–15.

121. Telephone conversation, JFK and Richard J. Daley, Oct. 28, 1963, Item 28A2, Pres. Recordings (Logs and Transcripts), Pres. Office File, JFK Papers; Schlesinger, *Robert Kennedy*, 299; Guthman, ed., *Robert F. Kennedy*, 197.

122. Wilkins Oral History, 12.

123. Garrow, *Bearing the Cross*, 220.

124. Guthman, ed., *Robert Kennedy*, 68–69, 71–72, 197, 230.

Chapter 6. Brave Knight

1. Strom Thurmond Oral History, May 7, 1979, p. 3, Lyndon B. Johnson Library, Austin, Tex.; John Lewis Oral History, Aug. 22, 1967, p. 131, Ralph J. Bunche Collection, Moorland-Spingarn Research Center, Howard University, Washington, D.C.; Clarence Mitchell Oral History, Dec. 11, 1968, pp. 66, 81, ibid. Malcolm is quoted in Richard Kluger, *Simple Justice* (New York: Knopf, 1975), 957.

2. Dictaphone recording, June 3, 1963, Subject—Civil Rights, Box 30, Theodore Sorensen Papers, John F. Kennedy Library, Boston, Mass.; Lee White Oral History, Sept. 28, 1970, p. 3, Johnson Library; John P. Roche Oral History, July 16, 1970, p. 41, ibid.; Richard M. Brown, *Strain of Violence* (New York: Oxford University Press, 1975), 294–95; Monroe Billington, "Lyndon B. Johnson and Blacks: The Early Years," *Journal of Negro History* 62 (Jan. 1977): 28–31; B. Joyce Ross, "Mary McLeod Bethune and the National Youth Administration," ibid., 60(Jan. 1975): 11–12.

3. Roy Wilkins, with Tom Mathews, *Standing Fast* (New York: Penguin ed., 1984), 243, 298; Roy Wilkins Oral History, April 1, 1969, p. 6, Johnson Library; Nicholas deB. Katzenbach Oral History, Nov. 11, 1968, p. 31, ibid.

4. Dictaphone recording, June 3, 1963, Subject—Civil Rights, Box 30, Sorensen Papers.

5. "Andrew Young," *Playboy*, July 1977, p. 75; A. Philip Randolph Oral History, Oct. 29, 1968, p. 11, Johnson Library; James Farmer Oral History, Oct. 1969, pp. 10–12, ibid.; David J. Garrow, *Bearing the Cross* (New York: Morrow, 1986), 308; Wilkins, *Standing Fast*, 294–95. See also the president's agenda in Civil Rights, White House Aides' Files—Robert Hardesty (Personal Files), Lyndon B. Johnson Papers, Johnson Library.

6. Robert C. Weaver Oral History, March 12, 1969, p. 9, Bunche Collection; Mitchell Oral History, 83; Whitney Young Oral History, June 18, 1969, p. 9, Johnson Library; Patrick J. Buchanan, *Right from the Beginning* (Boston: Little, Brown, 1988), 282–83; J. Edgar Hoover to Clyde Tolson, Cartha DeLoach, James H. Gale, William C. Sullivan, and Robert Wick, July 7, 1966, Folder 37, FBI–J. Edgar Hoover Official and Confidential File, J. Edgar Hoover FBI Building, Washington, D.C.

7. Edwin O. Guthman and Jeffrey Shulman, eds., *Robert Kennedy: In His Own Words* (New York: Bantam, 1988), 158, 381; Carl M. Brauer, "Kennedy, Johnson, and the War on Poverty," *Journal of American History* 69(June 1982): 105, 119; James T. Patterson, *America's Struggle Against Poverty, 1900–1980* (Cambridge, Mass.: Harvard University Press, 1981), 134.

8. Carl Rowan Oral History, Jan. 29, 1969, p. 35, Bunche Collection.

9. Wilkins, *Standing Fast*, 300–01; Jacob K. Javits, *Javits: The Autobiography of a Public Man* (Boston: Houghton Mifflin, 1981), 346; Burke Marshall Oral History, Feb. 27, 1970, pp. 33–34, Bunche Collection. Charles Whalen and Barbara Whalen, *The Longest Debate: A Legislative History of the 1964 Civil Rights Act* (Cabin John, Md.: Seven Locks

Press, 1985), emphasizes the role of House Republicans, particularly Ohio's William McCulloch. Charles Whalen served in the House from 1967–1979, representing Ohio's third district.

10. Gilbert C. Fite, *Richard B. Russell, Jr.* (Chapel Hill: University of North Carolina Press, 1991), 411. LBJ is quoted in Richard Harris, *Justice* (New York: Avon Books ed., 1970), 137; Mark Stern, *Calculating Visions: Kennedy, Johnson, and Civil Rights* (New Brunswick, N.J.: Rutgers University Press, 1992), 162.

11. Wilkins, *Standing Fast*, 299; Robert Moses, Aaron Henry, and David Dennis to Johnson, May 25, 1964, Miss. Summer Project Voter Registration, White House Aides' Files—Lee White, Johnson Papers; Robert Kennedy to Johnson, May 21, 1964, Ex HU2, WHCF, ibid.

12. Lee White to File, June 23, 1964, Miss. Summer Project Voter Registration, White House Aides' Files—White, Johnson Papers; interview, Lee White, July 9, 1987, Washington, D.C. The president also saw Schwerner's wife, Rita, on June 29, and Chaney's mother in early July.

13. Johnson to Hoover, July 13, 1964, FG35-6, WHCF, Johnson Papers. For the tap, see SAC New York to Director, Aug. 10, 1964, no. 100-3-116-not recorded, FBI–Communist Influence Racial Matters File. For LBJ's Klan order, see Don Whitehead, *Attack on Terror* (New York: Funk and Wagnalls, 1970), 91. For RFK, see Milton A. Jones to DeLoach, Nov. 19, 1964, no. 77-86882-124, FBI–Don Whitehead File.

14. U.S., National Commission on the Causes and Prevention of Violence, Task Force on Violent Aspects of Protest and Confrontation, *The Politics of Protest* (New York: Simon and Schuster ed., 1969), 224–25.

15. Ibid.

16. Lyndon B. Johnson, *The Vantage Point* (New York: Holt, Rinehart and Winston, 1971), 71.

17. Eric F. Goldman to Johnson, May 4, 1964, Ex LE/HU2, WHCF, Johnson Papers; S. Douglass Cater to Johnson, May 19, 1964, White House Aides' Files—S. Douglass Cater, ibid.

18. U.S., Congress, Senate, Select Committee to Study Governmental Operations with Respect to Intelligence Activities, *Final Report*, Book II, *Intelligence Activities and the Rights of Americans*, 94th Cong., 2d sess., 1976, p. 63.

19. *Jackson Daily News*, Aug. 26, 1964.

20. Guthman, ed., *Robert Kennedy*, 415.

21. Interview, Joseph L. Rauh, Jr., July 10, 1986, Washington, D.C.

23. E. T. Turner to W. A. Branigan, Aug. 23, 1964, no. 100-106670-440, FBI–Martin Luther King, Jr., File; DeLoach to Mohr, Aug. 29, 1964, in U.S., Congress, Senate, Select Committee to Study Governmental

Operations with Respect to Intelligence Activities, *Hearings—FBI*, vol. 6, 94th Cong., 1st sess., 1975, pp. 495–97.

24. Bill Moyers to Johnson, Aug. 19, 1964, Ex HU2/ST24, WHCF, Johnson Papers.

25. Rauh interview.

26. See, for example, DeLoach to Bill Moyers, Sept. 10, 1964, Name File—Cartha D. DeLoach, WHCF, Johnson Papers. King's comments are paraphrased in White to Johnson, Aug. 13, 1964, PL1/St24, WHCF, ibid.

27. Johnson, *Vantage Point*, 160.

28. Wilkins, *Standing Fast*, 303; Barry M. Goldwater, *The Conscience of a Conservative* (Shepherdsville, Ky.: Victor Publishing, 1960), 36; Richard Rovere, *The Goldwater Caper* (New York: Harcourt, Brace and World, 1965), 85; *New York Times*, Aug 4, 7, 13, and 14, 1964.

29. White to Johnson, Aug. 19, 1964, Ex HU2, WHCF, Johnson Papers.

30. Barry M. Goldwater, with Jack Casserly, *Goldwater* (Garden City, N.Y.: Doubleday, 1988), 172–73, and *With No Apologies* (New York: Morrow, 1979), 192–94; Theodore H. White, *The Making of the President 1964* (New York: Atheneum, 1965), 332–33n.

31. Myer Feldman to Johnson, July 23, 1964, Ex HU2, WHCF, Johnson Papers.

32. Wilkins, *Standing Fast*, 304. For Dewey, see the voluminous documents in the Thomas E. Dewey Folder, FBI–Hoover Official and Confidential File. For the report itself, see *New York Times*, Sept. 27, 1964.

33. Hoover to Moyers, Oct. 20, 1964, no. 100-106670-not recorded, FBI–King File.

34. Garrow, *Bearing the Cross*, 382. For "personal conduct," see, for an example, Hoover to Moyers, Dec. 21, 1964, no. 100-106670-650, FBI–King File. Moyers is quoted in U.S., Senate, Select Committee to Study Governmental Operations with Respect to Intelligence Activities, *Final Report*, Book III, *Supplemental Detailed Staff Reports on Intelligence Activities and the Rights of Americans*, 94th Cong., 2d sess., 1976, pp. 92–93.

35. Burke Marshall to Johnson, Dec. 9, 1964, Justice Dept., White House Aides' Files—Bill Moyers, Johnson Papers. Hoover is quoted in transcript, "Off the Record Remarks . . . for Editors of Georgia and Michigan Newspapers," April 15, 1965, Hoover FBI Building.

36. George Wallace, *Stand Up for America* (Garden City, N.Y.: Doubleday, 1976), 101–02; Johnson, *Vantage Point*, 163; Richard N. Goodwin, *Remembering America* (Boston: Little, Brown, 1988), 321.

37. Nicholas deB. Katzenbach to Joseph A. Califano, Jr., Dec. 13, 1965, Civil Rights 1965 (1), White House Aides' Files—Harry McPherson,

Johnson Papers. LBJ is quoted in Howell Raines, *My Soul Is Rested: Movement Days in the Deep South Remembered* (New York: G. P. Putnam's Sons, 1977), 337.

38. Wilkins, *Standing Fast*, 156.
39. Deborah Shapely, *Promise and Power: The Life and Times of Robert S. McNamara* (Boston: Little, Brown, 1993), 282.
40. Hoover to Tolson, Alan H. Belmont, DeLoach, and Alex Rosen, March 26, 1965, no. 44-28601-15 and -16, FBI–Viola Liuzzo File.
41. Hoover, "Off-the-Record Remarks."
42. George Reedy to Johnson, Sept. 7, 1965, Civil Rights—List of Orgs. and Pol. Leaders, White House Aides' Files—White, Johnson Papers; Eldridge Cleaver, *Soul On Ice* (New York: Random House, 1968), 201.
43. Doris Kearns, *Lyndon Johnson and the American Dream* (New York: Harper and Row, 1976), 305; Clifford L. Alexander, Jr., Oral History, Nov. 1, 1971, p. 13, Johnson Library.
44. Louis Martin to Marvin Watson, May 20, 1966, Civil Rights—Negroes (2), White House Aides' Files—Marvin Watson, Johnson Papers; White to Watson, Nov. 12, 1965, HU2, CF, ibid.; Harry McPherson Oral History, March 24, 1969, pp. 8–15, Johnson Library; *Christian Century*, Nov. 2, 1966, p. 1330. For the report, see U.S., Department of Labor, Office of Policy Planning and Research, *The Negro Family: The Case for National Action* (Washington, D.C.: Government Printing Office, 1965); Lee Rainwater and William L. Yancey, *The Moynihan Report and the Politics of Controversy* (Cambridge, Mass.: MIT Press, 1967).
45. Fred Dutton to Moyers, June 10, 1966, Name File—Ronald Reagan, WHCF, Johnson Papers; Reedy to Ivan Sinclair, Jan. 8, 1966, ibid.
46. Hoover to Tolson, DeLoach, and Wick, June 16 and July 6, 1966, no. 67-9524-not recorded, FBI–Clyde Tolson Personal File. A transcript of the CBS report is in the Moorland-Spingarn Research Center.
47. McPherson to Moyers, Aug. 15, 1966, Moyers/Valenti (1), White House Aides' Files—McPherson, Johnson Papers; Charles D. Roche to Lawrence O'Brien, March 11, 1966, Civil Rights, Charles Roche Office Files, ibid.
48. McPherson to Johnson, Sept. 12, 1966, Civil Rights (2), White House Aides' Files—McPherson, Johnson Papers.
49. Katzenbach to McPherson, Sept. 17, 1966, Civil Rights (2), White House Aides' Files—McPherson, ibid.; McPherson to Katzenbach, Sept. 20, 1966, White House Aides' Files—McPherson, ibid.; Martin Oral History, 32; telephone conversation, JFK and Allen C. Thompson, June 17, 1963, Item 22A4, Pres. Recordings (Logs and Transcripts), Pres. Office File, JFK Papers.

50. F. J. Baumgardner to Sullivan, July 7, 1965, no. 100-106670-1555, FBI–King File; Hoover to Dean Rusk, July 7, 1965, no. 100-106670-1538, ibid.; Hoover to Tolson, Belmont, Sullivan, and DeLoach, July 6, 1965, no. 100-106670-1551, ibid.

51. John P. Roche to Johnson, April 5, 1967, HU2, CF, WHCF, Johnson Papers. See also LBJ's note on John Criswell to Watson, March 23, 1967, Name File—Martin Luther King, WHCF, ibid.

52. Interview (telephone conversation), John P. Roche, Sept. 16, 1986, Medford, Mass.; James H. Cone, "Martin Luther King, Jr., and the Third World," *Journal of American History* 74(Sept. 1987): 462; Garrow, *Bearing the Cross*, 564, 581; Cleaver, *Soul on Ice*, 137; Wilkins, *Standing Fast*, 331. LBJ is quoted in Joseph A. Califano, Jr., *The Triumph and Tragedy of Lyndon Johnson* (New York: Simon and Schuster, 1991), 211.

53. Hubert H. Humphrey to Johnson, July 27, 1967, Ex HU2, WHCF, Johnson Papers; Humphrey to File, Aug. 23, 1967, George Romney, White House Aides' Files—Marvin Watson, ibid.; Roche to Johnson, July 6, 1967, FG11-8-1, CF, WHCF, ibid.; Ben Wattenberg to Johnson, Nov. 21, 1967, Civil Rights—Negroes, White House Aides' Files—Watson, ibid.; Cater, Wattenberg, and Ervin Duggan to Johnson, Aug. 9, 1967, Memos to the President, White House Aides' Files—Cater, ibid.

54. Jerome P. Cavanagh Oral History, March 22, 1971, p. 50, Johnson Library. See also Sidney Fine, *Violence in the Model City: The Cavanagh Administration, Race Relations, and the Detroit Riot of 1967* (Ann Arbor: University of Michigan Press, 1989), 212–17.

55. McPherson to Johnson, July 26, 1967, Ex HU2, WHCF, Johnson Papers.

56. Ibid.

57. McPherson to Johnson, Aug. 14, 1967, Riots (1), White House Aides' Files—McPherson, ibid. For McPherson's reference ("I am a neo-Malthusian if the purpose of our policy is to slow down the making of babies in conditions of squalor"), see McPherson to Moyers, March 16 and Dec. 13, 1965, Moyers—Valenti (1-2), ibid.

58. Hugh Davis Graham, "The Ambiguous Legacy of American Presidential Commissions," *Public Historian* 7(Spring 1985): 20.

59. U.S., National Advisory Commission on Civil Disorders, *Report of the National Advisory Commission on Civil Disorders* (Washington, D.C.: Government Printing Office, 1968). The Kerner Commission records are in RG 282, National Archives, Washington, D.C.

60. Note, LBJ, Aug. 28, 1967, Ex WE9, WHCF, Johnson Papers; Johnson, *Vantage Point*, 172–73; Harry C. McPherson, Jr., *A Political Education* (Boston: Little, Brown, 1972), 376–77.

61. McPherson to Johnson, March 13, 1968, FG690, CF, WHCF, Johnson Papers; note, LBJ, March 13, 1968, ibid.; McPherson to Califano, March 1, 1968, ibid.; Wilkins, *Standing Fast*, 328.

62. James Gaither to Califano, Oct. 17, 1967, Riots 1967, Pres. Task Forces—Subject File, White House Aides' Files—James Gaither, Johnson Papers; Charles M. Smith and E. Winslow Turner to Edmund Muskie, Sept. 13, 1967, Riots, Legislative—Subject File, Box 98, Robert F. Kennedy Papers, Kennedy Library; U.S., Congress, Senate, Committee on Government Operations, Permanent Subcommittee on Investigations, *Hearings on Riots, Civil and Criminal Disorders*, pts. 1–25, 90th Cong., 2d sess., 1967–1970.

63. Sargent Shriver to Johnson, Sept. 12, 1967, Ex WE9, WHCF, Johnson Papers; Padraic Kennedy to Shriver, July 31, 1967, Ex WE9, WHCF, ibid.; Willard Wirtz to Johnson, Aug. 11, 1967, Ex WE9, WHCF, ibid.; Shriver to Johnson, Sept. 15, 1967, FG11-15, CF, WHCF, ibid.; Shriver to Califano, July 29, 1967, Detroit Riots, White House Aides' Files—Gaither, ibid.; Gaither to Califano, July 27, 1967, Detroit Riots, White House Aides' Files—Gaither, ibid.; interview, Donald M. Baker, July 21, 1986, Washington, D.C.; interview, Sargent Shriver, July 25, 1986, Washington, D.C.

64. Shriver and Baker interviews.

65. Hoover to Mildred Stegall, Aug. 17, 1967, no. 62-109683-115, FBI–Alan McSurely File; Bland to Sullivan, Aug. 17, 1967, no. 62-109683-115, ibid.; memo, re Telephone Briefing, July 26, 1967, Goodpaster and Wheeler Briefings (1), Gettysburg—Indio, Post.-Pres., Dwight D. Eisenhower Papers, Dwight D. Eisenhower Library, Abilene, Ka.

66. Cater to Johnson, March 30, 1965, Memos to the President, White House Aides' Files—Cater, Johnson Papers; Charles L. Schultze to Johnson, Sept. 19, 1965, OEO (1), White House Aides' Files—Moyers, ibid.; McPherson to Johnson, Aug. 10, 1967, Ex WE9, WHCF, ibid.

67. Hobart Taylor to Johnson, Nov. 27, 1964, Ex HU2, WHCF, ibid.; Hoover to Watson, Jan. 20, 1967, no. 100-367743-53, FBI–National Lawyers Guild File.

68. James Rowe to Johnson, June 29, 1965, OEO (1), White House Aides' Files—Moyers, Johnson Papers; Baker interview.

69. McPherson, *Political Education*, 376; Kenneth O'Reilly, *"Racial Matters:" The FBI's Secret File on Black America, 1960–1972* (New York: Free Press, 1989), 241. Willis is quoted in Hugh T. Lovin, "Lyndon B. Johnson, the Subversive Activities Control Board, and the Politics of Anti-Communism," *North Dakota Quarterly* 27(Winter 1986): 567.

70. Hoover to Tolson, DeLoach, Sullivan, and Wick, July 26, 1967, no. not recorded, FBI–Tolson File; Roger Wilkins, *A Man's Life* (New York: Simon and Schuster, 1982), 230–31; Roche to Watson, Dec. 22, 1967, PU1-2, CF, WHCF, Johnson Papers.

71. DeLoach to Tolson, July 10, 1967, no. 100-106670-not recorded, FBI–King File. For the SACB, see note, LBJ, Aug. 27, 1964, Ex FG285, WHCF, Johnson Papers; Larry Temple to Johnson, Jan. 19, 1968, FG285, CF, WHCF, ibid.; Temple to Johnson, Jan. 10, 13, Feb. 6, April 30, May 4 and 28, and June 19, 1968, SACB, White House Aides' Files—Larry Temple, ibid.; Hoover to Tolson, DeLoach, and Sullivan, July 25, 1967, no. 157-6-959, FBI–Detroit Riot File.

72. DeLoach to Tolson, July 10, 1967, no. 100-106670-not recorded, FBI–King File.

73. McPherson Oral History, 8; George Reedy, *Twilight of the Presidency* (New York: New American Library, 1971), 17–18. The report is attached to Director to Attorney General, July 26, 1967, no. 157-6-956, FBI–Detroit Riot File. For McCarthy, see Hoover to Stegall, June 18, July 8, and Aug. 14, 1968, nos. 100-438794-2198, -2214, and -2290, FBI–SCLC File.

74. Califano to Johnson, Jan. 18, 1968, Ex HU2, WHCF, Johnson Papers; Ramsey Clark to Hoover, Sept. 14, 1967, Civil Disturbances 1967 (1), Box 10, Warren Christopher Papers, Johnson Library; Roche interview; Ramsey Clark Oral History, Oct. 30, 1968, p. 2, Johnson Library.

75. Director to SAC Albany et al., Aug. 25, 1967, no. 100-448006-1, and March 4, 1968, no. 100-448006-19, FBI–COINTELPRO (Black Nationalist) File; SAC Charlotte to Director, April 4, 1968, no. 100-448006-77, ibid. For the COINTELPRO supervisor and *ultra vires*, see Senate Select Committee, *Supplementary Detailed Staff Reports*, 4; U.S., Department of Justice, *Report of the Task Force to Review the FBI Martin Luther King, Jr., Security and Assassination Investigations* (Washington, D.C.: Government Printing Office, 1977), 141.

76. Clark Clifford, *Counsel to the President* (New York: Random House, 1991), 531.

77. SAC Indianapolis to Director, April 8, 1968, no. 77-51387-2007, FBI–Robert Kennedy File. Edelman is quoted in Calvin Tomkins, "A Sense of Urgency," *New Yorker*, March 27, 1989, p. 64.

78. Andrew Young Oral History, July 16, 1968, p. 24, Bunche Collection; Garry Wills, "The Hostage," *New York Review of Books*, Aug. 13, 1992, p. 23; Ralph Abernathy, *And the Walls Came Tumbling Down* (New York: Harper and Row, 1989), 514; Califano to Johnson, May 17, 1968, Riot Control—Poor People's March (1), White House Aides' Files—Gaither, Johnson Papers.

79. Matthew Nimetz to Califano, April 24, 1968, Riots and Riot Control General 1968 (2), White House Aides' Files—Gaither, Johnson Papers; McPherson to Johnson, June 14, 1968, Crime Message 1968, White House Aides' Files—McPherson, ibid.; Califano to Johnson, Feb. 9, 1968, Name File—John McClellan, WHCF, ibid.; Clark to Stanley R. Resor, May 9, 1968, Civil Disturbances 1968 (2–6), Box 12, Christopher Papers; Stephen J. Pollak to Clark, April 18, 1968, Anti-Riot Plans 1968, Box 61, Ramsey Clark Papers, Johnson Library.

80. Hoover to Tolson, DeLoach, Bishop, and Sullivan, Aug. 15, 1968, no. 62-77485-not recorded, FBI–Hubert Humphrey File.

81. SAC Jackson to Director, Sept. 5, 1968, no. 100-449698-54-5, FBI–COINTELPRO (New Left) File.

82. Charles Roche to Johnson, March 14, July 3, and Oct. 22, 1968, Memos to the President 1968, Roche Office Files, Johnson Papers; Joseph A. Califano, Jr., *Governing America* (New York: Simon and Schuster, 1981), 212; Kearns, *Lyndon Johnson*, 305.

83. Alan F. Westin and Trudy Hayden, "Presidents and Civil Liberties from FDR to Ford: A Rating by 64 Experts," *Civil Liberties Review* 3(Oct./Nov. 1976): 9–35.

84. McPherson interview; McPherson Oral History, 8.

85. Agenda, Nov. 1, 1967 (1), Cabinet, Johnson Papers.

Chapter 7. Demographer

1. Richard M. Nixon, *RN: Memoirs of Richard Nixon* (New York: Grossett and Dunlap, 1978), 19–20, 104–05.

2. Ibid., 106, 398.

3. Ibid., 268; Roger Morris, *Richard Milhous Nixon* (New York: Henry Holt, 1990), 592; Herbert S. Parmet, *Richard Nixon and His America* (Boston: Little, Brown, 1990), 269.

4. Nixon, *RN*, 301; Rowland Evans, Jr., and Robert D. Novak, *Nixon in the White House* (New York: Random House, 1971), 137.

5. Thomas Byrne Edsall and Mary D. Edsall, *Chain Reaction* (New York: Norton, 1991), 10, passim.

6. Garry Wills, *Nixon Agonistes* (New York: New American Library ed., 1971), 45; Jody Carlson, *George C. Wallace and the Politics of Powerlessness* (New Brunswick, N.J.: Transaction Books, 1981), 6; Marshall Frady, *Wallace* (New York: World, 1968), 6–7. See also Wayne Greenhaw, *Watch Out for Wallace* (Englewood Cliffs, N.J.: Prentice Hall, 1976), 155.

7. Reg Murphy and Hal Gulliver, *The Southern Strategy* (New York: Scribner, 1971), 1.

8. Nixon, *RN*, 268, and "What Has Happened to America," *Reader's Digest*, Oct. 1967, pp. 50, 54; Joseph A. Califano, Jr., *Governing America* (New York: Simon and Schuster, 1981), 216. See also Nixon's last book, *Beyond Peace* (New York: Random House, 1994), 222–27; Nicol C. Rae, *The Decline and Fall of the Liberal Republicans: From 1952 to the Present* (New York: Oxford University Press, 1989).

9. Wills, *Nixon Agonistes*, 205–06.

10. Ibid., 244, 272–73, 289.

11. Ibid., 244–45; Evans and Novak, *Nixon in the White House*, 136–37.

12. See Dewey W. Grantham, *The Life and Death of the Solid South* (Lexington: University Press of Kentucky, 1988); Earl Black and Merle Black, *The Vital South: How Presidents Are Elected* (Cambridge, Mass.: Harvard University Press, 1992).

13. Nixon, *RN*, 268; Tom Wicker, *One of Us: Richard Nixon and the American Dream* (New York: Random House, 1991), 418; Evans and Novak, *Nixon in the White House*, 137; Nadine Cohodas, *Strom Thurmond and the Politics of Southern Change* (New York: Simon and Schuster, 1993), 396–400.

14. Harry S. Dent to Nixon, Dec. 11, 1969, Handwriting, Pres. Office File, Richard M. Nixon Papers, Nixon Presidential Materials Project, National Archives, Washington, D.C.; Raymond Price, *With Nixon* (New York: Viking, 1977), 209; Harry S. Dent, *The Prodigal South Returns to Power* (New York: Wiley, 1978), 6, 75, 175; Roy Wilkins Oral History, April 29, 1970, p. 34, Ralph J. Bunche Oral History Collection, Moorland-Spingarn Research Center, Howard University, Washington, D.C.

15. Kevin P. Phillips, *The Emerging Republican Majority* (New Rochelle, N.Y.: Arlington House, 1969), 468; Wills, *Nixon Agonistes*, 249.

16. Phillips, *Emerging Republican Majority*, 286–87, 464, and *The Politics of Rich and Poor* (New York: Random House, 1990), 40–41; Wills, *Nixon Agonistes*, 248–49.

17. Wills, *Nixon Agonistes*, 247–48

18. Dent to Nixon, April 30, 1969, Handwriting, Pres. Office File, Nixon Papers; Jonathan Schell, *The Time of Illusion* (New York: Knopf, 1976), 62; Dent, *Prodigal South*, 136; Edsall, *Chain Reaction*, 85.

19. Wills, *Nixon Agonistes*, 31, 47, 67, 261, 263, 267–70. Agnew called his State Office Building statement "a lecture." Spiro Agnew, *Go Quietly— or else* (New York: Morrow, 1980), 147.

20. John Ehrlichman, *Witness to Power* (New York: Simon and Schuster, 1982), 149; Nixon to John Ehrlichman and H. R. Haldeman, Jan. 9, 1969, in Bruce Oudes, ed., *From: The President—Richard Nixon's Secret Files* (New York: Harper and Row, 1989), 2.

21. Roy Wilkins, invited to the inauguration, stayed home and watched it on television instead. Shortly thereafter he and his wife received a White House dinner invitation. "Minnie said she wouldn't go," he recalled. "I told her she had to. Minnie gave me a look that would have dropped a mule, but finally she agreed." Before issuing that second invitation Nixon had asked J. Edgar Hoover for name checks on both Roy and Minnie Wilkins. On this front he was truly indiscriminate, requesting FBI file checks as well on such wholesome whites as Billy Graham and Pat Boone. Roy Wilkins, with Tom Mathews, *Standing Fast* (New York: Penguin Books ed., 1984), 332; J. Edgar Hoover to Ehrlichman, July 2, 1969, no. 62-78270-42, FBI–Roy Wilkins File, J. Edgar Hoover FBI Building, Washington, D.C.; Hoover to Alexander P. Butterfield, March 16, 1970, no. 94-4-3169-not recorded, FBI–David Lawrence File.

22. Nicholas Lemann, *The Promised Land* (New York: Knopf, 1991), 208–09; Wills, *Nixon Agonistes*, 250–51.

23. J. J. Daunt to Thomas E. Bishop, July 18, 1970, no. 62-110834-not recorded, FBI–Law Enforcement Assistance Administration File; Richard Harris, *Justice* (New York: Avon Books ed., 1970), 152; Edward Jay Epstein, *Agency of Fear* (New York: Putnam's, 1977), 67–68.

24. Schell, *Time of Illusion*, 43.

25. Ovid Demaris, *The Director: An Oral Biography of J. Edgar Hoover* (New York: Harper's Magazine Press, 1975), 140.

26. Hoover to Clyde Tolson, Cartha DeLoach, Alex Rosen, and Bishop, June 5, 1970, no. not recorded, FBI–Clyde Tolson Personal File; Hoover to Tolson, DeLoach, James Gale, Rosen, William Sullivan, and Bishop, April 23, 1969, no. not recorded, ibid.

27. Hoover to Tolson, DeLoach, Gale, Rosen, Sullivan, and Bishop, April 23, 1969, no. not recorded, ibid.; Seymour Hersh, *The Price of Power* (New York: Simon and Schuster, 1983), 127.

28. Hoover to Tolson, DeLoach, Sullivan, and Bishop, May 9, 1969, in U.S., Congress, House, Committee on the Judiciary, *Statement of Information*, Book VII, *White House Surveillance and Campaign Activities*, 93d Cong., 2d sess., 1974, p. 143; Conor Cruise O'Brien, "The Theater of Southern Africa," *New York Review of Books*, March 23, 1978, p. 33; Chuck Stone, "Black Political Power in the Carter Era," *Black Scholar* 8(Jan.–Feb. 1977): 8; Hersh, *Price of Power*, 111. The president once told Haldeman "that there has never in history been an adequate black nation, and they are the only race of which this is true. Says Africa is hopeless." H. R. Haldeman, *The Haldeman Diaries: Inside the Nixon White House* (New York: G. P. Putnam's Sons, 1994), 53.

29. Roger Morris, *Uncertain Greatness* (New York: Harper and Row, 1977), 131–32; Hersh, *Price of Power*, 110–11.

30. "Andrew Young," *Playboy*, July 1977, p. 70.

31. S. B. Donahoe to DeLoach, March 12, 1969, no. 100-106670-3575, FBI–Martin Luther King, Jr., File; Hoover to John Mitchell, March 3, 1969, no. 100-106670-3571, ibid.; Hoover to Spiro Agnew, June 19, 1969, no. 100-106670-3602, ibid.; Hoover to Winton M. Blount, Aug. 28, 1969, no. 100-106670-3670, ibid.; George C. Moore to Sullivan, Jan. 22 and Aug. 27, 1969, no. 100-106670-3560 and -3670, ibid.; Hoover to Nixon, Jan. 23, 1969, no. 100-106670-3560, ibid.; interview (telephone), John Ehrlichman, Feb. 16, 1987; Dent, *Prodigal South*, 232; Todd R. Hullin to Egil Krogh, Nov. 13, 1970, FBI, FG17-5, WHCF, Nixon Papers.

32. Hoover to Mitchell, June 30 and Oct. 1, 1969, no. 100-392452-341 and -353, FBI–Stanley Levison File; Hoover to Mitchell, Feb. 5, 1969, no. 100-106670-3564, FBI–King File.

33. Stanley Kutler, *The Wars of Watergate* (New York: Knopf, 1990), 90.

34. Hoover to Tolson, DeLoach, Rosen, Sullivan, and Bishop, May 18, 1970, no. not recorded, FBI–Tolson File.

35. Ibid.; *The Report of the President's Commission on Campus Unrest* (Washington, D.C.: Government Printing Office, 1970), 458–59.

36. Hoover to Tolson, DeLoach, Rosen, Sullivan, and Bishop, May 18, 1970, no. not recorded, FBI–Tolson File.

37. Hoover to Tolson, DeLoach, Sullivan, and Bishop, April 20, 1970, no. 67-9524-not recorded, ibid.; Hoover to Tolson, Sullivan, Bishop, and Charles D. Brennan, Jan. 7, 1971, no. 67-9524-not recorded, ibid.

38. Harris, *Justice*, 139–41, 163.

39. Ibid., 188–89; Hugh Davis Graham, *The Civil Rights Era* (New York: Oxford University Press, 1990), 382; Dent to Nixon, Dec. 11, 1969, Handwriting, Pres. Office File, Nixon Papers; *Alexander v. Holmes County Board of Education*, 396 U.S. 19 (1969)

40. Schell, *Time of Illusion*, 43; Dent to John Sears, Feb. 10, 1969, Southern GOP, Staff Member—Harry Dent, Nixon Papers; Ehrlichman, *Witness*, 220.

41. Dent to Nixon, March 5, 1969, Handwriting, Pres. Office File, Nixon Papers; Dent to Harlow, Feb. 14, 1969, Southern GOP, Staff Member—Dent, ibid.; Dent to Mitchell, Feb. 19, 1969, Southern GOP, Staff Member—Dent, ibid.; Dent to Herb Klein, Feb. 25, 1969, Southern GOP, Staff Member—Dent, ibid.; Fred LaRue to Harlow, Feb. 18, 1969, Education—Schooling, HU2-1, CF, WHSF/WHCF, ibid.; Harris, *Justice*, 181–83; Murphy and Gulliver, *Southern Strategy*, 173.

42. Leonard is quoted in Harris, *Justice* 182; the Johnson official in Evans and Novak, *Nixon in the White House*, 157. For "corrective action," see Ehrlichman to Nixon, April 17, 1969, Handwriting, Pres. Office File,

Nixon Papers; Dent to Ehrlichman, March 28, 1969, ibid. For Carmichael, see Dent to Mitchell, Feb. 19, 1969, Southern GOP, Staff
Member—Dent, ibid.

43. Harris, *Justice*, 189.

44. John Brown to Ehrlichman, March 26, 1970, Education—Schooling,
HU2-1, CF, WHSF/WHCF, Nixon Papers.

45. Harris, *Justice*, 185.

46. Ibid., 187; Arthur M. Schlesinger, Jr., *The Imperial Presidency* (Boston:
Houghton Mifflin, 1973), 234–35.

47. Ehrlichman to Nixon, Feb. 5, 1969, Handwriting, Pres. Office File,
Nixon Papers; Dent to Haldeman and Ehrlichman, Feb. 3, 1969, ibid.;
Ehrlichman, *Witness*, 227, 229; Price, *With Nixon*, 206, 208.

48. Dent to Nixon, n.d., Handwriting, Pres. Office File, Nixon Papers.
Evers is quoted in Harris, *Justice*, 186.

49. Nixon, *RN*, 440; John R. Greene, *The Limits of Power: The Nixon and
Ford Administrations* (Bloomington: Indiana University Press, 1992);
clipping, Jan. 18, 1970, Annotated News Summaries, Pres. Office File,
Nixon Papers; Haldeman to Nixon, Aug. 4, 1970, Handwriting, Pres.
Office File, ibid.; Leonard Garment to Nixon, Aug. 5, 1970, Handwrit-
ing, Pres. Office File, ibid.; Brown to Ehrlichman, Jan. 20, 1970,
Education—Schooling, HU2-1, CF, WHSF/WHCF, ibid.

50. Edward L. Morgan to Nixon, Aug. 29, 1970, Handwriting, Pres. Office
File, Nixon Papers.

51. Sam Ervin Oral History, Jan. 29, 1971, p. 28, Bunche Collection; clipping, n.d. [ca. Jan. 13, 1970], Annotated News Summaries, Pres. Office
File, Nixon Papers.

52. Agnew to Nixon, May 16, 1969, Handwriting, Pres. Office File, Nixon
Papers; Ehrlichman, *Witness*, 224–27. For Panetta's account, see Leon
E. Panetta and Peter Gall, *Bring Us Together* (Philadelphia: J. B. Lippin-
cott Co., 1971).

53. "I don't think there's any compassion in the man, no love for blacks,"
Alexander said. "The man's a bigot." Clifford L. Alexander, Jr., Oral
History, Nov. 1, 1971, pp. 14, 34, Bunche Collection. See also Alexan-
der P. Butterfield to Harry Flemming, April 1, 1969, EEOC, FG109,
CF, WHSF/WHCF, Nixon Papers; Flemming to Staff Secretary,
April 4, 1969, ibid.

54. Brown to Ehrlichman, Feb. 5, 1970, Education—Schooling, HU2-1,
CF, WHSF/WHCF, Nixon Papers; Ehrlichman to Nixon, Oct. 21,
1970, Handwriting, Pres. Office File, ibid.

55. Morgan to Nixon, Oct. 6, 1970, Handwriting, Pres. Office File, ibid.;
Arthur A. Fletcher to Nixon, Jan. 5, 1971, Handwriting, Pres. Office
File, ibid.; Nixon, *RN*, 439–40; A. James Reichley, *Conservatives in an*

Age of Change (Washington, D.C.: Brookings Institution, 1981), 174; Ehrlichman, *Witness*, 230, 234.

56. Theodore H. White, *The Making of the President 1972* (New York: Bantam, 1973), 242; Ehrlichman, *Witness* 220–21; Nixon to Ehrlichman, Feb. 8, 1971, Education—Schooling, HU2-1, CF, WHSF/WHCF, Nixon Papers; Charles Colson to Nixon, May 19, 1972, Handwriting, Pres. Office File, ibid.

57. Haldeman to Timmons, Feb. 24, 1970, Education—Schooling, HU2-1, CF, WHSF/WHCF, Nixon Papers; Morgan to Cole, June 6, 1972, Education—Schooling, HU2-1, CF, WHSF/WHCF, ibid.; Colson to Nixon, May 19, 1972, Handwriting, Pres. Office File, ibid.

58. Dent to Nixon, Jan. 19, 1970, Education—Schooling, HU2-1, CF, WHSF/WHCF, ibid.; Ervin Oral History, 20; Hoover to Tolson, DeLoach, Gale, Rosen, and Sullivan, April 23, 1969, no. not recorded, FBI–Tolson File; Seymour M. Hersh, "Nixon's Last Cover-Up," *New Yorker*, Dec. 14, 1992, 81; Burke Marshall Oral History, Aug. 27, 1980, p. 39, Bunche Collection.

59. Hoover to Tolson, DeLoach, and Gale, July 1, 1969, no. 23, John Mitchell Folder, FBI–J. Edgar Hoover Official and Confidential File; Wilkins, *Standing Fast*, 334.

60. Dent to Ken Belieu, Oct. 17, 1969, Haynesworth, Staff Member—Dent, Nixon Papers.

61. Wicker, *One of Us*, 497–98; William W. Turner, *Hoover's F.B.I.* (New York: Dell ed., 1971), 91–92; Hoover to Tolson, DeLoach, Gale, and Bishop, Jan. 19, 1970, no. 67-9524-not recorded, FBI–Tolson File. For the "battery" charge, see Curt Gentry, *J. Edgar Hoover: The Man and the Secrets* (New York: Norton, 1991), 626.

62. Wilkins, *Standing Fast*, 334.

63. Nixon to Haldeman, April 13, 1970, in Oudes, ed., *From: The President*, 114–15. For Ford, see Kutler, *Wars of Watergate*, 150; Athan Theoharis and John Stuart Cox, *The Boss: J. Edgar Hoover and the Great American Inquisition* (Philadelphia: Temple University Press, 1988), 406; Gerald R. Ford, *A Time to Heal* (New York: Harper and Row/Reader's Digest, 1979), 90–94; Jerald F. terHorst, *Gerald Ford and the Future of the Presidency* (New York: Third Press/Joseph Okpaku Publishing, 1974), 122–26.

64. Patrick J. Buchanan to Nixon, Sept. 20 and 29, 1971, Pres. Memos, Staff Member—Patrick J. Buchanan, Nixon Papers.

65. Ibid.; "Research" to Mitchell and Haldeman, Oct. 5, 1971, in U.S., Congress, Senate, Select Committee on Presidential Campaign Activities, *Hearings on Watergate and Related Activities—Phase II*, Book 10, *Campaign Practices*, 93d Cong., 1st sess., 1973, p. 4199.

66. See John M. Huntsman to Buchanan, April 27, 1971, in Oudes, ed., *From: The President*, 243.

67. Buchanan to Haldeman, Sept. 20, 1971, ibid., 320–21; Schell, *Time of Illusion*, 181; Patrick J. Buchanan, *Right From the Beginning* (Boston: Little, Brown, 1988), 350, and *Conservative Votes, Liberal Victories* (New York: Quadrangle/New York Times Book Co., 1975), 52.

68. Buchanan, *Right From the Beginning*, 301–06, and *Conservative Votes*, 7, 52.

69. Buchanan to Nixon, Nov. 10, 1972, in Oudes, ed., *From: The President*, 566.

70. Ibid., 558–68.

71. Nixon to Haldeman, Sept. 22, 1969, ibid., 49; Ehrlichman to Nixon, Feb. 18, 1971, Handwriting, Pres. Office File, Nixon Papers; Notes of Meetings with the President, May 20 and 28, 1970, Staff Member—Ehrlichman Notes, ibid.; Arthur F. Burns to Staff Secretary, Jan. 17, 1970, Staff Secretary, Box A24, Arthur F. Burns Papers, Gerald Ford Library, Ann Arbor, Mi.; Hersh, "Nixon's Last Cover-up," 94.

72. Ehrlichman, *Witness*, 231.

73. U.S., Congress, Senate, Committee on the Judiciary, Subcommittee on Constitutional Rights, *Political Intelligence in the Internal Revenue Service*, 93d Cong., 2d sess., 1974.

74. Hoover to Tolson, DeLoach, Gale, Rosen, and Sullivan, April 23, 1969, no. not recorded, FBI–Tolson File; Hoover to Tolson, DeLoach, Sullivan, and Bishop, April 21, 1970, no. not recorded, ibid.; Hoover to Tolson, DeLoach, Rosen, Sullivan, and Bishop, May 14, 1970, no. not recorded, ibid.; Ehrlichman to Hoover, Dec. 22, 1969, Black Panther Party, WHSF, Nixon Papers.

75. Notes of Meetings with the President, Jan. 29, 1970, Staff Member—Ehrlichman Notes, Nixon Papers; Krogh to Hoover, June 27, 1969, Black Panther Party, WHSF, ibid.; Krogh to Mitchell, Jan. 28, 1970, Black Panther Party, WHSF, ibid.; Krogh to Haldeman, March 12, 1970, Black Panther Party, WHSF, ibid.; Herb Klein to Nixon, Jan. 29, 1970, Law Enforcement—Police, JL6, CF, WHSF/WHCF, ibid.; John Brown to Ehrlichman, Feb. 5, 1970, Equality, HU2, CF, WHSF/WHCF, ibid.; John Dean to Tom Huston and Jeff Donfeld, Aug. 25, 1970, Black Panthers, Staff Member—John Dean, ibid.; Krogh to File, Aug. 23, 1971, FBI, FG17-5, WHCF, ibid.; Krogh to Haldeman, Feb. 23, 1970, Alpha—Internal Security, Staff Member—Egil Krogh, ibid.; clipping, Jan. 12, 1970, Annotated News Summaries, Pres. Office File, ibid.; Haldeman to Klein, Jan. 17, 1970, in Oudes, ed., *From: The President*, 89; Haldeman to Buchanan, Feb. 19, 1971, ibid., 219–20; Hoover to Tolson, Sullivan, Brennan, Gale, Rosen, and Casper,

May 26, 1971, no. not recorded, FBI–Tolson File; Hoover to Tolson, DeLoach, Sullivan, and Bishop, July 14, 1969, no. not recorded, ibid. For Hampton, see Kenneth O'Reilly, *"Racial Matters:" The FBI's Secret File on Black America, 1960–1972* (New York: Free Press, 1989), 303–05, 310–15.

76. Moynihan to Nixon, Jan. 16, 1970, Handwriting, Pres. Office File, Nixon Papers (the president scribbled the note on this document); Moynihan to Ehrlichman, Peter Flanigan, and Donald Rumsfeld, Sept. 19, 1969, Alpha—Black Panther Party, Staff Member—Ehrlichman, ibid.

77. Nixon, *RN*, 469, 471.

78. Buchanan to Mitchell and Haldeman, Oct. 5, 1971, in Senate Watergate Committee, Book 10, *Campaign Practices*, pp. 4197–4203; Buchanan, *Right From the Beginning*, 350.

79. Haldeman, *Diaries*, 53; Nixon to Robert Finch, n.d. [ca. Feb. 1969], Handwriting, Pres. Office File, Nixon Papers; Ehrlichman to Nixon, March 19, 1969, ibid.; Burns to Nixon, March 21, 1969, ibid.

80. Bryce Harlow to Nixon, March 23, 1969, ibid. (for Nixon's scribbled order); Burns to Nixon, March 24, 1969, ibid.; Buchanan to Ehrlichman and Krogh, Dec. 13, 1971, in Oudes, ed., *From: The President*, 346; Buchanan to Nixon, Nov. 10, 1972, ibid., 562.

81. Notes of Meetings with the President, Nov. 14 and 28, and Dec. 1, 1972, Staff Member—Ehrlichman Notes, Nixon Papers; Colson to Larry Higby, Dec. 22, 1972, in Oudes, ed., *From: The President*, 576. See also Lemann, *Promised Land*, 218.

82. Schlesinger, *Imperial Presidency*, 235–36.

83. Hullin to Ken Clawson, March 15, 1973, Poverty Programs, WE10, CF, WHSF/WHCF, Nixon Papers; Nixon to Ehrlichman, March 14, 1973, ibid.; David Gergen to Hullin, March 21, 1973, ibid.; Clawson to Cole, March 26, 1973, ibid.; Kenneth L. Khachigian to Hullin, March 21, 1973, ibid.

84. Ehrlichman to Leonard Garment, April 23, 1970, Black Elected Officials, Staff Member—Bradley Patterson, ibid.; Moynihan to Nixon, May 12 and June 30, 1970, Handwriting, Pres. Office File, ibid. For the welfare reforms, see also Vincent J. Burke and Dee Burke, *Nixon's Good Deed* (New York: Columbia University Press, 1974); Daniel Patrick Moynihan, *The Politics of a Guaranteed Income* (New York: Random House, 1973); M. Kenneth Bowler, *The Nixon Guaranteed Income Proposals* (Cambridge, Mass.: Ballinger, 1974).

85. Ehrlichman, *Witness*, 235–36; Evans and Novak, *Nixon in the White House*, 135; Moynihan to Nixon, Jan. 16, 1970, Handwriting, Pres. Office File, Nixon Papers; Khachigian to Buchanan, July 26, 1971,

Pres. Memos, Staff Member—Buchanan, ibid.; John Andrews to Dick Howard, April 21, 1971, in Oudes, ed., *From: The President*, 242.

86. Nixon to Ehrlichman, Feb. 8, 1971, in Oudes, ed., *From: The President*, 214; Moynihan to Nixon, Feb. 1, 1969, and July 24, 1970, Handwriting, Pres. Office File, Nixon Papers; Dwight L. Chapin to Brown, Ehrlichman, Garment, and Finch, July 25, 1970, Equality, Ex HU2, WHCF, ibid.; Rumsfeld to Nixon, July 20, 1970, Equality, Ex HU2, WHCF, ibid.; Evans and Novak, *Nixon in the White House*, 134.

87. See the note on Moynihan to Nixon, Feb. 1, 1969, Handwriting, Pres. Office File, Nixon Papers.

88. Haldeman, *Diaries*, 128–29; Ehrlichman, *Witness*, 229.

89. Ibid., 55; clipping, Dec. 30, 1969, Annotated News Summaries, Pres. Office File, Nixon Papers; Nixon, *RN*, 436; Ralph Abernathy, *And the Walls Came Tumbling Down* (New York: Harper and Row, 1989), 554; Lemann, *Promised Land*, 217.

90. Graham, *Civil Rights Era*, 303.

91. Ehrlichman to Nixon, Oct. 21, 1970, Handwriting, Pres. Office File, Nixon Papers.

92. Harris, *Justice*, 136.

93. Ehrlichman to Nixon, Oct. 21, 1970, Handwriting, Pres. Office File, Nixon Papers.

94. George P. Shultz, *Turmoil and Triumph: My Years as Secretary of State* (New York: Charles Scribner's Sons, 1993), 1110. The Democrats had problems here. To appease the Kennedy/McCarthy forces at the 1968 Chicago convention, the DNC created a Special Commission on Party Structure and Delegate Selection requiring racial minorities, youth, and women in state delegations to be represented "in reasonable relationship to their presence in the population of the state." At the 1972 convention the Chicago delegation (Daley's machine) failed this criteria and the Credentials Committee voted it out (71–61). The new slate of 59 delegates had only 3 Poles and 1 Italian. "Anybody who would reform Chicago's Democratic party by dropping the white ethnic," *Chicago Sun-Times* columnist Mike Royko wrote, "would probably begin a diet by shooting himself in the stomach." Byron E. Shafer, *Quiet Revolution* (New York: Russell Sage Foundation, 1983), 465; Thomas B. Edsall, "Race," *Atlantic*, May 1991, pp. 66, 68.

95. Nixon, *RN*, 438.

96. Ehrlichman to Nixon, Oct. 21, 1970, Handwriting, Pres. Office File, Nixon Papers; Nixon, *RN*, 438; Ehrlichman, *Witness*, 228–29.

97. Senate Watergate Committee, Book 11, *Campaign Practices*, 4487.

98. Teeter to Haldeman, Nov. 2, 1972, Box 1, Teeter Papers; Moynihan to Nixon, Jan. 16, 1970, Handwriting, Pres. Office File, Nixon Papers;

Ehrlichman to Nixon, Nov. 24, 1970, Handwriting, Pres. Office File, ibid.; Garment to Nixon, Nov. 23, 1970, Handwriting, Pres. Office File, ibid.; Nixon to Alexander Haig, June 2, 1971, Pres. Personal File, ibid.; Nixon, *RN*, 436–37; Haldeman, *Diaries*, 31; Lemann, *Promised Land*, 205.

99. Colson to Nixon, Nov. 6, 1970, in Oudes, ed., *From: The President*, 167.

100. J. Anthony Lucas, *Nightmare: The Underside of the Nixon Years* (New York: Viking, 1976), 149; Jeb Stuart Magruder, *An American Life* (New York: Atheneum, 1974), 188–89.

101. Colson to File, May 16, 1972, in Oudes, ed., *From: The President*, 445–46; George Wallace, *Stand Up for America* (Garden City, N.Y.: Doubleday, 1976), 170.

102. Senate Watergate Committee, Book 10, *Campaign Practices*, 3966, 3983, 4055–58.

103. [Buchanan] to Mitchell and Haldeman, Oct. 5, 1971, ibid., 4201–02; Robert M. Teeter to Mitchell, April 11, 1972, Box 1, Robert M. Teeter Papers, Ford Library.

104. Nixon to Buchanan, June 10, 1972, in Oudes, ed., *From: The President*, 475; Nixon to Mitchell, June 6, 1972, ibid., 462.

105. Memo, Buchanan and Khachigian, June 8, 1972, ibid., 463–74.

106. Robert C. Mardian to Frederic V. Malek, June 26, 1972, in U.S., Congress, Senate, Select Committee on Presidential Campaign Activities, *Executive Session Hearings on Watergate and Related Activities*, Book 19, *Use of Incumbency—Responsiveness Program (Additional Documents)* 93d Cong., 2d sess., 1974, p. 8742; Jack Crawford to Mardian, June 23, 1972, ibid., Book 19, pp. 8743–47; Dent to Haldeman, Oct. 26, 1971, ibid., Book 19, p. 8613; John Clark to Malek, June 15, 1972, ibid., Book 18, pp. 8406–12; Malek to Brown et al., March 3, 1972, in *Hearings on Watergate and Related Activities—Phase III*, Book 13, *Campaign Financing*, 93d Cong., 1st sess., 1973, p. 5542; Bill Marumoto to Colson, March 17, 1972, ibid., Book 13, p. 5543.

107. Nixon to Haldeman, Nov. 15, 1972, in Oudes, ed., *From: The President*, 571.

108. Elmo R. Zumwalt, Jr., *On Watch* (New York: Quadrangle/New York Times Book Co., 1976), 221–42; Haldeman, *Diaries*, 533.

109. G. Gordon Liddy, *Will* (New York: St. Martin's Press, 1980), 296; Haldeman, *Diaries*, 587. Dent is quoted in Cohodas, *Strom Thurmond*, 434.

110. Stanley S. Scott to Buchanan et al., Jan. 21, 1974, Black Leadership, Vice-President, Gerald R. Ford Papers, Ford Library.

111. Andrew Young Oral History, Dec. 20, 1972, p. 10, Bunche Collection, and *Playboy* interview, 70.

112. Ehrlichman, *Witness*, 222–23. See also Lemann, *Promised Land*, 203. For "the moon," see Theodore H. White, *Breach of Faith* (New York: Atheneum, 1975), 163.

113. Parmet, *Richard Nixon*, 269; Buchanan, *Conservative Votes*, 49–50. See also Joan Hoff, *Nixon Reconsidered* (New York: Basic Books, 1994), 17–49, 77–114.

114. Nixon, *RN*, 435–36, 442.

115. U.S., Congress, Senate, Select Committee to Study Governmental Operations with Respect to Intelligence Activities, *Final Report*, Book IV, *Supplementary Detailed Staff Reports on Foreign and Military Intelligence*, 94th Cong., 2d sess., 1976, p. 157.

116. Nixon, *RN*, 268, 316.

117. *The White House Transcripts* (New York: Bantam ed., 1974), 276.

118. Richard M. Nixon, *In the Arena: A Memoir of Victory, Defeat, and Renewal* (New York: Simon and Schuster, 1990), 245.

Chapter 8. Accidentals

1. Chuck Stone, "Black Political Power in the Carter Era," *Black Scholar* 8(Jan.–Feb. 1977): 10–11; Gerald R. Ford, *A Time to Heal* (New York: Harper and Row/Reader's Digest, 1979), 52–53; Robert T. Hartman, *Palace Politics* (New York: McGraw-Hill, 1980), 215–16. For Ford's early years, see also James Cannon, *Time and Chance: Gerald Ford's Appointment with History* (New York: HarperCollins, 1994), 1–39. For the White House years, see John R. Greene, *The Presidency of Gerald R. Ford* (Lawrence: University Press of Kansas, 1995).

2. Roy Wilkins, with Tom Mathews, *Standing Fast* (New York: Penguin ed., 1984), 322; Jerald F. terHorst, *Gerald Ford and the Future of the Presidency* (New York: Third Press/Joseph Okpaku Publishing, 1974), 107–09, 112–13; Ford, *Time to Heal*, 115, 140.

3. Ford, *Time to Heal*, 115; Hartman, *Palace Politics*, 121n; Betty Ford, with Chris Chase, *The Times of My Life* (New York: Harper and Row/ Reader's Digest, 1978), 154.

4. terHorst, *Gerald Ford*, 126.

5. Press release, Oct. 25, 1974, in Black Caucus, Office of Domestic Council, Geoffrey Shepard Files, Gerald R. Ford Papers, Gerald R. Ford Library, Ann Arbor, Mich.; Stanley Scott to Donald Rumsfeld et al., Jan. 8, 1975, HU3–1, WHCF, ibid.; Ford to Scott, Oct. 31, 1974, Human Rights/Equality (1), Handwriting, ibid.; Richard Cheney to

Rumsfeld, Feb. 15, 1975, Voting Rights Extension, Richard Cheney Files, ibid.; Steven F. Lawson, *In Pursuit of Power: Southern Blacks and Electoral Politics, 1965–1982* (New York: Columbia University Press, 1985), 248–50.

6. John J. Casserly, *The Ford White House* (Boulder: Colardo Associated University Press, 1977), 149, 158–59, 236, 245.

7. Caspar Weinberger to Ford, March 4, 1975, HU2–2, WHCF, Ford Papers; William Simon to James M. Cannon, May 17, 1975, HU2, WHCF, ibid.

8. *Public Papers of the Presidents of the United States: Gerald Ford, 1976–1977* (Washington, D.C.: Government Printing Office, 1979), 657–58, 668, 1909–13; A. James Reichley, *Conservatives in an Age of Change* (Washington, D.C.: Brookings Institution, 1981), 279; note, May 27, 1976, Busing, John G. Carlson Files, Ford Papers. See also the documents in Busing/Alternatives to, Richard D. Parsons File, ibid.

9. Robert Goldwin to Edward Schmultz and Cannon, June 15, 1976, Busing—General (2), Edward C. Schmultz File, Ford Papers; Scott to Philip W. Buchen, Nov. 14, 1974, Minority Groups (2), Philip Buchen Files, ibid.; Roy Wilkins to Buchen, Oct. 28, 1974, Minority Groups (2), ibid.; Richard Parsons to Cannon and Buchen, Oct. 23, 1975, Busing (1), Arthur F. Quern Files, ibid.

10. Parsons to Cannon, March 13, 1975, HU2–1/St21, WHCF, ibid.; Cannon to Ford, March 22, 1975, ibid.; Bobbie Greene Kilbert to William Nicholson, Feb. 20 and June 30, 1976, ibid.; Edward Kennedy to William T. Kendall, June 14, 1976, ibid.; Christopher Lasch, *The True and Only Heaven* (New York: Norton, 1991), 409, 478.

11. Wilkins, *Standing Fast*, 339.

12. Ron Nessen, *It Sure Looks Different from the Inside* (Chicago: Playboy Press, 1978), 195; "Campaign Plan—Draft," July 17, 1976, p. 96, in Box 12, Michael Raoul-Duval Papers, Ford Library.

13. Ford, *A Time to Heal*, 412; Mike Duval to Cheney and Jerry Jones, Oct. 19, 1976, Debate Working Papers—Bedford-Stuyvesant, Box 28, Duval Papers.

14. Betty Glad, *Jimmy Carter: In Search of the Great White House* (New York: Norton, 1980), 323–25. Rosalynn Carter, *First Lady from Plains* (Boston: Houghton Mifflin, 1984), makes no mention of the campaign duty in black neighborhoods.

15. Stone, "Black Political Power," 6.

16. Wilkins, *Standing Fast*, 339–40.

17. "Andrew Young," *Playboy*, July 1977, p. 67.

18. Jimmy Carter, *Why Not the Best?* (Nashville, Tenn.: Broadman Press, 1975), 36–37; Bruce Mazlish and Edwin Diamond, *Jimmy Carter: A Character Portrait* (New York: Simon and Schuster, 1979), 21.

19. Carter, *Why Not the Best*, 36–37. For Carter's father, see also Jimmy Carter, *Turning Point: A Candidate, a State, and a Nation Comes of Age* (New York: Times Books, 1992), 16–19.

20. Carter, *Why Not the Best*, 66–67; Carter, *First Lady from Plains*, 45–46, 65; Pat Watters, "Probing Jimmy Carter's Civil Liberties Record," *Civil Liberties Review*, Aug./Sept. 1976, p. 8. For the 1970 campaign, see Mazlish and Diamond, *Jimmy Carter*, 176–92.

21. John Dumbrell, *The Carter Presidency: A Re-Evaluation* (Manchester: Manchester University Press, 1993), 88; Joseph Lelyveld, "Our New Voice at the U.N.," *New York Times Magazine*, Feb. 6, 1977, p. 56; Martin Schram, *Running for President 1976* (New York: Stein and Day, 1977), 122; Kandy Stroud, *How Jimmy Won* (New York: Morrow, 1977), 278–79.

22. Stroud, *How Jimmy Won*, 171–72, 280.

23. Note, Ford, April 13, 1976, Human Rights—Equality (2), Pres. Handwriting File, Ford Papers; James Reichley to Cheney, June 25, 1976, Constituency Analysis, James A. Reichley Files, ibid; David Gergen to Duval, June 8, 1976, Busing, Box 12, Raoul-Duval Papers; George Van Cleve to Gergen, June 4, 1976, Busing, Box 12, ibid.

24. Patrick Anderson, *Electing Jimmy Carter: The Campaign of 1976* (Baton Rouge: Louisiana State University Press, 1994), 31–33.

25. Schram, *Running*, 207.

26. Roger Wilkins, "Jimmy Carter's First Year," *Black Enterprise*, March 1978, p. 24; Stephen Birmingham, "The Clubs Griffin Bell Had to Quit," *New York Times Magazine*, Feb. 6, 1977, p. 20; Joseph A. Califano, Jr., *Governing America* (New York: Simon and Schuster, 1981), 241.

27. Clayborne Carson, *In Struggle: SNCC and the Black Awakening of the 1960s* (Cambridge, Mass.: Harvard University Press, 1981), 305; "Michigan's Cool Hand Luke," *National Review*, Nov. 7, 1986, p. 32. Coretta King is quoted in David J. Garrow, *The FBI and Martin Luther King, Jr.: From "SOLO" to Memphis* (New York: Norton, 1981), 212.

28. William Lee Miller, *Yankee from Georgia* (New York: New York Times Books, 1978), 49–50; Gerald Rafshoon Oral History, Sept. 12, 1979, p. 10, Jimmy Carter Library, Atlanta, Georgia; Hamilton Jordan to Senior Staff, Aug. 10, 1978, FG 6-1-1, WHCF, Jimmy Carter Papers, Carter Library. For the president's civil rights initiative, see Reorganization Plan No. 1 of 1978, Civil Rights Reform, Domestic Policy Staff (Civil Rights and Justice)—Frank White, ibid.

29. Vernon Jordan to Hamilton Jordan, April 3 and 18, 1978, Black Community, Box 39, Hamilton Jordan Papers, Carter Library. Hamilton Jordan wrote his note on the first document.

30. Kurt Schmoke to Stuart Eizenstat, Feb. 18, 1977, Desegregation, Domestic Policy Staff—Stuart Eizenstat, Carter Papers.

31. Karl Hess and David S. Broder, *The Republican Establishment* (New York: Harper and Row, 1967), 268.

32. 438 U.S. 265 (1978).

33. Derrick A. Bell, Jr., "Awakening After *Bakke*," *Harvard Civil Rights-Civil Liberties Law Review* 14(Spring 1979): 2.

34. Bunny Mitchell to Tim Kraft, Sept. 12, 1977, Domestic Policy Staff—Eizenstat, Carter Papers; Timothy J. O'Neill, Bakke *and the Politics of Equality* (Middletown, Conn.: Wesleyan University Press, 1985), 179–91.

35. Califano, *Governing America*, 213, 232–33, 238–40.

36. Eizenstat to Carter, Oct. 26, 1977, Bakke, Domestic Policy Staff—Eizenstat, Carter Papers; Jordan to Carter, n.d. [ca. Sept. 16, 1977], Bakke Case, Box 33, Hamilton Jordan Papers, Carter Library; O'Neill, *Bakke,* 187; Califano, *Governing America,* 242; Allan P. Sindler, Bakke, DeFunis, *and Minority Admissions* (New York: Longman, 1978), 252. See also McGeorge Bundy, "The Issue Before the Court: Who Gets Ahead in America?," *Atlantic,* Nov. 1977, pp. 41–54; Joel Dreyfuss and Charles Lawrence III, *The* Bakke *Case: The Politics of Inequality* (New York: Harcourt Brace Jovanovich, 1979); Bernard Schwartz, *Behind* Bakke: *Affirmative Action and the Supreme Court* (New York: New York University Press, 1988).

37. Zbigniew Brzezinski, *Power and Principle* (New York: Farrar Straus and Giroux, 1983), 139.

38. U.S., Congress, House, Select Committee on Intelligence, *Hearings on Domestic Intelligence Programs,* 94th Cong., 1st sess., 1975, pt. 3, pp. 1044–45; U.S., Congress, Senate, Select Committee to Study Governmental Operations with Respect to Intelligence Agencies, *Final Report,* Book II, *Intelligence Activities and the Rights of Americans,* 94th Cong., 2d sess., 1976, p. 240 n95.

39. Barry Goldwater, with Jack Casserly, *Goldwater* (Garden City, N.Y.: Doubleday, 1988), 298; Seymour M. Finger, "Andrew Young at the UN," *Foreign Service Journal* 57(July–Aug. 1980): 17, 20. See also Garry Wills, *Certain Trumpets: The Call of Leaders* (New York: Simon and Schuster, 1994), 70–78.

40. Finger, "Andrew Young," 40–41; Clayton Fritchey, "Free at Last: The Fall and Rise of Andy Young," *The Nation,* Sept. 15, 1979, p. 201.

41. Carter to Young, Aug. 15, 1979, in Name File (Andrew Young), WHCF, Carter Papers; Valerie Pinson to Frank Moore, Sept. 4, 1979, Cong. Black Caucus, Box 22, Louis Martin Papers, Carter Library; Jimmy Carter, *Keeping Faith: Memoirs of a President* (New York: Bantam, 1982), 491. Bell is quoted in Kenneth W. Thompson, ed., *The Carter Presidency* (Lanham, Md.: University Press of America, 1990), 65; Jackson in Arch Puddington, "Jesse Jackson, the Blacks, and American Foreign Policy," *Commentary*, April 1984, p. 20.

42. Memo, Ben Brown (Deputy Chair, Carter/Mondale Pres. Committee), June 9, 1980, PL/Jimmy Carter, WHCF, Carter Papers; Louis Martin to Landon Butler, Jan. 8, 1980, FG 6-1-1, ibid.

43. Elizabeth Drew, *Portrait of An Election: The 1980 Presidential Campaign* (New York: Simon and Schuster, 1981), 185–86, 318; Stone, "Black Political Power," 11.

44. Carl Rowan, *Breaking Barriers: A Memoir* (Boston: Little, Brown, 1919), 325; *New York Times*, Aug. 4, 1980; Walt Harrington, "On the Road With the President of Black America," *Washington Post Magazine*, Jan. 25, 1987, p. 19.

45. *New York Times*, Aug. 1, 1980; *Washington Post*, Aug. 7, 1980; *Christian Science Monitor*, Aug. 26, 1980; Jack W. Germond and Jules Witcover, *Blue Smoke and Mirrors* (New York: Viking, 1981), 220–21.

46. *New York Times*, Sept. 17, 1980; Carter, *Keeping Faith*, 556.

47. *New York Times*, Aug. 3, and Sept. 18, 19, and 22, 1980.

48. Ibid., Feb. 5, 1976; Hodding Carter III, "South Africa at Home: Reagan and the Revival of Racism," *Playboy*, Jan. 1986, p. 108.

49. Hamilton Jordan, *Crisis: The Last Year of the Carter Presidency* (New York: G. P. Putnam's Sons, 1982), 343.

50. Stephen Vaughn, *Ronald Reagan in Hollywood: Movies and Politics* (New York: Cambridge University Press, 1994), 171.

51. Eizenstat to David Rubenstein, Oct. 7, 1980, PL/Ronald Reagan, Carter Papers; Martin D. Franks to File, Sept. 10, 1980, Campaign 1980—Reagan Book (I), Staff Offices, Counsel—Lloyd Cutler, Carter Papers.

52. Sam Popkin to Eizenstat, Sept. 16, 1980, PL/Ronald Reagan, WHCF, Carter Papers.

53. Califano, *Governing America*, 230–31.

54. Carter, *Keeping Faith*, 542; Haynes Johnson, *In the Absence of Power: Governing America* (New York: Viking, 1980), 284; Louis Martin to Coretta King, Dec. 18, 1980, Name File (Coretta King), WHCF, Carter Papers; Garry Wills, *Reagan's America: Innocents at Home* (Garden City, N.Y.: Doubleday, 1987), 352–61.

55. Thompson, ed., *Carter*, 5; Martin to Carter, March 12, 1979, FG 6-1-1, WHCF, Carter Papers; Rafshoon to Carter, June 14, 1977, Press Office—Jody Powell, ibid.

Chapter 9. Quota Kings

1. Nancy Reagan, with William Novak, *My Turn: The Memoirs of Nancy Reagan* (New York: Random House, 1989), 107.
2. James Conway, "Looking at Reagan," *Atlantic*, Oct. 1980, p. 45; David L. Norman, "The Strange Career of the Civil Rights Division's Commitment to *Brown*," *Yale Law Journal* 93(May 1984): 989; Hodding Carter III, *The Reagan Years* (New York: Braziller, 1988), 67; Paul Delaney, "Voting: The New Black Power," *New York Times Magazine*, Nov. 27, 1983, pp. 35ff; *Wall Street Journal*, Oct. 22, 1985.
3. Ronald Reagan, with Richard G. Hubler, *Where's the Rest of Me?* (New York: Duell, Sloan and Pearce, 1965), 7–9; Ronald Reagan, *An American Life* (New York: Simon and Schuster, 1990), 30–31; Anne Edwards, *Early Reagan* (New York: Morrow, 1987), 53.
4. Reagan, *Where's the Rest of Me?*, 63–64, and *American Life*, 52; Lou Cannon, *President Reagan: The Role of a Lifetime* (New York: Simon and Schuster, 1991), 519–20.
5. *Los Angeles Times*, March 6, 1980; Cannon, *President Reagan*, 519.
6. Cannon, *President Reagan*, 519–20.
7. Reagan, *Where's the Rest of Me?*, 63; Robert Dallek, *Ronald Reagan: The Politics of Symbolism* (Cambridge, Mass.: Harvard University Press, 1984), 34.
8. Reagan, *American Life*, 385; Cannon, *President Reagan*, 520–21, 524.
9. Mayor Coleman Young, who brought the Republicans to Detroit, spent the next twelve years regretting it. He called the Reagan-Bush era "a bleak period of neglect and retrogression." Coleman Young, with Lonnie Wheeler, *Hard Stuff* (New York: Viking, 1994), 256.
10. Ralph Abernathy, *And the Walls Came Tumbling Down* (New York: Harper and Row, 1989), 591, 596–99.
11. Reagan, *American Life*, 402; Roger Wilkins, *A Man's Life* (New York: Simon and Schuster, 1982), 369–70.
12. Calvin Tomkins, "A Sense of Urgency," *New Yorker*, March 27, 1989, p. 69.
13. Jonathan Kozol, *Rachel and Her Children: Homeless Families in America* (New York: Crown, 1988), 59, 163; Cannon, *President Reagan*, 518–19.
14. David A. Stockman, *The Triumph of Politics* (New York: Harper and Row, 1986), 23. See also Michael B. Katz, *In the Shadow of the Poor-*

house (New York: Basic Books, 1986), 290, for the administration's abandonment of one of welfare's historic roles, preservation of social order, in favor of ghetto apartheid enforced by police and military hardware.

15. See Andrew Kull, *The Color-Blind Constitution* (Cambridge, Mass.: Harvard University Press, 1992).

16. Ronald Reagan, *A Time for Choosing: The Speeches of Ronald Reagan, 1961–1982* (Chicago: Regnery Gateway, 1983), 169.

17. *New York Times*, Oct. 20, 1983.

18. William Schneider, "An Insider's View of the Election," *Atlantic*, July 1988, pp. 35, 38.

19. See Reynolds's articles, "The Reagan Administration and Civil Rights: Winning the War Against Discrimination," *University of Illinois Law Review*, 1986(No. 4, 1987): 1001, 1023; "The Reagan Administration's Civil Rights Policy: The Challenge for the Future," *Vanderbilt Law Review* 42(May 1989): 995, 997; "Individualism vs. Group Rights: The Legacy of *Brown*," *Yale Law Journal* 93(May 1984): 996, 1003, 1005.

20. Charles Fried, *Order and Law: Arguing the Reagan Revolution—A Firsthand Account* (New York: Simon and Schuster, 1991), 27, 40–43, 105–06.

21. Ibid., 40; Edwin Meese, *With Reagan: The Inside Story* (Washington, D.C.: Regnery Gateway, 1992), 314–15; Juan Williams, "In His Mind, But Not His Heart," *Washington Post Magazine*, Jan. 10, 1988, pp. 12, 15, 17.

22. Williams, "In His Mind," 10.

23. Joel Selig, "The Reagan Justice Department and Civil Rights: What Went Wrong," *University of Illinois Law Review*, 1985(No. 4, 1986): 826; Drew Days, "Turning Back the Clock: The Reagan Administration and Civil Rights," *Harvard Civil Rights–Civil Liberties Law Review* 19(Summer 1984): 346; *Wall Street Journal*, Oct. 24, 1985.

24. For SPONGE, see Randall Kennedy, "Persuasion and Distrust: A Comment on the Affirmative Action Debate," *Harvard Law Review* 99(April 1986): 1345. Meese is quoted in *Wall Street Journal*, Oct. 24, 1985; Watt in Bob Schieffer and Gary Paul Gates, *The Acting President* (New York: Dutton, 1989), 152–53; Reynolds in Williams, "In His Mind," 17.

25. Fried, *Order and Law*, 89–90, 99–101, 220 n5.

26. Thomas Byrne Edsall and Mary D. Edsall, *Chain Reaction: The Impact of Race, Rights, and Taxes on American Politics* (New York: Norton, 1991), 182. See also the Edsalls' "Race," *Atlantic*, May 1991, pp. 53–86.

27. Edsall, *Chain Reaction*, 3–4.

28. Jon Wiener, "Reagan's Children: Racial Hatred on Campus," *The Nation*, Feb. 27, 1989, p. 260; Dinesh D'Souza, *Illiberal Education: The Politics of Race and Sex on Campus* (New York: Free Press, 1991).

29. Herman Schwartz, *Packing the Courts: The Conservative Campaign to Rewrite the Constitution* (New York: Charles Scribner's Sons, 1988), 73, 96, 98.

30. Ibid., 109–15. See also Jamie Kalven, "The Reagan Administration and the Federal Judiciary," in *Freedom at Risk: Secrecy, Censorship, and Repression in the 1980s*, ed. Richard O. Curry (Philadelphia: Temple University Press, 1988), 315–34.

31. Thurgood Marshall, "The Supreme Court and Civil Rights: Has the Tide Turned?," *USA Today*, March 1990, p. 20; Robert Bork, *The Tempting of America: The Political Seduction of the Law* (New York: Free Press, 1990), 337–43. See also Ethan Bronner, *Battle for Justice: How the Bork Nomination Shook America* (New York: Norton, 1989); Aaron Wildavsky, "Robert Bork and the Crime of Inequality," *Public Interest* 98(Winter 1990): 98–117.

32. See Abigail M. Thernstrom, *Whose Votes Count? Affirmative Action and Minority Voting Rights* (Cambridge, Mass.: Harvard University Press, 1987).

33. Douglas S. Massey and Nancy A. Denton, *American Apartheid: Segregation and the Making of the Underclass* (Cambridge, Mass.: Harvard University Press, 1993), 207.

34. Selig, "The Reagan Justice Department," 808; Stephen L. Carter, *Reflections of an Affirmative Action Baby* (New York: Basic Books, 1991), 155; *Wall Street Journal*, Oct. 22, 1985; Mark Hertsgaard, *On Bended Knee: The Press and the Reagan Presidency* (New York: Farrar Straus Giroux, 1988), 144.

35. Terrel H. Bell, *The Thirteenth Man: A Reagan Cabinet Memoir* (New York: Free Press, 1988), 38, 100, 104, 108–09, 112.

36. Cannon, *President Reagan*, 521–22.

37. *Bob Jones University v. United States*, 461 U.S. 574 (1983); U.S., Congress, Senate, Committee on Finance, *Hearings on Legislation to Deny Tax Exemptions to Racially Discriminatory Private Schools*, 97th Cong., 2d Sess., 1982; Selig, "The Reagan Justice Department," 820; Fried, *Order and Law*, 41–42, 102–03; Cannon, *President Reagan*, 522–23; William French Smith, *Law and Justice in the Reagan Administration: The Memoirs of an Attorney General* (Stanford, Cal: Hoover Institution Press, 1991), 103.

38. Mary Frances Berry, "Taming the Civil Rights Commission," *The Nation*, Feb. 2, 1985, pp. 106–08; Tom Pugh, "'White Minstrel Show,'" ibid., Aug. 6–13, 1983, p. 104; Jocelyn C. Frye et al., "The

Rise and Fall of the United States Commission on Civil Rights," *Harvard Civil Rights–Civil Liberties Law Review* 22(Spring 1987): 478–79.

39. Morris B. Abram, "Affirmative Action: Fair Shakers and Social Engineers," *Harvard Law Review* 99(April 1986): 1312–13, 1317.

40. Berry, "Taming the Civil Rights Commission," 106; Frye, "Rise and Fall," 47–78, 483–84; Pugh, "Minstrel Show," 104, 106; Barry Mehler, "Rightest on the Rights Panel," *The Nation*, May 7, 1988, pp. 640–42. For Speakes, see his memoir *Speaking Out* (New York: Charles Scribner's Sons, 1988).

41. Jane Mayer and Doyle McManus, *Landslide: The Unmaking of the President, 1984–1988* (Boston: Houghton Mifflin, 1988), 4.

42. Jonathan Kaufman, *Broken Alliance: The Turbulent Times Between Blacks and Jews in America* (New York: Charles Scribner's Sons, 1988), 256–65.

43. Anne Braden, *The FBI vs. Black Voting Rights* (Los Angeles: National Committee Against Repressive Legislation, 1989), 1–8, passim.

44. *Congressional Record*, 100th Cong., 2d sess., Jan. 27, 1988, pp. H3-32. See also Mary R. Sawyer, *Harassment of Black Elected Officials: Ten Years Later* (Washington, D.C.: Voter Education and Registration Action, Inc., 1987).

45. Carter, *Reflections*, 155; Mayer and McManus, *Landslide*, 131.

46. Cannon, *President Reagan*, 524–25.

47. Carter, "South Africa," 108.

48. Reagan, *American Life*, 401–02; *New York Times*, Feb. 12, 1986, and Dec. 20, 1988; Patricia J. Williams, *The Alchemy of Race and Rights* (Cambridge, Mass.: Harvard University Press, 1991), 48–49.

49. Donald T. Regan, *For the Record* (New York: Harcourt Brace Jovanovich, 1988), 238; *Wall Street Journal*, Oct. 22, 1985.

51. Michael Deaver arranged the 1985 trip to the Bitburg military cemetary where forty-seven Nazi Waffen SS troops were buried with ordinary soldiers. When criticized for this appearance Reagan said his "research" proved many SS officers fought Hitler. Nancy Reagan, seeking balance, suggested another stop at the Bergen-Belsen concentration camp. She consulted her astrologer about the precise timing of both visits. Michael Schaller, *Reckoning with Reagan: America and Its President in the 1980s* (New York: Oxford University Press, 1992), 63.

52. Michael K. Deaver, *Behind the Scenes* (New York: Morrow, 1987), 79.

53. George Bush, with Victor Gold, *Looking Forward* (New York: Bantam ed., 1988), 90–91; Jefferson Morley, "Bush and the Blacks: An Unknown Story," *New York Review of Books*, Jan. 16, 1992, pp. 19–21;

Fred Powledge, "Racism Revisted: George Bush Is Whistling Dixie," *The Nation*, Oct. 14, 1991, p. 447.

54. Bush, *Looking Forward*, 91–92.

55. Morley, "Bush and the Blacks," 25; Charles Colson to Richard Nixon, Nov. 6, 1970, in Bruce Oudes, ed., *From: The President—Richard Nixon's Secret Files* (New York: Harper and Row, 1989), 166–70. Nixon scribbled a note in response to Colson's observations: "Probably true."

56. Mary Matalin and James Carville, with Peter Knobler, *All's Fair: Love, War, and Running for President* (New York: Random House and Simon and Schuster, 1994), 359; Martin Schram, "The Odd Couple," *Washingtonian*, May 1989, p. 91; Eric Alterman, "Playing Hardball," *New York Times Magazine*, April 30, 1989, p. 66; Remnick, "Why," 280, 282, 288, 291; Marjorie Williams, "The New Lee Atwater Lies Low," *Washington Post Magazine*, Nov. 19, 1989, p. 24.

57. Williams, "The New Lee Atwater," 48, 50; Thomas Byrne Edsall, *Power and Money: Writing About Politics, 1971–1987* (New York: Norton, 1988), 297.

58. Kathleen Hall Jamieson, "Context and the Creation of Meaning in the Advertising of the 1988 Presidential Campaign," *American Behavioral Scientist* 32(March/April 1989): 418.

59. By far the best analysis of the Horton story is Kathleen Hall Jamieson, *Dirty Politics: Deception, Distraction, and Democracy* (New York: Oxford University Press, 1992), 15–42, passim.

60. Susan Estrich, "The Hidden Politics of Race," *Washington Post Magazine*, April 23, 1989, p. 23; Haynes Johnson, *Sleepwalking Through History: America in the Reagan Years* (New York: Norton, 1991), 399; Elizabeth Drew, *Election Journal: Political Events of 1987–1988* (New York: Morrow, 1989), 305, 333; Roger Simon, *Road Show* (New York: Farrar, Straus, Giroux, 1990), 306.

61. Steve Burkholder, "The Lawrence *Eagle-Tribune* and the Willie Horton Story," *Washington Journalism Review*, July/Aug. 1989, pp. 14–19; Jack W. Germond and Jules Witcover, *Whose Broad Stripes and Bright Stars? The Trivial Pursuit of the Presidency 1988* (New York: Warner Books, 1989), 12; Dick Kirschten, "How the Furlough Issue Grew," *National Journal*, Oct. 29, 1988, p. 2719; *Wall Street Journal*, April 19, 1988.

62. Germond and Witcover, *Whose Broad Stripes*, 12; Drew, *Election Journal*, 253; Kirschten, "How the Furlough Issue Grew," 2718–20.

63. Simon, *Road Show*, 218; Jamieson, *Dirty Politics*, 23.

64. Jeffrey M. Elliot, "The 'Willie' Horton Nobody Knows," *The Nation*, Aug. 23/30, 1993, pp. 201–05; Sidney Blumenthal, *Pledging Allegiance: The Last Campaign of the Cold War* (New York: HarperCollins, 1990),

265; Kirschten, "How the Furlough Issue Grew," 2719; Jamieson, "Context," 416–17.

65. Kristin Clark Taylor, *The First to Speak: A Woman of Color Inside the White House* (New York: Doubleday, 1993), 141, 143; Jamieson, "Context," 416–18; Kirschten, "How the Furlough Issue Grew," 2719; Drew, *Election Journal*, 305.

66. Blumenthal, *Pledging Allegiance*, 308–09.

67. Simon, *Road Show*, 227–28.

68. Ibid., 306; Garry Wills, *Under God: Religion and American Politics* (New York: Simon and Schuster, 1990), 175; James A. Barnes, "What Went Wrong?," *National Journal*, Oct. 29, 1988, pp. 2717, 2720; Kirschten, "How the Furlough Issue Grew," 2718; Jamieson, "Context," 417; Johnson, *Sleepwalking*, 480.

69. Tomkins, "A Sense of Urgency," 72; Arthur Kempton, "Native Sons," *New York Review of Books*, April 11, 1991, pp. 55–61; Andrew Hacker, "Black Crime, White Racism," ibid., March 3, 1988, pp. 36–41; Peter Brown, *Minority Party* (Washington, D.C.: Regnery Gateway, 1991), 133–34; Simon, *Road Show*, 226; Estrich, "Hidden Politics," 22–24; Richard Ben Cramer, *What It Takes: The Way to the White House* (New York: Random House, 1992), 1017.

70. Williams, "The New Lee Atwater," 24, 51; Schram, "The Odd Couple," 88; Alterman, "Playing Hardball," 73.

71. "Civil Wrongs," *National Review*, June 11, 1990, p. 13; Schram, "Odd Couple," 88; Kempton, "GOP Blues," 4. See also Louis Bolce, Gerald De Maio, and Douglas Muzzio, "Blacks and the Republican Party: The 20 Percent Solution," *Political Science Quarterly* 107(Spring 1992): 63–80, and "The 1992 Republican 'Tent': No Blacks Walked In," ibid. 108(Summer 1993): 255–70.

72. Matalin and Carville, *All's Fair*, 50; Schram, "Odd Couple," 88, 91, 93; Kempton, "GOP Blues," 4; Williams, "The New Lee Atwater," 48, 50; Drew, *Election Journal*, 332–33. Gray is quoted in Fitzhugh Green, *George Bush: An Intimate Portrait* (New York: Hippocrene Books, 1989), 193.

73. *New York Times*, April 3, 1989.

74. Estrich, "Hidden Politics," 23; "Black and Blue," *The Nation*, April 1, 1991, p. 400; "Lower Education," ibid., Jan. 7–14, 1991, pp. 3–4.

75. Paul M. Sniderman and Thomas Piazza, *The Scar of Race* (Cambridge, Mass.: Harvard University Press, 1993), 175–76. See also Steven A. Shull, *A Kinder, Gentler Racism? The Reagan-Bush Civil Rights Legacy* (Armonk, N.Y.: M. E. Sharpe, 1993).

76. *Newsweek*, Dec. 31, 1990, pp. 28–29.

77. "Rainbow Signs," *The Nation*, July 1, 1991, p. 5; "The Legal Rights Bill," ibid., June 24, 1991, p. 833; Elizabeth Drew, "Letter from Washington," *New Yorker*, June 17, 1991, pp. 102, 105.

78. Jamieson, *Dirty Politics*, 97–100; Joe Klein, "Race vs. Rich," *New York*, Dec. 10, 1990, p. 16; Drew, "Letter from Washington," 105. Helms also moved on Gantt by mailing 125,000 postcards to registered voters in eighty-six predominantly black North Carolina districts warning them that they might not be properly registered to vote and could be prosecuted for fraud if they showed up on election day. No Helms campaign official was fined or imprisoned for this. The campaign merely signed a Justice Department consent decree. Michael Duffy and Dan Goodgame, *Marching in Place: The Status Quo Presidency of George Bush* (New York: Simon and Schuster, 1992), 101–02.

79. *Time*, Dec. 24, 1990, 21–22; *Newsweek*, Dec. 3, 1990, p. 26, and Dec. 24, 1990, p. 19. See also William J. Bennett and Terry Eastland, *Counting by Race: Equality from the Founding Fathers to* Bakke *and* Weber (New York: Basic Books, 1979).

80. *Christian Science Monitor*, April 23 and 24, 1991; Drew, "Letter from Washington," 104–05, 109; Diane R. Gordon, "A Civil Rights Bill for Workers," *The Nation*, July 9, 1990, pp. 44–46; "What They Didn't Say," *National Review*, May 28, 1990, p. 33; *Newsweek*, April 1991, 35.

81. *New York Times*, May 3 and June 2, 1991; Alexander Cockburn, "Bush & PC—A Conspiracy So Immense," *The Nation*, May 27, 1991, pp. 685ff.

82. Lewis H. Lapham, "Justice Horatio Alger," *Harper's*, Sept. 1991, pp. 8, 11; Carter, *Reflections*, 136–37, 159.

83. Jane Mayer and Jill Abramson, *Strange Justice* (New York: Houghton Mifflin, 1994), 189–91; Ronald Dworkin, "Justice for Clarence Thomas," *New York Review of Books*, Nov. 7, 1991, pp. 41–42; *Clarence Thomas—Confronting the Future: Selections from the Senate Confirmation Hearings and Prior Speeches* (Washington, D.C.: Regnery Gateway, 1992).

84. Quoted in John Hope Franklin, *The Color Line: Legacy for the Twenty-First Century* (Columbia: University of Missouri Press, 1993), 15–16, from Transcript of Hearing in *Adams v. Bell*, Civil Action 3095–70 (Washington, D.C., March 121, 1982).

85. Dan Quayle, *Standing Firm* (New York: HarperCollins, 1994), 272. Quayle had more respect for Anita Hill than most of his colleagues, the result, he said, of a law school incident involving his wife: "Marilyn had been a victim of a professor's unwelcome attentions (her response to him is not printable) and we have been sensitive to the issue ever since." Ibid., 273.

86. U.S., Congress, Senate, Committee on the Judiciary, *Hearings on the Nomination of Judge Clarence Thomas*, 102d Cong., 1st sess., 1991; Michael Pertshuk and Wendy Schaetzel, *The People Rising: The Campaign Against the Bork Nomination* (New York: Thunder's Mouth Press, 1989), 207–15; Jeffrey Tobin, "The Burden of Clarence Thomas," *New Yorker*, Sept. 27, 1993, p. 51. See also Mayer and Abramson, *Strange Justice*; John C. Danforth, *Resurrection: The Confirmation of Clarence Thomas* (New York: Viking 1994); Timothy M. Phelps and Helen Winternitz, *Capitol Games* (New York: Hyperion, 1992); Robert Crisman and Robert L. Allen, *Court of Appeal: The Black Community Speaks Out on the Racial and Sexual Politics of Clarence Thomas v. Anita Hill* (New York: Ballantine, 1992); Toni Morrison, ed., *Race-ing Justice, En-gendering Power* (New York: Pantheon Books, 1992); David Brock, *The Real Anita Hill* (New York: Free Press, 1993); Ronald Suresh Roberts, *Clarence Thomas and the Tough Love Crowd* (New York: New York University Press, 1995), 115–70.

87. Quoted in Charles Kolb, *White House Daze* (New York: Free Press, 1994), 258.

88. Ibid., 252–56.

89. Garry Wills, "A Tale of Three Cities," *New York Review of Books*, March 28, 1991, p. 16; Bob Woodward, *The Commanders* (New York: Simon and Schuster, 1991), 47.

90. For Duke's story, see Tyler Bridges, *The Rise of David Duke* (Jackson: University Press of Mississippi, 1994); Douglas D. Rose, ed., *The Emergence of David Duke and the Politics of Race* (Chapel Hill: University of North Carolina Press, 1992); John Maginnis, *Cross to Bear* (Baton Rouge, La.: Darkhorse Press, 1992); Michael Zatarain, *David Duke: Evolution of a Klansman* (Gretna, La.: Pelican Publishing, 1990).

91. Kevin P. Phillips, *Boiling Point: Republicans, Democrats, and the Decline of Middle-Class Prosperity* (New York: Random House, 1993), 243.

92. Barbara Bush, *A Memoir* (New York: Charles Scribner's Sons, 1994), 459–60; *Report of the Independent Commission on the Los Angeles Police Department* (Los Angeles: Independent Commission on the Los Angeles Police Department, 1991).

93. Alexander M. Haig, Jr., with Charles McCarry, *Inner Circles: How America Changed the World* (New York: Warner Books, 1992), 566.

94. Duffy and Goodgame, *Marching in Place*, 101; Garry Wills, "The Born-Again Republicans," *New York Review of Books*, Sept. 24, 1992, p. 14.

95. Wills, "Born-Again Republicans," 9; Deaver, *Behind the Scenes*, 226.

96. Murray Kempton, "The Last Hurrah," *New York Review of Books*, Dec. 3, 1992, p. 32.

97. See Phillips's *Boiling Point, The Politics of Rich and Poor: Wealth and the American Electorate in the Reagan Aftermath* (New York: Random House, 1990); *Arrogant Capital: Washington, Wall Street, and the Frustration of American Politics* (Boston: Little, Brown, 1995).

98. Edsall, *Chain Reaction*, 30; *Newsweek*, March 25, 1991, p. 39.

99. Barbara Bush, *A Memoir*, 50–51; Pamela Kilian, *Barbara Bush: A Biography* (New York: St. Martin's Press, 1992), 61–62

Rectors and Souljas

1. *New York Times*, Nov. 1, 1992.

2. Sidney Blumenthal, "Firebell," *New Republic*, May 25, 1992, pp. 11–14; Charles F. Allen and Jonathan Portis, *The Comeback Kid: The Life and Career of Bill Clinton* (New York: Birch Lane Press, 1992), 16–17, 24, 32, 55; Robert E. Levin, *Bill Clinton: The Inside Story* (New York: S.P.I. Books, 1992), 88; Ernest Dumas, ed., *The Clintons of Arkansas* (Fayetteville: University of Arkansas Press, 1993), 39–40; Donnie Radcliffe, *Hillary Rodham Clinton: A First Lady for Our Time* (New York: Warner Books, 1993), 92–93. Brewster is quoted in *New York Times*, April 25, 1970.

3. Andrew Hacker, "The Blacks and Clinton," *New York Review of Books*, Jan. 28, 1993, 14; Jack W. Germond and Jules Witcover, *Mad as Hell: Revolt at the Ballot Box, 1992* (New York: Warner Books, 1993), 292–93; Blumenthal, "Firebell," 14; *New York Times*, Sept. 20, 1992; Bill Clinton and Al Gore, *Putting People First: How We Can All Change America* (New York: Times Books, 1992).

4. Mary Matalin and James Carville, with Peter Knobler, *All's Fair: Love, War, and Running for President* (New York: Random House and Simon and Schuster, 1994), 166; Gore Vidal, "Bedfellows Make Strange Politics," *New York Times Book Review*, Sept. 18, 1994, 24; Joan Didion, "Eye on the Prize," *New York Review of Books*, Sept. 24, 1992, p. 60; Germond and Witcover, *Mad as Hell*, 296.

5. *The Nation*, Aug. 17/24, 1992, p. 164.

6. Marshall Frady, "Death in Arkansas," *New Yorker*, Feb. 22, 1993, pp. 105–33; Tom Fox, "Bill Clinton's Dangerous Liaison Not With Flowers," *National Catholic Reporter*, Feb. 7, 1992, p. 2; Christopher Lydon, "Sex, War, and Death: Covering Clinton Becomes a Test of Character—For the Media," *Columbia Journalism Review* 32(May/June 1992): 57–60. Since 1988 the Willie Horton gambit has become a staple of GOP electioneering. David C. Anderson, "Expressive Justice is all the Rage," *New York Times Magazine*, Jan. 15, 1995, pp. 36–37.

7. Matalin and Carville, *All's Fair*, 155–56; Steven M. Gillon, *The Democrats' Dilemma: Walter F. Mondale and the Liberal Legacy* (New York: Columbia University Press, 1992), 350.

8. Gerald Horne, "Race: Ensuring a True Multiculturalism," in *State of the Union 1994*, ed. Richard Caplan and John Feffer (Boulder, Col.: Westview Press, 1994), 184; Harry S. Ashmore, *Civil Rights and Wrongs: A Memoir of Race and Politics, 1944–1994* (New York: Pantheon, 1994), 365; Peter Goldman et al., *Quest for the Presidency 1992* (College Station: Texas A&M University Press, 1994), 275; Germond and Witcover, *Mad as Hell*, 293–304. Souljah was the other winner, taking away some fame and a book contract. Sister Souljah, *No Disrespect* (New York: Times Books, 1994).

9. Matalin and Carville, *All's Fair*, 213–16.

10. *New York Times*, July 10, 1992; *Newsweek*, July 27, 1992, pp. 28–30.

11. *Los Angeles Times*, June 18, 1994; *New York Times*, Nov. 13, 1993; Hacker, "The Blacks and Clinton," 14.

12. Horne, "Race," 186–88.

13. Lani Guinier, "Who's Afraid of Lani Guinier?," *New York Times Magazine*, Feb. 27, 1994, 38ff; Elizabeth Drew, *On the Edge: The Clinton Presidency* (New York: Simon and Schuster, 1994), 198–211. For Guinier's scholarship, see *The Tyranny of the Majority* (New York: Free Press, 1994). For the Civil Rights Division under Patrick, see "Civil Rights on the Move," *The Nation*, Jan. 23, 1995, pp.88–90.

14. Michael Kelly, "You Say You Want a Revolution," *New Yorker*, Nov. 21, 1994, p. 58.

15. *New York Times*, April 8, 1996.

16. *Newsweek*, Feb. 13, 1995, pp. 36–37; *U.S. News & World Report*, Feb. 13, 1995, pp. 32–38.

INDEX

503